Fodors

New
EDITION

Eastern and Central Europe

"When it comes to information on regional history, what to see and do, and shopping, these guides are exhaustive."

—*USAir Magazine*

"Usable, sophisticated restaurant coverage, with an emphasis on good value."

—Andy Birsh, *Gourmet Magazine* columnist

"Valuable because of their comprehensiveness."

—*Minneapolis Star-Tribune*

"Fodor's always delivers high quality...thoughtfully presented...thorough."

—*Houston Post*

"An excellent choice for those who want everything under one cover."

—*Washington Post*

Fodor's Travel Publications, Inc.
New York • Toronto • London • Sydney • Auckland
http://www.fodors.com/

Fodor's Eastern and Central Europe

Editor: Matthew Lore

Editorial Contributors: Steven K. Amsterdam, Robert Andrews, Mark Baker, Christopher Billy, Robert Blake, David Brown, Audra Epstein, Janet Foley, Emma Harris, Gregory A. Hedger, Charlie Hornberger, Christina Knight, Ky Krauthamer, Martha Lagace, Alan Levy, Rebecca Miller, Witold Orzechowski, Heidi Sarna, Helayne Schiff, Mary Ellen Schultz, M. T. Schwartzman (Gold Guide editor), Timea Špitková, Dinah Spritzer, Julie Tomasz, Ivanka Tomova

Creative Director: Fabrizio La Rocca

Associate Art Director: Guido Caroti

Photo Researcher: Jolie Novak

Cartographer: David Lindroth, Inc.

Cover Photograph: David Hanson/Tony Stone Images

Text Design: Between the Covers

Copyright

Seventeenth Edition

ISBN 0–679–03199–5

Special Sales

CONTENTS

as you can, and reconfirm when you get to town. Unless otherwise noted, the restaurants listed are open daily for lunch and dinner. We mention dress only when men are required to wear a jacket or a jacket and tie. Look for an overview of local habits in the Pleasures and Pastimes section that follows each chapter introduction.

Credit Cards

The following abbreviations are used: **AE,** American Express; **D,** Discover; **DC,** Diners Club; **MC,** MasterCard; and **V,** Visa.

Please Write to Us

You can use this book in the confidence that all prices and opening times are based on information supplied to us at press time; Fodor's cannot accept responsibility for any errors. Time inevitably brings changes, so always confirm information when it matters—especially if you're making a detour to visit a specific place. In addition, when making reservations be sure to mention if you have a disability or are traveling with children, if you prefer a private bath or a certain type of bed, or if you have specific dietary needs or any other concerns.

Were the restaurants we recommended as described? Did our hotel picks exceed your expectations? Did you find a museum we recommended a waste of time? If you have complaints, we'll look into them and revise our entries when the facts warrant it. If you've discovered a special place that we haven't included, we'll pass the information along to our correspondents and have them check it out. So send your feedback, positive *and* negative, to the Eastern and Central Europe editor at 201 East 50th Street, New York, New York 10022—and have a wonderful trip!

Karen Cure

Karen Cure
Editorial Director

Eastern Europe Railways

Hamburg
Rostock
Słupsk
Koszalin
Gdynia
Gdańsk
Malbork
Olsztyn
Bremen
Szczecin
Bydgoszcz
Toruń
Hannover
Gorzów
Wielkopolski
Berlin
Poznań
Włocławek
GERMANY
Leipzig
Zielona
Góra
POLAND
Kalisz
Łódź
Erfurt
Dresden
Wrocław
Piotrków
Tyrb.
Legnica
Częstochowa
Karlovy
Vary
Hradec-
Králové
Wałbrzych
Bytom
Sosnowiec
Prague
Gliwice
Plzeň
Katowice
Kraków
Nürnberg
CZECH REPUBLIC
Ostrava
Tarnów
Telč
Brno
Kroměříž
Prešov
České
Budějovice
Banská-
Bystricaо
Košice
Linz
Vienna
Nitra
SLOVAKIA
Munich
Salzburg
Bratislava
Miskolc
AUSTRIA
Sopron
Győr
Debrec
Tatabánya
Budapest
Graz
Veszprém
Kecskemét
Lake
Balaton
HUNGARY
SLOVENIA
Békéscsaba
Ljubljana
Pécs
Szeged
Venézia
Zagreb
CROATIA
Novi
Sad
Bologna
BOSNIA
AND
HERZEGOVINA
Belgrade
Adriatic
Sea
Sarajevo
SERBIA
ITALY
MONTENEGRO
Rome
ALBANIA

R
FEI

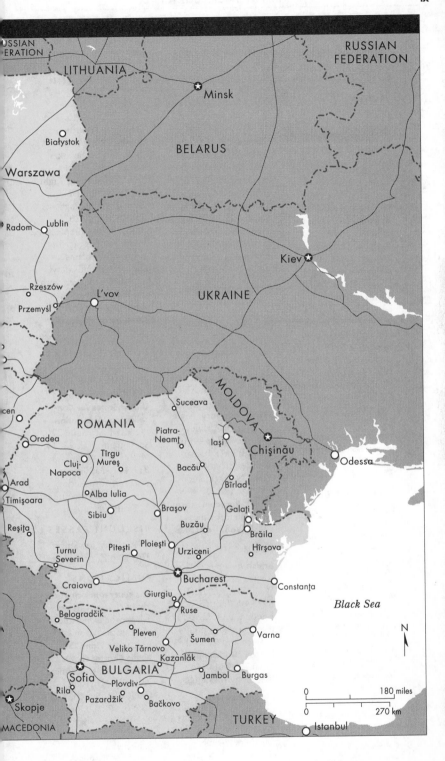

IMPORTANT CONTACTS A TO Z

An Alphabetical Listing of Publications, Organizations, and Companies That Will Help You Before, During, and After Your Trip

A

AIR TRAVEL

The major gateways to Eastern and Central Europe include Bulgaria (**Sofia International Airport,** ☎ 011–359–2/720672); the Czech Republic (**Ruzyně Airport,** about 20 mi northwest of Prague, ☎ 011–42–2/367760); Slovakia (**Ivanka Airport,** near Bratislava, ☎ 011–42–7/522–3003); Hungary (**Ferihegy Airport,** about 14 mi southeast of Budapest, ☎ 011–36–1/579213); Poland (**Okecie Airport,** just southwest of Warsaw, ☎ 011–48–22/461731); and Romania (**Otopeni International Airport,** just outside Bucharest, ☎ 011–40–2/121602).

FLYING TIME

Depending on your flight connections and layovers, flights from the West Coast to Prague will take about 19 hours and to Bucharest about 22 hours. From the East Coast you can expect travel to Prague to take about 12 hours and to Bucharest about 15 hours. Chicago–Warsaw is a 10-hour nonstop flight. Flying from Australia to Central Europe is a trek of about a day and a half.

CARRIERS

U.S. airlines that serve Eastern and Central European cities include **Continental** (☎ 800/231–0856), **Delta** (☎ 800/241–4141), **Northwest** (☎ 800/447–4747), and **United** (☎ 800/538–2929). In most cases, a European co-carrier provides a connecting flight from a gateway in Europe.

These European national airlines offer nonstop service from the United States to their own countries and connecting flights to others: **Bulgaria:** Balkan Air (☎ 212/573–5530); **the Czech Republic and Slovakia:** Czech Air (CSA; ☎ 212/765–6022); **Hungary:** Malév Hungarian Airlines (☎ 212/757–6446); **Poland:** LOT Polish Airlines, from New York, Newark, and Chicago (☎ 212/869–1074); **Romania:** Tarom Romanian Airlines (☎ 212/687–6013).

FROM THE U.K

British Airways (✉156 Regent St., London W1R 5TA, ☎ 0181/897–4000; outside London, 0345/222-111) flies to various points in Eastern and Central Europe. **British Midland** (☎ 0345/554–554) flies daily to Prague.

COMPLAINTS

To register complaints about charter and scheduled airlines, contact the U.S. Department of Transportation's **Aviation Consumer Protection Division.** Only recorded messages can be taken via the phone, so have the details of your flight handy if calling in. (✉ C-75, Washington, DC 20590, ☎ 202/366–2220). Complaints about lost baggage or ticketing problems and concerns about safety may also be logged with the **Federal Aviation Administration (FAA) Consumer Hotline** (☎ 800/322–7873).

CONSOLIDATORS

For the names of reputable air-ticket consolidators, contact the **United States Air Consolidators Association** (✉ 925 L St., Suite 220, Sacramento, CA 95814, ☎ 916/441–4166, FAX 916/441–3520). For discount air-ticketing agencies, *see* Discounts & Deals, *below.*

DISCOUNT PASSES

☞ Air Travel *in* Smart Tips A to Z, *below.*

PUBLICATIONS

For general information about charter carriers, ask for the Department of Transportation's free brochure **"Plane Talk: Public Charter Flights"** (✉ Aviation Consumer Protection Division, C-75, Washington, DC 20590, ☎ 202/366–2220). The Department of Transportation also publishes a 58-page booklet, **"Fly Rights,"** available from the

Consumer Information Center (⊠ Dept. 136C, Pueblo, CO 81009; $1.75).

For other tips and hints, consult the Consumers Union's monthly **"Consumer Reports Travel Letter"** (⊠ Box 53629, Boulder, CO 80322, ☎ 800/234–1970; $39 1st yr).

WITHIN EASTERN & CENTRAL EUROPE

Czech Air (☞ *above*; ☎ 02/2010–4111 in Prague) and **Balkan Air** (☞ *above*; ☎ 2/79–321 in Sofia) offer flights within Eastern and Central Europe from Prague and Sofia, respectively. **Malév Hungarian Airlines** (☞ *above*; ☎ 1/267–4333 in Budapest) has regular nonstop flights between Budapest and major Eastern and Central European cities. **LOT** (☞ *above*; ☎ 22/953 or 22/952 in Warsaw) has flights between Polish cities and from Warsaw to 27 destinations in Eastern and Central Europe. **Tarom** (☞ *above*; ☎ 01/6594125 or 01/6594185 in Romania), the Romanian national airline, provides flights to most major cities within Romania and Eastern and Central European destinations.

B

BETTER BUSINESS BUREAU

For local contacts in the hometown of a tour operator you may be considering, consult the **Council of Better Business Bureaus** (⊠ 4200 Wilson Blvd., Suite 800, Arlington, VA 22203,

☎ 703/276–0100, FAX 703/525–8277).

BOAT TRAVEL

MAHART (International Shipping Station, Belgrád rakpart, ☎ 1/118–1704 or 1/118–1586; in Vienna, 01/729–2161 or 01/729–2162), Hungary's national shipping company, operates hydrofoils on the Danube between Budapest and Vienna, which make stops in Bratislava on advance order. **Polske Linie Oceaniczne** (Polish Ocean Lines, ☎ 022/629–28–95) will occasionally book you (and your car) onto cargo boats to and from Scandinavian or British ports.

BUS TRAVEL

FROM THE U.K.

Unless you latch onto a real deal on airfare, a bus ticket from London's **Victoria Terminal** (☎ 0171/730–0202) is probably the cheapest transit from the United Kingdom to Eastern and Central Europe, although it may take a little research, as regularly scheduled routes to all cities except Berlin and Warsaw are practically nonexistent. Check newspaper ads for eastbound passage.

WITHIN EASTERN & CENTRAL EUROPE

See Arriving and Departing by Bus in the A to Z section at the end of each country chapter.

C

CAR RENTAL

The major car-rental companies represented in Eastern and Central

Europe are **Avis** (☎ 800/331–1084; in Canada, 800/879–2847), **Budget** (☎ 800/472–3325; in the U.K., 0800/181181), **Dollar** (☎ 800/800–6000; in the U.K., 0990/565656, where it is known as Eurodollar), **Hertz** (☎ 800/654–3001; in Canada, 800/263–0600; in the U.K., 0345/555888), and **National InterRent** (sometimes known as Europcar InterRent outside North America; ☎ 800/227–3876; in the U.K., 0345/222–525).

For additional country-specific information, *see* Car Rental in the A to Z section at the end of each country chapter, or in the A to Z section for its capital city.

RENTAL WHOLESALERS

Contact **Auto Europe** (☎ 207/828–2525 or 800/223–5555) or the **Kemwel Group** (☎ 914/835–5555 or 800/678–0678).

CHILDREN & TRAVEL

FLYING

Look into **"Flying with Baby"** (⊠ Third Street Press, Box 261250, Littleton, CO 80163, ☎ 303/595–5959; $4.95 includes shipping), cowritten by a flight attendant. **"Kids and Teens in Flight,"** free from the U.S. Department of Transportation's Aviation Consumer Protection Division (⊠ C-75, Washington, DC 20590, ☎ 202/366–2220), offers tips on children flying alone. Every two years the February issue of *Family Travel Times* (☞ Know-How, *below*) details children's services on three dozen airlines. **"Flying Alone, Handy Advice for Kids Traveling Solo"** is available free from the American Automobile Association (AAA; Send stamped, self-addressed, legal-size envelope: ✉ Flying Alone, Mail Stop 800, 1000 AAA Dr., Heathrow, FL 32746).

KNOW-HOW

Family Travel Times, published quarterly by Travel with Your Children (✉ TWYCH, 40 5th Ave., New York, NY 10011, ☎ 212/477–5524; $40 per yr), covers destinations, types of vacations, and modes of travel.

LOCAL INFORMATION

The Adventures of Mickey, Taggy, Pupo, and Cica and How They Discover Budapest, by Kati Rekai (Canadian Stage Arts Publications, Toronto), is an animal fantasy story for children set in Budapest, written by a Hungarian-born author.

LODGING

The **Novotel** chain (☎ 800/221–4542), which has hotels in Budapest, Warsaw, and five other Polish cities, and Sofia and Plovdiv in Bulgaria, allows up to two children under 12 to stay free in their parents' room. Many Novotel properties also have playgrounds. The **Budapest Hilton** (☎ 1/214–3000) has an unusual policy allowing children of *any* age—even middle-aged

adults—to stay for free in their parents' room.

Young visitors to the Czech Republic will enjoy staying at one of Prague's picturesque floating "botels." For further information contact **Čedok.**

IN THE U.S.

The **U.S. Customs Service** (✉ Box 7407, Washington, DC 20044, ☎ 202/927–6724) can answer questions on duty-free limits and publishes a helpful brochure, "Know Before You Go." For information on registering foreign-made articles, call 202/927–0540 or write U.S. Customs Service, Resource Management, 1301 Constitution Ave. NW, Washington DC, 20229.

Complaints➤ Note the inspector's badge number and write to the commissioner's office (✉ 1301 Constitution Ave. NW, Washington, DC 20229).

CANADIANS

Contact **Revenue Canada** (✉ 2265 St. Laurent Blvd. S, Ottawa, Ontario K1G 4K3, ☎ 613/993–0534) for a copy of the free brochure **"I Declare/Je Déclare"** and for details on duty-free limits. For recorded information (within Canada only), call 800/461–9999.

U.K. CITIZENS

HM Customs and Excise (✉ Dorset House, Stamford St., London SE1 9NG, ☎ 0171/202–4227) can answer questions about U.K.

customs regulations and publishes a free pamphlet, **"A Guide for Travellers,"** detailing standard procedures and import rules.

D

COMPLAINTS

To register complaints under the provisions of the Americans with Disabilities Act, contact the U.S. Department of Justice's **Disability Rights Section** (✉ Box 66738, Washington, DC 20035, ☎ 202/514–0301 or 800/514–0301, FAX 202/307–1198, TTY 202/514–0383 or 800/514–0383). For airline-related problems, contact the U.S. Department of Transportation's **Aviation Consumer Protection Division** (☞ Air Travel, *above*). For complaints about surface transportation, contact the Department of Transportation's **Civil Rights Office** (✉ 400 7th St. SW, Room 10215, Washington DC, 20590, ☎ 202/366–4648).

LOCAL INFORMATION

Visitors to Hungary may want to contact the **Mozgáskorlátozottak Egyesületeinek Országos Szövetsége** (National Association of People with Mobility Impairments, or MEOSZ; ✉ 1032 Budapest, San Marco u. 76, ☎ 1/188–2388) for information on special services and accommodations.

ORGANIZATIONS

TRAVELERS WITH HEARING IMPAIRMENTS➤ The **American Academy of Otolaryngology** (✉ 1 Prince St., Alexandria, VA 22314, ☎ 703/836–4444, FAX 703/683–5100, TTY 703/519–1585) publishes a brochure, "Travel Tips for Hearing Impaired People."

TRAVELERS WITH MOBILITY PROBLEMS➤ Contact **Mobility International USA** (✉ Box 10767, Eugene, OR 97440, ☎ and TTY 541/343–1284, FAX 541/343–6812), the U.S. branch of a Belgium-based organization (☞ *below*) with affiliates in 30 countries; **MossRehab Hospital Travel Information Service** (☎ 215/456–9600, TTY 215/456–9602), a telephone information resource for travelers with physical disabilities; the **Society for the Advancement of Travel for the Handicapped** (✉ 347 5th Ave., Suite 610, New York, NY 10016, ☎ 212/447–7284, FAX 212/725–8253; membership $45); and **Travelin' Talk** (✉ Box 3534, Clarksville, TN 37043, ☎ 615/552–6670, FAX 615/552–1182), which provides local contacts worldwide for travelers with disabilities.

TRAVELERS WITH VISION IMPAIRMENTS➤ Contact the **American Council of the Blind** (✉ 1155 15th St. NW, Suite 720, Washington, DC 20005, ☎ 202/467–5081, FAX 202/467–5085) for a list of travelers' resources or the **American Founda-**tion for the Blind** (✉ 11 Penn Plaza, Suite 300, New York, NY 10001, ☎ 212/502–7600 or 800/232–5463, TTY 212/502–7662), which provides general advice and publishes "Access to Art" ($19.95), a directory of museums that accommodate travelers with vision impairments.

IN THE U.K.

Contact the **Royal Association for Disability and Rehabilitation** (✉ RADAR, 12 City Forum, 250 City Rd., London EC1V 8AF, ☎ 0171/250–3222) or **Mobility International** (✉ Rue de Manchester 25, B-1080 Brussels, Belgium, ☎ 00–322–410–6297, FAX 00–322–410–6874), an international travel-information clearinghouse for people with disabilities.

PUBLICATIONS

Several publications for travelers with disabilities are available from the **Consumer Information Center** (✉ Box 100, Pueblo, CO 81009, ☎ 719/948–3334). Call or write for its free catalog of current titles. The Society for the Advancement of Travel for the Handicapped (☞ Organizations, *above*) publishes the quarterly magazine **"Access to Travel"** ($13 for 1-yr subscription).

The 500-page **Travelin' Talk Directory** (✉ Box 3534, Clarksville, TN 37043, ☎ 615/552–6670, FAX 615/552–1182; $35) lists people and organizations that help travelers with disabilities. For travel agents worldwide, consult the **Directory of Travel Agencies for the Disabled** (✉ Twin Peaks Press, Box 129, Vancouver, WA 98666, ☎ 360/694–2462 or 800/637–2256, FAX 360/696–3210; $19.95 plus $3 shipping).

TRAVEL AGENCIES & TOUR OPERATORS

The Americans with Disabilities Act requires that all travel firms serve the needs of all travelers. That said, you should note that some agencies and operators specialize in making travel arrangements for individuals and groups with disabilities, among them **Access Adventures** (✉ 206 Chestnut Ridge Rd., Rochester, NY 14624, ☎ 716/889–9096), run by a former physical-rehab counselor.

TRAVELERS WITH MOBILITY PROBLEMS➤ Contact **Hinsdale Travel Service** (✉ 201 E. Ogden Ave., Suite 100, Hinsdale, IL 60521, ☎ 708/325–1335), a travel agency that benefits from the advice of wheelchair traveler Janice Perkins; and **Wheelchair Journeys** (✉ 16979 Redmond Way, Redmond, WA 98052, ☎ 206/885–2210 or 800/313–4751), which can handle arrangements worldwide.

TRAVELERS WITH DEVELOPMENTAL DISABILITIES➤ Contact the nonprofit **New Directions** (✉ 5276 Hollister Ave., Suite 207, Santa Barbara, CA 93111, ☎ 805/967–2841).

THE GOLD GUIDE / IMPORTANT CONTACTS

TRAVEL GEAR

The **Magellan's** catalog (☎ 800/962–4943, FAX 805/568–5406) includes a section devoted to products designed for travelers with disabilities.

DISCOUNTS & DEALS

AIRFARES

For the lowest airfares to Eastern and Central Europe, call 800/FLY–4–LESS.

CLUBS

Contact **Entertainment Travel Editions** (⊠ Box 1068, Trumbull, CT 06611, ☎ 800/445–4137; $28–$53, depending on destination), **Great American Traveler** (⊠ Box 27965, Salt Lake City, UT 84127, ☎ 800/548–2812; $49.95 per yr), **Moment's Notice Discount Travel Club** (⊠ 7301 New Utrecht Ave., Brooklyn, NY 11204, ☎ 718/234–6295; $25 per yr, single or family), **Privilege Card International** (⊠ 3391 Peachtree Rd. NE, Suite 110, Atlanta, GA 30326, ☎ 404/262–0222 or 800/236–9732; $74.95 per yr), **Travelers Advantage** (⊠ CUC Travel Service, 49 Music Sq. W, Nashville, TN 37203, ☎ 800/548–1116 or 800/648–4037; $49 per yr, single or family), or **Worldwide Discount Travel Club** (⊠ 1674 Meridian Ave., Miami Beach, FL 33139, ☎ 305/534–2082; $50 per yr for family, $40 single).

HOTEL ROOMS

For hotel room rates guaranteed in U.S. dollars, call **Steigenberger Reservation Service** (☎ 800/223–5652).

PASSES

See Train Travel, *below,* and Air Travel *in* Smart Tips A to Z, *below;* and Getting Around by Train in the A to Z section at the end of each country chapter.

STUDENTS

Members of Hostelling International–American Youth Hostels (☞ Students, *below*) are eligible for discounts on car rentals, admissions to attractions, and other selected travel expenses.

PUBLICATIONS

Consult *The Frugal Globetrotter,* by Bruce Northam (⊠ Fulcrum Publishing, 350 Indiana St., Suite 350, Golden, CO 80401, ☎ 800/992–2908; $16.95 plus $4 shipping). For publications that tell how to find the lowest prices on plane tickets, *see* Air Travel, *above.*

DRIVING

AUTO CLUBS

To become a member of AAA, call 800/564–6222. In the United Kingdom, contact the Automobile Association (AA) or the Royal Automobile Club (RAC).

The **Hungarian Automobile Club** (⊠ XIV, Francia út 38/B, ☎ 1/252–8000; when outside Budapest, ☎ 088) runs a 24-hour "Yellow Angels" breakdown service from Budapest. There are repair stations in all major Hungarian towns and emergency telephones on the main highways.

The **Polish Motoring Association** (PZMot) provides free breakdown and repair services for members of affiliated organizations. Check details with Orbis. It is a good idea to carry spare parts, which can still be difficult to get for Western models. There are no motor-rail services in Poland. For emergency road help, dial ☎ 981.

In Romania, the **Automobil Clubul Roman** (ACR; ⊠ Str. Take Ionescu 27, Bucharest, ☎ 01/6507076, FAX 01/3120434) offers mechanical assistance in case of breakdowns and medical and legal assistance at fixed rates in case of accidents. For breakdowns, call 927 in Bucharest and 01/927 elsewhere. Spare parts are scarce, so carry extras. Thefts of parts from vehicles under repair are frequent.

MAPS

In the Czech Republic, **Čedok,** the ubiquitous travel agency, is a good first stop for city maps. In Prague, the **Jan Kanzelsberger** bookshop on Wenceslas Square (⊠ Václavské nám. 42, ☎ 02/2421–7335) has a good selection of hiking maps and auto atlases. In Hungary, good maps are sold at most large gas stations. In Budapest, the **Globe Térképbolt** (Globe Map Store; ⊠ VI, Bajcsy-Zsilinszky út 37, ☎ 1/112–6001) has an excellent supply of domestic and foreign maps. In Poland, check at large bookshops for driving maps, produced by the State Cartographic Publishers and with keys in

English; major hotels will also supply them, and gas stations in cities often have them. Esso driving maps are available at Esso gas stations and sometimes elsewhere. Maps of Bucharest and Romania can be obtained from bookstores, travel agencies, and sidewalk vendors. They may also be obtained from the **Romanian National Tourist Office (ONT)** (☞ Visitor Information, *below*).

E
EMERGENCIES

For country-specific emergency numbers, *see* Emergencies in the A to Z section at the end of each country chapter.

F
FERRIES

In Hungary, ferries operate on the Danube River and on Lake Balaton. Contact **MA-HART** (✉ V, Belgrád rakpart, ☎ 1/118–1704) in Budapest for information. In Poland, you can take ferries or hydrofoils between various points on the Baltic coast, two of the more popular routes being Szczecin to Świnoujście, near the German border on the coast; and Sopot to Hel, farther east near Gdańsk. Ferries also travel daily from Gdańsk to Helsinki and to Oxelösund, Sweden. In Gdańsk contact **Orbis** office in the Hotel Hevelius (✉ Ul. Heweliusa 22, ☎ 058/31–34–56) or the **Polish Baltic Shipping Co.** (✉ Ul. Przemysłowa 1, Gdańsk, ☎ 058/43–18–87 or 058/43–69–78).

G
GAY & LESBIAN TRAVEL

ORGANIZATIONS

The **International Gay Travel Association** (✉ Box 4974, Key West, FL 33041, ☎ 800/448–8550, FAX 305/296–6633), a consortium of more than 1,000 travel companies, can supply names of gay-friendly travel agents, tour operators, and accommodations.

In Poland, contact **Lambda** (✉ Ul. Śniadeckich 1/15, Warszawa, ☎ 022/628–52–22).

PUBLICATIONS

The 16-page monthly newsletter **"Out & About"** (✉ 8 W. 19th St., Suite 401, New York, NY 10011, ☎ 212/645–6922 or 800/929–2268, FAX 800/929–2215; $49 for 10 issues and quarterly calendar) covers gay-friendly resorts, hotels, cruise lines, and airlines.

In Budapest, *Budapest Week* and the *Budapest Sun,* both English-language weekly newspapers, include gay clubs in their nightlife listings; *Mások* is a monthly gay magazine in Hungarian that may be helpful, as well.

TOUR OPERATORS

Toto Tours (✉ 1326 W. Albion Ave., Suite 3W, Chicago, IL 60626, ☎ 312/274–8686 or 800/565–1241, FAX 312/274–8695) offers group tours to worldwide destinations.

TRAVEL AGENCIES

The largest agencies serving gay travelers are **Advance Travel** (✉ 10700 Northwest Fwy., Suite 160, Houston, TX 77092, ☎ 713/682–2002 or 800/292–0500), **Club Travel** (✉ 8739 Santa Monica Blvd., W. Hollywood, CA 90069, ☎ 310/358–2200 or 800/429–8747), **Islanders/Kennedy Travel** (✉ 183 W. 10th St., New York, NY 10014, ☎ 212/242–3222 or 800/988–1181), **Now Voyager** (✉ 4406 18th St., San Francisco, CA 94114, ☎ 415/626–1169 or 800/255–6951), and **Yellowbrick Road** (✉ 1500 W. Balmoral Ave., Chicago, IL 60640, ☎ 312/561–1800 or 800/642–2488). **Skylink Women's Travel** (✉ 2460 W. 3rd St., Suite 215, Santa Rosa, CA 95401, ☎ 707/570–0105 or 800/225–5759) serves lesbian travelers.

H
HEALTH

FINDING A DOCTOR

For its members, the **International Association for Medical Assistance to Travellers** (IAMAT, membership free; ✉ 417 Center St., Lewiston, NY 14092, ☎ 716/754–4883; ✉ 40 Regal Rd., Guelph, Ontario N1K 1B5, ☎ 519/836–0102; ✉ 1287 St. Clair Ave. W, Toronto, Ontario M6E 1B8, ☎ 416/652–0137; ✉ 57 Voirets, 1212 Grand-Lancy, Geneva, Switzerland, no phone) publishes a worldwide directory of English-

THE GOLD GUIDE / IMPORTANT CONTACTS

speaking physicians meeting IAMAT standards.

MEDICAL ASSISTANCE COMPANIES

The following companies are concerned primarily with emergency medical assistance, although they may provide some insurance as part of their coverage. For a list of full-service travel insurance companies, *see* Insurance, *below.*

Contact **International SOS Assistance** (⊠ Box 11568, Philadelphia, PA 19116, ☎ 215/244–1500 or 800/523–8930; ⊠ Box 466, Pl. Bonaventure, Montréal, Québec H5A 1C1, ☎ 514/874–7674 or 800/363–0263; ⊠ 7 Old Lodge Pl., St. Margarets, Twickenham TW1 1RQ, England, ☎ 0181/744–0033), **Medex Assistance Corporation** (⊠ Box 5375, Timonium, MD 21094, ☎ 410/453–6300 or 800/537–2029), **Near Travel Services** (⊠ Box 1339, Calumet City, IL 60409, ☎ 708/868–6700 or 800/654–6700), **Traveler's Emergency Network** (⊠ 1133 15th St. NW, Suite 400, Washington DC, 20005, ☎ 202/828–5894 or 800/275–4836, ☎ 202/828–5896), **TravMed** (⊠ Box 5375, Timonium, MD 21094, ☎ 410/453–6380 or 800/732–5309), or **Worldwide Assistance Services** (⊠ 1133 15th St. NW, Suite 400, Washington, DC 20005, ☎ 202/331–1609 or 800/821–

2828, ☎ 202/828–5896).

PUBLICATIONS

The Safe Travel Book, by Peter Savage (⊠ Jossey-Bass Publishers, Inc., 350 Sansome St., San Francisco, CA 94104, ☎ 800/956–7739, ☎ 800/605–2665; $12.95 plus $5 shipping) is authoritative.

I
INSURANCE

IN CANADA

Contact **Mutual of Omaha** (⊠ Travel Division, 500 University Ave., Toronto, Ontario M5G 1V8, ☎ 416/598-4083; in Canada, 800/465–0267.

IN THE U.S.

Travel insurance covering baggage, health, and trip cancellation or interruptions is available from **Access America** (⊠ 6600 W. Broad St., Richmond, VA 23230, ☎ 804/285–3300 or 800/334–7525), **Carefree Travel Insurance** (⊠ Box 9366, 100 Garden City Plaza, Garden City, NY 11530, ☎ 516/294–0220 or 800/323–3149), **Tele-Trip** (⊠ Mutual of Omaha Plaza, Box 31716, Omaha, NE 68131, ☎ 800/228–9792), **Travel Guard International** (⊠ 1145 Clark St., Stevens Point, WI 54481, ☎ 715/345–0505 or 800/826–1300), **Travel Insured International** (⊠ Box 280568, East Hartford, CT 06128, ☎ 203/528–7663 or 800/243–3174), and **Wallach & Company** (⊠ 107 W. Federal St., Box 480, Middleburg, VA

22117, ☎ 540/687–3166 or 800/237–6615).

IN THE U.K.

The **Association of British Insurers** (⊠ 51 Gresham St., London EC2V 7HQ, ☎ 0171/600–3333) gives advice by phone and publishes the free pamphlet **"Holiday Insurance and Motoring Abroad,"** which sets out typical policy provisions and costs.

L
LODGING

For information on hotel consolidators, *see* Discounts, *above.* For country-specific lodging contacts, *see* Lodging in the A to Z section at the end of each country chapter.

APARTMENT & VILLA RENTAL

Among the companies to contact are **Europa-Let/Tropical Inn-Let, Inc.** (⊠ 92 N. Main St., Ashland, OR 97520, ☎ 541/482–5806 or 800/462–4486, ☎ 541/482–0660), **Interhome** (⊠ 124 Little Falls Rd., Fairfield, NJ 07004, ☎ 201/882–6864, ☎ 201/808–1742), and **Property Rentals International** (⊠ 1008 Mansfield Crossing Rd., Richmond, VA 23236, ☎ 804/378–6054 or 800/220–3332, ☎ 804/379–2073).

M
MAIL

For country-specific mail information, *see* Mail in the A to Z section at the end of each country chapter.

MONEY

For country-specific money information, *see* Money and Expenses in the A to Z section at the end of each country chapter.

ATMS

For specific foreign **Cirrus** locations, call 800/424–7787; for foreign **Plus** locations, consult the Plus directory at your local bank.

CURRENCY EXCHANGE

If your bank doesn't exchange currency, contact **Thomas Cook Currency Services** (☎ 800/287–7362 for locations). **Ruesch International** (☎ 800/424–2923 for locations) can also provide you with foreign banknotes before you leave home and publishes a number of useful brochures, including a "Foreign Currency Guide" and "Foreign Exchange Tips."

TAXES & VAT REFUNDS

For country-specific tax and VAT information, *see* Money and Expenses in the A to Z section at the end of each country chapter.

WIRING FUNDS

Funds can be wired via **MoneyGram**[SM] (for locations and information in the U.S. and Canada, ☎ 800/926–9400), which has subagents in Warsaw (American Express Travel Limited, ☎ 22/635–2002), Prague (American Express Czech, ☎ 22/421–686), and Budapest (American Express Hungary, ☎ 1/266–8680); or **Western Union** (for agent locations or to send money using MasterCard or Visa, ☎ 800/325–6000; in Canada, 800/321–2923; in the U.K., 0800/833833; or visit the Western Union office at the nearest major post office).

P

PACKING

For strategies on packing light, get a copy of *The Packing Book,* by Judith Gilford (✉ Ten Speed Press, Box 7123, Berkeley, CA 94707, ☎ 510/559–1600 or 800/841–2665, FAX 510/524–4588; $7.95 plus $3.50 shipping).

PASSPORTS & VISAS

For country-specific information, *see* Passports and Visas in the A to Z section at the end of each country chapter.

IN THE U.S.

For fees, documentation requirements, and other information, call the State Department's **Office of Passport Services** information line (☎ 202/647–0518).

CANADIANS

For fees, documentation requirements, and other information, call the Ministry of Foreign Affairs and International Trade's **Passport Office** (☎ 819/994–3500 or 800/567–6868).

U.K. CITIZENS

For fees, documentation requirements, and to request an emergency passport, call the **London Passport Office** (☎ 0990/210410).

PHOTO HELP

The **Kodak Information Center** (☎ 800/242–2424) answers consumer questions about film and photography. The *Kodak Guide to Shooting Great Travel Pictures* (available in bookstores; or contact Fodor's Travel Publications, ☎ 800/533–6478; $16.50 plus $4 shipping) explains how to take expert travel photographs.

S

SAFETY

"Trouble-Free Travel," from the AAA, is a booklet of tips for protecting yourself and your belongings when away from home. Send a stamped, self-addressed, legal-size envelope to Trouble-Free Travel (✉ Mail Stop 75, 1000 AAA Dr., Heathrow, FL 32746).

SENIOR CITIZENS

CLUBS

Sears's **Mature Outlook** (✉ Box 10448, Des Moines, IA 50306, ☎ 800/336–6330; annual membership $14.95) includes a lifestyle/travel magazine and membership in the ITC-50 travel club, which offers discounts of up to 50% at participating hotels and restaurants. (☞ Discounts & Deals *in* Smart Travel Tips A to Z).

DISCOUNTS

In Hungary, non-Hungarian senior citizens (men over 60, women over 55) are eligible for a 20% discount on rail travel. Contact or visit

MÁV Passenger Service
(✉ Andrassy út 35,
Budapest VI, ☎ 1/322–
8275) for information.
In Poland, travelers
over 60 receive dis-
counts up to 40% on
LOT air tickets.

EDUCATIONAL TRAVEL

The nonprofit **Elderhos-
tel** (✉ 75 Federal St.,
3rd floor, Boston, MA
02110, ☎ 617/426–
7788), for people 55
and older, has offered
inexpensive study
programs since 1975.
Courses cover every-
thing from marine
science to Greek
mythology and cowboy
poetry. Costs for two-
to three-week interna-
tional trips—including
room, board, and
transportation from the
United States—range
from $1,800 to $4,500.

Interhostel (✉ University of New Hampshire,
6 Garrison Ave., Dur-
ham, NH 03824,
☎ 603/862–1147 or
800/733–9753), for
travelers 50 and older,
has two- to three-
week trips; most last
two weeks and cost
$2,000–$3,500, includ-
ing airfare.

ORGANIZATIONS

Contact the **American
Association of Retired
Persons** (✉ AARP, 601
E St. NW, Washington,
DC 20049, ☎ 202/
434–2277; annual dues
$8 per person or cou-
ple). Its Purchase Privi-
lege Program secures
discounts for members
on lodging, car rentals,
and sightseeing.

HOSTELING

In the United States,
contact **Hostelling**

**International–American
Youth Hostels** (✉ 733
15th St. NW, Suite 840,
Washington, DC
20005, ☎ 202/783–
6161, FAX 202/783–
6171); in Canada,
**Hostelling Interna-
tional–Canada** (✉ 205
Catherine St., Suite 400,
Ottawa, Ontario K2P
1C3, ☎ 613/237–
7884); and in the
United Kingdom, the
**Youth Hostel Association
of England and Wales**
(✉ Trevelyan House,
8 St. Stephen's Hill, St.
Albans, Hertfordshire
AL1 2DY, ☎ 01727/
855215 or 01727/
845047). Membership
(in the U.S., $25; in
Canada, C$26.75; in
the U.K., £9.30) gives
you access to 5,000
hostels in 77 countries
that charge $5–$40 per
person per night.

ORGANIZATIONS

A major contact is the
**Council on International
Educational Exchange**
(✉ Mail orders only:
CIEE, 205 E. 42nd St.,
16th floor, New York,
NY 10017, ☎ 212/
822–2600, FAX 212/
822–2699, info@ciee.
org). The **Educational
Travel Centre** (✉ 438
N. Frances St., Madi-
son, WI 53703, ☎
608/256–5551 or 800/
747–5551, FAX 608/
256–2042) offers rail
passes and low-cost
airline tickets, mostly
for flights that depart
from Chicago.

In Canada, also contact
Travel Cuts (✉ 187
College St., Toronto,
Ontario M5T 1P7, ☎
416/979–2406 or 800/
667–2887).

PUBLICATIONS

Check out the **Berkeley
Guide to Eastern Europe**

(available in book-
stores; or contact
Fodor's Travel Publica-
tions, ☎ 800/533–
6478; $19.50 plus $4
shipping).

T

Country and select city
codes are as follows:
Bulgaria (359), Sofia
(2); Czech Republic
(42), Prague (2);
Hungary (36), Budapest
(1); Poland (48), War-
saw (22); Romania
(40), Bucharest (0);
Slovakia (42),
Bratislava (7).

For local access num-
bers abroad, contact
AT&T USADirect (☎
800/874–4000), **MCI**
Call USA (☎ 800/444–
4444), or **Sprint** Express
(☎ 800/793–1153).

For additional country-
specific telephone
information, *see* Tele-
phones in the A to Z
section at the end of
each country chapter.

Among the companies
that sell tours and
packages to Eastern and
Central Europe, the
following are nationally
known, have a proven
reputation, and offer
plenty of options. For
additional country-
specific tour informa-
tion, *see* Guided Tours
in the A to Z section at
the end of each country
chapter.

GROUP TOURS

SUPER-DELUXE➤ **Aber-
crombie & Kent** (✉
1520 Kensington Rd.,
Oak Brook, IL 60521-
2141, ☎ 708/954–
2944 or 800/323–7308,
FAX 708/954–3324) and
Travcoa (✉ Box 2630,

2350 S.E. Bristol St., Newport Beach, CA 92660, ☎ 714/476–2800 or 800/992–2003, FAX 714/476–2538).

DELUXE➤ **Globus** (✉ 5301 S. Federal Circle, Littleton, CO 80123, ☎ 303/797–2800 or 800/221–0090, FAX 303/795–0962), **Maupintour** (✉ Box 807, 1515 St. Andrews Dr., Lawrence, KS 66047, ☎ 913/843–1211 or 800/255–4266, FAX 913/843–8351), and **Tauck Tours** (✉ Box 5027, 276 Post Rd. W, Westport, CT 06881, ☎ 203/226–6911 or 800/468–2825, FAX 203/221–6828).

FIRST CLASS➤ **Brendan Tours** (✉ 15137 Califa St., Van Nuys, CA 91411, ☎ 818/785–9696 or 800/421–8446, FAX 818/902–9876), **Caravan Tours** (✉ 401 N. Michigan Ave., Chicago, IL 60611, ☎ 312/321–9800 or 800/227–2826), **Cedok Travel** (10 E. 40th St., #3604, New York, NY 10016, ☎ 212/725–0948 or 800/800–8891), **Collette Tours** (✉ 162 Middle St., Pawtucket, RI 02860, ☎ 401/728–3805 or 800/832–4656, FAX 401/728–1380), **General Tours** (✉ 53 Summer St., Keene, NH 03431, ☎ 603/357–5033 or 800/221–2216, FAX 603/357–4548), **Insight International Tours** (✉ 745 Atlantic Ave., #720, Boston, MA 02111, ☎ 617/482–2000 or 800/582–8380, FAX 617/482–2884 or 800/622–5015), **Scantours** (✉ 1535 6th St., #205, Santa Monica, CA 90401-2533, ☎ 310/451–0911 or 800/223–7226, FAX 310/

395–2013), and **Trafalgar Tours** (✉ 11 E. 26th St., New York, NY 10010, ☎ 212/689–8977 or 800/854–0103, FAX 800/457–6644).

BUDGET➤ **Cosmos** (☞ Globus, *above*) and **Trafalgar** (☞ *above*).

PACKAGES

Independent vacation packages that include round-trip airfare and hotel accommodations are available from major airlines and tour operators. Among U.S. carriers, contact **United Vacations** (☎ 800/328–6877). Leading tour operators include **DER Tours** (✉ 11933 Wilshire Blvd., Los Angeles, CA 90025, ☎ 310/479–4140 or 800/782–2424) and **General Tours** (☞ Group Tours, *above*).

THEME TRIPS

Travel Contacts (✉ Box 173, Camberley, GU15 1YE, England, ☎ 0127/667–7217, FAX 0127/66–3477), which represents 150 tour operators, can satisfy travelers to Eastern and Central Europe who have just about any special interest.

ART AND ARCHITECTURE➤ For a variety of educational programs, contact **Smithsonian Study Tours and Seminars** (✉ 1100 Jefferson Dr. SW, Room 3045, MRC 702, Washington, DC 20560, ☎ 202/357–4700, FAX 202/633–9250).

BALLOONING➤ **Buddy Bombard European Balloon Adventures** (✉ 855 Donald Ross Rd., Juno Beach, FL 33408,

☎ 407/775–0039 or 800/862–8537, FAX 407/775–7008) operates balloon holidays in the Czech Republic.

BARGE/RIVER CRUISES➤ Contact **KD River Cruises of Europe** (✉ 2500 Westchester Ave., Purchase, NY 10577, ☎ 914/696–3600 or 800/346–6525, FAX 914/696–0833).

BEER/WINE➤ **MIR Corporation** (✉ 85 S. Washington St., #210, Seattle, WA 98104, ☎ 206/624–7289 or 800/424–7289, FAX 206/624–7360, mir@igc.apc.org) leads you to the finest beers and wines in the Czech Republic and Hungary.

BICYCLING➤ Bike tours are available from **Backroads** (✉ 1516 5th St., Berkeley, CA 94710-1740, ☎ 510/577–1555 or 800/462–2848, FAX 510/527–1444, goactive@Backroads.com).

CRUISING➤ **EuroCruises** (✉ 303 W. 13th St., New York, NY 10014, ☎ 212/691–2099 or 800/688–3876) represents more than 20 European-based cruise lines, with ships of all sizes available.

HISTORY➤ History buffs should contact **Herodot Travel** (✉ 775 E. Blithedale, Box 234, Mill Valley, CA 94941, ☎ FAX 415/381–4031).

HORSEBACK RIDING➤ **FITS Equestrian** (✉ 685 Lateen Rd., Solvang, CA 93463, ☎ 805/688–9494 or 800/666–3487, FAX 805/688–2943) has tours in the Czech Republic and Hungary.

NATURAL HISTORY➤ **Questers** (✉ 381 Park Ave. S, New York, NY 10016, ☎ 212/251–0444 or 800/468–8668, FAX 212/251–0890) explores the wild side of Eastern and Central Europe in the company of expert guides. **Earthwatch** (✉ Box 403, 680 Mt. Auburn St., Watertown, MA 02272, ☎ 617/926–8200 or 800/776–0188, FAX 617/926–8532, info@earthwatch.org, http://www.earthwatch.org) recruits volunteers to serve in its EarthCorps as short-term assistants to scientists on research expeditions.

PERFORMING ARTS➤ **Dailey-Thorp Travel** (✉ 330 W. 58th St., #610, New York, NY 10019-1817, ☎ 212/307–1555 or 800/998–4677, FAX 212/974–1420) specializes in classical-music and opera programs throughout Europe.

SINGLES AND YOUNG ADULTS➤ Travelers 18–35 looking to join a group should try. **Club Europa** (✉ 802 W. Oregon St., Urbana, IL 61801, ☎ 217/344–5863 or 800/331–1882, FAX 217/344–4072) and **Contiki Holidays** (✉ 300 Plaza Alicante, #900, Garden Grove, CA 92640, ☎ 714/740–0808 or 800/266–8454, FAX 714/740–0818).

SPAS➤ Contact **Great Spas of the World** (✉ 211 E. 43rd St., #1404, New York, NY 10017, ☎ 212/599–0382 or 800/826–8062) and **Spa-Finders** (✉ 91 5th Ave., #301, New York, NY 10003-3039, ☎ 212/924–6800 or 800/255–7727).

TRAIN TOURS➤ **Abercrombie & Kent** (☞ Group Tours, *above*) can arrange packages that include rail travel, stays in first-class and deluxe hotels, and a traveling bellhop so you don't have to lug your own bags.

WALKING/HIKING➤ For walking and hiking tours in Eastern and Central Europe, contact **Above the Clouds Trekking** (✉ Box 398, Worcester, MA 01602-0398, ☎ 508/799–4499 or 800/233–4499, FAX 508/797–4779) and **Uniquely Europe** (✉ 2819 1st Ave., #280, Seattle, WA 98121-1113, ☎ 206/441–8682 or 800/426–3615, FAX 206/441–8862).

ORGANIZATIONS

The **National Tour Association** (✉ NTA, 546 E. Main St., Lexington, KY 40508, ☎ 606/226–4444 or 800/755–8687) and the **United States Tour Operators Association** (✉ USTOA, 211 E. 51st St., Suite 12B, New York, NY 10022, ☎ 212/750–7371) can provide lists of members and information on booking tours.

PUBLICATIONS

Contact the USTOA (☞ Organizations, *above*) for its **"Smart Traveler's Planning Kit."** Pamphlets in the kit include the "Worldwide Tour and Vacation Package Finder," "How to Select a Tour or Vacation Package," and information on the organization's consumer protection plan. Also get copy of the Better Business Bureau's **"Tips on Travel**

Packages"** (✉ Publication 24-195, 4200 Wilson Blvd., Arlington, VA 22203; $2).

TRAIN TRAVEL

DISCOUNT PASSES

East Passes are available through travel agents and **Rail Europe** (✉ 226–230 Westchester Ave., White Plains, NY 10604, ☎ 914/682–5172 or 800/438–7245; ✉ 2087 Dundas E., Suite 105, Mississauga, Ontario L4X 1M2, ☎ 416/602–4195), **DER Tours** (✉ Box 1606, Des Plaines, IL 60017, ☎ 800/782–2424, FAX 800/282–7474), or **CIT Tours Corp.** (✉ 342 Madison Ave., Suite 207, New York, NY 10173, ☎ 212/697–2100 or 800/248–8687; in western U.S., 800/248–7245).

FROM THE U.K.

For timetable information on trains bound for Eastern and Central Europe, consult **Cook's European Timetable,** about £10 from Thomas Cook (✉ 378 Strand, London WC2 O2R, ☎ 0171/836–5200, and major branches).

TRAVEL AGENCIES

For names of reputable agencies in your area, contact the **American Society of Travel Agents** (✉ ASTA, 1101 King St., Suite 200, Alexandria, VA 22314, ☎ 703/739–2782), the **Association of Canadian Travel Agents** (✉ Suite 201, 1729 Bank St., Ottawa, Ontario K1V 7Z5, ☎ 613/521–0474, FAX 613/521–0805), or the **Association of British Travel Agents** (✉ 55–57 Newman St., London

W1P 4AH, ☎ 0171/
637–2444, FAX 0171/
637–0713).

TRAVEL GEAR

For travel apparel,
appliances, personal-
care items, and other
travel necessities, get a
free catalog from
Magellan's (☎ 800/
962–4943, FAX 805/
568–5406), **Orvis
Travel** (☎ 800/541–
3541, FAX 540/343–
7053), or **TravelSmith**
(☎ 800/950–1600, FAX
415/455–0554).

ELECTRICAL
CONVERTERS

Send a self-addressed,
stamped envelope to the
Franzus Company (✉
Customer Service, Dept.
B50, Murtha Industrial
Park, Box 142, Beacon
Falls, CT 06403, ☎
203/723–6664) for a
copy of the free bro-
chure "Foreign Electric-
ity Is No Deep, Dark
Secret."

U

U.S.
GOVERNMENT
TRAVEL BRIEFINGS

The U.S. Department
of State's American
Citizens Services office
(✉ Room 4811, Wash-
ington, DC 20520;
enclose SASE) issues
**Consular Information
Sheets** on all foreign
countries. These cover
issues such as crime,
security, political cli-
mate, and health risks
as well as listing em-
bassy locations, entry
requirements, and
currency regulations
and providing other
useful information. For
the latest information,
stop in at any U.S.
passport office, con-
sulate, or embassy; call

the interactive hot line
(☎ 202/647–5225, FAX
202/647–3000); or
with your PC's modem,
tap into the depart-
ment's computer bul-
letin board (☎ 202/
647–9225).

V

VISITOR
INFORMATION

BULGARIAN NATIONAL
TOURIST OFFICE➣ In
the United States and
Canada: **Balkan Holi-
days** (authorized
agent), ✉ 41 E. 42nd
St., Suite 508, New
York, NY 10017, ☎
212/573–5530, FAX
212/573–5538. In the
United Kingdom: The
**Bulgarian National
Tourist Office** no longer
exists; for information
contact **Balkan Holi-
days** (✉ 19 Conduit
St., London W1R 9TD,
☎ 0171/491–4499).

CZECH REPUBLIC➣
The tourist desk of the
Czech Cultural Center,
a state-run informa-
tion service, dispenses
brochures, maps, and
the like. In the United
States: ✉ 1109–1111
Madison Ave., New
York, NY 10028,
☎ 212/288–0830,
FAX 212/288–0971.
In Canada: ✉ Box 198,
Exchange Tower, 2
First Canadian Place,
14th floor, Toronto,
Ontario M5X 1A6,
☎ 416/367–3432, FAX
416/367–3492. In the
United Kingdom: **Czech
Centre** (✉ 95 Great
Portland St., London
W1N5RA, ☎ 0171/
291–9922, FAX 0171/
436–8300).

HUNGARIAN NATIONAL
TOURIST OFFICE
(IBUSZ)➣ In the
United States and

Canada: ✉ 150 E. 58th
St., New York, NY
10155, ☎ 212/355–
0240, FAX 212/207–
4103. In Canada,
contact the **Hungarian
Consulate General
Office** (✉ 121 Bloor St.
E, Suite 1115, Toronto
M4W3M5, Ontario,
☎ 416/923–8981, FAX
416/923–2732). In the
United Kingdom:
**Hungarian National
Tourist Board** (✉ Box
4336, London, SW18
4XE, ☎ 0181/871–
4009). Calls cost 49p
per minute peak rate or
39p per minute cheap
rate.

POLISH NATIONAL
TOURIST OFFICE➣ In
the United States and
Canada: ✉ 275 Madi-
son Ave., Suite 1711,
New York, NY 10016,
☎ 212/338–9412,
FAX 212/338–9283. In
the United Kingdom: ✉
Remo House, 1st floor,
310–312 Regent St.,
London W1R 5AJ,
☎ 0171/580–8811,
FAX 0171/580–8866.

ROMANIAN NATIONAL
TOURIST OFFICE➣ In
the United States and
Canada: ✉ 342 Madi-
son Ave., Suite 210,
New York, NY 10173,
☎ 212/697–6971,
FAX 212/697–6972. In
the United Kingdom:
✉ 83A Marylebone
High St., London
W1M 3DE, ☎ FAX
0171/224–3692).

SLOVAKIA➣ In the
United States: **The
Slovak Information
Center** (✉ 406 E. 67th
St., New York, NY
10021, ☎ 212/
737–3971, FAX 212/
737–3454) has a walk-
in information center
and can also provide
travel information via
phone, fax, or e-mail.

THE GOLD GUIDE / IMPORTANT CONTACTS

In Canada: **Slovak Culture and Information Center** (✉ 12 Birch Ave., Toronto, Ontario M4V 1C8, ☎ 416/925–0008, FAX 416/925–0009). In the United Kingdom: ✉ Embassy of the Slovak Republic, Information Dept., 25 Kensington Palace Gardens, London W8 4QY, ☎ 0171/243–0803, FAX 0171/727–5824.

W

WEATHER

For current conditions and forecasts, plus the local time and helpful travel tips, call the **Weather Channel Connection** (☎ 900/932–8437; 95¢ per minute) from a Touch-Tone phone.

The *International Traveler's Weather Guide* (✉ Weather Press, Box 660606, Sacramento, CA 95866, ☎ 916/974–0201 or 800/972–0201; $10.95 includes shipping), written by two meteorologists, provides month-by-month information on temperature, humidity, and precipitation in more than 175 cities worldwide.

SMART TRAVEL TIPS A TO Z

Basic Information on Traveling in Eastern and Central Europe and Savvy Tips to Make Your Trip a Breeze

A

AIR TRAVEL

If time is an issue, **always look for nonstop flights,** which require no change of plane. If possible, **avoid connecting flights,** which stop at least once and can involve a change of plane, even though the flight number remains the same; if the first leg is late, the second waits.

For better service, **fly smaller or regional carriers,** which often have higher passenger-satisfaction ratings. Sometimes they have such in-flight amenities as leather seats or greater legroom, and they often have better food.

CUTTING COSTS

The Sunday travel section of most newspapers is a good place to look for deals. *See also* Travel Passes, *below.*

MAJOR AIRLINES➤ The least-expensive airfares from the major airlines are priced for round-trip travel and are subject to restrictions. Usually, you must **book in advance and buy the ticket within 24 hours** to get cheaper fares, and you may have to **stay over a Saturday night.** The lowest fare is subject to availability, and only a small percentage of the plane's total seats is sold at that price. It's smart to **call a number of airlines, and**

when you are quoted a good price, book it on the spot—the same fare may not be available on the same flight the next day. Airlines generally allow you to change your return date for a $25 to $50 fee. If you don't use your ticket, you can apply the cost toward the purchase of a new ticket, again for a small charge. However, most low-fare tickets are nonrefundable. To get the lowest airfare, **check different routings.** If your destination has more than one gateway, **compare prices to different airports.**

FROM THE U.K.➤ To save money on flights, **look into an APEX or Super-PEX ticket.** APEX tickets must be booked in advance and have certain restrictions. Super-PEX tickets can be purchased right at the airport.

CONSOLIDATORS➤ Consolidators buy tickets for scheduled flights at reduced rates from the airlines, then sell them at prices below the lowest available from the airlines directly—usually without advance restrictions. Sometimes you can even get your money back if you need to return the ticket. Carefully read the fine print detailing penalties for changes and cancellations. If you doubt the reliability of a consolidator, **confirm your**

reservation with the airline.

ALOFT

AIRLINE FOOD➤ If you hate airline food, **ask for special meals when booking.** These can be vegetarian, low cholesterol, or kosher, for example; commonly prepared to order in smaller quantities than standard fare, they can be tastier.

JET LAG➤ To avoid this syndrome, which occurs when travel disrupts your body's natural cycles, try to maintain a normal routine. At night, **get some sleep.** By day, move about the cabin to **stretch your legs; eat light meals, and drink water—not alcohol.**

SMOKING➤ Smoking is not allowed on flights of six hours or less within the continental United States. Smoking is also prohibited on flights within Canada. For U.S. flights longer than six hours or international flights, **contact your carrier regarding their smoking policy.** Some carriers have prohibited smoking throughout their system; others allow smoking only on certain routes or even certain departures of that route.

TRAVEL PASSES

You can **save on air travel** within Europe if you plan on traveling to and from Prague aboard Czech Airlines. As part of their Euro Flyer program, you can then buy between three and nine flight coupons, which are valid on flights to more than 100 European cities. At $120 each, these coupons are a good deal, and the fine print still allows you plenty of freedom.

LOT also offers discounts of from 20% to 40% for young people under 25 and those over 60. The LOT Voyager Club allows members to collect air miles and to use Polish VIP lounges.

AIRPORT TRANSFERS

For the best way to get between the airport and a your destination, *see* Arriving and Departing in the A to Z section at the end of each country chapter, or in the A to Z section of the city you are flying into.

B
BUS TRAVEL

Bus travel is generally more costly than travel by train, although this varies by country. In some instances, especially where trains are largely local (and stop seemingly every 100 feet), buses are actually speedier than rail travel. Comfort is minimal, though; roads tend to be bumpy and seats lumpy. Buses are generally tidier; train bathrooms are notoriously rank. It's a bit of a gamble; seats on buses are a rarity during prime traveling hours, and drivers don't always stop where they should, although most

leave promptly on time (especially when you're still waiting in line for a ticket). Comfort and fares vary drastically by nation; *see* chapters on individual countries for more information.

BUSINESS HOURS

For country-specific opening and closing times and business hours, *see* Opening and Closing Times in the A to Z section at the end of each country chapter.

C
CAMERAS, CAMCORDERS, & COMPUTERS

IN TRANSIT

Always **keep your film, tape, or disks out of the sun**; never put these on the dashboard of a car. Carry an extra supply of batteries, and **be prepared to turn on your camera, camcorder, or laptop computer for security personnel** to prove that it's real.

X RAYS

Always **ask for hand inspection at security.** Such requests are virtually always honored at U.S. airports and are usually accommodated abroad. Photographic film becomes clouded after successive exposure to airport X-ray machines. Videotape and computer disks are not harmed by X rays, but **keep your tapes and disks away from metal detectors.**

CUSTOMS

Before departing, **register your foreign-made camera or laptop with U.S. Customs.** If your equipment is U.S.-made, call the consulate of the

country you'll be visiting to find out whether it should be registered with local customs upon arrival.

CAR RENTAL

The big drawback here is price—rentals can rival airfare for the most expensive transport alternative. The pluses are a freewheeling itinerary and lots of luggage space. Two restrictions to keep in mind: **Don't plan on renting a car in Western Europe and dropping it off in Eastern Europe.** Such one-way rentals are usually prohibited (or prohibitively expensive). Second, **try to get a car that takes leaded gas, because unleaded can be rare.**

CUTTING COSTS

To get the best deal, **book through a travel agent who is willing to shop around.** Ask your agent to **look for fly-drive packages,** which also save you money, and **ask if local taxes are included** in the rental or fly-drive price. These can be as high as 20% in some destinations. Don't forget to find out about required deposits, cancellation penalties, drop-off charges, and the cost of any required insurance coverage.

Also **ask your travel agent about a company's customer-service record.** How has it responded to late plane arrivals and vehicle mishaps? Are there often lines at the rental counter, and—if you're traveling during a holiday period—does a confirmed reservation guarantee you a car?

Always **find out what equipment is standard** at your destination before specifying what you want; automatic transmission and air-conditioning are usually optional—and very expensive.

Be sure to **look into wholesalers**—companies that do not own their own fleets but rent in bulk from those that do and often offer better rates than traditional car-rental operations. Prices are best during off-peak periods; rentals booked through wholesalers must be paid for before you leave the United States.

INSURANCE

When driving a rented car, you are generally responsible for any damage to or loss of the rental vehicle. Before you rent, **see what coverage you already have** under the terms of your personal auto-insurance policy and credit cards.

If you do not have auto insurance or an umbrella insurance policy that covers damage to third parties, purchasing CDW or LDW is highly recommended.

Collision policies that car-rental companies sell for European rentals typically do not cover stolen vehicles. Before you buy additional coverage for theft, find out if your credit card or personal auto insurance will cover the loss.

LICENSE REQUIREMENTS

In most Eastern and Central European countries, U.S. and Canadian driver's licenses are acceptable. An International Driver's Permit, available from the American or Canadian Automobile Association, is a good idea and a requirement for British citizens.

SURCHARGES

Ask whether the car-rental rate includes the VAT. Before you pick up a car in one city and leave it in another, **ask about drop-off charges or one-way service fees,** which can be substantial. Note, too, that some rental agencies charge extra if you return the car before the time specified on your contract. To avoid a hefty refueling fee, **fill the tank just before you turn in the car**—but be aware that gas stations near the rental outlet may overcharge.

CHILDREN & TRAVEL

When traveling with children, **plan ahead** and **involve your youngsters** as you outline your trip. When packing, **include a supply of things to keep them busy** en route (☞ Children & Travel *in* Important Contacts A to Z, *above*). On sightseeing days, try to **schedule activities of special interest to your children,** like a trip to a zoo or a playground. If you **plan your itinerary around seasonal festivals,** you'll never lack for things to do. In addition, **check local newspapers for special events** mounted by public libraries, museums, and parks.

BABY-SITTING

For recommended local sitters, **check with your hotel desk.**

DRIVING

If you are renting a car, don't forget to **arrange for a car seat when you reserve.** Sometimes they're free.

FLYING

As a general rule, infants under two not occupying a seat fly at greatly reduced fares and occasionally for free. If your children are two or older, **ask about special children's fares.** Age limits for these fares vary among carriers. Rules also vary regarding unaccompanied minors, so again, check with your airline.

BAGGAGE> In general, the adult baggage allowance applies to children paying half or more of the adult fare. If you are traveling with an infant, **ask about carry-on allowances** before departure. In general, for infants charged 10% of the adult fare, you are allowed one carry-on bag and a collapsible stroller, which may have to be checked; you may be limited to less if the flight is full.

SAFETY SEATS> According to the FAA, it's a good idea to **use safety seats aloft** for children weighing less than 40 pounds. Airline policies vary. U.S. carriers allow FAA-approved models but usually require that you buy a ticket, even if your child would otherwise ride free, since the seats must be strapped

SMART TRAVEL TIPS / THE GOLD GUIDE

into regular seats. However, some U.S. and foreign-flag airlines may require you to hold your baby during takeoff and landing—defeating the seat's purpose. Other foreign carriers may not allow infant seats at all or may charge a child fare rather than an infant fare for their use.

FACILITIES➤ When making your reservation, **request children's meals or freestanding bassinets** if you need them; the latter are available only to those seated at the bulkhead, where there's enough legroom. If you don't need a bassinet, **think twice before requesting bulkhead seats**—the only storage space for in-flight necessities is in inconveniently distant overhead bins.

GAMES

Milton Bradley and Parker Brothers have travel versions of some of their most popular games, including Yahtzee, Trouble, Sorry, and Monopoly. Prices run $5 to $8. Look for them in the travel section of your local toy store.

LODGING

Most hotels allow children under a certain age to stay in their parents' room at no extra charge; others charge them as extra adults. Be sure to **ask about the cutoff age.**

CUSTOMS & DUTIES

To speed your clearance through customs, **keep receipts for all your purchases abroad** and **be ready to show the inspector what you've bought.** If you feel that you've been incorrectly or unfairly charged a duty, you can **appeal assessments in dispute.** First ask to see a supervisor. If you are still unsatisfied, **write to the port director** at your point of entry, sending your customs receipt and any other appropriate documentation. The address will be listed on your receipt. If you still don't get satisfaction, you can take your case to customs headquarters in Washington.

IN EASTERN & CENTRAL EUROPE

You may import duty-free into the Czech Republic, Slovakia, Hungary, Poland, or Bulgaria 250 cigarettes or the equivalent in tobacco, 1 liter of spirits, and 2 liters of wine (in Poland, ½ liter of spirits and 2 liters of wine). In addition to the above, you are permitted to import into the Czech Republic gifts valued at up to 1,000 Kčs (approximately $35); to Poland, gifts valued at up to $200; and to Hungary, gifts valued up to 8,000 Ft. You may bring into Romania 200 cigarettes, 2 liters of spirits, 4 liters of wine or beer, 2 cameras only and 20 rolls of film, and one small movie camera, though you may be charged duty on electronic goods.

If you are bringing into any of these countries any valuables or foreign-made equipment from home, such as cameras, it's wise to carry the original receipts with you or register the items with U.S. Customs before you leave (Form 4457). Otherwise you could end up paying duty upon your return. When traveling to Romania, you should declare video cameras, personal computers, and expensive jewelry upon arrival.

IN THE U.S.

You may bring home $400 worth of foreign goods duty-free if you've been out of the country for at least 48 hours and haven't already used the $400 allowance, or any part of it, in the past 30 days.

Travelers 21 or older may bring back 1 liter of alcohol duty-free, provided the beverage laws of the state through which they reenter the United States allow it. In addition, regardless of their age, they are allowed 100 non-Cuban cigars and 200 cigarettes. Antiques, which the U.S. Customs Service defines as objects more than 100 years old, are duty-free. Original works of art done entirely by hand are also duty-free. These include, but are not limited to, paintings, drawings, and sculptures.

Duty-free, travelers may mail packages valued at up to $200 to themselves and up to $100 to others, with a limit of one parcel per addressee per day (and no alcohol or tobacco products or perfume valued at more than $5); on the outside, the package must be labeled as either for personal use or as an unsolicited gift, and a list of its contents and their retail value must be attached. Mailed items do not affect your duty-free allowance on your return.

IN CANADA

If you've been out of Canada for at least seven days, you may bring in C$500 worth of goods duty-free. If you've been away for fewer than seven days but for more than 48 hours, the duty-free allowance drops to C$200; if your trip lasts between 24 and 48 hours, the allowance is C$50. You cannot pool allowances with family members. Goods claimed under the C$500 exemption may follow you by mail; those claimed under the lesser exemptions must accompany you.

Alcohol and tobacco products may be included in the seven-day and 48-hour exemptions but not in the 24-hour exemption. If you meet the age requirements of the province or territory through which you reenter Canada, you may bring in, duty-free, 1.14 liters (40 imperial ounces) of wine or liquor *or* 24 12-ounce cans or bottles of beer or ale. If you are 16 or older, you may bring in, duty-free, 200 cigarettes, 50 cigars or cigarillos, and 400 tobacco sticks or 400 grams of manufactured tobacco. Alcohol and tobacco must accompany you on your return.

An unlimited number of gifts with a value of up to C$60 each may be mailed to Canada duty-free. These do not affect

your duty-free allowance on your return. Label the package "Unsolicited Gift—Value Under $60." Alcohol and tobacco are excluded.

IN THE U.K.

From countries outside the EU, including the countries covered in this book, you may import, duty-free, 200 cigarettes, 100 cigarillos, 50 cigars, or 250 grams of tobacco; 1 liter of spirits or 2 liters of fortified or sparkling wine or liqueurs; 2 liters of still table wine; 60 milliliters of perfume; 250 milliliters of toilet water; plus £136 worth of other goods, including gifts and souvenirs.

D
DINING

For country-specific dining information, *see* Dining *in* Pleasures and Pastimes at the beginning of each country chapter. Additional city-specific dining information may also be found at the start of a city's dining listings.

DISABILITIES & ACCESSIBILITY

Provisions for travelers with disabilities in Eastern and Central Europe are extremely limited; probably the best solution is to **travel with a nondisabled companion.** While many hotels, especially large American or international chains, offer some wheelchair-accessible rooms, special facilities at museums, restaurants, and on public transportation are difficult to find. In

Poland wheelchairs are available at all airports, and most trains have special seats designated for people with disabilities, but it is wise to notify ahead. Generally speaking, Romania is not very friendly toward travelers with disabilities. Some of the newer hotels are wheelchair accessible, but beyond that, a traveler with a disability will have a difficult time here.

When discussing accessibility with an operator or reservationist, **ask hard questions.** Are there any stairs, inside *or* out? Are there grab bars next to the toilet *and* in the shower/tub? How wide is the doorway to the room? To the bathroom? For the most extensive facilities, meeting the latest legal specifications, **opt for newer accommodations,** which more often have been designed with access in mind. Older properties or ships must usually be retrofitted and may offer more limited facilities as a result. Be sure to **discuss your needs before booking.**

DISCOUNTS & DEALS

You shouldn't have to pay for a discount. In fact, you may already be eligible for all kinds of savings. Here are some time-honored strategies for getting the best deal.

LOOK IN YOUR WALLET

When you **use your credit card to make travel purchases,** you may get free travel accident insurance, collision damage insurance, and medical or legal assistance, depending on the card and the bank that issued it. American Express, Visa, and MasterCard provide one or more of these services, so **get a copy of your card's travel benefits.** If you are a member of the AAA or an oil-company-sponsored road-assistance plan, always **ask hotel or car-rental reservationists for auto-club discounts.** Some clubs offer additional discounts on tours, cruises, or admission to attractions. And don't forget that auto-club membership entitles you to free maps and trip-planning services.

SENIORS CITIZENS & STUDENTS

As a senior-citizen traveler, you may be eligible for special rates, but you should mention your senior-citizen status up front. If you're a student or under 26, you can also get discounts, especially if you have an official ID card (☞ Senior-Citizen Discounts *and* Students on the Road, *below*).

DIAL FOR DOLLARS

To save money, **look into "1-800" discount reservations services,** which often have lower rates. These services use their buying power to get a better price on hotels, airline tickets, and sometimes even car rentals. When booking a room, always **call the hotel's local toll-free number** (if one is available) rather than the central reservations number—you'll often get a better price. Ask the reservationist about

special packages or corporate rates, which are usually available even if you're not traveling on business.

JOIN A CLUB?

Discount clubs can be a legitimate source of savings, but you must use the participating hotels and visit the participating attractions in order to realize any benefits. Remember, too, that you have to pay a fee to join, so **determine if you'll save enough to warrant your membership fee.** Before booking with a club, **make sure the hotel or other supplier isn't offering a better deal.**

GET A GUARANTEE

When shopping for the best deal on hotels and car rentals, **look for guaranteed exchange rates,** which protect you against a falling dollar. With your rate locked in, you won't pay more, even if the price goes up in the local currency.

DRIVING

The plus side of driving is an itinerary free from the constraints of bus and train schedules and lots of trunk room for extra baggage. The negatives are many, however (☞ Car Rental, *above*), not the least of which are shabbily maintained secondary roads, the risk of theft and vandalism, and difficulty finding gas. However, car travel does make it much easier to get to out-of-the-way monasteries and other sights not easily accessible by public transportation.

Good road maps are usually available.

A word of caution: If you have any alcohol whatsoever in your body, **do not drive after drinking in Eastern and Central Europe.** Penalties are fierce, and the blood-alcohol limit is practically zero. (In Hungary, it *is* zero.)

ROADS & GASOLINE

Eastern and Central Europe's main roads are built to a fairly high standard. There are now quite substantial stretches of highway on main routes, and a lot of rebuilding is being done. Gas stations are fewer than in the West, sited at intervals of about 48 kilometers (30 miles) along main routes and on the outskirts of large towns. Very few stations remain open after 9:30 PM. At least two grades of gasoline are sold in Eastern and Central European countries, usually 90–93 octane (regular) and 94–98 octane (super). Lead-free gasoline is available in most gas stations in Poland and Hungary, but in few elsewhere. In Romania, the supply of gas to filling stations is by no means regular, so there are sometimes long lines and considerable delays. **Get into the habit of filling your tank whenever you see a gas station** to avoid being stranded.

For additional country-specific information relating to roads, gasoline, and insurance, *see* Getting Around By Car in the A to Z section at the end of each country chapter.

FROM THE U.K.

Theoretically it's possible to travel by car from the United Kingdom to Eastern and Central Europe, although it's really not recommended due to lack of parts and mechanical know-how. However, if you do choose to drive your own vehicle, **don't leave home without the car registration, third-party insurance, driver's license, and (if you're not the car's owner) a notarized letter of permission from the owner.** The vehicle must bear a country ID sticker.

The best ferry ports for Eastern and Central Europe are Rotterdam, Holland, or Ostende, Belgium, from which you drive to Cologne (Köln), Germany, and then through either Dresden or Frankfurt and on to Prague.

F

FERRIES

Ferries offer a pleasant and cheap mode of transportation to Eastern and Central Europe, although you have to be fairly close to your destination already to hop a Europe-bound ferry or hydrofoil. Flying into the appropriate hub, however, is an option. Water bookings connect Denmark and Sweden to eastern Germany, and Copenhagen, Denmark, to Świnoujście and Gdańsk, Poland. A hydrofoil shuttles visitors from Vienna to Bratislava, Slovakia, or Budapest, Hungary. For

further country-specific information, *see* Arriving and Departing in the A to Z section in Budapest (Chapter 4); Gdańsk and the Northeast (Chapter 5), and the Poland A to Z section; the Black Sea Golden Coast (Chapter 6), and the Bulgaria A to Z section; and the Black Sea Coast and Danube Delta (Chapter 7).

G

GAY & LESBIAN TRAVEL

Even in Budapest, Hungary's gay population keeps a fairly low profile. Budapest's thermal baths are popular meeting places, as are the city's several gay bars and clubs, which you can find listed in English-language newspapers and the monthly magazine, *Mások*.

Gay and lesbian organization is a relatively new thing in Poland, and clubs and meeting points change addresses frequently. One of the longest-standing gay organizations is Lambda (☞ Gay and Lesbian Travel *in* Important Contacts A to Z, *above*).

H

HEALTH

You may gain weight, but there are few other serious health hazards for the traveler in Eastern and Central Europe. Tap water tastes bad but is generally drinkable; when it runs rusty out of the tap or the aroma of chlorine is overpower-

ing, it might help to **have some iodine tablets or bottled water handy.** Vegetarians and those on special diets may have a problem with the heavy local cuisine, which is based almost exclusively on pork and beef. To keep your vitamin intake above the danger levels, **buy fresh fruits and vegetables at seasonal street markets**—regular grocery stores often don't sell them. Milk in Romania or Bulgaria may not be pasteurized and can make Westerners sick; **stick to cheese to satisfy calcium cravings.**

In Romania you should avoid drinking tap water when outside of Bucharest, as it is often contaminated with such things as cholera. When traveling with children, avoid drinking tap water completely, as there is a heavy lead content.

SHOTS & MEDICATIONS

No vaccinations are required for entry into any of the Eastern and Central European countries covered in this book, but selective vaccinations are recommended by the International Association for Medical Assistance to Travellers (☞ Health *in* Important Contacts A to Z, *above*). Those traveling in forested areas of most Eastern and Central European countries should consider vaccinating themselves against Central European, or tick-borne, encephalitis. Schedule vaccinations well in advance of departure because some require several doses, and others may cause uncomfortable side effects.

To avoid problems clearing customs, diabetic travelers carrying needles and syringes should have on hand a letter from their physician confirming their need for insulin injections.

I
INSURANCE

Travel insurance can protect your monetary investment, replace your luggage and its contents, or provide for medical coverage should you fall ill during your trip. Most tour operators, travel agents, and insurance agents sell specialized health-and-accident, flight, trip-cancellation, and luggage insurance as well as comprehensive policies with some or all of these coverages. Comprehensive policies may also reimburse you for delays due to weather—an important consideration if you're traveling during the winter months. Some health-insurance policies do not cover preexisting conditions, but waivers may be available in specific cases. Coverage is sold by the companies listed in Important Contacts A to Z; these companies act as the policy's administrators. The actual insurance is usually underwritten by a well-known name, such as The Travelers or Continental Insurance.

Before you make any purchase, **review your existing health and home-owner policies** to find out whether they cover expenses incurred while traveling.

BAGGAGE

Airline liability for baggage is limited to $1,250 per person on domestic flights. On international flights, it amounts to $9.07 per pound or $20 per kilogram for checked baggage (roughly $640 per 70-pound bag) and $400 per passenger for unchecked baggage. Insurance for losses exceeding the terms of your airline ticket can be bought directly from the airline at check-in for about $10 per $1,000 of coverage; note that it excludes a rather extensive list of items, shown on your airline ticket.

COMPREHENSIVE

Comprehensive insurance policies include all the coverages described above plus some that may not be available in more specific policies. If you have purchased an expensive vacation, especially one that involves travel abroad, comprehensive insurance is a must; **look for policies that include trip-delay insurance,** which will protect you in the event that weather problems cause you to miss your flight, tour, or cruise. A few insurers will also sell you a waiver for preexisting medical conditions. Some of the companies that offer both these features are Access America, Carefree Travel, Travel Insured International, and TravelGuard (☞ Insurance *in* Important Contacts A to Z).

FLIGHT

You should **think twice before buying flight insurance.** Often purchased as a last-minute impulse at the airport, it pays a lump sum when a plane crashes, either to a beneficiary if the insured dies or sometimes to a surviving passenger who loses his or her eyesight or a limb. Supplementing the airlines' coverage described in the limits-of-liability paragraphs on your ticket, it's expensive and basically unnecessary. Charging an airline ticket to a major credit card often automatically provides you with coverage that may also extend to travel by bus, train, and ship.

HEALTH

Medicare generally does not cover health care costs outside the United States; nor do many privately issued policies. If your own health-insurance policy does not cover you outside the United States, **consider buying supplemental medical coverage.** It can reimburse you for $1,000–$150,000 worth of medical and/or dental expenses incurred as a result of an accident or illness during a trip. These policies also may include a personal-accident, or death-and-dismemberment, provision, which pays a lump sum ranging from $15,000 to $500,000 to your beneficiaries if you die or to you if you lose one or more limbs or your eyesight, and a medical-assistance provision, which may either reimburse you for the cost of referrals, evacuation, or repatriation and other services, or automatically enroll you as a member of a particular medical-assistance company. (☞ Health *in* Important Contacts A to Z, *above*.)

Due to the poor conditions of most medical facilities in Eastern and Central Europe, travelers should **consider evacuation insurance** to help get them out of the country in the event of an emergency.

U.K. TRAVELERS

You can buy an annual travel-insurance policy, valid for most vacations during the year in which it's purchased. If you are pregnant or have a preexisting medical condition, make sure you're covered before buying such a policy.

TRIP

Without insurance, you will lose all or most of your money if you cancel your trip, regardless of the reason. Especially if your airline ticket, cruise, or package tour is nonrefundable and cannot be changed, it's essential that you **buy trip-cancellation-and-interruption insurance.** When considering how much coverage you need, look for a policy that will cover the cost of your trip plus the nondiscounted price of a one-way airline ticket should you need to return home early. Read the fine print carefully, especially sections that define "family member" and "preexisting medical conditions." Also **consider default or**

bankruptcy insurance, which protects you against a supplier's failure to deliver. Be aware, however, that if you buy such a policy from a travel agency, tour operator, airline, or cruise line, it may not cover default by the firm in question.

L
LANGUAGE

For country-specific information about language issues, *see* Language in the A to Z section at the end of each country chapter.

LODGING

If your experience of Eastern and Central European hotels is limited to capital cities such as Prague and Budapest, you may be pleasantly surprised. There are baroque mansions turned guest houses and elegant high-rise resorts, not to mention bed-and-breakfast inns presided over by matronly babushkas. Many facilities throughout the region are being upgraded.

Outside major cities, hotels and inns are more rustic than elegant. Standards of service generally do not suffer, but in most rural areas the definition of "luxury" includes little more than a television and a private bathroom. In some instances, you may have no choice but to stay in one of the cement high-rise hotels that scar skylines from Poland to the Czech Republic to Romania. It's hard to say why Communists required their hotels to be as big and impersonal as

possible, but they did, and it may take a few more years to exorcise or "beautify" these ubiquitous monsters.

In rural Eastern and Central Europe, you may have difficulty parting with more than $25–$30 per night for lodgings. Reservations are vital if you plan to visit Prague, Budapest, Warsaw, or most other major cities during the summer season. Reservations are a good idea but aren't imperative if you plan to strike out into the countryside.

For country-specific lodging information, *see* Lodging in Pleasures and Pastimes at the beginning of each country chapter. Additional city-specific lodging information may also be found at the start of a city's lodging listings.

APARTMENT & VILLA RENTAL

If you want a home base that's roomy enough for a family and comes with cooking facilities, **consider taking a furnished rental.** This can also save you money, but not always—some rentals are luxury properties (economical only when your party is large). Home-exchange directories list rentals—often second homes owned by prospective house swappers—and some services search for a house or apartment for you (even a castle if that's your fancy) and handle the paperwork. Some send an illustrated catalog; others send photographs only of specific properties, sometimes at a charge;

THE GOLD GUIDE / SMART TRAVEL TIPS

up-front registration fees may apply.

HOME EXCHANGE

If you would like to find a house, an apartment, or some other type of vacation property to exchange for your own while on holiday, **become a member of a home-exchange organization,** which will send you its updated listings of available exchanges for a year and will include your own listing in at least one of them. Arrangements for the actual exchange are made by the two parties involved, not by the organization.

M

MAIL

For country-specific information, *see* Mail in the A to Z section at the end of each country chapter.

MEDICAL
ASSISTANCE

No one plans to get sick while traveling, but it happens, so **consider signing up with a medical assistance company.** These outfits provide referrals, emergency evacuation or repatriation, 24-hour telephone hot lines for medical consultation, cash for emergencies, and other personal and legal assistance. They also dispatch medical personnel and arrange for the relay of medical records. Coverage varies by plan, so **read the fine print carefully.**

MONEY

In addition to the information below, for country-specific information about all issues relating to money and expenses, *see* Money and Expenses in the A to Z section at the end of each country chapter.

ATMS

CASH ADVANCES➣ Before leaving home, **make sure your credit cards have been programmed for ATM use in Eastern and Central Europe.** Note that Discover is accepted mostly only in the United States. Local bank cards often do not work overseas either; **ask your bank about a Visa debit card,** which works like a bank card but can be used at any ATM displaying a Visa logo.

TRANSACTION FEES➣ Although fees charged for ATM transactions may be higher abroad than at home, Cirrus and Plus exchange rates are excellent because they are based on wholesale rates offered only by major banks.

COSTS

Prices in Eastern and Central Europe continue to escalate, as most countries experiment with "economic shock therapy," the radical transformation of state-controlled economies into market economies. Poland, for example, had a stunning 2,000% hyperinflation rate in January 1990. Current Polish inflation rates are running at about 30% per year. What all this means to the Western traveler is that quoted restaurant, hotel, and transportation costs will almost certainly have changed by the time

you read this. Use the prices given as a rough and relative guide. Be advised that many hotel and other tourist-oriented enterprises in Eastern and Central Europe list prices in deutsche marks.

TAXES

VAT➣ With the exception of Bulgaria and Romania, most Eastern and Central European countries have some form of value-added tax (VAT); rates vary from 7% in Poland to 25% in Hungary. VAT rebate rules vary by country, but you'll need to present your receipts on departure. (There are no VAT rebates in Poland.)

TRAVELER'S CHECKS

Whether or not to buy traveler's checks depends on where you are headed; **take cash to rural areas and small towns, traveler's checks to cities.** The most widely recognized checks are issued by American Express, Citicorp, Thomas Cook, and Visa. These are sold by major commercial banks for 1%–3% of the checks' face value—it pays to **shop around.** Both American Express and Thomas Cook issue checks that can be countersigned and used by either you or your traveling companion. So you won't be left with excess foreign currency, **buy a few checks in small denominations** to cash toward the end of your trip. Before leaving home, **contact your issuer for information on where to cash your checks** without a incurring a transaction fee. Record the numbers of all your checks and keep this listing in a separate place, crossing off the numbers of checks you have cashed.

WIRING MONEY

For a fee of 3%–10%, depending on the amount of the transaction, you can have money sent to you from home through Money-Gram^SM or Western Union (☞ Money *in* Important Contacts A to Z, *above*). The transferred funds and the service fee can be charged to a Master-Card or Visa account.

P
PACKING FOR
EASTERN AND
CENTRAL EUROPE

Don't worry about packing lots of formal clothing. Fashion was all but nonexistent under 40 years of Communist rule, although residents of Budapest, Prague, and even Bucharest—catching up with their counterparts in other European capitals—are considerably more fashionably dressed than even a few years ago. Still, Western dress of virtually any kind is considered stylish: A sports jacket for men and a dress or pants for women are appropriate for an evening out. Everywhere else, you'll feel comfortable in casual pants or jeans.

Eastern and Central Europe enjoy all the extremes of an inland climate, so plan accordingly. In the higher elevations winter can

last until April, and even in summer the evenings will be on the cool side.

Many areas are best seen on foot, so take a pair of sturdy walking shoes and be prepared to use them. High heels will present considerable problems on the cobblestone streets of Prague, Warsaw, and towns in Hungary. If you plan to visit the mountains, make sure your shoes have good traction and ankle support, as some trails can be quite challenging.

Many items that you take for granted at home are occasionally unavailable or of questionable quality in Eastern and Central Europe. Take your own toiletries and personal-hygiene products with you. Women traveling in Bulgaria or Romania should pack tampons or sanitary napkins, which are in chronic short supply. Few places provide sports equipment for rent; an alternative to bringing your own equipment would be to buy what you need locally and take it home with you. In general, sporting goods are relatively cheap and of good quality.

Bring an extra pair of eyeglasses or contact lenses in your carry-on luggage. Contact lens wearers should bring enough saline and disinfecting solution with them, as they are expensive and in short supply. If you have a health problem, **pack enough medication** to last the trip or have your doctor write you a prescription using the

drug's generic name, because brand names vary from country to country (you'll then need a duplicate prescription from a local doctor). It's important that you **don't put prescription drugs or valuables in luggage to be checked,** for it could go astray. To avoid problems with customs officials, carry medications in the original packaging. Also, don't forget the addresses of offices that handle refunds of lost traveler's checks.

ELECTRICITY

To use your U.S.-purchased electric-powered equipment, **bring a converter and an adapter.** The electrical current in Eastern and Central Europe is 220 volts, 50 cycles alternating current (AC); wall outlets generally take plugs with two round prongs.

If your appliances are dual-voltage, you'll need only an adapter. Hotels sometimes have 110-volt outlets for low-wattage appliances near the sink, marked FOR SHAVERS ONLY; don't use them for high-wattage appliances like blow-dryers. If your laptop computer is older, carry a converter; new laptops operate equally well on 110 and 220 volts, so you only need an adapter.

LUGGAGE

Airline baggage allowances depend on the airline, the route, and the class of your ticket; ask in advance. In general, on domestic flights and on international flights between the United States and foreign destinations, you are entitled to check two bags. A third piece may be brought on board, but it must fit easily under the seat in front of you or in the overhead compartment. In the United States, the FAA gives airlines broad latitude regarding carry-on allowances, and they tend to tailor them to different aircraft and operational conditions. Charges for excess, oversize, or overweight pieces vary.

If you are flying between two foreign destinations, note that baggage allowances may be determined not by piece but by weight—generally 88 pounds (40 kilograms) in first class, 66 pounds (30 kilograms) in business class, and 44 pounds (20 kilograms) in economy. If your flight between two cities abroad *connects* with your transatlantic or transpacific flight, the piece method still applies.

SAFEGUARDING YOUR LUGGAGE➤ Before leaving home, **itemize your bags' contents** and their worth and label them with your name, address, and phone number. (If you use your home address, cover it so that potential thieves can't see it readily.) Inside each bag, **pack a copy of your itinerary.** At check-in, **make sure that each bag is correctly tagged** with the destination airport's three-letter code. If your bags arrive damaged—or fail to arrive at all—file a written report with the airline before leaving the airport.

PASSPORTS & VISAS

If you don't already have one, **get a passport.** It is advisable that you **leave one photocopy of your passport's data page** with someone at home and keep another with you, separated from your passport, while traveling. If you lose your passport, promptly call the nearest embassy or consulate and the local police; having the data page information can speed replacement.

For additional country-specific information about passports and visas, *see* Passports and Visas in the A to Z section at the end of each country chapter.

IN THE U.S.

All U.S. citizens, even infants, need a valid passport to enter the Czech Republic, Slovakia, or Romania for stays of up to 30 days, and to enter Bulgaria, Hungary, and Poland for stays of up to 90 days. New and renewal application forms are available at any of the 13 U.S. Passport Agency offices and at some post offices and courthouses. Passports are usually mailed within four weeks; allow five weeks or more in spring and summer.

CANADIANS

You need a valid passport to enter the Czech Republic, Slovakia, or Romania for stays of up to 30 days, and to enter Bulgaria, Hungary, and Poland for stays of up to 90 days. Application forms are available at 28 regional passport offices as well as post offices and travel agencies. Whether for a first or a subsequent passport, you must apply in person. Children under 16 may be included on a parent's passport but must have their own to travel alone. Passports are valid for five years and are usually mailed within two to three weeks of application.

U.K. CITIZENS

Citizens of the United Kingdom need a valid passport to enter the Czech Republic and Slovakia for stays of up to 30 days, and to enter Bulgaria, Hungary, and Poland for stays of up to 90 days. Applications for new and renewal passports are available from main post offices as well as at the passport offices, located in Belfast, Glasgow, Liverpool, London, Newport, and Peterborough. You may apply in person at all passport offices or by mail to all except the London office. Children under 16 may travel on an accompanying parent's passport. All passports are valid for 10 years. Allow a month for processing.

Citizens of the United Kingdom must have a visa to enter Bulgaria. Visas may be obtained at the border or at the nearest embassy or consulate.

S
SAFETY

Crime rates are still relatively low in Eastern

and Central Europe, but travelers should **beware of pickpockets in crowded areas,** especially on public transportation, at railway stations, and in big hotels. In general, always keep your valuables with you—in open bars and restaurants, purses hung on or placed next to chairs are easy targets. **Make sure your wallet is safe in a buttoned pocket, or watch your handbag.**

To qualify for age-related discounts, **mention your senior-citizen status up front** when booking hotel reservations, not when checking out, and before you're seated in restaurants, not when paying the bill. Note that discounts may be limited to certain menus, days, or hours. When renting a car, **ask about promotional car-rental discounts**—they can net even lower costs than your senior-citizen discount.

For country-specific information, *see* Student and Youth Travel in the A to Z section at the end of each country chapter.

To save money, **look into deals available through student-oriented travel agencies.** To qualify, you'll need to have a bona fide student ID card. Members of international student groups are also eligible (☞ Students *in* Important Contacts A to Z, *above*).

T
TELEPHONES

For country-specific information, *see* Telephones in the A to Z section at the end of each country chapter.

LONG-DISTANCE

The long-distance services of AT&T, MCI, and Sprint make calling home relatively convenient, but in many hotels you may find it impossible to dial the access number. The hotel operator may also refuse to make the connection. Instead, the hotel will charge you a premium rate—as much as 400% more than a calling card—for calls placed from your hotel room. To avoid such price gouging, travel with more than one company's long-distance calling card—a hotel may block Sprint but not MCI. If the hotel operator claims you cannot use any phone card, ask to be connected to an international operator, who will help you to access your phone card. You can also dial the international operator yourself. If none of this works, try calling your phone company collect in the United States. If collect calls are also blocked, call from a pay phone in the hotel lobby. Before you go, **find out the local access codes** for your destinations.

TIPPING

For country-specific information, *see* Tipping in the A to Z section at the end of each country chapter.

A package or tour to Eastern and Central Europe can make your vacation less expensive and more hassle-free. Firms that sell tours and packages reserve airline seats, hotel rooms, and rental cars in bulk and pass some of the savings on to you. In addition, the best operators have local representatives available to help you at your destination.

A GOOD DEAL?

The more your package or tour includes, the better you can predict the ultimate cost of your vacation. Make sure you know exactly what is covered and **beware of hidden costs.** Are taxes, tips, and service charges included? Transfers and baggage handling? Entertainment and excursions? These can add up.

Most packages and tours are rated deluxe, first-class superior, first class, tourist, or budget. The key difference is usually accommodations. Remember, tourist class in the United States might be a comfortable chain hotel, but in Eastern and Central Europe you might share a bath and do without hot water. If the package or tour you are considering is priced lower than in your wildest dreams, **be skeptical.** Also, **make sure your travel agent knows the accommodations** and other services. Ask about the hotel's location, room size, beds, and whether it has a pool, room service, or programs for children, if you care about these. Has your agent been there in person or sent others you can contact?

BUYER BEWARE

Each year a number of consumers are stranded or lose their money when operators—even very large ones with excellent reputations—go out of business. To avoid becoming one of them, take the time to **check out the operator**—find out how long the company has been in business and ask several agents about its reputation. Next, **don't book unless the firm has a consumer-protection program.** Members of the USTOA and the NTA are required to set aside funds for the sole purpose of covering your payments and travel arrangements in case of default. Non-member operators may instead carry insurance; look for the details in the operator's brochure—and for the name of an underwriter with a solid reputation. Note: When it comes to tour operators, **don't trust escrow accounts.** Although there are laws governing those of charter-flight operators, no governmental body prevents tour operators from raiding the till.

Next, **contact your local Better Business Bureau and the attorney general's offices** in both your own state and the operator's; have any complaints been filed? Finally, **pay with a major credit card.** Then you can cancel payment, provided that you can document your complaint. Always **consider trip-cancella-tion insurance** (☞ Insurance, *above*).

BIG VS. SMALL➤ Operators who handle several hundred thousand travelers per year can use their purchasing power to give you a good price. Their high volume may also indicate financial stability. But some small companies provide more personalized service; because they tend to specialize, they may also be more knowledgeable about a given area.

USING AN AGENT

Travel agents are excellent resources. In fact, large operators accept bookings made only through travel agents. But it's good to **collect brochures from several agencies** because some agents' suggestions may be skewed by promotional relationships with tour and package firms that reward them for volume sales. If you have a special interest, **find an agent with expertise in that area**; ASTA can provide leads in the United States. (Don't rely solely on your agent, though; agents may be unaware of small-niche operators, and some special-interest travel companies only sell direct.)

SINGLE TRAVELERS

Prices are usually quoted per person, based on two sharing a room. If traveling solo, you may be required to pay the full double-occupancy rate. Some operators eliminate this surcharge if you agree to be matched up with a roommate of the same sex, even if one is not found by departure time.

Although standards have improved during the past few years, on the whole they are far short of what is acceptable in the West. Trains are very busy, and it is rare to find one running less than full or almost so. All six countries operate their own dining, buffet, and refreshment services. Always crowded, they tend to open and close at the whim of the staff. Couchette cars are second class only and can be little more than a hard bunk without springs and adequate bed linen. This is not true of Poland, where Express and Intercity trains are reservation-only, are rarely overcrowded, and have acceptable buffet facilities.

Although trains in Eastern and Central Europe are usually crowded and aren't always comfortable, traveling by rail is very inexpensive (it's much cheaper than renting a car in this part of Europe). Rail networks in all the Eastern and Central European countries are very extensive, though trains can be infuriatingly slow. You'll invariably enjoy interesting and friendly traveling company, however; most Eastern and Central Europeans are eager to hear about the West and to discuss the enormous changes in their own countries.

DISCOUNT PASSES

To save money, **look into rail passes** (☞

Train Travel *in* Important Contacts A to Z, *above,* and Getting Around by Train in the A to Z section at the end of each country chapter). But be aware that if you don't plan to cover many miles, you may come out ahead by buying individual tickets.

You can **use the East Pass** on the national rail networks of the Czech Republic, Hungary, Poland, and Slovakia. You can choose between five days of unlimited first-class travel within a 15-day period for $195 or 10 days of first-class travel within a one-month period for $299.

You can also **combine the East Pass with a national rail pass.** The Bulgarian Flexipass costs $70 for three days of unlimited first-class travel within a one-month period. A pass for the Czech Republic costs $69 for five days of train travel within a 15-day period. The Hungarian Flexipass costs $55 for five days of unlimited first-class train travel within a 15-day period or $69 for 10 days within a one-month period. The Romanian Pass costs $60 for three days of first-class train travel in a 15-day period.

Many travelers assume that rail passes guarantee them seats on the trains they wish to ride. Not so. You need to **book seats ahead, even if you are using a rail pass**; seat reservations are required on some European trains, particularly high-speed

trains, and are a good idea on trains that may be crowded—particularly in summer on popular routes. You will also need a reservation if you purchase sleeping accommodations.

FROM THE U.K.

There are no direct trains from London. You can take a direct train from Paris to Warsaw or via Frankfurt to Prague (daily) or from Berlin to Warsaw or via Dresden to Prague (three times a day). Vienna is a good starting point for Prague, Brno, or Bratislava. There are three trains a day from Vienna's Franz Josefsbahnhof to Prague via Třeboň and Tábor (5½ hours) and one from the Südbahnhof (South Station) via Brno (5 hours). Bratislava can be reached from Vienna by a 67-minute shuttle service, which runs every two hours during the day. You should check out times and routes before leaving.

TRAVEL GEAR

Travel catalogs specialize in useful items that can **save space when packing** and make life on the road more convenient. Compact alarm clocks, travel irons, travel wallets, and personal-care kits are among the most common items you'll find. They also carry dual-voltage appliances, currency converters and foreign-language phrase books. Some catalogs even carry miniature coffeemakers and water purifiers.

U
U.S. GOVERNMENT

The U.S. government can be an excellent source of travel information. Some of this is free and some is available for a nominal charge. When planning your trip, **find out what government materials are available.** For just a couple of dollars, you can get a variety of publications from the Consumer Information Center in Pueblo, Colorado. Free consumer information also is available from individual government agencies, such as the Department of Transportation or the U.S. Customs Service. For specific titles, see the appropriate publications entry in Important Contacts A to Z, *above.*

W
WHEN TO GO

The tourist season generally runs from April or May through October; spring and fall combine good weather with a more bearable level of tourism. The ski season lasts from mid-December through March. Outside the mountain resorts you will encounter few other visitors; you'll have the opportunity to see the region covered in snow, but many of the sights are closed, and it can get very, very cold. If you're not a skier, try visiting the Giant Mountain of Bohemia or the High Tatras in Slovakia and Poland in late spring or fall; the colors are dazzling, and you'll

THE GOLD GUIDE / SMART TRAVEL TIPS

have the hotels and restaurants pretty much to yourself. Bear in mind that many attractions are closed November through March.

Prague and Budapest are beautiful year-round, but avoid midsummer (especially July and August) and the Christmas and Easter holidays, when the two cities are choked with visitors. Warsaw, too, suffers a heavy influx of tourists during the summer season, though not on quite the same grand scale. Lake Balaton in Hungary becomes a mob scene in July and August. At the opposite end of the spectrum, Bucharest and Sofia are rarely crowded, even at the height of summer. In July and August, however, the weather in these capitals sometimes borders on stifling.

For additional country-specific information, *see* When to Tour following the Great Itineraries at the beginning of each country chapter.

CLIMATE

The following are the average daily maximum and minimum temperatures for major cities in the region.

BRATISLAVA

Jan.	36F	2C	May	70F	21C	Sept.	72F	22C
	27	– 3		52	11		54	12
Feb.	39F	4C	June	75F	24C	Oct.	59F	15C
	28	– 2		57	14		45	7
Mar.	48F	9C	July	79F	26C	Nov.	46F	8C
	34	1		61	16		37	3
Apr.	61F	16C	Aug.	79F	26C	Dec.	39F	4C
	43	6		61	16		32	0

BUCHAREST

Jan.	34F	1C	May	74F	23C	Sept.	78F	25C
	19	– 7		51	10		52	11
Feb.	38F	4C	June	81F	27C	Oct.	65F	18C
	23	– 5		57	14		43	6
Mar.	50F	10C	July	86F	30C	Nov.	49F	10C
	30	– 1		60	16		35	2
Apr.	64F	18C	Aug.	85F	30C	Dec.	39F	4C
	41	5		59	15		26	– 3

BUDAPEST

Jan.	34F	1C	May	72F	22C	Sept.	73F	23C
	25	– 4		52	11		54	12
Feb.	39F	4C	June	79F	26C	Oct.	61F	16C
	28	– 2		59	15		45	7
Mar.	50F	10C	July	82F	28C	Nov.	46F	8C
	36	2		61	16		37	3
Apr.	63F	17C	Aug.	81F	27C	Dec.	39F	4C
	25	– 4		61	16		30	– 1

PRAGUE

Jan.	36F	2C	May	66F	19C	Sept.	68F	20C
	25	– 4		46	8		50	10
Feb.	37F	3C	June	72F	22C	Oct.	55F	13C
	27	– 3		52	11		41	5
Mar.	46F	8C	July	75F	24C	Nov.	46F	8C
	32	0		55	13		36	2
Apr.	58F	14C	Aug.	73F	23C	Dec.	37F	3C
	39	4		55	13		28	– 2

SOFIA

Jan.	35F	2C	May	69F	21C	Sept.	70F	22C
	25	– 4		50	10		52	11
Feb.	39F	4C	June	76F	24C	Oct.	63F	17C
	27	– 3		56	14		46	8
Mar.	50F	10C	July	81F	27C	Nov.	48F	9C
	33	1		60	16		37	3
Apr.	60F	16C	Aug.	79F	26C	Dec.	38F	4C
	42	5		59	15		28	– 2

WARSAW

Jan.	32F	0C	May	68F	20C	Sept.	66F	19C
	21	– 6		48	9		50	10
Feb.	32F	0C	June	73F	23C	Oct.	55F	13C
	21	– 6		54	12		41	5
Mar.	43F	6C	July	75F	24C	Nov.	43F	6C
	28	– 2		59	15		34	1
Apr.	54F	12C	Aug.	73F	23C	Dec.	36F	2C
	37	3		57	14		27	– 3

THE GOLD GUIDE / SMART TRAVEL TIPS

1 Destination: Eastern and Central Europe

CATCHING UP TO THE PRESENT

"The city was changing."

—Jachým Topol, *A Trip to the Train Station*

AT THE TABLES of a few select pubs in the Smíchov district of Prague, you can occasionally find Jachým Topol, the Czech Republic's most highly prized young novelist and poet, quietly passing away the afternoon hunched in a rickety wooden chair. His literary reputation aside, Topol seems much like any other young Czech who, for one reason or another, passes a weekday afternoon in a corner pub, sipping beer and smoking his way through a pack of Spartas or Petras or some such horrible brand of local cigarettes.

Like many here who divide their time neatly between "pubbing" and working, Topol has produced some of the Czech Republic's most vivid chronicles of late 20th-century, post-communist society, although his reputation is far less prominent than that of novelists like Ivan Klíma, whose recent novel, *The Judge,* is also among the few "new" pieces of serious literature produced since 1989. One of Topol's more recent novellas, *A Trip to the Train Station,* published locally in a dual-language, Czech-English paperback edition, is a stream-of-consciousness look at the new Prague. It is a fine introduction to a fascinating city: Topol introduces readers to the excited world of black marketeers and concentration camp survivors, incompetent hit men and journalists on the take, and even takes a poke at the thousands of young Americans who have taken up residence in Prague. Its pages walk the streets of his "city of a thousand faces," passing beneath its baroque and Gothic towers, staring up at the art-nouveau, stained glass canopy of its main train station, browsing its second-hand bookstores, and strolling past its tiny shops, ten to a block.

That multitude of faces and facades—the ones that Jachým says replaced the "mask of rotting Bolshevism"—is perhaps the most fascinating part of the new Eastern and Central Europe. Like others in the region, the Czech capital city has teemed with activity, some of it legal and much of it not, ever since the revolutions of 1989.

And what Jachým writes about Prague—its palpable history, its free-for-all capitalism, its strange perch between East and West—holds true for Budapest, Warsaw, and to a lesser extent Kraków. Though the years between World War II and the fall of communism have left a vicious economic and social hangover, these awakened cities are alive with a frenetic brand of commerce, with a rapidly changing and still-young street culture, with jazz trios that play Thelonious Monk, art galleries that exhibit avant-garde conceptualist sculpture, and performances of Mozart's *Don Giovanni* in the same house that saw its premiere two centuries ago.

The countries of what were once known collectively as the Soviet bloc are now divided quite cleanly into two groups: Central Europe and Eastern Europe. Central Europe these days means basically four countries: Poland, the Czech Republic, Slovakia, and Hungary, plus the often forgotten former Yugoslav republic of Slovenia. Occasionally, Germany and Austria are included as part of Central Europe, a sign that these four formerly communist states have, in the minds of many, rejoined the rest of Europe.

The countries of Eastern Europe have had dramatically less success in joining the community of nations to their west. Though *Fodor's Eastern and Central Europe* covers only Bulgaria and Romania, the countries that make up the former Yugoslavia as well as Ukraine and the Baltic states are also members of this group. The major cities of this part of the region, while fascinating in their own ways, for the most part lack the growing cosmopolitanism and buzzing economies that characterize those of their neighbors.

It is to the former set of nations—the ones known as Central Europe—that most visitors travel. Millions upon millions of tourists have poured through the wide-open borders of these countries since 1989. Prague, for one, became one of the most visited cities in the world in 1994. What visitors to Central Europe enter are profoundly historic lands that are hurriedly catching up to the present. In some senses, these countries are the true "heart of Europe," as their citizens and politicians like to remind visitors. They have been at the center of European civilization from the Middle Ages to the present, from the days of the medieval Bulgarian Empire, which stretched far north to include a few of them, to the Austro-Hungarian Empire of the 18th and 19th centuries, in which they often served as servant states that lined the coffers of Viennese bureaucrats, to the national Europe of the 20th century.

PRAGUE—since the Czech revolution one of the world's most popular tourist destinations—made its debut as a European metropolis in the 9th century but spent several hundred years languishing under the dominance of more powerful states. It was not until the arrival of King Charles in the 14th century that Prague ascended to its height as the political and cultural center of Europe, when Charles became the Holy Roman Emperor and founded Central Europe's first university. The university survives in buildings along the banks of the Vltava River—known to many as the Moldau, the name it was given by Germans who lived here and administrated local government under the Hapsburgs. To the chagrin of contemporary Czechs, the glory of Prague's half-century reign as the seat of the Holy Roman Empire and Europe's putative capital has yet to be revived.

Hungary, too, has its claims to fame. Aside from the obvious strength and influence that allowed it to carve its own chunk out of the Hapsburg Empire, Hungarians can boast of more recent achievements, including the construction of the first underground subway on the Continent and the development of one of the first stock exchanges in Europe. It is also in Hungary that one finds perhaps the most distinct Turkish flavor in Europe: Its occupation by the Turks, from the early 16th century to the latter half of the 17th, left it with Eastern architectural accents, as well as the famous Turkish baths, which draw tourists to their mineral-rich, warm waters.

It is difficult when traveling in Central Europe not to encounter some aspect of the past pushing its way into the present. Busts of famous composers decorate the buildings where they once lived, and concert halls contain the instruments on which they played. Even the physical geography of the places themselves evoke their rich cultural histories. There is Prague's Vltava River, its banks lined with castles, small palaces, and fresco-covered apartment buildings that glow gold in the afternoon, for which composer Bedřich Smetana created the symphonic poem *The Moldau,* and the stunning countryside of Hungary, in which Béla Bartók found the Gypsy songs that he incorporated into his quartets and symphonies.

Upon that past, Central Europeans are creating Central Europe anew. Although six or so years are—especially in Central European terms—a short while indeed, the events since 1989 promise a grand reshaping of Central European societies. This is most true, of course, in the cities, where the many effects, both large and small, of open borders and free societies tend to accumulate most rapidly. The cosmopolitan feel that was stamped out among all but the intellectuals under communism has been revived. And while the joie de vivre that characterized many cities for the year or two following the 1989 revolutions has given way to a more stolid optimism, these cities can now be compared in many ways to Paris or Berlin.

There are many obvious indications of the rapid changes that have occurred: In downtown Budapest, Thai restaurants serve shrimp soup spiced with coconut milk and lemongrass alongside traditional pubs that specialize in goulash and dumplings. Men and women chat on mobile telephones—which have been an enormous hit in Hungary—while having coffee at a sidewalk café on a bustling city boulevard. Staying in Budapest, or any of the other major cities of the region, can now be as amenity enriched—or as bare bones—as you please. Finding a four-star hotel, a quaint bed-and-breakfast, or a private apartment—which Central Europeans still tend to rent out at bargain rates—is a snap. And a traveler in the city can choose to indulge, at a price that's generally paid in cholesterol, in either standard pork-and-potatoes fare or a sumptuous Mediterranean meal at an upscale restaurant.

In the countryside less than two hours away, the country's long and famous equestrian tradition continues at weather-beaten stables where guides have learned enough English, German, French, and whatever other language is necessary to carry on at least some conversation during a ride through green foothills. Resorts along Lake Balaton, Central Europe's largest lake, are crowded with visitors touring medieval churches, browsing in art galleries, and passing the time in coffee-houses along the water's edge.

In Kraków, the pristine southern Polish city whose magnificent buildings were among the few major structures to escape the devastation of World War II—its defenders turned away Nazi troops in one of Poland's few victories during the war—tourists marvel at the town's medieval town square and browse at shop windows that are jammed full of everything from food to footwear.

In a less glamorous sign of the times, the summer of 1996 saw a move by Poland's privatization minister to declare bankrupt the famous Gdańsk shipyard, birthplace of the Solidarity labor movement that was largely responsible for the country's overthrow of communism. Although shipyard workers saw revenge in the decision—the ministry is part of a government run by former Communists—the minister's own explanation seemed likelier: The shipyard is collapsing under the weight of its debts, and market forces dictate that it should be closed.

In Bulgaria and Romania, the same transformations are unarguably taking place, but at a much different pace. In Sofia, a traveler who hadn't been there in a decade remarked that he returned to stay in a hotel room that looked just as had in 1986, complete with a sign that still bore the admonition NO SMOKING IN BED. Host to the European Bank for Reconstruction and Development's 1996 annual meeting, Sofia is badly in need of both. Three major earthquakes during the last century have damaged, in some cases ruined, many of its buildings. Its roads, like those of many East European nations,

are a web of potholes and ditches through which even taxi drivers don't dare to speed. Cars, what few there are, crawl through town at 15 kilometers (9 miles) per hour.

However, the lack of development and interaction with the outside world also means that Bulgaria is sometimes a more welcoming, if less well equipped, host to travelers. Where the people of tourist hot spots like Budapest, Prague, Warsaw and Kraków can be decidedly cool to visitors, a Sofia shopkeeper, taxi driver, or concierge will go decidedly out of his or her way to help a befuddled foreigner, whether the visitor is looking for a hotel, a lost wallet, or a restaurant recommendation.

T HESE COUNTRIES are also politically fascinating—some more so than others. For instance, the Czech Republic's widely acclaimed government, which has inflicted the least pain and enjoyed the most stable support of any former Soviet bloc country during its economic transformation, is much more stable than even the government of Slovakia, the nation with which it was federated until the split of Czechoslovakia at the end of 1992. Whereas the Czech Republic is led—for the time being at least—by a prime minister, Václav Klaus, who appears firmly committed to free markets and free elections, and a president, the playwright and former dissident Václav Havel, who appears to be more of a philosopher than a politician, Slovakia is still struggling with democracy. Its leaders often show less than perfect tolerance for the compromises needed to create an "open society," to use a term favored by one of the most famous living Central Europeans, Hungarian-born financier, multibillionaire, and philanthropist George Soros. Freedom of the press and minority rights, for instance, can sometimes mean very little to government ministers in this small nation.

Hungary, which recently elected former Communists to power in the guise of the Hungarian Socialist party, is more politically stable than Slovakia but still exhibits some signs of the lingering nationalism and cross-border enmities that have plagued it for centuries. Socialist party leaders tend to anguish over decisions about privatization and economic reform, but in the end, usually manage to work out a solution that is palatable to even the country's economic conservatives.

In terms of political stability and occasional national unease, Poland is probably most like Hungary. Like many other former Soviet bloc states, Poland has its own batch of former Communists and Socialists in power, but they give few signs that they are any more leftist than the Social Democratic parties of Western Europe. Poland's famous former president, the dissident and Solidarity leader Lech Wałesa, made headlines in early 1996 by announcing that he would go back to work at his old job at the Gdańsk shipyard because the government that replaced him wouldn't give him a pension. Soon afterward, the government relented, giving Wałesa a monthly check that, combined with his other income, will make him quite well off by Polish standards. Such a battle against the powers-that-be is a far cry from the political struggles Wałęsa endured for so many years. Such minor political dramas, in fact, aren't so very far from what Westerners are used to reading in their own newspapers—yet another sign that Polish society has quickly become quite similar to the ones in which Western tourists live.

In Bulgaria and Romania, the political scene is less refined, a situation that may be attributed to the two countries' heavy reliance on the Soviet Union prior to 1989 and to their continuing poverty. By far the most gruesome case has been Romania's, which has seen crude internal repression, crushing inflation and poverty, and the lack, in general, of any plan to revive the country's economy or repair its politics. Such problems have ensured that Romania and Bulgaria, despite their magnificent countrysides, mountains, and stretches of Black Sea coast, do not swarm with tourists during the summer months like their neighbors to the north, and that foreign investors, whose money has helped revitalize much of the region, approach with caution.

Much, of course, still remains to be done to build the Western European future to which these countries aspire. A thin-skinned tourist here will notice much of it immediately, in the form of pollution, inconvenience, or simply the scarcity of fresh vegetables. Politically and economically, these are not fully mature societies by late 20th-century standards.

Mention that to someone who lives here, however, and he or she will likely agree. But they might also point out what has been done, not only in the few years since Central and Eastern Europe rejoined the rest of Europe, but during the last 10 centuries. It is true that for 40 long years, people in Central and Eastern Europe were closed off from the rest of the world. But now that it is open to them, they are embracing it. And their deep cultural history—with the lessons it has taught and the legacy it has left—may turn out to be the strongest asset they have as a Westernized world closes in around them.

—*Charlie Hornberger*

WHAT'S WHERE

Czech Republic

Planted firmly in the heart of Central Europe—Prague is some 250 miles north*west* of Vienna—the Czech Republic is culturally and historically more closely linked to Western, particularly Germanic, culture than any of its former "East bloc" brethren. Encompassing some 79,000 square kilometers (30,500 square miles), the Czech Republic is made up of the regions of Bohemia in the west (sharing long borders with Germany and Austria) and Moravia in the east. Moravia's White Carpathian Mountains (Biele Karpaty) form the border with the young Slovak Republic, which broke its 74-year-old union with the Czechs in 1993 to establish itself as an independent nation. With a population of 1,212,000, the Czech Republic is one of the most densely populated countries of Eastern/Central Europe.

The capital city of **Prague** sits on the Vltava (Moldau) River, roughly in the middle of Bohemian territory. A stunning city of human dimensions, Prague offers the traveler a lesson in almost all the major architectural styles of Western European history; relatively unscathed by major wars, most of Prague's buildings are remarkably well preserved. **Southern Bohemia** is dotted with several well-preserved and stunning walled towns, many of which played important roles in the Hussite religious wars of the 15th century. The two most notable towns are **Tábor** and **Český Krumlov. Western Bohemia,** especially the far western hills near the German border, remains justly famous for its mineral springs and spa towns, in particular **Karlovy Vary, Mariánské Lázně,** and **Františkový Lázně. Northern Bohemia,** with its rolling hills, and on the frontier with Poland, the **Krkonoše** (White Mountains) is a hiker's and camper's delight.

Slovakia

Having declared its independence from the Czech Republic in 1993, the smaller and more agrarian Slovak Republic has been struggling to revive its economic life and adjust to new post–Cold War realities. The 49,000 square kilometers (19,000 square miles) of Slovak territory are both less urbanized and less industrialized than that of the country's Moravian and Bohemian neighbors to the west. **Bratislava,** the capital, lies on the Danube in the southwestern corner of the country, just a few miles away from both the Austrian and Hungarian borders. Its small Old Town is charming and contains several buildings and churches of interest (especially to those interested in the history of the Austrio-Hungarian Empire), but Slovakia's real assets are to the north and east. **Central Slovakia,** a hilly region crossed by hiking trails, is rich in folklore and traces of medieval history. The **High Tatra Mountains** attract skiers, campers, and mountaineers from all across Europe; these days they are a real meeting ground for tourists from east and west. And relatively undiscovered **eastern Slovakia** lures travelers with its country lanes—watch out for herds of sheep and gaggles of geese—fairy-tale-like villages, castles, and wooden churches.

Hungary

Sandwiched between Slovakia and Romania, Hungary was the Austro-Hungarian Empire's eastern frontier. Measuring approximately 93,000 square kilometers (36,000 square miles), with a population of 10,238,000, it is the geographical link between the Slavic regions of Central Europe and the Black Sea region's amalgam of Orthodox and Islamic cultures. The heart of the nation is **Budapest,** in the northwest on the Danube,

just an hour from Bratislava in Slovakia and two hours from Vienna. Just north of Budapest, the Danube River forms a gentle, heart-shaped curve along which lie the romantic and historic towns of the region called the **Danube Bend.** Southwest of Budapest are the vineyards, quaint villages, and popular, developed summer resorts around **Lake Balaton,** the largest lake in Central Europe. The more rural and gently mountainous stretch of **northern Hungary** also includes the handsome, vibrant town of Eger and the famous wine village of Tokaj; the contrastingly flat and dry expanses of the **Great Plain,** in the east, are spiced with legendary traditions of horsemanship and agriculture and anchored by the interesting and lively cities of Kecskemét and Debrecen. The verdant, rolling countryside of **Transdanubia** stretches west of the Danube to the borders of Austria, Slovenia, and Croatia; in the northern hills nestle the gemlike, beautifully restored towns of Sopron and Kőszeg, and in the south, the culturally rich, dynamically beautiful city of Pécs.

Poland

The northernmost country in the region, Poland has a long coastline on the Baltic Sea. A vast nation of 313,000 square kilometers (121,000 square miles), Poland is made up primarily of a great plain in the north and central region and a small but dramatic stretch of mountainous territory to the south (on its border with Slovakia and the Czech Republic). **Warsaw,** just to the east of the country's center, has rebuilt itself several times over the course of its tumultuous history and since the end of communism has been changing faster than any other city or region in Poland.

Travelers interested in art and architecture shouldn't miss **Kraków** in the south (it's one of UNESCO's 12 great historic cities of the world) and the historic small towns of the surrounding region known as Little Poland. Outdoor enthusiasts will want to move on to the west and south, to the **Podhale** region and the **Tatra Mountains.** Many of the natural wonders and recreational areas of these two regions are within two hours' drive of downtown Kraków.

Gdańsk and the north offer wide-open vistas, long stretches of coast, great lakes, and historic cities and castles rising up from the plain. This is a great area for water sports and also for hiking and camping.

Lublin and the east offer a trip back into the traditional way of life of rural Central Europe: small towns, whose great age was in the Renaissance but which have slept since, vast palaces of the nobility, and gently varied countryside where the tractor has not yet replaced the horse.

Apart from the far southwest, and a few park areas around **Poznań** and **Wrocław,** the countryside of western Poland is flat and somewhat monotonous—lots of dairy farms and hay fields. Poznań and Wrocław have fine historic centers and a thriving cultural life.

Bulgaria

The southernmost frontier of Eastern/Central Europe, Bulgaria borders Turkey to the south and the Black Sea to the east; to the west are the territories of the former Yugoslavia. Covering a territory of approximately 111,000 square kilometers (43,000 square miles), Bulgaria has a population of 8,454,000. **Sofia,** the capital, sits on the so-called Sofia Plain in western Bulgaria and is surrounded by rugged mountain ranges. The wooded and mountainous interior is sprinkled with attractive "museum" villages and ancient towns. In the **Balkan Range** in the north is the old Bulgarian capital of **Veliko Târnovo.** South of there, in the foothills of the Balkan Range, you'll find the verdant **Valley of Roses** and beyond that, **Plovdiv,** the country's second-largest city. The sunny, sandy beaches of Bulgaria's **Black Sea coast** attract visitors from all over Europe; the historic port city of **Varna** makes a good base for exploring the region.

Romania

Romania is one of the poorest countries in Europe, second only to Albania, but it's also one of the most beautiful. The same factors that kept Romania from developing economically during the Communist era also helped to preserve the country as one of the last bastions of medieval Europe. The country covers approximately 238,000 square kilometers (92,000 square miles) and has a population of 22,687,000. **Bucharest,** the capital city, in the southeast just two hours or so from the Black Sea coast, was once known as the "Paris of the East." From Bucharest you can set out on a journey of the villages of **Transylvania.** Many of the towns here have preserved their medieval core and still show traces of the Latin and Germanic traders who passed through on their way to the Black Sea.

Bucovina, a remote region in the north, provides an unspoiled view of medieval Europe: Farmers still tend fields with handmade plows and hoes, and horse-drawn wagons are as numerous as cars. This region is home to the painted churches, a collection of monasteries built during the Middle Ages notable for their vividly colored frescoes.

In contrast to the rest of Romania, the **Black Sea** region has always been a major center of tourism. The main attraction here is the warm beaches. The area also bears historical significance, with ruins in the area dating to the conquest of the region during the period of the Roman Empire. From the coast travelers can journey to the **Danube Delta,** Europe's largest wetland and home to 300 bird species, including the common pelican.

NEW AND NOTEWORTHY

Czech Republic

The Czech Republic continues along its path of economic and cultural revitalization, which began with the peaceful revolution of 1989 and accelerated following the breakup of the Czechoslovak state in 1993. Far from hurting the country, the Czech-Slovak split has freed officials to concentrate on the rapid economic changes of Bohemia and Moravia without having to worry about Slovakia. Their eventual goal is incorporation into the European Union (EU) by the year 2000. Tourism remains one of the brightest sectors of the economy, and visitors from the West will find the country is still quite affordable. Everywhere, castles, palaces, and dusty old museums are spiffing themselves up and throwing open their doors to visitors.

One tangible impact of the country's economic reforms has been an acceleration in the pace of architectural renovations. Many hotels, old private houses, and churches are installing new fixtures and applying a fresh coat of paint. One of the areas to get a face-lift over the past few years is Staroměstské náměstí (Old Town Square), one of the jewels of the "new" Prague, lined by such landmarks as the Týn Church and the Old Town Hall. Brightly painted facades and gleaming shopfronts now fan out from Old Town Square in all directions; the change will astonish visitors who last saw the city as recently as the early 1990s.

The number of hotels and restaurants keeps pace with the growing number of visitors. This is even true of Prague, which has become one of Europe's leading tourist destinations. Like the number of new large hotels, the number of smaller, privately owned hotels and pensions is also on the rise. The arrival of visitors and long-term residents from all over the world has brought forth new restaurants offering Cajun, Mexican, vegetarian, and other exotic fare alongside the traditional ones serving pork and dumplings.

Prague's cultural life continues to thrive, and the city in particular is a classical-music lover's dream, with a plethora of concerts to choose from almost every hour of the day in high season. Opera fans should also not be disappointed. The annual mid-May–early June Prague Spring Music Festival, which even before the collapse of the Communist government was one of the great events on the European calendar, is attracting record numbers of music lovers.

Slovakia

Slovakia continues steadily along the path to economic and democratic restructuring, with the eventual goal of incorporation into the EU by the year 2000. New hotels, pensions, and restaurants are springing up all over the country, but not fast enough to eliminate the shabby government-owned establishments that still dominate certain parts of the scene. Almost all cities now have pensions, often housed in beautifully renovated historic buildings. Keep an eye out for the new chain of Slovak restaurants called Slovenská Restauracia, where you can get typical Slovak food in a lovely rustic environment at dirt cheap prices. Eastern Slovakia, known for its natural beauty and unusual architecture, remains uncharted territory and can now offer accommodations that are up to Western standards.

Hungary

Last year marked Hungary's 1,100th birthday—the anniversary of the Magyar settlement of the Carpathian Basin. In the wake of celebratory sprucings-up and restorations, many museums have updated historical exhibits, and monuments sparkle like new. Riding the mille-centennial momentum, improvements and restoration work on important sites will continue through the year 2000, when Hungary celebrates the 1,000th anniversary of its founding as a state.

Slowly but surely, Hungary is improving its infrastructure, helping it fill its increasingly important role as a link between Eastern and Western Europe. Over the next several years, major highways will be upgraded and extended, the airport in Budapest will undergo a major expansion, and the antiquated telephone system will be overhauled. Travelers may witness these changes taking place but should not expect to reap their full benefits for some time to come.

Travelers will still find Hungary a bargain compared to Western Europe, but strictly rock-bottom prices are a thing of the past. Restaurant and hotel rates are steadily creeping upward, and at press time, the annual inflation rate was at more than 25% and still rising.

Poland

Gdańsk celebrates its 1,000th anniversary in 1997 with a wide variety of special events and festivals running from mid-April to the end of October. Highlights include a World Expo–like exhibition and the International Organ Music Festival, both in June; a crafts fair and street theater performances during July; in August, a Shakespeare week, sailing competitions, and a street feast sponsored by local restaurateurs; and extensive exhibitions on Solidarity, the anti-Communist union movement that was born in the shipyards of Gdańsk.

Poland's range of accommodations continues to broaden and improve. Older fine hotels are being renovated in Warsaw; there are also many new small, private, and relatively inexpensive hotels and pensions countrywide. 1997 should see the effects of the privatization of the hotel chain run by Orbis, the old state travel giant.

The second terminal at Warsaw airport, opened in the 1990s, has greatly improved the speed and comfort of arrival at Poland's capital; LOT now also offers more domestic flights—at least one daily to most major cities from Warsaw. Getting around within Poland is also becoming easier: Public transportation has now been expanded by a network of Express buses that serve the bigger cities. Major highways are being widened and improved very quickly, gasoline is now readily available, and all the major car-rental companies are competing to offer better prices.

The financial services and banking industries have been relatively slow to change and innovate, but credit cards are now finally being accepted in almost all hotels and restaurants, as well as in major retail outlets throughout the country. In big cities it is now also much easier to cash travelers checks and to use cash cards like American Express or Eurocheque.

Bulgaria

More than most other former Soviet-bloc countries of Eastern Europe, Bulgaria's state-controlled economy remains dominated by clunky Soviet-era companies. As a result, at press time, a major government-sponsored economic-reform effort sparked protests and minor social unrest, as Bulgarians anticipated large-scale job cuts and further economic uncertainty. Overall, however, the country's economic difficulties should not affect foreign tourists, and the exchange rate continues to be favorable for visitors.

Bulgaria's tourist industry, at least, is undergoing a slow process of privatization. International hotel chains are showing special interest in the resort areas now attracting tourists who once frequented resorts in Yugoslavia. The first hotels to go private were Hotel Sofia and Hotel Bulgaria in Sofia and Hotel Trimontzium in Plovdiv. During this transition period, many hotels and restaurants are temporarily closed for reconstruction and modernization by their new owners. Facilities not up to Western standards are expected to be upgraded and to acquire more distinctive features. At the same time, hundreds of new hotels, hostels, and taverns are opening throughout the country.

The pace of change is fastest in Sofia: New art galleries exhibiting works by contemporary Bulgarian painters and sculptors have opened, as have new restaurants, often with menus in English and better service than in the past. A new telephone system is being installed in Sofia and its suburbs; many numbers are likely to change by the end of 1996. Also slated for a 1996 year-end opening: the first stations in the capital's new subway.

Romania

Change is moving more rapidly through Bucharest than elsewhere in post-Ceauşescu Romania. Bucharest sports dozens of new restaurants; new shops offer imported and locally made items. Shabby, state-run accommodations lacking the type of service expected by most Western travelers are being replaced by private, service-oriented hotels and facilities. (This edition of *Fodor's Eastern and Central Europe* includes only four state-run hotels that were able to meet basic Western expectations.)

Outside Bucharest, Romania is developing at a slower pace. In some areas state-run hotels and restaurants are still the rule, but wherever possible, new and improved choices have replaced those of lesser quality. In some outlying cities, like Sibiu and Sinaia, new private hotels and restaurants have finally begun to be introduced and are included for the first time in this edition.

In addition to improved dining and lodging choices, new areas are covered: Most prominent among these is the Bucovina. Probably one of the best kept secrets of Europe, the Bucovina is home to a collection of monasteries erected during the Middle Ages, many of which have painted frescoes adorning their interior and exterior walls; they are included in UNESCO's *Catalogue of the World's Greatest Monuments.*

Transylvania has been expanded to include Sinaia, where it is now possible to tour one of the best-preserved royal palaces in Europe, hike the private mountain trail once reserved for Ceauşescu, and ride a cable car to the top of the mountain for an exceptional view of the Transylvanian Alps.

FODOR'S CHOICE

Dining

Czech Republic

★**V Zátiši, Prague.** In one of the city's oldest and calmest squares—the restaurant's name means "in a quiet corner"—this refined dining room offers tantalizing international specialties served with care. $$$$

★**Lobkovická, Prague.** An atmospheric 17th-century wine bar with an imaginative menu. $$$

Slovakia

★**Kláštorná vináreň, Bratislava.** Sample the best of the happy—and spicy—merger of Hungarian and Slovak cuisines at this dark and intimate monastery wine cellar not far from the banks of the Danube. $$$

★**Restaurant Koliba, Starý Smokovec.** This charming, rustic spot on the slopes of the Tatra Mountains serves up grilled specialties to the accompaniment of Gypsy folk music. $$

★**Slovenská Reštauracia, Poprad.** The very best of eastern Slovakian comfort food served in a convivial village-style atmosphere. $

Hungary

★**Gundel, Budapest.** Established at the turn of the century, Budapest's most famous restaurant continues its legacy of impeccable Old World grandeur and exquisite cuisine. $$$$

★**Náncsi Néni, Budapest.** Hearty, creative home cooking in a rustic, grandma's-country-kitchen atmosphere makes this a favorite with locals. $$–$$$

★**Aranysárkány, Szentendre.** This top-notch eatery's small size and open kitchen give it a decidedly convivial atmosphere. $$

★**Hortobágyi Csárda, Hortobágy.** A favorite of wayfarers since it opened in 1699, the Great Plain's legendary old inn consistently serves excellent, inexpensive traditional fare. $

Poland

★**Belvedere, Warsaw.** Enjoy exquisitely prepared Polish cuisine in an elegant candlelit orangerie in Warsaw's serene Łazienki Park. $$$$

★**Wierzynek, Kraków.** Poland's most famous restaurant, in a room glittering with chandeliers and silver, has a reputation for fine food that goes back to the 14th century. $$$$

★**Pod Łososiem, Gdańsk.** The fish and the service at this historic Old Town inn in Gdańsk, which dates to 1598, are both first-rate. $$$

★**Zajazd Napoleoński, Warsaw.** This 18th-century inn with Napoleonic associations serves traditional Polish specialties like *barszcz* and *bigos*. $$$

Bulgaria

★**The House, Sofia.** International cuisine and, in good weather, garden seating make this a worthy new addition to Sofia's restaurant scene. $$$

Romania

★**Coliba Haiducilor, Poina Braşov.** This updated version of a traditional Romanian hunting lodge—you'll feel as if you just got back from a wild-boar hunt—specializes in grilled game. Be sure to request a view of the refrigerator; they'll let you pick out your own cut of meat. $$$$

★**Darclee, Bucharest.** A new cozy French restaurant in the Hotel Sofitel, the Darclee's kitchen actually draws on both French and Romanian traditions. $$$$

★**Bistro Atheneum, Bucharest.** A charming spot in the former residence of the royal family, the Atheneum serves up traditional Romanian specialties to the accompaniment of live classical music. $$

Lodging

Czech Republic

★**Dvořák, Karlovy Vary, Bohemia.** This elegant hotel right in the center of a beautiful spa town has all the modern amenities but plenty of Old World charm to spare. $$$$

★**Růže, Český Krumlov, Bohemia.** Some rooms in this refurbished monastery on a hill facing Krumlov Castle afford stunning views of the loveliest of Bohemian towns. *$$$*

★**U Páva, Prague.** A rare find among Prague's hotels, this little inn has a splendid location on a charming, gaslit street, friendly service, and rooms with individual character and homey comfort. *$$$*

★**Bican Pension, Tábor, Bohemia.** This lovely family-run pension dates from the 14th century but has all the modern conveniences you've come to expect at the end of the 20th; its cool cellar lounge provides a perfect retreat on scorching summer days. *$$*

Slovakia

★**Danube, Bratislava.** This gleaming French-run hotel on the banks of the Danube has a sterling reputation. *$$$$*

★**Grandhotel Praha, Tatranská Lomnica.** This multiturreted mansion in the foothills of the Tatras has retained the elegance and gentility of an earlier age. *$$$*

★**Arkada Hotel, Levoča.** The bright and comfortable rooms in this jewel of an antique boutique hotel belie the building's 13th-century origins. *$$*

Hungary

★**Epona Rider Village, Máta.** You don't have to rough it to spend a night out on the wide open spaces of Hungary's Great Plain; this luxurious modern complex offers sparkling facilities and world-class equestrian entertainment. *$$$$*

★**Gellért, Budapest.** This grand 1918 art-nouveau hotel on the Danube at the foot of Gellért Hill is the pride of Budapest. Housing an extensive, elegant complex of marble bathing facilities fed by ancient curative springs, it is also one of Europe's most famous Old World spas. *$$$$*

★**Hotel Palota, Miskolc-Lillafüred.** This turreted castle in a magical setting in the forested hills of northern Hungary provides modest, comfortable lodging and a perfect base for winter sports. *$$–$$$*

★**Kulturinov, Budapest.** Set on one of historic Castle Hill's most famous cobblestone squares, this neo-baroque castle houses budget accommodations in a priceless location. *$*

Poland

★**Grand Hotel, Sopot.** This legendary late-19th-century luxury hotel fronts directly onto Sopot Beach and stands in its own gorgeous gardens. *$$$$*

★**Hotel Bristol, Warsaw.** Warsaw's only truly legendary hotel, the Bristol has emerged from a decade of extensive refurbishing and is once again pampering guests with luxurious service. *$$$$*

★**Marriott, Warsaw.** This American-run hotel—a relative newcomer on the Warsaw skyline—has much to recommend it: outstanding service, the best health club in the city, and on a clear day, spectacular views. *$$$$*

★**Hotel Grand, Kraków.** At the heart of Kraków's Old Town sits this beautifully restored Regency hotel with some fine art-nouveau touches. *$$$*

★**Zajazd Napoleoński, Warsaw.** This family hotel in a lovingly restored wayside inn is reputed to have hosted Napoléon on his way to Moscow in 1812. *$$$*

Bulgaria

★**Sheraton Sofia Hotel Balkan, Sofia.** It's hard to beat the central location of this first-class hotel. *$$$$*

★**Grand Hotel Varna, Sveti Konstantin.** The best hotel on Bulgaria's Black Sea coast, the Varna offers its guests spa services in addition to lodging. *$$$*

Romania

★**Mara Sinaia, Sinaia.** The new Mara Sinaia, in the mountains northwest of Bucharest, is quite possibly the grandest hotel outside the capital. *$$$$*

★**Sofitel, Bucharest.** An island of serenity and attentive service in the Romanian capital. *$$$$*

Castles and Churches

Czech Republic

★**Chrám svatého Víta, Prague Castle, Prague.** Soaring above the castle walls and dominating the city at its feet, St. Vitus Cathedral is among the most beautiful sights in Europe.

★**Chrám svaté Barbory, Kutná Hora, Bohemia.** Arguably the best example of the Gothic impulse in Bohemia, St. Barbara's

Cathedral lifts the spirit and gives the town of Kutná Hora its unmistakable skyline.

⭐**Týn Church, Staré Město, Prague.** The gold-tipped spires of this 15th-century cathedral beckon people from all corners of Prague to the center of Old Town Square.

⭐**Vranov Castle, Vranov, Moravia.** Perched on a bluff overlooking the Austrian border, this dramatic castle flaunts Gothic, Renaissance, and baroque details.

Slovakia

⭐**Dóm svätej Alžbety, Košice.** Inside this 15th-century Gothic cathedral—the largest in Slovakia—stands a monumental piece of wood carving, the 35-foot Altar of the Holy Elizabeth.

⭐**Kostol svätého Jakuba, Levoča.** The most impressive memorial to Gothic art in Eastern Europe; front and center on the main altar is wood-carver Pavol of Levoča's breathtaking masterpiece, *The Last Supper.*

⭐**Krásna Hôrka, Krásnohradské Podhradie.** Visible from miles around, this fairy-tale castle on a hill is one of Slovakia's best-preserved fortifications from the Middle Ages.

⭐**Wooden churches of eastern Slovakia.** Even the nails are made of wood in these handsome structures that combine elements of Byzantine and baroque styles; religious paintings and icons line the interior walls of many.

Hungary

⭐**Esztergom Cathedral.** The imposing neoclassical dome of Hungary's largest church looming over the village and river below is one of the Danube Bend's best sights.

⭐**Eszterházy Palace, Fertőd.** Known as the Hungarian Versailles, this yellow, 18th-century baroque gem near Sopron in northern Transdanubia was a residence of the noble Eszterházy family.

⭐**Fellegvár, Visegrád.** Crowning the hill above the Danube Bend village of Visegrád, this mighty late-medieval fortress forms one of Hungary's most postcard-perfect images.

⭐**Festetics Kastély, Keszthely.** Dating from the mid-18th century and set on the pic-turesque northern shore of Lake Balaton, this is one of the finest baroque complexes in Hungary.

⭐**Mátyás Templon (Matthias Church), Budapest.** Castle Hill's soaring Gothic church is colorfully ornate inside with lavishly frescoed Byzantine pillars.

⭐**Nagy Zsinagóga (Great Synagogue), Budapest.** Europe's largest synagogue is fresh out of a massive, nearly decade-long restoration. Built in the mid 1800s, this giant Byzantine-Moorish beauty was ravaged by Hungarian and German Nazis during World War II.

⭐**Pécs Bazilica (Pécs Basilica), Pécs.** This four-spired cathedral is one of Europe's most magnificent, its breathtaking interior resplendent with shimmering frescoes and ornate statuary.

⭐**Szent István Bazilika (St. Stephen's Basilica), Budapest.** Inside this massive neo-Renaissance beauty, the capital's biggest church, is a rich collection of mosaics and statuary, as well as the mummified right hand of Hungary's first king and patron saint, St. Stephen.

Poland

⭐**Kościół Najświętszej Marii Panny (Church of Our Lady), Gdańsk.** Dating from the 14th-century, the largest church in Poland and the largest brick-built church in the world is capable of holding 25,000 people.

⭐**Kościół Mariacki (Church of Our Lady), Kraków.** This church on Kraków's central marketplace holds a magnificent wooden altarpiece with more than 200 carved figures, works of the 15th-century master Wit Stwosz.

⭐**Pauline monastery at Jasna Góra, Częstochowa.** The 14th-century church in this monastic complex holds Poland's holiest religious image, the famous Black Madonna of Częstochowa, a destination for pilgrims from around the world.

⭐**Puławy Palace, Puławy.** The home of the powerful Czartoryski family, this neoclassical palace became a cultural focal point in the 18th century.

⭐**Wilanów Palace, Warsaw.** A baroque gem on the outskirts of the capital, this palace was home to several Polish kings and queens; when you get tired of royal portraits and gilt, explore the Romantic gardens with their pagodas, summer-houses, and bridges overlooking a lake.

★ **Zamek Królewski (Royal Castle), Wawel Hill, Kraków.** Stroll the courtyards and chambers of Krakow's 14th-century Royal Castle, built when Kraków was Poland's capital, for a compact lesson in the trials and tribulations of Polish history and to view fine collections of artwork, arms and armor, and tapestries.

Bulgaria

★ **Hram-pametnik Alexander Nevski (Alexander Nevski Memorial Church), Sofia.** A modern, neo-Byzantine structure with glittering onion domes, this memorial to the Bulgarians' Russian neighbors/liberators can hold some 5,000 worshipers; the Crypt Museum holds an outstanding collection of icons and religious artifacts.

Romania

★ **Biserica Ortodoxă, Bucharest.** Inside this Orthodox church are superb examples of Romanian folk-style wood-and-stone carvings and a richly ornate iconostasis.

★ **Vornet Monastery, Bucovina.** The walls of the church at the most famous of all of the Bucovina monasteries are lined with detailed and vivid frescoes depicting scenes from the Bible; the peculiarly deep and penetrating shade of blue used in the frescoes is known to art historians and artists as "vornet blue."

Museums

Czech Republic

★ **Národní galérie (National Gallery), Prague.** Spread among a half-dozen branches around the city, the National Gallery's collections span most major periods of European art, from medieval and baroque masters to a controversial new display of 20th-century Czech works.

★ **The Jewish Museum of Prague.** Actually a collection of several must-see sights and exhibits, Prague's Jewish Museum includes the dramatic and unforgettable Old Jewish Cemetery and several synagogues.

★ **Theresienstadt Memorial Museum, Terezín, Bohemia.** The grounds and buildings of the most notorious Nazi concentration camp on Czech territory have been preserved as a testament to the horrific legacy of the Holocaust.

Slovakia

★ **Museum of Jewish Culture in Slovakia, Bratislava.** Housed in a mid-17th-century Renaissance mansion, this exhibition covers the history of Jews in Slovakia from the time of the Great Moravian Empire to the present.

★ **Šariš Icon Museum, Bardejov.** A captivating collection of Russian Orthodox artwork from the region's churches.

★ **Warhol Family Museum of Modern Art, Medzilaborce.** Original Andy Warhol silkscreens, including two from the famous Campbell's Soup series, as well as portraits of Lenin and singer Billie Holiday.

Hungary

★ **Néprajzi Múzeum (Museum of Ethnography), Budapest.** A majestic 1890s structure across from the Parliament building—the lavish marble entrance hall alone is worth a visit—houses an impressive exhibit on Hungary's historic folk traditions.

★ **Szépművészeti Múzeum (Museum of Fine Arts), Budapest.** Hungary's best collection of fine art includes esteemed groups of works by Dutch and Spanish masters.

★ **Zsolnay Múzeum, Pécs.** Pécs's oldest surviving building houses an extensive collection of the world-famous Zsolnay family's exquisite porcelain art.

Poland

★ **Czartoryski Collection, Kraków.** Part of the National Museum's holdings, housed in Municipal Arsenal, the is one of the best art collections in Poland; among its highlights are works by da Vinci, Raphael, and Rembrandt.

★ **Muzeum Narodowe (National Museum), Warsaw.** A remarkable collection of contemporary Polish and European paintings and ceramics, as well as Gothic icons and works from antiquity.

★ **Oświęcim (Auschwitz-Birkenau), near Kraków.** A million Jews, Gypsies, and others were killed by the Nazis at this concentration camp, which more than any other has come to be seen as the epicenter of the moral collapse of the West; it has been preserved as a museum.

Bulgaria

★**Natzionalen Archeologicheski Musei (National Archaeological Museum), Sofia.** Housed in the former Great Mosque, this collection is devoted to the various peoples who have inhabited Bulgarian territory over the centuries.

★**Natzionalen Istoricheski Musei (National History Museum), Sofia.** Considered the city's most important museum, it houses priceless Thracian treasures, Roman mosaics, and enameled jewelry from the First Bulgarian Kingdom.

Romania

★**Muzeul Satului Romanesc, Bucharest.** This fascinating open-air museum near Herăstrău Lake comprises some 300 authentic, fully furnished peasants' houses.

Towns and Villages

Czech Republic

★**Český Krumlov, Bohemia.** The repainted facades and the new shops and pensions that now crowd the lanes have banished much of Krumlov's charming old decay, but the hard-earned dignity of the houses and the sweet melancholy of the streetscapes abide in this lovely southern Bohemian town.

★**Telč, Moravia.** The perfectly preserved town square, clustered with superb examples of Gothic, Renaissance, and baroque architecture, resembles a scene from a fairy tale.

Slovakia

★**Ždiar, High Tatras.** This tiny mountain village is notable for its enchanting, vibrantly painted wood houses built in traditional peasant designs.

★**Špania Dolina, central Slovakia.** Set in the midst of the Low Tatras, this beautiful village is renowned for its lace making; if you arrive in summer, you'll see older women making tablecloths and lace on their front porches.

★**Levoča, eastern Slovakia.** The medieval capital of the Spiš region seems frozen in time; between the 14th and 17th centuries it flourished as an important center of trade, crafts, and art.

Hungary

★**Sopron, Transdanubia.** Boasting a sparkling inner city of Gothic, baroque, and Renaissance architecture, and bordered by verdant forested hills, this beautifully and faithfully restored town near the Austrian border is one of Hungary's most picturesque towns.

★**Szentendre, the Danube Bend.** A tremendously popular day-trip destination from Budapest, this quaint town offers cobblestone streets for strolling and numerous art galleries for browsing and buying.

★**Szigliget, Lake Balaton.** A tranquil, delightfully picturesque little village on the lakeshore, Szigliget is a collection of traditional thatched-roof houses clustered together on narrow streets at the base of a hill crowned by a 13th-century fortress; the views of the lake from the ruins are exceptional.

Poland

★**Kazimierz Dolny (Lublin and the east).** Perched on a steep, hilly bank above the Vistula River, Kazimierz Dolny is a cluster of whitewashed facades and red-tiled roofs; known in an earlier incarnation as the "Pearl of the Renaissance," the town is something of an artists' colony.

★**Toruń (western Poland).** The birthplace of Nicolas Copernicus, this beautiful medieval city has a charming Old Town packed with ancient churches and residences.

★**Zakopane (Małopolska).** Poland's leading mountaineering and ski resort is nestled at the foot of the Tatra Mountains on the border with Slovakia.

Bulgaria

★**Koprivshtitsa (Inland Bulgaria).** Situated among mountain pastures and pine forests in the Sredna Gora Range, Koprivshtitsa is a showcase of the architectural style known as Bulgarian Renaissance.

Romania

★**Sighişora, Transylvania.** The birthplace of Vlad Tepes, the real Dracula, Sighişora hasn't been developed as a tourist attraction, which makes its medieval citadel particularly inviting.

FURTHER READING

Since the revolutions of 1989–90, a number of leading journalists have produced highly acclaimed books detailing the tumultuous changes experienced by Eastern and Central Europeans and the dramatic effects these changes have had on individual lives. Timothy Garten Ash's eyewitness account, *The Magic Lantern: The Revolution of '89 Witnessed in Warsaw, Budapest, Berlin, and Prague,* begins with Václav Havel's ringing words from his 1990 New Year's Address: "People, your government has returned to you!" Winner of both a National Book Award and a Pulitzer Prize, *The Haunted Land* is Tina Rosenberg's wide-ranging, incisive look at how Poland, the Czech Republic, and Slovakia (as well as Germany) are dealing with the memories of 40 years of communism.

Also essential reading is *Balkan Ghosts,* by Robert Kaplan, which traces his journey through the former Yugoslavia, Albania, Romania, Bulgaria, and Greece; it is an often chilling political travelogue, which fully deciphers the Balkans' ancient passions and intractable hatred for outsiders. In *Exit into History: A Journey Through the New Eastern Europe,* Eva Hoffman returns to her Polish homeland and five other countries—Hungary, Romania, Bulgaria, the Czech Republic, and Slovakia—and captures the texture of everyday life of a world in the midst of change. Isabel Fonseca's *Bury Me Standing: The Gypsies and Their Journey* is an unprecedented and revelatory look at the Gypsies—or Romany—of Eastern and Central Europe, the large and landless minority whose history and culture has long been obscure.

Travelogues worth reading, though less recent, include Claudio Magris's widely regarded *Danube,* which follows the river as it flows from its source in Germany to its mouth in the Black Sea; Brian Hall's *Stealing from a Deep Place,* a lively account of a solo bicycle trip through Romania and Bulgaria in 1982, followed by a stay in Budapest; Patrick Leigh Fermor's *Between the Woods and the Water,* which relates his 1934 walk through Hungary and Romania and captures life in these lands before their transformation during World War II and under the Soviets. Though its emphasis is on the countries on the eastern side of the Black Sea, Neal Ascherson's recent, widely acclaimed *Black Sea* does touch on Bulgaria and Romania.

Forty-three writers from 16 nations of the former Soviet bloc are included in *Description of a Struggle: The Vintage Book of Contemporary Eastern European Writing,* edited by Michael March. Focusing on novels, poetry, and travel writing, the *Traveller's Literary Companion to Eastern and Central Europe* is a thorough guide to the vast array of literature from this region available in English translation. It includes country-by-country overviews, dozens of excerpts, reading lists, biographical discussions of key writers that highlight their most important works, and guides to literary landmarks.

Czech Republic and Slovakia

With the increased interest in the Czech Republic in recent years, English readers now have an excellent range of both fiction and nonfiction about the country at their disposal. The most widely read Czech author of fiction in English is probably Milan Kundera, whose well-crafted tales illuminate both the foibles of human nature and the unique tribulations of life in Communist Czechoslovakia. *The Unbearable Lightness of Being* takes a look at the 1968 invasion and its aftermath through the eyes of a strained young couple. *The Book of Laughter and Forgetting* deals in part with the importance of memory and the cruel irony of how it fades over time; Kundera was no doubt coming to terms with his own forgetting as he wrote the book from his Paris exile. *The Joke,* Kundera's earliest work available in English, takes a serious look at the dire consequences of humorlessness among Communists.

Born and raised in the German-Jewish enclave of Prague, Franz Kafka scarcely left the city his entire life. *The Trial* and *The Castle* strongly convey the dread and mystery he detected beneath the 1,000 golden spires of Prague. Kafka worked as a bureaucrat for 14 years, in a job he detested; his books are, at least in part, an indictment of the bizarre bureaucracy of the Austro-Hungarian empire, though they now seem eerily prophetic of the even crueler and more arbitrary Communist system that was to come. Until recently, most of his works could not be purchased in his native country.

The most popular Czech authors today were those banned by the communists after the Soviet invasion of 1968. Václav Havel and members of the Charter 77 illegally distributed self-published manuscripts, or *samizdat* as they were called, of these banned authors—among them, Bohumil Hrabel, Josef Škvorecký, and Ivan Klíma. Hrabel, perhaps the most beloved of all Czech writers, never left his homeland; many claim to have shared a table with him at his favorite pub in Prague, U Zlatéyho tygra. His books include *I Served the King of England* and the lyrical *Too Loud a Solitude,* narrated by a lonely man who spends his days in the basement compacting the world's greatest works of literature along with bloodied butcher paper into neat bundles before they get carted off for recycling and disposal. Škvorecký sought refuge and literary freedom in Toronto in the early 1970s. His book *The Engineer of Human Souls* reveals the double censorship of the writer in exile—censored in the country of his birth and unread in his adopted home. Still, Škvorecký did gain a following thanks to his translator, Paul Wilson—who lived in Prague in the 1960s and '70s until he was ousted for his assistance in dissident activities. Wilson also set up 68 Publishers, which is responsible for the bulk of Czech literature translated into English. Novelist, short story writer, and playwright Ivan Klíma is now one of the most widely read Czech writers in English; his books include the novels *Judge on Trial* and *Love and Garbage,* and *The Spirit of Prague,* a collection of essays about life in the Czech Republic today.

Václav Havel, one-time dissident playwright and now president of the Czech Republic, is essential nonfiction reading. The best place to start is probably *Living in Truth,* which provides an absorbing overview of his own political philosophy and of Czechoslovak politics and history over the last 30 years. Other recommended books by Havel include *Disturbing the Peace* (a collection of interviews with him) and *Letters to Olga.* Havel's plays explore the absurdities and pressures of life

under the former Communist regime; the best example of his absurdist dramas is *The Memorandum,* which depicts a Communist bureaucracy more twisted than the streets of Prague's Old Town.

A new wave of young writers pick up where the dissident writers leave off. Among the most prominent are Jáchym Topol, whose *A Visit to the Train Station* (cited at the start of this guide's introductory essay; ☞ Chapter 1) documents the creation of a new Prague with a sharp wit that cuts the false pretenses of American youth currently occupying Prague.

Hungary

Hungarians have played a central role in the intellectual life of the 20th century, although their literary masters are less well known to the west than those who have excelled in other arts, such as Béla Bartok in music, and Andre Kertesz and Robert and Cornell Capa in photography (the latter two founded New York's International Center for Photography).

Worth discovering is novelist and essayist György Konrád, one of Hungary's leading 20th-century dissidents, whose *The Loser* is a disturbing reflection on intellectual life in a totalitarian state. The English writer Tibor Fischer's novels *Under the Frog* and *The Thought Gang* deal with life in contemporary Hungary. John Lukacs's *Budapest 1900: A Historical Portrait of a City and Its Culture* is an oversize, illustrated study of Hungary's premier city at a particularly important moment in its history. For a more in-depth look at the city, András Török's *Budapest: A Critical Guide* offers detailed historical and architectural information, and is illustrated with excellent drawings.

For a selection of books on Hungary or written by Hungarians, visit or contact the **Püski Corvin Bookstore** (✉ 251 E. 82nd St., New York, NY 10028, ☎ 212/879–8893) or, in Canada, **Pannonia Books** (✉ 472 Bloor St. W, 2nd floor, Toronto, M5S 1X8 Ontario, ☎ 416/535–3963).

Poland

Neal Ascherson's *The Struggles for Poland* deals with the history and politics of modern Poland, as does *Heart of Europe, A Short History of Poland,* by Norman Davies, a clear, readable account of modern Polish history.

Bruno Schulz wrote two volumes of stories—*The Street of Crocodiles* and *Sanatorium Under the Sign of the Hourglass*—about life in a Polish shtetl before World War II that, in their fantastical aspect, are not unlike something Kafka could have written. Australian Thomas Keneally's *Schindler's List* (originally titled *Schindler's Ark*)—half fiction, half documentary—tells the dramatic, moving story of Oskar Schindler, a Kraków businessman who saved the lives of a thousand Polish Jews. The novel won the Booker Prize; Stephen Spielberg's 1993 Academy Award®–winning film based on the book became perhaps the most widely seen movie about the Holocaust. Louis Begley's haunting 1991 *Wartime Lies* is the story of how a young Jewish boy and his aunt manage to stay one step ahead of the Nazis during the war. Tadeusz Borowski's *This Way for the Gas, Ladies and Gentleman* wryly explores the fate of the Jews in Polish concentration camps under the Nazis.

Andrzej Szczypiorski's *The Beautiful Mrs. Seidenman* is a highly praised exploration of the Polish psyche, complex Polish-Jewish history, and notions of East Central Europe and Polish nationalism. The poet, essayist, and novelist Czesław Miłosz, winner of the Nobel Prize for Literature in 1980, is one of Poland's greatest living writers. His major prose works include *Native Realm,* his moral and intellectual autobiography from childhood to the 1950s, and *The Captive Mind,* an exploration of the power of Communist ideology over Polish intellectuals.

Jerzy Andrzejewski's *Ashes and Diamonds*—the first of a trilogy and the basis for the Andrzej Wajda film of the same name—is a poignant account of Poland in the mid-1940s. Andrzejewski vividly captures this window in Polish history immediately after the war when partisans were still hiding in the fields and before the Soviets and their regime had fully entered the scene. For a glimpse of life in modern Poland, read Janine Wedel's *The Private Poland,* an account of three years' living among the Polish people. Denis Hills' *Return to Poland,* an idiosyncratic look at the country in the 1980s from an author who first lived in Poland during the 1930s and had many adventures, is entertaining and revealing. Another excellent memoir is Eva Hoffman's *Lost in Translation,* an account of her Jewish-Polish childhood and subsequent sense of dislocation when she and her family moved to British Columbia.

Bulgaria

Bulgarian writers are less well known than their counterparts in other Eastern and Central European countries. Though their work is not specifically illuminating of Bulgarian life and culture, intellectuals such as Julia Kristeva, Tzvetan Todorov, and Elias Canetti (winner of the 1981 Nobel Prize for Literature, the first Bulgarian to be so honored) are all Bulgarian-born.

Romania

Gregor von Rezzori, born in the Bucovina region of Romania to Austrian-German parents, has written two of the most moving memoirs of the 20th century: *Memoirs of an Anti-Semite* and *The Snows of Yesteryear.* Both offer richly detailed, coruscatingly honest recollections of his childhood and young adult life in Romania between the two world wars.

National Public Radio commentator Andrei Codrescu returned to his homeland to witness the December '89 revolution and offers his wry appraisal in *The Hole in the Flag: A Romanian Exile's Story of Return and Revolution.* One of the few Romanian novels available in English is Zaharia Stancu's *Barefoot,* a national classic about a turn-of-the-century peasant uprising. For an outsider's view of the country—one disputed by most Romanians—see Saul Bellow's novel *The Dean's December,* which alternates between Bucharest and Chicago. For profiles of Romania's most notorious character, read Radu R. Florescu's *Dracula: Prince of Many Faces* and Raymond T. McNally's *In Search of Dracula,* the first comprehensive histories of the myth and the actual historical figure.

Edward Behr's *Kiss the Hand You Cannot Bite: The Rise and Fall of the Ceauşescus* is a riveting account of the notorious Romanian dictator. Also worth discovering: Norman Manea's *Compulsory Happiness,* an absurdist's view of Romania under the Ceauşescu regime, and his collection of short stories, *October Eight O'clock.*

FESTIVALS AND SEASONAL EVENTS

Czech Republic

DECEMBER➤ **Christmas fairs and programs** take place in most towns and cities; among those particularly worth catching are: **Christmas in Valašsko,** in Rožnov pod Radhoštěm, and the **Arrival of Lady Winter Festival** in Prachatice.

MARCH➤ **Prague City of Music Festival; Czech Alpine Skiing Championships.**

APRIL➤ **Brno's International Consumer Goods Fair; Easter Spiritual Music Festival,** also in Brno; the massive **Flora Flower Show.**

MAY➤ **Prague Spring Music Festival; Prague Marathon; Prague Writers' Festival** offers dramatic readings by major writers from around the world; **International Children's Film Festival** (Zlín).

JUNE➤ **Prague International Film Festival; Smetana National Opera Festival** in the composer's hometown; **International Festival of Mime** (Mariánské Lázně); **Festival of World Records and Curiosities** (Pelhřimov).

JULY➤ **Prague Summer Culture Festival; Karlovy Vary Film Festival.**

AUGUST➤ **Chopin Festival** (Mariánské Lázně); **Baroque Opera Festival** (Valtice); **Český Krumlov's International Music Festival.**

SEPTEMBER➤ **Brno's International Engineering Fair; Smetana International Music Festival; Mikulov Vintage Wine Festival; Prague Autumn International Music Festival; Brno**

Beer Days; Mělník Vintage Wine Festival.

OCTOBER➤ **AghaRTA International Jazz Festival** (Prague); **Velká Pardubická Steeplechase,** considered one of Europe's toughest racing events; **Prague's Festival of 20th Century Music.**

Slovakia

In addition to the events noted below, many villages also host annual folklore festivals, usually on a weekend in late summer or early fall, which are often filled with singing, dancing, and drinking.

MARCH➤ **Musical Spring** (Bardejov); **Folk Song Festival** (Liptovský Mikuláš).

APRIL➤ The **International Festival of Ghosts and Phantoms** is held every year at the end of April in the striking castle in Bojnice.

MAY➤ **Košice Musical Spring** takes place in May.

JUNE➤ **International Folklore Festival** (Košice).

SEPTEMBER➤ **Puppeteers' Festival** (Banská Bystrica).

OCTOBER➤ **Bratislava Music Festival** attracts national and international musicians to venues throughout the capital late in the month.

Hungary

For contact information about most of these festivals, see the city or town's Nightlife and the Arts section or inquire at the local visitor information center.

MID-MARCH TO EARLY APRIL➤ The season's first

and biggest arts festival, the **Budapest Spring Festival,** showcases Hungary's best opera, music, theater, fine arts, and dance, as well as visiting foreign artists. Other towns—including Kecskemét, Szentendre, and Szombathely—also participate.

MAY➤ The **Balaton Festival** in Keszthely features high-caliber classical concerts and other festivities held in venues around town and outdoors on Kossuth Lajos utca.

JUNE➤ The **World Music Festival** in Budapest features several days of world music concerts by local and international artists. Kőszeg's biggest cultural event, held midmonth, is the annual **East West Folk Festival**—a weekend of open-air international folk music and dance performances. Szombathely's gala **Savaria International Dance Competition** (one day in early June) features a full day of elegant ballroom dancing by competing pairs from around the world. **Old Music Days** in and around Sopron features concerts of early music.

LATE JUNE–EARLY JULY➤ Pécs's **Nemzetközi Zenei Fesztivál** (International Music Festival) features concerts by the Pécs Symphony Orchestra and international guests. The **Sopron Festival Weeks** bring music, dance, and theater performances and art exhibits to churches and other venues around town.

JULY➤ The **Szentendre Summer Days** festival

offers open-air theater performances and jazz and classical concerts. Equestrian fans will not want to miss the **Hortobágy International Horse Festival**, held in Máta (and in neighboring Hortobágy) annually the first week of July. During the first two weeks of July, **Celebration Weeks in Baroque Eger** presents classical concerts, dance programs, and more, in Eger's picturesque venues and streets and squares.

Jazz fans can hear local ensembles as well as groups from around Hungary and abroad during the **Debrecen Jazz Festival** in mid-July; around the same time, the **Visegrád International Palace Games** includes medieval jousting tournaments and festivities. Late in the month, the Sárospatak cultural center hosts a **dixieland and blues festival**, while in Balatonfüred the **Anna Ball** is a traditional ball and beauty contest. In Vác the last weekend in July, the **Váci Világi Vigalom** (Vác World Jamboree) festival is held, with folk dancing, music, crafts fairs, and other festivities throughout town.

Every two years in early July, Kecskemét hosts a giant children's festival, **Európa Jövője Gyermektalálkozó** (Future of Europe Children's Convention), during which children's groups from some 25 countries put on colorful folk-dance and singing performances. Debrecen's biannual **Béla Bartók International Choral Festival**, held in 1996 and scheduled again for early July 1998, is a competition for choirs from around the world.

JULY–AUGUST➤ Established in the 1930s, the annual **Szegedi Szabadtéri Napok** (Open-Air Days) offers a gala series of dramas, operas, operettas, classical concerts, and folk-dance performances by Hungarian and international artists. Tickets are always hot commodities; plan far ahead.

AUGUST➤ Early in the month, Budapest hosts a **Formula 1** car race, while the weeklong **BudaFest** opera and ballet festival takes place mid-month at the opera house after the opera season ends. St. Stephen's Day (August 20) is a major national holiday. Two highlights are the **fireworks** in Budapest and Debrecen's **Flower Carnival**, which features a festive parade of flower-encrusted floats and carriages. Held annually around August 20, **Hortobágy Bridge Fair** brings horse shows, a folk-art fair, ox roasts, and festive crowds to the plot beneath the famous Nine-Arch Bridge.

Every two years Esztergom hosts the **Nemzetközi Gitár Fesztivál** (International Guitar Festival), during which renowned classical guitarists from around the world hold master classes and workshops for participants. The festival runs for two weeks early in the month; the next one will be held in 1997.

SEPTEMBER➤ The **Eger Harvest Festival** early in the month celebrates the grape harvest with a traditional parade and wine tastings.

SEPTEMBER–EARLY OCTOBER➤ Tokaj's annual **Szüreti Hetek** celebrates the autumn grape harvest

with a parade, street ball, folk-art markets, and a plethora of wine-tasting opportunities from the local vintners' stands set up on and around the main square.

Poland

DECEMBER➤ **St. Nicholas Day** (December 6), when children receive gifts and dress as mummers, particularly in the south; Kraków's **Christmas crèche competition** features nativity crèches handcrafted by artists countrywide.

JANUARY➤ **Warsawskie Spotkania Teatralne** (Polish theater festival).

MAY➤ **Chamber Music Festival** (Łańcut); **Festival of Contemporary Drama** (Wrocaw); the **Warsaw International Book Fair** is Central and Eastern Europe's largest fair of books, magazines, and manuscripts.

MAY–JUNE➤ The **International Festival of Short Feature Films** (Kraków) presents hundreds of short, video, documentary, animated, and experimental films.

JUNE➤ **International Trade Fair** (Poznań); **Polish Song Festival** (Opole); **Jan Kiepura Song Festival** (Krynica); **midsummer ceremonies** (June 23), which include throwing candlelit wreaths into the Vistula (Warsaw); **Sunday morning open-air Chopin concerts** at the Chopin Memorial in Warsaw's Łazienki Park and at Żelazowa Wola (runs until October); **Festival of Folk Dance and Music Ensembles** (Kazimierz Dolny); **Łowicz Fair**.

JUNE–JULY➤ Poznan's **International Theater Festival** offers performances in various outdoor venues.

JULY–AUGUST➤ **Organ Music Festival** (Gdańsk–Oliwa).

AUGUST➤ Artisans, folk dancers, and musicians take over the streets of Gdańsk for the **Dominican Fair and Festival,** the annual commemoration of St. Dominic. The **International Festival of Highland Folklore** in Zakopane celebrates highland cultures with folk-art and costume exhibits, poetry competitions, and musical concerts. The **International Country Music Festival** in Mrągowo features local and foreign performers. Other August festivals include the **International Song Festival** (Sopot) and the **International Chopin Festival** (Duszniki Zdrój).

SEPTEMBER➤ **Wratislavia Cantans** in Wrocław features oratorio and cantata music. The **"Warsaw Autumn" festival of contemporary music** showcases symphony and chamber concerts, opera, ballet, and electronic-music performances. Other festivals: the **festival of Karol Szymanowski's music** (Zakopane); **Festival of Highland Folklore** (Zakopane).

OCTOBER➤ **Warsaw's Jazz Jamboree** is the oldest jazz festival in

Europe. The same month, Kraków hosts its own **Jazz Festival.**

NOVEMBER➤ Thousands of candles are placed on graves in cemeteries on **All Saints' Day** (November 1).

Bulgaria

For exact dates of annual events and for more information, check with any local tourist agency or contact Balkan Holidays International (✉ 5 Triaditsa, Sofia, ☎ 2/86–861).

DECEMBER–JANUARY➤ **Sofia International New Year's Music Festival** is a winter version of the summer Music Days (☞ *below*).

MAY–JUNE➤ **Sofia Music Days,** focusing on classical and contemporary orchestral repertoire, attracts internationally recognized musicians, conductors, orchestras, and choruses. Concerts are held at the Bulgaria Concert Hall (☎ 2/87–15–88) and the National Palace of Culture (☎ 2/80–10–23). The **Albena Chess Festival and International Masters' Tournament** is held annually at the Black Sea resort of Albena. The **Rose Festival** in the Valley of the Roses is held in the town of Kazanlak. Dancers and singers perform after the predawn gathering of rosebuds by "rose maidens."

JUNE–JULY➤ **Varna Summer International Music Festival** is held in Varna and Golden Sands. It also incorporates the **International Ballet Festival,** held in July.

JUNE–AUGUST➤ The **International Windsurfing Regatta** takes place at the Black Sea resorts of Golden Sands, Sunny Beach, and Sozopol.

AUGUST➤ **Rozhen Sings National Fair,** held in Rozhen near the Pamporovo mountain resort, features Bulgarian folk singers, dancers, and revelers outfitted in traditional costumes.

SEPTEMBER➤ **Apollonia Festival of the Arts,** held in Sozopol, includes art exhibitions, theater, poetry readings, and street events.

Romania

JULY➤ **The Golden Stag,** Braşov's annual music festival, attracts local and international musicians for a weeklong festival of music. Performers have included James Brown and Kenny Rogers.

EARLY OCTOBER➤ In a nod to its Germanic ancestry, the town of Braşov holds an annual **Octoberfest,** with food, local and imported beer, and traditional folk activities

you should certainly seek them out. A fourth dining option, the *lahůdky* (snack bar or deli), is the quickest and cheapest option.

Lunch, usually eaten between noon and 2, is the main meal for Czechs and offers the best deal for tourists. Many restaurants put out a special luncheon menu (*denní lístek*), usually printed only in Czech, with more appetizing selections at better prices. If you don't see it, ask your waiter. Dinner is usually served from 5 until 9 or 10, but don't wait too long to eat. First of all, most Czechs eat only a light meal or a cold plate of meat and cheese in the evening. Second, restaurant cooks frequently knock off early on slow nights, and the later you arrive, the more likely it is that the kitchen will be closed. In general, dinner menus do not differ substantially from lunch offerings, except the prices are higher.

CATEGORY	PRAGUE*	OTHER AREAS*
$$$$	over $25	over $20
$$$	$15–$25	$10–$20
$$	$7–$15	$5–$10
$	under $7	under $5

per person for a three-course meal, excluding wine and tip

Hiking

The Czech Republic is a hiker's paradise, with 40,000 kilometers (25,000 miles) of well-kept, marked, and signposted trails both in the mountainous regions and leading through beautiful countryside from town to town. The best areas for ambitious mountain walkers are the Beskydy range in northern Moravia and the Krkonoše range (Giant Mountains) in northern Bohemia. The rolling Šumava Hills of southern Bohemia are excellent for less ambitious walkers. You'll find the colored markings denoting trails on trees, fences, walls, rocks, and elsewhere. The main paths are marked in red, others in blue and green, while the least important trails are marked in yellow. Hiking maps covering the entire country can be found in almost any bookstore; look for the large-scale *Soubor turistických* maps.

Lodging

The number of hotels and pensions has increased dramatically throughout the Czech Republic, in step with the influx of tourists. Finding a suitable room should pose no problem, although it is highly recommended that you book ahead during the peak tourist season (July and August, and the Christmas and Easter holidays). Hotel prices, in general, remain high. This is especially true in Prague and in the spa towns of western Bohemia. Better value can often be found at private pensions and with individual homeowners offering rooms to let. In the outlying towns, the best strategy is to inquire at the local tourist information office or simply fan out around the town and look for room-for-rent signs on houses (usually in German: ZIMMER FREI or PRIVAT ZIMMER).

Outside Prague and the major tourist centers, hotels tend to fall into two categories: the old-fashioned hotel on the main square, with rooms above a restaurant, no private bathrooms, and a price lower than you can imagine; or the modern, impersonal, and often ugly high-rise with all the basic facilities and a reasonable price. Nevertheless, you'll rarely find a room that is not clean, and some hotels (of both varieties) can be quite pleasant. Hostels are understood to mean dormitory rooms and are probably best avoided. In the mountainous areas you can often find little *chaty* (chalets), where pleasant surroundings compensate for a lack of basic amenities. *Autokempink* parks (campsites) generally have a few bungalows.

The Czech Republic's official hotel classification now follows the international star system. These ratings correspond closely to our categories as follows: deluxe or five-star plus four-star ($$$$); three-star ($$$); two-star ($$). The $ category will most often be met by private rooms. Often you can book rooms—both at hotels and in private homes—through Čedok or visitor bureaus. Otherwise, try calling or writing the hotel directly.

The prices quoted below are for double rooms during high season, generally not including breakfast. At certain periods, such as Easter or during festivals, prices can jump 15%–25%; as a rule, always ask the price before taking a room.

As for camping, there are hundreds of sites for tents and trailers throughout the country, but most are open only in summer (May to mid-September). You can get a map from Čedok of all the sites, with addresses, opening times, and facilities. Camping outside official sites is prohibited. Some campgrounds also offer bungalows. Campsites are divided into Categories A and B according to facilities, but both have hot water and toilets.

CATEGORY	PRAGUE*	OTHER AREAS*
$$$$	over $200	over $100
$$$	$100–$200	$50–$100
$$	$50–$100	$25–$50
$	under $50	under $25

All prices are for a standard double room during peak season.

Outdoor Activities and Sports

Bicycling: Czechs are avid cyclists. The flatter areas of southern Bohemia and Moravia are ideal for biking. Outside the larger towns, quieter roads stretch out for miles. The hillier terrain of northern Bohemia makes it popular with mountain-biking enthusiasts. Not many places rent bikes, though. Inquire at Čedok or at your hotel for rental information. **Boating and Sailing:** The country's main boating area is the enormous series of dams and reservoirs along the Vltava south of Prague. The most popular lake is Slapy, where it is possible to rent small paddleboats as well as to relax and swim on a hot day. If you have your own kayak, you can test your skills on one of the excellent rivers near Český Krumlov. **Skiing:** The two main skiing areas in the Czech Republic are the Krkonoše range in northern Bohemia and the Šumava hills of southern Bohemia (lifts at both operate from January through March). In the former, you'll find a number of organizations renting skis—although supplies may be limited. Both places are also good for cross-country skiing.

Shopping

In Prague, Karlovy Vary, and elsewhere in Bohemia, look for elegant and unusual crystal and porcelain. Bohemia is also renowned for the quality and deep-red color of its garnets; keep an eye out for beautiful garnet rings and brooches, set in either gold or silver. You can also find excellent ceramics, especially in Moravia, as well as other folk artifacts, such as printed textiles, lace, hand-knit sweaters, and painted eggs. There are attractive crafts stores throughout the Czech Republic. Karlovy Vary is blessed with a variety of unique items to buy, including the strange pipelike drinking mugs used in the spas; roses; vases left to petrify in the mineral-laden water; and *oplatky*, crispy wafers sometimes covered with chocolate. Here you'll also find *Becherovka*, a tasty herbal aperitif that makes a nice gift to take home.

Wine

Best known as a nation of beer makers, the Czechs also produce quite drinkable wines: peppy, fruity whites and mild, versatile reds. Southern Moravia, with comparatively warm summers and rich soil, grows the bulk of the wine harvest; look for the Mikulov and Znojmo regional designations. Favorite white varietals are **Müller Thurgau,** with a fine muscat bouquet and light flavor that go well with fish and veal, and **Neuburské,** yellow-green in color and with a dry, smoky bouquet, delicious with roasts. **Rulandské bílé,** a semidry Burgundy-like white, has a flowery bouquet and full-bodied flavor. It's a good complement to poultry and veal. The dry, smooth flavor of **Ryzlink Rýnský** (the Rhine Riesling grape) is best enjoyed with cold entrées and fish. **Veltlínské zelené,** distinguished by its beautiful light-green color, also goes well with cold entrées.

Belying the notion that northerly climes are more auspicious for white than red grapes, northern Bohemia's scant few hundred acres of vineyards produce reliable reds and the occasional jewel. The leading wineries are found in the towns of Roudnice and Mělník, near the confluence of the Vltava and Labe (Elbe) rivers. **Frankovka,** fiery red and slightly acidic, is well suited to game and grilled meats. **Rulandské červené,** cherry red in color and flavor, makes an excellent dry companion to poultry and game. **Vavřinecké,** the country's favorite red, dark and slightly sweet, also stands up well to red meats.

Exploring the Czech Republic

Great Itineraries

Numbers in the text correspond to numbers in the margin and on the maps.

IF YOU HAVE 3 DAYS

Make Prague your base. This will allow you plenty of time to explore the beauties and wonders of the Old Town and Hradčany, as well as to make a day trip to one of the country's fascinating smaller cities: the splendid spa town of **Karlovy Vary** ⑨, nestled in the western Bohemia hills, makes a good one-day destination.

IF YOU HAVE 5 DAYS

Plan to spend three full days exploring Prague. You could easily spend a day each in the Old Town, Malá Strana, and the castle and the other two days visiting the well-preserved medieval mining town of **Kutná Hora** (59) and the unforgettable concentration camp **Terezín** (76). Or you could spend a day amid the Renaissance charm of **Český Krumlov** (65).

When to Tour

Prague is beautiful year-round, but avoid midsummer (especially July and August) and the Christmas and Easter holidays, when the city is overrun with tourists. Spring and fall generally combine good weather with a more bearable level of tourism. During the winter months you'll encounter few other visitors and have the opportunity to see Prague breathtakingly covered in snow; but it can get very cold. The same guidelines generally apply to traveling in the rest of Bohemia and Moravia, although even in August, the peak of the high season, the number of visitors to these areas is far smaller than in Prague. The Giant Mountains of Bohemia come into their own in winter (December–February), when skiers from all over the country crowd the slopes and resorts. If you're not a skier, try visiting the mountains in late spring (May or June) or fall, when the colors are dazzling and you'll have the hotels and restaurants nearly to yourself. Bear in mind that many castles and museums are closed November through March.

PRAGUE

In the seven years since Prague's students took to the streets to help bring down the 40-year-old Communist regime, the city has enjoyed an unparalleled cultural renaissance. Much of the energy has come from planeloads of idealistic young Americans, but the enthusiasm has been shared in near-equal measure by their Czech counterparts and by the many newcomers who have arrived from all over the world. Amid Prague's cobblestone streets and gold-tipped spires, new galleries, cafés, and clubs teem with bright-eyed "expatriates" and perplexed locals, who must wonder how their city came to be Eastern Europe's new Left Bank. New shops and, perhaps most noticeably, scads of new restaurants have opened, expanding the city's culinary reach far beyond the traditional roast pork and dumplings. Many have something to learn in the way of presentation and service, but Praguers still marvel at a variety that was unthinkable only a few years ago.

The arts and theater are also thriving in the "new" Prague. Young playwrights, some writing in English, regularly stage their own works. Weekly poetry readings are standing room only. The city's dozen or so rock clubs are jammed nightly; bands play everything from metal and psychedelic to garage and grunge.

All of this frenetic activity plays well against a stunning backdrop of towering churches and centuries-old bridges and alleyways. Prague achieved much of its present glory in the 14th century, during the long reign of Charles IV, king of Bohemia and Moravia and Holy Roman Emperor. It was Charles who established a university in the city and laid out the New Town (Nové Město), charting Prague's growth.

During the 15th century, the city's development was hampered by the Hussite Wars, a series of crusades launched by the Holy Roman Empire to subdue the fiercely independent Czech noblemen. The Czechs were eventually defeated in 1620 at the Battle of White Mountain (Bílá Hora) near Prague and were ruled by the Hapsburg family for the next 300 years. Under the Hapsburgs, Prague became a German-speaking city and an important administrative center, but it was forced to play second fiddle to the monarchy's capital of Vienna. Much of the Lesser Town (Malá Strana), across the river, was built up at this time, becoming home to Austrian nobility and its baroque tastes.

Prague regained its status as a national capital in 1918, with the creation of the modern Czechoslovak state, and quickly asserted itself in the interwar period as a vital cultural center. Although the city escaped World War II essentially intact, it and the rest of Czechoslovakia fell under the political and cultural domination of the Soviet Union until the 1989 popular uprisings. The election of dissident playwright Václav Havel to the post of national president set the stage for the city's renaissance, which has since proceeded at a dizzying, quite Bohemian rate.

Exploring Prague

The spine of the city is the river Vltava (also known as the Moldau), which runs through the city from south to north with a single sharp curve to the east. Prague originally comprised five independent towns, represented today by its main historic districts: **Hradčany** (Castle Area), **Malá Strana** (Lesser Quarter), **Staré Město** (Old Town), **Nové Město** (New Town), and **Josefov** (the Jewish Quarter).

Hradčany, the seat of Czech royalty for hundreds of years, has as its center the **Pražský Hrad** (Prague Castle), which overlooks the city from its hilltop west of the Vltava. Steps lead down from Hradčany to Malá Strana, an area dense with ornate mansions built by 17th- and 18th-century nobility.

Karlův Most (Charles Bridge) connects Malá Strana with Staré Město. Just a few blocks east of the bridge is the focal point of the Old Town, **Staroměstské náměstí** (Old Town Square). Staré Město is bounded by the curving Vltava and three large commercial avenues: **Revoluční** to the east, **Na příkopě** to the southeast, and **Národní třída** to the south.

Beyond lies the Nové Město; several blocks south is **Karlovo náměstí,** the city's largest square. Roughly 1 kilometer (½ mile) farther south is **Vyšehrad,** an ancient castle high above the river.

On a promontory to the east of Wenceslas Square stretches **Vinohrady,** once the favored neighborhood of well-to-do Czechs; below Vinohrady lie the crumbling neighborhoods of **Žižkov** to the north and **Nusle** to the south. On the west bank of the Vltava south and east of Hradčany lie many older residential neighborhoods and enormous parks. About 3 kilometers (2 miles) from the center in every direction, Communist-era housing projects begin their unsightly sprawl.

Numbers in the text correspond to numbers in the margin and on the Prague map.

The Old Town

A GOOD WALK

Václavské náměstí (Wenceslas Square) ①, marked by the **Statue of St. Wenceslas** ② and convenient to hotels and transportation, is an excellent place to begin a tour of the Old Town (Staré Město). A long, gently sloping boulevard rather than a square in the usual sense, Václavské náměstí is bounded at the top (the southern end) by the **Národní Muzeum** (Czech National Museum) ③ and at the bottom by the pedestrian shopping areas of **Národní třída** and **Na příkopě.** Today Wenceslas Square comprises Prague's liveliest street scene. Don't miss the dense maze of arcades tucked away from the street in buildings that line both sides. You'll find an odd assortment of cafés, discos, ice cream parlors, and movie houses, all seemingly unfazed by the passage of time. At night the square changes character somewhat as dance music pours out from the crowded discos and leather-jacketed cronies crowd around the taxi stands. One eye-catching building on the square is the **Hotel Europa** ④, at No. 25, a riot of art nouveau that recalls the glamorous world of turn-of-the-century Prague.

To begin the approach to the Old Town proper, walk past the tall, art-deco Koruna complex and turn right onto the handsome pedestrian zone called **Na příkopě.** Turn left onto Havířská ulice and follow this small alley to the glittering green-and-cream splendor of the newly renovated **Stavovské Divadlo** (Estates Theater) ⑤.

Return to Na příkopě, turn left, and continue to the end of the street. On weekdays between 8 AM and 5 PM, it's well worth taking a peek at the stunning interior of the **Živnostenská banka** (Merchants' Bank) ⑥, at No. 20.

Na příkopě ends abruptly at the **Náměstí Republiky** (Republic Square) ⑦, an important New Town transportation hub (with a metro stop). The severe Depression-era facade of the **Česka Národní banka** (Czech National Bank; ⊠ Na příkopě 30) makes the building look more like a fortress than the nation's central bank. Close by stands the stately **Prašná brána** (Powder Tower), its festive Gothic spires looming above the square. Adjacent to the dignified Powder Tower, the **Obecní dům** (Municipal House), under reconstruction until 1997, looks decidedly decadent.

Walk through the arch at the base of the Powder Tower and down the formal **Celetná ulice,** the first leg of the so-called Royal Way. Monarchs favored this route primarily for its stunning entry into **Staroměstské**

30

Exploring Prague

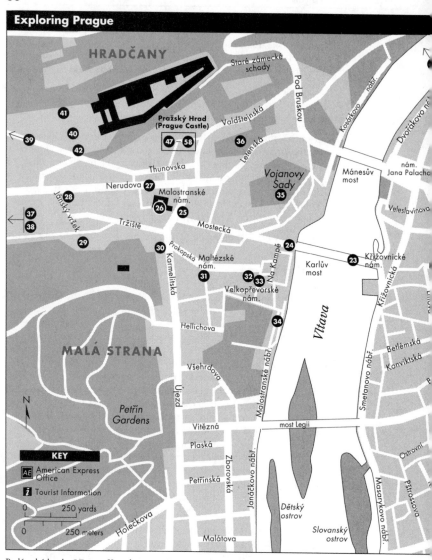

Betlémská kaple, **17**

Bretfeld palác, **28**

Chrám sv.
Mikuláše, **26**

Clam-Gallas palota, **15**

Hotel Europa, **4**

Hradčanské
náměstí, **40**

Jan Hus
monument, **11**

Kampa Island, **34**

Karlův Most
(Charles Bridge), **23**

Kostel sv. Jiljí, **16**

Kostel sv. Martina
ve zdi, **18**

Kostel
sv. Mikuláše, **13**

Kostel Nejsvětějšího
Srdce Páně, **45**

Lennon Peace Wall, **33**

Letenské sady, **43**

Loreto Church, **39**

Maislova synagóga, **22**

Malá Strana Bridge
Towers, **24**

Malé náměstí, **14**

Malostranské
náměstí, **25**

Maltézské náměstí, **31**

Náměstí Republiky, **7**

Národní galerie, **41**

Národní Muzeum, **3**

Nerudova ulice, **27**

Pohořelec, **37**

Schönbornský
palác, **29**

Schwarzenberský
palác, **42**

Sixt House, **8**

Staroměstská
radnice, **12**

Staroměstské
náměstí (Old Town
Square), **9**

Staronová
synagóga, **20**

Starý židovský
hřbitov, **21**

Statue of
St. Wenceslas, **2**

Stavovské Divadlo, **5**

Strahovský
klášter, **38**

Týn Church, **10**

Václavské náměstí
(Wenceslas Square), **1**

Veletržní palác
(Muesum of
Modern Art), **44**

Velkopřevorské
náměstí, **32**

Vojanovy sady, **35**

Vrtbovský palác, **30**

Vysoká synagóga, **19**

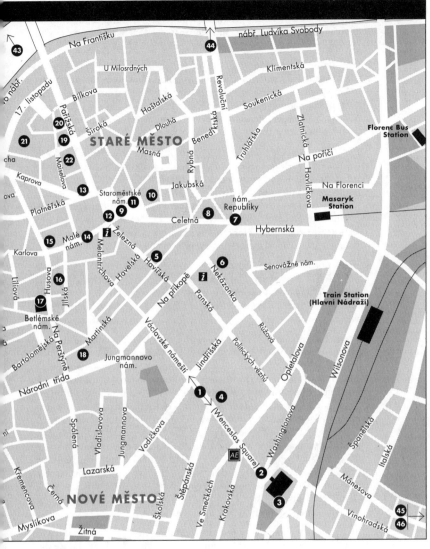

Zahrada
Valdštejnského
paláca, **36**
Židovské hřbitovy, **46**
Živnostenská banka, **6**

náměstí (Old Town Square) and because the houses along Celetná were among the city's finest, providing a suitable backdrop to the coronation procession. The pink **Sixt House** ⑧, at Celetná 2, sports one of the street's handsomest, if restrained, baroque facades.

Staroměstské náměstí (Old Town Square) ⑨, at the end of Celetná, is dazzling, thanks partly to the double-spired **Týn Church** (Kostel Panny Marie před Týnem) ⑩, which rises over the square from behind a row of patrician houses. To the immediate left of Týn Church is **U Zvonů** (No. 13), a baroque structure that has been stripped down to its original Gothic elements.

A short walk away stands the gorgeous pink-and-ocher **Palác Kinských** (Kinský Palace). At this end of the square, you can't help noticing the expressive **Jan Hus monument** ⑪. Opposite the Týn Church is the Gothic **Staroměstská radnice** (Old Town Hall) ⑫, which with its impressive 200-foot tower, gives the square its sense of importance. As the hour approaches, join the crowds milling below the tower's 15th-century **astronomical clock** for a brief but spooky spectacle taken straight from the Middle Ages, every hour on the hour.

Walk north along the edge of the small park beside Town Hall to reach the baroque **Kostel svatého Mikuláše** (Church of St. Nicholas) ⑬, not to be confused with the Lesser Town's St. Nicholas Church, on the other side of the river (☞ A Good Walk *in* Charles Bridge and Malá Strana, *below*).

Franz Kafka's birthplace is just to the left of St. Nicholas on U radnice. A small plaque can be found on the side of the house. Continue southwest from Old Town Square until you come to **Malé náměstí** (Small Square) ⑭, a nearly perfect ensemble of facades dating from the Middle Ages. Look for tiny **Karlova ulice,** which begins in the southwest corner of Malé náměstí, and take another quick right to stay on it (watch the signs—this medieval street seems designed to confound the visitor). Turn left at the T intersection where Karlova seems to end in front of the Středočeská Galérie and continue left down the quieter Husova Street (if you want to go on directly to A Good Walk 3, veer to the right for the Charles Bridge and the other side of the river). Pause and inspect the exotic **Clam-Gallas palota** (Clam-Gallas Palace) ⑮, at Husova 20. You'll recognize it easily: Look for the Titans in the doorway holding up what must be a very heavy baroque facade.

Return to the T and continue down Husova. For a glimpse of a less successful baroque reconstruction, take a close look at the **Kostel svatého Jiljí** (Church of St. Giles) ⑯, across from No. 7.

Continue walking along Husova třída to Na Perštýně and turn right at tiny Betlémská ulice. The alley opens up onto a quiet square of the same name (Betlémská náměstí) and upon the most revered of all Hussite churches in Prague, the **Betlémská kaple** (Bethlehem Chapel) ⑰.

Return to Na Perštýně and continue walking to the right. As you near the back of the buildings of the busy **Národní třída** (National Boulevard), turn left at Martinská ulice. At the end of the street, the forlorn but majestic church **Kostel svatého Martina ve zdi** (St. Martin-in-the-Wall) ⑱ stands like a postwar ruin. Walk around the church to the left and through a little archway of apartments onto the bustling Národní třída. To the left, a five-minute walk away, lies Wenceslas Square and the starting point of the walk.

TIMING

Now that Prague is such a popular travel destination, the Wenceslas Square and Old Town Square areas are busy with activity around-the-clock almost all year round. Visitors in search of a little peace and quiet will find the streets at their most subdued on early weekend summer mornings or right after a sudden downpour; otherwise, expect to share Prague's pleasures. The streets in this walking tour are reasonably close together and can be covered in half a day, or in a full day if you have more time.

SIGHTS TO SEE

🄗 Betlémská kaple (Bethlehem Chapel). The church's elegant simplicity is in stark contrast to the diverting Gothic and baroque of the rest of the city. The original structure dates from the end of the 14th century, and Jan Hus himself was a regular preacher here from 1402 until his death in 1415. After the Thirty Years' War the church fell into the hands of the Jesuits and was finally demolished in 1786. Excavations carried out after World War I uncovered the original portal and three windows, and the entire church was reconstructed during the 1950s. Although little remains of the first church, some remnants of Hus's teachings can still be read on the inside walls. ⊠ *Betlémské nám. 5.* 💷 *Admission charged.* ☉ *Apr.–Sept., daily 9–6; Oct.–Mar., daily 9–5.*

Celetná ulice (Celetna Street). Most of the facades indicate the buildings are from the 17th or 18th century, but appearances are deceiving: Many of the houses in fact have foundations dating from the 12th century or earlier. **Sixt House**, at Celetná 2, dates from the 12th century— its Romanesque vaults are still visible in the wine restaurant in the basement.

🄖 Clam-Gallas palota (Clam-Gallas Palace). The palace dates from 1713 and is the work of Johann Bernhard Fischer von Erlach, the famed Viennese architectural virtuoso of the day. Enter the building (push past the guard as if you know what you're doing) for a glimpse of the finely carved staircase, the work of the master himself, and of the Italian frescoes featuring Apollo that surround it. The Gallas family was prominent during the 18th century but has long since died out. The building now houses the municipal archives and is rarely open to visitors. ⊠ *Husova 20.*

Franz Kafka's birthplace. For years this memorial to Kafka's birth (July 3, 1883) was the only public acknowledgment of the writer's stature in world literature, reflecting the traditionally ambiguous attitude of the Czech government to his work. The Communists were always too uncomfortable with Kafka's themes of bureaucracy and alienation to sing his praises too loudly, if at all. As a German and a Jew, moreover, Kafka could easily be dismissed as standing outside the mainstream of Czech literature. Following the 1989 revolution, however, Kafka's popularity soared, and his works are now widely available in Czech. A fascinating little museum has been set up in the house of his birth. ⊠ *U radnice 5.* 💷 *20 Kč.* ☉ *Tues.–Sat. 10–6 (until 7 in summer).*

🄐 Hotel Europa. An art-nouveau gem, it has elegant stained glass and mosaics in the café and restaurant. The terrace, serving drinks in the summer, is an excellent spot for people-watching. ⊠ *Václavské nám. 25.*

🄑 Jan Hus monument. Few memorials have elicited as much controversy as this one, which was dedicated in July 1915, exactly 500 years after Hus was burned at the stake in Constance, Germany. Some maintain that the monument's Secessionist style (the inscription seems to come right from turn-of-the-century Vienna) clashes with the Gothic and baroque of the square. Others dispute the romantic depiction of Hus, who appears here in flowing garb as tall and bearded. The real Hus, historians maintain, was short and had a baby face. Still, no one can take issue with the influence of this fiery preacher, whose ability to transform doctrinal disputes, both literally and metaphorically, into the language of the common man made him into a religious and national symbol for the Czechs. ⊠ *Staroměstské nám.*

Karlova ulice. The character of Karlova ulice has changed in recent years to meet the growing number of tourists. Galleries and gift shops now occupy almost every storefront. But the cobblestones, narrow alleys, and crumbling gables still make it easy to imagine what life was like 400 years ago.

⑯ Kostel svatého Jiljí (Church of St. Giles). This baroque church was another important outpost of Czech Protestantism in the 16th century. The exterior is a powerful example of Gothic architecture, including the buttresses and a characteristic portal; the interior, surprisingly, is baroque, dating from the 17th century. ⊠ *Across from Husova 7.*

⑱ Kostel svatého Martina ve zdi (St. Martin-in-the-Wall). It was here in 1414 that Holy Communion was first given to the Bohemian laity—with both bread and wine, in defiance of the Catholic custom of the time, which dictated that only bread was to be offered to the masses, with wine reserved for the priests and clergy. From then on, the chalice came to symbolize the Hussite movement.

⑬ Kostel svatého Mikuláše (Church of St. Nicholas). Designed in the 18th century by Prague's own master of late baroque, Kilian Ignaz Dientzenhofer, this church is probably less successful than its namesake across town in capturing the style's lyric exuberance. Still, Dientzenhofer utilized the limited space to create a structure that neither dominates nor retreats from the imposing square. The interior is compact, with a beautiful but small chandelier and an enormous black organ that seems to overwhelm the rear of the church. The church often hosts afternoon and evening concerts.

⑭ Malé náměstí (Small Square). Note the Renaissance iron fountain dating from 1560 in the center of the square. The sgraffito on the house at No. 3 is not as old (1890) as it looks, but here and there you can find authentic Gothic portals and Renaissance sgraffiti that betray the square's true age.

Na příkopě. The name means "at the moat," harking back to the time when the street was indeed a moat separating the Old Town on the left from the New Town on the right. Today the pedestrian zone Na příkopě is prime shopping territory, its smaller boutiques considered far more elegant than the motley collection of stores on Wenceslas Square. But don't expect much real elegance here: After 40 years of Communist orthodoxy in the fashion world, it will be many years before the boutiques really can match Western European standards.

❼ Náměstí Republiky (Republic Square). Although an important New Town transportation hub (with a metro stop), the square has never really come together as a vital public space, perhaps because of its jarring architectural eclecticism. Taken one by one, each building is interesting in its own right, but the ensemble is less than the sum of the parts.

❸ Národní Muzeum (Czech National Museum). This imposing structure, designed by Prague architect Josef Schulz and built between 1885 and 1890, does not come into its own until it is bathed in nighttime lighting. By day the grandiose edifice seems an inappropriate venue for a musty collection of stones and bones, minerals, and coins. This museum is only for dedicated fans of the genre. ⊠ *Václavské nám. 68,* ☎ *02/2423–0485.* ▨ *40 Kč.* ⊙ *Daily 9–5; closed 1st Tues. of month.*

Obecní dům (Municipal House). When reconstruction ends, this building should return to its former glory as a center for concerts and fash-

finest collection of Torah wrappers and mantles, silver pointers, breast-plates, spice boxes, candleholders (the eight-branched *Hanukkiah* and the seven-branched menorah), and Levite washing sets. ⊠ *Maislova 10.* 🖃 *For admission information to this and other synagogues, see entry under Státní židovské muzeum.*

Obřadní síň (Ceremony Hall). It now houses drawings made by children at the Nazi concentration camp Terezín. During the early years of the war the Nazis used the camp for propaganda purposes to demonstrate their "humanity" toward the Jews, and prisoners were given relative freedom to lead "normal" lives. Transports to death camps in Poland began in earnest in the final months of the war, however, and many thousands of Terezín prisoners, including many of these children, eventually perished. 🖃 *For admission information to the hall, see entry under Státní židovské muzeum.*

Pařížská Street. The buildings on this street date from the end of the 19th century, and their elegant facades reflect the prosperity of the Czech middle classes at the time. Here and there you can spot the influence of the Viennese Jugendstil, with its emphasis on mosaics, geometric forms, and gold inlay. The look is fresh against the busier 19th-century revival facades of most of the other structures.

Pinkasova synagóga (Pinkas Synagogue). Further testimony to the appalling crimes perpetrated against the Jews during World War II can be seen in this newly renovated synagogue. The names of 77,297 Bohemian and Moravian Jews murdered by the Nazis were inscribed in rows on the walls inside (many of the names, sadly, have been destroyed by water damage). The building's foundation dates from the 11th century. Enter the synagogue from Şiroká Street on the other side of the cemetery, or through the cemetery. 🖃 *For admission information to this and other synagogues, see entry under Státní židovské muzeum.*

㉚ Staronová synagóga (Old-New Synagogue). Dating from the mid-13th century, it is one of the most important works of early Gothic in Prague. The odd name recalls the legend that the synagogue was built on the site of an ancient Jewish temple and that stones from the temple were used to build the present structure. The synagogue has not only survived fires and the razing of the ghetto at the end of the last century but also emerged from the Nazi occupation intact; it is still in active use. The oldest part of the synagogue is the entrance, with its vault supported by two pillars. The grille at the center of the hall dates from the 15th century. Note that men are required to cover their heads inside and that during services men and women sit apart. ⊠ *Červená 2.*

★ ㉛ Starý židovský hřbitov (Old Jewish Cemetery). An unforgettable sight, this melancholy space not far from the busy city was, from the 14th century to 1787, the final resting place for all Jews living in Prague. Some 12,000 graves in all are piled atop one another in 12 layers. Walk the paths amid the gravestones. The relief symbols represent the name or profession of the deceased. The oldest marked grave belongs to the poet Avigdor Kara, who died in 1439. The best-known marker is probably that of Jehuda ben Bezalel, the famed Rabbi Loew, who is credited with having created the mythical Golem in 1573. Even today, small scraps of paper bearing wishes are stuffed into the cracks of the rabbi's tomb in the hope he will grant them. Loew's grave lies just a few steps from the entrance, near the western wall of the cemetery.

Státní židovské muzeum (State Jewish Museum). All the synagogues and the Old Jewish Cemetery are under the auspices of this museum. In a bit of irony, the holdings are vast thanks to Hitler, who had planned to open a museum here documenting the life and practices of what he had hoped would be an "extinct" people. The cemetery and most of the synagogues are open to the public. Each synagogue specializes in certain artifacts, and you can buy tickets for all the buildings at either Maislova synagóga, Pinkasova synagóga, Vysoká synagóga, or in front of the Old Jewish Cemetery. ☎ 02/231–0681. ✉ *Combined ticket to Jewish Museum collections and Old Jewish Cemetery 270 Kč; museum collections only, 150 Kč; Old Jewish Cemetery only, 120 Kč.* ⊙ *Apr.–May, Sun.–Fri. 9–6; June–Oct., Sun.–Fri. 9–6:30; Nov.–Mar., Sun.–Fri. 9–4:30; closed Jewish holidays.*

⑲ **Vysoká synagóga** (High Synagogue). This striking building features rich Torah mantles and silver. It was ordered built in the second half of the 16th century by the banker and businessman Mordecai Maisel (☞ Jewish Town Hall, *below*) and was expanded at the end of the 17th century. ✉ *Červená ul. (enter at No. 101).* ✉ *For admission information to this and other synagogues, see entry under Státní židovské muzeum.*

★ **Židovská radnice** (Jewish Town Hall). The hall was the creation of Mordecai Maisel, an influential Jewish leader at the end of the 16th century. It was restored in the 18th century and given its clock and bell tower at that time. A second clock, with Hebrew numbers, keeps time counterclockwise. Now home to the Jewish Community Center, the building also houses Prague's only kosher restaurant, Shalom. ✉ *Maislova 18.*

Charles Bridge and Malá Strana

A GOOD WALK

Prague's **Malá Strana** (the so-called Lesser Quarter, or Little Town) is not for the methodical traveler. Its charm lies in the tiny lanes, the sudden blasts of bombastic architecture, and the soul-stirring views that emerge for a second before disappearing behind the sloping roofs.

Begin the tour on the Old Town side of **Karlův most** (Charles Bridge) ㉓, which you can reach by foot in about 10 minutes from the Old Town Square. Rising above it is the majestic **Old Town Bridge Tower;** the climb of 138 steps is worth the effort for the views it affords of the Old Town and, across the river, of Malá Strana and Prague Castle.

It's worth pausing to take a closer look at some of the statues as you walk across Charles Bridge toward Malá Strana. Approaching Malá Strana, you'll see the Kampa Island below you, separated from the Lesser Town by an arm of the Vltava known as Čertovka (Devil's Stream).

By now you are almost at the end of the bridge. In front of you is the striking conjunction of the two **Malá Strana bridge towers** ㉔, one Gothic, the other Romanesque. Together they frame the baroque flamboyance of St. Nicholas Church in the distance. At night this is an absolutely wondrous sight. If you didn't climb the tower on the Old Town side of the bridge, it's worth scrambling up the wooden stairs inside the Gothic tower **Mostecká věž** for the views over the roofs of the Malá Strana and of the Old Town across the river.

Walk under the gateway of the towers into the little uphill street called **Mostecká ulice.** You have now entered the **Malá Strana** (Lesser Quarter). Follow Mostecká ulice up to the rectangular **Malostranské náměstí** (Lesser Quarter Square) ㉕, now the district's traffic hub rather than its heart. On the left side of the square stands **Chrám svatého Mikuláše** (St. Nicholas Church) ㉖.

Nerudova ulice ㉗ runs up from the square toward Prague Castle. Lined with gorgeous houses (and in recent years an ever-larger number of places to spend money), it's sometimes burdened with the moniker "Prague's most beautiful street." A tiny passageway at No. 13, on the left-hand side as you go up, leads to **Tržiště ulice** and the **Schöbornský palác** ㉙, once Franz Kafka's home, now the Embassy of the United States. The street winds down to the quarter's noisy main street, **Karmelitská,** where the famous "Infant of Prague" resides in the **Kostel Panny Marie vítězné.** Tiny **Prokopská ulice** leads off of Karmelitská, past the former Church of St. Procopius, now converted, oddly, into an apartment block, and into **Maltézské náměstí** ㉛, a characteristically noble compound. Nearby, **Velkopřevorské náměstí** ㉜ boasts even grander palaces.

A tiny bridge at the cramped square's lower end takes you across the little backwater called Čertovka to **Kampa Island** ㉞ and its broad lawns, cafés, and river views. Winding your way underneath the Charles Bridge and along the street **U lužického semináře** brings you to a quiet walled garden, **Vojanovy sady** ㉟. Another, more formal garden, with an unbeatable view of Prague Castle looming above, the **Zahrada Valdštejnského paláca** ㊱ hides itself off busy Letenská ulice near the Malostranská metro station.

TIMING

The area is at its best in the evening, when the softer light hides the crumbling facades and brings you into a world of glimmering beauty. The basic walk described here could take as little as half a day—longer if you'd like to explore the area's lovely nooks and crannies.

SIGHTS TO SEE

㉘ **Bretfeld palác** (Bretfeld Palace). It's worth taking a quick look at this rococo house on the corner of Nerudova ulice and Jánský vršek. The relief of St. Nicholas on the facade is the work of Ignaz Platzer, but the building is valued more for its historical associations than for its architecture: This is where Mozart, his lyricist partner Lorenzo da Ponte, and the aging but still infamous philanderer and music lover Casanova stayed at the time of the world premiere of *Don Giovanni* in 1787. The Malá Strana gained a new connection with Mozart when its streets were used to represent 18th-century Vienna in the filming of Miloš Forman's *Amadeus.* ⊠ *Nerudova 33.*

The archway at Nerudova 13, more or less opposite the Santini-designed **Kostel Panny Marie ustavičné pomoci u Kajetánů** (Church of Our Lady of Perpetual Help at the Theatines), hides one of the many winding passageways that give the Malá Strana its enchantingly ghostly character at night. Follow the dogleg curve downhill, past two restaurants, vine-covered walls, and some broken-down houses. The alleyway really comes into its own only in the dark, the dim lighting hiding the grime and highlighting the mystery.

★ ㉖ **Chrám svatého Mikuláše** (St. Nicholas Church). With its dynamic curves, this church is one of the purest and most ambitious examples of high baroque. The celebrated architect Christoph Dientzenhofer began the Jesuit church in 1704 on the site of one of the more active Hussite churches of 15th-century Prague. Work on the building was taken over by his son Kilian Ignaz Dientzenhofer, who built the dome and presbytery; Anselmo Lurago completed the whole in 1755 by adding the bell tower. The juxtaposition of the broad, full-bodied dome with the slender bell tower is one of the many striking architectural contrasts that mark the Prague skyline. Inside, the vast pink-and-green space is impossible to take in with a single glance; every corner bristles with movement, guiding the eye first to the dramatic statues, then to the hectic frescoes, and on to the shining faux-marble pillars. Many of the statues are the work of Ignaz Platzer; they constitute his last blaze of success. When the centralizing and secularizing reforms of Joseph II toward the end of the 18th century brought an end to the flamboyant baroque era, Platzer's workshop was forced to declare bankruptcy. ⊠ *Malostranské nám.* ⌕ *20 Kč.* ☉ *Daily 9–4 (until 5 or 6 in summer).*

㉞ Kampa Island. Prague's largest island is cut off from the "mainland" by the narrow Čertovka streamlet. The name Čertovka translates as Devil's Stream and reputedly refers to a cranky old lady who once lived on Maltese Square (given the river's present filthy state, however, the name is ironically appropriate). The unusually well-kept lawns of the **Kampa Gardens** that occupy much of the island are one of the few places in Prague where sitting on the grass is openly tolerated. If it's a warm day, spread out a blanket and bask for a while in the sunshine. The row of benches that line the river to the left is also a popular spot from which to contemplate the city. At night this stretch along the river is especially romantic.

★ ㉓ Karlův most (Charles Bridge). The view from the foot of the bridge on the Old Town side is nothing short of breathtaking, encompassing the towers and domes of Malá Strana and the soaring spires of St. Vitus Cathedral to the northwest. This heavenly vision, one of the most beautiful in Europe, changes subtly in perspective as you walk across the bridge, attended by the host of baroque saints that decorate the bridge's peaceful Gothic stones. At night its drama is spellbinding: St. Vitus Cathedral lit in a ghostly green, the castle in monumental yellow, and the Church of St. Nicholas in a voluptuous pink, all viewed through the menacing silhouettes of the bowed statues and the Gothic towers. If you do nothing else in Prague, you must visit the Charles Bridge at night. During the day the pedestrian bridge buzzes with activity. Street musicians vie with artisans hawking jewelry, paintings, and glass for the hearts and wallets of the passing multitude. At night the crowds thin out a little, the musicians multiply, and the bridge becomes a long block party—nearly everyone brings a bottle.

When the Přemyslide princes set up residence in Prague in the 10th century, there was a ford across the Vltava at this point, a vital link along one of Europe's major trading routes. After several wooden bridges and the first stone bridge had washed away in floods, Charles IV appointed the 27-year-old German Peter Parler, the architect of St. Vitus Cathedral, to build a new structure in 1357. After 1620, following the defeat of Czech Protestants by Catholic Hapsburgs at the Battle of White Mountain, the bridge and its adornment became caught up in the Catholic-Hussite (Protestant) conflict. The many baroque statues that began to appear in the late 17th century, commissioned by Catholics, eventually came to symbolize the totality of the Austrian (hence Catholic) triumph. The Czech writer Milan Kundera sees the statues from this perspective: "The thousands of saints looking out from all sides, threatening you, following you, hypnotizing you, are the raging hordes of occupiers who invaded Bohemia three hundred and fifty years ago to tear the people's faith and language from their hearts."

The religious conflict is less obvious nowadays, leaving only the artistic tension between baroque and Gothic that gives the bridge its allure. It's worth pausing to take a closer look at some of the statues as you walk toward Malá Strana. The third on the right, a brass crucifix with Hebrew lettering in gold, was mounted on the location of a wooden cross destroyed in the battle with the Swedes (the golden lettering was reputedly financed by a Jew accused of defiling the cross). The eighth statue on the right, St. John of Nepomuk, is the oldest of all; it was designed by Johann Brokoff in 1683. On the left-hand side, sticking out from the bridge between the 9th and 10th statues (the latter has a wonderfully expressive vanquished Satan), stands a Roland statue. This knightly figure, bearing the coat of arms of the Old Town, was once a reminder that this part of the bridge belonged to the Old Town before Prague became a unified city in 1784.

In the eyes of most art historians, the most valuable statue is the 12th, on the left. Mathias Braun's statue of St. Luitgarde depicts the blind saint kissing Christ's wounds. The most compelling grouping, however, is the second from the end on the left, a work of Ferdinand Maximilien Brokov from 1714. Here the saints are incidental; the main attraction is the Turk, his face expressing extreme boredom while guarding Christians imprisoned in the cage at his side. When the statue was erected, just 29 years after the second Turkish invasion of Vienna, it scandalized the Prague public, who smeared the statue with mud.

Kostel Panny Marie vítězné (Church of Our Lady Victorious). Just down the street from the ☞ **Vrtbovský palác**, this comfortably ramshackle church makes the unlikely home of one of Prague's best-known religious artifacts, the *Pražské Jezulátko* (Infant Jesus of Prague). Originally brought to Prague from Spain in the 16th century, this tiny porcelain doll (now bathed in neon lighting straight out of Las Vegas) is renowned worldwide for showering miracles on anyone willing to kneel before it and pray. Nuns from a nearby convent arrive at dawn each day to change the infant's clothes; pieces of the doll's extensive wardrobe have been sent by believers from around the world. ⊠ *Karmelitská 9a.* 🎫 *Free.*

33 **Lennon Peace Wall.** Amid the pompous display of baroque finery stands a peculiar monument to the passive rebellion of Czech youth against the strictures of the former Communist regime. Under the Communists, Western rock music was officially discouraged, and students adopted the former Beatle as a symbol of resistance. Paintings of John Lennon and lyrics from his songs in Czech and English began to appear on the wall sometime in the 1980s. Even today, long after the Communists have departed, new graffiti still turns up regularly. It's not clear how long the police or the owners of the wall will continue to tolerate the massive amount of writing (which has started to spread to other walls around the neighborhood), but the volume of writing suggests that the Lennon myth continues to endure.

Malá Strana (Lesser Quarter). One of Prague's most exquisite neighborhoods, Malá Strana was established in 1257 and for years was home to the merchants and craftsmen who served the royal court.

24 **Malá Strana bridge towers.** The lower, Romanesque tower formed a part of the earlier wooden and stone bridges, and its present appearance stems from a renovation in 1591. The Gothic tower, **Mostecká věž**, was added to the bridge a few decades after its completion. ⊠ *Mostecká ul.* 🎫 *20 Kč.* 🕐 *Apr.–Oct., daily 9–6.*

25 **Malostranské náměstí** (Lesser Quarter Square). The arcaded houses on the left, dating from the 16th and 17th centuries, exhibit a mix of baroque and Renaissance elements.

31 **Maltézské náměstí** (Maltese Square). Peaceful and grandiose, this square was named for the Knights of Malta. In the middle is a sculpture depicting John the Baptist. This work, by Ferdinand Brokov, was erected in 1715 to commemorate the end of a plague. The relief on the far side shows Salome engrossed in her dance of the seven veils while John is being decapitated. There are two intricately decorated palaces on this square: to the right the rococo Turba Palace, now the Japanese Embassy, and at the bottom the Nostitz Palace, the Dutch Embassy.

㉗ Nerudova ulice. This steep little street used to be the last leg of the Royal Way, walked by the king before his coronation, and it is still the best way to get to Prague Castle. It was named for the 19th-century Czech journalist and poet Jan Neruda (after whom Chilean poet Pablo Neruda renamed himself). Until Joseph II's administrative reforms in the late 18th century, house numbering was unknown in Prague. Each house bore a name, depicted on the facade, and these are particularly prominent on Nerudova ulice. House No. 6, U červeného orla (At the Red Eagle), proudly displays a faded painting of a red eagle. Number 12 is known as U tří housliček (At the Three Violins). In the early 18th century, three generations of the Edlinger violin-making family lived here. Joseph II's scheme numbered each house according to its position in Prague's separate "towns" (here Malá Strana) rather than according to its sequence on the street. The red plates record these original house numbers; the blue ones are the numbers used in addresses today—except, oddly enough, in some of the newer suburbs—while, to confuse the tourist, many architectural guides refer to the old, red number plates.

NEED A BREAK?

Nerudova ulice is filled with little restaurants and snack bars and offers something for everyone. **U zeleného čaje,** at No. 19, is a fragrant little tearoom, offering fruit and herbal teas as well as light salads and sweets. **U Kocoura** at No. 2 is a traditional pub that hasn't caved in to touristic niceties.

Two palaces break the unity of the burghers' houses on Nerudova ulice. Both were designed by the adventurous baroque architect Giovanni Santini, one of the Italian builders most in demand by wealthy nobles of the early 18th century. The **Morzin Palace,** on the left at No. 5, is now the Romanian Embassy. The fascinating facade, with an allegory of night and day, was created in 1713 and is the work of F. M. Brokov of Charles Bridge statue fame. Across the street at No. 20 is the **Thun-Hohenstein Palace,** now the Italian Embassy. The gateway with two enormous eagles (the emblem of the Kolovrat family, who owned the building at the time) is the work of the other great Charles Bridge statue sculptor, Mathias Braun. Santini himself lived at No. 14, the so-called **Valkoun House.**

Old Town Bridge Tower. This was where Peter Parler (the architect of St. Vitus Cathedral) began his bridge building. The carved facades he designed for the sides of the bridge were destroyed by Swedish soldiers in 1648, at the end of the Thirty Years' War. The sculptures facing the square, however, are still intact; they depict an old and gout-ridden Charles IV with his son, who later became Wenceslas IV. ▣ 20 Kč. ☉ Daily 9–7.

㉙ Schönbornský palác (Schönborn Palace). Franz Kafka had an apartment in this massive baroque building at the top of Tržiště ulice from March through August 1917, after moving out from Zlatá ulička (Golden Lane) (☞ Prague Castle, below). The U.S. Embassy now occupies this prime location. If you look through the gates, you can see the beautiful formal gardens rising up to the Petřín hill; they are unfortunately not open to the public. ⊠ Tržiště at Vlašská.

U tří pštrosů (the Three Ostriches). The original building stems from the 16th century, when one of the early owners was a supplier of ostrich feathers to the royal court and had the house's three unmistakable emblems painted on the facade. The top floors and curlicue gables were early baroque additions from the 17th century. The ancient inn functions as a hotel to this day. It was the site of the first coffeehouse in Prague, opened by the Armenian Deodat Damajian in 1714. ✉ *Dražického nám. 12.*

NEED A BREAK? At the corner of Na Kampě, right next to the arches of the Charles Bridge, the small stand-up café **Bistro Bruncvík** serves hot wine and coffee in winter and cold drinks in summer. Its slices of pizza are also satisfying.

㉜ Velkopřevorské náměstí (Grand Priory Square). The palace fronting the square is considered one of the finest baroque buildings in the Malá Strana, though it is now part of the Embassy of the Knights of Malta and no longer open to the public. Opposite is the flamboyant orange-and-white stucco facade of the Buquoy Palace, built in 1719 by Giovanni Santini and the present home of the French Embassy. From the street you can glimpse an enormous twinkling chandelier through the window, but this is about all you'll get to see of the elegant interior.

㉟ Vojanovy sady. Once the gardens of the Monastery of the Discalced Carmelites, later taken over by the Order of the English Virgins and now part of the Ministry of Finance, this walled garden, with its weeping willows, fruit trees, and benches, makes another peaceful haven in summer. Exhibitions of modern sculptures are often held here, contrasting sharply with the two baroque chapels and the graceful Ignaz Platzer statue of John of Nepomuk standing on a fish at the entrance. The park is surrounded by the high walls of the old monastery and new Ministry of Finance buildings, with only an occasional glimpse of a tower or spire to remind you that you're in Prague. ✉ *U lužického semináře, between Letenská and Míšeňská Sts.* ⊘ *Daily 8–5 (until 7 in summer).*

㉚ Vrtbovský palác (Vrtba Palace and Gardens). An unobtrusive door on noisy Karmelitská hides the entranceway to an intimate courtyard. Walk between the two Renaissance houses, the one to the left built in 1575, the one to the right in 1591. The owner of the latter house was one of the 27 Bohemian nobles executed by the Hapsburgs in 1621 before the Old Town Hall. The house was given as confiscated property to Count Sezima of Vrtba, who bought the neighboring property and turned the buildings into a late-Renaissance palace. The Vrtbovská zahrada (Vrtba Gardens), created a century later, boasts one of the best views over the Malá Strana rooftops and is a fascinating oasis from the tourist beat. Unfortunately, the gardens are perpetually closed for renovation, even though there is no sign of work in progress. The powerful stone figure of Atlas that caps the entranceway dates from 1720 and is the work of Mathias Braun. ✉ *Karmelitská ul. 25.*

OFF THE BEATEN PATH **VILLA BERTRAMKA** – Mozart fans won't want to pass up a visit to this villa, where the great composer lived when in Prague. The small, well-organized museum is packed with memorabilia, including the program from that exciting night in 1787 when *Don Giovanni* had its world premiere in Prague. Also on hand is one of the master's pianos. Take Tram No. 12 from Karmelitská south to the Anděl metro station (or ride Metro Line B), walk down Plzeňská ulice a few hundred yards, and take a left at Mozartova ulice. ✉ *Mozartova ul. 169, Smíchov,* ⊘ *02/543893.* 🎫 *60Kč.* ⊘ *Daily 10–5.*

★ ㊱ Zahrada Valdštejnského paláca (Wallenstein Palace Gardens). Albrecht von Wallenstein, onetime owner of the house and gardens, began a meteoric military career in 1624 when the Austrian emperor Ferdinand II retained him to save the empire from the Swedes and Protestants during the Thirty Years' War. Wallenstein, wealthy by marriage, offered to raise 20,000 men at his own cost and lead them personally.

Ferdinand II accepted and showered Wallenstein with confiscated land and titles. Wallenstein's first acquisition was this enormous area. Having knocked down 23 houses, a brick factory, and three gardens, in 1623 he began to build his magnificent palace with its idiosyncratic high-walled gardens and superb Renaissance *sala terrena*. Walking around the formal paths, you'll come across numerous statues, an unusual fountain with a woman spouting water from her breasts, and a lava-stone grotto along the wall. Most of the palace itself is earmarked to serve the Czech Senate. The only part open to the public, the cavernous *Jízdárna,* or riding school (not to be confused with the Prague Castle Riding School), hosts occasional art exhibitions. ⊠ *Garden entrance at Letenská 10.* ▣ *Free.* ☉ *May–Sept., daily 9–7.*

The Castle District

To the west of Prague Castle is the residential **Hradčany** (Castle District), the town that during the early 14th century emerged out of a collection of monasteries and churches. The concentration of history packed into one small area makes Prague Castle and the Castle District challenging objects for visitors not versed in the ups and downs of Bohemian kings, religious uprisings, wars, and oppression. The picturesque area surrounding Prague Castle, with its breathtaking vistas of the Old Town and Malá Strana, is ideal for just wandering; but the castle itself, with its convoluted history and architecture, is difficult to appreciate fully without investing a little more time.

A GOOD WALK

Begin on **Nerudova ulice** ㉗, which runs east–west a few hundred yards south of Prague Castle. At the western foot of the street, look for a flight of stone steps guarded by two saintly statues. The stairs lead up to Loretánská ulice, affording panoramic views of St. Nicholas Church and Malá Strana. At the top of the steps, turn left and walk a couple hundred yards until you come to a dusty elongated square named **Pohořelec** ㊱. Go through the inconspicuous gateway at No. 8 and up the steps, and you'll find yourself in the courtyard of one of the city's richest monasteries, the **Strahovský klášter** ㊳.

Retrace your steps to Loretánské náměstí, which is flanked by the feminine curves of the baroque **Loreto Church** ㊴. Across the road, the 29 half pillars of the **Černínský palác** now mask the Czech Ministry of Foreign Affairs. At the bottom of Loretánské náměstí, a little lane trails to the left into the area known as **Nový Svět**; the name means "new world," though the district is as Old World as they come. Turn right onto the street Nový Svět. Around the corner you get a tantalizing view of the cathedral through the trees. Walk past the Austrian Embassy to Kanovnická ulice, a winding street lined with the dignified but melancholy **Kostel svatého Jana Nepomuckého.** At the top of the street on the left, the rounded, Renaissance corner house **Martinický palác** (Martinic Palace) catches the eye with its detailed sgraffito drawings. Martinic Palace opens onto **Hradčanské náměstí** ㊵ with its grandiose gathering of Renaissance and baroque palaces. To the left of the bright yellow Archbishop's Palace on the square is an alleyway leading down to the **Národní galérie** ㊶ and its collections of European art. Across the square, the handsome sgraffito sweep of **Schwarzenberg palác** ㊷ beckons; this is the building you saw from the back side at the beginning of the tour.

TIMING

Brisk-paced sightseers could zip through Hradčany in an hour, but to do it justice, allow at least an hour just for ambling and admiring the passing buildings and views of the city. The Strahov Monastery's halls need about a half hour to take in, and the Loreto Church and its treasures at least that length of time. The National Gallery in the Šternberský palá deserves at least a couple of hours.

Černínský palác (Chernin Palace). While the Loreto Church represents the softer side of the Counter-Reformation, this ungainly, overbearing structure seems to stand for the harsh political fate that met the Czechs after their defeat at the battle of Bílá Hora in 1620. During World War II it was the seat of the occupying German government.

40 **Hradčanské náměstí** (Hradčany Square). With its fabulous mixture of baroque and Renaissance housing, topped by the castle itself, the square featured prominently (ironically, disguised as Vienna) in the film *Amadeus,* directed by the then-exiled Czech director Miloš Forman. The house at No. 7 was the set for Mozart's residence, where the composer was haunted by the masked figure he thought was his father. Forman used the flamboyant rococo **Arcibiskupský palác** (Archbishop's Palace), at the top of the square on the left, as the Viennese archbishop's palace. The plush interior, shown off in the film, is open to the public only on Maundy Thursday.

39 **Loreto Church.** The church's seductive lines were a conscious move on the part of Counter-Reformation Jesuits in the 17th century who wanted to build up the cult of Mary and attract the largely Protestant Bohemians back to the church. According to legend, angels had carried Mary's house in Nazareth and dropped it in a patch of laurel trees in Ancona, Italy; known as *Loreto* (from the Latin for laurel), it immediately became a center of pilgrimage. The Prague Loreto was one of many re-creations of this scene across Europe, and it worked: Pilgrims came in droves. The graceful facade, with its voluptuous tower, was built in 1720 by Kilian Ignaz Dientzenhofer, the architect of the two St. Nicholas churches in Prague. Most spectacular of all is a small exhibition upstairs displaying the religious treasures presented to Mary in thanks for various services, including a monstrance studded with 6,500 diamonds. ✉ *Loretánské nám. 7,* ☎ *02/2451–0789.* 🎟 *30 Kč.* 🕐 *Tues.–Sun. 9–12:15 and 1–4:30.*

★ **41** **Národní galérie** (National Gallery); housed in the 18th-century Šternberský palác (Sternberg Palace). You'll need at least an hour to view the palace's impressive art collection—one collection in Prague you should not miss. On the first floor there's an exhibition of icons and other religious art from the 3rd through the 14th centuries. Up a second flight of steps is an entire room full of Cranachs and an assortment of paintings by Holbein, Dürer, Brueghel, Van Dyck, Canaletto, and Rubens. Other branches of the National Gallery are scattered around town, notably, the modern art collections in the Veletržní palác (☞ Letná and Holešovice, *below*). ✉ *Hradčanské nám. 15,* ☎ *02/2451–0594.* 🎟 *50 Kč.* 🕐 *Tues.–Sun. 10–6.*

Nový Svět. This picturesque, winding little alley, with facades from the 17th and 18th centuries, once housed Prague's poorest residents; now many of the homes are used as artists' studios. The last house on the street, No. 1, was the home of the Danish-born astronomer Tycho Brahe. Living so close to the Loreto, so the story goes, Tycho was constantly disturbed during his nightly stargazing by the church bells. He ended up complaining to his patron, Emperor Rudolf II, who instructed the Capuchin monks to finish their services before the first star appeared in the sky.

37 **Pohořelec** (Scene of Fire), suffered tragic fires in 1420, 1541, and 1741. The 1541 calamity sparked into life on Malostranské náměstí and spread up the hill, ravaging much of Malá Strana and the castle as it raged. Many Gothic houses burned down, opening up large plots for the Renaissance and especially the Baroque houses and palaces that dominate the quarter's architectural face.

㊷ Schwarzenberský palác (Schwarzenberg Palace). This boxy palace with its extravagant sgraffito facade was built for the Lobkowicz family between 1545 and 1563; today it houses the **Vojenské historické muzeum** (Military History Museum), one of the largest of its kind in Europe. Of more general interest are the jousting tournaments held in the courtyard in summer. ✉ *Hradčanské nám. 2.* 🔳 *20 Kč.* ⊙ *Apr.–Oct., Tues.–Sun. 10–6.*

★ **㊳ Strahovský klášter** (Strahov Monastery). Founded by the Premonstratensian order in 1140, the monastery remained in their hands until 1952, when the Communists abolished all religious orders and turned the entire complex into the **Památník národního písemnictví** (Museum of National Literature). The major building of interest is the **Strahov Library,** with its collection of early Czech manuscripts, the 10th-century Strahov New Testament, and the collected works of famed Danish astronomer Tycho Brahe. Also of note is the late-18th-century **Philosophical Hall.** Engulfing its ceilings is a startling sky-blue fresco completed by the Austrian painter Franz Anton Maulbertsch in just six months. The fresco depicts an unusual cast of characters, including Socrates' nagging wife Xanthippe, Greek astronomer Thales with his trusty telescope, and a collection of Greek philosophers mingling with Descartes, Diderot, and Voltaire. ✉ *Strahovské nádvoří 1/132.* 🔳 *20 Kč.* ⊙ *Daily 9–noon and 1–5.*

OFF THE **PETŘÍN –** For a superb view of the city—from a mostly undiscovered,
BEATEN PATH tourist-free perch—stroll over from the Strahov Monastery along the paths toward Prague's own miniature version of the Eiffel Tower. The tower and its breathtaking view, the hall of mirrors, and the seemingly abandoned church are beautifully peaceful and well worth an afternoon's wandering. You can also walk up from Karmelitská ulice or Újezd down in Malá Strana or ride the funicular railway from U lanové dráhy ulice, off Újezd. Regular public-transportation tickets are valid. For the descent, take the funicular or meander on foot down through the stations of the cross on the pathways leading back to Malá Strana.

Prague Castle

Numbers in the text correspond to numbers in the margin and on the Prague Castle (Pražský hrad) map.

Despite its monolithic presence, Pražský hrad (Prague Castle) is a collection of buildings dating from the 10th to the 20th centuries, all linked by internal courtyards. The most important structures are **Chrám svatého Víta** (St. Vitus Cathedral) ㊾, clearly visible soaring above the castle walls, and the **Královský palác** (Royal Palace) ㊿, the official residence of kings and presidents and still the center of political power in the Czech Republic. The castle is compact and easy to navigate in. Visitors can easily design a walking tour to fit their interests and the time they have for sightseeing. Be forewarned: In summer, St. Vitus Cathedral and Golden Lane take the brunt of the heavy sightseeing traffic, while all of the castle is hugely popular.

TIMING
The castle is at its mysterious best in early morning and late evening, and it is incomparable when it snows. You can charge through the castle in 10 minutes, but that would be criminal. The cathedral deserves

an hour, as does the Royal Palace, while you can easily spend an entire day taking in the many other museums and their architectural details, the views of the city, and the hidden nooks of the castle.

SIGHTS TO SEE

⑤④ Bazilika svatého Jiří (St. George's Basilica). This church was originally built in the 10th century by Prince Vratislav I, the father of Prince (and St.) Wenceslas. It was dedicated to St. George (of dragon fame), who it was believed would be more agreeable to the still largely pagan people. The outside was remodeled during early baroque times, although the striking rusty-red color is in keeping with the look of the Romanesque edifice. The interior, following substantial renovation, looks more or less as it did in the 12th century and is the best-preserved Romanesque relic in the country. The effect is at once barnlike and peaceful, the warm golden yellow of the stone walls and the small triplet arched windows exuding a sense of enduring harmony. The house-shaped, painted tomb at the front of the church holds the remains of the founder, Vratislav I. Up the steps, in a chapel to the right, is the tomb Parler designed for St. Ludmila, the grandmother of St. Wenceslas. ⊠ *Náměstí U sv. Jiří.*

④⑨ Castle Information Office. Empress Maria Theresa's court architect, Nicolò Pacassi, received the imperial approval to remake the castle in the 1760s. The castle took heavy damage from Prussian shelling during the War of the Austrian Succession in 1757. The **Druhé nádvoří** (Second Courtyard) was the main victim of his attempts at imparting classical grandeur to what had been a picturesque collection of Gothic and Renaissance styles. Except for the view of the spires of St. Vitus Cathedral towering above the palace, there's little for the eye to feast upon here. The main reason to come is to visit the main castle information office for entrance tickets, headphones for listening to recorded tours, tickets to cultural events, and changing money. ⊠ *Druhé nádvoří.* 🎫 *Tickets (80 Kč, valid for 3 consecutive days) give admission to older parts of St. Vitus Cathedral, Royal Palace, St. George's Basilica, and Mihulka Tower. ☉ These sites open Nov.–Mar., daily 9–5; Apr.–Oct., daily 9–4. Castle gardens Apr.–Oct., Tues.–Sun. 10–6 (free admission).*

The Second Courtyard also houses the reliquary of Charles IV inside the **Kaple svatého Kříže** (Chapel of the Holy Cross). Displays include Gothic silver busts of the major Bohemian patron saints and bones and vestments that supposedly belonged to various saints.

Built in the late-16th and early 17th centuries, the Second Courtyard was part of a reconstruction program commissioned by Rudolf II, under whom Prague enjoyed a period of unparalleled cultural development. Once the Prague court was established, the emperor gathered around him some of the world's best craftsmen, artists, and scientists, including the brilliant astronomers Johannes Kepler and Tycho Brahe.

Rudolf also amassed a large collection of art, surveying instruments, and coins. The bulk of the collection was looted by the Swedes and Hapsburgs during the Thirty Years' War or auctioned off during the 18th century, but a small part of the collection was rediscovered in unused castle rooms in the 1960s. It used to be displayed, and will be again when slow-moving repairs are completed, in the **Obrazárna** (Picture Gallery), on the left side of the Second Courtyard. The passageway at the gallery entrance forms the northern entrance to the castle and leads out over a luxurious ravine known as the **Jelení příkop** (Stag Moat).

★ ⑤② Chrám svatého Víta (St. Vitus Cathedral). With its graceful, soaring towers, this Gothic cathedral—among the most beautiful in Europe—

Prague Castle (Pražský hrad)

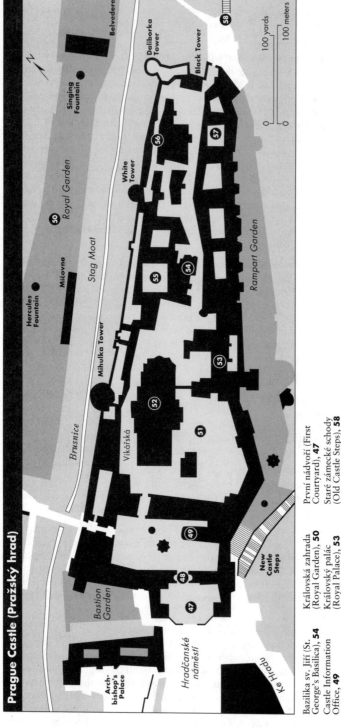

Brusnice

Bastion Garden

Archbishop's Palace

Hradčanské náměstí

Ke Hradu

Hercules Fountain

Míčovna

Mihulka Tower

Vikářská

Royal Garden

Stag Moat

Rampart Garden

White Tower

Singing Fountain

Belvedere

Daliborka Tower

Black Tower

New Castle Steps

100 yards

100 meters

N

Bazilika sv. Jiří (St. George's Basilica), **54**

Castle Information Office, **49**

Chrám sv. Víta (St. Vitus Cathedral), **52**

Klášter sv. Jiří (St. George's Convent), **55**

Královská zahrada (Royal Garden), **50**

Královský palác (Royal Palace), **53**

Lobkovický palác, (Lobkowicz Palace) **57**

Matyášova brána (Matthias Gate), **48**

První nádvoří (First Courtyard), **47**

Staré zámecké schody (Old Castle Steps), **58**

Třetí Nádvoří (Third Courtyard), **51**

Zlatá ulička (Golden Lane), **56**

the museum at St. George's Convent), and the peculiar golden ball topping the eagle fountain near the eastern end of the courtyard.

56 **Zlatá ulička** (Golden Lane). An enchanting collection of tiny, ancient, brightly colored houses crouches under the fortification wall looking remarkably like a Disney set for *Snow White and the Seven Dwarfs*. Legend has it that these were the lodgings of the international group of alchemists whom Rudolf II brought to the court to produce gold. The truth is a little less romantic: The houses were built during the 16th century for the castle guards, who supplemented their income by practicing various crafts outside the jurisdiction of the powerful guilds. By the early 20th century, Golden Lane had become the home of poor artists and writers. Franz Kafka, who lived at No. 22 in 1916 and 1917, described the house on first sight as "so small, so dirty, impossible to live in and lacking everything necessary." But he soon came to love the place. As he wrote to his fiancée: "Life here is something special . . . to close out the world not just by shutting the door to a room or apartment but to the whole house, to step out into the snow of the silent lane." The lane now houses tiny stores selling books, music, and crafts.

Letná and Holešovice

From above the Vltava's left bank, the large grassy plateau called Letná affords one of the classic views of the Old Town and the many bridges crossing the river. Beer gardens, tennis, and Frisbee attract people of all ages, while amateur soccer players emulate the professionals of Prague's top team, Sparta, which plays in the stadium just across the road. Ten minutes' walk from Letná, down into the residential neighborhood of Holešovice, brings you to a massive, gray-blue pile of a building that might have been designed by a young postmodernist architect. In fact it dates to the 1920s, and the cool exterior gives no hint of the cavernous halls within or of the treasures of Czech and French modern art that line its corridors. Just north along Dukelských hrdinů Street, Stromovka—a royal hunting preserve turned gracious park—offers quiet strolls under huge old oaks and chestnuts.

Numbers in the margin correspond to numbers on the Prague map.

43 **Letenské sady** (Letna Gardens). Come to this large, shady park for an unforgettable view from on high of Prague's bridges. From the enormous cement pedestal at the center of the park, the largest statue of Stalin in Eastern Europe once beckoned to citizens on the Old Town Square far below. The statue was ripped down in the 1960s, when Stalinism was finally discredited. The walks and grass that stretch out behind the pedestal are perfect for relaxing on a warm afternoon. On sunny Sundays expatriates often meet up here to play ultimate Frisbee. ⊠ *Prague 7. To get to Letna, cross the Čechův Bridge, opposite the Hotel Inter-Continental, and climb the stairs.*

44 **Veletržní palác Museum of Modern Art.** The National Gallery's newest museum, housed in a trade-fair hall in the Holešovice neighborhood, set off a furor when it opened in 1995. The lighting, the exhibit design, the unused empty spaces in the building's two enormous halls, even the selection of paintings and sculpture—all came under critics' scrutiny. The negative voices couldn't deny, though, that the palace—itself a key work of constructivist architecture—serves a vital purpose in making permanently accessible hundreds of pieces of 20th-century Czech art. Much of the collections languished in storage for decades, either because some cultural commissar forbade its public display or for simple lack of exhibition space. The collection of 19th- and 20th-century French art, including an important group of early cubist paintings by Picasso and Braque, is also here, moved from the Šternberský

Palace (☞ The Castle District, *above*). ⊠ *Veletržní at Dukelských hrdinů, Prague 7.* 🎟 *80 Kč.* ⊙ *Tues.–Sun. 10–6.*

OFF THE
BEATEN PATH **ZOOLOGICKÁ ZAHRADA** – Prague's small but delightful zoo is north of the city in Troja, under the shadow of the Troja Castle. Take the metro Line C to Nádraží Holešovice and change to Bus 112. ⊠ *U trojského zámku 3, Prague 7,* ☎ *02/688-0480.* 🎟 *30 Kč.* ⊙ *May–Sept., daily 9–6; Oct.–Apr., daily 9–4.*

Vinohrady

From Riegrovy sady and its sweeping view of the city from above the National Museum, the elegant residential neighborhood called Vinohrady extends its streets of eclectic apartment houses and villas eastward and southward. The pastel-tinted ranks of turn-of-the-century apartment houses—many crumbling after years of neglect—are slowly but unstoppably being transformed into upscale flats, slick offices, eternally packed new restaurants, and a range of shops unthinkable only a half decade ago. Much of the development lies on or near Vinohradská, the main street, which extends from the top of Wenceslas Square to a belt of enormous cemeteries about two miles eastward. Yet the flavor of daily life persists: Smoky old pubs still ply their trade on the quiet side streets; the stately theater, Divadlo na Vinohradech, keeps putting on excellent shows as it has for decades; and on the squares and in the parks nearly everyone still practices Prague's favorite form of outdoor exercise—walking the dog.

㊺ Kostel Nejsvětějšího Srdce Páně (Church of the Most Sacred Heart). If you've had your fill of Romanesque, Gothic, and baroque, take the metro to the Jiřího z Poděbrad station (Line A) for a look at a startling art-deco edifice. Designed in 1927 by Slovenian architect Josip Plečnik (the same architect commissioned to update Prague Castle), the church resembles a luxury ocean liner more than a place of worship. The effect was conscious; during the 1920s and '30s, the avant-garde imitated mammoth objects of modern technology. Plečnik used many modern elements on the inside: Notice the hanging speakers, seemingly designed to bring the word of God directly to the ears of each worshiper. You may be able to find someone at the back entrance of the church who will let you walk up the long ramp into the fascinating glass clock tower. ⊠ *Nám. Jiřího z Poděbrad, Prague 3.*

㊻ Židovské hřbitovy (New Jewish Cemetery). Tens of thousands of Czechs find eternal rest in Vinohrady's cemeteries. The modest **tombstone of Franz Kafka** in the newest of the city's half-dozen Jewish cemeteries, situated where Vinohrady's elegance peters out into more mundane districts, seems grossly inadequate to Kafka's stature but oddly in proportion to his own modest ambitions. The cemetery is usually open for visitors, although guards sometimes inexplicably seal off the grounds. Turn right at the main cemetery gate and follow the wall for about 100 yards. Dr. Franz Kafka's thin, white tombstone lies at the front of Section 21. ⊠ *Vinohradská at Jana Želivského, Prague 3 (metro station Želivského).* 🎟 *Free.* ⊙ *Summer, Sun.–Thurs. 8–5; winter Sun.–Thurs. 9–4 (closes at 3 on Sun. in winter).*

A much smaller, but older, Jewish burial ground huddles at the foot of the soaring rocket ship–like television tower that broke ground in the last years of communism and used to be dubbed, in mockery, "Big Brother's Finger." The cemetery once spread where the tower now stands, but Jewish community leaders agreed, or were pressured, into letting it be dug up and the most historic tombstones crammed into one corner of the large square. The stones date back as far as the 17th century; a little neoclassical mausoleum stands forlornly just outside the fence. The cemetery gate is almost never unlocked. ⊠ *Fibichova at Kubelíkova, Prague 3.*

Dining

Dining choices in Prague have increased greatly in the past year as hundreds of new places have opened to cope with the increased tourist demand. Quality and price vary widely, though. Be wary of tourist traps; cross-check prices of foreign-language menus with Czech versions. Also ask if there is a *denní lístek* (daily menu). These menus, usually written only in Czech, generally list cheaper and often fresher selections (though many places provide daily menus for the midday meal only).

The crush of visitors has placed tremendous strain on the more popular restaurants. The upshot: Reservations are nearly always required; this is especially true during peak tourist periods. If you don't have reservations, try arriving a little before standard meal times: 11:30 AM for lunch or 5:30 PM for dinner.

For a cheaper and quicker alternative to the sit-down establishments listed below, try a light meal at one of the city's growing number of street stands and fast-food places. Look for stands offering *párky* (hot dogs) or *smažený sýr* (fried cheese). McDonald's, with several locations in the city, heads the list of Western imports. For more exotic fare, try a gyro (made from pork) at the stand on the Staromětské náměstí or the very good vegetarian fare at **Country Life** (⊠ Melantrichova ul. 15, ☎ 02/2421–3366), open Sunday to Friday. The German coffeemaker **Tchibo** has teamed up with a local bakery and now offers tasty sandwiches and excellent coffee at convenient locations on the Staromětské náměstí and at the top of Wenceslas Square.

Old Town

$$$$ ✕ **Potomac.** Chef Jörn Heinrich lends imagination and creativity to Potomac's fresh imported ingredients, and discerning diners can't ask for anything more. The two-pepper soup proves a superb starter for main courses of grilled sea bass, and beef fillet with roasted cashews, green beans, and kidney beans. ⊠ *Renaissance Hotel, V celnici 7, Prague 1 (near Námůstí Republiky),* ☎ *02/2182–2431. Jacket required. AE, DC, MC, V.*

$$$$ ✕ **V Zátiší.** White walls and casual grace accentuate the subtle flavors
★   of smoked salmon, plaice, beef Wellington, and other non-Czech specialties. Order the house *Rulandské červené,* a fruity Moravian red wine that meets the exacting standards of the food. In behavior unusual for the city, the benign waiters fairly fall over each other to serve diners. ⊠ *Liliová 1, Betlémské nám., Staré Město,* ☎ *02/2422–8977. AE, DC, MC, V.*

$$$ ✕ **Fakhreldine.** This elegant Lebanese restaurant, crowded with diplomats who know where to find the real thing, has an excellent range of Middle Eastern appetizers and main courses. For a moderately priced meal, try several appetizers—hummus and garlic yogurt, perhaps—instead of a main course. ⊠ *Klimentská 48, Prague 1,* ☎ *02/232–7970. AE, DC, MC, V.*

$$ ✕ **U Rychtáře** (The Landlord's). A contender for best Italian restaurant in Prague, there's plenty to tempt here, from 20 pasta dishes to nine pizzas, fish courses, and flavorful omelets. Especially tasty are the linguine with chicken breast, ginger, shallots, and parsley and farfalle with broccoli and pepper sauce. The classic Italian desserts, *tiramisù* and *tartuffo,* are crafted with love. ⊠ *Dlouhá 2, Prague 1,* ☎ *02/232–7207. AE, MC, DC, V.*

Prague Dining and Lodging

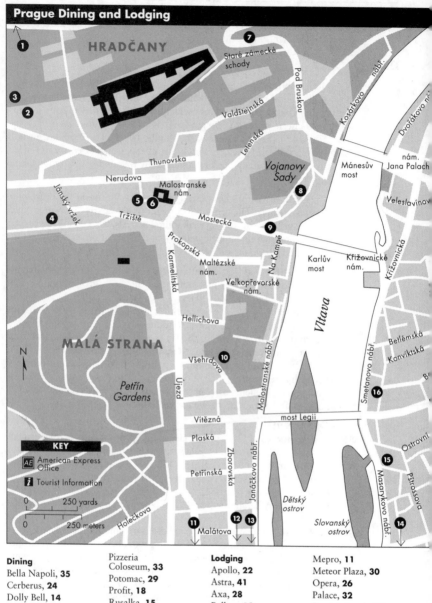

Dining
Bella Napoli, **35**
Cerberus, **24**
Dolly Bell, **14**
Fakhreldine, **25**
Kogo Pizzeria-
Caffeteria, **20**
Lobkovická, **4**
Myslivna, **40**
Na Zvonařce, **39**
Parnas, **16**
Penguin's, **12**
Pezinok, **34**

Pizzeria
Coloseum, **33**
Potomac, **29**
Profit, **18**
Rusalka, **15**
Taj Mahal, **38**
U Mecenáše, **5**
U Počtů, **7**
U Rychtáře, **21**
U Tří Zlatých Hvězd, **6**
U Zlaté Hrušky, **2**
V Krakovské, **37**
V Zátiší, **19**

Lodging
Apollo, **22**
Astra, **41**
Axa, **28**
Balkan, **13**
City Hotel Moráň, **36**
Diplomat, **1**
Grand Hotel
Bohemia, **31**
Harmony, **27**
Kampa, **10**

Mepro, **11**
Meteor Plaza, **30**
Opera, **26**
Palace, **32**
Pension Louda, **23**
Pension Unitas, **17**
Pension U Raka, **3**
U Páva, **8**
U Tří Pštrosů, **9**

room, are fitted in velvety pinks and greens cribbed straight from an Alfons Mucha print. Two rooms are set aside for travelers with disabilities. The ground-floor buffet boasts the city's finest salad bar. ⊠ *Panská 12, 110 00 Prague 1,* ☎ *02/2409–3111,* 🖷 *02/2422– 1240. 125 rooms with bath. 2 restaurants, bar, café, snack bar, minibars, sauna, satellite TV. AE, DC, MC, V.*

$$$$ 🏨 **U Tří Pštrosů.** The location could not be better—a romantic corner in the Malá Strana only a stone's throw from the river and within arms' reach of the Charles Bridge. The airy rooms, dating back 300 years, still have their original oak-beamed ceilings and antique furniture; many also have views over the river. Massive walls keep out the noise of the crowds on the bridge. An excellent in-house restaurant serves traditional Czech dishes to guests and nonguests alike. ⊠ *Dražického nám. 12, 118 00 Prague 1,* ☎ *02/2451–0779,* 🖷 *02/2451–0783. 18 rooms with bath. Restaurant. AE, MC, V (no credit cards in restaurant).*

$$$ 🏨 **Axa.** Funky and functional, this modernist high-rise, built in 1932, was a mainstay of the budget-hotel crowd until a makeover forced substantial price hikes. The rooms, now with color television sets and modern plumbing, are certainly improved; however, the lobby and public areas look decidedly tacky, with plastic flowers and glaring lights. ⊠ *Na poříčí 40, 113 03 Prague 1,* ☎ *02/2481–2580,* 🖷 *02/2481– 2067. 109 rooms, most with bath. Restaurant, bar, pool, exercise room, nightclub. AE, DC, MC, V.*

$$$ 🏨 **City Hotel Morán.** This 19th-century town house was tastefully renovated in 1992; now the lobby and public areas are bright and inviting, made over in an updated Jugendstil style. The modern if slightly bland rooms are a cut above the Prague standard for convenience and cleanliness; ask for one on the sixth floor for a good view of Prague Castle. ⊠ *Na Moráni 15, 120 00 Prague 2 (corner of Václavská),* ☎ *02/2491–5208,* 🖷 *02/297533. 53 rooms, most with bath. Restaurant, bar. AE, DC, MC, V.*

$$$ 🏨 **Harmony.** This is one of the newly renovated, formerly state-owned standbys. The stern 1930s facade clashes with the bright, nouveau riche–type 1990s interior, but cheerful receptionists and big, clean rooms compensate for the aesthetic flaws. Ask for a room away from the bustle of one of Prague's busiest streets. ⊠ *Na poříčí 31, 110 00 Prague 1,* ☎ *02/232–0720,* 🖷 *02/231–0009. 60 rooms with bath. Restaurant, snack bar. AE, DC, MC, V.*

$$$ 🏨 **Kampa.** This early baroque armory turned hotel is tucked away on ★ a leafy corner at the southern end of Malá Strana. The rooms are clean, if sparse, though the bucolic setting makes up for any discomforts. Note the late-Gothic vaulting in the massive dining room. ⊠ *Všehrdova 16, 118 00 Prague 1,* ☎ *02/2451–0409,* 🖷 *02/2451–0377. 85 rooms with bath. Restaurant, café. AE, DC, MC, V.*

$$$ 🏨 **Meteor Plaza.** This popular Old Town hotel, operated by the Best Western chain, combines the best of New World convenience and Old World charm (Empress Maria Theresa's son, Joseph, stayed here when he was passing through in the 18th century). The setting is ideal: a newly renovated baroque building that is only five minutes on foot from downtown. There is a good, if touristy, in-house wine cellar. ⊠ *Hybernská 6, 110 00 Prague 1,* ☎ *02/2422–0664,* 🖷 *02/2421–3005. 86 rooms with bath. Restaurant, business center. AE, DC, MC, V.*

$$$ 🏨 **Pension U Raka.** This private guest house offers the peace and co- ★ ziness of an alpine lodge, plus a quiet location on the ancient, winding streets of Nový Svět, just behind the Loreto Church and a 10-minute walk from Prague Castle. The dark-wood building has only five rooms, but if you can get a reservation (try at least a month in advance), you will gain a wonderful base for exploring Prague. ⊠ *Černínská ul.*

10/93, 118 00 Prague 1, ☎ *02/351453 or 02/2051–1100,* ℻ *02/353074 or 02/2051–0511. 5 rooms. AE, DC, MC, V.*

$$$ ⊡ **U Páva.** This neoclassical inn, on a quiet gaslit street in Malá Strana,
★ offers upstairs suites that afford an unforgettable view of Prague Cas-
tle. Best of all, the U Páva is small and intimate—the perfect escape
for those who've had their fill of cement high-rise resorts. The staff is
courteous and helpful, while the reception and public areas are elegant
and discreet. ⊠ *U lužického semináře 32, 118 00 Prague 1,* ☎ *02/2451–
0922,* ℻ *02/533379. 11 rooms with bath. Restaurant, bar. AE, DC,
MC, V.*

$$ ⊡ **Apollo.** This is a standard, no-frills, square-box hotel where clean
rooms come at a fair price. Its primary flaw is its location: roughly 20
minutes by metro or bus from the city center. ⊠ *Kubišova 23, 182 00
Prague 8 (metro Holešovice, Line C, then Tram 5, 17, or 25 to the
Hercovka stop),* ☎ *02/688–0628,* ℻ *02/688–4570. 35 rooms with
bath. AE, MC, V.*

$$ ⊡ **Astra.** The location best serves drivers coming in to town from the
east, although the nearby metro station makes this modern hotel easy
to reach from the center. It's good value at the price. ⊠ *Mukařovská
1740/18, 100 00 Prague 10 (from metro station Skalka, Line A, walk
south on Na padesátém about 5 mins to Mukařovská),* ☎ *02/781–
3595,* ℻ *02/781–0765. 50 rooms with bath. Restaurant, in-room satel-
lite TVs, nightclub. AE, DC, MC, V.*

$$ ⊡ **Mepro.** Standard rooms and service and a reasonably central location make this small hotel worth considering. The Smíchov neighbor-
hood offers a good range of restaurants (for one, the U Mikuláše
Dačického wine tavern, across the street from the hotel) and nice
strolls along the river or up the Petřín hill. ⊠ *Viktora Huga 3, 150 00
Prague 5,* ☎ *02/549167,* ℻ *02/561–8587. 26 rooms with bath. Snack
bar, in-room satellite TVs. AE, MC, V.*

$$ ⊡ **Opera.** Once the lodging of choice for divas performing at the
nearby State Theater, the Opera greatly declined under the Commu-
nists. New owners, however, are working hard to restore the hotel's
former luster. Until then, the clean (but smallish) rooms, friendly staff,
and fin-de-siècle charm are still reason enough to recommend it. Rooms
without bath are half price. ⊠ *Těšnov 13, 110 00 Prague 1,* ☎ *02/
231–5609,* ℻ *02/231–1477. 66 rooms, some with bath. Restaurant,
bar. AE, DC, MC, V.*

$ ⊡ **Balkan.** One of the few central hotels that can compete in cost with
private rooms, the spartan Balkan is on a busy street, not far from
Malá Strana and the National Theater. ⊠ *Svornosti 28, 150 00 Prague
5,* ☎ ℻ *02/540777. 24 rooms with bath. Breakfast not included.
Restaurant. AE.*

$ ⊡ **Pension Louda.** The friendly owners of this family-run guest house,
★ set in a suburb roughly 20 minutes by tram from the city center, go
out of their way to make you feel welcome. The large, spotless rooms
are an unbelievable bargain, and the hilltop location offers a stunning
view of greater Prague. ⊠ *Kubišova 10, 182 00 Prague 8 (metro
Holešovice, Line C, then Tram 5, 17, or 25 to the Hercovka stop),*
☎ *02/688–1491,* ℻ *02/688–1488. 9 rooms with bath. No credit cards.*

$ ⊡ **Pension Unitas.** Operated by the Christian charity Unitas in an Old
Town convent, the spartan rooms at this well-run establishment used
to serve as interrogation cells for the Communist secret police. Con-
ditions are much more comfortable nowadays, if far from luxurious.
Alcohol and tobacco are not permitted. ⊠ *Bartolomějská 9, 110 00
Prague 1,* ☎ *02/232–7700,* ℻ *02/232–7709. 40 rooms, none with
bath. AE, MC, V.*

Nightlife and the Arts

Nightlife

CABARET

For adult stage entertainment (with some nudity) try the **Lucerna Bar** (⊠ Štěpánská ul. 61, at Wenceslas Sq.) or **Varieté Praga** (⊠ Vodičkova ul. 30, ☎ 02/2421–5945).

DISCOS

Dance clubs come and go with predictable regularity. The longtime favorite is **Radost FX** (⊠ Bělehradská 120, Prague 2, ☎ 02/251210), featuring imported DJs playing the latest dance music and techno from London. The café on the ground floor is open all night and serves wholesome vegetarian food. Two popular discos for dancing the night away with fellow tourists are **Lávká** (⊠ Novotného lávká 1, near the Charles Bridge), featuring open-air dancing by the bridge on summer nights, and the **Corona Club and Latin Café** (⊠ Novotného lávká, Prague 1), which highlights Latin, Gypsy, and other dance-friendly live music. Discos catering to a very young crowd blast sound onto lower Wenceslas Square.

JAZZ CLUBS

Jazz gained notoriety under the Communists as a subtle form of protest, and the city still has some great jazz clubs, featuring everything from swing to blues and modern. **Reduta** (⊠ Národní 20, ☎ 02/2491–2246) features a full program of local and international musicians. **AghaRTA** (⊠ Krakovská 5, ☎ 02/2421–2914) offers a variety of jazz acts in an intimate café/nightclub atmosphere. Music starts around 9 PM, but come earlier to get a seat. Check posters around town or any of the English-language newspapers for current listings.

PUBS, BARS, AND LOUNGES

Bars or lounges are not traditional Prague fixtures; social life, of the drinking variety, usually takes place in pubs (*pivnice* or *hospody*), which are liberally sprinkled throughout the city's neighborhoods. Tourists are welcome to join in the evening ritual of sitting around large tables and talking, smoking, and drinking beer. Before venturing in, however, it's best to familiarize yourself with a few points of pub etiquette. Always ask if a chair is free before sitting down. To order a beer (*pivo*), do not wave the waiter down or shout across the room; he will usually assume you want beer and bring it over to you without asking. He will also bring subsequent rounds to the table without asking. To refuse, just shake your head or say no thanks. At the end of the evening, usually around 10:30 or 11:00, the waiter will come to tally the bill. Some of the most popular pubs in the city center include **U Medvidků** (⊠ Na Perštýně 7), **U Vejvodů** (⊠ Jilská 4), and **U Zlatého Tygra** (⊠ Husova ul. 17). All can get impossibly crowded.

One of the oddest phenomena of Prague's post-1989 renaissance is the sight of travelers and tour groups from the United States, Britain, Australia, and even Japan descending on this city to experience the life of—American expatriates. There are a handful of bars guaranteed to ooze Yanks and other native English speakers. **Jo's Bar** (⊠ Malostranské nám. 7) is a haven for younger expats, serving bottled beer, mixed drinks, and good Mexican food. The **James Joyce Pub** (⊠ Liliová 10) is authentically Irish, with Guinness on tap and excellent food. **U Malého Glena** puts on live jazz, folk, and rock (⊠ Karmelitská 23, ☎ 02/535–8115). The major hotels also run their own bars and nightclubs. The **Piano Bar** (⊠ Hotel Palace, Panská ul. 12) is the most pleasant of the lot; jacket and tie are suggested.

ROCK CLUBS

Prague's rock scene is thriving. Hard-rock enthusiasts should check out the **Rock Café** (⊠ Národní 20, ☎ 02/2491–4416) or **Strahov 007** (⊠ Near Strahov Stadium; take Bus 218 2 stops from Anděl metro station). **RC Bunkr** (⊠ Lodecká 2, ☎ 02/2481–0665) was the first post-revolutionary underground club. The **Malostranska Beseda** (⊠ Malostranské nám. 21, ☎ 02/539024) and the **Belmondo Revival Club** (⊠ Bubenská 1, Prague 7, ☎ 02/791–4854) are dependable bets for some-times bizarre, but always good, musical acts from around the country.

The Arts

Prague's cultural flair is legendary, though performances are usually booked far in advance by all sorts of Praguers. The concierge at your hotel may be able to reserve tickets for you. Otherwise, for the cheap-est tickets go directly to the theater box office a few days in advance or immediately before a performance. The biggest ticket agency, **Tiket-pro,** has outlets all over town and accepts credit cards (main branch at ⊠ Štěpánská 61, Lucerna passage, ☎ 02/2481–4020). **Bohemia Ticket International** (⊠ Na příkopě 16, ☎ 02/2421–5031; ⊠ Václavské nám. 25, ☎ 02/2422–7253) sells tickets for major cultural events, though at semi-inflated prices. Tickets can also be purchased at **American Express** (⊠ Václavské nám. 56).

For details of cultural events, look for the English-language news-paper the *Prague Post* or the monthly *Velvet* magazine, or the monthly *Prague Guide,* available at hotels and tourist offices.

FILM

If a film was made in the United States or Britain, the chances are good that it will be shown with Czech subtitles rather than dubbed. (Film titles, however, are usually translated into Czech, so your only clue to the movie's country of origin may be the poster used in advertisements.) Popular cinemas are **Blaník** (⊠ Václavské nám. 56, ☎ 02/2421–6698), **Hvěda** (⊠ Václavské nám 38, ☎ 02/264545), **Praha** (⊠ Václavské nám. 17, ☎ 02/262035), and **Světozor** (⊠ Vodičkova ul. 39, ☎ 02/263616). Prague's English-language publications carry film re-views and full timetables.

MUSIC

Classical concerts are held all over the city throughout the year. The best orchestral venues are the resplendent art-nouveau **Obecní dům** (⊠ Smetana Hall, Nám. Republiky 5, scheduled to reopen in the spring of 1997), home of the Prague Symphony Orchestra, and **Dvořák Hall** (⊠ In the Rudolfinum, nám. Jana Palacha, ☎ 02/2489–3111). The latter concert hall is home to one of Central Europe's best orchestras, the Czech Philharmonic, which has been racked in recent years by bit-ter disputes among players, conductors, and management but still plays sublimely.

Performances also are held regularly in the **Garden on the Ramparts** below Prague Castle (where the music comes with a view), the two **churches of St. Nicholas** (on Old Town Square and Malostranské náměstí), the **Church of Sts. Simon and Jude** (⊠ Dušní ul., in the Old Town, near the Hotel Inter-Continental), the **Church of St. James** (⊠ Malá Štupartská, near Old Town Square), the **Zrcadlová kaple** (⊠ Mirror Chapel, Klementinum, Mariánské náměstí, Old Town), the **Lobkowicz Palace** at Prague Castle, and plenty more palaces and churches. Dozens of classical ensembles survive off the tourist-concert trade at these and many other venues. The standard of performance ranges from adequate to superb, though the programs tend to take few risks. Serious fans of baroque music have the opportunity to hear works of little-known Bohemian composers at these concerts. Some of the best chamber ensembles are the **Talich Chamber Orchestra,** the **Guarneri Trio,** the **Wihan Quartet,** the **Czech Piano Trio,** and the **Agon** contemporary music group.

Concerts at the **Villa Bertramka** (✉ Mozartova 169, Smíchov, ☎ 02/543893) emphasize the music of Mozart and his contemporaries (☞ Off the Beaten Path *in* Charles Bridge and Malá Strana, *above*).

Fans of organ music will be delighted by the number of recitals held in Prague's historic halls and churches. Popular programs are offered at **St. Vitus Cathedral** in Hradčany, **U Křížovníků** near the Charles Bridge, the **Church of St. Nicholas** in Malá Strana, and **St. James's Church** on Malá Štupartská in the Old Town, where the organ plays amid a complement of baroque statuary.

OPERA AND BALLET
The Czech Republic has a strong operatic tradition, and performances at the **Národní divadlo** (✉ National Theater, Národní třída 2, ☎ 02/2491–2673) and the **Statní Opera Praha** (✉ State Opera House, Wilsonova 4, ☎ 02/265353), near the top of Wenceslas Square, can be excellent. It's always worthwhile to buy a cheap ticket (for as little as 10 Kč) just to take a look at these stunning 19th-century halls; appropriate attire is recommended. Now, unlike the Communist period, operas are almost always sung in their original tongue, and the repertoire offers plenty of Italian favorites and the Czech national composers Janaček, Dvořák, and Smetana. The historic **Stavovské divadlo** (✉ Estates' Theater, Ovocný trh. 1, ☎ 02/2421–5001), where *Don Giovanni* premiered in the 18th century, plays host to a mix of operas and dramatic works. Simultaneous translation into English via a microwave transmitter and headsets is usually offered at drama performances. The National and State theaters also occasionally have ballets.

PUPPET SHOWS
This traditional form of Czech popular entertainment has been given new life thanks to the productions mounted at the **National Marionette Theater** (✉ Žatecká 1) and the **Magic Theater of the Baroque World** (✉ Celetná 13). Traditionally, children and adults alike enjoy the hilarity and pathos of these performances.

THEATER
Theater thrives in the Czech Republic as a vibrant art form. A dozen or so professional companies play in Prague to ever-packed houses; the language barrier can't obscure the players' artistry. Tourist-friendly, nonverbal theater abounds as well, notably Black Theater, a melding of live acting, mime, video, and stage trickery, which continues to draw crowds despite signs of fatigue. The famous **Laterna Magika** (Magic Lantern) puts on a similar extravaganza (✉ Národní třída 4, ☎ 02/2491–4129). Performances usually begin at 7 or 7:30 PM. Several English-language theater groups operate sporadically in Prague; pick up a copy of the *Prague Post* for complete listings.

Outdoor Activities and Sports

Fitness Clubs
The best fitness clubs in town are at the **Forum Hotel** (✉ Kongresova ul. 1, ☎ 02/6119–1111; Vyšehrad metro station), the **Hilton Hotel** (✉ Pobřežní 1, ☎ 02/2484–1111; Florenc metro station), and the **AXA Hotel** (✉ Na Poříčí 12, ☎ 2481–2580; Florenc metro station). All three are open to nonresidents, but call first to inquire about rates.

Golf

You can golf year-round at Prague's only course, located outside the city at the **Stop Motel** (⊠ Plzeňská ul. 215, ☎ 02/523251). Take a taxi to the motel or Tram 7 to the end of the line.

Jogging

The best place for jogging is the **Letenské sady,** the large park across the river from the Hotel Inter-Continental. Cross the Svatopluka Çecha Bridge, climb the stairs, and turn to the right for a good, long run far away from the car fumes. The **Riegrový sady,** a park in Vinohrady behind the main train station, is also nice, but it is small and a bit out of the way.

Spectator Sports

Prague plays host to a wide variety of spectator sports, including world-class ice hockey, handball, tennis, and swimming. Most events, however, are held at irregular intervals. The best place to find out what's going on (and where) is the weekly sports page of the *Prague Post,* or you can inquire at your hotel.

SOCCER

National and international matches are played regularly at the Sparta Stadium in Holešovice, behind the Letenské Sady (☞ Jogging, *above*). To reach the stadium, take Tram 1, 25, or 26 to the Sparta stop.

Swimming

The best public swimming pool in Prague is at the **Podolí Swimming Stadium** in Podolí, easily reached from the city center via Tram 3 or 17. The indoor pool is 50 meters long, and the complex also includes two open-air pools, a sauna, a steam bath, and a wild-ride water slide. (A word of warning: Podolí, for all its attractions, is notorious as a local hot spot of petty thievery; don't entrust any valuables to the lockers—it's best to either check them in the safe with the *vrátnice* (superintendent) or better yet, don't bring them at all.) The pool at the **Hilton Hotel** is smaller, but the location is more convenient (☞ Fitness Clubs, *above*). Another pool to try is in the **Hotel Olšanka** (⊠ Táboritská 23, Prague 3, ☎ 6709–2111).

Tennis

There are public courts at the **Strahov Stadium** in Břevnov. Take Tram 8 to the end from the Hradčanská metro stop and change to Bus 143, 149, or 217. The **Hilton Hotel** (☞ Fitness Clubs, *above*) has two indoor courts available for public use.

Shopping

Despite the relative shortage of quality clothes—Prague has a long way to go before it can match shopping meccas Paris and Rome—the capital is a great place to pick up gifts and souvenirs. Bohemian crystal and porcelain deservedly enjoy a worldwide reputation for quality, and plenty of shops offer excellent bargains. The local market for antiques and artworks is still relatively undeveloped, while dozens of antiquarian bookstores can yield some excellent finds, particularly German and Czech books and graphics. Another bargain is recorded music: CD prices are about half what you would pay in the West.

Shopping Districts

The major shopping areas are **Národní třída,** running past Můstek to Na příkopě, and the area around **Staroměstské náměstí** (Old Town Square). **Pařížská ulice, Karlova ulice** (on the way to the Charles Bridge), and the area just south of **Josefov** (the Jewish Quarter) are also good places to find boutiques and antiques shops. In the Malá Strana, try **Nerudova ulice,** the street that runs up to the Castle Hill district.

Department Stores

These are not always well stocked and often have everything except the one item you're looking for, but a stroll through one may yield some interesting finds and bargains. The best are **Kotva** (⊠ Nám. Republiky 8), **Tesco** (⊠ Národní třída 26), **Bílá Labut'** (⊠ Na poříčí 23), and **Krone** (⊠ Václavské nám. 21).

Street Markets

For fruits and vegetables, the best street market in central Prague is on **Havelská ulice** in the Old Town. But arrive early in the day if you want something a bit more exotic than tomatoes and cucumbers. The best market for nonfood items is the flea market in **Holešovice,** north of the city center, although there isn't really much of interest here outside of cheap tobacco and electronics products. Take the metro Line C to the Vltavská station and then ride any tram heading east (running to the left as you exit the metro station). Exit at the first stop and follow the crowds.

Specialty Stores

ANTIQUES

Starožitnosti (antiques shops) are everywhere in Prague, but you'll need a sharp eye to distinguish truly valuable pieces from merely interesting ones. Many dealers carry old glassware and vases. Antique jewelry, many pieces featuring garnets, is also popular. Remember to retain your receipts as proof of legitimate purchases, otherwise you may have difficulty bringing antiques out of the country. Comparison shop at stores along Karlova ulice in the Old Town. Also check in and around the streets of the former Jewish ghetto for shops specializing in Jewish antiques and artifacts. **Art Program** (⊠ Nerudova ul. 28) in the Malá Strana has an especially beautiful collection of art-deco jewelry and glassware.

BOOKS AND PRINTS

It's hard to imagine a more beautiful bookstore than **U Karlova Mostu** (⊠ Karlova ul. 2, Staré Město, ☎ 02/2422–9205), with its impressive selection of old maps, prints, and rare books.

One shop that comes close in appeal to U Karlova Mostu is **Antikvariát Karel Křenek** (⊠ Celetná 31, ☎ 02/231–4734), near the Powder Tower in the Old Town. It stocks prints and graphics from the 1920s and '30s, in addition to a small collection of English books.

If you'd just like a good read, be sure to check out the **Globe Bookstore and Coffeehouse** (⊠ Janovského 14, Prague 7, ☎ 02/6671–2610), which is one of Prague's meccas for the local English-speaking community.

U Knihomola Bookstore and Café (⊠ Mánesova 79, Prague 2, ☎ 02/627–7770) is a close contender to the Globe for the best place to find the latest in English literature, plus it stocks the best selection of new English-language art books and guidebooks. It's near the metro stop Jiřího z Poděbrad.

CRYSTAL AND PORCELAIN

Moser (⊠ Na příkopě 12, ☎ 02/2421–1293), the flagship store for the world-famous Karlovy Vary glassmaker, is the first address for stylish, high-quality lead crystal and china. Even if you're not in the market to buy, stop by the store simply to browse through the elegant wood-paneled salesrooms on the second floor. The staff will gladly pack goods for traveling. **Bohemia** (⊠ Pařížska 2, ☎ 02/2481–1023) carries a wide selection of porcelain from Karlovy Vary. If you still can not find anything, have no fear: There is a crystal shop on just about every street in central Prague.

FOOD

Specialty food stores have been slow to catch on in Prague. **Fruits de France** (✉ Jindřišská 9, Nové Město, ☎ 02/2422–0304) stocks Prague's freshest fruits and vegetables imported directly from France at Western prices. The bakeries at the **Krone** and **Kotva** department stores sell surprisingly delicious breads and pastries. Both stores also have large, well-stocked basement grocery stores.

FUN THINGS FOR CHILDREN

Children enjoy the beautiful watercolor and colored-chalk sets available in nearly every stationery store at rock-bottom prices. The Czechs are also master illustrators, and the books they've made for young "pre-readers" are some of the world's loveliest. Many stores also offer unique wooden toys, sure to delight any young child. For these, look in at **Obchod Vším Možným** (✉ Nerudova 45, ☎ 02/536941). For older children and teens, it's worth considering a Czech or Eastern European watch, telescope, or set of binoculars. The quality/price ratio is unbeatable.

JEWELRY

The **Granát** shop at Dlouhá 30 in the Old Town has a comprehensive selection of garnet jewelry, plus contemporary and traditional pieces set in gold and silver. Several shops specializing in gold jewelry line Wenceslas Square.

MUSICAL INSTRUMENTS

Melodia (✉ Jungmannova nám. 17, ☎ 02/2422–2500) carries a complete range of quality musical instruments at reasonable prices. **Capriccio** (✉ Újezd 15, Prague 1, ☎ 02/532507) is a great place to find sheet music of all kinds.

SPORTS EQUIPMENT

Adidas has an outlet at Na Příkopě 8. Department stores also sometimes carry medium-quality sports equipment.

Prague A to Z

Arriving and Departing

BY BUS

The Czech complex of regional bus lines known collectively as **ČSAD** operates its dense network from the sprawling main bus station on Křižíkova (metro stop: Florenc, Lines B or C). For information about routes and schedules call 02/2421–1060, consult the confusingly displayed timetables posted at the station, or visit the information window, situated at the bus unloading area (⊙ Mon.–Fri. 6–7:45, Sat. 6–4, Sun. 8–6). The helpful private travel agency Tourbus, in the pedestrian overpass above the station, dispenses bus information daily until 8 PM. If the ticket windows are closed, you can usually buy a ticket from the driver.

BY CAR

Prague is well served by major roads and highways from anywhere in the country. On arriving in the city, simply follow the signs to CENTRUM (city center). During the day, traffic can be heavy, especially on the approach to Wenceslas Square. Pay particular attention to the trams, which enjoy the right-of-way in every situation. Note that parts of the historic center of Prague, including Wenceslas Square itself, are closed to private vehicles.

Krumlov). Farther north and an easy drive east of Prague is the old silver-mining town of Kutná Hora, once a rival to Prague for the royal residence.

The major towns of southern Bohemia offer some of the best accommodations in the Czech Republic. (This is also true of western Bohemia; ☞ *below*.) Towns with private rooms available are noted below; here, as in many parts of Bohemia, the only real options for dining are the restaurants and cafés at the larger hotels and resorts.

Numbers in the margin correspond to numbers on the Bohemia map.

Kutná Hora

59 *70 km (44 mi) east of Prague.*

The approach to Kutná Hora looks much as it has for centuries. The long economic decline of this town, once Prague's chief rival in Bohemia for wealth and beauty, spared it the postwar construction that has blighted the outskirts of so many other Czech cities. Though it is undeniably beautiful, with an intact Gothic and baroque townscape, Kutná Hora can leave one feeling a bit melancholy. The town owes its illustrious past to silver, discovered here during the 12th century. For some 400 years the mines were worked with consummate efficiency, the wealth going to support grand projects throughout Bohemia. Charles IV used the silver to finance his transformation of Prague from a market town into the worthy capital of the Holy Roman Empire during the 14th century. As the silver began to run out during the 16th and 17th centuries, however, Kutná Hora's importance faded. What remains is the paradox you see today: poor inhabitants dwarfed by the splendors of the Middle Ages.

Forget the town center for a moment and walk to the ★**Chrám svaté Barbory** (St. Barbara's Cathedral), a 10-minute stroll from the main Palackého náměstí along Barborská ulice. The approach to the cathedral, overlooking the river, is magnificent. Statues line the road, and the baroque houses vie with each other for attention. In the distance, the netted vaulting of the cathedral resembles a large, magnificent tent more than a religious center; the effect gives the cathedral a cheerier look than that of the dignified Gothic towers of Prague. St. Barbara's is undoubtedly Kutná Hora's masterpiece and a high point of the Gothic style in Bohemia. Built in the 14th and 15th centuries, it drew on the talents of the Peter Parler workshop as well as on other Gothic luminaries, such as Matthias Rejsek and Benedikt Ried.

St. Barbara is the patron saint of miners, and silver-mining themes dominate the interior. Gothic frescoes depict angels carrying shields with mining symbols. The town's other major occupation, minting, can be seen in frescoes in the **Mintner's Chapel.** A statue of a miner, donning the characteristic smock and dating from 1700, stands proudly in the nave. But the main attraction of the interior is the vaulting itself—attributed to Ried (also responsible for the fabulous vaulting in Prague Castle's Vladislav Hall)—which carries the eye effortlessly upward. ⊠ *Barborská ul.* 🎫 *20 Kč.* ☉ *Tues.–Sun. 9–noon and 2–4.*

The romantic view over the town from the cathedral area, marked by the visibly tilting 260-foot tower of St. James Church, is impressive, and few modern buildings intrude. As you descend into town, the **Hrádek** (Little Castle), on your right along Barborská ulice, was once part of the town's fortifications and now houses a museum of mining and coin production and a claustrophobic medieval mine tunnel. ⊠ *Barborská ul.* 🎫 *20 Kč.* ☉ *Apr.–Oct., Tues.–Sun. 9–noon and 1–5.*

Bohemia

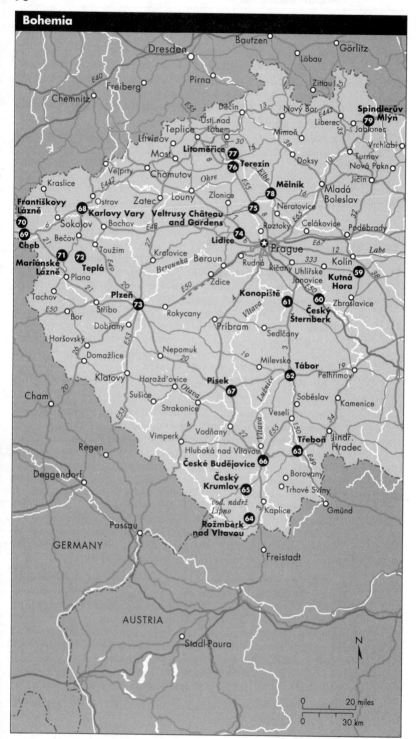

Bautzen
Görlitz
Dresden
Löbau
Freiberg
E40
Pirna
Zittau
Chemnitz
Děčín
13
Nový Bor
E442
Spindlerův
79 Mlýn
Ústí nad
Labem
Teplice
30
Liberec
Jablonec
Litvínov
Litoměřice 77
Mimoň
38
Vrchlabí
Most
76 Terezín
Doksy
Turnov
Nová Pakn
Vejprty
Chomutov
Ohre
Elbe
Jičín
Kraslice
E442
Ostrov
Louny
Zlonice
Mělník
Mladá
Boleslav
Frantíškovy
Lázně
68
Karlovy Vary
Zatec
78
Neratovice
70
Sokolov
Bochov
Veltrusy Château
and Gardens
75
Celákovice
Poděbrady
69
Bečov
E48
Roztoky
Cheb
71 72
Touzim
Kralovice
74 Lidice
E67
12
Labe
Mariánské
Lázně
Teplá
E40
Plana
Berounka
Beroun
Prague
333
Kolín
59
Tachov
E50
Štříbro
Plzeň
Zdice
Rudná
Uhlířske
Jonovice
E50
Kutná
Hora
60
Zbraslavice
E50
Bor
73
Rokycany
Konopiště
61
Český
Sternberk
Dobřany
Nepomuk
Příbram
Sedlčany
Horšovský
20
Domažlice
Milevsko
Tábor
62
Pelhřimov
19
Cham
Klatovy
Horažd'ovice
Otava
Písek
67
Soběslav
Kamenice
Sušice
Veselí
Strakonice
34
Vimperk
Vodňany
22
Třeboň
63
Jindř.
Hradec
Regen
Hluboká nad Vltavou
66
Vltava
Deggendorf
České Budějovice
Borovany
Český
Krumlov
65
Trhové Sviny
vod. nádrž
Lipno
64
Kaplice
Gmünd
Passau
Rožmberk
nad Vltavou
GERMANY
Freistadt
AUSTRIA
Stadl-Paura
N
0   20 miles
0   30 km

NEED A
BREAK?

The **Café U Hrádku** is a pleasant place to stop for refreshments or a light home-cooked meal. Lamps and furnishings from the 1920s add a period touch. ⊠ *Barborská ul. 33,* ☎ *0327/4277.* ☉ *Tues.–Sun. 10–5. No credit cards.*

You'll easily find the **Vlašský dvůr** (Italian Court), the old mint, by following the signs through town. Coins were first minted here in 1300, struck by Italian artisans brought in from Florence—hence the mint's odd name. It was here that the famed Prague groschen, one of the most widely circulated coins of the Middle Ages, was minted until 1726, and here, too, that the Bohemian kings stayed on their frequent visits. Something of the court's former wealth can be glimpsed in the formal Gothic interiors of the chapel and tower rooms. A **coin museum,** open in spring and summer, allows you to see the small, silvery groschen being struck and gives you a chance to buy replicas. Small wooden triptychs can be purchased in the chapel. ⊠ *Havlíčkovo nám.* ☎ *30 Kč.* ☉ *Apr.–Oct., daily 10–6; Nov.–Mar., daily 10–4.*

If the door to the **Chrám svatého Jakuba** (St. James Church) next door is open, peek inside. Originally a Gothic church dating from the early 1400s, the structure was almost entirely transformed into baroque during the 17th and 18th centuries. The characteristic onion dome on the tower was added in 1737. The paintings on the wall include works of the best baroque Czech masters; the *Pietà* is by the 17th-century painter Karel Škréta. Pause to admire the simple Gothic beauty of the 12-sided **kamenná kašna** (stone fountain) at Rejskovo náměstí, just off Husova ulice. This unique work, some 500 years old, is supposedly the creation of Rejsek, one of the architects of St. Barbara's.

Before leaving the city, stop in the nearby suburb of Sedlec for a bone-chilling sight: a chapel decorated with the bones of some 40,000 people. The All Saints' Cemetery Chapel, or **Bone Church,** at the site of the former Sedlec Monastery, came into being in the 14th century, when development forced the clearing of a nearby graveyard. Monks of the Cistercian order came up with the bright idea of using the bones for decoration; the most recent creations date from the end of the last century. ☎ *20 Kč.* ☉ *Daily 9–noon and 2–4.*

Lodging

$$$ 🏨 **Medínek.** This is one of the few hotels in town with modern conveniences, so book in advance or risk being squeezed out by German and Austrian tour groups. The location, on the main square, puts you at an easy stroll from the sights, and the ground-floor restaurant offers decent Czech cooking in an atmosphere more pleasant than that found in the local beer halls. Yet, as with many of the hotels built during the 1960s and 1970s, the modern architecture blights the surrounding square. ⊠ *Palackého nám. 316, 284 01 Kutná Hora,* ☎ *0327/2741,* 📠 *0327/2743. 90 rooms, some with bath. Restaurant, café. AE, MC, V.*

$$ 🏨 **U Hrnčíře.** This is a picturesque little inn situated next to a potter's shop near the town center. The quaintness doesn't make up for the very standard, plain rooms, but the friendly staff gives the hotel a decidedly homey feel. The restaurant in the back garden features a beautiful view overlooking the valley. ⊠ *Barborská 24, 284 01 Kutná Hora,* ☎ *0327/2113. 5 rooms with bath. Restaurant. AE, MC, V.*

Český Šternberk

⑥⓪   *40 km (24 mi) from Kutná Hora, 24 km (15 mi) from Benešov.*

At night this 13th-century castle looks positively evil, occupying a forested knoll over the Sázava River. By daylight, the structure, last renovated in the 17th century, is less haunting but still impressive. Although the castle became the property of the Czechoslovak state following the Communist coup, Count Šternberk (the former owner) was permitted to occupy it until his death in 1966 as a reward for not cowering to the occupying German forces. Ownership returned to the Šternberk family in 1991. In season, you can tour some of the rooms fitted out with period furniture (mostly rococo); little of the early Gothic has survived the many renovations. ✉ *Český Šternberk,* ☎ *0303/55101.* 🎫 *75 Kč.* ⏲ *May–June and Sept., Tues.–Sun. 9–5; July–Aug., Tues.–Sun. 9–6; Apr. and Oct., weekends 9–4.*

Konopiště

61 *25 km (15 mi) west of Český Šternberk, 45 km (27 mi) southeast of Prague.*

Given its remote location, Český Šternberk is ill equipped for a meal or an overnight stay. Instead, continue on to the superior facilities of Konopiště (via the industrial town of Benešov). Konopiště is best known for its 14th-century castle, which served six centuries later as the residence of the former heir to the Austrian crown, Franz Ferdinand d'Este. Scorned by the Austrian nobility for having married a commoner, Franz Ferdinand wanted an impressive summer residence to win back the envy of his peers, and he spared no expense in restoring the castle to its original Gothic form, filling its 82 rooms with outlandish paintings, statues, and curiosities. Franz Ferdinand's dream came to a fateful end in 1914 when he was assassinated at Sarajevo, an event that precipitated World War I. The Austrian defeat in the war ultimately led to the fall of the Hapsburgs. Ironically, the destiny of the Austrian Empire had been sealed at the castle a month before the assassination, when Austrian emperor Franz Joseph I met with Germany's Kaiser Wilhelm II and agreed to join forces with him in the event of war.

★ To visit **Zámek Konopiště** (Konopiště Castle), start from the Konopiště Motel, about a kilometer (½ mile) off Route 3, and walk straight for about 2 kilometers (1 mile) along the trail through the woods. Before long, the rounded, neo-Gothic towers appear through the trees, and you reach the formal garden with its almost mystical circle of classical statues. Built by the wealthy Beneschau family, the castle dates from around 1300 and for centuries served as a bastion of the nobility in their struggle for power with the king. In what must have been a great affront to royal authority at the end of the 14th century, Catholic nobles actually captured the weak King Wenceslas (Václav) IV in Prague and held him prisoner in the smaller of the two rounded towers. To this day the tower is known affectionately as the Václavka. Several of the rooms, reflecting the archduke's extravagant taste and lifestyle, are open to the public during the tourism season. A valuable collection of weapons from the 16th to 18th centuries can be seen in the Weapons Hall on the third floor. Less easy to miss are the hundreds of stuffed animals, rather macabre monuments to the archduke's obsession with hunting. ✉ *Zá mek Konopiště, Benešov, about 3 km (2 mi) west of train and bus stations on red- or yellow-marked paths).* 🎫 *Each tour 90–200 Kč.* ⏲ *Apr. and Oct., Tues.–Sun. 9–3; May–Aug., Tues.–Sun. 9–5; Sept., Tues.–Sun. 9–4.*

Dining and Lodging

$$$$ ✕ **Stodola.** It's a little cabin, next to the Konopiště Motel, with a reputation as one of the best exemplars of Bohemian-style grilled meats, chicken, and fish dishes. The live folk music in the evenings is romantic

rather than obtrusive; the wines and service are excellent. ⊠ *Benešov,* ☎ *0301/22732. No lunch. AE, MC, V.*

$$$ 🏨 **Konopiště Motel.** Long a favorite with diplomats in Prague, who come for the fresh air and outdoor sports, the motel is about 2 kilometers (1 mile) from Konopiště Castle, on a small road about a kilometer from the main Prague–Tabor highway (Route 3). The rooms are small but well appointed (ask for one away from the main road). The castle and gardens are an easy 20-minute walk through the woods; a campground is nearby. ⊠ *256 01 Benešov,* ☎ *0301/22732,* 📠 *0301/22053. 40 rooms with bath. 2 restaurants, in-room satellite TV, minigolf, parking. Breakfast not included. AE, DC, MC, V.*

Tábor

㉒ *40 km (25 mi) south of Konopiště down Route 3.*

It's hard to believe this dusty Czech town was built to receive Christ on his return to Earth in the Second Coming. But that's what the Hussites intended when they flocked here by the thousands in 1420 to construct a society modeled on the communities of the early Christians. Tábor's fascinating history is unique among Czech towns. It started out not as a mercantile or administrative center but as a combination utopia and fortress.

Following the execution of Jan Hus, a vociferous religious reformer who railed against the Catholic Church and the nobility, reform priests drawing on the support of poor workers and peasants took to the hills of southern Bohemia. These hilltop congregations soon grew into permanent settlements, wholly outside the feudal order. The most important settlement, on the Lužnice River, became known in 1420 as Tábor. Tábor quickly evolved into the symbolic and spiritual center of the Hussites (now called Taborites) and, together with Prague, served as the bulwark of the reform movement.

The early 1420s in Tábor were heady days for religious reformers. Private property was denounced, and the many poor who made the pilgrimage to Tábor were required to leave their possessions at the town gates. Some sects rejected the doctrine of transubstantiation (the belief that the Eucharist becomes the Body and Blood of Christ), making Holy Communion into a bawdy, secular feast of bread and wine. Still other reformers considered themselves superior to Christ—who by dying had shown himself to be merely mortal. Few, however, felt obliged to work for a living, and the Taborites had to rely increasingly on raids of neighboring villages for survival.

War fever in Tábor at the time ran high, and the town became one of the focal points of the ensuing Hussite wars (1419–34), which pitted reformers against an array of foreign crusaders, Catholics, and noblemen. Under the brilliant military leadership of Jan Žižka, the Taborites enjoyed early successes, but the forces of the established church proved too mighty in the end. Žižka was killed in 1424, and the Hussite uprising ended at the rout of Lipany 10 years later. But even after the fall, many of the town's citizens resisted recatholicization. Fittingly, following the Battle of White Mountain in 1620 (the final defeat for the Czech Protestants), Tábor was the last city to succumb to the conquering Hapsburgs.

Begin a walking tour of the town at the **Žižkovo náměstí** (Žižka Square), named for the gifted Hussite military leader. A large bronze statue of Žižka from the 19th century dominates the square, serving as a reminder of the town's fiery past. The stone tables in front of the

Gothic town hall and the house at No. 6 date from the 15th century and were used by the Hussites to give daily Communion to the faithful. Follow the tiny streets around the square, which seemingly lead nowhere. They curve around, branch off, and then stop; few lead back to the main square. The confusing street plan was purposely laid during the 15th century to thwart incoming invasions.

The **Museum of the Hussite Movement,** just behind the town hall, documents the history of the reformers. Note the elaborate network of tunnels carved by the Hussites below the Old Town for protection in case of attack. ⊠ *Křivkova ul. 31.* 🖭 *20 Kč.* ☺ *Daily 8:30–5; closed weekends Nov.–Mar. and Mon. Apr.–Oct.*

Leave the square along **Pražská ulice,** a main route to the newer part of town, and note the beautiful Renaissance facades from the 16th century. Turn right at Divadelní and head to the Lužnice River to see the remaining walls and fortifications of the 15th century, irrefutable evidence of the town's vital function as a stronghold. **Kotnov hrad** (Kotnov Castle), rising above the river in the distance to the right, dates from the 13th century and was part of the earliest fortifications. The large pond to the northeast of Tábor was created as a reservoir in 1492; since it was used for baptism, the fervent Taborites named the lake Jordan.

Dining and Lodging

$$ 🏨 **Palcát.** A 10-minute walk from the Old Town Square, the slightly rundown Palcát is quite a contrast. The architecture is overwhelmingly drab, but the rooms, though plain, are bright and comfortable; those on the upper floors have a dazzling view of the Old Town. ⊠ *Tř. 9, Května 2467, 390 01 Tábor,* ☎ *0361/252901,* 𝔽𝔸𝕏 *0361/252905. 65 rooms with shower. Restaurant, bar, café, conference hall. Breakfast included. AE, MC, V.*

$–$$ 🏨 **Bican Pension.** Highly recommended. This lovely family-run pen-
★ sion is sure to inspire you to linger in Tábor. The staff couldn't be nicer, nor could the view from either side of the pension: One side faces the Old Town, the other offers a soothing view of the river and the rolling landscape beyond. The premises date from the 14th century, and the Bicans will gladly oblige with a minitour of the house's own catacombs. The chilly basement lounge is a godsend on sweltering summer days. ⊠ *Hradební 189/16, 390 01 Tábor,* ☎ *0361/252109. 6 rooms with bath. Lounge, sauna, use of kitchen. Breakfast included. No credit cards.*

Třeboň

⑥ *48 km (28 mi) south of Tábor.*

Amid a plethora of ponds rests another jewel of a town with a far different historical heritage than Tábor's. Třeboň was settled during the 13th century by the Wittkowitzes (later called the Rosenbergs), once Bohemia's noblest family. From 1316 to the end of the 16th century, the dynasty dominated southern Bohemia. You can see their emblem, a five-petaled rose, on castles, doorways, and coats of arms all over the region. The Rosenbergs' wealth was based on silver and real estate. Their official residence was 40 kilometers (25 miles) to the southwest, in Český Krumlov, but Třeboň was an important second residence and repository of the family archives.

Thanks to the Rosenberg family, this unlikely landlocked town has become the center of the Czech Republic's fishing industry. During the 15th and 16th centuries, the Rosenbergs peppered the countryside with 6,000 enormous ponds, partly to drain the land and partly to breed fish. Carp breeding is still big business, and if you are in the area in the late autumn, you may be lucky enough to witness the great carp harvests, when tens of thousands of the glittering fish are netted. The largest pond, bearing the Rosenberg name, lies just north of Třeboň. The **Rybník Svět** (Svět Pond) is closest to town, along the southern edge. Join the locals on a warm afternoon for a stroll along its banks and enjoy the mild breezes.

Begin a walking tour of Třeboň from the park outside the town walls, with the Svět Pond at your back. From here, the simple sgraffito Renaissance exterior of the castle, with its deep turrets, is highly impressive. The intact town walls, built during the 16th century, are among the best in the Czech Republic. Continue along the park, turning left at the first of the three gates into town. An 18th-century brewery, still producing outstanding beer, is off to the right. First brewed in 1379, as the redbrick tower proudly boasts, beer enjoys nearly as long a tradition here as in Plzeň or České Budějovice. Continue straight ahead to arrive at the main square, with its familiar collection of arcaded Renaissance and baroque houses. Look for the **Bílý Koníček** (Little White Horse), the best-preserved Renaissance house on the square, dating from 1544. The large rectangular gable on the roof is composed of numerous tiny towers.

The entrance to **Zámek Třeboň** (Třeboň Château) lies at the southwest corner of the square. From here it looks plain and sober, with its stark white walls, but the rooms (open to the public) are sumptuous recreations of 16th-century life. The castle also houses a permanent exhibition of pond building. The last of the Rosenbergs died in 1611, and the castle eventually became the property of the Schwarzenberg family, who built their family tomb in a grand park on the other side of Svět Pond. It is now a monumental neo-Gothic destination for Sunday-afternoon picnickers. ⊠ *Zámek Třeboň,* ☎ *0333/721193.* 🎫 *40 Kč.* ☉ *Apr. and Oct., weekends 9–4; May and Sept., Tues.–Sun. 9–4; June–Aug., Tues.–Sun. 9–5.*

In the **Augustine Monastery,** adjacent to the castle, take a look at the famous Altar of the Masters of Wittingau, dating from the late 14th century. The altar was removed in 1781 from St. Giles Church (Chrám svatého Jiljí), on Husova třída. The paintings themselves, the most famous example of Bohemian Gothic art, are now in the National Gallery in Prague.

NEED A BREAK?	Before leaving Třeboň, sample some of the excellent local beer at the **Bílý Koníček** (☎ 0333/2818), now a modest hotel and restaurant on the square. You can also get a variety of nonalcoholic beverages as well as good local dishes at reasonable prices.

Lodging

$ 🏨 **Bílý Koníček.** This old-style hotel occupies one of the most striking Renaissance buildings on the main square. With the nearby Zlatá Hvězda being remodeled, it's a very acceptable alternative. The rooms fail to measure up to the splendid facade but are suitably clean. ⊠ *Masarykovo nám. 97, 379 01 Třeboň,* ☎ *0333/721213,* 📠 *0333/721136. 10 rooms with bath. Restaurant. Breakfast not included. V.*

Swimming

You can swim in most of the larger carp ponds around town. The Svět Pond is particularly appealing because of its little sandy beaches, although these are generally crowded in summer.

Rožmberk nad Vltavou

★ ⑥   *60 km (36 mi) southwest of Třeboň.*

This little village, just a few kilometers from the former Iron Curtain, was forgotten in the postwar years. It seems like a ghost town, especially at night with the darkened **Rosenberg hrad** (Rosenberg Castle) keeping lonely vigil atop the hill overlooking the Vltava River. A barely visible German sign, WIRTSCHAFT ZUM GOLDENEN BÄREN (Inn at the Golden Bear), on the battered facade of a beer hall across the bridge, adds to the feeling of abandonment, as if nothing has happened here in decades. Take a moment to enjoy the silence and walk up the hill to the castle. The slender tower, the Jakobinka, dates from the 13th century, when the Rosenberg family built the original structure. Most of the exterior, however, is neo-Gothic from the last century. In summer you can tour some of the rooms, admiring the weapons and Bohemian paintings. From the castle gates, the Romanesque-Gothic church below, standing beside the lone figure of St. Christopher on the bridge, looks especially solemn. ⊠ *Rožmberk nad Vltavou,* ☎ *0337/9838.* ⌨ *50 Kč.* ☉ *Apr. and Oct., weekends 9–3; May and Sept., Tues.–Sun. 9–3:15; June–Aug., Tues.–Sun. 9–4:15.*

Český Krumlov

★ ⑥   *22 km (13 mi) north of Rožmberk nad Vltavou.*

Český Krumlov, the official residence of the Rosenbergs for some 300 years, is an eye-opener: None of the surrounding towns or villages, with their open squares and mixtures of old and new buildings, will prepare you for the beauty of the Old Town. Here the Vltava works its wonders as nowhere else but in Prague itself, swirling in a nearly complete circle around the town. Across the river stands the proud castle, rivaling any in the country in size and splendor.

For the moment, Český Krumlov's beauty is still intact, even though the dilapidated buildings that lend the town its unique atmosphere are slowly metamorphosizing into boutiques and expensive pensions. In peak months, when visitors from Austria and Germany pack the streets, the existing facilities for visitors can be woefully overburdened. But overlook any minor inconveniences and enjoy a rare, unspoiled trip through time.

Begin a tour of the Old Town from the main **Svornosti náměstí.** The square itself is disappointing; the arcades hide the richness of the buildings' architecture. The **town hall,** at No. 1, built in 1580, is memorable for its Renaissance friezes and Gothic arcades. Tiny alleys fan out from the square in all directions. Horní ulice begins just opposite the Hotel Krumlov. A quick visit to the **Městské muzeum** (City Museum) at No. 152 is a good way to familiarize yourself with the rise and fall of the Rosenberg dynasty.

Just opposite the museum, at No. 154, are the Renaissance facades, complete with lively sgraffiti, of the former **Jesuit school**—now the semi-luxurious Růže Hotel Český Krumlov, which owes its abundance of Renaissance detailing to its location on the main trading routes to Italy and Bavaria—a perfect site for absorbing incoming fashions. The tower of the nearby late-Gothic **St. Vitus Church,** built in the late 1400s, rises from its position on Kostelní ulice to offset the larger, older tower of the castle across the river. The view over the Old Town and castle is at its most spectacular from here.

Ⓒ   To get to **Krumlov hrad** (Krumlov Castle), make your way from St. Vitus to the main street, Radniční, via either Masná or Kostelní ulice, both of which form a big ring around the square. Cross the peaceful Vltava and enter at one of two gates along the Latrán. The oldest and most striking part of the castle is the round 12th-century tower, renovated, like the rest of the building in the 16th century, to look something like a minaret, with its delicately arcaded Renaissance balcony. The tower is part of the old border fortifications, guarding the Bohemian frontiers from Austrian incursion.

The castle passed out of the Rosenbergs' hands when the last of the line, the dissolute Petr Vok, sold castle and town to Rudolf II in 1601 to pay off his debts. The castle's Renaissance and baroque features and its most sumptuous furnishings were added later by the Eggenberg and Schwarzenberg families.

As you enter the castle area, look into the old moats, where two playful brown bears now reside—unlikely to be of much help in protecting the castle from attack. In season, the castle rooms are open to the public. The **Hall of Masks** is the most impressive interior, with its richly detailed 18th-century frescoes. After proceeding through a series of courtyards, you'll come to a wonderfully romantic elevated passageway with spectacular views of the huddled houses of the Old Town. The Austrian expressionist painter Egon Schiele often stayed in Český Krumlov in the early years of this century and liked to paint this particular view over the river. He called his now famous Krumlov series *The Dead Town*. From the river down below, the elevated passageway is revealed in all its Renaissance glory as part of a network of tall arches, looking like a particularly elaborate Roman viaduct. On top runs a narrow three-story residential block (still inhabited), dressed in gray-and-white Renaissance stripes. At the end of the passageway you'll come to the luxuriously appointed castle gardens (open only in summer). In the middle is an open-air theater, one of Bohemia's first such theaters and remarkable for its still-intact gold stage. Performances are held here in July and August. ✉ *Český Krumlov hrad,* ☎ *0337/3135.* 🎫 *70 Kč.* ⊙ *Apr. and Oct., Tues.–Sun. 9–noon and 1–3; May–Aug., Tues.–Sun. 9–noon and 1–5, Sept., Tues.–Sun. 9–noon and 1–4.*

The **Egon Schiele Center** exhibits the work of Schiele and other 20th-century artists in a rambling Renaissance house near the river. ✉ *Široká 70–72.* 🎫 *100 Kč.* ⊙ *Daily 10–6.*

Dining and Lodging
Český Krumlov is crammed with pensions and private rooms for rent, many priced around $15 per person per night. The best place to look is along the tiny Parkán ulice, which parallels the river just off the main street. A safe bet is the house at Parkán No. 107, blessed with several nice rooms and friendly management (☎ 0337/4396).

$ ✕🏨 **Na louži.** Wood floors and exposed-beam ceilings lend a traditional
★ touch to this warm, inviting, family-run pub, which also has rooms for rent upstairs. The atmosphere is cozy and the service attentive. The quality extends to the food, which is as close to homemade as you'll find. This is a rare treat among the inns of Bohemia. ✉ *Kájovská 66, 381 01 Český Krumlov,* ☎ 🖷 *0337/5495. 5 rooms with bath. Restaurant. No credit cards.*

$$$ 🏨 **Růže.** This Renaissance monastery has been renovated and trans-
★ formed into an excellent luxury hotel, only a five-minute walk from the main square. The rooms are spacious and clean—some also have drop-dead views of the town below, so ask to see several before choosing. The restaurant, too, is top-rate; the elegant dining room is formal without being oppressive, and the menu draws from traditional Czech

and international cuisines. ⊠ *Horní ul. 153, 381 01 Český Krumlov,* ☎ *0337/2245,* 🆉🆇 *0337/3881. 50 rooms, most with bath. Restaurant, nightclub. AE, MC, V.*

Nightlife and the Arts
An outdoor theater in the castle gardens in **Český Krumlov** is a popular venue for plays and concerts throughout the summer.

České Budějovice

🟢 *22 km (13 mi) from Çeský Krumlov: Follow Route 159, then Route 3.*

After the glories of Çeský Krumlov, any other town would be a letdown—and Çeské Budějovice, known as Budweis under the Hapsburgs and famous primarily for its beer, is no exception. The major attraction of what is basically an industrial town is the enormously proportioned main square, lined with arcaded houses and worth an hour or two of wandering. To get a good view over the city, it's well worth climbing the 360 steps up to the Renaissance gallery of the **Černá Věž** (Black Tower), at the northeast corner of the square next to St. Nicholas Cathedral. 🎟 *10 Kč.* ⊗ *Apr.–Oct., Tues.–Sun. 9–5.*

Lodging

$$$ 🏨 **Gomel.** This modern high-rise, a 15-minute walk from the main square along the road to Prague, is probably best suited to business travelers. The rooms are plain, but the hotel does offer a reasonable range of facilities and has an English-speaking staff. ⊠ *Pražská tř. 14, 307 01 Çeské Budějovice,* ☎ *038/7311390,* 🆉🆇 *038/7311365. 180 rooms with bath or shower. 3 restaurants, café, nightclub, conference hall. Breakfast included. AE, DC, MC, V.*

$$$ 🏨 **Zvon.** Old-fashioned, well-kept, and comfortable, the Zvon has an ideal location, right on the main town square. The rooms are bright, and the period bathrooms have large bathtubs. The price is high, however, for the level of facilities. ⊠ *Nám. Přemysla Otakara II 28, 307 01 Çeské Budějovice,* ☎ *038/7311383,* 🆉🆇 *038/7311385. 75 rooms, most with bath. Restaurant. Breakfast not included. AE, MC, V.*

Hluboká nad Vltavou

★ *9 km (6 mi) north of Çeské Budějovice.*

This is one of the Czech Republic's most curious castles. Although the structure dates from the 13th century, what you see is pure 19th-century excess, perpetrated by the wealthy Schwarzenberg family as proof of their "good taste." If you think you've seen it somewhere before, you're probably thinking of Windsor Castle, near London, on which it was carefully modeled. Take a tour; 41 of the 140 rooms are open to the public. The rather pompous interior reflects the no-holds-barred tastes of the time, but many individual pieces are interesting in their own right. The wooden Renaissance ceiling in the large dining room was removed by the Schwarzenbergs from the castle at Çeský Krumlov and brought here in the 19th century. Also look for the beautiful late-baroque bookshelves in the library, holding some 12,000 books. If your interest in Czech painting wasn't satisfied in Prague, have a look at the **Aleš Art Gallery** in the Riding Hall, featuring the works of southern Bohemian painters from the Middle Ages to the present. The collection is the second largest in Bohemia. 🎟 *Admission to castle and gallery 100 Kč.* ⊗ *Apr.–Oct., daily (except Mon. in May, Sept., and Oct.) 9–4:30 (until 5 June–Aug.).*

In summer the castle grounds make a nice place for a stroll or a picnic. If you're in the mood for a more strenuous walk, follow the yellow trail signs 2 kilometers (1¼ miles) to the **Ohrada hunting lodge,** which houses a museum of hunting and fishing and also has a small zoo for children. ☎ 038/965340. ⏲ Apr.–Oct., daily 9–noon and 1–4; May–Aug., daily 1–5.

Písek

⑥⑦ 60 km (37 mi) northwest of České Budějovice.

If it weren't for Písek's 700-year-old **Gothic bridge,** peopled with baroque statues, you could easily bypass the town and continue on to Prague. After the splendors of Český Krumlov or even Třeboň, Písek's main square is admittedly plain, despite its many handsome Renaissance and baroque houses. The bridge, a five-minute walk from the main square along Karlovo ulice, was commissioned in 1254 by Přemysl Otakar II, who sought a secure crossing over the difficult Otava River for his salt shipments from nearby Prachatice. Originally one of the five major Hussite strongholds, as early as the 9th century Písek stood at the center of one of the most important trade routes to the west, linking Prague to Passau and the rest of Bavaria. The baroque statues of saints were not added until the 18th century.

Return to the town square and look for the 240-foot tower of the early Gothic **Mariánský chrám** (Church of Mary). Construction was started at about the time the bridge was built. The tower was completed in 1487 and got its baroque dome during the mid-18th century. On the inside, look for the *Madonna from Písek,* a 14th-century Gothic altar painting. On a middle pillar is a rare series of early Gothic wall paintings dating from the end of the 13th century.

OFF THE BEATEN PATH

ZVÍKOV – If you've got room for still another castle, head for Zvíkov Castle, about 18 kilometers (11 miles) north of town. The castle, at the confluence of the Otava and Vltava rivers, is impressive for its authenticity. Unlike many other castles in Bohemia, Zvíkov survived the 18th and 19th centuries unrenovated and still looks just as it did 500 years ago. The side trip also brings you to the dams and man-made lakes of the Vltava, a major swimming and recreation area that stretches all the way back to Prague.

Southern Bohemia A to Z

Arriving and Departing

Prague is the main gateway to southern Bohemia (☞ Arriving and Departing *in* Prague A to Z, *above*). Several trains a day run from Vienna to Prague; most of these travel via Třeboň and Tábor. To drive from Vienna, take the E49 from Gmünd.

Getting Around

BY BUS

All the major sights are reachable from Prague using ČSAD's dense bus network. Service between the towns, however, is far less frequent and will require some forethought.

BY CAR

Car travel affords the greatest ease and flexibility in this region. The major road from Prague south to Tábor and Çeské Budějovice, though often crowded, is in relatively good shape.

BY TRAIN

Benešov (Konopiště), Tábor, and Třeboň all lie along the major southern line in the direction of Vienna, and train service to these cities from Prague is frequent and comfortable. Good connections also exist from Prague to Çeské Budějovice. For other destinations, you may have to combine the train and bus.

Contacts and Resources

EMERGENCIES

Police (☎ 158). **Ambulance** (☎ 155).

GUIDED TOURS

Čedok (☎ 02/2419–7111) offers several specialized tours that include visits to Çeské Budějovice, Hluboka Castle, Çeský Krumlov, Kutná Hora, and Çeský Šternberk. Çedok also offers a full-day excursion to Moser, the oldest glassworks in Central Europe, south of Prague. Prague departure points include the Çedok offices at Na příkopě 18 and Bílkova ulice 6 and the Panorama, Forum, and Hilton hotels.

VISITOR INFORMATION

Čedok is the first stop for general tourist information and city maps:

České Budějovice (Čedok České Budějovice, ⊠ Nám. Přemysla Otakára II 39, ☎ 038/7352127). **Český Krumlov** (Čedok, ⊠ Latrá 79, ☎ 0337/2189; Infocentrum, ⊠ Nám. Svornosti 1, ☎ 0337/5670). **Kutná Hora** (Kulturní a Informační Centrum, ⊠ Palackého 377, ☎ 0327/2378). **Písek** (Čedok, ⊠ Velké nám. 1, ☎ 0362/212988). **Třeboň** (Informační středisko, ⊠ Masarykovo nám. 103, ☎ 0333/721169).

WESTERN BOHEMIA

Until World War II, western Bohemia was the playground of Central Europe's rich and famous. Its three well-known spas, Karlovy Vary, Mariánské Lázně, and Františkový Lázně (better known by their German names: Karlsbad, Marienbad, and Franzensbad, respectively) were the annual haunts of everybody who was anybody—Johann Wolfgang von Goethe, Ludwig van Beethoven, Karl Marx, and England's King Edward VII, to name but a few. Although strictly "proletarianized" in the Communist era, the spas still exude a nostalgic aura of a more elegant past and, unlike most of Bohemia, offer a basic tourist infrastructure that makes dining and lodging a pleasure.

Karlovy Vary

★ ⑱ *132 km (79 mi) due west on Route 6 (E48) from Prague. By car the trip takes about two hours.*

Karlovy Vary, better known outside the Czech Republic by its German name, Karlsbad, is the most famous Bohemian spa. It is named for Emperor Charles (Karl) IV, who allegedly happened upon the springs in 1358 while on a hunting expedition. As the story goes, the emperor's hound—chasing a harried stag—fell into a boiling spring and was scalded. Charles had the water tested and, familiar with spas in Italy, ordered baths to be established in the village of Vary. The spa reached its heyday in the 19th century, when royalty came here from all over Europe for treatment. The long list of those who "took the cure" includes Goethe (no fewer than 13 times, according to a plaque on one house in the Old Town), Schiller, Beethoven, and Chopin. Even Karl Marx, when he wasn't decrying wealth and privilege, spent time at the resort and wrote some of *Das Kapital* here between 1874 and 1876.

The shabby streets of modern Karlovy Vary, though, are vivid reminders that those glory days are long over. Aside from a few superficial changes, the Communists made little new investment in the town for 40 years; many of the buildings are literally crumbling behind their beautiful facades. Today officials face the daunting tasks of financing the town's reconstruction and carving out a new role for Karlovy Vary, in an era when few people can afford to set aside weeks or months at a time for a leisurely cure. To raise some quick cash, many sanatoriums have turned to offering short-term accommodations to foreign visitors (at rather expensive rates). It's even possible at some spas to receive "treatment," including carbon-dioxide baths and massage. For most visitors, though, it's enough simply to stroll the streets and parks and allow the eyes to feast awhile on the splendors of the past.

Whether you're arriving by bus, train, or car, your first view of the town on the approach from Prague will be of the ugly new section on the banks of the Ohře River. Don't despair: Continue along the main road—following the signs to the Grandhotel Pupp—until you reach the lovely main street of the older spa area, situated gently astride the banks of the little Teplá River. The walk from the New Town to the spa area is about 20 minutes; take a taxi if you're carrying a heavy load. The **Old Town** is still largely intact. Tall 19th-century houses, boasting decorative and often eccentric facades, line the spa's proud, if dilapidated, streets. Throughout you'll see colonnades full of the healthy and the not-so-healthy sipping the spa's hot sulfuric water from odd pipe-shaped drinking cups. At night the streets fill with steam escaping from cracks in the earth, giving the town a slightly macabre feel.

Karlovy Vary's jarringly modern **Vřídlo Colonnade,** home of the spring of the same name, is the town's hottest and most dramatic spring. The Vřídlo is indeed unique, shooting its scalding water to a height of some 40 feet. Walk inside the arcade to watch the hundreds of patients here take the famed Karlsbad drinking cure. You'll recognize them promenading somnambulistically up and down, eyes glazed, clutching a drinking glass filled periodically at one of the five "sources." The waters are said to be especially effective against diseases of the digestive and urinary tracts. They're also good for the gout-ridden (which probably explains the spa's former popularity with royals!). If you want to join the crowds and take a sip, you can buy your own spouted cup from vendors within the colonnade.

Walk in the direction of the New Town, past the wooden **Market Colonnade.** Continue down the winding street until you reach the **Mill Colonnade.** This neo-Renaissance pillared hall, built in 1871–81, offers four springs bearing the romantic names of Rusalka, Libussa, Prince Wenceslas, and Millpond. If you continue down the valley, you'll soon arrive at the very elegant **Park Colonnade,** a white wrought-iron construction built in 1882 by the Viennese architectural duo of Fellner and Helmer, who sprinkled the Austro-Hungarian Empire with many such edifices during the late 19th century and who also designed the town's theater (1886), the Market Colonnade (1883), and one of the old bathhouses (1895), now a casino.

The 20th century emerges at its most disturbing a little farther along the valley across the river, in the form of the huge, bunkerlike **Thermal Hotel,** built in the late 1960s. Although the building is a monstrosity, the view of Karlovy Vary from the rooftop pool is nothing short of spectacular. Even if you don't feel like a swim, it's worth taking the winding road up to the baths for the view.

The **Imperial Sanatorium** is a perfect example of turn-of-the-century architecture, with its white facade and red-roofed tower. The Imperial was once the haunt of Europe's wealthiest financiers. Under the Communists, though, the sanatorium was used to house visiting Soviet dignitaries—a gesture of "friendship" from the Czech government. The Imperial has recently reopened as a private hotel, but it will be many years before it can again assume its former role.

You'll find the steep road **Zámecký vrch** by crossing over the little Gogol Bridge near the Hotel Otova, then following the steps leading behind the colonnade. Walk uphill until you come to the redbrick **Victorian Church,** once used by the local English community. A few blocks farther along Petra Velikeho Street, you'll come to a splendiforous **Russian Orthodox church,** once visited by Czar Peter the Great. Return to the English church and take a sharp right uphill on the redbrick road. Then turn left onto a footpath through the woods, following the signs to **Jeleni Skok** (Stag's Leap). After a while you'll see steps leading up to a bronze statue of a deer towering over the cliffs, the symbol of Karlovy Vary. From here a winding path leads up to a little red **gazebo** (Altán Jeleni Skok), opening onto a fabulous panorama of the town.

NEED A BREAK?	Reward yourself for making the climb with a light meal at the nearby restaurant **Jeleni Skok.** You may have to pay an entrance fee if there is a live band (but you'll also get the opportunity to polka). If you don't want to walk up, you can drive from the church.

The **Grandhotel Pupp** is the former favorite of the Central European nobility and longtime rival of the Imperial. The Pupp's reputation was tarnished somewhat during the years of Communist rule (the hotel was renamed the Moskva-Pupp), but the hotel's former grandeur is still in evidence. Even if you're not staying here, be sure to stroll around the impressive facilities and have a drink in the elegant cocktail bar.

Diagonally across from the Grandhotel Pupp, behind a little park, is the pompous Fellner and Helmer **Imperial Spa,** now known as **Lázně I** and housing the local casino. As you walk back into town along the river, you'll pass a variety of interesting stores, including the Moser glass store and the Elefant, one of the last of a dying breed of sophisticated coffeehouses in the Czech Republic. Across the river is the Fellner and Helmer theater. Continue on to the right of the Vřídlo, where the tour began, and walk up the steps to the white **Kostel svatej Maří Magdaleny** (Church of Mary Magdalene). Designed by Kilian Dientzenhofer (architect of the two St. Nicholas churches in Prague), this church is the best of the few baroque buildings still standing in Karlovy Vary.

Dining and Lodging

$$$ ✕ **Embassy.** This cozy wine restaurant, conveniently located near the Grandhotel Pupp, serves an innovative range of pastas, seafoods, and meats: Tagliatelle with smoked salmon in cream sauce makes an excellent main course. Highlights of the varied dessert menu include plum dumplings with *fromage blanc* (white cheese). ⊠ *Nová Louka 21,* ☎ *017/23049,* FAX *017/23146. DC.*

$$ ✕ **Karel IV.** Its location atop an old castle not far from the main colon-
★   nade affords diners the best view in town. Good renditions of traditional Czech standbys—mostly pork and beef entrées—are served in small, secluded dining areas that are particularly intimate after sunset. ⊠ *Zámecký vrch 2,* ☎ *017/27255. AE, MC.*

$ ✕ **Vegetarian.** This is a tiny, mostly meat-free oasis not far from the Hotel Thermal in the New Town. Look for a small but tempting array of vegetarian standards and nontraditional variations of Czech dishes. ⊠ *I. P. Pavlova 25,* ☎ *017/29021. No credit cards.*

$$$$ ⊞ **Dvořák.** Consider a splurge here if you're longing for Western stan-
★ dards of service and convenience. Opened in late 1990, this Austrian-
owned hotel occupies three renovated town houses a five-minute walk
from the main spas. The staff is helpful, and the rooms are spotlessly
clean. If possible, request a room with a bay-window view of the
town. ⊠ *Nová Louka 11, 360 21 Karlovy Vary,* ☎ *017/3224145,* FAX
*017/3222814. 87 rooms with bath. Restaurant, café, in-room satellite
TVs, pool, beauty parlor, massage, sauna, exercise room. Breakfast included. AE, DC, MC, V.*

$$$$ ⊞ **Grandhotel Pupp.** This enormous 300-year-old hotel, perched on
★ the edge of the spa district, is one of Central Europe's most famous resorts. Standards and service slipped under the Communists (when the
hotel was known as the Moskva-Pupp), but the highly professional management is working hard to atone for the decades of neglect. Ask for
a room furnished in 19th-century period style. The food in the ground-
floor restaurant is passable, but the elegant setting makes the hotel worth
a splurge. ⊠ *Mírové nám. 2, 360 21 Karlovy Vary,* ☎ *017/209111,*
FAX *017/24032. 298 rooms with bath. 4 restaurants, lounge, in-room
satellite TVs, sauna, exercise room, 2 nightclubs. Breakfast included.
AE, DC, MC, V.*

$$$ ⊞ **Elwa.** Renovations have successfully integrated modern comforts
into this older, elegant spa resort located midway between the Old and
New Towns. Modern features include clean, comfortable rooms (most
with television) and an on-site fitness center. ⊠ *Zahradní 29, 360 21
Karlovy Vary,* ☎ *017/3228472,* FAX *017/3228473. 30 rooms with
bath. Restaurant, bar, beauty parlor, health club. Breakfast included.
AE, DC, MC, V.*

Nightlife and the Arts

In Karlovy Vary, the action centers on the two nightclubs of the **Grand-
hotel Pupp.** The "little dance hall" is open daily 8 PM–1 AM. The second
club is open Wednesday through Sunday 7 PM–3 AM. **Club Propaganda**
(⊠ Jaltska 7) is Karlovy Vary's best venue for live rock and new music.

Outdoor Activities and Sports

Karlovy Vary's warm open-air pool (on top of the Thermal Hotel) of-
fers the unique experience of swimming comfortably even in the coolest
weather; the view over the town is outstanding.

Shopping

In western Bohemia, Karlovy Vary is best known to glass enthusiasts
as home of the **Moser** glass company, one of the world's leading pro-
ducers of crystal and decorative glassware. In addition to running the
flagship store at Na Příkopě 12 in Prague, the company operates an
outlet in Karlovy Vary on Stará Louka, next to the Cafe Elefant. A num-
ber of outlets for lesser-known, although also high-quality makers of
glass and porcelain can also be found along Stará Louka.

For excellent buys in porcelain, try the **Pirkenhammer** outlet below the
Hotel Atlantic (⊠ Tržiště 23).

A cheaper but nonetheless unique gift from Karlovy Vary would be a
bottle of the ubiquitous bittersweet (and potent) Becherovka, a liqueur
produced by the town's own Jan Becher distillery. Always appreciated
as gifts are the unique pipe-shaped ceramic drinking cups used to take
the drinking cure at spas. Find them at the colonnades in Karlovy Vary
and Mariánské Lázně. You can also buy boxes of tasty Oplatky wafers,
sometimes covered with chocolate, at shops in all of the spa towns.

Cheb

 42 km (26 mi) southwest of Karlovy Vary.

Known for centuries by its German name of Eger, the old town of Cheb lies on the border with Germany in the far west of the Czech Republic. The town has been a fixture of Bohemia since 1322 (when the king purchased the area from German merchants), but as you walk around the beautiful medieval square, it's difficult not to think you're in Germany. The tall merchants' houses surrounding the square, with their long, red-tiled sloping roofs dotted with windows like droopy eyelids, are more Germanic in style than anything else in Bohemia. You'll also hear a lot of German on the streets—but more from the many German visitors than from the town's residents.

Germany took full possession of the town in 1938 under the terms of the notorious Munich Pact. But following World War II, virtually the entire German population was expelled, and the Czech name of Cheb was officially adopted. A more notorious German connection has emerged in the years following the 1989 revolution. Cheb has quickly become the unofficial center of prostitution for visiting Germans. Don't be startled to see young women, provocatively dressed, lining the highways and bus stops on the roads into town. The legal status of prostitution remains unsettled, and its level of toleration varies from town to town. The police have been known to crack down periodically on streetwalkers and their customers.

Begin a tour of the town in the bustling central square, **Náměstí Krále Jiřího z Poděbrad,** where the ubiquitous Vietnamese vendors have reestablished its original marketplace function. The statue in the middle, similar to the Roland statues you see throughout Bohemia and attesting to the town's royal privileges, represents the town hero, Wastel of Eger. Look carefully at his right foot, and you'll see a small man holding a sword and a head—this denotes the town had its own judge and executioner.

Walk downhill from the square to see two rickety groups of timbered medieval buildings, 11 houses in all, divided by a narrow alley. The houses, forming the area known as **Špalíček**, date from the 13th century and were home to many Jewish merchants. **Židovská ulice** (Jews' Street), running uphill to the left of the Špalíček, served as the actual center of the ghetto. Note the small alley running off to the left of Židovská. This calm street, with the seemingly inappropriate name ulička Zavražděných (Lane of the Murdered), was the scene of an outrageous act of violence in 1350. Pressures had been building for some time between Jews and Christians. Incited by an anti-Semitic bishop, the townspeople finally chased the Jews into the street, closed off both ends, and massacred them. Only the name attests to the slaughter.

NEED A BREAK?   Cheb's main square abounds with cafés and little restaurants, all offering a fairly uniform menu of schnitzel and sauerbraten aimed at visiting Germans. The **Kavárna Špalíček,** nestled in the Špalíček buildings, is one of the better choices and has the added advantage of a unique architectural setting.

History buffs, particularly those interested in the Hapsburgs, will want to visit the **Chebský muzeum** (Cheb Museum) in the Pachelbel House, behind the Špalíček on the main square. It was in this house that the great general of the Thirty Years' War, Albrecht von Wallenstein (Valdštejn), was murdered in 1634 on the orders of his own emperor, the Hapsburg Ferdinand II. According to legend, Wallenstein was on his way to the Saxon border to enlist support to fight the Swedes when his own officers barged into his room and stabbed him through the heart with a stave. The stark bedroom with its four-poster bed and dark-red velvet curtains has been left as it was in his memory. The museum is also interesting in its own right: It has a section on the history of Cheb and a collection of minerals (including one discovered by Goethe). ⊠ *Nám. Krále Jiřího z Poděbrad.* ☉ *Tues.–Sun. 9–noon and 1–5.*

The **art gallery** in the bright-yellow baroque house near the top of the square, open daily 9–5, offers an excellent small collection of Gothic sculpture from western Bohemia and a well-chosen sampling of modern Czech art. One of the country's best-known private galleries of photography, **Gallery G4,** is just off the square at ⊠ *Kamenná 4.*

In the early 1820s, Goethe often stayed in the **Gabler House,** on the corner of the square at the museum. He shared a passionate interest in excavation work with the town executioner, and they both worked on the excavation of the nearby extinct volcano Komorní Hůrka. In 1791 Germany's second most famous playwright, Friedrich Schiller, lived at No. 2, at the top of the square next to the "new" town hall, where he planned his famous *Wallenstein* trilogy.

If you follow the little street on the right side of the square at the Gabler House, you will quickly reach the plain but imposing **Kostel svatého Mikuláše** (St. Nicholas Church). Construction began in 1230, when the church belonged to the Order of the Teutonic Knights. You can still see Romanesque windows under the tower; renovations throughout the centuries added an impressive Gothic portal and a baroque interior. Just inside the Gothic entrance is a wonderfully faded plaque commemorating the diamond jubilee of Hapsburg emperor Franz Josef in 1908.

From here walk down the little alley onto Kammená and turn left onto Křižovnická. Follow the road up to **Chebský hrad** (Cheb Castle), on a cliff overlooking the Ohře River. The castle was built in the late 12th century for Holy Roman Emperor Frederick Barbarossa. The square black tower was built with blocks of lava taken from the nearby Komorní Hůrka volcano; the redbrick walls were added during the 15th century. Inside the castle grounds is the carefully restored double-decker chapel, built in the 12th century. The rather dark ground floor, still in Romanesque style, was used by commoners. The bright ornate top floor, with pointed Gothic windows, was reserved for the emperor and his family and has a wooden bridge leading to the royal palace. ⊠ *Hradní ul.* ☉ *Apr. and Oct., Tues.–Sun. 9–4; May and Sept., Tues.–Sun. 9–5; June–Aug., Tues.–Sun. 9–6.*

Dining and Lodging

$$ ✕ **Eva.** Of the many restaurants opened on and around the main square since the tourism boom began in the early 1990s, the Eva is certainly one of the best. A decent array of mostly Czech and German dishes is served in a stylish, contemporary setting that is carefully maintained by a troop of attentive waiters. ⊠ *Jateční 4,* ☎ *0166/22498. No credit cards.*

Cheb's hotels have failed to keep pace with the times. For a short stay, a room in a private home is a better bet. Owners of an older home at Valdstejnova 21 offer two clean and comfortable rooms (☎ 0166/33088). Several houses along Přemysla Otakara Street north of the city have rooms available. Try the house at No. 7 (☎ 0166/22270).

$$ ⊞ **Hvězda.** This turn-of-the-century hotel was last renovated in the 1970s, which partly accounts for its present disheveled look. The location at the top of the main square is excellent, but the dilapidated facilities do not justify the prices. ⊠ *Nám. Krále Jiřího 4–6, 351 01 Cheb,* ☏ *0166/22549,* 𝔽𝔸𝕏 *0166/22546. 38 rooms, most with bath. Restaurant, café, in-room TVs. MC, V.*

$$ ⊞ **Hradní Dvůr.** This somewhat cramped older hotel is due for a renovation; until then, the plain rooms are kept acceptably clean. The hotel's prime asset is location, on a side street that runs parallel to the main square. Request a room on the top floor, above the noisy reception area. ⊠ *Dlouhá ul. 12, 350 02 Cheb,* ☏ *0166/22006,* 𝔽𝔸𝕏 *0166/22444. 21 rooms, some with bath. Breakfast not included. Restaurant, nightclub. AE, MC.*

Františkovy Lázně

70 *6 km (4 mi) from Cheb.*

This little spa town couldn't make a more distinct contrast to nearby Cheb's slightly seedy, hustling air and medieval streetscapes. You might like to ease the transition by walking the red-marked path from Cheb's main square, westward along the river and then north past **Komorní Hůrka.** The extinct volcano is now a tree-covered hill, but excavations on one side have laid bare the rock, and one tunnel is still open. Goethe instigated and took part in the excavations, and you can still barely make out a relief of the poet carved into the rock face.

Františkovy Lázně, or Franzensbad, the smallest of the three main Bohemian spas, isn't really in the same league as the other two (Karlovy Vary and Mariánské Lázně). Built on a more modest scale at the start of the 19th century, the town's ubiquitous kaiser-yellow buildings have been prettified after their neglect under the previous regime and now present cheerful facades, almost too bright for the few strollers. The poorly kept parks and the formal, yet human-scale neoclassical architecture retain much of their former charm. Overall, a pleasing torpor reigns in Františkovy Lázně. There is no town to speak of, just **Národní ulice,** the main street, which leads down into the spa park. The waters, whose healing properties were already known in the 16th century, are used primarily for curing infertility—hence the large number of young women wandering the grounds.

The most interesting sight in town may be the small **Spa Museum,** just off Národní ulice. There is a wonderful collection of spa antiques, including copper bathtubs and a turn-of-the-century exercise bike called a Velotrab. The guest books (*Kurbuch*) provide an insight into the cosmopolitan world of pre–World War I Central Europe. The book for 1812 contains the entry "Ludwig van Beethoven, composer from Vienna." ⊠ *Ul. Doktora Pohoreckého 8.* 🎟 *15 Kč.* ☉ *Weekdays 9–noon and 2–5; June–Sept., also open weekends 9–4.*

Exploration of the spa itself should start on Národní ulice. Wander down the street to the main spring, **Františkuv pramen,** under a little gazebo filled with brass pipes. The colonnade to the left was decorated with a bust of Lenin that was replaced in 1990 by a memorial to the American liberation of the town in April 1945. Walk along the path to the left until you come to the Lázeňská poliklinika, where you can arrange for a day's spa treatment for around 350 Kč. The park surrounding the town is good for aimless wandering, interrupted by empty pedestals for discarded statues of historical figures no longer considered worthy of memorial.

Only insipid pop music (the scourge of eating and drinking places everywhere in the country) spoils the mood in the little café of the **Hotel Slovan** on Národní. The tiny gallery and lively frescoes make it a cheerful spot for cake, coffee, or alcoholic drinks.

Dining and Lodging

$$$ ✕🏠 **Slovan.** A quaint and gracious establishment—the perfect com-
★ plement to this relaxed little town. The eccentricity of the original turn-of-the-century design survived a thorough renovation during the 1970s; the airy rooms are clean and comfortable, and some come with a balcony overlooking the main street. The main-floor restaurant serves above-average Czech dishes; consider a meal here even if you're staying elsewhere. ✉ *Národní 5, 35101 Františkovy Lázně,* ☎ *0166/942841,* ☏ *0166/942843. 25 rooms, most with bath. Restaurant, café, wine bar. DC, V.*

$$$ 🏠 **Centrum.** Renovations have left the rooms clean and well appointed if a bit sterile. Still, it is among the best-run hotels in town and only a short walk from the main park and central spas. ✉ *Anglická 41, 351 01 Františkovy Lázně,* ☎ *0166/943156,* ☏ *0166/942843. 30 rooms with bath. Restaurant, wine bar, in-room TVs. MC, V.*

$$$ 🏠 **Tři Lilie.** Reopened in 1995 after an expensive refitting, it once accommodated the likes of Goethe, Metternich, and Hapsburg emperor Ferdinand V ("the Benign"). Though too new to have developed a style of its own, the "Three Lilies" has certainly become the best-equipped hotel in town. Spa treatments are conducted off-premises. ✉ *Máchova at Libušina (off Národní),* ☎ *0166/942415. 31 rooms with bath. Restaurant, brasserie, café. No credit cards. Reservations are made through the town's spa management: Obchodní oddělení, Lázně Františkovy Lázně a.s., Jiráskova 17, 351 01 Františkovy Lázně,* ☏ *0166/942970.*

$$ 🏠 **Bajkal.** This is an offbeat, older hotel with acceptably clean rooms and a friendly staff. It is on the far side of the park from the main spas, roughly a 10-minute walk from the city center. The travel agency in the building also books private accommodations. ✉ *Americká ul. 84/4, 351 01 Františkovy Lázně,* ☎ *0166/942501,* ☏ *0166/942503. 25 rooms, most with bath. Restaurant. V.*

Mariánské Lázně

★ ⑦ *30 km (18 mi) southeast of Cheb, 47 km (29 mi) south of Karlovy Vary.*

Visitors' expectations of what a spa resort should be come nearest to full reality here. It's far larger and better maintained than Františkovy Lázně and is greener and quieter than Karlovy Vary. This was the spa favored by Britain's Edward VII; Goethe and Chopin, among other luminaries, also repaired here frequently. Mark Twain, on a visit to the spa in 1892, labeled the town a "health factory" and couldn't get over how new everything looked. Indeed, at that time everything was new. The sanatoriums, all built in the middle of the last century in a confident, outrageous mixture of "neo" styles, fan out impressively around a finely groomed oblong park. Cure takers and curiosity seekers alike parade through the two stately colonnades, both placed near the top of the park. Buy a spouted drinking cup (available at the colonnades) and join the rest of the sippers taking the drinking cure. Be forewarned, though: The waters from the Rudolph, Ambrose, and Caroline springs, though harmless, all have a noticeable diuretic effect. For this reason they're used extensively in treating disorders of the kidney and bladder. Several spa hotels offer more extensive treatment for visitors, including baths and massage. Prices are usually reckoned in U.S. dollars or German marks. For more information, inquire at the main spa offices at ✉ *Masarykova 22*, ☎ *0165/2170*, ℻ *0165/2982*.

A stay in Mariánské Lázně, however, can be healthful even without special treatment. Special walking trails of all difficulty levels surround the resort in all directions. The best advice is simply to put on comfortable shoes, buy a hiking map, and head out. One of the country's few golf courses lies 3 or 4 kilometers (2 or 3 miles) from town to the east. Hotels can also help to arrange special activities, such as tennis and horseback riding. For the less intrepid, a simple stroll around the gardens, with a few deep breaths of the town's famous air, is enough to restore a healthy sense of perspective.

Dining and Lodging

$$ ✕ **Filip.** This bustling wine bar is where locals come to find relief from the sometimes large horde of tourists. A tasty selection of traditional Czech dishes—mainly pork, grilled meats, and steaks—is served by a friendly and efficient staff. ✉ *Poštovní 96*, ☎ *0165/2639. No credit cards.*

$$ ✕ **Koliba.** This combination hunting lodge and wine tavern, set in the
★ woods roughly 20 minutes on foot from the spas, is an excellent alternative to the hotel restaurants in town. Grilled meats and shish kebobs, plus tankards of Moravian wine (try the cherry-red Rulandské Červené), are served with traditional gusto. ✉ *Dusíkova, on the road to Karlovy Vary*, ☎ *0165/5169. AE, DC, MC, V.*

$ ✕ **Classic.** This small, trendy café on the main drag serves fine sandwiches and light meals throughout the day. Unusual for this part of the world, it also offers a full breakfast menu until 11 AM. ✉ *Hlavní tř. 131/50*, ☎ *0165/2807. Reservations not accepted. AE, DC, MC, V.*

The best place to look for private lodgings is along Paleckého ulice and Hlavní třída, south of the main spa area. Private accommodations can also be found in the neighboring villages of Zádub and Závišín and along roads in the woods to the east of Mariánské Lázně.

$$$$ 🏨 **Excelsior.** This lovely older hotel is on the main street and is convenient to the spas and colonnade. The renovated rooms are clean and comfortable, and the staff is friendly and helpful. The food in the adjoining restaurant is only average, but the romantic setting provides adequate compensation. ✉ *Hlavní tř. 121, 353 01 Mariánské Lázně*, ☎ *0165/2705 or 0165/622705*, ℻ *0165/5346 or 0165/625346. 64 rooms with bath. Restaurant, café. AE, DC, MC, V.*

$$$$ 🏨 **Hotel Golf.** Book in advance to secure a room at this stately villa situated 3½ kilometers (2 miles) out of town on the road to Karlovy Vary. A major renovation in the 1980s left the large, open rooms with a cheery, modern look. The restaurant on the main floor is excellent, but the big draw is the 18-hole golf course on the premises, one of the few in the Czech Republic. ✉ *Zádub 55, 353 01 Mariánské Lázně*, ☎ *0165/2651 or 0165/2652*, ℻ *0165/2655. 25 rooms with bath. Restaurant, in-room satellite TVs, pool, golf, tennis. AE, DC, MC, V.*

$$$ 🏨 **Bohemia.** This renovated spa resort is definitely worth the splurge;
★ beautiful crystal chandeliers in the main hall set the stage for a comfortable and elegant stay. The rooms are well appointed and completely equipped, though you may want to be really decadent and request one of the enormous suites overlooking the park. The helpful staff can arrange spa treatments and horseback riding. ✉ *Hlavní tř. 100, 353 01 Mariánské Lázně*, ☎ *0165/3251*, ℻ *0165/2943. 77 rooms with bath. Restaurant, in-room TVs and phones. AE, DC, MC, V.*

Nightlife and the Arts

Mariánske Lázně sponsors a music festival each June, with numerous concerts featuring Czech and international composers and orchestras.

The town's annual Chopin festival each autumn brings in fans of the Polish composer's work from around the world.

Mariánské Lázně's **Casino Marienbad** (☎ 0165/3292) is at Anglická 336 and is open daily 6 AM–2 AM. For late-night drinks, try the **Hotel Golf** (☞ Lodging, *above*), which has a good nightclub with dancing in season.

Teplá

72 *15 km (9 mi) from Mariánské Lázně.*

It is worth making a detour to the little town of Teplá and its 800-year-old monastery, which once played an important role in Christianizing pagan Central Europe. If you don't have a car, a special bus departs daily in season from Mariánské Lázně (inquire at the information office in front of the Hotel Excelsior). The sprawling monastery, founded by the Premonstratensian order of France in 1193 (the same order that established Prague's Strahov Monastery), once controlled the farms and forests in these parts for miles around. The order even owned the spa facilities at Mariánské Lázně and until 1942 used the proceeds from the spas to cover operating expenses. The complex you see before you today, however, betrays none of this earlier prosperity. Over the centuries, the monastery was plundered dozens of times during wars and upheavals, but history reserved its severest blow for the night of April 13, 1950, when security forces employed by the Communists raided the grounds and imprisoned the brothers. The monastery's property was given over to the Czech army, and for the next 28 years the buildings were used as barracks to house soldiers. In 1991 the government returned the monastery buildings and immediate grounds (but not the original land holdings) to the order, and the brothers began the arduous task of picking up the pieces—physically and spiritually.

The most important building on the grounds from an architectural point of view is the Romanesque **basilica** (1197), with its unique triple nave. The rest of the monastery complex was originally Romanesque, but it was rebuilt in 1720 by baroque architect K. I. Dientzenhofer. There are several wall and ceiling paintings of interest here, as well as some good sculpture. The most valuable collection is in the **Nová knihovna** (New Library), where you will find illuminated hymnals and rare Czech and foreign manuscripts, including a German translation of the New Testament that predates Luther's by some 100 years. Tours of the church and library are given daily (English notes are available). The monastery also offers short-term accommodations to visitors (inquire directly at the monastery offices on the grounds). ⊠ *Klášter, 364 61 Teplá,* ☎ *0169/92264.* ▣ *Monastery 80 Kč.* ☉ *Tues.–Sun. 9–3 (until 4:30 in summer).*

Plzeň

73 *92 km (55 mi) from Prague.*

The sprawling industrial city of Plzeň is hardly a tourist mecca, but it's worth stopping off for an hour or two on the way back to Prague. Two sights here are of particular interest to beer fanatics. The first is the **Pilsner-Urquell Brewery,** to the east of the city near the railway station. Group tours of the 19th-century redbrick building are offered weekdays at 12:30 PM, during which you can taste the valuable brew, exported around the world. The beer was created in 1842 using the excellent Plzeň water, a special malt fermented on the premises, and hops grown in the region around Žatec. ⊠ *U Prazdroje,* ☎ *019/7062888.* ▣ *50 Kč.*

You can continue drinking and find some cheap traditional grub at the large **Na Spilce** beer hall just inside the brewery gates. The pub is open daily from 10 AM to 10 PM.

The second stop on the beer tour is the **Pivovarské muzeum** (Brewery Museum), in a late-Gothic malt house one block northeast of the main square. ✉ *Veleslavinova ul. 6,* ☎ *019/7235574.* 🎫 *40 Kč.* ⊙ *Tues.–Sun. (daily in summer) 10–6.*

The city's architectural attractions center on the main square, **Náměstí Republiky.** The square is dominated by the enormous Gothic **Chrám svatého Bartoloměja** (Church of St. Bartholomew). Both the square and the church towers hold size records: The former is the largest in Bohemia, and the latter, at 102 meters (335 feet), the highest in the Czech Republic. The church was begun in 1297 and completed almost 200 years later. Around the square, mixed in with its good selection of stores, are a variety of other architectural jewels, including the town hall, adorned with sgraffiti and built in the Renaissance style by Italian architects during the town's heyday in the 16th century.

Dining and Lodging

$$$ ✕🏨 **Continental.** Just five minutes on foot from the main square, the fin-de-siècle Continental remains the best hotel in Pzleň, a relative compliment considering the hotel is slightly rundown and the rooms, though large, are exceedingly plain. The restaurant, however, serves dependably satisfying traditional Czech dishes. ✉ *Zbojnická 8, 305 31 Plzeň,* ☎ *019/7236477,* 🆗 *019/7221746. 46 rooms, 23 with bath or shower. Restaurant, café. Breakfast included. AE, DC, MC, V.*

$$$ 🏨 **Central.** This angular 1960s structure (named the Ural until 1990) is recommendable for its sunny rooms, friendly staff, and great location, right on the main square. Indeed, even such worthies as Czar Alexander of Russia stayed here in the days when the hotel was a charming inn known as the Golden Eagle. ✉ *Nám. Republiky 33, 305 31 Plzeň,* ☎ *019/7226757,* 🆗 *019/7226064. 77 rooms with shower. Restaurant, café, wine bar. Breakfast not included. AE, DC, MC, V.*

$$ 🏨 **Slovan.** A gracious off-white facade, sweeping stairways, and large, elegant rooms attest to the Slovan's former grandeur, and there's a pleasant, English-speaking staff to boot. The restaurant still occupies the once beautiful ballroom, but the experience is spoiled by mediocre food and the rock-music accompaniment. The Slovan's best asset may be its location, on a lovely square of its own, a short walk from the main square. ✉ *Smetanový Sady 1, 305 31 Plzeň,* ☎ *019/7227256,* 🆗 *019/7227012. 100 rooms, most with bath or shower. Restaurant, café. Breakfast included. AE, DC, MC, V.*

Western Bohemia A to Z

Arriving and Departing

Prague is the main gateway to western Bohemia (☞ Arriving and Departing *in* Prague A to Z, *above*). Major trains from Munich and Nürnberg stop at Cheb and some of the spa towns. It is also an easy drive across the border from Bavaria on the E48 to Cheb and from there to any of the spas.

Getting Around

Good, if slow, train service links all the major towns west of Prague. The best stretches are from Františkovy Lázně to Plzeň and from Plzeň to Prague. The Prague–Karlovy Vary run takes far longer than it should but has a romantic charm all its own. Note that most trains heading west to Germany (in the direction of Nürnberg) stop at Mariánské Lázně.

Most trains leave from Prague's Hlavní nádraží (main station), but be sure to check on which station if in doubt.

Contacts and Resources

EMERGENCIES
Police (☎ 158). **Ambulance** (☎ 155).

GUIDED TOURS
Čedok (☎ 02/2419–7111) offers several specialized tours covering western Bohemia's major sights. Tour "G-O" combines a trip to Lidice in northern Bohemia (☞ *below*) with a visit to the spa town of Karlovy Vary. The trip takes a full day and departs three times weekly. Prague departure points are at the Çedok offices at Na příkopě 18 and Bílkova ulice 6, and the Panorama, Forum, and Hilton hotels.

VISITOR INFORMATION
Čedok is the first stop for general tourist information and city maps:

Cheb (✉ Májova 31, ☎ 0166/30650). **Mariánské Lázně** (✉ Třebízského 2/101, ☎ 0165/2254; Infocentrum, ✉ Hlavní 47, ☎ 0165/2474; City Service, ✉ Hlavní 626/1, ☎ 0165/3816).

NORTHERN BOHEMIA

Northern Bohemia is a paradox: While much of it was despoiled over the past 40 years by rampant, postwar industrialization, here and there you can still find areas of great natural beauty. Particularly along the Labe (Elbe River), rolling hills, perfect for walking, guard the country's northern frontiers with Germany and Poland. Hikers and campers head for the Giant Mountains (Krkonoše) on the Polish border (the only region which has good hotels); this range is not so giant, actually, though it is very pretty. As you move toward the west, the interest is more historical, in an area where the influence of Germany was felt in less pleasant ways than in the spas. You needn't drive too far to reach the Sudetenland, the German-speaking border area that was ceded to Hitler by the British and French in 1938. Indeed, the landscape here is riddled with the tragic remains of the Nazi occupation of Czech lands from 1939 to 1945. Most drastically affected was Terezín, better known as the infamous concentration camp, Theresienstadt, where the Nazis converted the redbrick fortress town into a Jewish ghetto and prison camp during World War II.

In the area around Terezín and Litoměřice, tourist amenities are practically nonexistent; if you do choose to stay overnight, you'll generally be able to find a room in a primitive inn or a rather unwelcoming modern hotel. In many parts of Bohemia the only real options for dining are the restaurants and cafés at the larger hotels and resorts.

Lidice

⑦⑭ *18 km (11 mi) from Prague on Route 7 (the road to Ruzyně Airport). Head in the direction of Slaný. Turn off at the Lidice exit and follow the country road for 3 km (1¼ mi).*

The **Lidice museum and monument** are unforgettable sights. The empty field to the right, with a large cross at the bottom, is where the town of Lidice stood until 1942, when it was viciously razed by the Nazis in retribution for the assassination of German district leader Reinhard Heydrich.

The Lidice story really begins with the notorious Munich Pact of 1938, according to which the leaders of Great Britain and France permitted Hitler to occupy the largely German-speaking border regions of

Czechoslovakia (the so-called Sudetenland). Less than a year later, in March 1939, Hitler used his forward position to occupy the whole of Bohemia and Moravia, making the area into a protectorate of the German Reich. To guard his new possessions, Hitler appointed ruthless Nazi Reinhard Heydrich as Reichsprotektor. Heydrich immediately implemented a campaign of terror against Jews and intellectuals while currying favor with average Czechs by raising rations and wages. As a result, the Czech army-in-exile, based in Great Britain, soon began planning Heydrich's assassination. In the spring of 1942 a small band of parachutists was flown in to carry out the task.

The assassination attempt took place just north of Prague on May 27, 1942, and Heydrich died from his injuries on June 4. Hitler immediately ordered the little mining town of Lidice, west of Prague, "removed from the face of the earth," since it was alleged (although later found untrue) that some of the assassins had been sheltered by villagers there. On the night of June 9, a Gestapo unit entered Lidice, shot the entire adult male population (199 men), and sent the 196 women to the Ravensbruck concentration camp. The 103 children in the village were sent either to Germany to be "Aryanized" or to death camps. On June 10, the entire village was razed. The assassins and their accomplices were found a week later in the Orthodox Church of Sts. Cyril and Methodius in Prague's New Town, where they committed suicide after a shootout with Nazi militia.

The monument to these events is a sober place. The arcades are graphic in their depiction of the deportation and slaughter of the inhabitants. The museum itself is dedicated to those killed, with photographs of each person and a short description of his or her fate. You'll also find reproductions of the German documents ordering the village's destruction, including the Gestapo's chillingly bureaucratic reports on how the massacre was carried out and the peculiar problems encountered in Aryanizing the deported children. The exhibits highlighting the international response (a suburb of Chicago was even renamed for the town) are heartwarming. An absorbing 18-minute film in Czech (worthwhile even for non-Czech speakers) tells the Lidice story. ⊠ *Museum: ul. 10. června 1942.* ⊡ *20 Kč.* ☉ *Daily 9–5.*

Lidice was rebuilt after the war on the initiative of a group of miners from Birmingham, England, who called their committee "Lidice Must Live." Between New Lidice and the museum is a rose garden with some 3,000 bushes sent from all over the world. The wooden cross in the field to the right of the museum, starkly decorated with barbed wire, marks the place in Old Lidice where the men were executed. Remains of brick walls are visible here, left over from the Gestapo's dynamite and bulldozer exercise. Still, Lidice is a sad town, not a place to linger.

Veltrusy Château and Gardens

🄰 *25 km (15 mi) north of Prague.*

The aristocratic retreat of Veltrusy contrasts vividly with the ordinariness of nearby Kralupy, an industrial town better left unexplored. The mansion's late-baroque splendor lies hidden in a carefully laid out English park full of old and rare trees and scattered with 18th-century architectural follies. The château itself has been turned into a museum showcasing the cosmopolitan lifestyle of the imperial aristocracy, displaying Japanese and Chinese porcelain, English chandeliers, and 16th-century tapestries from Brussels. ⊡ *20 Kč.* ☉ *Apr. and*

*Oct.–Dec., weekends 9–4; May–Aug., Tues.–Sun. 8–5; Sept.,
Tues.–Sun. 9–5.*

Nelahozeves

*2½ km (1½ mi) on foot by marked paths from Veltrusy Château. By
car, the route is more circuitous: Turn right out of Veltrusy onto the
highway and over the river, then make a sharp left back along the river
to Nelahozeves.*

Nelahozeves was the birthplace in 1841 of Antonín Dvořák, the Czech
Republic's greatest composer. Dvořák's pretty corner house on the main
road (No. 12), with its tidy windows and arches, has a small memorial museum. In Dvořák's time, the house was an inn run by his parents, and it was here that he learned to play the violin. 🎫 *Free.* ☉
Tues.–Thurs. and weekends 9–noon and 2–5.

For those not enamored of the spirit of Dvořák's youth, the main attraction in town is the brooding Renaissance **chateau,** with its black-
and-white sgraffito, once the residence of the powerful Lobkowitz
family. The castle now houses an excellent collection of fine art. ☎
0205/22995. 🎫 *80 Kč.* ☉ *Tues.–Sun. 10–5 (until 3 in winter).*

Terezín

76 *36 km (22 mi) from Nelahozeves on Route 8.*

★ The old garrison town of Terezín gained notoriety under the Nazis as
the nefarious Nazi concentration camp **Theresienstadt,** though the
enormity of Theresienstadt's role in history is difficult to grasp at first.
The Czechs have put up few signs to tell you what to see; the town's
buildings, parks, and buses resemble those of any of a hundred other
unremarkable places, built originally by the Austrians and now inhabited
by Czechs. You could easily pass through it and never learn any of the
town's dark secrets.

Part of the problem is that **Malá Pevnost** (Small Fortress), the actual
prison and death camp, is 2 kilometers (1¼ miles) south of Terezín. Visitors to the strange redbrick complex see the prison more or less as it
was when the Nazis left it in 1945. Above the entrance to the main
courtyard stands the cynical motto ARBEIT MACHT FREI (Work will
make you free). Take a walk around the various rooms, still housing
a sad collection of rusty bedframes, sinks, and shower units. At the far
end of the fortress, opposite the main entrance, is the special wing built
by the Nazis when space became tight. The windowless cells are horrific; try going into one and closing the door—and then imagine being
crammed in with 14 other people. In the center of the fortress is a museum and a room where films are shown. ☎ *0416/92225.* 🎫 *90 Kč.*
☉ *Daily 8–4 (until 5 in summer).*

During World War II, Terezín served as a detention center for thousands of Jews and was used by the Nazis as an elaborate prop in a nefarious propaganda ploy. The large barracks buildings around town,
once used in the 18th and 19th centuries to house Austrian soldiers,
became living quarters for thousands of interred Jews. But in 1942, to
placate international public opinion, the Nazis cynically decided to transform the town into a showcase camp—to prove to the world their
"benevolent" intentions toward the Jews. To give the place the image
of a spa town, the streets were given new names such as Lake Street,
Bath Street, and Park Street. Numerous elderly Jews from Germany
were taken in by the deception and paid large sums of money to come
to the new "retirement village." Just before the International Red

Cross inspected the town in early 1944, Nazi authorities began a beautification campaign: painted the buildings, set up stores, laid out a park with benches in front of the town hall, and arranged for concerts and sports. The map just off the main square shows the town's street plan as the locations of various buildings between 1941 and 1945. The Jews here were able, with great difficulty, to establish a cultural life of their own under the limited "self-government" that was set up in the camp. The inmates created a library and a theater, and lectures and musical performances were given on a regular basis.

Once it was clear that the war was lost, however, the Nazis dropped any pretense and quickly stepped up transport of Jews to the Auschwitz death camp in Poland. Transports were not new to the ghetto; to keep the population at around 30,000, a train was sent off every few months or so "to the east" to make room for incoming groups. In the fall of 1944, these transports were increased to one every few days. In all, some 87,000 Jews were murdered in this way, and another 35,000 died from starvation or disease. The town's horrific story is told in words and pictures at the **Ghetto Museum,** just off the central park in town.

For all its history, Terezín is no place for an extended stay. Locals have chosen not to highlight the town's role during the Nazi era, and hence little provision has been made for visitors.

Litoměřice

77 *4 km (2½ mi) from Terezín, 70 km (42 mi) north of Prague.*

The decrepit state of the houses and streets belies this riverside town's medieval status as one of Bohemia's leading towns and a rival to Prague. It has remained largely untouched by modern development. Even today, although the food industry has established several factories in the surrounding area, much of central Litoměřice is like a living museum.

The best way to get a feel for Litoměřice is to start at the excellent **Městské muzeum** (City Museum), on the corner of the main square and Dlouhá ulice in the Old Town Hall building. The building itself deserves notice as one of the first examples of the Renaissance style in Bohemia, dating from 1537–39. Unfortunately, the museum's exhibits are described in Czech (with written commentary in German available from the ticket seller); but even if you don't understand the language, you'll find this museum fascinating. Despite its position near the old border with Germany, Litoměřice was a Czech and Hussite stronghold, and one of the museum's treasures is the brightly colored, illuminated gradual, or hymn book, depicting Hus's burning at the stake in Constance. Note also the golden chalice nearby, the old symbol of the Hussites. Farther on you come to an exquisite Renaissance pulpit and altar decorated with painted stone reliefs. On the second floor the most interesting exhibit is from the Nazi era, when Litoměřice became a part of Sudeten Germany and a border town of the German Reich, providing soldiers for nearby Theresienstadt. ⊠ *Mírové nám.* ⚏ *10 Kč.* ☉ *Tues.–Sun. 10–5.*

After leaving the museum, stroll along the busy but decaying central square, which sports a range of architectural styles from Renaissance arcades to baroque gables and a Gothic bell tower. The town's trademark, though, is the chalice-shaped tower at No. 7, the **Chalice House,** built in the 1560s for an Utraquist patrician. The Utraquists were moderate Hussites who believed that laymen should receive wine as well as bread in the sacrament of Holy Communion. On the left-hand corner of the Old Town Hall is a replica of a small and unusual Roland statue (the original is in the museum) on a high stone pedestal. These statues, found throughout Bohemia, signify the town as a "royal free town," due all the usual privileges of such a distinction. This particular statue is unique because instead of showing the usual handsome knight, it depicts a hairy caveman wielding a club. Even in the 15th century, it seems, Czechs had a sense of humor.

NEED A
BREAK?

For an ice cream, a fruit drink, or a cup of coffee, try the little stand-up **Atropic Cafe,** next to the museum on the main square (⊠ Mírové nám). Good beer and passable Czech food are served up daily in clean surroundings at the **Pivnice Kalich** (⊠ Lidická 9), a block from the main square.

A colorful, two-story baroque house with a facade by the 18th-century Italian master-builder Octavio Broggio houses the **Galerie výtvarného umění** (Art Gallery). Its strong collection of Czech art from the Gothic to the baroque and its temporary shows of living artists, make it one of the country's best provincial art museums. ⊠ *Michalská 7.* 🎫 *16 Kč.* ☉ *Tues.–Sun. 10–6 (until 5 in winter).*

More of Broggio's work can be seen in the facade and interior of the **All Saints' Church,** to the right of the town hall, while the church's high tower keeps its 16th-century appearance. Broggio also remade the monastery **Church of St. Jacob** (⊠ Ul. Velká Dominikánská), whose exterior sorely needs restoration. His most beautiful work, though, is the small **Kostel svatého Václava** (St. Wenceslas Chapel), squeezed into an unwieldy square to the north of town on the cathedral hill and now an Orthodox church. **Dóm svatého Štěpána** (St. Stephen's Cathedral), farther up the hill, is monumental but uninspired. Its one real treasure is a Lucas Cranach painting of St. Anthony—but unfortunately the cathedral door is often locked. There are also a number of paintings by the famed 17th-century Bohemian artist Karel Škréta.

Lodging

$$ 🏨 **Roosevelt.** The Secession-style town bathhouse was converted into a small hotel in 1994, adding to this area's limited supply of decent accommodations. On a 19th-century residential street, the Roosevelt is a couple minutes' walk from the town center. ⊠ *Rooseveltova 18, 412 01 Litoměřice,* ☎ *0416/8061,* 𝙵𝙰𝚇 *0416/8062. 30 rooms with bath. Restaurant, in-room TVs. Breakfast not included. AE, MC, V.*

OFF THE
BEATEN PATH

STŘEKOV CASTLE – The Vltava River north of Litoměřice flows through a long, unspoiled winding valley, packed in by surrounding hills, which has something of the look of a 16th-century landscape painting. As you near heavily industrialized Ústí nad Labem, your eyes are suddenly assaulted by the towering mass of Střekov Castle, perched precariously on huge cliffs and rising abruptly above the right bank. The fortress was built in 1319 by King Johann of Luxembourg to control the rebellious nobles of northern Bohemia. During the 16th century it became the residence of Wenceslas of Lobkowicz, who rebuilt the castle in the Renaissance style. The lonely ruins have served to inspire many German artists and poets, including Richard Wagner, who came here on a moonlit night in the summer of 1842. But if you arrive on a dark night, about the only classic that comes to mind is Mary Shelley's *Frankenstein.* Inside there is a small historical exhibit relating to the Lobkowicz family, which owns the castle, and on winemaking. ⊠ *400 03 Ústí nad Labem,* ☎ *047/31553.* ☉ *Apr.–Oct., Tues.–Sun. 9–5.* 🎫 *30 Kč.*

Mělník

78 *50 km (31 mi) south from Střekov; continue on Route 261 through the picturesque hills of the Elbe banks back through Litoměřice and on to Mělník. Follow Route 9 south about 30 km (20 mi) to return to Prague.*

If coming by car, park on the small streets just off the pretty but hard-to-find main square (head in the direction of the towers to find it). Mělník is a lively town, known best perhaps as the source of the special Ludmila wine, the country's only decent wine not produced in southern Moravia. The town's **zámek,** a smallish castle a few blocks from the main square, majestically guards the confluence of the Elbe River with two arms of the Vltava. The view here is stunning, and the sunny hillsides are covered with vineyards. As the locals tell it, Emperor Charles IV was responsible for bringing wine production to the area. Having a good eye for favorable growing conditions, he encouraged vintners from Burgundy to come here and plant their vines.

The courtyard's three dominant architectural styles, reflecting alterations to the castle over the years, fairly jump out at you. On the north side, note the typical arcaded Renaissance balconies, decorated with sgraffiti; to the west, a Gothic tract is still easy to make out. The southern wing is clearly baroque (although also decorated with arcades). Inside the castle at the back, you'll find a *vinárna* with mediocre food but excellent views overlooking the rivers. On the other side is a museum devoted to wine making and folk crafts. ⊠ *Museum 20 Kč.* ☉ *May–Oct., Tues.–Sun. 10–5 (June–Aug. until 6).*

Lodging

$$ ☷ **Ludmila.** Though the hotel is an inconvenient 4 kilometers (2½ miles) outside town, the Ludmila's pleasant English-speaking staff keeps the plain but cozy rooms impeccably clean, and the restaurant is better than many you will find in Mělník itself. ⊠ *Pražská 2639,* ☎ *0206/622423. 79 rooms with shower or bath. Restaurant, souvenir shop. Breakfast included. AE, MC, V.*

Špindlerův Mlýn and the Krkonoše Range

79 *To get to the Krkonoše area from Prague, take the D11 freeway 55 km (33 mi) east to Poděbrady, then via Freeway 32 through Jičín, Nová Paka (switch to Route 16), and Vrchlabí (a total distance of 152 km [91 mi], finally reaching Špindlerův Mlýn on the stretch of Freeway 295. Excellent bus connections link Prague with the towns of Špindlerův Mlýn, Vrchlabí, and Pec pod Sněžkou.*

If you're not planning to go to the Tatras in Slovakia but nevertheless want a few days in the mountains, head for the **Krkonoše range**—the so-called Giant Mountains—near the Polish frontier. Here you'll find the most spectacular scenery in Bohemia, although it oversteps linguistic convention to call these rolling hills "giant" (the highest point is 1,602 meters, or 5,256 feet). Not only is the scenery beautiful, but the local architecture is refreshingly rural after all the towns and cities; the steep-roofed timber houses, painted in warm colors, look just right pitched against sunlit pinewoods or snowy pastures.

Dining and Lodging

$$$ ☷ **Montana.** This "modern" 1970s hotel is ill suited to the rustic setting, and the rooms are more spartan than luxurious; but the service is attentive, and the staff can offer good advice for planning walks around this popular resort town. ⊠ *54351 Špindlerův Mlýn,* ☎ *0438/93551,* FAX *0438/93556. 70 rooms with bath. Restaurant, bar, café, in-room TVs. Breakfast included. AE, DC, MC, V.*

\$\$ ✕🖫 **Savoy.** This Tudor-style chalet, more than 100 years old but thor-
★   oughly renovated in the early 1980s, is rich in alpine atmosphere and
very comfortable—its cozy reception area is more typical of a family
inn than a large hotel. The rooms, although on the smallish side and
sparsely furnished, are immaculately clean. The restaurant serves fine
traditional Czech dishes in a comfortably polished setting. ✉ *54351
Špindlerův Mlýn,* ☎ *0438/93521,* 🖷 *0438/93641. 50 rooms, most with
bath or shower. Restaurant, bar. Breakfast included. AE, DC, MC, V.*

\$ 🖫 **Nechanicky.** At this private, older hotel near the bridge in the cen-
ter of town, the management is working to improve the structure's somewhat tarnished appearance. The rooms are bright, clean, and well
proportioned; front-facing rooms enjoy an excellent view overlooking
the town. ✉ *54351 Špindlerův Mlýn,* ☎ *0438/93263,* 🖷 *0438/93315.
16 rooms with bath. Restaurant. Breakfast included. No credit cards.*

Outdoor Activities and Sports

Janské Lázně (another spa), **Pec pod Sněžkou,** and **Špindlerův Mlýn**
are the principal resorts of the area, the last the most sophisticated in
its accommodations and facilities. **Špindlerův Mlýn** is attractively
placed astride the rippling Labe (Elbe) River, here in its formative
stages. To get out and experience the mountains, a good trip is to take
a bus from Špindlerův Mlýn via Janské Lázně to Pec pod Sněžkou—a
deceptively long journey by road of around 50 kilometers (31 miles).
From there, embark on a two-stage chairlift to the top of **Sněžka** (the
area's highest peak) and then walk along a ridge overlooking the Polish countryside, eventually dropping into deep, silent pinewoods and
returning to Špindlerův Mlýn. If you walk over the mountain instead
of driving around it, the return trip is just 11 kilometers (7 miles)—a
comfortable walk of about three to four hours. The path actually
takes you into Poland at one point; you won't need a visa, but take
your passport along just in case.

The source of the Labe also springs from the heights near the Polish
border. From the town of **Harrachov,** walkers can reach it by a marked
trail. The distance is about 10 kilometers (6 miles). From Špindlerův
Mlýn, a beautiful but sometimes steep trail follows the Labe Valley up
to the source near **Labská Bouda.** Allow about three hours for this walk
and take good shoes and a map.

Northern Bohemia A to Z

Arriving and Departing

Prague is the gateway to northern Bohemia (☞ Arriving and Departing *in* Prague A to Z, *above*). If you are driving, the E55 leads directly
into the Czech Republic from Dresden and winds down to Prague via
the old spa town of Teplice.

Getting Around

Motorists driving through northern Bohemia are rewarded with a particularly picturesque drive along the Labe (Elbe) River on the way to
Střekov Castle near Ústí nad Labem (☞ *above*). Train connections in
the north are spotty at best; bus is the preferred means of travel. Regular train service connects Prague with Ústí nad Labem, but to reach
other towns you'll have to take slower local trains or the bus.

Contacts and Resources

EMERGENCIES
Police (☎ 158). **Ambulance** (☎ 155).

GUIDED TOURS

Čedok (☎ 02/2419–7111) offers several specialized tours covering the major sights in northern Bohemia. Tour "G-O" combines a trip to Lidice with a visit to the spa town of Karlovy Vary. The trip takes a full day and departs three times weekly. Prague departure points are the Čedok offices at Na příkopě 18 and Bílkova ulice 6 and the Panorama, Forum, and Hilton hotels.

Several private companies also offer trips to Lidice and Terezín (Theresienstadt) in northern Bohemia. For the latter, try **Wittmann Tours** (☎ 02/439–6293 or 02/251235). Bus tours leave from Pařížska 28 daily at 10 AM, returning around 5 PM (950 Kč adults).

VISITOR INFORMATION

Northern Bohemia's main tourist center is in **Litoměřice:** Infocentrum (⌧ Mírové nám., ☎ 0416/2136). It's open daily in summer, closed Sunday in winter.

SOUTHERN MORAVIA

Lacking the turbulent history of Bohemia to the west or the stark natural beauty of Slovakia farther east, Moravia, the easternmost province of the Czech Republic, is frequently overlooked as a travel destination. Still, although Moravia's cities do not match Prague for beauty, and its gentle mountains hardly compare with Slovakia's strikingly rugged Tatras, Moravia's colorful villages and rolling hills certainly do merit a few days of exploration. After you've seen the admittedly superior sights of Bohemia and Slovakia, come here for the good wine, the folk music, the friendly faces, and the languid pace.

Moravia has a bit of both Bohemia and Slovakia. It is closer culturally to Bohemia: The two were bound together as one kingdom for some 1,000 years, following the fall of the Great Moravian Empire (Moravia's last stab at Slavonic statehood) at the end of the 10th century. All the historical and cultural movements that swept through Bohemia, including the religious turbulence and long period of Austrian Hapsburg rule, were felt strongly here as well. But, oddly, in many ways Moravia resembles Slovakia more than its cousin to the west. The colors come alive here in a way that is seldom seen in Bohemia: The subdued earthen pinks and yellows in towns such as Telč and Mikulov suddenly erupt into the fiery reds, greens, and ⌐urples of the traditional folk costumes farther to the east. Folk music, all but gone in Bohemia, is still very much alive in Moravia. You'll hear it, ranging from the foot stomping to the tear-jerking, sung with pride by young and old alike.

Southern Moravia's highlands define the "border" with Bohemia. Here, towns such as Jihlava and Telč are virtually indistinguishable from their Bohemian counterparts. The handsome squares, with their long arcades, bear witness to the prosperity enjoyed by this part of Europe several hundred years ago. The tour then heads south along the frontier with Austria—until recently a heavily fortified expanse of the Iron Curtain. Life is just starting to return to normal in these parts, as the towns and people on both sides of the border seek to reestablish ties going back centuries. One of their common traditions is wine making; and Znojmo, Mikulov, and Valtice are to the Czech Republic what the small towns of the *Weinviertel* on the other side of the border are to Austria.

Don't expect gastronomic delights in Moravia. The food—especially outside Brno—is reasonably priced, but the choices are usually limited to roast pork, sauerkraut, and dumplings or fried pork and french fries. Moravia's hotels are only now beginning to recover from 40 years of state ownership, and excellent hotels are few and far between. In many larger towns, private rooms are preferred. In mountainous areas inquire locally about the possibility of staying in a *chata* (cabin). These are abundant and often a pleasant alternative to the faceless modern hotels. Many lack modern amenities, though, so be prepared to rough it.

Numbers in the margin correspond to numbers on the Moravia map.

Jihlava

⓼ *100 km (62 mi) from Prague.*

On the Moravian side of the rolling highlands that mark the border between Bohemia and Moravia, and just off the main highway from Prague to Brno, lies the old mining town of Jihlava, a good place to begin an exploration of Moravia. If the silver mines here had held out just a few more years, the townspeople claim, Jihlava could have become a great European city—and a household name to foreign visitors. Indeed, during the 13th century, the town's enormous **main square** was one of the largest in Europe, rivaled in size only by those in Cologne and Kraków. But history can be cruel: The mines went bust during the 17th century, and the square today bears witness only to the town's once oversize ambitions.

The **Kostel svatého Ignáce** (St. Ignace Church) in the northwest corner of the square is relatively young for Jihlava, built at the end of the 17th century, but look inside to see a rare Gothic crucifix, created during the 13th century for the early Bohemian king Přemysl Otakar II. The town's most striking structure is the Gothic **Kostel svatého Jakuba** (St. James Church) to the east of the main square, down the Farní ulice. The church's exterior, with its uneven towers, is Gothic; the interior is baroque; and the font is a masterpiece of the Renaissance style, dating from 1599. Note also the baroque **Chapel of the Holy Virgin**, sandwiched between two late-Gothic chapels, with its oversize 14th-century pietà. Two other Gothic churches worth a look are the **Kostel svatého Kříža** (Church of the Holy Cross), north of the main square, and the **Minoritský kostel** (Minorite Church), to the west of the square. Just next to the latter is the last remaining of the original five medieval town gates.

Dining and Lodging

$$ ✕⊡ **Zlatá Hvězda.** Centrally located on the main square, this reconstructed old hotel in a beautiful Renaissance house is comfortable and surprisingly elegant. You're a short walk from Jihlava's restaurants and shops, though the on-site café and wine bar are among the best in town. ⊠ *Nám. Míru 32, 58601,* ☎ *066/29421,* 𝐅𝐀𝐗 *066/29426. 17 rooms with bath. Restaurant, café, wine bar. Breakfast included. AE, MC, V.*

Telč

★ **⓼** *30 km (19 mi) to the south from Jihlava, via Route 406.*

The little town of Telč has an even more impressive main square than that of Jihlava. But what strikes the eye most here is not its size but the unified style of the buildings. On the lowest levels are beautifully vaulted Gothic halls, just above are Renaissance floors and facades, and all of it is crowned with rich baroque gables. The square is so perfect you feel more as if you've entered a film set rather than a living town. The town allegedly owes its architectural unity to Zacharias of Neuhaus, for whom the main square is now named. During the 16th century, so the story goes, the wealthy Zacharias had the castle—orig-

Moravia

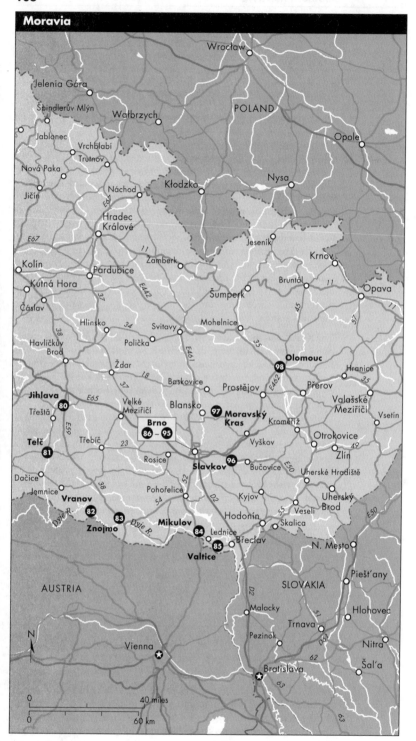

inally a small fort overlooking the Bohemian border with Hungary—rebuilt in the Renaissance style. But the contrast between the new castle and the town's rather ordinary buildings was so great that Zacharias had the square rebuilt to match the castle's splendor. Luckily for architecture fans, the Neuhaus dynasty died out shortly thereafter, and succeeding nobles had little interest in refashioning the town according to the vogue of the day.

It's best to approach Telč's main square on foot. If you've come by car, park outside the main walls on the side south of town and walk through the **Great Gate,** part of the original fortifications dating to the 13th century. The tiny Palackého ulice takes you past the 160-foot Romanesque tower of the **Kostel svatého Ducha** (Church of the Holy Ghost) on your right. This is the oldest standing structure in Telč, dating from the first quarter of the 13th century. As you walk up Palackého ulice, the **square** unfolds nobly in front of you, with the castle at the top and beautiful houses, bathed in pastel reds and golds, gracing both sides. If you're a fan of Renaissance reliefs, note the black-and-white sgraffito corner house at No. 15, which dates from the middle of the 16th century. The house at No. 61, across from the Černý Orel Hotel, is also noteworthy for its fine detail.

At the northern end of the square, the **château** forms a complex with the former **Jesuit college** and **St. James Church.** The château, originally Gothic, was built during the 14th century, when Telč first gained importance as a town bordering the old Hungarian kingdom. It was given its current Renaissance appearance by Italian masters between 1553 and 1568. In season, you can tour the castle and admire the rich Renaissance interiors, equally as impressive as the Italian palaces on which the château was modeled. Given the reputation of nobles for lively banquets lasting for hours, the sgraffito relief in the dining room depicting gluttony (in addition to the six other deadly sins) seems odd indeed. Other interesting rooms with sgraffiti include the Treasury, the Armory, and the Blue and Gold chambers.

NEED A BREAK?
The restaurant of the **Černý Orel** Hotel on the main square is a good place to have coffee or a meal; the hotel itself is a fine place to spend the night (☞ *below*). If you're looking for sweets, you can get good homemade cakes at a little private café, **Cukrárna u Matěje,** at Na baště 2 (no phone).

Dining and Lodging

$$ ✕🏠 **Černý Orel.** Here you'll get a very rare treat: an older, refined hotel
★ that combines modern amenities in a traditional setting. The public areas are functional but elegant, and the basic but inviting rooms are well balanced and comfortably furnished. The hotel, with its baroque facade, is a perfect foil to the handsome main square outside; ask for a room overlooking it. Even if you don't stay here, take a meal at the hotel restaurant, one of the best in town. ⊠ *Nám. Zachariase z Hradce 7, 588 56 Telč,* ☎ FAX *066/962220. 30 rooms, most with bath. Restaurant, wine bar, 24-hour exchange. Breakfast included. AE, DC, MC, V.*

$$ 🏠 **Telč.** This is a slightly upscale alternative to the Černý Orel, even though the bright, polished appearance of the reception area doesn't quite carry over to the functional but pleasant rooms. Some rooms open up onto a pleasant courtyard. The location, in a corner of the main square, is ideal. ⊠ *Na Můstku 37, 588 56 Telč,* ☎ *066/962109,* FAX *066/96887. 10 rooms with bath. Restaurant. Breakfast included. AE, MC, V.*

Vranov

82 *55 km (34 mi) southeast of Telč.*

Leave Telč and continue farther south into the heart of Moravian wine country. Follow the signs first to the picturesque little town of **Dačice,** then along Route 408 through **Jemnice,** and finally to the chain of recreation areas along the man-made lakes of the **Dyje (Thaya) River.** Turn right at Šumná and follow the signs to the little town of Vranov, nestled snugly between hill and river.

★   As a swimming and boating center for southern Moravia, Vranov would be a good place to stop in its own right. But what makes the town truly noteworthy is the enormous and colorful **Vranov Castle,** rising 200 feet from a rocky promontory. For nearly 1,000 years, this was the border between Bohemia and Austria and therefore worthy of a fortress of these dimensions. You'll either love or hate this proud mongrel of a building, as its multicolored Gothic, Renaissance, and baroque elements vie for your attention. In the foreground, the solemn Renaissance tower rises over some Gothic fortifications. The structure is shored up on its left by a golden baroque church, with a beautiful pink-and-white baroque dome to the back. Each unit is spectacular, but the overall effect of so many styles mixed together is jarring.

Take your eyes off the castle's motley exterior and tour its mostly baroque (and more harmonious) interior. The most impressive room is certainly the 43-foot-high elliptical **Hall of Ancestors,** the work of the Viennese master Johann Bernhard Fischer von Erlach (builder of the Clam-Gallas Palace in Prague and the Hofburg in Vienna). The frescoes, added by the Salzburg painter Johann Michael Rottmayr, depict scenes from Greek mythology. Look inside the **castle church** as well. The rotunda, altar, and organ were designed by Fischer von Erlach at the end of the 17th century. ☎ *0624/97215.* ✉ *50 Kč.* ☉ *Apr.–May, weekends 9– 6; June–Oct., Tues.–Sun. 9–6.*

Znojmo

83 *20 km (12 mi) east of Vranov. Follow Route 408 and turn right on the busier Route 38.*

Znojmo enjoys a long history as an important frontier town between Austria and Bohemia and is the cultural center of southern Moravia. The Přemyslide prince Břetislav I had already built a fortress here in the 11th century, and in 1226 Znojmo became the first Moravian town (ahead of Brno) to receive town rights from the king. But, alas, modern Znojmo, with its many factories and high-rises, isn't really a place for lingering. Plan on spending no more than a few hours walking through the Old Town, admiring the views over the Dyje River, and visiting the remaining fortifications and churches that stand between the New Town and the river.

Znojmo's tumbledown **main square,** now usually filled with peddlers selling everything from butter to cheap souvenirs, isn't what it used to be when it was crowned by Moravia's most beautiful **town hall.** Unfortunately, the 14th-century building was destroyed in 1945, just before the end of the war, and all that remains of the original structure is the 250-foot Gothic tower you see at the top of the square—looking admittedly forlorn astride the modern department store that now occupies the space.

For a cheerier sight, follow the rundown Zelinářská ulice, which trails from behind the Town Hall Tower to the southwest in the direction of the Old Town and the river. The grand, Gothic **Kostel svatého Mikuláše**

(St. Nicholas Church), on the tiny Old Town square (Staré Město), dates from 1338, but its neo-Gothic tower was not added until the last century, when the original had to be pulled down. If you can get into the church (it's often locked), look for the impressive sacraments house, which was built around 1500 in late-Gothic style.

The curious, two-layered **Kostel svatého Václava** (St. Wenceslas Church), built at the end of the 15th century, stands just behind St. Nicholas. The upper level of this tiny white church is dedicated to St. Anne, the lower level to St. Martin. Farther to the west, along the medieval ramparts that separate the town from the river, stands the original 11th-century **Rotunda svatej Kateřiny** (St. Catherine's Rotunda), still in remarkably good condition. Step inside to see a rare cycle of restored frescoes from 1134 depicting various members of the early Přemyslide dynasty.

The **Jihomoravské Muzeum** (South Moravian Museum), just across the way in the former town castle, houses an extensive collection of artifacts from the area, dating from the Stone Age to the present. Unless you're a big fan of museums, though, there's little point in making a special visit to this one; and unless you can read Czech, you'll have difficulty making sense of the collection. ⊠ *Přemyslovců ul. 6,* ☎ *0625/224961.* ▨ *10 Kč.* ☉ *Tues.–Sun. 9–5; closed weekends in winter.*

Dining and Lodging

Znojmo's other claims to fame have endeared the town to the hearts (and palates) of Czechs everywhere. The first is the Znojmo gherkin, first cultivated in the 16th century. You'll find this tasty accompaniment to meals at restaurants all over the country. Just look for the *Znojmo* prefix—as in *Znojemský guláš*, a tasty stew spiced with pickles. Znojmo's other treat is wine. As the center of the Moravian wine industry, this is an excellent place to pick up a few bottles of your favorite grape at any grocery or beverage store. But don't expect to learn much about a wine from its label: Oddly, you'll search in vain for the vintage or even the name of the vineyard on labels, and about the only information you can gather is the name of the grape and the city in which the wine was bottled. The best towns to look for, in addition to Znojmo, are Mikulov and Valtice. Some of the best varieties of grapes are Rulandské and Vavřinecké (for red) and Ryslink and Müller Thurgau (for white).

$$ 🏨 **Pension Inka.** Rather than stay in a hotel, you might consider staying in this tiny, family-run pension not far from the center of town. The facilities are modest, but the rooms are bright and well kept. The kitchen is available for the use of guests. ⊠ *Jarošova ul. 27, 669 02 Znojmo,* ☎ *0624/224059. 3 rooms with bath. Breakfast not included. No credit cards.*

$ 🏨 **Pension Havelka.** Though it is tiny, the charms of this family-run
★ pension's tastefully folksy furnishings and ideal location in the center of Old Town can only be topped by its friendly, obliging management. They'll gladly set you up at one of the family's two other pensions if this one happens to be full. ⊠ *Nám. Mikulášské 3, 669 02 Znojmo,* ☎ 🆂 *0624/220138. 2 rooms with shared bath. Restaurant, café, use of kitchen. Breakfast included. No credit cards.*

Mikulov

④ *Leave Znojmo by heading northeast on Route 54 in the direction of Pohořelice. Make a right turn when you see signs to Mikulov, eventually arriving in town along Route 52 after a semicircuitous drive of 54 km (34 mi).*

Mikulov is known today chiefly as the border crossing on the Vienna–Brno road. If you want to leave the Czech Republic for a day to stock up on Western supplies, this is the place to do it. The nearest Austrian town, Poysdorf, is just 7 kilometers (4½ miles) away.

In many ways, Mikulov is the quintessential Moravian town. The soft pastel pinks and yellows of its buildings look almost mystical in the afternoon sunshine against the greens of the surrounding hills. But aside from the busy wine industry, not much goes on here. The main sight is the striking **château,** which dominates the tiny main square and surrounding area. The château started out as the Gothic residence of the noble Liechtenstein family in the 13th century and was given its current baroque appearance some 400 years later. The most famous resident was Napoléon, who stayed here in 1805 while negotiating peace terms with the Austrians after winning the battle of Austerlitz (Slavkov, near Brno). Sixty-one years later, Bismarck used the castle to sign a peace treaty with Austria. The castle's darkest days came at the end of World War II, when retreating Nazi SS units set the town on fire. In season, take a walk from the main square up around the side of the castle into the **museum** of wine making. The most remarkable exhibit is a wine cask made in 1643, with a capacity of more than 22,000 gallons. This was used for collecting the vintner's obligatory tithe. ⌦ 20 Kč. ☉ Apr.–Oct., Tues.–Sun. 9–4 (9–5 in summer).

If you happen to arrive at grape-harvesting time in October, head for one of the many private *sklípeks* (wine cellars) built into the hills surrounding the town. The tradition in these parts is simply to knock on the door; more often than not, you'll be invited in by the owner to taste a recent vintage.

Dining and Lodging

$$$ ✕🏨 **Rohatý Krokodýl.** This is a prim, nicely renovated hotel on a quaint
★   street in the Old Town. The standards and facilities are the best in Mikulov, particularly the ground-floor restaurant, which serves a typical but delicately prepared selection of traditional Czech dishes. ⌂ Husova 8, 692 00 Mikulov, ☏ 0625/2692, FAX 0625/3887. 13 rooms with bath. Restaurant. Breakfast included. MC, V.

Shopping
The secret of Moravian wine is only now beginning to extend beyond the country's borders. A vintage bottle from one of the smaller but still excellent vineyards in Bzenec, Velké Pavlovice, or Hodonín would be appreciated by any wine connoisseur.

Valtice

⑧⑤ *9 km (6 mi) to the east of Mikulov along Route 414.*

This small town would be wholly nondescript except for the fascinating **château,** just off the main street, built by the Liechtenstein family in the 19th century. Next to the town's dusty streets, with their dilapidated postwar storefronts, the castle looks positively grand, a glorious if slightly overexuberant holdover from a long-lost era. But the best news of all is that you can also spend the night there if you like. Unusual for the country, the left wing of the castle has been converted into the Hubertus Hotel. The rooms aren't luxurious, but the setting is inspiring (especially if the standard high-rise hotels are getting you down). The castle boasts some 365 windows, painted ceilings, and much ornate woodwork. A small museum on the ground floor demonstrates how the town and castle have changed over the years according to aristocratic and political whim. Even if you're just passing through, enjoy a drink on the terrace behind the hotel, an ideal spot in which to relax

on a warm afternoon. The Valtice winery is behind and to the right of
the castle, but it is not open to the public. ☎ *0627/94423*. 🖼 *Chateau
60 Kč.* ⊘ *Apr.–Oct., Tues.–Sun. 9–4.*

Dining and Lodging

$$ ✕🖼 **Hubertus.** This comfortable hotel, tucked away in one wing of a
★   neo-Renaissance palace, is not hard to find. Just look for the only palace
in town; the hotel is on the left-hand side. Though the rooms are nei-
ther palatial nor furnished in period style, they are nevertheless gen-
erously proportioned and comfortable. The restaurant, with garden
terrace, serves reasonable Moravian cooking and good wine. Book ahead
in summer, as the hotel is popular with Austrians who like to slip across
the border for an impromptu holiday. ⊠ *Zámek, 69142,* ☎ *0627/94537,*
℻ *0627/94538. 62 rooms, 13 rooms with bath. Restaurant, wine bar.
Breakfast included. AE, MC, V.*

NEED A   The little mountain town of Pavlov, a short drive or bus ride from Mikulov
BREAK?   or Valtice, has several wine cellars built into the hills and makes for a
           good refreshment stop. At **U Venuše** (⊠ Česká 27), be sure to sample
           some of the owner's wine, which comes from his private *sklípek* across
           the lake in Strachotín. After dinner, stroll around the village, perched ro-
           mantically overlooking a man-made lake.

Lednice

7 km (4½ mi) northwest of Valtice.

The Liechtenstein family peppered the countryside with neoclassical
temples and follies, such as Lednice, throughout the 19th century as a
display of their wealth and taste. An abandoned summer palace lies
just to the north of Valtice, not far from the tiny town of **Hlohovec.** In
winter you can walk or skate across the adjoining Hlohovec Pond to
the golden-yellow building; otherwise follow the tiny lane to Hlo-
hovec, just off Route 422 outside Valtice. Emblazoned across the front
of the palace is the German slogan ZWISCHEN ÖSTERREICH UND MÄHREN
(Between Austria and Moravia), another reminder of the proximity of
the border and the long history that these areas share.

The extravagantly neo-Gothic château at **Lednice,** though obviously
in disrepair, affords stunning views of the surrounding grounds and
ponds. Be sure to tour the sumptuous interior; particularly resplendent
with the afternoon sunshine streaming through the windows are the
blue-and-green silk wallcoverings embossed with the Moravian eagle
in the formal dining room and bay-windowed drawing room. The
grounds, now a pleasant park open to the public, even boast a 200-
foot minaret and a massive greenhouse filled with exotic flora. ⊠
Zámek, ☎ *0627/98306.* 🖼 *90 Kč.* ⊘ *Apr.–Oct., Tues.–Sun. 9–4 (until
6 in summer).*

Dolní Věstonice

18 km (11 mi) northwest from Lednice.

From Lednice, follow the Dyje River to the northwest through the vil-
lages of Bulhary and Milovice and on to the tiny town of Dolní Věston-
ice, perched alongside another giant artificial lake. Although the town
has little going for it today, some 20,000 to 30,000 years ago the area
was home to a thriving prehistoric settlement, judging from ivory and
graves found here by archaeologists in 1950. Some of the world's ear-
liest ceramics were also discovered, among them a curvaceous figurine
of ash and clay that has become known as the Venus of Věstonice. The

original is kept in Brno, but you can see replicas, real mammoth bones, and much else of archaeological interest at the excellent **museum** in the center of town along the main road. ⊠ *20 Kč.* ☉ *Apr.–Sept., Tues.–Sun. 8–noon and 1–4.*

Outdoor Activities and Sports

For walking enthusiasts, the **Pavlovské vrchy** (Pavlov Hills), where the settlement was found, offers a challenging climb. Start out by ascending the **Děvín Peak** (1,800 feet), just south of Dolní Věstonice. A series of paths then follows the ridges the 10 kilometers (6 miles) to Mikulov.

Southern Moravia A to Z

Arriving and Departing

BY BUS

Bus connections from Prague to Jihlava are excellent and inexpensive, and, in lieu of a car, the best way to get to Moravia. Southern Moravian destinations are also well served from Bratislava and other points in Slovakia.

BY CAR

Southern Moravia is within easy driving distance of Prague, Bratislava, and eastern Slovakia. Jihlava, the starting point for touring the region, is 124 kilometers (78 miles) southeast of Prague along the excellent D1 freeway. Southern Moravia is also easily reached by car from Austria; there are major border crossings at Háté (below Znojmo) and Mikulov.

Getting Around

☞ Getting Around *in* Czech Republic A to Z, *below.*

Contacts and Resources

EMERGENCIES

Police (☎ 158). **Ambulance** (☎ 155). **Breakdowns** (☎ 154 or 123 [in some areas 0123]).

VISITOR INFORMATION

Telč (⊠ Nám. Zachariáše z Hradce 10).

BRNO

Moravia's cultural and geographic center, Brno (pronounced *burrno*) grew rich in the 19th century and doesn't look or feel like any other Czech or Slovak city. Beginning with a textile industry imported from Germany, Holland, and Belgium, Brno became the industrial heartland of the Austro-Hungarian Empire during the 18th and 19th centuries— hence its nickname "Manchester of Moravia." You'll search in vain for an extensive old town; you'll also find few of the traditional arcaded storefronts that typify other historic Czech towns. What you will see instead are fine examples of Empire and neoclassical styles, their formal, geometric facades more in keeping with the conservative tastes of the 19th-century middle class.

In the early years of this century, the city became home to the best young architects working in the cubist and constructivist styles. And experimentation wasn't restricted to architecture. Leoš Janáček, an important composer of the early modern period, also lived and worked in Brno. The modern tradition continues even today, and the city is considered to have the best theater and performing arts in Moravia.

It's best to avoid Brno at trade-fair time (the biggest are in early spring and early autumn), when hotel and restaurant facilities are strained.

If the hotels are booked, Čedok or the accommodation services at the town hall or main station will help you find a room.

Numbers in the text correspond to numbers in the margin and on the Brno map.

Exploring Brno

A Good Walk

Begin the walking tour at the triangular **Náměstí Svobody** (Freedom Square) ⑧⑥ in the heart of the commercial district. Then walk up the main Masarykova ulice toward the train station and make a right through the little arcade at No. 6 to see the animated Gothic portal of the **Stará radnice** (Old Town Hall) ⑧⑦. Leave the town hall by Pilgram's portal and turn right into the old **Zelný trh** (Cabbage Market) ⑧⑧. On the far side of the market, dominating the square, stands the severe Renaissance **Dietrichstein Palace** ⑧⑨ at No. 8. From the garden, walk down the stairs to the baroque **Kostel Nalezení svatého Kříže** (Church of the Holy Cross) ⑨⓪.

Towering above the church and market is the **Chrám sv. Petra a Pavla** (Cathedral of Sts. Peter and Paul) ⑨①, Brno's main church and a fixture of the skyline. The best way to get to the cathedral is to return to the Cabbage Market (via the little street off the Kapucínské náměstí), make a left at the market, and walk up the narrow Petrská ulice, which begins just to the right of the Dietrichstein Palace. Before leaving the cathedral area, stroll around the park and grounds. The view of the town from here is pretty, and the mood is restful. Continue the tour by walking down the continuation of the Petrská ulice to Biskupská ulice. Turn left at the Starobrněnská ulice and cross the busy Husova třída onto Pekařská ulice, which planners are hoping to someday transform into a lively area of boutiques and shops. At the end of the street is the Mendlovo náměstí (Mendel Square) and the **Monastery of Staré Brno** ⑨②.

Continue the tour along the busy and somewhat downtrodden Úvoz ulice (in the direction of Špilberk Castle). Take the first right and climb the stairs to the calmer residential street of Pellicova. If there's a unique beauty to Brno, it's in neighborhoods such as this one, with its attractive houses, each in a different architectural style. Many houses incorporate cubist and geometric elements of the early modern period (1920s and '30s). Begin the ascent to **Špilberk hrad** (Špilberk Castle) ⑨④. There is no direct path to the castle; just follow your instincts (or a detailed map) upward, and you'll get there. From the top, look over to the west at the gleaming art-deco pavilions of the Brno **Výstaviště** (exhibition grounds) ⑨③ in the distance. The earliest buildings were completed in 1928, in time to hold the first cultural exhibition to celebrate the 10th anniversary of the Czech state. The grounds are now the site of annual trade fairs. Before leaving Brno, try to visit Ludwig Mies van der Rohe's **Villa Tugendhat** ⑨⑤, though you will need to travel there by car, taxi, or tram.

Timing

The tour should take two or three hours at a leisurely pace. Allow an extra hour to explore Špilberk Castle. Museum enthusiasts could easily spend a half day or more browsing the city's many collections.

Sights to See

⑨① **Chrám sv. Petra a Pavla** (Cathedral of Sts. Peter and Paul). Sadly, Sts. Peter and Paul is one church that probably looks better from a distance. The interior, a blend of baroque and Gothic, is light and tasteful but hardly overwhelming. Still, the slim neo-Gothic twin spires, added in this century to give the cathedral more of its original Gothic dignity,

Brno

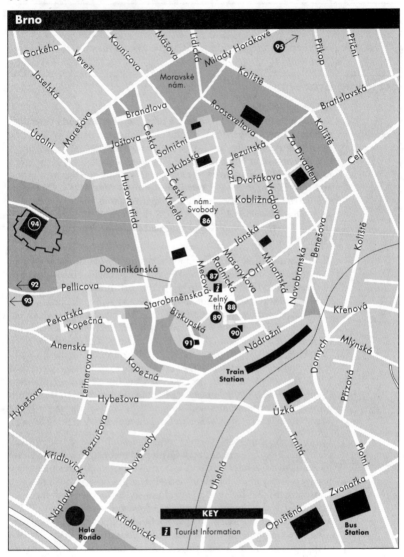

Chrám sv. Petra a Pavla, **91**

Dietrichstein Palace, **89**

Kostel Nalezení svatého Kříže, **90**

Monastery of Staré Brno, **92**

Náměstí Svobody, **86**

Špilberk hrad, **94**

Stará radnice, **87**

Villa Tugendhat, **95**

Výstaviště, **93**

Zelný trh, **88**

are a nice touch. Don't be surprised if you hear the noon bells ringing from the cathedral at 11 o'clock. The practice dates from the Thirty Years' War, when Swedish troops were massing for an attack outside the town walls. Brno's resistance had been fierce, and the Swedish commander decreed that he would give up the fight if the town could not be taken by noon the following day. The bell ringer caught wind of the decision and the next morning, just as the Swedes were preparing a final assault, rang the noon bells—an hour early. The ruse worked, and the Swedes decamped. Ever since, the midday bells have been rung an hour early as a show of gratitude. While the city escaped, the cathedral caught a Swedish cannon shot and suffered severe damage in the resulting fire. ⊠ *Petrov at Petrská.* 🖻 *Free.* ◉ *During daylight hrs, except during services.*

89 Dietrichstein Palace. The building was once home to Cardinal Count Franz von Dietrichstein, who led the Catholic Counter-Reformation in Moravia following the Battle of White Mountain in 1620. Today the palace and the adjoining **Biskupský dvůr** (Bishop's Court) house the **Moravské muzeum** (Moravian Museum), with its mundane exhibits of local history, artifacts, and wildlife. To enter the Bishop's Court, walk through the little gate to the left of the Dietrichstein Palace and then through the lovely Renaissance garden. Note the arcades, the work of 16th-century Italian craftsmen. ⊠ *Zelný trh 8.* ◉ *Tues.–Sun. 9–5 (Bishop's Court closes at 5).*

90 Kostel Nalezení svatého Kříže (Church of the Holy Cross). This plain-looking baroque church was formerly part of the Capuchin Monastery. If you've ever wondered what a mummy looks like without its bandages, then enter the door to the monastery's *hrobka* (crypt). In the basement are the mummified remains of some 200 nobles and monks from the late 17th and the 18th centuries, ingeniously preserved by a natural system of air circulating through vents and chimneys. The best-known mummy is Colonel František Trenck, commander of the brutal Pandour regiment of the Austrian army, who, at least in legend, spent several years in the dungeons of Špilberk Castle before finding his final rest here in 1749. Even in death the hapless colonel has not found peace—someone made off with his head several years ago. A note of caution about the crypt: The graphic displays may frighten small children, so ask at the admission desk for the small brochure (10 Kč) with pictures that preview what's to follow. ⊠ *Kapucínské nám.* 🖻 *20 Kč.* ◉ *Tues.–Sat. 9–11:45 and 2–4:30, Sun. 11–11:45 and 2–4:30.*

92 Monastery of Staré Brno. The uninspiring location seems to confirm the adage that genius can flourish anywhere, for in the 19th century this was home to Gregor Mendel, the shy monk who became the father of modern genetic research. If you recall from high-school science, it was Mendel's experiments with crossing pea and bean plants, from which he figured out dominant and recessive traits, that led to the first formulations of the laws of heredity. A small statue to his memory can be found in the garden behind the monastery. ⊠ *Mendlovo nám. 1.* ◉ *Sept.–May, weekdays 8–5; June–Aug., daily 9–6.*

86 Náměstí Svobody (Freedom Square). The square itself is architecturally undistinguished, but here and along the adjoining streets you'll find the city's best stores and shopping opportunities. A certain air of friendly provinciality reigns here amid the hurrying crowds of shoppers and schoolchildren, and the relatively small numbers of tourists have yet to make much of an impact on the city center.

94 Špilberk hrad (Špilberk Castle). Once among the most feared places in the Hapsburg Empire, this fortress-cum-prison still broods over the town from behind its menacing walls. Špilberk's advantageous location was no secret to the early kings, who moved here during the 13th century from neighboring Petrov Hill. Successive rulers gradually converted the old castle into a virtually impregnable fortress. Indeed, it successfully withstood the onslaughts of Hussites, Swedes, and Prussians over the centuries; only Napoléon, in 1809, succeeded in occupying the fortress. But the castle is best known for its gruesome history as a prison for the Austro-Hungarian monarchy and, later, for the Nazis in World War II. Although tales of torture during the Austrian period are probably legendary (judicial torture had been prohibited prior to the first prisoners' arrival in 1784), conditions for the hardest offenders were hellish: shackled day and night in dark, dank catacombs and fed only bread and water. The most brutal corrections ended with the death of the harsh, rationalist ruler Joseph II in 1790. The casemates (passages within the walls of the castle) have been turned into an exhibition of the late-18th-century prison and their Nazi-era use as an air-raid shelter. Parents should note that young children can easily become lost in the spooky, dim casemates. More dangerous, the low parapets atop the castle walls near the restaurant provide little security for overcurious climbers. The castle is still being renovated, and there are plans for more displays on the German occupation during World War II. In summertime, temporary historical exhibitions are installed in the west wing. ☎ *05/4221–4145.* 🖼 *Casemates 20 Kč.* ⊙ *Tues.–Sun. 9– 4:45 (until 6 June–Sept.).*

NEED A BREAK?

After a long walk and a good climb, what could be better than one of the best beers you'll ever have? The **Stopkova pivnice**, at Česka 5, will set you up with one, or a soft drink, in clean, comfortable surroundings. If you're hungry, try the house goulash, a tangy mixture of sausage, beef, rice, egg, and dumpling. For something more substantial, head for the restaurant on the second floor.

---

⑧⑦ Stará radnice (Old Town Hall). The oldest secular building in Brno has an important Gothic portal. The door is the work of Anton Pilgram, architect of Vienna's St. Stephen's Cathedral, and was completed in 1510; the building itself is about 200 years older. Look above the door to see a badly bent pinnacle that looks as if it wilted in the afternoon sun. This isn't the work of vandals but was apparently done by Pilgram himself out of revenge against the town. According to legend, Pilgram had been promised an excellent commission for his portal, but when he finished, the mayor and city councillors reneged on their offer. So angry was Pilgram at the duplicity, he purposely bent the pinnacle and left it poised, fittingly, over the statue of justice.

Just inside the door are the remains of two other famous Brno legends, the **Brno Dragon** and the **wagon wheel.** The dragon—a female alligator to be anatomically correct—apparently turned up at the town walls one day in the 17th century and began eating children and livestock. A gatekeeper came up with the novel idea of filling a sack with limestone and placing it inside a freshly slaughtered goat. The dragon devoured the goat, swallowing the limestone as well, and went to quench its thirst at a nearby river. The water mixed with the limestone, bursting the dragon's stomach (the scars on the dragon's stomach are still clearly visible). The story of the wagon wheel, on the other hand, concerns a bet placed some 400 years ago that a young wheelwright, Jiří Birk, couldn't chop down a tree, fashion the wood into a wheel, and roll it from his home at Lednice (33 miles away) to the town walls of Brno—all between sunup and sundown. The wheel stands as a lasting tribute to his achievement (the townspeople, however, became convinced that Jiří had enlisted the help of the devil to win the bet, so they stopped frequenting his workshop; poor Jiří died penniless).

No longer the seat of the town government, the Old Town Hall holds exhibitions and performances. To find out what's on, look for a sign on the door of the exhibition room. The view from the top of the tower is one of the best in Brno, but the climb (five flights) is strenuous. What catches the eye is not so much any single building—although the cathedral does look spectacular—but the combination of old and new that defines modern Brno. In the distance, next to the crooked roofs and baroque onion domes, a power plant looks startlingly out of place. ⊠ *Radnická ul. 8.* 🎫 *Tower 10 Kč.* ◷ *Apr.–Sept., daily 9–5.*

⑨⑤ Villa Tugendhat. Designed by Ludwig Mies van der Rohe and completed in 1930, this austere white villa, built in the Bauhaus style, counts among the most important works of the modern period. The emphasis here is on function and the use of geometric forms, but you be the judge as to whether the house fits the neighborhood. The Tugendhat family fled before the Nazis, and their original furnishings vanished during the war or the house's subsequent heavy handed remodeling. Replicas of Mies's cool, functional designs have been installed in the downstairs living area. Some of the original exotic wood paneling and an eye-stopping onyx screen remain in place. The best way to get there is to take a taxi or Tram 3, 5, or 11 to the Dětská nemocnice stop and then walk up the unmarked Černopolní Street for 10 minutes or so. ⊠ *Černopolní 45,* ☏ *05/4521–2118.* 🎫 *80 Kč.* ◷ *Wed.–Sun. 10–5.*

⑨③ Výstaviště (exhibition grounds). The earliest buildings were completed in 1928, in time to hold the first cultural exhibition to celebrate the 10th anniversary of the Czech state. The Brno-born modern architect Adolf Loos designed the interior of the 19th-century mansion on the grounds, and Bohuslav Fuchs—another modernist linked to Brno—created the City of Brno Pavilion. The enormous circular Pavilion Z dates from 1959. The grounds are now the site of annual trade fairs, and the grounds may be closed between fairs. ⊠ *Výstaviště 1,* ☏ *05/4115 3101. From main train station, take Tram 1 or 18 west to the 5th stop.*

⑧⑧ Zelný trh (Cabbage Market). The only place where Brno begins to look like a typical Czech town, the Cabbage Market is immediately recognizable, not just for the many stands from which farmers still sell vegetables but also for the unique **Parnassus Fountain** that adorns its center. This baroque pile of rocks (you either love it or hate it) couldn't be more out of place amid the formal elegance of most of the buildings on the square. But when Johann Bernhard Fischer von Erlach created the fountain in the late 17th century, it was important for a striving town like Brno to display its understanding of the classics and of ancient Greece. Thus, Hercules slays a three-headed dragon, while Amphitrite on top awaits the arrival of her lover—all incongruously surrounded by farmers hawking turnips and onions.

OFF THE BEATEN PATH

MORAVSKÝ KRUMLOV – Admirers of art-nouveau meister Alfons Mucha may want to make a short detour off the main highway linking Mikulov and Brno. The town museum is the unlikely home of one of Mucha's most celebrated works, his 20-canvas *Slav Epic*. This enormous work, which tells the story of the emergence of the Slav nation, was not well received when it was completed in 1928; painters at the time were more interested in imitating modern movements and considered Mucha's representational art to be old-fashioned. Interest in Mucha's lyrical style has grown in recent years, however, and the museum annually attracts some

15,000 visitors. *Museum:* ✉ *Zámecká 1,* ☎ *0621/2789–2225.* ⊙ *Apr.–Oct. Tues.–Sun. 9–noon and 1–4.*

Dining and Lodging

$$$ ✕ **Černý Medvěd.** Undoubtedly Brno's most comfortable dining room, it has plush red upholstery and, weather permitting, a fire crackling on the open hearth. Wild game is the key ingredient in a menu that focuses on Czech specialties. ✉ *Jakubské nám. 1,* ☎ *05/4221–4548. MC, V.*

$$ ✕ **Baroko vinárna.** This 17th-century wine cellar housed in a Minorite monastery offers excellent cooking in a fun, if touristy, setting. Try the roast beef Slavkov, named for the site of Napoléon's triumph not far from Brno. Mystery of Magdalene is a potato pancake stuffed with pork, liver, mushrooms, and presumably anything else the cook could get his hands on. ✉ *Orlí 17,* ☎ *05/4221–1344. No credit cards. No lunch.*

$$ ✕ **Maccaroni.** Delicious pastas and pizzas (a welcome alternative to the heavy local fare) are served here in a casual, unhurried setting. Take a taxi, walk the 15 minutes from the center, or ride Tram 5 or 6 to the stop called Nemocnice u sv. Anny. ✉ *Pekařská 80,* ☎ *05/4321–4528. MC.*

$$ ✕ **Modrá Hvězda.** Liberal opening hours and a convenient location just to the west of Náměstí Svobody make this cheery restaurant a good choice for a quick lunch or off-hours snack. ✉ *Starobrněnská 20,* ☎ *05/4221–5292. AE, DC, MC, V.*

$$$$ 🏨 **Grand.** Though not really grand, this hotel, built in 1870 and thoroughly remodeled in 1988, is certainly comfortable and the best in Brno. High standards are maintained through the hotel's association with an Austrian chain. The reception and public areas are clean and modern; service is attentive; and the rooms, though small, are well appointed. Ask for a room at the back, overlooking the town, as the hotel is on a busy street opposite the railroad station. ✉ *Benešova 18/20, 657 83 Brno,* ☎ *05/4232–1287,* 𝙵𝙰𝚇 *05/4221–0345. 113 rooms with bath. 3 restaurants, minibars, in-room satellite TVs, casino, nightclub. AE, DC, MC, V.*

$$$$ 🏨 **Holiday Inn.** Opened in 1993, this modern but handsome representative of the American chain has become the hotel of choice for business travelers in town for a trade fair. It has all you'd expect for the price, including a well-trained, multilingual staff, clean and well-appointed rooms, and a full range of business services. The location, at the exhibition grounds about a mile from the city center, is inconvenient for those who don't have a car. ✉ *Křížkovského 20, 603 00 Brno,* ☎ *05/4312–2111,* 𝙵𝙰𝚇 *05/4115–9081. 205 rooms with bath. Restaurant, café, sauna, conference rooms. AE, DC, MC, V.*

$$$ 🏨 **Pegas.** This little inn makes an excellent choice given its reasonable
★ price and central location. The plain rooms are snug and clean, and the staff is helpful and friendly. Even if you don't stay here, be sure to have a meal at the house pub-microbrewery. ✉ *Jakubská 4, 602 00 Brno,* ☎ *05/4221–0104,* 𝙵𝙰𝚇 *05/4221–1232. 15 rooms with bath. Restaurant. AE, DC, MC, V.*

$$$ 🏨 **Slavia.** The century-old Slavia, just off the main Česká ulice, was thoroughly renovated in 1987, giving the public areas an efficient, up-to-date look and leaving the rooms plain but clean. The café, with adjacent terrace, is a good place to enjoy a cool drink on a warm afternoon. ✉ *Solniční 15/17, 622 16 Brno,* ☎ *05/4221–5080,* 𝙵𝙰𝚇 *05/4221–1769. 81 rooms with shower or bath. Restaurant, café, minibars, parking. AE, DC, MC, V.*

$$ ⬚ **U svatého Jakuba.** Little seems to have changed here for several decades, including the behavior of the staff (who operate on the premise that the customer may always be right, but should also be grateful for any services rendered). It used to be classed as a "moderate" hotel, but the cheaper establishments of the central city have vanished into the precapitalist past, leaving this one to keep up tradition by offering basic accommodation at reasonable rates. ⌧ *Jakubské nám. 6, 602 00 Brno,* ☎ *05/4221–0795,* ℻ *05/4221–0797. 37 rooms, most with bath. Restaurant, wine bar. MC, V.*

Nightlife and the Arts

Brno is renowned throughout the Czech Republic for its theater and performing arts. The two main locales for jacket-and-tie cultural events are the **Mahen Theater** (for drama) and the modern **Janáček Theater** (for opera and ballet). Both are slightly northwest of the center of town, just off Rooseveltova ul. Check the schedules at the theater or pick up a copy of *KAM*, Brno's monthly bulletin of cultural events. Buy tickets directly at the theater box office 30 minutes before showtime. One of the country's best-known fringe theater companies, **Divadlo Husa na provázku** (Goose on a String Theater), has its home where Petrská Street enters Zelný trh (⌧ Zelný trh 9, ☎ 05/4221–0099).

For more sophisticated entertainment than talk and drink at the local pivnice or vinárna, head for the **casinos** at the **Grand Hotel** (⌧ Benešova 18/20, across from the main station, ☎ 05/4232–1287) and the **International Hotel** (⌧ Husova 16, ☎ 05/4212–2111); the tables usually stay open until 3 AM or 4 AM. Both hotels also have bars that serve drinks until very late. The "casinos" on Náměstí Svobody are glorified video gambling parlors with a mixed clientele of clueless tourists and all-too-streetwise locals.

Klub Alterna (⌧ Kounicova 48, a few blocks north of the city center) puts on good Czech jazz and folk performers.

Shopping

Moravia produces very attractive folk pottery, painted with bright red, orange, and yellow flower patterns. You can find these products in stores and hotel gift shops throughout the region. For more modern art objects, including paintings, stop by **Dílo** (⌧ Kobližná 4). **Merkuria** (down the street at ⌧ Kobližná 10) stocks a beautiful selection of crystal and porcelain from Karlovy Vary. You can buy English paperbacks including a huge range of travel guidebooks, should Central America suddenly seem more alluring than Central Europe, at the **Zahraniční literatura** shop (⌧ Nám. Svobody 18).

Brno A to Z

Arriving and Departing

BY BUS

Bus connections from Prague to Brno are excellent and inexpensive, and, in lieu of a car, the best way to get here. Buses also run daily between Brno's main bus station and Vienna's Wien-Mitte station, leaving Brno at 7:30 AM and 5:30 PM. Round-trip tickets cost about $27.

BY CAR

Brno, within easy driving distance of Prague, Bratislava, and eastern Slovakia, is 196 kilometers (122 miles) from Prague and 121 kilometers (75 miles) from Bratislava.

BY PLANE

The private carrier **Air Ostrava** links Prague with Brno and Ostrava (Prague, ☏ 02/2403–2731 or 02/0601–533003 [mobile phone]). The distances between the cities are short, however, and it's ultimately cheaper and quicker to drive or take a bus. During the two large Brno trade fairs, in April and September, foreign carriers also connect the city with Frankfurt and Vienna. These flights are usually crowded with businessmen, so you'll have to book well in advance.

BY TRAIN

Several trains daily make the three-hour run from Prague to Brno. Most use Prague's **Hlavní nádraží** (main station), but some depart from and arrive at the suburban station **Holešovice nádraží** (Holešovice station) or at **Masarykovo nádraží** (Masaryk station), on Hybernská ulice in the city center. Trains leaving Prague for Budapest and Bucharest (and some Vienna-bound trains) also frequently stop in Brno (check timetables to be sure).

Getting Around

BY BUS

The Brno bus station is a 10-minute walk behind the train station. To find it, simply go to the train station and follow the signs to ČSAD.

BY TRAIN

Comparatively good trains run frequently on the Prague–Brno–Břeclav main line.

Contacts and Resources

B&B RESERVATION AGENCIES

If you've arrived at Brno's main station and are stuck for a room, try the accommodations service on the far left of the main hall, open every day (closes at 10 AM Sun.); you can place a sports bet there too.

EMERGENCIES

Police (☏ 158). **Ambulance** (☏ 155). **Breakdowns** (☏ 154 or 123 [in some areas 0123]).

LATE-NIGHT PHARMACIES

Brno has a 24-hour pharmacy at Kobližná ulice 7.

TRAVEL AGENCIES

American Express representative (✉ Starobrněnská 20); **CKM** (youth travel bureau; ✉ Česká 11, ☏ 05/4221–2677).

VISITOR INFORMATION

Čedok (✉ Nádražní 10/12, ☏ 05/4232–1267); **Kulturní a informační Centrum** (✉ Radnická 8 [Old Town Hall], ☏ 05/4221–1090). ☞ Visitor Information *in* Czech Republic A to Z, *below.*

NORTHERN MORAVIA

Just north of Brno is the **Moravian Karst,** a beautiful wilderness area with an extensive network of caves, caverns, and underground rivers. Many caves are open to the public, and some tours even incorporate underground boat rides. Farther to the north lies Moravia's "second capital," **Olomouc,** an industrial but still charming city with a long history as a center of learning. Paradoxically, despite its location far from the Austrian border, Olomouc remained a bastion of support for the Hapsburgs and the empire at a time when cries for independence could be heard throughout Bohemia and Moravia. In 1848, when revolts everywhere threatened to bring the monarchy down, the Hapsburg family fled here for safety. Franz Joseph, who went on to personify the stodgy permanence of the empire, was even crowned here as Austrian emperor that same year.

The green foothills of the **Beskydy range** begin east of Olomouc, perfect for a day or two of walking in the mountains. Farther to the east you'll find the spectacular peaks of the Tatras, and the tour is a good jumping-off point for exploring eastern Slovakia or southern Poland. Similarly, if you're coming from Slovakia, you could easily begin in Olomouc and conduct the tour in reverse order.

Slavkov

96 *20 km (12 mi) east of Brno.*

Slavkov, better known as **Austerlitz,** was the scene of one of the great battlefields of European history, where the armies of Napoléon met and defeated the combined forces of Austrian emperor Franz II and Czar Alexander I in 1805. If you happen to have a copy of *War and Peace* handy, you will find no better account of it anywhere. Scattered about the rolling agricultural landscapes are a museum, a garden, and the memorial chapel of the impressive **Cairn of Peace.** In the town of Slavkov itself, the baroque château houses more memorabilia about the battle; it's well worth visiting. ⊠ *Slavkov U Brna,* ☎ *05/941204.*

Moravský Kras

97 *30 km (19 mi) north of Brno.*

If it's scenic rather than military tourism you want, however, take a short trip north from Brno up the Svitava Valley and into the Moravský Kras (Moravian Karst), an area of limestone formations, underground stalactite caves, rivers, and tunnels. The most interesting part is near **Blansko** and includes the **Kateřinská jeskyně** (Catherine Cave), **Punkevní jeskyně** (Punkva Cave), and the celebrated **Macocha Abyss,** the deepest drop of the karst (more than 400 feet). Several caves can be visited: Try the 90-minute Punkva tour, which includes a visit to the Macocha Abyss and a boat trip along an underground river. In a controversial decision, the state turned over some of the area's tourist services to a private firm, which operates the *Eco-Express* train-on-wheels linking the Skalní Mlýn Hotel to the Punkva Cave, and the funicular from Punkva to the Macocha Abyss. ▦ *20 Kč to Kateřinská jeskyně, 60 Kč to Punkevní jedkyně, including underground boat ride.* ☉ *Daily 8–2. Funicular:* ▦ *50 Kč.* ☉ *Daily 8–5 (until 3 Oct.–Apr.).*

Hiking

Underground or on the surface, the walking is excellent in the karst, and if you miss one of the few buses running between the town of Blansko and the cave region, you may have to hoof it anyway. Try to obtain a map in Brno or from the tourist information office in Blansko, which is across the road from the train station and 300 yards from the bus station (☎ 0506/53635). It's 8 kilometers (5 miles) from the unattractive outskirts of Blansko to the Skalní Mlýn Hotel and nearby Catherine Cave, set amid thickly forested ravines. Look out for Devil's Bridge (*Čertův most*), a natural bridge high over the road just past the entrance to Catherine Cave; or follow the yellow-marked path from the cave for another couple of miles to the Macocha Abyss. Before setting out, check with the information office or at the bus station for current bus schedules; for much of the year the last bus from Skalní Mlýn back to Blansko leaves at around 3 PM.

Olomouc

★ 🏛 98   *77 km (48 mi) northeast of Brno.*

Olomouc is a paradox—so far from Austria yet so supportive of the empire. The Hapsburgs always felt at home here, even when they were being violently opposed by Czech nationalists and Protestants throughout Bohemia and much of Moravia. During the revolutions of 1848, when the middle class from all over the Austro-Hungarian Empire seemed ready to boot the Hapsburgs out of their palace, the royal family fled to Olomouc, where they knew they could count on the population for support. The 18-year-old Franz Joseph was even crowned emperor here in 1848 because the situation in Vienna was still too turbulent.

Despite being overshadowed by Brno, Olomouc, with its proud square and prim 19th-century buildings, still retains something of a provincial imperial capital, not unlike similarly sized cities in Austria. The focal point here is the triangular **Horní náměstí** (Upper Square), marked at its center by the bright and almost flippantly colored Renaissance **radnice** (town hall) with its 220-foot tower. The tower was begun in the late 14th century and given its current appearance in 1443; the astronomical clock on the outside was built in 1422, but its inner mechanisms and modern mosaic decorations date from immediately after World War II. Be sure to look inside at the beautiful Renaissance stairway. There's also a large Gothic banquet room in the main building, with scenes from the city's history, and a late-Gothic chapel.

The eccentric **Trinity Column** in the northwest corner of the square, at more than 100 feet, is the largest of its kind in the Czech Republic and houses a tiny chapel. Four baroque fountains, depicting Hercules (1687), Caesar (1724), Neptune (1695), and Jupiter (1707), dot the main square and the adjacent **Dolní náměstí** (Lower Square) to the south, as if to reassure us that this Moravian town was well versed in the humanities.

NEED A BREAK?   The wooden paneling and floral upholstery in the **Café Mahler** recall the taste of the 1880s, when Gustav Mahler briefly lived just around the corner while working as a conductor at the theater on the other side of the Upper Square. It makes a good spot for ice cream, cake, or coffee. ⊠ *Horní nám. 11.*

Just north of the Horní náměstí, along the small Jana Opletalova ulice, stands the **Chrám svatého Mořice** (Church of St. Maurice), the town's best Gothic building. Construction began in 1412, but a fire 40 years later badly damaged the structure; its current fierce, gray exterior dates from the middle of the 16th century. The baroque organ inside, the largest in the Czech Republic, contains 2,311 pipes.

The interior of triple-domed **Kostel svatého Michala** (St. Michael's Church) casts a dramatic spell. The frescoes, the high, airy central dome, and the shades of rose, beige, and gray marble on walls and arches blend to a harmonious, if dimly glimpsed, whole. The decoration followed a 1709 fire, which came 30 years after the original construction. Architect and builder are not known, but it's surmised they are the same team that put up the Church of the Annunciation on Svatý Kopeček (Holy Hill), a popular Catholic pilgrimage site just outside Olomouc. ⊠ *Žerotínovo nám., 1 block uphill from the Upper Square along Školní ul.*

Between the main square and the **Dóm svatého Václava** (Cathedral of St. Wenceslas) lies a peaceful neighborhood given over to huge buildings, done in baroque or later styles, mostly belonging either to the university or the archbishopric. As it stands today, the cathedral is just another example of the overbearing neo-Gothic enthusiasm of the late 19th century, having passed through just about every other architectural fad since its true Gothic days. To the left of the church, however, is the entrance to the **Přemyslide Palace,** now a museum, where you can see early 16th-century wall paintings decorating the Gothic cloisters and, upstairs, a wonderful series of two- and three-arched Romanesque windows. This part of the building was used as a schoolroom some 700 years ago, and you can still make out drawings of animals engraved on the walls by early young vandals. You can get an oddly phrased English-language pamphlet to help you around the building. ⊠ *Dómská ul.* 🎫 *20 Kč.* ☉ *Tues.–Sun. 9–12:30 and 1–5.*

The **deacon's house** opposite the cathedral, now part of Palácký University, has two unusual claims to fame. Here, in 1767, the young musical prodigy Wolfgang Amadeus Mozart, age 11, spent six weeks recovering from a mild attack of chicken pox. The 16-year-old King Wenceslas III suffered a much worse fate here in 1306, when he was murdered, putting an end to the Přemyslide dynasty.

OFF THE BEATEN PATH

PŘÍBOR – Fans of dream interpretation and psychoanalysis shouldn't leave Moravia without stopping at this little town, the birthplace of Sigmund Freud. To find it, drive east out of Olomouc along Route 35, following the signs first to Lipník, then Hranice, Nový Jičín, and finally Příbor—about 50 kilometers (31 miles) in all. Park at the Náměstí Sigmunda Freuda (Sigmund Freud Square). The seemingly obvious name for the main square is actually new; the former Communist regime was not in favor of Freudians. The comfortable, middle-class house, marked with a plaque, where the doctor was born in 1856 is a short walk away along Freudova ulice. At present, the house is still inhabited, so you can't go inside. ⊠ *Freudova ul. 117.*

Dining and Lodging

$$$ 🏨 **Flora.** Don't expect luxury at this 1960s cookie-cutter high-rise, about a 15-minute walk from the town square. To its credit, the staff is attentive (English is spoken), and the pleasant if anonymous rooms are certainly adequate for a short stay. ⊠ *Krapkova ul. 34, 779 00 Olomouc,* ☎ *068/412021,* 📠 *068/412221. 175 rooms, most with bath or shower. Restaurant. AE, DC, MC, V.*

$$ 🏨 **Národní Dům.** Built in 1885 and a block from the main square, this is a better choice than the Flora for evoking a little of Olomouc's 19th-century history. The handsome building recalls the era's industriousness, as does the large, gracious café on the main floor. Standards have slipped in the intervening years, though, and signs of decline are evident. ⊠ *Třída 8. května 21, 772 00 Olomouc,* ☎ *068/522–4806,* 📠 *068/522–4808. 63 rooms, most with bath or shower. Restaurant, café, snack bar. AE, DC, MC, V.*

$$ 🏨 **U Dómu sv. Václava.** A pleasant place that well represents a new class of Czech hotel and pension, you'll find modernized fittings installed in an old, often historic, house. This pension's six small suites all have kitchenettes. It's just down the street from the sleepy Cathedral Square. ⊠ *Dómská 4, 772 00 Olomouc,* ☎ *068/522–0502,* 📠 *068/522–0501. 6 rooms with bath. In-room TVs, kitchenettes. MC, V.*

Hiking and Cross-Country Skiing

The gentle, forested peaks of the **Beskydy Mountains** are popular destinations for hill walking, berry picking, and cross-country skiing; several resorts have ski lifts as well. The year-round resort town of Rožnov pod Radhoštěm has bus connections to all major cities in the country. Stay the night at one of the modest but comfortable mountain chalets in the area. You'll find a good one, the **Chata Soláň,** along the road between Rožnov and Velké Karlovice (✉ 756 06 Velké Karlovice, ☎ 0657/94365). The latter settlement lies at the end of a rail line from Vsetín. But be sure to take along a good map before venturing along the tiny mountain roads. Also, some roads may be closed during the winter.

Northern Moravia A to Z

Arriving and Departing

Brno is the gateway to northern Moravia, whether by bus, car, plane, or train. ☞ Arriving and Departing *in* Brno A to Z, *above.*

Getting Around

Comparatively good trains run frequently on the Prague–Olomouc–Vsetín main lines. In any event, you'll sometimes have to resort to the bus to reach the smaller, out-of-the-way places throughout northern Moravia. ☞ Getting Around *in* the Czech Republic A to Z, *below.*

Contacts and Resources

EMERGENCIES

Police (☎ 158). **Ambulance** (☎ 155). **Breakdowns** (☎ 154 or 123 [in some areas 0123]).

VISITOR INFORMATION

Olomouc: Information Center (✉ Horní nám. [Town Hall], ☎ 068/551–3385), ☉ daily 9–7.

THE CZECH REPUBLIC A TO Z

Arriving and Departing

By Bus

Several bus companies run direct services between London and Prague. Two with almost daily service are Kingscourt Express (London, ☎ 0181/673–7500) and Eurolines, both operating out of London's Victoria Coach Station. The trip takes 20–24 hours and costs around $85 one-way.

By Car

The most convenient ferry ports for Prague are Hoek van Holland and Ostend. To reach Prague from either ferry port, drive first to Cologne (Köln) and then through either Dresden or Frankfurt.

By Plane

FROM NORTH AMERICA

All international flights to the Czech Republic fly into Prague's **Ruzyně Airport,** about 20 kilometers (12 miles) northwest of downtown. The airport is small and easy to negotiate.

ČSA (Czech Airlines), the Czech and Slovak national carrier (☎ 718/656–8439), maintains regular direct flights to Prague from New York's JFK Airport, and twice-weekly flights from Chicago, Los Angeles, and Montréal.

Several other international airlines have good connections from cities in the United States and Canada to European bases and from there to Prague. **British Airways** (☎ 800/247–9297) flies daily via London; and **SwissAir** (☎ 718/995–8400), daily via Zurich.

FLYING TIME

From New York, a nonstop flight to Prague takes 9–10 hours; with a stopover, the journey will take at least 12–13 hours. From Montreal nonstop it is 7½ hours; from Los Angeles, 16 hours.

FROM THE UNITED KINGDOM

British Airways (☎ 0171/897–4000) has daily nonstop service to Prague from London (with connections to major British cities); **ČSA** (☎ 0171/255–1898) flies five times a week nonstop from London. The flight takes around three hours.

By Train

There are no direct trains from London. You can take a direct train from Paris via Frankfurt to Prague (daily) or from Berlin via Dresden to Prague (three times a day). Vienna is a good starting point for Prague, Brno, or Bratislava. There are three trains a day from Vienna's Franz Josefsbahnhof to Prague via Třeboň and Tábor (5½ hours) and two from the Südbahnhof (South Station) via Brno (5 hours).

Getting Around

By Bus

The Czech Republic's extremely comprehensive state-run bus service, **ČSAD,** is usually much quicker than the normal trains and more frequent than express trains, unless you're going to the major cities. (The wait between buses can sometimes be very, very long.) Prices are reasonable—essentially the same as those for second-class rail tickets. Buy your tickets from the ticket window at the bus station or directly from the driver on the bus. Long-distance buses can be full, so you might want to book a seat in advance; Čedok will help you do this. The only drawback to traveling by bus is figuring out the timetables. They are easy to read, but beware of the small letters denoting exceptions to the time given. If in doubt, inquire at the information window or ask someone for assistance.

By Car

Traveling by car is the easiest and most flexible way of seeing the Czech Republic. There are few four-lane highways, but most of the roads are in reasonably good shape, and traffic is usually light. The road can be poorly marked, however, so before you start out, buy one of the multilingual, inexpensive auto atlases available at any bookstore. The Czech Republic follows the usual Continental rules of the road. A right turn on red is permitted only when indicated by a green arrow. Signposts with yellow diamonds indicate a main road where drivers have the right of way. The speed limit is 110 kph (68 mph) on four-lane highways, 90 kph (56 mph) on open roads, and 60 kph (37 mph) in built-up areas. The fine for speeding is 300 Kč, payable on the spot. Seat belts are compulsory, and drinking before driving is absolutely prohibited.

A permit is required to drive on expressways and other four-lane highways. They cost 400 Kč and are sold at border crossings and some service stations.

Don't rent a car if you intend to visit only Prague. Most of the city center is closed to traffic, and you'll save yourself a lot of hassle by sticking to public transportation.

For accidents, call the emergency number (☎ 154 or 123). In case of repair problems, get in touch with the 24-hour **Autoturist Servis** (✉ Limuzská 12, Prague 10, ☎ 02/773455). Autoturist (ÚAMK) offices throughout the Czech Republic can provide motoring information of all kinds.

By Plane

ČSA (Czech Airlines) no longer operates any internal routes in its home country. Small, private lines have filled some of the holes; one is **Air Ostrava** (Prague, ☎ 02/2403–2731), which links Prague, Ostrava, and Brno. ČSA still flies to Slovak destinations including Poprad (High Tatras) and Košice. Reservations can be made through Čedok offices abroad or ČSA in Prague (✉ Revoluční 1, ☎ 02/2431–4271).

By Train

Trains vary in speed, but it's not really worth taking anything less than an express train, marked in red on the timetable. Tickets are relatively cheap; first class is considerably more spacious and comfortable and well worth the 50% increase over standard tickets. If you don't specify "express" when you buy your ticket, you may have to pay a supplement on the train. If you haven't bought a ticket in advance at the station, it's easy to buy one on the train for a small extra charge. On timetables, departures (*odjezd*) appear on a yellow background; arrivals (*příjezd*) are on white. It is possible to book sleepers (*lůžkový*) or the less-roomy *couchettes* (*lehátkový*) on most overnight trains. Since tickets are so inexpensive, most rail passes cost more than what you'd spend buying tickets on the spot. The European East Pass and the InterRail Pass—but not the EurailPass or Eurail Youthpass—are valid for unlimited train travel within the Czech Republic.

Contacts and Resources

B&B Reservation Agencies

Most offices of Čedok and local information offices also book rooms in hotels, pensions, and private accommodations. Travelers usually do not need to resort to reservation agencies and fare quite well by simply keeping a sharp eye out for signs reading ZIMMER FREI or UBYTOVÁNÍ. **In Britain:** Czechbook Agency (✉ Jopes Mill, Trebrownbridge, near Liskeard, Cornwall PL14 3PX, ☎ FAX 01503/240629) arranges stays in B&Bs, self-catering apartments, and hotels.

Car Rentals

There are no special requirements for renting a car in the Czech Republic, but be sure to shop around, as prices can differ greatly. **Avis** and **Hertz** offer Western makes for as much as $500–$700 per week. Smaller local companies, on the other hand, can rent Czech cars for as little as $130 per week, but the service is of dubious quality and sometimes not worth the savings.

Customs and Duties

ON ARRIVAL

You may import duty-free into the Czech Republic 200 cigarettes or the equivalent in tobacco, 50 cigars, 1 liter of spirits, 2 liters of wine, and ½ liter of perfume. You may also bring up to 1,000 Kč worth of gifts and souvenirs.

If you take into the Czech Republic valuables or foreign-made equipment from home, such as cameras, carry the original receipts with you or register the items with U.S. Customs before you leave (Form 4457). Otherwise you could end up paying duty upon your return.

ON DEPARTURE

From the Czech Republic you can take out gifts and souvenirs valued at up to 1,000 Kč. Theft of antiques—particularly baroque pieces from churches—continues to despoil the Czech cultural heritage. Only antiques bought at specially appointed shops may be exported. If there's any doubt about a piece's history, it's likely to have been stolen.

Emergencies

Police (☎ 158). **Ambulance** (☎ 155). **Breakdowns** (☎ 154 or 123 [in some areas, 0123]).

Language

Czech, a Slavic language closely related to Slovak and Polish, is the official language of the Czech Republic. Learning English is popular among young people, but German is still the most useful language for tourists. Don't be surprised if you get a response in German to a question asked in English. If the idea of attempting Czech is daunting, you might consider bringing a German phrase book.

Mail

POSTAL RATES

Postcards to the United States cost 6 Kč; letters up to 20 grams in weight, 10 Kč; to Great Britain a postcard is 5 Kč; a letter, 8 Kč. You can buy stamps at post offices, hotels, and shops that sell postcards.

RECEIVING MAIL

If you don't know where you'll be staying, **American Express** mail service is a great convenience, available at no charge to anyone holding an American Express credit card or carrying American Express traveler's checks. The American Express office is at Václavské náměstí. 56 (Wenceslas Square) in central Prague. You can also have mail held *poste restante* (general delivery) at post offices in major towns, but the letters should be marked *Pošta 1,* to designate the city's main post office. The poste restante window is No. 28 at the main post office in Prague (✉ Jindřišská ul. 14). You will be asked for identification when you collect your mail.

Money and Expenses

CURRENCY

The unit of currency in the Czech Republic is the *koruna,* or crown (Kč), which is divided into 100 haléř, or halers. There are (little-used) coins of 10, 20, and 50 halers; coins of 1, 2, 5, 10, 20, and 50 Kč; and notes of 20, 50, 100, 200, 500, 1,000, and 5,000 Kč. The 1,000-Kč note may not always be accepted for small purchases, because the proprietor may not have enough change.

Try to avoid exchanging money at hotels or private exchange booths, including the ubiquitous Čekobanka and Exact Change booths. They routinely take commissions of 8%–10%. The best places to exchange are at bank counters, where the commissions average 1%–3%, or at ATMs. The koruna became fully convertible late in 1995 and can now be purchased outside the country and exchanged into other currencies. Ask about current regulations when you change money, however, and keep your receipts. At press time the exchange rate was around 27 Kč to the U.S. dollar, 19 Kč to the Canadian dollar, and 41 Kč to the pound sterling.

WHAT IT WILL COST

Despite rising inflation, the Czech Republic is still generally a bargain by Western standards. Prague remains the exception, however. Hotel prices, in particular, frequently meet or exceed the average for the United States and Western Europe—and are higher than the standard of facilities would warrant. Nevertheless, you can still find bargain private accommodations. The prices at tourist resorts outside the capital are lower and, in the outlying areas and off the beaten track, incredibly low. Tourists can now legally pay for hotel rooms in crowns, although some hotels still insist on payment in "hard" (i.e., Western) currency.

SAMPLE COSTS

A cup of coffee will cost about 15 Kč; museum entrance, 20 Kč–150 Kč; a good theater seat, up to 200 Kč; a cinema seat, 30 Kč–50 Kč; ½ liter (pint) of beer, 15 Kč–25 Kč; a 1-mile taxi ride, 60 Kč–100 Kč; a bottle of Moravian wine in a good restaurant, 100 Kč–150 Kč; a glass (2 deciliters or 7 ounces) of wine, 25 Kč.

National Holidays

January 1; Easter Monday; May 1 (Labor Day); May 8 (Liberation Day); July 5 (Sts. Cyril and Methodius); July 6 (Jan Hus); October 28 (Czech National Day); and December 24, 25, and 26.

Opening and Closing Times

Though hours vary, most banks are open weekdays 8–5, with an hour's lunch break. Private exchange offices usually have longer hours. Museums are usually open daily except Monday (or Tuesday) 9–5; they tend to stop selling tickets an hour before closing time. Outside the large towns, many sights, including most castles, are open daily except Monday only from May through September and in April and October are open only on weekends and holidays. Stores are open weekdays 9–6; some grocery stores open at 6 AM. Department stores often stay open until 7 PM. On Saturday, most stores close at noon. Nearly all stores are closed on Sunday.

Passports and Visas

American and British citizens require only a valid passport for stays of up to 30 days in the Czech Republic. No visas are necessary. The seesaw situation for Canadian citizens seemed to come down in their favor when visa requirements for the Czech Republic were dropped on April 1, 1996. It's advisable to contact the Czech Embassy, however, for changes in the rules (✉ Embassy of the Czech Republic, 541 Sussex Dr., Ottawa, Ontario K1N 6Z6, ☎ 613/562–3875, ☒ 613/562–3878). U.S. citizens can receive additional information from the Czech Embassy (✉ 3900 Spring of Freedom St. NW, Washington, DC 20008, ☎ 202/274–9100, ☒ 202/966–8540).

Rail Passes

The **European East Pass** is good for unlimited first-class travel on the national railroads of Austria, the Czech Republic, Slovakia, Hungary, and Poland. The pass allows five days of travel within a 15-day period ($169) or 10 days of travel within a 30-day period ($275). Apply through your travel agent or through **Rail Europe** (✉ 226–230 Westchester Ave., White Plains, NY 10604, ☎ 914/682–2999 or 800/848–7245). The **EurailPass** and **Eurail Youthpass** are not valid for travel within the Czech Republic. The **InterRail Pass** (£249), available to European citizens only through local student or budget travel offices, is valid for one month of unlimited train travel in the Czech Republic and the other countries covered in this book. For more information, *see* Rail Passes *in* Important Contacts A to Z *and* Smart Travel Tips A to Z.

Student and Youth Travel

In the Czech Republic, **CKM Youth Travel Service** (✉ Žitná 12, Prague 1, ☎ 02/2491–5767) provides information on student hostels and travel bargains within the Czech Republic and issues IYH cards (200 Kč). For general information about student identity cards, work-abroad programs, and youth hostels, *see* Student and Youth Travel *in* Smart Travel Tips A to Z.

Telephones

The country code for the Czech Republic is 42.

LOCAL CALLS

The few remaining coin-operated telephones take 1-, 2-, and 5-Kč coins. Most newer public phones operate only with a special telephone card, available from newsstands and tobacconists in denominations of 100 Kč and 190 Kč. A call within Prague costs 2 Kč. The dial tone is a series of short and long buzzes.

INTERNATIONAL CALLS

To reach an English-speaking operator in the United States, dial 00–420–00101 (**AT&T**), 00–420–00112 (**MCI**), or 0420–87187 (**Sprint**). For **CanadaDirect,** dial 00420–00151; for **B.T.Direct** to the United Kingdom, 00420–04401. The operator will connect your collect or credit-card call at the carrier's standard rates. In Prague, many phone booths allow direct international dialing; if you can't find one, the main post office (Hlavní pošta, ⊠ Jindřišská ul. 14), open 24 hours, is the best place to try. There you can use the public phones in the lobby or ask one of the clerks in the 24-hour telephone room, to the left as you enter, for assistance. Twenty-four-hour fax and telex service is handled from the office to the right of the entrance. The international dialing code is 00. For international inquiries, dial 0132 for the United States, Canada, or the United Kingdom. Otherwise, ask the receptionist at any hotel to put a call through for you, though beware: The more expensive the hotel, the more expensive the call will be.

Tipping

To reward good service in a restaurant, round the bill up to the nearest multiple of 10 (if the bill comes to 83 Kč, for example, give the waiter 90 Kč); 10% is considered appropriate on very large tabs. If you have difficulty communicating the amount to the waiter, just leave the money on the table. Tip porters who bring bags to your rooms 20 Kč. For room service, a 20-Kč tip is enough. In taxis, round the bill up by 10%. Give tour guides and helpful concierges between 20 Kč and 30 Kč for services rendered.

Visitor Information

Čedok, the former state-run travel bureau, went private in 1995 and is now a travel agent rather than a tourist information office. It will supply you with hotel and travel information, and book air and rail tickets, but don't expect much in the way of general information.

Most major towns have a local or private information office, usually in the central square and identified by a lowercase "i" on the facade. These offices are often good sources for maps and historical information and can usually help visitors book hotel and private accommodations. Most are open during normal business hours, with limited hours on Saturday (until noon), and are closed on Sunday and holidays. Out-of-season hours are severely reduced. For individual centers, *see* Visitor Information *in* each of this chapter's A to Z sections, *above.*

3 Slovakia

Despite a long period of common statehood with the Czechs (which ended in 1993), Slovakia (Slovensko) differs from the Czech Republic in many aspects. Its mountains are higher and more rugged, its veneer less sophisticated, its folklore and traditions richer. Observers of the two regions like to link the Czech Republic geographically and culturally with the orderly Germans, while they put Slovakia with Ukraine and Russia, firmly in the east. This is a simplification, yet it contains more than a little bit of truth.

By Mark Baker

Updated by
Timea Špitková

SLOVAKIA BECAME AN INDEPENDENT STATE on January 1, 1993, when Czechoslovakia—formerly comprised of what is today Slovakia and the Czech Republic—ceased to exist. To the east of the Czech Republic, Slovakia is about one-third as large as its neighbor. Although the Slovaks speak a language closely related to Czech, they managed to maintain a strong sense of national identity throughout the more than 70 years of common statehood. Indeed, the two Slavic groups developed quite separately: Though united in the 9th century as part of the Great Moravian Empire, the Slovaks were conquered a century later by the Magyars and remained under Hungarian and Hapsburg rule. Following the Tartar invasions in the 13th century, many Saxons were invited to resettle the land and develop the economy, including the region's rich mineral resources. In the 15th and 16th centuries, Romanian shepherds migrated from Wallachia through the Carpathians into Slovakia, and the merging of these varied groups with the resident Slavs bequeathed to the region a rich folk culture and some unique forms of architecture, especially in the east.

In the end, it was this very different history that split the Slovaks from the Czechs, ending the most successful experiment in nation building to follow World War I.

For many Slovaks, the 1989 revolution provided for the first time an opportunity not only to bring down the Communists, but also to establish a fully independent state—thus ending what many Slovaks saw as a millennium of subjugation by Hungary and the Hapsburgs, Nazi Germany, Prague's Communist regimes, and ultimately the Czechs. Although few Slovaks harbored any real resentment toward the Czechs, Slovak politicians were quick to recognize and exploit the deep, inchoate longing for independence. Slovak nationalist parties won more than 50% of the vote in the crucial 1992 Czechoslovak elections, and once the results were in, the end came quickly: On January 1, 1993, Slovakia became the youngest country in Europe.

The outside world witnessed the demise of the Czechoslovak federation in 1993 with some sadness; the split seemed just another piece of evidence to confirm that tribalism and nationalism continue to play the deciding role in European affairs. Yet there is something hopeful to be seen in the peaceful nature of the separation. Despite lingering differences about the division of the federation's assets, no Czechs or Slovaks have yet died in nationalistic squabbles. For the visitor, the changes may in fact be positive. The Slovaks have been long overshadowed by their cousins to the west; now they have the unfettered opportunity to tell their story to the world.

Most visitors to Slovakia head first for the great peaks of the High Tatras (Vysoké Tatry), which rise magnificently from the foothills of northern Slovakia. The tourist infrastructure here is very good, catering especially to hikers and skiers. Visitors who come to admire the peaks, however, often overlook the exquisite medieval towns of Spiš, in the plains and valleys below the High Tatras, and the beautiful 18th-century country churches farther east. (Removed from main centers, these areas are short on tourist amenities, so if creature comforts are important to you, stick to the High Tatras.)

Bratislava, the capital of Slovakia, is at first a disappointment to many visitors. The last 40 years of communism left a clear mark on the city, hiding its ancient beauty with hulking, and now dilapidated, futurist structures. Yet despite its gloomy appearance, Bratislava tries hard to project the cosmopolitanism of a European capital, bolstered by the fact that it is filled with good restaurants and wine bars, opera and art. The Old Town, though still needing more renovation, is beginning to recapture some of its lost charm.

Pleasures and Pastimes

Bicycling

Slovaks are avid cyclists, and the flatter areas to the south and east of Bratislava and along the Danube are ideal for biking. Outside large towns, quieter roads stretch out for many kilometers. A special bike trail links Bratislava and Vienna, paralleling the Danube for much of its 40-kilometer (25-mile) length. For the more adventurous bikers, the Low Tatras (Nízke Tatry) have scenic biking trails along the small secluded rivers surrounding Banská Bystrica. There is a hiking map of the Low Tatras, which includes routes for cyclists, available at the tourist office in Banská Bystrica. Not many places rent bikes, however; inquire at tourist information centers or at your hotel for rental information.

Boating and Sailing

Slovaks with boats head to the man-made lakes of Zemplínska Šírava (east of Košice near the Ukrainian border) or Orava (northwest of the Tatras near the Polish border). River rafting has been hampered in recent years by dry weather, which has also reduced river levels. However, raft rides are still given in summer at Červený Kláštor, north of Kežmarok (☞ Eastern Slovakia, *below*).

Camping

There are hundreds of camping sites for tents and trailers throughout Slovakia, but most are open only in summer (May to mid-September). You can get a map of all the sites, with addresses, opening times, and facilities, from Satur; auto atlases also identify campsites. Camping outside official sites is prohibited. Some camping grounds also offer bungalows. Campsites are divided into Categories A and B according to facilities, but both have hot water and toilets.

Dining

Slovak food is an amalgam of its neighbors' cuisines. As in Bohemia and Moravia, the emphasis is on meat, particularly pork and beef. But you will seldom find the Czechs' traditional (and often bland) roast pork and dumplings on the menu. The Slovaks, betraying their long link to Hungary, prefer to spice things up a bit, usually with paprika and red peppers. Roast potatoes or french fries are often served in place of dumplings, although occasionally you'll find a side dish of tasty *halušky* (noodles similar to Italian gnocchi or German spaetzle) on the menu. No primer on Slovak eating would be complete without mention of *bryndzové halušky*, the country's unofficial national dish, a tasty and filling mix of halušky, sheep's cheese, and a little bacon fat for flavor (it seldom makes it onto the menu at elegant restaurants, so look for it instead at roadside restaurants and snack bars). For dessert, the emphasis comes from upriver, in Vienna: pancakes, fruit dumplings (if you're lucky), poppy-seed dumplings, and strudel.

Eating out is still not a popular pastime among Slovaks, particularly since prices have risen markedly in the past few years. As a result, you will find relatively few restaurants about; and those that do exist generally cater to foreigners or a wealthy business clientele. Restaurants known as *vináreň* specialize in serving wines, although you can order beer virtually anywhere. The Slovaks, however, do not have many bars equivalent to the Czech *pivnice* (beer hall).

Slovaks pride themselves on their wines, and to an extent they have a point. Do not expect much subtlety, though, for the typical offering is hearty, sometimes heavy, but always very drinkable wines that complement the region's filling and spicy food. This is especially true of the reds. The most popular is *Frankovka*, which is fiery and slightly acidic. *Vavrinecké*, a relatively new arrival, is dark and semisweet and stands up well to red meats. Slovakia's few white wines are similar in character to the Moravian wines and, on the whole, unexceptional.

Lunch, usually eaten between noon and 2, is the main meal for Slovaks and offers the best deal for tourists. Many restaurants put out a special luncheon menu, with more appetizing selections at better prices. Dinner is usually served from 5 until 9 or 10, but don't wait too long to eat. Cooks frequently knock off early on slow nights. The dinner menu does not differ substantially from lunch offerings, except the prices are higher.

CATEGORY	COST*
$$$$	over $20
$$$	$15–$20
$$	$7–$15
$	under $7

per person for a three-course meal, excluding wine and tip

Festivals and Seasonal Events

Many villages host annual folklore festivals, usually in late summer or early fall (☞ Festivals and Seasonal Events *in* Chapter 1). These frequently take place in the town center and are accompanied by lots of singing, dancing, and drinking. Every year, the Slovak Ministry of Economy puts out a calendar of events in English, available in travel agencies and tourist information centers. Try visiting Košice during June, when the International Folklore Festival is in full swing. Singing and dancing groups from all over show off their rich traditions and colorful costumes on the streets of this eastern Slovakia town.

Fishing

There are hundreds of lakes and rivers suitable for fishing, often amid striking scenery. Demanovská dolina, a picturesque valley near Liptovský Mikuláš in central Slovakia, offers some excellent places to catch trout. Some other freshwater fish include catfish, eel, pike, and carp. You should bring your own tackle or be prepared to buy it locally because rental equipment is scarce. To legally cast a line, you must have a fishing license (valid for one year) plus a fishing permit (valid for a day, week, month, or year for the particular body of water on which you plan to fish). Both are available from Satur offices.

Hiking

Slovakia is a hiker's paradise, with more than 20,000 kilometers (15,000 miles) of well-kept, marked, and signposted trails in both the mountainous regions and the agricultural countryside. You'll find the colored markings denoting trails on trees, fences, walls, rocks, and elsewhere. The colors correspond to the path marking on the large-scale *Soubor turistickych* maps available at many bookstores and tobacconists. The main paths are marked in red, others in blue and green; the least important trails are marked in yellow. The best areas for ambitious mountain walkers are the Low Tatras in the center of the country near Banská Bystrica and the High Tatras to the north. *Slovenský Raj,* or Slovak Paradise, in eastern Slovakia is an ideal place for hikers—a wild, romantic area, you'll see cliffs, caves, and waterfalls. If you have to stick closer to Bratislava, the Small Carpathians and the Fatra range in western Slovakia offer good hiking trails as well.

Lodging

Slovakia's hotel industry has been slow to react to the political and economic changes that have taken place since 1989. Few new hotels have been built, and many of the older establishments are still mostly owned by the state and often give shabby service. On the bright side, small, private hotels and pensions in beautifully renovated buildings have been springing up all over the country. While some may be a few rooms in someone's house, others provide the amenities of a hotel in a much more beautiful setting. Banská Bystrica's Arcade Hotel and Hotel Salamander in Banská Štavnica have both transformed 16th-century historical sites into stylish accommodations. The facilities in the Tatras remain good though a bit expensive, and Bratislava has added a few new hotels, but there still remains a shortage of good inexpensive accommodations. Elsewhere in the country, you'll find everything from a cheap fairy-tale-like villa, such as the 13th-century Arkada Hotel in Levoča, to a nightmarishly gloomy apartment building with tiny rooms and rude clerks, charging outrageous prices to foreigners.

In general, hotels can be divided into two categories: edifices built in the 1960s or '70s that offer modern amenities but not much character; and older, more central establishments that are heavy on personality but may lack basic conveniences. Hostels are understood to be cheap dormitory rooms and are probably best avoided. In the mountainous areas, you can often find little *chata* (chalets), where pleasant surroundings compensate for a lack of basic amenities. *Autokempink* (campsites) generally have a few bungalows available for visitors.

Slovakia's official hotel classification, based on letters (Deluxe, A*, B*, C), is gradually being changed over to the international star system, although it will be some time before the old system is completely replaced. These ratings correspond closely to our categories as follows: Deluxe or five-star (\$\$\$\$); A* or four-star (\$\$\$); B* or three- to two–star (\$\$–\$). We've included C hotels in our listings where accommodations are scarce or when the particular hotel has redeeming qualities. In any case, prices for hotels in Slovakia do not always mesh with the quality. As a rule, always ask the price before taking a room.

Slovakia is a bargain by Western standards, particularly in the outlying areas. The exception is the price of accommodations in Bratislava, where hotel rates often meet or exceed both U.S. and Western European averages. Accommodations outside the capital, with the exception of the High Tatras resorts, are significantly lower. Tourists can pay for hotel rooms in Slovak crowns, although payment in "hard" (i.e., Western) currency is still welcomed by some hotels.

The prices quoted below are for double rooms, generally not including breakfast. Prices at the lower end of the scale apply to low season. At certain periods, such as Christmas, Easter, or during festivals, there may be an increase of 15%–25%.

CATEGORY	COST*
\$\$\$\$	over \$100
\$\$\$	\$50–\$100
\$\$	\$15–\$50
\$	under \$15

All prices are for a standard double room, including tax and service.

Shopping

Among the most interesting finds in Slovakia are batik-painted Easter eggs, corn-husk figures, delicate woven table mats, hand-knit sweaters, and folk pottery. The best buys are folk-art products sold at stands along the roads and in Slovart or folk art stores in most major towns. There are also several Dielo stores, which sell paintings, some wooden toys, and great ceramic pieces by Slovak artists at very reasonable prices. The local brands of firewater—*slivovice* (plum brandy) and *borovička* (a spirit made from juniper berries)—also make excellent buys.

Skiing

Slovakia is one of the best countries in the region for downhill skiers, both amateurs and experts. The two main skiing areas are the Low Tatras and the High Tatras. The Low Tatras are more pleasant if you want to avoid crowds, but the High Tatras offer more reliable conditions (good snow throughout winter) and superior facilities, including places where you can rent equipment. The High Tatras are also blessed with high peaks such as Skalnaté Pleso (1,751 meters above sea level) and are host to several world championships. Lifts in both regions generally operate from January through March, though cross-country skiing is a popular alternative.

Exploring Slovakia

Slovakia can best be divided into four regions of interest to tourists: Bratislava, the High Tatra Mountains, central Slovakia, and eastern Slovakia. Despite being the capital, Bratislava, in the western part of the country, is probably the least alluring of these spots. The country's true beauty lies among the peaks of the High Tatras in the northern part of central Slovakia. The remainder of central Slovakia, also a striking mountainous region with great hiking trails, is rich in folklore and is home to fascinating medieval mining towns. Few tourists have yet discovered the eastern region, with its fairy-tale villages, castles, and wooden churches, or the caves, cliffs, and plateaus of the national park known as Slovenský Raj.

Great Itineraries

Numbers in the text correspond to numbers in the margin and on the maps.

Although Slovakia is relatively small, its mountains and poor roads make it difficult to explore in a short period of time. Driving or taking the train from Bratislava to the eastern town of Košice will take you a minimum of seven hours. A more convenient option is to fly. From Košice, it's easy to explore the surrounding region, with the High Tatras less than three hours away. In 10 days you can travel through the country at a leisurely pace, exploring both the mountains in central Slovakia and the towns and villages of the eastern region. Unless you are flying, five days will allow you time in the High Tatras and a brief visit to a few historic towns in the surrounding area. If you only have three days, you can either stay in Bratislava and explore some of the vineyards and small villages in the outlying areas or get on the first plane headed for the High Tatras. Although the trip may be a bit rushed, the second option of a trip to the mountains will probably be far more rewarding, especially if the weather is pleasant enough for hiking.

IF YOU HAVE 3 DAYS

If you only have a few days to see Slovakia, spend a maximum of a few hours walking through the Old Town and the castle in **Bratislava** ①–⑱, then head straight for the **High Tatras.** Once you get to the mountains, you can settle down in a comfortable hotel or a pension in one of the resort towns. 🏠 **Smokovec** ㉑ and 🏠 **Tatranská Lomnica** ㉓ are probably the most convenient places from which to explore the area and go hiking in summer or skiing in winter. You can also visit nearby **Ždiar** ㉔, a typical Slovak village high up in the mountains. If you can pull yourself away from the High Tatras on the second day, take a brief

excursion slightly south to the beautiful Spiš town of 🔯 **Levoča** ㉞. Spend
the night here, and on your last day, head back to Bratislava via **Poprad** ⑳ and **Banská Bystrica** ㉕.

IF YOU HAVE 5 DAYS
Do not linger too long in **Bratislava** ①–⑱ before heading out to
🔯 **Smokovec** ㉑ or 🔯 **Taranská Lomnica** ㉓, which offer easy access to
the **High Tatras.** Spend your second day hiking in the mountains. On
your third day, head east toward 🔯 **Levoča** ㉞, where you an spend the
day (and the night). From here, you can also explore the Špis Castle
and the caves and gorges in the area. The following day, head south
toward 🔯 **Košice** ㉝. Take a look at some of the historic sights in the
Old Town of this region's capital, and if there is still time, take an excursion to **Herłany Geyser,** about 20 miles outside the city. Overnight
in Košice, and on your last day, make your way back home. From Košice,
it's possible to fly to Bratislava or Prague or to take a direct day or
night train to one of the two cities.

When to Tour Slovakia

Slovakia, which experiences all four seasons, is beautiful throughout
the year. The High Tatras are loveliest in winter (January–March). However, the area does get crowded when thousands of skiers descend on
the major resorts. A smaller summer season in the mountains attracts
mostly walkers and hikers looking to escape the heat and noise of the
cities. Because of the snow, many hiking trails, especially those that
cross the peaks, are open only between June and October.

Bratislava is at its best in the temperate months of spring and autumn.
July and August, though not especially crowded, can be unbearably
hot. In winter, when many tourist attractions are closed, expect lots
of rain and snow in the capital. Note that temperatures are always much
cooler in the mountains. Even in summer, expect to wear a sweater or
jacket in the High Tatras.

BRATISLAVA

Many visitors are initially disappointed when they see Europe's newest
capital city, Bratislava—or "Blava" as it is affectionately known by residents. Expecting a Slovak version of Prague or Vienna, they discover
instead a busy industrial city that seems to embody the Communists'
blind faith in modernity rather than the stormy history of this once
Hungarian and now Slovak capital. The problem, of course, is that
Bratislava has more than its fair share of high-rise housing projects,
faded supermodern structures, and less-than-inspiring monuments to
carefully chosen acts of heroism. Even the handsome castle on the hill
and the winding streets of the Old Town look decidedly secondary in
their crumbling beauty.

The jumble of modern Bratislava, however, masks a long and regal history that rivals Prague's in importance and complexity. Settled by a
variety of Celts and Romans, the city became part of the Great Moravian Empire around the year 900 under Prince Břetislav. After a short
period under the Bohemian Přemysl princes, Bratislava was brought
into the Hungarian kingdom by Stephan I at the end of the 10th century and given royal privileges in 1217. Following the Tatar invasion
in 1241, the Hungarian kings brought in German colonists to repop-
ulate the town. The Hungarians called the town Pozsony; the German
settlers referred to it as Pressburg; and the original Slovaks called it
Bratislava after Prince Břetislav.

Slovakia

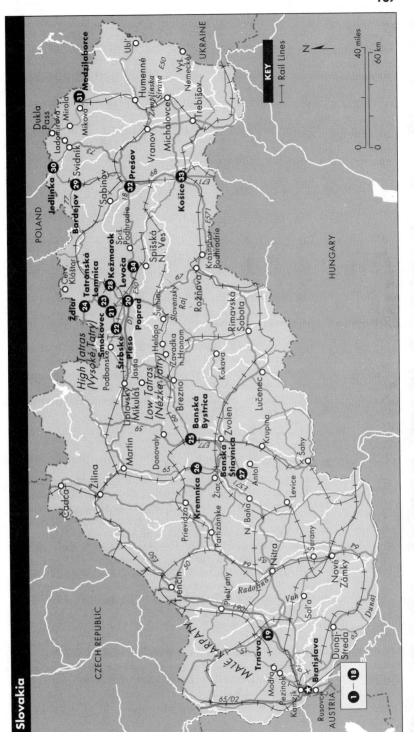

KEY
† Rail Lines

N

0 — 40 miles
0 — 60 km

POLAND

UKRAINE

HUNGARY

CZECH REPUBLIC

AUSTRIA

1 — **18**

19

20 Poprad

21

22 Štrbské Pleso

23 Tatranská Lomnica

24 Ždiar

25 Banská Bystrica

26 Kremnica

27 Banská Štiavnica

28 Kežmarok

29 Bardejov

30 Jedlinka

31 Medzilaborce

32 Prešov

33 Košice

34 Levoča

Ubľa
Humenné
Vyš.
Nemecké
Trebišov
Michalovce
Vranov
Zemplínska
Strava
E50
Dukla Pass
Mirola
Ladomirová
Svidník
Sabinov
Spiš.
Podhradie
Spišská N Ves
Krásnohor.
Podhradie
Rožňava
Kokava
Rimavská Sobota
Lučenec
Šahy
Levice
Šurany
Nové Zámky
Nitra
Dunaj
Dunaj-Streda
Šaľa
Vah
Radošina
Piešťany
N. Baňa
Partizánske
Prievidza
Trenčín
Trnava
Modra
Pezinok
Kamzík
Rusovce
Bratislava
Žilina
Čadca
Martin
Donovaly
Žiar
Antol
Krupina
Zvolen
Brezno
Zavadka
n.Hronom
Heľpa
Šumiac
Slovenský Raj
Liptovský Mikuláš
Jasná
Podbanské
High Tatras (Vysoké Tatry)
Low Tatras (Nízke Tatry)
Smokovec
Spišská
MALÉ KARPATY
Červ
Kláštor

E50
E58
E571
E77
E571
E77
D1
E50

18
77
68
67
65
66
50
51
61
62
64
63
75
65/D2

When Pest and Buda were occupied by the Turks, in 1526 and 1541, respectively, the Hungarian kings moved their seat to Bratislava, which remained the Hungarian capital until 1784 and the coronation center until 1835. At this time, with a population of almost 27,000, it was the largest Hungarian city. Only in 1919, when Bratislava became part of the first Czechoslovak republic, did the city regain its Slovak identity. In 1939, with Germany's assistance, Bratislava infamously exerted its yearnings for independence by becoming the capital of the puppet Slovak state, under the fascist leader Josef Tiso. In 1945 it became the provincial capital of Slovakia, still straining under the powerful hand of Prague (Slovakia's German and Hungarian minorities were either expelled or repressed). Leading up to the 1989 revolution, Bratislava was the site of numerous anticommunist demonstrations; many of these were carried out by supporters of the Catholic Church, long repressed by the regime then in power. Following the "Velvet Revolution" in 1989, Bratislava gained importance as the capital of the Slovak Republic within the new Czech and Slovak federal state, but rivalries with Prague persisted. It was only following the breakup of Czechoslovakia on January 1, 1993, that the city once again became a capital in its own right. But don't come to Bratislava expecting beauty or bustle. Instead, plan to spend a leisurely day or two sightseeing before setting off for Slovakia's superior natural splendors.

Exploring Bratislava

If you want to discover the greater part of Bratislava's charms, you should travel the city by foot. Imagination is also helpful, as some of the Old Town's more potentially interesting streets are often covered with scaffolding or look as though they've recently gone through a war. Nevertheless, many areas have been reconstructed and are packed with interesting historical sights.

Numbers in the text correspond to numbers in the margin and on the Bratislava map.

A Good Walk

Begin your tour at the modern **Námestie SNP** (SNP Square) ①. SNP stands for *Slovenské Národné Povstanie* (Slovak National Uprising), an anti-Nazi resistance movement. In the middle of the square are three larger-than-life statues: a dour partisan with two strong, sad women in peasant clothing. From here walk up the square toward Hurbanovo námestie, where you can glance at the **Kostol svätej Trojice** ②. Across the road, unobtrusively located between a shoe store and a bookstore, is the enchanting entrance to the Old Town. A small bridge, decorated with wrought-iron railings and statues of St. Michael and St. John Nepomuk, takes you over a former moat, now blossoming with trees and fountains, into the intricate barbican, a set of gates and houses that composed Bratislava's medieval fortifications. After passing through the first archway, you'll come to the narrow promenade of Michalská ulica (Michael Street). In front of you is **Michalská brána** (Michael's Gate) ③. Before going through the gate, you'll find the **Farmaceutické múzeum** (Pharmaceutical Museum). After a visit there, walk through the gate, and in an adjoining tower is a small museum, the **Múzeum zbraní a mestského opevnenia** (Museum of Weapons and Fortifications). You'll get a good view over the city from here.

Take a stroll down Michalská ulica. Many of the more interesting buildings along the street are undergoing renovation, but notice the eerie blue **Kaplnka svätej Kataríny** (Chapel of St. Catherine) at No. 6 on the left, built in 1311 but now graced with a sober classical facade. Opposite, at No. 7, is the **Renaissance Segnerova kúria** (Segner House),

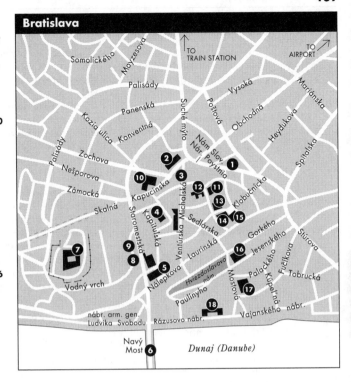

built for a wealthy merchant in 1648. Farther down on the right is the **Palác Uhorskej kráľ'ovskej komory** (Hungarian Royal Chamber), a baroque palace that housed the Hungariean nobles' parliament from 1802 until 1848; it is now the University Library. Go through the arched passageway at the back of the building, and you'll emerge in a tiny square dominated by the **Kostol Klarisiek** (Church and Convent of the Poor Clares), which is now the Slovak Pedagogical Library.

Stretched along Farská ulica ahead of you is the 14th-century **Klariský kostol** (Klariský Church) ④. Follow Farská up to the corner and turn left on Kapitulská ulica (noticing the paving stone depicting two kissing lizards). This street could be the most beautiful in Bratislava, but its array of Gothic, Renaissance, and baroque buildings is in such disrepair that the effect is almost lost. Renovation has begun, and at No. 15 you can see that the remains of a wall painting have been uncovered on the stone facade. At the bottom of the street on the right is the late-Renaissance Jezuitské kolégium (Jesuit College), which has been a theological seminary since 1936. Ahead of you on the right is the side wall of the **Dóm svätého Martina** (St. Martin's Cathedral) ⑤, one of the more impressive churches in the city, despite the freeway built across its front doors in the 1970s.

As you leave the church and walk around to the front, the first thing you see is the freeway leading to the futuristic spaceship bridge, **Nový Most** (New Bridge) ⑥, formerly called Most SNP (Bridge of the Slovak National Uprising). When the highway was built, a row of old houses and a synagogue in the former Jewish quarter outside the city walls were destroyed. The only good thing to be said for the road is that its construction led to the discovery of remnants of the city's original walls, which have been partially restored and now line the freeway on the right. Follow the steps under the passageway and up the other side in the direction of the castle.

Continue up the steps, through a Gothic arched gateway built in 1480, and climb up to the **hrad** (castle) ⑦ area. From the top, there is an excellent view over the Danube to the endless apartment blocks on the Petržalka side of the river. On a good day you can see over to Austria to the right. In the castle, you'll find the **Slovenské národné múzeum** (Slovak National Museum), which is worth a brief visit. Leave the castle by the same route, but instead of climbing the last stairs by the Arkadia restaurant, continue down Old World Beblavého ulica. Now home to stylish galleries and restaurants, this route to the castle was once one of the city's infamous red-light districts.

At the bottom of the street on the right is the **Múzeum umeleckých remesiel** (Handicraft Museum) ⑧. Next, go around the House at the Good Shepherd and continue along Židovská ulica (Jews' Street), marred by the freeway and dominated by a rash of buildings under construction. The street name recalls that this area was the former Jewish ghetto. You can visit the **Múzeum Židovskej Kultúry** (Museum of Jewish Culture in Slovakia) ⑨ in a Renaissance mansion, the only reminder that before World War II Jews made up more than 10% of Bratislava's population.

Continue on Židovská ulica until you come to a thin concrete bridge that crosses the freeway to the reconstructed city walls. Standing in the middle of this bridge, looking toward the river, you'll get one of the best views of the incongruous and contradictory jumble of buildings that make up Bratislava. Directly to the south is the Nový Most, surrounded by housing blocks; to the east (left) are the city walls, leading into St. Martin's Cathedral; to the west (right) are a little rococo house backed by construction and the towers of the castle. If you turn left and walk along the city walls, you will come, after negotiating a series of steps, to the main road, Kapucínska ulica.

Across the road on the left is the small, golden-yellow **Kostol kapucínov** (Capuchin Chapel) ⑩. Cross the street and take the steps leading down into the Old Town. Turn left at the bottom into little Baštová ulica. Go through the arch at the end, and you'll find yourself back at Michael's Gate. Continue straight along Zámočnícka ulica, which turns right heading in the direction of Františkánske námestie. To the left is the oldest preserved building in Bratislava, the **Františkánsky kostol** (Franciscan Church) ⑪. Across from the church is the beautifully detailed rococo **Mirbachov palác** (Mirbach Palace) ⑫, which today houses the Municipal Gallery.

Go across the Františkánske námestie, with its statues of little-known Slovak World War II heroes, onto the adjoining square, Hlavné námestie. The latter is lined with old houses and palaces representing a spectrum of architectural styles, from Gothic (No. 2), baroque (No. 4), and rococo (No. 7), to a wonderfully decorative example of art nouveau at No. 10. To your immediate left as you come into the square is the richly decorated **Jezuitský kostol** (Jesuit Church) ⑬. Next to the church is the colorful agglomeration of old bits and pieces of structures that make up the **Stará radnica** (Old Town Hall) ⑭. Walk through the arched passageway, still with its early Gothic ribbing, into a cheery Renaissance courtyard with romantic arcades and gables. Toward the back of the courtyard is the entrance to the **Mestské múzeum** (City Museum).

Leaving by the back entrance of the Old Town Hall, you'll come to the Primaciálne námestie (Primates' Square), dominated by the glorious pale-pink **Primaciálny palác** (Primates' Palace) ⑮, where you should take some time to explore. After you're done, walk down Uršulínska ulica and turn right at the bottom onto Laurinská ulica. If you continue to the left down Rybárska brána, you will emerge into the more modern part of the Old Town, with businesses and hotels stretched along the rectangular Hviezdoslavovo námestie (Hviezdoslav Square). To your right is the **Slovenské národné divadlo** (Slovak National Theater) ⑯, Bratislava's opera house. Behind the theater you can buy tickets to performances.

Across the Hviezdoslav Square, on the corner of Mostová ulica and Palackého ulica, is the **Reduta** ⑰, home to the Slovak Philharmonic Orchestra. If you can't make it to a concert, take a look inside. Continue down Mostová ulica to the banks of the Danube. To the right is the baroque onetime barracks, transformed by the Communists to house the modern **Slovenská národná galéria** (Slovak National Gallery) ⑱, which features a conglomeration of past and present works by Slovak artists.

TIMING

If you get an early morning start, you can complete a leisurely walking tour of the Old Town in a day (make sure you have on comfortable shoes). With the exception of the Slovak National Gallery, which deserves some time, most of the museums are small and won't detain you long. If you have more than one day to explore Bratislava, save the Museum of Jewish Culture and the castle, two of the more interesting sights, for their own day. Avoid touring on Mondays, as many sights are closed. On other days, plan to break around lunchtime, because many museums close between noon and 1.

SIGHTS TO SEE

❺ Dóm svätého Martina (St. Martin's Cathedral). Construction of this massive Gothic church, with its 280-foot steeple twinkling beneath a layer of golden trim, began in the 14th century. The cathedral was finally consecrated in 1452, and between the 16th and 19th centuries it hosted the coronations of 17 Hungarian royals. Numerous additions made over the centuries were unfortunately removed in the 19th century, when the church was re-Gothicized. Nowadays, the three equal-size naves give an impression of space and light, but the uplifting glory found in Bohemia's Gothic cathedrals is definitely missing. ⊠ *Kapitulská 9,* ☎ *07/3309504.* ☺ *Weekdays 10–11:45 and 2–4:45, Sat. 10–noon and 2–4:45, Sun. 2–4:45.*

Farmaceutické múzeum (Pharmaceutical Museum). Housed in the barbican wall on the site of the former Red Crab Pharmacy, this small museum is worth visiting if only to see the beautifully carved wood shelves and imaginative pharmaceutical receptacles. Next to the museum, a small arched gateway topped with the symbol of a crab leads down through an apartment building to the moat-side garden, which has good views of the looming fortifications. ⊠ *Michalská ul. 26,* ☎ *07/5333596.* ☜ *10 Sk.* ☺ *Tues.–Sun. 10–4:30.*

⓫ Františkánsky kostol (Franciscan Church). Consecrated in 1297, this church was funded by the Hungarian king László IV to celebrate his victory over the Bohemian king Přemysl Otakar II at the Battle of the Marchfeld, near Vienna. Only its presbytery is still in early Gothic style, the rest having been destroyed in an earthquake in the 17th century and rebuilt in a mixture of baroque and Gothic. Just around the corner, built onto the church, is another quite different and much more stunning Gothic building, the 14th-century **Chapel of St. John the Evangelist,** the burial chapel for Mayor Jakub. Art historians believe that Peter Parler, architect of Prague's Charles Bridge and St. Vitus Cathedral, may have worked on this Gothic gem. You can take a look around before or after services at 7 AM and 5 PM. ⊠ *Františká nám.*

7 **Hrad** (castle). Bratislava's castle has been continually rebuilt since its foundations were laid in the 9th century. The Hungarian kings expanded it into a large royal residence, and the Hapsburgs further developed its fortifications, turning it into a very successful defense against the Turks. Its current design, square with four corner towers, stems from the 17th century, although the existing castle had to be completely rebuilt after a disastrous fire in 1811. Inside you'll find the **Slovenské národné múzeum** (Slovak National Museum), with exhibits featuring furniture, arts, folklore costumes, medieval warfare, and minting. ⊠ *Hrad, Zámocká ul.,* ☎ *07/5311444.* 🖾 *40 Sk.* ☼ *Tues.–Sun. 10–5.*

NEED A
BREAK?
Snuggle up to a mug of beer or a glass of wine at **Judy's Gallery Bar** (⊠ Beblavého ul. 4, ☎ 07/516968) and contemplate the offbeat local art hanging from the walls. Judy's is open daily 4 PM to 1 AM.

OFF THE
BEATEN PATH
PETRŽALKA GARDENS – On a balmy summer's day you can take a short ferry ride to this pleasant park on the water. However, if you'd rather spend more time cruising the Danube, stay on the ferry and enjoy the 10-kilometer (6-mile) ride up the river. The ferry operates between April and October and costs 10 Sk.; the ferry offices are on Fajnorovo nábrežie near the Slovak National Museum.

13 **Jezuitský kostol** (Jesuit Church). This church was originally built by Protestants who, in 1636, were granted an imperial concession to build a place of worship on the strict condition that it have no tower. The Jesuits took over the towerless church in 1672 and to compensate for its external simplicity, went wild with baroque detailing on the inside. ⊠ *Hlavné nám.* ☼ *Service at 4:30.*

4 **Klariský kostol** (Klariský church). This 14th-century church is simple but inspiring, with a wonderfully peaceful early Gothic interior. The small High Gothic steeple was added in an unusually secondary position at the back of the church during the 15th century; as a mendicant order, the Poor Clares were forbidden to build a steeple atop the church, so they sidestepped the rules and built it against a side wall. Unfortunately, the church is now a concert hall—and usually locked, but you may be able to get in for a concert or during rehearsals. ⊠ *Farská ul.*

10 **Kostol kapucínov** (Capuchin Chapel). A pillar of Mary, which commemorates the plague, stands in front of this small chapel, dating from 1717. The baroque chapel is of little artistic interest, but its peaceful interior is always filled with worshipers—something not often seen in Bratislava. You can sneak a peek inside the chapel before or after the services held early in the morning or in the evening 5–7. ⊠ *Kapucínska ul.*

2 **Kostol svätej Trojice** (Church of the Holy Trinity). This golden-yellow baroque church has space-expanding frescoes on the ceiling, which are the work of Antonio Galli Bibiena in the early 18th century. ⊠ *Hurbanovo nám.* ☼ *Services at 9 AM and 6 PM.*

OFF THE
BEATEN PATH
DEVÍN – Just west of the city atop a hill overlooking both the Danube and the Morava rivers is the ruined castle of Devín. The oldest section of the present castle dates from the 13th century, but most of the castle was destroyed by Napoléon's soldiery in 1809. A reconstructed basement of the Renaissance palace houses a small but interesting historical exhibition. Take Bus 29 from under the Nový Most to Devín and follow the

marked path up the hill to the castle. ⊠ *Devín,* ☏ *07/776346.* ▣ *10 Sk.* ☉ *Tues.–Fri. 10–5.*

❸ Michalská brána (Michael's Gate). This is the last remaining of the city's three original gates. The bottom part of the adjoining tower, built in the 14th century, retains its original Gothic design; the octagonal section was added in the early 16th century; and the flamboyant, copper onion tower, topped with a statue of St. Michael, is an addition from the 18th century. A small museum—**Múzeum zbraní a mestského opevnenia** (Museum of Weapons and Fortifications)—is housed in the tower. The museum itself is not really worth a lot of time, but the *veža* (tower) has a good view over the city. ⊠ *Michalská veža, Michalská ul. 24,* ☏ *07/5333044.* ▣ *5 Sk.* ☉ *Wed.–Mon. 10–5.*

⓬ Mirbachov palác (Mirbach Palace). This rococo palace with original stucco decor was built in 1770. Today it houses the **Municipal Gallery,** which has a small collection of 18th- and 19th-century Slovak and European art. ⊠ *Františkánske nám.,* ☏ *07/5331556.* ▣ *10 Sk.* ☉ *Summer, Tues.–Sun. 10–6; winter, Tues.–Sun. 10–3.*

★ **❾ Museum of Jewish Culture in Slovakia.** This small but stirring museum is housed in a large, white mid-17th-century Renaissance mansion that's been reconstructed twice after fires in the 18th and 19th centuries. The exhibits celebrate the history and culture of the Jews living on the territory of Slovakia since the Great Moravian Empire. A section is devoted to the victims of the Holocaust in Slovakia. ⊠ *Židovská ul. 17,* ☏ *07/5318507.* ▣ *30 Sk.* ☉ *Sun.–Fri. 11–5.*

❽ Múzeum umeleckých remesiel (Handicraft Museum). In a baroque burgher house, this tiny museum displays a few nice works of arts and crafts from the 12th to 18th centuries, including ceramics, silverware, and furniture. ⊠ *Beblavého ul. 1.* ▣ *10 Sk.* ☉ *Wed.–Mon. 10–5.*

❶ Námestie SNP (SNP Square). The square, formerly known as Stalinovo námestie (Stalin Square), was and still remains the center for demonstrations in Slovakia.

OFF THE BEATEN PATH
SLAVÍN MEMORIAL – This group of socialist-realist statues is a monument to the 6,000 who died during the Soviet liberation of Bratislava in 1945. You can get a dose of Communist Bratislava seeing this memorial. Even if you're not interested in the sculpture, the monument has fine views over Bratislava. Take a taxi for about 200 Sk.; or ride Bus 27, 43, 47, or 104 (from Hodžovo námestie up from Námestie SNP) to Puškinová, where you can climb the many steps to the top.

❻ Nový Most (New Bridge). Although it would make a splendid sight for an alien flick, the modern bridge is a bit of an eyesore for anyone who doesn't appreciate futuristic designs. The bridge is difficult to miss if you're anywhere near the Danube River.

NEED A BREAK?
Unless you are squirmish about heights, have a coffee at the **Vyhliadková Kaviaren** (☏ 07/850042) on Nový Most. This spaceship-like café—reached via speedy glass-faced elevators for a minimal charge—is perched on top of pylons, 80 meters above the Danube River. One of Prague's English-language newspapers has dubbed the café's retro-Socialist interior *"Starship Enterprise-*gone-cocktail lounge." However you may feel about the architecture, it's not a bad place for a reasonable snack and an excellent view of the city. Be warned that during stronger winds the café does sway.

⑮ **Primaciálny palác** (Primates' Palace). This is one of the most valuable architectural monuments in Bratislava. Don't miss the dazzling Hall of Mirrors, with its six 17th-century English tapestries depicting the legend of the lovers Hero and Leander. In this room Napoléon and Hapsburg emperor Francis I signed the Bratislava Peace of 1805, following Napoléon's victory at the Battle of Austerlitz. In the revolutionary year of 1848, when the citizens of the Hapsburg lands revolted against the imperial dominance of Vienna, the rebel Hungarians had their headquarters in the palace; ironically, following the failed uprising, the Hapsburg general Hainau signed the rebels' death sentences in the very same room. ⊠ *Primaciálne nám. 1,* ☎ *07/5331473.* 🎟 *10 Sk.* ⊙ *Tues.–Sun. 10–5.*

⑰ **Reduta.** Bratislava's classical musical center, this extravagantly decorated building is home to the Slovak Philharmonic Orchestra. Built in neobaroque style but dating from 1914, the Reduta deserves a visit. ⊠ *Medená ul. 3,* ☎ *07/5333351.*

⑱ **Slovenská národná galéria** (Slovak National Gallery). This gallery is in a conspicuously modern restoration of old 18th-century barracks. However you feel about the strange additions to the old building, the museum itself has an interesting collection of Slovak Gothic, baroque, and contemporary art, along with a small number of European masters. ⊠ *Rázusovo nábrežie 2,* ☎ *07/5332081.* 🎟 *30 Sk.* ⊙ *Tues.–Sun. 10–6.*

⑯ **Slovenské národné divadlo** (Slovak National Theater). You can see performances of Bratislava's opera, ballet, and theater at this striking theater, which was built in the 1880s by the famous Central European architectural duo of Hermann Helmer and Ferdinand Fellner. If you get a feeling of déjà vu looking at the voluptuous neobaroque curves, it's not surprising: The two men also built opera houses in Vienna, Prague, and Karlovy Vary, to name but a few. Don't bother trying to tour the theater; buy a ticket to a performance instead. ⊠ *Hviezdoslavovo nám. 1,* ☎ *07/5330069 or 07/5321146.*

⑭ **Stará radnica** (Old Town Hall). One of the more interesting buildings in Bratislava, it developed gradually over the 13th and 14th centuries out of a number of burghers' houses. The imaginative roofing stems from the end of the 15th century, and the wall paintings from the 16th century. The strangely out-of-place baroque onion tower was a revision of the original tower. During the summer concerts are held here. You may want to stop in the **Mestské múzeum** (City Museum) here, which documents Bratislava's varied past. ⊠ *Primaciálne nám. 3,* ☎ *07/5334742.* 🎟 *10 Sk.* ⊙ *Tues.–Sun. 10–5.*

Dining

Prague may have its Slovak rival beat when it comes to architecture, but when it's time to eat, you can thank your lucky stars that you're in Bratislava. The long-shared history with Hungary gives Slovak cuisine an extra fire that Czech cooking admittedly lacks. Geographic proximity to Vienna, moreover, has lent something of grace and charm to the city's eateries. What does this add up to? You'll seldom see pork and dumplings on the menu. Instead, prepare for a variety of shish kebabs, grilled meats, steaks, and pork dishes, all spiced to warm the palate and served (if you're lucky) with those special noodles Slovaks call halušky. Wash it all down with a glass or two of red wine from nearby Modra or Pezinok.

The city's many street stands provide a price-conscious alternative to restaurant dining. In addition to the ubiquitous hot dogs and hamburgers (no relation to their American namesakes), try some *langoš*—flat, deep-fried, and delicious pieces of dough, usually seasoned with garlic.

$$$$ ✕ **Arkadia.** The elegant setting here, at the threshold to the castle, sets the tone for a luxurious evening. There are several dining rooms, ranging from intimate to more boisterous, all decorated with 19th-century furnishings. A standard repertoire of Slovak and international dishes, which include shish kebabs and steaks, is prepared to satisfaction. It is a 15-minute walk from the town center; take a taxi here and enjoy the mostly downhill walk back into town. ✉ *Zámocké schody,* ☎ 07/5335650. Jacket and tie. AE, DC, MC, V.

$$$$ ✕ **Rybársky cech.** The name means Fisherman's Guild, and fish is the unchallenged specialty at this refined but comfortable eatery on a quiet street by the Danube. Freshwater fish is served upstairs, with pricier saltwater varieties offered on the ground floor. ✉ *Žižkova 1,* ☎ 07/5313049. AE, DC, MC, V.

$$$ ✕ **Kláštorná vináreň.** In the wine cellar of a former monastery, this restau-
★ rant with its wine-barrel-shaped booths is pleasantly dark and intimate. The Hungarian-influenced spiciness of traditional Slovak cooking comes alive in such dishes as *Cíkos tókeň,* a fiery mixture of pork, onions, and peppers; or try the milder *Bravcové Ražnicí,* a tender pork shish kebab served with fried potatoes. ✉ *Frantíškanská ul.,* ☎ 07/5330430. No credit cards. Closed Sun.

$$$ ✕ **Veľkí Františkáni.** Housed in a beautiful 13th-century building, this wine cellar has a menu and an atmosphere similar to that at the Kláštorná (☞ *above*). However, the Veľkí's expansive dining area, which includes a garden patio, nurtures a more raucous, giddy clientele. Try one of the local specialties, *Prešporská Pochúdka* (sautéed beef with vegetables and potato pancakes). ✉ *Františkánske nám. 10,* ☎ 07/5333073. AE, MC, V.

$$ ✕ **Korzo.** Here you'll find delicious Slovak specialties—try a shish kebab or spicy grilled steak—served in a clean, cozy cellar setting. After dinner take a stroll along the Danube, right next door. The Korzo's ground-floor café is a great spot for people-watching or writing postcards. ✉ *Hviezdoslavovo nám. 11,* ☎ 07/5334974. No credit cards.

$$ ✕ **Modrá Hviezda.** The first of a new breed of small, family-owned wine
★ cellars, this popular eatery serves old Slovak specialties from the village as well as some imaginative dishes; try the sheep-cheese pie. ✉ *Beblavého 14,* ☎ 07/5332747. No credit cards. Closed Sun.

$$ ✕ **Pekná Brána.** With more than 75 main-course meals to choose
★ from, this is not the place to go if you have trouble making up your mind. The menu includes Chinese and vegetarian dishes and traditional Slovak cuisine. You can also dine in the cellar, which is open until sunrise. The restaurant is open daily 9 AM to midnight. ✉ *Obchodná ul. 39,* ☎ 07/5323008. AE, MC, V.

$$ ✕ **Spaghetti and Co.** This local representative of an American chain serves good pizzas and pasta in a pleasant, tourist-friendly setting—a godsend if you're traveling with children. The adjacent food court, right out of your local shopping mall, has booths selling Greek, Chinese, and health foods. ✉ *Gorkého l,* ☎ 07/5332303. No credit cards.

$ ✕ **Gremium.** This trendy restaurant caters to the coffee-and-cigarette crowd and to anyone in search of an uncomplicated light meal. Choose from a small menu of pastries, sandwiches, and some local specialties including *brynzové halušky* (tasty noodles with goat cheese) and *pytliacky guláš* (creamy goulash with halušky topped with blueberries)—though a bizarre combination, it's scrumptious. The regulars are mostly students or, owing to the proximity of a ceramics gallery, Bratislava's self-styled art crowd. ✉ *Gorkého 11,* ☎ 07/521818. Reservations not accepted. AE, MC, V.

$ ✕ **Stará Sladovňa.** To Bratislavans, this gargantuan beer hall is known
★ lovingly, and fittingly, as *mamut* (mammoth). Locals come here for the
Bohemian brews on tap, but it is also possible to get an inexpensive
and filling meal. ⊠ *Cintorínska 32,* ☎ *07/5321151. No credit cards.*

Lodging

The lodging situation in Bratislava is improving, though not fast enough
to rid the city of some pretty shabby establishments. The few decent
hotels that do exist are very expensive; the cheaper hotels tend to be
rundown and utterly depressing. However, small, privately owned hotels and pensions continue to materialize and put the old establishments
to shame. Make reservations in advance or arrive in Bratislava before
4 PM and ask tourist information (☞ Bratislava A to Z, *below*) for help
finding a room. If all decent hotels are booked, consider renting an apartment. Beware of individuals offering apartments at train stations, or you
may be going back home with a much lighter load.

$$$$ 🏨 **Danube.** Opened in 1992, this French-run hotel on the banks of the
★ Danube has quickly developed a reputation for superior facilities and
service. The modern rooms are decorated in pastel colors; the gleaming public areas are everything you expect from an international hotel
chain. ⊠ *Rybné nám. 1,* ☎ *07/5340833,* 🅵🅰🆇 *07/5314311. 280 rooms
with bath. 2 restaurants, pool, sauna, health club, nightclub, convention center. AE, DC, MC, V.*

$$$$ 🏨 **Forum.** If creature comforts are an important factor, the Forum is
for you. Bratislava's most expensive hotel, built in 1989 right in the center of town, offers a complete array of services and facilities. The staff
is efficient and friendly, and the functional rooms are pleasantly, if in-
nocuously, decorated. ⊠ *Hodžovo nám. 2,* ☎ *07/348111,* 🅵🅰🆇 *07/314645.
219 rooms with bath. 2 restaurants, 2 bars, 2 cafés, indoor pool, beauty
salon, sauna, health club, casino, nightclub. AE, DC, MC, V.*

$$$ 🏨 **Bratislava.** This bland but suitably clean cement-block hotel in the
suburb of Ružinov has rooms with televisions and private bathrooms.
It offers few facilities beyond a standard restaurant and lounge, but
there is a large department store nearby where you can stock up on
supplies. From the city center take Bus 34 or Tram 8. Breakfast is in-
cluded. ⊠ *Urxova ul. 9,* ☎ *07/239000,* 🅵🅰🆇 *07/236420. 344 rooms with
bath. Restaurant, lobby lounge, snack bar. AE, DC, MC, V.*

$$$ 🏨 **Devín.** This boxy 1950s hotel set on the banks of the Danube has
managed to create an air of elegance in its reception area that doesn't
translate into much else, despite its five-star status. The furniture is poorly
arranged in the small rooms, and the service is on the gruff side. Nevertheless, the hotel is clean, with a variety of restaurants and cafés that
serve dependably satisfying food; breakfast is included. ⊠ *Riečna ul.
4,* ☎ *07/5330851,* 🅵🅰🆇 *07/5330682. 98 rooms with bath. 3 restaurants,
2 bars, café. AE, DC, MC, V.*

$$$ 🏨 **Hotel Pension No. 16.** This cozy pension in a quiet residential haven
★ close to the castle is a nice alternative to the big chain hotels—it pro-
vides all the conveniences, but with character. The apartments are suit-
able for families; breakfast is included. ⊠ *Partizánska ul. 16,* ☎
07/5311672, 🅵🅰🆇 *07/5311298. 10 rooms with bath, 5 apartments. Kitch-
enettes. AE, MC, V.*

$$$ 🏨 **Perugia.** Finished in 1993, this stunning postmodern jewel is in a
renovated building in the center of Old Town. The light and airy in-
terior contrasts sharply with the dark, drab ones of many of the city's
buildings. The clean, colorful rooms are an eye-opener. Breakfast is included. ⊠ *Zelená 5,* ☎ *07/5331818.* 🅵🅰🆇 *07/5331821. 11 rooms with
bath. Restaurant. AE, DC, MC, V.*

$$ 🏨 **Hotel Echo.** This small, pink, modern hotel, not far from the center of Bratislava, looks more like a health club than a hotel, but it's a great place to stay, especially if you have a car. It has a friendly staff, large bright rooms—and a great breakfast, which is included in the price of a room. ✉ *Presovská ul. 39,* ☎ *07/329170,* 🅵🅰🆇 *07/329174. Restaurant. MC, V.*

Nightlife and the Arts

Nightlife

BARS AND LOUNGES

Bratislava doesn't offer much in the way of bars and lounges; after-dinner drinking takes place mostly in wine cellars and beer halls. Two of the former are **Kláštorná vináreň** or **Veľkí Františkáni** (☞ Dining, *above*), both in vaulted, medieval cellars. For beer swilling, the best address in town is the mammoth **Stará Sladovňa** (☞ Dining, *above*).

JAZZ CLUBS

Bratislava hosts an annual jazz festival in the fall, but the city lacks a good venue for regular jazz gigs. That said, **Mefisto Club** (✉ Panenska 24, no phone) occasionally features local jazz acts.

ROCK CLUBS

Bratislava's live-music and club scene is expanding; new bands, running the spectrum from folk and rock to rap, are constantly turning up. The venues are changing just as rapidly; check the English-language *Slovak Spectator,* a Bratislava-based newspaper with regular features on the city's cultural life, for the lowdown on the latest clubs. Dependable hot spots are the **Rock Fabrik Danubius** (✉ Komanárska ul. 3, no phone), featuring loud and sweaty Czech and Slovak acts nightly; and the **U Club** (✉ Pod Hradom ul., no phone), where hard-core rock can be fun if you're into that sort of thing.

The Arts

Bratislava does not have a roaring nightlife scene so stick to the classics. The celebrated **Slovak Philharmonic Orchestra** plays regularly throughout the year, and chamber-music concerts are held at irregular intervals in the stunning Gothic **Church of the Poor Clares.** In summer the Renaissance courtyard of the **Old Town Hall** is also used for concerts. Slovenské národné divadlo offers high quality opera and ballet performances at bargain prices. Call BIS or Satur (☞ Bratislava A to Z, *below*) for program details and tickets; the *Slovak Spectator* is another good source for information.

CONCERTS

The **Slovak Philharmonic Orchestra** plays a full program, featuring Czech and Slovak composers as well as European masters, at its home in the Reduta. ✉ *Medená 3,* ☎ *07/5333351. Buy tickets at the theater box office (*☉ *Weekdays 1–5).*

FILM

Most new releases are shown in their original language with Slovak subtitles. **Charlie Centrum** regularly shows American classics, in English, in a friendly, artsy environment. ✉ *Špitálska 4,* ☎ *07/363430.*

OPERA AND BALLET

The **Slovenské národné divadlo** (Slovak National Theater) is the place for high-quality opera and ballet. Buy tickets at the theater office on the corner of Jesenského and Komenského streets weekdays between noon and 6 PM or 30 minutes before showtime. ✉ *Hviezdoslavovo nám. 1,* ☎ *07/5321146.*

THEATER

Traditional theater is usually performed in Slovak and is therefore incomprehensible to most visitors. For non-Slovak speakers, the **Stoka Theater** blends nontraditional theater with performance art in a provocative and entertaining way. For details, contact the theater box office. ⊠ *Pribinova 1,* ☎ *07/364961.*

Shopping

Bratislava is an excellent place to find Slovak arts and crafts of all types. You will find plenty of folk-art and souvenir shops along **Obchodná ulica** (Shopping Street) as well as on **Námestie SNP.** Stores still come and go in this rapidly changing city, so don't be too surprised if some of the listed stores have vanished.

Antikvariat Steiner. This shop stocks beautiful old books, maps, graphics, and posters. ⊠ *Venturská ul. 20,* ☎ *07/52834.*

Dielo. This large store (☞ Pleasures and Pastimes, *above*) has designer jewelry and clothing in addition to very unusual and fun ceramic pieces and other works of art. ⊠ *Námestie SNP 12,* ☎ *07/5334568. Two smaller locations are:* ⊠ *Obchodná ul. 27,* ☎ *07/5334568, and* ⊠ *Obchodná 33,* ☎ *07/5330688.*

Folk, Folk. Here you'll find a large collection of Slovak folk art, including pottery, handwoven tablecloths, wooden toys, and dolls with Slovak folk costumes. ⊠ *Obchodná ul. 10,* ☎ *07/5334292.*

Folk Art. This spot has a nice selection of hand-painted table pottery and vases, wooden figures, and village folk clothing and numerous types of small corn-husk figures, which are dirt cheap and can be very beautiful, though not easy to transport. ⊠ *Námestie SNP 12,* ☎ *07/323802.*

Gremium Café. Try here for original pieces of art and pottery. ⊠ *Gorkého 11,* ☎ *07/51818.*

Bratislava A to Z

Arriving and Departing

BY BOAT

Hydrofoils travel the Danube between Vienna and Bratislava from April to December. Boats depart in the morning from Bratislava, on the eastern bank of the Danube just down from the Devin Hotel, and return from Vienna in the evening. Tickets cost $40–$70 per person and should be purchased in person at the dock.

BY BUS

There are numerous buses from Prague to Bratislava; the five-hour journey costs around 250 Sk. From Vienna, there are four buses a day from Autobusbahnhof Wien Mitte. The journey takes 1½–2 hours and costs about AS150. Bratislava's main bus terminal, **Autobus Stanica,** is roughly 2 kilometers (1¼ miles) from the city center; to get downtown, take Trolley (*trolej*) 217 to Mierové námestie or Bus 107 to the castle (*hrad*); or flag down a taxi.

BY CAR

There are good freeways from Prague to Bratislava via Brno (D1 and D2); the 325-kilometer (202-mile) journey takes about 3½ hours. From Vienna, take the A4 and then Route 8 to Bratislava, just across the border. Depending on the traffic at the border, the 60-kilometer (37-mile) journey should take about 1½ hours.

BY PLANE

Although few international airlines provide direct service to Bratislava, **ČSA** (☎ 07/361042 or 07/361045), the Czech and Slovak national carrier, offers frequent connections to Bratislava via Prague. You can also fly into Vienna's Schwechat Airport, about 50 kilometers (30 miles) to the west, and proceed to Bratislava by either bus or train—a one-hour journey.

BY TRAIN

Reasonably efficient train service regularly connects Prague and Bratislava. Trains leave from Prague's Hlavní nádraží (main station) or from Holešovice station, and the journey takes five to six hours. The Intercity trains are slightly more expensive but faster. From Vienna, four trains daily make the one-hour trek to Bratislava. Bratislava's train station, **Hlavná Stanica,** is about 2 kilometers (1¼ miles) from the city center; to travel downtown from the station, take Streetcar 1 or 13 to Poštová ulica or jump in a taxi.

Getting Around

Bratislava is compact, and most sights can be covered easily on foot. Taxis are reasonably priced and easy to hail; at night, they are the best option for returning home from wine cellars and clubs.

BY BUS AND TRAM

Buses and trams in Bratislava run frequently and connect the city center with outlying sights. Tickets cost 5 Sk. and are available from large hotels, news agents, and tobacconists. Validate tickets on board (watch how the locals do it). The fine for riding without a validated ticket is 200 Sk., payable on the spot.

BY TAXI

Meters start at 10 Sk. and jump 10 Sk. per kilometer (½ mile). The number of dishonest cabbies, sadly, is on the rise; to avoid being ripped off, watch to see that the driver engages the meter. If the meter is broken, negotiate a price with the driver before even getting in the cab. Taxis are hailable on the street, or call 07/311311.

Contacts and Resources

EMBASSIES

United States: ✉ Hviezdoslavovo 4, ☎ 07/5330861. **British:** ✉ Grösslingova 35, ☎ 07/364420.

EMERGENCIES

Police: ☎ 158. **Ambulance:** ☎ 155.

ENGLISH-LANGUAGE BOOKSTORES

Several Slovak bookstores stock English-language titles. Try **Big Ben Bookshop** (✉ Michalská 1, ☎ 07/5333632) or the beautiful second-hand bookstore **Antikvariat Steiner** (✉ Venturská ul. 20, ☎ 07/52834). A small magazine shop at Laurinská 9 is a good source for English-language newspapers and periodicals. The well-stocked reading room of the U.S. Embassy (☞ *above*) is open to the general public Tuesday through Friday 9 to 2 and Monday noon to 5. Bring a passport.

GUIDED TOURS

The best tours of Bratislava are offered by **BIS** (☞ Visitor Information, *below*), although tours during the off-season are conducted in German and only on weekends. Tours typically take two hours and cost 270 Sk. per person. **Satur** (☞ Visitor Information, *below*) also offers tours of the capital from May through September. You can sometimes combine these with an afternoon excursion through the Small Carpathian Mountains, including dinner at the Zochová chata.

The pharmacy at Špitálska 3, near the Old Town, maintains 24-hour service; other pharmacies hold late hours on a rotating basis.

Tatratur (✉ Bajkalská 25, ☎ 07/5233259 or 07/5211219, FAX 07/5213624) is a large, dependable agency that can help arrange sightseeing tours throughout Slovakia. Its office at Františkánske námestie 7 (☎ 07/335012) also acts as an official representative of American Express in Slovakia. **Satur** (☞ *below*) can also provide basic travel-agency services, such as changing traveler's checks and booking bus and train tickets to outside destinations.

Bratislava's tourist information service, **Bratislavská Informačná Služba** (BIS; ✉ Panská 18, ☎ 07/5333715 or 07/5334370), can assist in finding a hotel or private accommodation. The office, open weekdays 8 to 4:30 (until 6 in summer) and Saturday 8 to 1, is also a good source for maps and basic information. If you are arriving by train, the small **BIS** office in the station, open daily 8 to 8, can be very helpful.

The country's national travel agency **Satur Tours and Travel** (formerly known as Čedok; ✉ Jesenského 5, ☎ 07/367613 or 07/367624, FAX 07/323816; ✆ Weekdays 9 to 6, Sat. 9 to noon) can help find accommodations in one of its hotels across the country and can book air, rail, and bus tickets.

SIDE TRIPS FROM BRATISLAVA

The Wine Country

Much of the country's best wine is produced within a 30-minute drive of Bratislava, in a lovely mountainous region that offers a respite from the noise and grime of the capital. Two neighboring towns, Pezinok and Modra, vie for the distinction of being Slovakia's wine capital.

Pezinok, the larger of the two, is home to the Small Carpathian vineyards, the country's largest wine producer. In this quaint, red-roofed town you can find enough to keep you busy for an entire day without ever stepping off its busy main street, Stefanika ulica. Take in the wine-making exhibits at the **Malokarpatksé muzeum** (Small Carpathian Museum, ✉ Stefanika ul.), closed Monday, and then head next door to the outstanding bakery. Leave some room for lunch at the **Zámocka wine cellar,** open daily 11–11, in the town's castle at the end of the street. The castle also serves as a winery; around the side you'll find a sales counter offering a variety of locally produced wines.

Modra is a typical one-horse town, with some pretty folk architecture and a few comfortable wine gardens. Combine a visit here with a night at the nearby Zochová Chata (☞ Lodging, *below*).

The Renaissance castle **Červený Kameň** (Red Rock) is a great hiking destination from Modra. You can begin the trail at Zochová Chata. On the prettier yellow-marked trail, the walk takes upwards of 2½ hours; on the blue-and-green trail, around 1½ hours. You can visit the most fascinating parts of the structure with a guide. These include the vast storage and wine cellars, with their movable floors and high, arched ceilings, and the bastions, constructed with an intricate ventilation system and hidden passageways in the middle of the thick slate walls. ✉ 10 Sk. ✆ May–Oct., daily 11–3; Nov.–Apr., Tues.–Sun. 11–3. Tours on the hr.

Dining and Lodging

$$ ✕⛺ **Zochová Chata.** This attractive 1920s-style hunting chalet near
★ Modra, 32 kilometers (20 miles) outside Bratislava, is a comfortable al-
ternative to the latter's large luxury hotels. The rooms here are small but
very comfortable, and the food served in the adjoining tavern a few doors
down is top-rate. ✉ *Modra-Piesok,* ☎ *070492/2956,* ℻ *070492/2991.*
10 rooms with bath. Restaurant, wine tavern. No credit cards.

The Wine Country A to Z

ARRIVING AND DEPARTING

Infrequent buses link Bratislava with Modra and Pezinok; most leave
early in the morning, so contact **ČSAD** (Bratislava, ☎ 07/63213), the
national bus carrier, at least a day in advance. By car from Bratislava,
take Route 502, 4 kilometers (2½ miles) past the village of Jur pri
Bratislave, and turn right down a smaller road in the direction of the
villages Slovenský Grob and Viničné. At the latter, turn left onto Route
503 to reach Pezinok, a few kilometers beyond. Modra lies 4 kilome-
ters (2½ miles) farther along the same road.

Trnava

19 *45 km (28 mi) from Bratislava on the D61 highway.*

Trnava, with its silhouette of spires and towers, is the oldest town in
Slovakia; it received royal town rights in 1238. Trnava was the main
seat of the Hungarian archbishop until 1821 and a principal Hungar-
ian university center during the 17th and 18th centuries, until Maria
Theresa shifted the scholarly crowd to Budapest. That Trnava's "golden
age" coincided with the baroque period is readily apparent in its ar-
chitecture, beneath the neglected facades and pervasive industrial
decay. Look for the enormous **University Church of John the Baptist,**
designed by Italian baroque architects, with fabulous carved-wood al-
tars. Look for **St. Nicholas Cathedral,** which dominates the town with
its large onion towers.

Trnava A to Z

ARRIVING AND DEPARTING

Bratislava and Trnava are connected by frequent bus and train service.

CONTACTS AND RESOURCES

For tourist and lodging information contact the **Trnavský Informačný
Servis.** ✉ *Trojičné nám. 1,* ☎ *0805/20203,* ℻ *0805/42268.* ☉
June–Sept., weekdays 8–7, weekends 10–6; Oct.–May, daily 10–6.

THE HIGH TATRAS

Visiting the *Vysoké Tatry* (High Tatras) alone would make a trip to
Slovakia worthwhile. Although the range is relatively compact as
mountains go (just 32 kilometers, or 20 miles, from end to end), its
peaks seem wilder and more starkly beautiful than even those of Eu-
rope's other great range, the Alps. Some 20 Tatras peaks exceed 8,000
feet, with the highest Gerlachovský Štít at 8,710 feet. The 35 moun-
tain lakes are remote and clear and, according to legend, can impart
the ability to see through doors and walls to anyone who bathes in them;
however, they are also very cold, sometimes eerily deep, and swimming
is not permitted in the cold glacier lakes of the Tatras.

Man is a relative latecomer to the Tatras. The region's first town,
Schmecks (today Starý Smokovec), was founded in the late 18th cen-
tury, and regular visitors began coming here only after 1871, with the
construction of a mountain railroad linking the resort to the bustling
junction town of Poprad. In the late 19th and early 20th centuries, with

the founding of Štrbské pleso and Tatranská Lomnica, the Tatras finally came into their own as an elegant playground for Europe's elite.

But the post–World War II Communist era was hard on the Tatras. Almost overnight, the area became a mass resort for the mountain-starved, fenced-in peoples of the Eastern bloc, prompting much development and commercialization. But don't despair: The faded elegance of these mountain retreats and spa resorts remains intact, despite the sometimes heavy winter- and summertime crowds.

Most of the tourist facilities in the High Tatras are concentrated in three neighboring resort towns: Štrbské pleso to the west, Smokovec in the middle, and Tatranská Lomnica to the east. Each town is pretty similar in terms of convenience and atmosphere, and all provide easy passage to the hills, so it makes little difference where you choose to begin you explorations of the mountains.

Finding a satisfying meal in the Tatras is about as tough as making the 1,000-foot climb from Starý Smokovec to Hrebienok, especially in the fall when some restaurants close completely. The good news is that a couple of entrepreneurs have recently jumped on the opportunity and created the best places to eat in the region. Don't leave the Tatras without eating in one of the restaurants with an open-face grill. An alternative to the restaurants are local grocery stores—try the one in Starý Smokovec—which stock basic sandwich fixings.

If you are looking to splurge on accommodations, you'll find no better place than the Tatras. In older hotels, ask to see several rooms before selecting one, as room interiors can be quite quirky. Prices are highest in January and February, when there is snow on the ground. They are lower during the off-season (late fall and early spring), but the mountains are just as beautiful.

Hiking

The best way to see these beautiful mountains is on foot. Three of the best Tatras walks (three to five hours each) are outlined below, arranged according to difficulty (with the easiest and prettiest first), although a reasonably fit person of any age will have little trouble with any of the three. Yet even though the trails are well marked, it is very important to buy a walking map of the area—the detailed *Vysoké Tatry, Letná Turistická Mapa* is available for around 20 Sk. at newspaper kiosks. If you're planning to take any of the higher-level walks, be sure to wear proper shoes with good ankle support. Also use extreme caution in early spring, when melting snow can turn the trails into icy rivers. And don't forget drinking water, sunglasses, and sunscreen.

Since the entire area is a national park, the trails are well marked in different colors. Mountain climbers who do not want a guide have to be members of a climbing club. There are climbs of all levels of difficulty (although Grade 1 climbs may be used only as starting points), the best are the west wall of **Lomnický Štít,** the north wall of the **Kežmarský Štít,** and the **Široká veža.**

Skiing

The entire region is crisscrossed with paths ideal for cross-country skiing. You can buy a special ski map at newspaper kiosks. The season lasts from the end of December through April, though the best months are traditionally January and February. Renting ski equipment is not much of a problem, and it is reasonably priced. Ždiar, toward the Polish border, has a good ski area for beginners.

Numbers in the margin correspond to numbers on the Slovakia map.

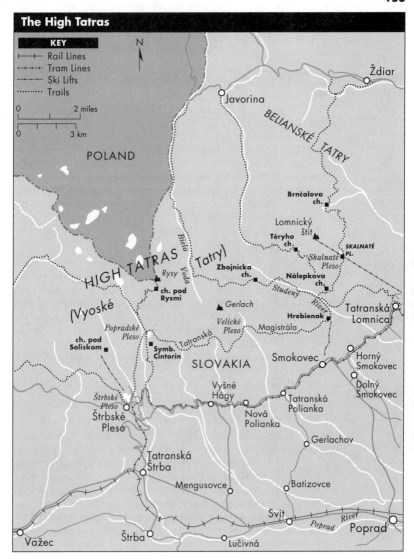

The High Tatras

KEY
- ┼──┼ Rail Lines
- ┼─┼─┼ Tram Lines
- ┼─·─┼ Ski Lifts
- ·········· Trails

0 ——— 2 miles
0 ——— 3 km

POLAND

HIGH TATRAS (Vyoské Tatry)

BELIANSKÉ TATRY

Žďiar

Javorina

Brnčalova ch.

Lomnický štít

Téryho ch.

SKALNATÉ PL.

Skalnaté Pleso

Zbojnicka ch.

Rysy

ch. pod Rysmi

Biela Voda

Nálepkova ch.

Gerlach

Studený River

Tatranská Lomnica

Velické Pleso

Hrebienok

Magistrála

Popradské Pleso

ch. pod Soliskom

Symb. Cintorin

Tatranská

SLOVAKIA

Smokovec

Horný Smokovec

Dolný Smokovec

Štrbské Pleso

Vyšné Hágy

Tatranská Polianka

Nová Polianka

Gerlachov

Tatranská Štrba

Mengusovce

Batizovce

Svit

Poprad River

Poprad

Važec

Štrba

Lučivná

Poprad

㉕ *329 km (204 mi) east of Bratislava along Highways E75 and E50.*

Poprad, the gateway to the Tatras, is a good place to begin exploring the region. But don't expect a beautiful mountain village. Poprad fell victim to some of the most insensitive Communist planning perpetrated in the country after the war, and as a result you'll see little more than row after row of apartment blocks, interspersed with factories and power plants. There's no need to linger here. Instead, drive or take the electric railroad to the superior sights and facilities of the more rugged resorts just over 30 kilometers (20 miles) to the north.

Dining and Lodging

$ ✕ **Slovenská Reštauracia.** If you have to spend a few hours in Poprad,
★ having a meal in this charming rustic restaurant is the best way of doing so. Try the *brynzové halušky* (dumplings with goat cheese) or *strapačky skapustou* (homemade noodles with sauerkraut). The English version

of the menu translates some of these delightful items as balls, bags, and pillows, but don't get frightened off—they really are delicious. ✉ *Ul. 1 May 216,* ☎ *092/722870. No credit cards.*

$$ 🏨 **Gerlach.** This modern structure a couple of blocks away from the station is as dreary as Poprad itself. The rooms are cheerier than the public areas, but the bathrooms are only just acceptable. If you're not satisfied with your room, ask to see an apartment (about double the standard room price). One is attractively, if incongruously, decorated with antique furniture. ✉ *Hviezdoslavova ul. 3,* ☎ *092/721945,* ℻ *092/63663. 120 rooms, most with bath. Restaurant, café, barbershop. No credit cards.*

$ 🏨 **Europa.** This cozy little hotel is next to the train station. From the reception area to the modest, old-fashioned rooms (with neither bathrooms nor TVs), the place exudes a faint elegance. In season, the bar and restaurant on the ground floor buzz with activity in the evenings. ✉ *Wolkerová ul.,* ☎ *092/721883. 50 rooms without bath. Restaurant, bar. No credit cards.*

En Route   A kilometer and a half (1 mile) northeast of Poprad is the medieval hamlet of **Spišská Sobota,** now a suburb of Poprad but formerly one of the main centers of the historic Spiš Empire. Sobota's lovely old square features a Romanesque church, rebuilt in Gothic style in the early 16th century, with an ornate altar carved by master Pavol of Levoča. The Renaissance belfry dates from the end of the 16th century. The square itself is a nearly perfect ensemble of Renaissance houses. But the most impressive of all is the setting, a 16th-century oasis amid the cultural desert of socialist realism.

Smokovec

㉑ *32 km (20 mi) north of Poprad.*

The first town you'll reach by road or rail from Poprad is Smokovec, the undisputed center of the Slovak Tatras resorts and the major bene-ficiary of postwar development. Smokovec is divided into two principal areas, Starý Smokovec (Old Smokovec) and Nový Smokovec (New Smokovec), which are within a stone's throw of each other. Stay in Starý Smokovec if you want to be near grocery stores, bars, and the local Satur office. The town is also a good starting point for many mountain ex-cursions (from here, for example, a funicular can take you the 4,144 feet up to Hrebienok and its many marked trails).

The Tatras are tailor-made for hikers of all levels. The best way to take in the scenery, of course, is on foot. **Starý Smokovec** is a great start-ing point for a trek that parallels a cascading waterfall for much of its three-hour length. From Starý Smokovec, walk out along the main road in the direction of Tatranská Lomnica for roughly 1 kilometer (½ mile). In Tatranská Lesná, follow the yellow-marked path that winds gently uphill through the pines and alongside a swift-running stream. In winter the walk is particularly lovely; the occasional burst of sun-shine warms your cheeks and transforms the cold running water to a tropical blue-green.

Farther along there are red markers leading to the funicular at Hrebi-enok, which brings you back to the relative comforts of Starý Smokovec. However, if you're in good physical shape and there is *plenty* of daylight left, consider extending your hike by four hours. (The extension is strik-ing, but avoid it during winter, when you may find yourself neck-deep in snow). Just before the Bilková chata, turn right along the green path and then follow the blue, red, and then green trails in the direction of windswept **Tery chata,** a turn-of-the-century chalet perched amid five lonely alpine lakes. The scenery is a few notches above dazzling. Once you reach the chalet after two strenuous hours of hiking, backtrack to Bilková chata and follow the signs to the funicular at Hrebienok.

A more adventurous and rigorous five-hour walk starts in Starý Smokovec behind and to the west of the Grand Hotel (☞ *below*). Begin by ascending to the tree line along the blue path. Thirty minutes of up-hill hiking will take you to the Magistrale Trail; follow the trail to the left, and after 20 minutes or so of moderate climbing, the trees thin out—leaving nothing but dwarf pines, rocks, and breathtaking peaks.

Sliezsky Dom, a 1960s cookie-cutter prefab (surely Slovakia's highest-elevation housing project), lies an hour down the trail. Forgive the building's architectural sins and head inside for a cup of tea and a bite to eat. The descent to Starý Smokovec along the green and then yellow trails is long and peaceful: Nothing breaks the silence save the snapping of twigs or, in winter, the crunch of snow underfoot.

Dining and Lodging

$$ ✕ **Restaurant Koliba.** This charming restaurant with rustic decor and
★ an open-face grill serves up tasty local fare. Try *kapustová polievka,* sauerkraut soup with mushrooms and sausage. If you're lucky, you may get serenaded by a local Gypsy band that plays here most nights. ☒ *Starý Smokovec,* ☎ *0969/2204. No credit cards. Closed Sun.*

$$ ✕🏨 **Villa Dr. Szontagh.** Away from the action in Nový Smokovec, this
★ steepled little chalet offers mostly peace and quiet. The darkly furnished rooms and public areas are well maintained, and the courtly staff goes out of its way to please. The decent restaurant has an extensive wine cellar. ☒ *Nový Smokovec,* ☎ *0969/2061,* ℻ *0969/2062. 11 rooms with bath. Restaurant, wine cellar. No credit cards. Closed Dec.*

$$$ 🏨 **Bellevue.** This modern hotel, just outside Starý Smokovec along the road to Tatranská Lomnica, lacks the atmosphere of the Grand (☞ *below*) but nevertheless offers top services and clean, functional rooms. However, you'll be a good 15-minute walk away from Starý Smokovec's grocers and bars. Breakfast is included with your room. For skiers and sports enthusiasts, a sporting-goods rental shop is right next door. ☒ *Starý Smokovec,* ☎ *0969/2941,* ℻ *0969/2719. 110 rooms with bath. Restaurant, pool. AE, DC, MC, V.*

$$$ 🏨 **Grand Hotel.** Along with its sister hotel in Tatranská Lomnica
★ (Grandhotel Praha), this hotel epitomizes Tatra luxury at its turn-of-the-century best. The hotel's golden Tudor facade rises majestically over the town of Starý Smokovec, with the peaks of the Tatras looming in the background. The location, at the commercial and sports center of the region, is a mixed blessing. In season, skiers and hikers crowd the reception area, and the hallways are filled with guests and visitors alike. The rooms themselves are quiet. Breakfast is included. ☒ *Starý Smokovec,* ☎ *0969/2154,* ℻ *0969/2157. 83 rooms with bath. Restaurant, café, pool, sauna. AE, DC, MC, V.*

Outdoor Activities and Sports

PARAGLIDING

Local sports shops provide equipment for many sports, including paragliding and paraskiing. The rates, surprisingly, are very reasonable. For information, consult the sporting-goods store, **Športcentrumin** (☒ Pekná vyhliadka, ☎ 0969/2953), in Horný Smokovec. It's a 10-minute walk along the highway, to the east of Starý Smokovec.

SKIING

For renting equipment, try the **Sport Centrum** (☏ 0969/2953) in Horný Smokovec or the Ski Service in the **Švajčiarský Dom,** next to the Grand Hotel (☞ *above*), open 8 to noon and 12:30 to 4. Arrive early—the equipment rents quickly when it snows. You can buy skis and equipment at the **Mladosť** department store in Starý Smokovec.

SLEDDING

🐧 If there's snow on the ground and the children are too young to ski, you'll find a good sledding slope at **Hrebienok,** just above Starý Smokovec. To get here, take the funicular from behind the Grand Hotel; you can rent sleds from the Ski Service near the Grand or purchase them for 200 Sk.–300 Sk. from local sporting-goods stores.

Shopping

The Tatras resorts are short on shopping places. Still, you'll find good-quality, reasonably priced hiking and camping equipment at several sporting-goods stores and at the **Mladosť** store in Starý Smokovec.

Štrbské Pleso

㉒ *18 km (11 mi) west of Smokovec.*

Štrbské pleso is the main center in the Tatras for active sports. As such, it's best suited for skiers and those who thrive on crowds and commotion. The best ski slopes are not far away, and the fine mountain lake is a perfect backdrop for a leisurely stroll—many excellent hiking trails are within easy reach, too. As for facilities, the town has not only the most modern hotels but also the most jarringly modern hotel architecture. This large resort presides over the finest panoramas in the Tatras. For a breathtaking view of the valley and mountains, head for the lawn of the town's sanatorium.

Dining and Lodging

$$$ ✕▦ **Panoráma.** The architects of Štrbské pleso must have had a ball designing hotels. This one, built in the 1960s, resembles an upside-down staircase. The rooms are small and plain, with clean bathrooms. What is special, though, is the truly panoramic view of the High and Low Tatras. Nevertheless, the public areas are unimpressive, and the hotel is too expensive for what it offers. The cozy wine cellar, Cengálka, is worth a visit. ⊠ *Across from bus and rail station,* ☏ *0969/92111,* 🆎 *0969/92810. 96 rooms with bath. Restaurant, bar. AE, DC, MC, V.*

$$$ ▦ **Patria.** This modern, slanting pyramid on the shores of a mountain
★ lake has two obvious advantages: location and view. Ask for a room on a higher floor; those overlooking the lake have balconies, and the other side opens onto the mountains. The rooms are functional, bright, and clean. Sadly, the hotel managers have opted for darker interiors in the public areas (except for the top-floor restaurant), with thick blinds that block out the marvelous view. Don't bother trying the Slovenka tavern on the side of the hotel—both the food and the atmosphere are abominable. ⊠ *Štrbské pleso,* ☏ *0969/92591,* 🆎 *0969/92590. 150 rooms with bath. 3 restaurants, café. AE, DC, MC, V.*

$$ ▦ **Fis.** Right next to the ski jump, within easy reach of several slopes, this hotel is for young, athletic types. It makes no pretense to elegance, preferring a busy jumble of track suits, families with young children, and teenagers on the make. The rooms, each with a balcony, are pleasant if a little institutional. The hotel also has bungalows for rent. ⊠ *Štrbské pleso,* ☏ *0969/92221,* 🆎 *0969/92422. 2 restaurants, pool, sauna, exercise room. No credit cards.*

Nightlife and the Arts

Despite the crowds, nightlife in the Tatras is usually little more than a good meal and an evening stroll before bed. The best option is an evening at one of the small rustic restaurants listening to a live Gypsy band. For discos, check out the **Patria** and **Panoráma** hotels (☞ *above*).

Outdoor Activities and Sports

SKIING

You can buy skis and equipment, plus a thousand other things, in the department store **Javor** (☎ 0969/92835). The **Patria Hotel** (☞ *above*) also rents skis.

SLEDDING

There is a gentle slope for sledding at the Hotel Fis (☞ *above*). Although there is no place to rent sleds, you can buy one (or an easily transportable rubber coaster) at any department store.

Tatranská Lomnica

㉓ *16 km (10 mi) southwest of Štrbské pleso.*

Tatranská Lomnica, on the eastern end of the electric rail line, offers a near-perfect combination of peace, convenience, and atmosphere. Spread out and relatively remote, the town is frequently overlooked by the masses of students and merrymakers, so it has been more successful in retaining a feel of "exclusivity" without being any more expensive than the other towns. Moreover, the lift behind the Grandhotel Praha brings some of the best walks in the Tatras to within 10 minutes or so of your hotel door.

If you want to brush up on the area's varied flora and fauna, visit the ☺ **Museum Tatranského Národného Parku** (Museum of the Tatras National Park). Children will love the startlingly realistic stuffed animals on the first floor. The upper floor documents the life of local peasants, who still wear vibrantly colored traditional dress in many villages.⊠ *Tatranská Lomnica,* ☎ *0969/96795.* ▨ *10 Sk.* ☉ *Weekdays 8:30–1 and 2–5; weekends 9–noon.*

The **Magistrale,** a 24-kilometer (15-mile) walking trail that skirts the peaks just above the tree line, offers some of the best views for the least amount of exertion. A particularly stunning stretch of the route— which is marked by red signposts—begins in Tatranská Lomnica and ends 5 kilometers (3 miles) away in Starý Smokovec. The total walking time is three or four hours.

To start the walk, take the aerial gondola behind the Grandhotel Praha in Tatranská Lomnica to Skalnaté pleso—a 10-minute proposition. From here you can access the trail immediately; or if you are really adventurous, consider a 30-minute detour via cable car (25 Sk.) to the top of Lomnický Štít (8,635 feet), the second-highest peak in the range. Because of the harsh temperatures (be sure to dress warmly even in summer) you're permitted to linger at the top for only 30 minutes, after which you take the cable car back down.

Return to the cable-car station at Skalnaté pleso and follow the red markers of the Magistrale Trail to the right (as you stand facing Tatranská Lomnica below). The first section of the trail cuts sharply across the face of the Lomnický Mountain just above the tree line. Note the little dwarf pines to the right and left of the trail. The trail then bends around to the right and again to the left through a series of small valleys, each view more outstanding than the last. Finally, you'll begin a small descent into the woods. Continue by following the signs to Hrebienok.

NEED A
BREAK?

Don't pass up the chance to have a snack and a hot or cold drink at the rustic **Bilková Chata** (☎ 0969/2266) in a little clearing just before you reach Hrebienok. This cozy cabin is a veritable oasis after the long walk. It's open 7 AM to 8 PM.

From Hrebienok, take the funicular down to Starý Smokovec. It runs at 45-minute intervals beginning at 6:30 AM and ending at 7:45 PM, but check the schedule posted at the Bilková Chata for any schedule changes. The funicular drops you off in the center of Starý Smokovec, just behind the Grand Hotel close to the electric rail, which connects all the resort towns and can take you back to Tatranská Lomnica.

Dining and Lodging

$$ ✕ **Zbojnická Koliba.** This stylish cottage restaurant serves up savory shish kebab made on an open-face grill in a romantic setting, though the portions are snack-size. Stock up on the tasty bread and cheese appetizers. ⊠ *Tatranská Lomnica,* ☎ *0969/967630. No credit cards. Closed Sun. No lunch.*

$$$ ✕▥ **Grandhotel Praha.** This large, multiturreted mansion, dating from
★   the turn of the century and resting in the foothills of the Lomnický Ştít, is one of the wonders of the Tatras. Although it is no longer filled with the rich and famous, the hotel has managed to retain an air of relaxed elegance. The staff is polite and attentive. The rooms are large and nicely decorated—ask for a large corner room with a view of the mountains. Since the hotel is far from the action, the price remains reasonable for what's offered. If you're planning on eating in the restaurant—where more attention is paid to atmosphere than food—be sure to arrive well before the 9 PM closing, or you'll be hustled out the door. As an added compensation, the cable car to the peak is only a five-minute walk away. ⊠ *Tatranská Lomnica,* ☎ *0969/967941,* ☏ *0969/967891. Restaurant, sauna, health club, nightclub. AE, MC, V.*

Nightlife and the Arts

For a night out, there's live dance music and a floor show in the **Grandhotel Praha** (☞ *above*) nightclub.

Outdoor Activities and Sports

SKIING

Moderately challenging slopes are found at the **Skalnaté pleso,** above Tatranská Lomnica.

Ždiar

❷ *17 km (11 mi) from Tatranská Lomnica. To reach the village, leave Tatranská Lomnica heading east on Route 537 and turn left at Route 67 along the road to the Polish border.*

This tiny traditional village where you can still find horse-drawn carriages, high up in the mountains, is a welcome respite from the stale resort towns. The village is noted for its unique folk architecture—mostly enchanting, vibrantly painted wooden houses built in traditional peasant designs. If you'd like to spend the night here, you can stay in one of the handful of private bed-and-breakfasts scattered along Ždiar's two streets. The population of Ždiar is Polish in origin (the Polish border is less than 16 kilometers [10 miles] away), but the people have long considered themselves Slovak.

Stop in one of the houses that has been converted into a small folk museum, the **Ždiarska Izba,** which is by the church. ☎ *0969/98135.* ۞ *Nov.–Apr., weekdays 9–4; May–Oct., weekdays 9–5, weekends 9–2.*

From Ždiar, you can continue along Route 67 and cross over to Poland to visit the village's twin, **Javorina,** also known for its unique folk architecture. Along the way you may want to stop in some of the outlying towns around Ždiar, which are good sources for lace and other types of folk arts and crafts.

The High Tatras A to Z

Arriving and Departing

BY BUS

Daily bus service connects Prague and Bratislava with Poprad, but on this run trains tend to be quicker and more comfortable. From Prague the journey will take 10 hours or longer, depending on the route.

BY CAR

Poprad, the gateway to the Tatras, is 328 kilometers (205 miles) from Bratislava, with a four-lane stretch between the capital and Trenčín and a well-marked, two-lane highway thereafter. The drive to Poprad from Prague takes the main east–west highway about 560 kilometers (350 miles) from the Czech capital in the direction of Hradec Králové. The eight-hour drive from Prague is relatively comfortable, very scenic, and can be broken up easily with an overnight stay in Olomouc, in the Czech Republic province of Moravia. The road is well marked, with some four-lane stretches.

BY PLANE

ČSA, the Czech and Slovak national carrier, offers service to the Tatras city of Poprad from Prague and Bratislava. The flight from Prague takes a little over an hour. Unfortunately, at press time ÇSA had temporarily halted its flights directly to Poprad and instead was flying passengers to Košice and shuttling them to Poprad, about two hours away. If ÇSA is still not flying to the High Tatras, try Air Ostrava, which offers direct flights from Prague to Poprad. On arrival, take a taxi to your hotel or to the Poprad train station, where you can catch an electric train to the Tatras resorts.

BY TRAIN

Regular rail service connects both Prague and Bratislava with Poprad, but book ahead: The trains are often impossibly crowded, especially in August and during the skiing season. The journey from Prague to Poprad takes about 10 hours; several night trains depart from Prague's Hlavní nádraží (main station) and from Holešovice station.

Getting Around

BY BUS

The bus network links all the towns in the High Tatras, but unless you are traveling to a town not directly on an electric rail route, the train service is faster.

BY CAR

Having a car is more of a hindrance than a help if you're just going to the High Tatras. Traveling the electric railway is much quicker than taking the winding roads that connect the resorts, and hotel parking fees can add up quickly. However, if you plan to tour the region's smaller towns and villages, or if you are continuing on to eastern Slovakia, a car will prove nearly indispensable.

BY TRAIN

An efficient electric railway connects Poprad with the High Tatras resorts, and the resorts with one another. If you're going only to the Tatras, you won't need any other form of transportation.

Contacts and Resources

EMERGENCIES

Police: ☎ 158. **Medical emergencies:** ☎ 2444. **Car repair:** ☎ 2704.

GUIDED TOURS

From Poprad airport, **Slovair** offers a novel biplane flight over the Tatras region; contact the Satur office in Poprad (☞ *below*). The Satur office in Starý Smokovec (☞ *below*) is also helpful in arranging tours of the Tatras and surrounding area. In summer, Satur offers a bargain tour of Levoča, Kežmarok, and Markušovice on Wednesday.

LATE-NIGHT PHARMACIES

Pharmacies (*lekárna*) are in all three major resorts and in the neighboring town of Ždiar. The pharmacy in Nový Smokovec (☎ 0969/2577) maintains late hours.

VISITOR INFORMATION

There are tourist information centers in all the resort towns listed above: **Starý Smokovec** (✉ Dom Služieb—House of Services, ☎ 0969/3440); **Štrbské pleso** (✉ Športový Areál—Sport Hall, ☎ 0969/92824); and **Tatranská Lomnica** (✉ Múseum, ☎ 0969/967951). **Slovakoturist** (☎ 0969/2827), a half kilometer east of Starý Smokovec in Horný Smokovec, can arrange private accommodations, including stays in mountain cottages.

You'll find **Satur offices** in **Poprad** (✉ Námestie sv. Egídia 2950, ☎ 092/721740 or 092/721353, ☒ 092/63619); **Tatranská Lomnica** (☎ 0969/967451); and **Starý Smokovec** (☎ 0969/2950), where you can change money, get hiking and driving maps, and find assistance in booking hotels (but not private rooms).

For more in-depth information on routes, mountain chalets, and weather conditions, contact the **Mountain Rescue Service** (✉ Horská služba, ☎ 0969/2820) in Starý Smokovec. This office can also provide guides for the more difficult routes for around 500 Sk. per day.

Few books or pamphlets on the Tatras are available in English. One good overview of the area, including a list of services, hotels, and restaurants, is provided in the hard-to-find booklet *Everyman's Guide to the High Tatras*. Look for it at hotel gift shops.

CENTRAL SLOVAKIA

Though generally overlooked by tourists, central Slovakia is the country's heart and soul. This is where the nation was born and where Slovak folklore and deep-rooted traditions continue to flourish. The people of the towns and villages of this mountainous region have been cut off from the world and continue to live in much the same way they have for hundreds of years. Not surprisingly, the people of central Slovakia are highly patriotic, and the region is home to the country's more nationalistic leaders as well as the Matica Slovenská, a less-than-liberal organization set up to protect Slovak language and culture.

Formerly a medieval mining town, Banská Bystrica lies at the heart of the region and is the ideal base from which to explore the towns and villages surrounding it. The city has been successfully reviving some of its former beauty, but as in the country's other large cities, it is unable to lose the rows of apartments and factories, which haunt an otherwise attractive landscape. The region's two other historical mining towns, Banská Štavnica and Kremnica, have remained more or less frozen in time since their glory days in the Middle Ages. Don't overlook the wooden churches in the villages; the most interesting is perhaps the large 17th-century church at Hronsek.

The beauty of central Slovakia, however, lies not so much in its architecture as in its inspiring natural landscapes. The region is not only home to the High Tatras (☞ *above*), it also contains the Low Tatras, the second-highest mountain range in Slovakia and largest by area. With a range stretching from Banská Bystrica and Ružomberok in the west to Poprad and Švermovo in the east, the area is largely undeveloped, with only an occasional isolated village with wooden houses. If you like to get away from the crowds, this is the place to do it. The thick pine forests that cover the lower slopes are populated by bears, lynx, and wolves. In winter, some of the best skiing slopes in the country can be found in the Low Tatras, which are mostly free from the hordes of tourists migrating to the High Tatras. In summer, the area offers wonderful hiking trails, caves, and scenic valleys.

Unfortunately, in central Slovakia you will also find some of the worst crimes against nature. In an effort to enrich the region in the 1950s, the Communist regime built many large steel- and tank-producing factories, which litter some of the most beautiful valleys in the country. Many of the worst can be seen while heading east from Banská Bystrica in the direction of Brezno, though to call them an eyesore would be an understatement. Some of the hills that surround the area are blackened with ash, and while the factories now operate at a fraction of their previous levels, breathing the region's air remains far from pleasurable. So unless you'd like to become a revolutionary environmentalist overnight, stick to exploring the area north and south of Banská Bystrica.

Banská Bystrica

㉕ *124 km (77 mi) southwest of Poprad, 205 km (128 mi) east of Bratislava.*

Banská Bystrica is handsome despite the rows of concrete apartments and factories that plague the outlying area and detract from the rolling hills that engulf the town. Surrounded by three mountain ranges—the Low Tatras, the Fatras, and the Slovak Rudohorie—Banská Bystrica is in an ideal starting point for exploring the beauty of the region. The town's historical sites are few and are mostly on the massive main square, which always brims with life.

Banská Bystrica has been around since the 13th century, acquiring its wealth from the nearby mines. Following the Tatar invasion in 1241, the Hungarian king Belo IV granted special privileges to encourage the immigration of German settlers, who together with the natives developed the prosperous mining of copper and precious metals. Once the mines had been fully exploited, Banská Bystrica became known in Slovakia for its role in the revival of the Slovak language and culture. In 1785, Slovak writers gathered here to found the first Slovak literary review. During the 19th century, the town was a major focus of Slovak national life, and it was from a school here that the teaching of the Slovak language originated and spread to the rest of the country.

The city is also famous as the center of the Slovak National Uprising during World War II. It was here that the underground Slovak National Council initiated the revolt on August 29, 1944. For some two months, thousands of Slovaks valiantly rose up against the Slovak puppet regime and their Nazi oppressors, forcing the Germans to divert critically needed troops and equipment from the front lines. Though the Germans eventually quashed the uprising on October 27, the costly operation is credited with accelerating the Allied victory and gaining Slovakia the short-lived appellation of ally.

You'll find reminders of the uprising (known in Slovak by the initials SNP) just about everywhere. The mecca for fans is the **Múzeum Slovenského Národného Povstania** (Museum of the Slovak National Uprising), which stands in a large field just outside the center of town, between Horný ulica and Ulica Dukelských Hrdinov. It's difficult to miss the monument's massive concrete wings—surprisingly evocative of a captive people rising up to freedom. The effect is particularly striking at night. The museum itself isn't of much interest, however. At press time, it was busily changing its commentary, which until recently was exceedingly dull and heavily biased toward a Communist perspective. More telling, perhaps, is the absence of Slovak visitors; since the locals are no longer required to visit, the corridors are often empty. More interesting are the historic planes and tanks parked on the museum's front lawn. ⊠ *Kapitulská ul. 23,* ☎ *088/723558.* 🎫 *10 Sk.* ☉ *Tues.–Sun. 9–4 (summer 9–6).*

If you're partial to less recent history, head for the main square, the Námestie SNP, with its cheery collection of Renaissance and baroque houses. The most impressive is the **Thurzo House,** an amalgamation of two late-Gothic structures built in 1495 by the wealthy Thurzo family. The genuine Renaissance sgraffiti on the outside were added during the 16th century, when the family's wealth was at its height. Today the building houses the **City Museum,** which is more interesting for the chance to see inside the house than for its artifacts. ⊠ *Námestie SNP 4,* ☎ *088/725897.* 🎫 *10 Sk.* ☉ *Weekdays 8–noon and 1–4, Sun. 9–noon and 1–4; in summer, until 5.*

Cross the main square in front of the leaning 16th-century Hodinová veža (Clock Tower) and venture up the Jána Bakoša ulica to see the **Parish Church of the Virgin Mary,** near the town walls. The church was built in 1255 by prosperous German mine owners. Inside the church, in **St. Barbara's Chapel,** you'll find the town's greatest treasure: a beautiful late-Gothic altar, another wooden masterpiece carved by Pavol of Levoča. At the altar's center stands the figure of St. Barbara, the patron saint of miners. The church forms a unit with the other surviving structures of the former castle complex: the Gothic royal palace and the Praetorium (the former city hall).

OFF THE
BEATEN PATH
ŠPANIA DOLINA – One of the more beautiful areas in Slovakia, Špania Dolina is in a valley of the same name in the Low Tatras National Park. This village is renowned for its lace making, and if you're there in the summer, you can see older women making tablecloths and other lace articles on their front porches. Špania Dolina is 8 miles (13 kilometers) north of Banská Bystrica along Route 59.

Dining and Lodging

$$ ✕ **Starobystrická Pivnica.** Grilled food is the house specialty at this classic wine cellar that features a spicy version of Slovak cuisine. Try an excellent pepper steak with spicy sauce, or if you want to go all out, call in a day ahead and treat yourself to an elaborate fondue meal. ⊠ *Námestie SNP 89,* ☎ *088/54326. AE, MC, V.*

$ ✕ **Slovenská Restauracia.** This homey restaurant serves hearty meals ★ in classic Slovak pottery in a village-style atmosphere. You can have the usual specialties—*brinzové halušsky* or *strapačky plnene s kyslou kapustou*—but under no circumstances should you leave the restaurant without trying the *buchty na pare s kakaom.* This heavenly treat— plump, doughnut-size dumplings filled with fruit and covered with chocolate—is eaten as a main course, but feel free to have it as a dessert instead. ⊠ *Lazovná 18,* ☎ *088/53716. No credit cards.*

$$$ ✗⊞ **Arcade Hotel.** This 16th-century building on the main square is
★ an ideal place to stay in Banská Bystrica. The rooms and apartments vary in size, comfort, and cost, but all are equipped with the basic creature comforts, including a fridge and satellite TV. Check out the bar for its bizarre interior, then head down to the beautifully designed stone wine cellar for a drink or a meal. ⊠ *Námestie SNP 5,* ☎ *088/702111,* ℻ *088/723126. Restaurant, bar, café, wine cellar, meeting room. AE, DC, MC, V.*

$$ ⊞ **Lux.** On the edge of town, the Lux is one of the few successful highrise hotels in Slovakia, managing to combine modernity with some semblance of style. The rooms (especially on the upper floors facing town) have a magnificent view over the mountains, enlivened at night by the Museum of the Slovak National Uprising glowing in the foreground. The elegant restaurant serves a good range of Slovak specialties. Breakfast is included. ⊠ *Nové nám. 2,* ☎ *088/724141,* ℻ *088/743853. 120 rooms with bath. Restaurant, bar, café. AE, DC, MC, V.*

$$ ⊞ **Urpín.** Here you'll find clean rooms in an older, somewhat neglected hotel a block away from the city center. Breakfast is included. ⊠ *Ul. Jána Cikkera 5,* ☎ *088/724556,* ℻ *088/23731. 45 rooms, some with shower. No credit cards.*

$ ⊞ **Motel Uľanka.** This inexpensive motel, 6 kilometers (4 miles) outside town on the road to Ružomberok, is a good alternative for budget-minded travelers with a car. The surrounding mountain scenery is magnificent, but the rooms are only adequate. The motel has strict rules similar to a youth hostel. ⊠ *Uľanská cesta,* ☎ *088/53657. 50 rooms without bath. No credit cards.*

Outdoor Activities and Sports

The mountainous region surrounding Banská Bystrica is ideal for all sorts of outdoor activities, from walking to skiing. In summer, the mountains have beautiful hiking and biking trails that link caves and natural lakes. The most attractive hiking trails are to the north of Banská Bystrica and in the area between Banská Bystrica and Kremnica. There is a hiking map of the Low Tatras, which includes routes for cyclists, available at tourist information (you can inquire here about bike rentals, too, since not many places rent them).

Nightlife and the Arts

The best bet for entertainment is seeing an opera or a ballet at the **Štátna Opera** (⊠ Národná 11, ☎ 088/724418) or seeing a puppet show at the **Bábkové Divadlo na Rázcestí** (⊠ Kollárova 18, ☎ 088/24567 or 088/193724). Another option is spending an evening in one of the city's wine cellars, listening to Gypsy music.

En Route   South of Banská Bystrica in the direction of Zvolen is the tiny village of **Hronsek.** This hamlet certainly warrants a stop—it has a wooden church built without a single piece of metal. The builders of this Protestant church, which was constructed at the time of the Counter-Reformation, abided by strict guidelines stipulating that wood was the only material to be used for building a church—even nails had to be made of wood!

Kremnica

㉖ *Head south out of Banská Bystrica via busy Route 66. Bypass Zvolen, following the signs in the direction of Žiar, turning finally to the right on Route 65 when you see the sign to Kremnica. The drive through the mountains is about 50 km (31 mi) and can be done in under an hour.*

Kremnica, known as the Golden City, was one of the most famous mining towns in Slovakia and one of the richest gold mines in medieval Europe. But the city never developed any political or cultural ambitions, and most of the wealth generated here was carted away to build glorious structures elsewhere in the then-Hungarian kingdom. What you'll find today is a beautifully preserved medieval town, surrounded by sturdy walls and gates that guarded the gold once stored in Kremnica's vaults. You can enter the town through the impressive **Dolná Brána** (Lower Gate), dating from 1441. Past the gate you'll come to the grassy main square. Here you'll see some of the best-kept merchant houses in Slovakia.

You can learn about the town's 650-year history as a mining and minting center at the **Kremnica Museum.** For coin enthusiasts, the second floor has fascinating exhibits of coins in use in Central Europe from Celtic and Roman times to the modern day. The 30-minute English commentary on tape (ask the attendant), which booms throughout the museum as you walk from room to room, is helpful but hard to follow. ✉ *Štefánikové nám. 10,* ☎ *0857/742696.* 🎫 *4 Sk.* ◷ *Tues.–Sat. 8–4:30 (summer Tues.–Sat. 8:30–1 and 1:30–5; Sun. 9–1 and 1:30–3).*

The town square is dominated by the former **town castle,** dating from the 13th century and once used for storing gold. The castle is one of the finest in Slovakia and includes a late-Romanesque tower and a Gothic two-aisle church. At press time, parts of the castle were under construction. ✉ *Hrad,* ☎ *0857/743968.* 🎫 *20 Sk.* ◷ *May–Sept., Tues.–Sun. 9–5; Oct.–Apr., Tues.–Sat. 8:30–4:30.*

Dining

$ ✕ **Jelen.** For a delicious lunch or dinner, try this unassuming restaurant in the new part of town, outside the walls. Although it looks like any ordinary beer hall, the food is several notches above the usual fare. Start out with the delicious lentil soup, then try the roast beef with paprika sauce and dumplings. ✉ *Dolná ul. 22,* ☎ *0857/744003.*

Banská Štiavnica

㉗ *42 km (26 mi) south of Kremnica, 45 km (28 mi) south of Banská Bystrica, along small but well-marked roads.*

Picturesque Banská Štiavnica is in a small valley among rolling hills. Since the 11th century, the town has earned its wealth from mining, and today it is essentially one large mining museum. German miners arrived here to exploit rich gold and silver deposits, and their success is apparent in some of the town's remaining monuments, such as the golden Trinity column and the impressive Lutheran church. The area surrounding the city, especially to the south, has some great hiking trails.

Built on the rocks above town, the **Old Castle** dates back to the early 13th century and has additions in practically every subsequent building style. It served as a fortress to protect the wealth of the local bigwigs against the Turkish invaders. After much reconstruction, it partially opened its doors to the public in May 1996. ✉ *Starozámocká 11,* ☎ *0859/23103.* 🎫 *10 Sk.* ◷ *June–Aug., daily 8–4.*

The **New Castle** was built between 1564 and 1571 as part of an effort to strenghten fortification of the town against invasions from the Turks. The six-story Renaissance building was used as a watch tower and later it became the town's live clock—the exact time was announced every quarter hour by a trumpet. Inside you'll find historical exhibits of the Turkish invasions in the 16th and 17th centuries, including life-size statues of Turks dressed in full battle regalia. ⊠ *Novozámocká 22,* ☎ *0859/21543.* ☜ *20 Sk.* ☉ *May–Sept., daily 8–4; Oct.–Apr., weekdays 8–3.*

You can view some of the town's original mining buildings and machinery dating back to the early 13th century at the **Open Air Mining Museum.** There is also a tour of a mining shaft, which lets you see the conditions under which medieval miners worked. The museum is about 2 kilometers from town in the direction of Štavnické Bane. ☎ *0859/22971.* ☜ *30 Sk.* ☉ *May–Sept., Tues.–Sun. 8–4.*

OFF THE BEATEN PATH

CHATEAU AT ANTOL – Don't miss this charming late-baroque château, which was built in 1750 on the site of a 15th-century castle in the small village of Antol, just outside Banská Štavnica. The château displays its original furnishings and has an exhibition on hunting arms and game. Take a look at the fresco paintings in the interior of the chapel. If the weather's agreeable, walk through the park and see the giant sequoia planted in 1878. ⊠ *Antol,* ☎ *0859/239.* ☉ *May–Sept., Tues.–Sun. 8:30–4; Oct.–Apr., Tues.–Sat. 8–3.*

Dining and Lodging

\$\$ ✕🏠 **Antolský Mlín.** This small family-run pension, in a tiny village just outside Banská Štavnica near the château at Antol, is a pleasant place to overnight. The owners are so attentive you'll feel as if you're visiting a dear aunt or uncle. Though small, the rooms are modern and have new, clean bathrooms. The homey restaurant will serve anything you wish (within reason) according to your taste—that means local cuisine, of course, no burger and fries here! ⊠ *Antol,* ☎ *0859/621011. Restaurant. No credit cards.*

\$\$ ✕🏠 **Salamander.** This brand new hotel, in a beautifully renovated 16th-
★ century building, has everything you would expect from a first-class establishment, including impeccable service. The rooms are large and bright, and the public areas are decorated with antiques. Don't let the cheap price here fool you. This hotel draws many glamorous guests, including the president of Slovakia. ⊠ *Paláriková 1,* ☎ *0859/23992,* FAX *0859/621262, Restaurant, ice cream parlor, outdoor café, wine cellar. AE, MC, V.*

Central Slovakia A to Z

Arriving and Departing

Unless you have a car, the best means of arriving in Banská Bystrica is by rail. There are daily trains from Bratislava, and the journey takes almost three hours. The trip from Kosice to Banská Bystrica, one of the most scenic railway routes in the country (take the northern, not the southern, route), lasts about five hours.

Getting Around

For those without a car, Banská Bystrica is an especially convenient spot from which to discover the region, since it serves as a hub for the complex rail and bus system and allows for easier access to the smaller destinations.

Contacts and Resources

EMERGENCIES

Police: ☎ 158. **Ambulance:** ☎ 155.

GUIDED TOURS

The **Satur** office in Banská Bystrica (✉ Nám. Slobody 4, ☎ 088/742525) can book hotels and arrange tours at a reasonable cost.

VISITOR INFORMATION

Banská Bystrica: ✉ Nám. SNP 1, ☎ 088/54369. ☉ June–Aug., weekdays 7:30–6; Oct.–May, 7:30–4:30; **Kremnica:** ✉ Štefánikovo nám. 35/44, ☎ 0857/742856. ☉ Weekdays 9–5; **Banská Štavnica:** ✉ Radničné nám. 1, ☎ 0859/21859. ☉ Late May–early Sept., Mon.–Sun. 8–6; late Sept.–early May, weekdays 8–4.

EASTERN SLOVAKIA

To the east of the High Tatras lies an expanse of Slovakia that seldom appears on tourist itineraries. Here, the High Tatras' mountains become hills that gently stretch to the Ukrainian border, with few "musts" for visitors in between.

However, eastern Slovakia is an especial must for the outdoorsman. The region is a veritable hiker's paradise. In addition to the offerings at Slovenský Raj, trails fan out in all directions in the area known as Spišská Magura, to the north and east of Kežmarok. Good outdoor swimming can be found in the lakes in Slovenský Raj and in Michalovce, east of Košice.

For 1,000 years, eastern Slovakia was isolated from the West; much of the region was regarded simply as the hinterland of Greater Hungary. The great movements of European history—the Reformation and the Renaissance—made their impact here as elsewhere on the continent, but in an muted and diluted form.

Isolation can have its advantages, however, and therein may lie the special charm of this area for the visitor. The baroque and Renaissance facades that dominate the towns of Bohemia and Moravia make an appearance in eastern Slovakia as well, but early artisans working in the region often eschewed the stone and marble preferred by their western counterparts in favor of wood and other local materials. Look especially for the wooden altars in Levoča and other towns.

The relative isolation also fostered the development of an entire civilization in medieval times, the Spiš, with no counterpart in the Czech Republic or even elsewhere in Slovakia. The territory of the kingdom, which spreads out to the east and south of the High Tatras, was originally settled by Slavonic and later by German immigrants who came here in medieval times to work the mines and defend the western kingdoms against invasion. Some 24 towns eventually came to join the Spiš group, functioning as a miniprincipality within the Hungarian monarchy. The group had its own hierarchies and laws, which were quite different from those brought in by Magyar or Saxon settlers. They also enjoyed many privileges denied to other cities and could choose their own count to represent them before the Hungarian king.

As the mines thrived, Spiš power and influence reached its height. But the confederation also had its bad times. In 1412, the Holy Roman Emperor Sigismund, king of Hungary, decided to sell 13 of the towns to his brother-in-law, the king of Poland, in order to finance a war with Venice. The split lasted until 1769, when the towns were reunited with one another. In 1876, the last of the Spiš towns lost its privileges, and the German speakers in the area were forced to learn Hungarian or emigrate—mainly to the United States. In 1919, when Slovakia became part of the new Czechoslovak state, the German speakers were again allowed to establish German schools, but in 1945 almost all of them were forced to leave the country because of their real or suspected collaboration with the Nazis.

Although the last Spiš town lost its independence 100 years ago, much of the group's architectural legacy remains—another fortuitous by-product of isolation, namely economic stagnation. Spiš towns are predominantly Gothic beneath their graceful Renaissance overlays. Their steep shingled roofs, high timber-framed gables, and brick-arched doorways have survived in a remarkable state of preservation. Gothic churches with imposing Renaissance bell towers are other major features of the area, as are some quite stunning altarpieces and exquisite wood carvings. Needless to say, Spiš towns are worth seeking out when you see them on a map; look for the prefix "Spišsky" preceding a town name.

Farther to the northeast, the influences of Byzantium are strongly felt, most noticeably in the form of the simple wooden churches that dominate the villages along the frontier with Poland and Ukraine. This area marks a border in Europe that has stood for a thousand years: the ancient line between Rome and Constantinople, between Western Christianity and the Byzantine Empire. Many churches here were built by members of the Uniat Church, Christians who acknowledge the supremacy of the Pope but retain their own organization and liturgy.

The busy industrial cities of Prešov and Košice, with their belching factories and rows of housing projects, quickly bring you back to the 20th century. Although these cities do bear signs of the region's historical complexity, come here instead for a taste of modern Slovakia, of a relatively poor country that is just beginning to shed a long legacy of foreign domination.

When visiting the region, keep in mind that more expensive does not necessarily mean better when it comes to food. Stay clear of the large hotels, some of which are state-owned, and instead, look to innovative, privately owned restaurants. Eastern Slovakia has successfully borrowed the best dishes and techniques from the Hungarians, the Ukrainians, and the Poles to create an original and delicious cuisine. Treat yourself to a some local specialties—try *palacinky* (crepes with fruit or jam stuffing) or *buchty* (puffy homemade doughnuts filled with fruit). You may gain a few pounds on your travels, but it's well worth it. Besides, hiking in the mountains will balance everything out.

Kežmarok

28 *15 km (9 mi) from Poprad driving northeast via Route 67, 320 km (199 mi) east of Bratislava.*

Kežmarok was once the great "second town" of the Spiš region. Founded by German settlers in the 12th century, the town for years competed—ultimately unsuccessfully—with Levoča to become the capital of this minikingdom. The main sights of Kežmarok today, however, have less to do with the Spiš tradition than with the town's later role within Greater Hungary.

You can't miss the enormous Gothic-Renaissance **Tokolyho hrad** (Tököly Palace), east of the main square. It was from here in the late 17th century that Count Imre Tököly launched his unsuccessful uprising against the Hapsburgs to form an independent Hungarian state in "Upper Hungary" (present-day Slovakia). The count initially enjoyed great success and soon united all of Upper Hungary, but he made the fateful decision to depend on the Ottoman Empire for support in his war. When the Turks were finally defeated by the Hapsburgs in 1683 at the city walls of Vienna, the Hapsburgs had the count condemned to death. Tököly escaped to Turkey, where he died in exile in 1705.

In the 19th century, the castle served as a barracks and was even used for a time as a textile factory. Today it houses a small museum of the town's history, with a cozy wine cellar in the basement. In summer, concerts are held in the castle chapel and courtyard. ⊠ *Hradné nám. 42,* ☎ *0968/2698.* 🎫 *28 Sk.* ⊙ *Summer, tours every ½ hr, Tues.–Sun. 9– noon and 1:30–4; rest of yr, tours every hr, Tues.–Sat. 9–11 and 1–4.*

The **Kostol svätého kríža** (Church of the Holy Cross) is a Gothic structure with impressive netted vaulting that dates from the beginning of the 15th century. The designs on the 16th-century bell tower, with its tin crown, are characteristic of the so-called Spiš Renaissance style. The large and handsome main square, befitting Kežmarok's history as a leader among the Spiš towns, is just a couple of minutes' walk from the church. ⊠ *Nová ul.* 🎫 *Free.* ⊙ *Weekdays 9–noon and 2–5.*

The wooden **Protestant Church** stands just outside the former city walls a few blocks west of the main square. The church owes its existence to a congress held in 1681 in Sopron, Hungary, where it was decided that Protestants living on then-Hungarian lands could have their own churches only if the churches were outside the town boundaries and were constructed completely of wood (without even iron nails or stone foundations). In 1717, Kežmarok's Protestants lovingly built this structure from red pine and yew, fashioning its gracious vaulting from clay. The church could accommodate some 1,000 worshipers. But the once idyllic setting has long since yielded to urban sprawl, and the church itself has been covered over in stone to protect the interior, so what you see today is something of a letdown. Still, next to the pompous pink-and-green Evangelical Church next door, built at the end of the last century in neo–*Arabian Nights* style, the church's elegant simplicity is still affecting. ⊠ *Hlavné nám.* ⊙ *Daily 8–noon and 1–5.*

Dining and Lodging

$$ ✕ 🏨 **Hotel Club.** This bright, pinkish-blue hotel in the center of Kežmarok is a decent place to stay. The rooms are plainly furnished, but have modern bathrooms. Try the restaurant (look up to see the ornate carved-wood ceilings) or the cozy wine cellar, both of which serve good Slovak and Continental fare at reasonable prices. ⊠ *MUDr. Alexandra 24,* ☎ *968/4051,* ☎ *968/4053. Restaurant, wine cellar. No credit cards.*

Bardejov

㉙ *88 km (55 mi) east of Kežmarok.*

Bardejov is a great surprise, tucked away in this remote corner of Slovakia yet possessing one of the nation's most enchanting squares. Indeed, Bardejov owes its splendors precisely to its location astride the ancient trade routes to Poland and Russia. It's hard to put your finger on exactly why the square is so captivating. Maybe it's the lack of arcades in front of the houses, which while impressive, can sometimes overburden the squares of Bohemian and Moravian towns. It could also be the pointed roofs of the houses, which have a lighter, almost comic effect.

The exterior of the Gothic **Kostol svätého Egídia** (St. Egidius Church), built in stages in the 15th century, is undeniably handsome, but take a walk inside for the real treasure. The nave is lined with 11 priceless Gothic side altars, all carved between 1460 and 1510 and perfectly preserved. Here you get pure Gothic, with no Renaissance or Baroque details to dampen the effect.

The most famous of the altars is to the left of the main altar (look for the number 1 on the side). The intricate work of Stefan Tarner, it depicts the birth of Christ and dates from the 1480s. Other noteworthy carvings are the figure of St. Barbara and the *Vir dolorum,* both to the right of the main altar, but in fact all of them are vividly detailed and merit close inspection. The Gothic pulpit, to the side of the nave, is as old as the church itself. The early baroque pews, with their sensuous curves, must have caused quite a sensation when they were added in about 1600. ⊠ *Radničné nám.*

The modest building with late-Gothic portals and Renaissance detailing in the center of the town square is the **town hall** (Radnice). Compared to the dark and imposing Gothic town halls in Bohemia and Moravia, this smaller, more playful structure is a breath of fresh air.

★ You may want to visit the pink **Šariš Icon Museum** on the south side of the main square to view its collection of 16th-century icons and paintings, taken from the area's numerous Russian Orthodox churches. The museum provides a fascinating look at the religious motifs of the surrounding area from between the 16th and 19th centuries. Pick up the short but interesting commentary in English (5 Sk.) when you buy your ticket. Many of the icons feature the story of St. George slaying the dragon (for the key to the princess's chastity belt!). The legend of St. George, which probably originated in pre-Christian mythology, was often used to attract the peasants of the area to the more abstemious myths of Christianity.

Take a close look at the icon of the Last Judgment on the second floor for what it reveals of this area's practices and fashions in the 16th century. The complex morality of the subject matter reflects quite sophisticated beliefs. Also on the second floor are models of the wooden churches that dot the surrounding countryside, the sources of many of these icons and paintings. ⊠ *Radničné nám. 13,* ☎ *0935/2009.* 🖾 *10 Sk.* ⊙ *Tues.–Sun. 8:30–11:30 and 12:30–4:30 (summer 9–6).*

The **Rhody House** is Bardejov's best remaining example of Renaissance relief work. The structure, essentially Gothic but with reliefs added in the 16th century, was one of the few in the city center to survive the great fire of 1878. Continue down the Rhodyho to Na Hradbach to see the town walls, built in the middle of the 14th century. Some eight of the 23 original bastions are still standing, mostly along the south and east walls.

En Route Leave the Bardejov area along Route 77, heading north and east in the direction of Svidník. This is really where *eastern* Slovakia, with its strong Byzantine influence, begins. The colors seem wilder here; the villages also look poorer, reflecting the area's physical—and cultural—insularity. Both the Orthodox and Uniat faiths are strong in these parts, echoing the work of Byzantine missionaries more than a millennium ago.

Dining and Lodging

$ ✕ **Republika.** This depressing socialist-realist structure is an acceptable alternative for travelers without a car. The hallways are cluttered with mismatched furniture; and the rooms, though clean, show a similar lack of forethought. The big advantage is location: A couple of steps and you're in Bardejov's beautiful medieval square. ⊠ *Nám. Oslo-boditel'ov,* ☎ *0935/2721,* 🖾 *0935/2657. 30 rooms, some with shower. Restaurant. No credit cards.*

Bardejovské Kúpele

6½ km (4 mi) north of Bardejov, off Route 77.

Though it is no longer the favorite haunt of Hungarian counts, this old spa town is still a pleasant enough place to stroll around and take in the fresh air from the surrounding hills. Don't expect lots of beautiful architecture unless you're a fan of "postwar modern." The town was built up rapidly after the war to serve as a retreat for the proletariat, and little of its aristocratic heritage remains. Be sure to walk behind the space-age colonnade to view a lovely wooden Russian Orthodox church from the 18th century along with some older wooden houses that form an open-air museum. The church was brought here in 1932 as a specimen of the "primitive" age. Ironically, the 226-year-old structure is holding up markedly better than the 20-year-old buildings from the "advanced" culture surrounding it.

Dining and Lodging

$$ ✕⊞ **Mineral.** Despite its location in a 19th-century spa town, this aging 1970s structure is fairly charmless. Yet as Bardejov lacks decent hotels, there aren't many choices. The rooms, some with a nice view over the spa area, are acceptably clean, and the restaurant serves a good breakfast. ⊠ *Bardejovské Kúpele,* ☎ *0935/724122. 50 rooms with bath. Restaurant, nightclub. No credit cards.*

Jedlinka

㉚ *13 km (8 mi) north of Bardejov along the road to Svidník, 12 km (7½ mi) from Bardejovské Kúpele.*

The area's great delights are unquestionably the old wooden churches still in use in their original village settings. Like most, the one in Jedlinka dates from the 18th and 19th centuries and combines Byzantine and baroque architectural elements. Its three onion-domed towers rise above the west front. Inside, the north, east, and south walls are painted with Biblical scenes; the west wall was reserved for icons (many of which now hang in the icon museum in Bardejov). The churches are usually locked, and you'll need some luck to see the inside. If you happen across a villager, ask him or her (with appropriate key-turning gestures) to let you in. More often than not, someone will turn up with a key, and you'll have your own guided tour. If you see a collection plate inside, make a small donation—though there is no pressure to do so.

OFF THE   **DUKELSKÝ PRIESMYK –** World War II buffs will want to complete the drive
BEATEN PATH   north of Svidník to the Dukelský Priesmyk (Dukla Pass) on the Polish border. It was here in late 1944 that Soviet troops, along with detachments of Czech and Slovak resistance fighters, finally made their long-awaited advance to liberate Czechoslovakia from the Nazis. Most of the fighting took place between the town of Krajná Pol'ana and the border. Alongside the many war monuments, which are in odd juxtaposition to the tranquil loveliness of the wooden churches, you'll find bunkers, trenches, and watchtowers. The Germans mustered far more resistance than expected during the battle, and the number of dead on both sides grew to more than 100,000. Near the top of the pass, a great monument and cemetery commemorate the fallen Slovaks; their leader, General Ludvík Svoboda, went on to become president of the reborn Czechoslovak state.

En Route   There are about a score of Uniat churches in the countryside north of Svidník, itself an uninteresting town destroyed during World War II and completely rebuilt in the 1960s. Consider seeking out the churches in the villages of **Ladomirová, Hunkovce,** and **Nižný Komárnik.** Venture off the main road to see more churches at **Bodružal, Mirol'a, Príkra,** and **Šemetkovce**—but be sure to take along a good map.

Medzilaborce

③ *40 km (25 mi) east of Svidník, 70 km (43 mi) east of Bardejov.*

The sleepy border town of Medzilaborce is quickly becoming the unlikely mecca for fans of pop-art guru Andy Warhol. It was here in 1991, near the birthplace of Warhol's parents, that the country's cultural authorities, in conjunction with the Andy Warhol Foundation for Visual

★ Arts in New York, opened the **Warhol Family Museum of Modern Art.** In all, the museum holds 17 original Warhol silkscreens, including two from the famous Campbell's Soup series, and portraits of Lenin and singer Billie Holiday. The Russian Orthodox church across the street lends a suitably surreal element to the setting. ☜ *10 Sk.* ☉ *Daily 10–5.*

Prešov

㉜ *85 km (53 mi) southwest of Medzilaborce.*

Prešov is a lively town and the center of Ukrainian culture in Slovakia. Its other claim to fame is a little controversial now that the Communists have been ousted from power. It was here in 1919, from the black wrought-iron balcony at Hlavná ulica 73, that enthusiastic Communists proclaimed their own Slovak Soviet Republic in 1919, just 17 months after the Bolshevik Revolution in Russia. This early attempt at communism lasted three weeks. The balcony is still lit up at night, but in 1990 the name of the square—Slovak Soviet Republic (SSR for short)—was quickly changed back to Main Street.

Dining and Lodging

$$ ✕☷ **Dukla.** Just down the main road from the center of town and right next to the theater, this hotel is a modern structure that works. The staff is friendly; the rooms, though nothing special, are comfortable and clean, with very immaculate bathrooms. Some rooms have balconies. ✉ *Nám. Legionárov 2,* ☎ *091/22741–2,* ℻ *091/32134. 89 rooms with bath. Restaurant, snack bar.*

$ ✕☷ **Šariš.** Though it is a little removed from the city center, the Šariš has facilities—including bike rentals—that you do not often find at a budget hotel. The staff is friendly and helpful, and the rooms, though small, have refrigerators. The bathrooms, however, are a bit on the old and worn side. ✉ *Sabinovská ul. 1,* ☎ *091/46351,* ℻ *091/46551. 110 rooms. Restaurant, bar. No credit cards.*

Košice

㉝ *30 km (19 mi) south of Prešov, 418 km (259 mi) east of Bratislava.*

In Košice you'll leave rural Slovakia behind. Traffic picks up, the smog settles in, and the high-rise apartment buildings of the suburbs suddenly seem to stretch out for miles. Though rich historically, Košice is a sprawling, modern city, the second largest in Slovakia after Bratislava. The city has always had an antagonistic relationship with the capital. No celebrations were held here when Slovakia became independent; the locals, who see themselves as more cosmopolitan, preferred the rule of Prague to that of Bratislava.

Positioned along the main trade route between Hungary and Poland, the city was the second largest in the Hungarian Empire (after Buda) during the Middle Ages. With the Turkish occupation of the Hungarian homeland in the 16th and 17th centuries, the town became a safe haven for the Hungarian nobility. Inevitably, however, it fell into economic decline as trade with Hungary came to a standstill. Relief did not come until 1861, with the advent of the railroad.

In this century the city has been shuttled between Hungary, Czechoslovakia, and now Slovakia. Sadly, Slovak efforts to eliminate Hungarian influence in Košice after World War II were remarkably successful. As you walk around, you'll be hard-pressed to find evidence that this was once a great Hungarian city—even with the Hungarian frontier just 20 kilometers (12 miles) away. Still, many of the older generation speak Hungarian, and the small Hungarian community in Košce is putting up a strong fight to retain Hungarian schools and maintain some of the diminishing government support for cultural activities. The city remains home to a popular Hungarian theater, as well as a successful Romany (Gypsy) theater, the only one of its kind in the world.

★ You won't see many Westerners strolling Košice's enormous medieval square, the **Hlavná ulica**; most of the tourists here are Hungarians on a day trip to shop and sightsee. The town square is dominated on its southern flank by the huge tower of the Gothic **Dóm svätej Alžbety** (Cathedral of St. Elizabeth). Built in the 15th century and finally completed in 1508, the cathedral is the largest in Slovakia. First walk over to the north side (facing the square) to look at the famed Golden Door. The reputed friend of the sick and aged, St. Elizabeth stands in the middle of the portal. The reliefs above her depict her good works.

Inside the church is one of Europe's largest Gothic altarpieces, 35 feet tall. It is a monumental piece of medieval wood carving attributed to the master Erhard of Ulm. You can also pay a visit to the great Hungarian leader Francis Rakóczi II, most of whose remains (he left his heart in Paris) were placed in a crypt under the north transept of the cathedral. Although generally open to worshipers, the church is under renovation, and you may not be able to wander at will. ✉ *Hlavná ul.* ☉ *Daily services at 7* PM.

The **Urbanová veža** (Urbans' Tower), next door to the Cathedral of St. Elizabeth, is a 14th-century bell tower remodeled in Renaissance style in 1612. But much of what you see today isn't much more than 30 years old. In 1966 the tower burned and had to be rebuilt. It now houses a permanent exhibition of bell making, but don't waste your time climbing to the top unless you're interested in forging and casting techniques. The view is disappointing and can't compensate for the eight floors of bell and iron exhibits you'll be subjected to on your way there. ✉ *Hlavná ul.* 🎫 *5 Sk.* ☉ *Tues.–Sat. 9–5, Sun. 9–1.*

Kaplnka svätého Michala (St. Michael's Chapel) dates from around 1260. A relief on the portal shows the archangel Michael weighing the souls of the dead. On the east side of the town square is the **Dom Košického vládneho programu** (House of the Košice Government Program), which played an important role in the final days of World War II. It was from here that the Košice Program was proclaimed on April 5, 1945, announcing the reunion of the Czech lands and Slovakia into one national state.

The **Štátne divadlo** (State Theater), a mishmash of neo-Renaissance and neobaroque elements built at the end of the last century, dominates the center of the town square. The deliberate imitation of earlier architectural styles was all the rage in the Hapsburg Empire at the time; indeed, the building would be equally at home on Vienna's Ringstrasse. The theater's interior is elaborately decorated with plaster ornaments. Notice the paintings on the ceilings by Viennese artist P. Gastgeb. For a town this size, the quality of theater, ballet, and opera productions is very impressive. Tickets are reasonably priced and can be bought at the theater box office. ✉ *Hlavná ul. 58,* ☎ *095/6221231.* ☉ *Weekdays 1–6, or 1 hr before performances.*

To the right of the State Theater, the impressive **rococo palace** at Hlavná ulica 59, which once housed the city's wealthiest nobility, was the unlikely site of a Slovak Soviet Republic congress in 1919, just a week before the revolutionary movement was aborted. The relief on the house has nothing to do with communism but recalls the stay here of the Russian commander Mikhail Kutuzov, who in 1805 led the combined Russian-Austrian forces in battle against Napoléon at Austerlitz.

On the main street between the theater and the cathedral is the **Music Fountain.** Water from this elaborate fountain springs in harmony with music (generally classical), accompanied by colored lights. It's worth a visit in the evening just to see all the pairs of lovers huddled around it.

NEED A BREAK?	To feel like you've really stepped into turn-of-the-century Vienna, have a cup of coffee and dessert in the elegant art-nouveau confines of the **Café Slavia** (✉ Hlavná ul. 63, ☎ 095/6224395).

Take a glance at the beautifully painted **Beggar's House** (✉ Hlavná ul. 71). According to legend, the owner of the house, who was once a beggar, had a statue made of himself. Look to the top of the house, where he tips his hat to everyone who ever gave him money.

From the town square, take a right at E. Adyho ulica and continue to the end of the street to the town walls. In the 16th and 17th centuries, these bastions—which date from the 1200s—helped secure Košice as a safe haven for the Hungarian nobility; it was from here that they launched their attacks on the Turks occupying the Hungarian motherland.

The **Miklusova väznica** (Nicholas Prison), an old Gothic building used as a prison and torture chamber until 1909, now houses a museum with exhibits on Košice's history. The underground premises of the former torture chamber are open to the public. ✉ *Pri Mikluśovej väznici 10,* ☎ *095/6222856.* 🎫 *20 Sk.* ☉ *Tues.–Sat. 9–5 (summer also Sun. 1–5).*

OFF THE BEATEN PATH	**HERL'ANY GEYSER** – This geyser, with water shooting up nearly 130 feet for about 20 minutes, is an interesting day trip from Košice—it's about 30 kilometers (20 miles) from the city. The geyser has an eruption interval of 32 to 36 hours. Check with the **Satur** office in Košice (☞ Eastern Slovakia A to Z, *below*) for the expected eruption times. To get here, follow Route 50 east out of the city, making a right at Route 576 and following the signs.
	KRÁSNA HÔRKA – Sitting on top of a hill, this fairy-tale castle can be seen from miles around. It is one of the best-preserved fortifications from the Middle Ages in Slovakia. The museum houses a valuable collection of paintings and a wide assortment of furniture and weapons from the 15th through 17th centuries. Below the castle is a beautiful art-nouveau mausoleum. To get here, head west on E57 in the direction of Rožnava and turn right at Krásnohradské Podhradie from where you can follow signs up to the castle; it takes about an hour from Košice. ✉ *Krásnohradské Podhradie,* ☎ *0942/24769.* ☉ *Tues.–Sun. 8–5:30.*

Dining and Lodging

$ ★ ✕ **Slovenská Reštauracia.** This tiny restaurant, decorated as an old country cottage complete with wooden tables, a pitchfork, and a picket fence, serves mouthwatering local specialties. If you don't mind rolling out of the establishment, try one of the meals for two. You'll receive an enormous plate piled high with various meats and either rice, mushrooms, and cheese or dumplings and red and white cabbage.✉ *Biela 3,* ☎ *095/6220402. No credit cards.*

$$$ ✕▥ **Pensión pri Radnici.** This small pension is ideal for business travel-
★ ers—modern apartments come with studies and fax machines. The upstairs restaurant is a bit upscale. If you want a quick lunch, try the buffet downstairs, which serves tasty local food at dirt-cheap prices. ✉ *Bačíková 18,* ☎ *095/6228601,* ℻ *095/6227824. 3 apartments. Restaurant, beer garden, café, cafeteria. AE, MC, V.*

$$$ ▥ **Hotel Cobra.** This hotel is a breath of fresh air when compared to
★ the concrete-block hotels that still plague much of Slovakia. The rooms are bright and the bathrooms pleasant. The hotel is outside the city center in a quiet residential area. ✉ *Jiskrova 3,* ☎ *095/6225809,* ℻ *095/6225918. 10 rooms, 3 apartments, Restaurant, bar, beer garden. AE, MC, V.*

$$$ ▥ **Slovan.** This unsightly high-rise surprisingly does many things well—
  the English-speaking staff is attentive, and the decor here is tasteful. Choose a room on one of the upper floors for a beautiful view of Košice's main square, just a few minutes' walk from the hotel. Breakfast is included. ✉ *Hlavná ul. 1,* ☎ *095/622–7378,* ℻ *095/622–8413. 212 rooms with bath. Restaurant, café, minibars. AE, DC, MC, V.*

Nightlife and the Arts

NIGHTLIFE

If you're looking for a lively evening, **Jazz Club,** a cozy basement bar, is a popular hangout for locals. The name is a bit misleading though, as the club features not only live and taped jazz music, but disco, country, and rap music as well. ✉ *Kováčská 39.*

Levoča

★ ㉞ *From Košice travel via Route 547, following the signs in the direction of Spišská Nová Ves. The road quickly turns hilly, offering beautiful panoramas over several central Slovak ranges. Follow Route 547 to Spišské Podhradie, turning left on Route 18 in the direction of Levoča.*

You'll enter Levoča, the center of the Spiš kingdom and the quintessential Spiš town, through the medieval Košice Gate. A few hundred yards beyond the gate you come to the beautiful main square, surrounded by colorful Renaissance facades. Some are in appalling disrepair, and others are undergoing renovation, but this detracts little from the honest Old World feel. This medieval capital of the Spiš region was founded around 1245 and flourished between the 14th and 17th centuries, when it was an important trade center for art and crafts.

Today, Levoča and the surrounding area continue to follow many of the old traditions. Thousands of people come every year to a pilgrimage held in the first week of June. The worshipers take a long walk up the Mariánska Hora, where they pray to Virgin Mary, who is said to have appeared on the mountain.

The main sights in the town are lined along and in the middle of the square. Take a closer look at the golden sgraffiti-decorated **Thurzo House** (at No. 7), named for the powerful mining family. The wonderfully ornate gables are from the 17th century, though the sgraffiti were added in the 19th-century. At the top of the square is the **Small Committee House** (No. 60), the former administrative center of the Spiš region. Above the doorway, in sgraffito, is the coat of arms of the Spiš alliance. The monumental classical building next door, the **Large Committee House,** was built in the early 19th century by Anton Povolný, who was also responsible for the Evangelical Church at the bottom of the square.

★ The most impressive sight in town is the **Kostol svätého Jakuba** (St. Jacob Church), a huge Gothic structure begun in the early 14th century but not completed in its present form until a century later. The interior is a breathtaking concentration of Gothic religious art. It was here in the early 16th century that the greatest Spiš artist, Pavol of Levoča, created his most unforgettable pieces. The carved-wood high altar, said to be the world's largest and incorporating a truly magnificent carving of the Last Supper in limewood, is his most famous work. The 12 disciples are in fact portraits of Levoča merchants. Two of the Gothic side altars are also the work of master Pavol. The wall paintings on the left wall are fascinating for their detail and inventiveness; one depicts the seven deadly sins, each riding a different animal into hell. For 2 Sk., a tape recording in an iron post at the back of the church gives you detailed information in English. ⊠ *Nám. Majstra Pavla.* 🎫 *20 Sk.* ⊘ *Tues.–Sun. 8:30–4.*

Mestská radnica (town hall), with its fine example of whitewashed Renaissance arcades, gables, and clock tower, was built in 1551 after the great fire of 1550 destroyed the old Gothic building along with much of the town. The clock tower, which was added in 1656, now houses an excellent museum, with exhibits of guild flags and a good collection of paintings and wood carvings. Here you can also look at the 18th-century *Lady in White,* painted on a doorway through which, as legend has it, she let in the enemy for a promise of wealth and a title. For this act of treason, the 24-year-old beauty's head was chopped off. ⊠ *Nám. Majstra Pavla,* ☎ *0966/2449.* 🎫 *10 Sk.* ⊘ *May–Oct., Tues.–Sun. 9–5; Nov.–Apr., Tues.–Sun. 8–4.*

The wooden cage **Klietka Hamby** (the Cage of Shame), which sits beside Evangelical church, is not much to look at, but has an interesting history. In the 16th century, single women were placed in here if they were caught wandering outside after 10 PM. Additionally, if a woman was caught in flagrante delicto with a man she wasn't married to, she was put in the cage for everyone to look at, the man was tied to a pole (no longer there), and the two were then married and banished from the town forever.

OFF THE
BEATEN PATH
SPIŠSKÝ HRAD (Spiš Castle) – A former administrative center of the kingdom, this is the largest castle in Slovakia (and one of the largest in Europe). Spiš overlords occupied this site starting in 1209; the castle soon proved its military worth by surviving the onslaught of the Mongol hordes in the 13th century. The castle later came under the domination of the Hungarians. Now, however, it's firmly in Slovak hands and in season is open to the general public. The museum has a good collection of torture devices, and the castle has a beautiful view of the surrounding hills and town. From Levoča, it's worth taking the short 16-kilometer (10-mile) detour east along Route 18 to this magnificent spot. ⊠ *Spišský hrad,* ☎ *0966/512786.* 🎫 *30 Sk.* ⊘ *May–Oct., Tues.–Sat. 9–6.*

En Route From Levoča, head south on Route 533 through Spišská Nová Ves, continuing along the twisting roads to the junction with Route 535. Turn right onto Route 535, following the signs to Mlynky and beyond, through the tiny villages and breathtaking countryside of the national park known as **Slovenský Raj** (Slovak Paradise). It is a wild and romantic area of cliffs and gorges, caves and waterfalls. Once the refuge for Spiš villagers during the Tatar invasion of 1241–42 and now a national park, the area is perfect for adventurous hikers. The gorges are accessible by narrow but secure iron ladders. The main tourist centers are Čingov in the north and Dedinky in the south.

Dining and Lodging

$ ✕ **U Janusa.** This family-owned restaurant is the perfect place to get a taste of Slovak culture as well as cuisine. Here you'll have no choice but to try one of the local specialties such as homemade sausage or dumplings with goat cheese. In summer, you can enjoy the garden patio. ⊠ *Kláštorská 22,* ☎ *0966/4592. No credit cards.*

$$ ✕⊞ **Arkada Hotel.** Arkada, with large, bright rooms, is one of the few
★ near-perfect hotels in the country. This hotel is housed in a 13th-century building that in the 17th century became the first printing shop in the Austro-Hungarian Empire. ⊠ *Nám. Majstra Pavla 26,* ☎ *0966/ 512255,* 𝔽𝔸𝕏 *0966/512372. Restaurant, café, wine cellar. AE, MC, V.*

$$$ ⊞ **Hotel Satel.** Levoča should win an award for having two of the best
★ hotels in the country. This beautiful 18th-century mansion is built around a picturesque courtyard. The rooms are large and bright, though some of the furniture, especially the peach-colored sofa chairs, are a bit gaudy. The glossy modern lobby area can be disappointing too, but it's all made up for in the service, which is impeccable. ⊠ *Nám. Majstra Pavla 55,* ☎ *0966/512943,* 𝔽𝔸𝕏 *0966/514486. Restaurant, bar, wine cellar, AE, MC, V.*

Eastern Slovakia A to Z

Arriving and Departing

BY BUS

Daily bus service connects Prague and Bratislava with Košice, but on this run, trains tend to be quicker and more comfortable.

BY CAR

Poprad, a good starting point for a tour of eastern Slovakia, lies on Slovakia's main east–west highway about 560 kilometers (350 miles) from Prague in the direction of Hradec Králové. The seven- to eight-hour drive from Prague can be broken up easily with an overnight in Olomouc. The drive from Bratislava to Poprad is 328 kilometers (205 miles), with a four-lane stretch from Bratislava to Trenčín and a well-marked two-lane highway thereafter.

BY PLANE

ČSA offers regular flights from Prague and Bratislava to Košice at reasonable prices.

BY TRAIN

Trains regularly connect Košice with Prague (12 hours) and Bratislava (six hours), but book in advance to ensure a seat on these sometimes crowded routes. Several night trains make the run between Košice and Prague's main stations Hlavní nádraží and Holešovice.

Getting Around

BY BUS

Most of the region is reachable via the extensive bus network. The only exceptions are some of the smaller towns in northeastern Slovakia. Most buses run only on weekdays; plan carefully or you may end up getting stuck in a small town that is ill equipped for visitors.

BY CAR

A car is essential for reaching some of the smaller towns along the tour. Roads are of variable quality. Try to avoid driving at night, as routes are not well marked. A good four-lane highway links Prešov with Košice.

BY TRAIN

Regular trains link Poprad with Košice and some of the other larger towns, but you'll have to resort to the bus to reach smaller villages.

Contacts and Resources

EMERGENCIES

Police: ☎ 158. **Ambulance:** ☎ 155.

LATE-NIGHT PHARMACIES

Lekárna (pharmacies) take turns staying open late and on Sunday. Look for the list posted on the front door of each pharmacy. For after-hours service, ring the bell; you will be served through a little hatch door.

TRAVEL AGENCIES

The **Satur offices** in eastern Slovakia are the best—and sometimes the only—places providing basic assistance and information. They offer tours of the region and can book you a room at one of their hotels. There are branch offices in the following towns: **Košice** (⊠ Rooseveltová ul. 1, ☎ 095/6223123 or 095/6223847); **Prešov** (⊠ Hlavná ul. 1, ☎ 091/724041); and **Kežmarok** (⊠ Hlavné nám. 64, ☎ 0968/3121).

VISITOR INFORMATION

There are offices in the following towns: **Košice** (⊠ Hlavná ul. 8, ☎ 095/186); **Prešov** (⊠ Hlavná ul. 67, ☎ 091/722594), **Kežmarok** (⊠ Hlavné nám. 46, ☎ 0968/4046); **Levoča** (⊠ Nám. Majstra Pavla 58, ☎ 0966/3763); and **Bardejov** (⊠ Radničné nám. 21, ☎ 0935/551064).

SLOVAKIA A TO Z

Arriving and Departing

By Bus

There is no direct bus service from the United Kingdom to Slovakia; the closest you can get is Vienna. **International Express** (⊠ Coach Travel Center, 13 Lower Regent St., London SW1Y 4LR, ☎ 0171/439–9368) operates daily in summer.

By Car

Hoek van Holland and Ostend are the most convenient ferry ports for Bratislava. From either, drive to Cologne (Köln) and then through Dresden or Frankfurt to reach Bratislava.

By Plane

At press time, few international airlines provided direct service to Bratislava, hence the best airports for traveling to Slovakia remain **Prague's Ruzyně Airport** and **Vienna's Schwechat Airport. ČSA,** the Czech and Slovak national carrier (in the U.S., ☎ 718/656–8439), offers regular service to Prague from New York's JFK Airport, Chicago, Los Angeles, and Montréal. Many of these flights have direct connections from Prague to Bratislava ($60–$75 each way); the trip takes about an hour. ČSA also offers regular air service between Prague and Košice. Vienna's Schwechat Airport is a mere 50 kilometers (30 miles) west of Bratislava. Four buses a day stop at Schwechat en route to Bratislava; the journey takes just over an hour. Numerous trains and buses also run daily between Vienna and Bratislava. From New York, a flight to

Bratislava (with a stopover in Prague) takes 11–12 hours. From Montréal it is 8½ hours; from Los Angeles, 17 hours.

British Airways (in the U.K., ☎ 0171/897–4000) has daily nonstop service to Prague from London; **ČSA** (in the U.K., ☎ 0171/255–1898) flies five times a week nonstop from London. Numerous airlines offer service between London and Vienna.

By Train
There are no direct trains from London. You can take a direct train from Paris via Frankfurt to Vienna (and connect to another train or bus), or from Berlin via Dresden and Prague (en route to Budapest). Vienna is a good starting point for Bratislava. There are several trains that make the 70-minute run daily from Vienna's Südbahnhof.

Getting Around
By Bus
S.A.D. (Slovenská autobusová doprava; Bratislava, ☎ 07/7211667), the national bus carrier for Slovakia, maintains a comprehensive network in Slovakia. Buses are usually much quicker than the normal trains and more frequent than express trains, though prices are comparable with train fares. Buy your tickets from the ticket window at the bus station or directly from the driver on the bus. Long-distance buses can be full, so you might want to book a seat in advance; any Satur office will help you do this. The only drawback to traveling by bus is figuring out the timetables. They are easy to read, but beware of the small letters denoting exceptions to the times given.

By Car
Slovakia has few multilane highways, but the secondary road network is in reasonably good shape, and traffic is usually light. Roads are poorly marked, however, so an essential purchase is the *Auto Atlas SR,* which is inexpensive and available at bookstores throughout Slovakia.

Slovakia follows the usual Continental rules of the road. A right turn on red is permitted only when indicated by a green arrow. Signposts with yellow diamonds indicate a main road where drivers have the right of way. The speed limit is 110 kph (70 mph) on four-lane highways; 90 kph (55 mph) on open roads; and 60 kph (40 mph) in built-up areas. The fine for speeding is roughly 300 Sk., payable on the spot. Seat belts are compulsory, and drinking before driving is prohibited.

To report an accident, call the emergency number (☎ 155); in case of car failure call rescue service (☎ 154 or 124) in Poprad.

By Plane
Despite the splintering of the Czechoslovak federation, **ČSA** maintains a remarkably good internal air service within Slovakia, linking Bratislava with Poprad (Tatras) and Košice. Reservations can be made through Satur offices abroad or ČSA in Bratislava (☎ 07/311205).

By Train
Trains vary in speed, but it's not really worth taking anything less than an "express" train, marked in red on the timetable. Tickets are relatively cheap; first class is considerably more spacious and comfortable and on full trains well worth the 50% increase over the price of standard tickets. If you don't specify "express" when you buy your ticket, you may have to pay a supplement on the train. If you haven't bought a ticket in advance at the station, it's easy to buy one on the train for a small extra charge. On timetables, departures appear on a yellow background; arrivals are on white. It is possible to book *couchettes* (sleepers) on most overnight trains, but don't expect much in the way of

comfort. The European East Pass and InterRail Pass are valid for all rail travel within Slovakia.

Contacts and Resources

Car Rentals

There are no special requirements for renting a car in Slovakia, but be sure to shop around, as prices can differ greatly. **Hertz** offers Western makes for as much as $1,000 per week. Smaller local companies, on the other hand, may rent local cars for as low as $130 per week.

The following agencies are in Bratislava: **Auto Danubius** (✉ Trnavská 31, ☎ 07/273754); **Hertz** (✉ Hotel Forum, ☎ 07/5334441); and **Recar** (✉ Svetoplukova 1, ☎ 07/5266436).

Europcar InterRent (✉ Ivanka Airport, ☎ 07/522–0285; ✉ Hotel Danube, ☎ 07/534–0841 or 07/534–0847).

Customs and Duties

You may import duty-free into Slovakia 250 cigarettes or the equivalent in tobacco, 1 liter of spirits, 2 liters of wine, ½ liter of perfume, and up to 1,000 Sk. worth of gifts and souvenirs.

As with the Czech Republic, if you take into Slovakia any valuables or foreign-made equipment from home, such as cameras, it's wise to carry the original receipts with you or register the items with U.S. Customs before you leave (Form 4457). Otherwise you could end up paying duty upon your return.

Language

Slovak, a western-Slavic tongue closely related to both Czech and Polish, is the official language of Slovakia. English is popular among young people, but German is still the most useful language for tourists.

Mail

POSTAL RATES

Postcards to the United States cost 6 Sk.; letters, 11 Sk. Postcards to Great Britain cost 4 Sk.; a letter, 6 Sk. Prices are due for an increase in 1997, so check with your hotel for current rates.

RECEIVING MAIL

If you don't know where you'll be staying, you can have mail held *poste restante* (general delivery) at post offices in major towns, but the letters should be marked Pošta 1 to designate a city's main post office. You will be asked for identification when you collect mail. The poste restante window in Bratislava is at Námestie SNP 35.

Money and Expenses

CURRENCY

The unit of currency in Slovakia is the crown, or koruna, written as Sk., and divided into 100 halierov. There are bills of 20, 50, 100, 200, 500, 1,000, and 5,000 Sk., and coins of 10, 20, and 50 halierov and 1, 2, 5, and 10 Sk.

At press time, the rate of exchange was around 30 Sk. to the American dollar, 21 Sk. to the Canadian dollar, and 46 Sk. to the pound sterling.

SAMPLE COSTS

A cup of coffee, 15 Sk.; museum entrance, 10 Sk.–30 Sk.; a good theater seat, from 60 to 750 Sk. (some theaters, including the Slovak National Theater, charge foreigners a hefty fee and locals pay only a margin of this price); a half liter (pint) of beer, 15 Sk.; a 1-mile taxi ride, 100 Sk.; a bottle of Slovak wine in a good restaurant, 100 Sk.–150 Sk.; a glass (2 deciliters, or 7 ounces) of wine, 25 Sk.

National Holidays

January 1; Easter Monday; May 1 (Labor Day); July 5 (Sts. Cyril and Methodius); August 29 (anniversary of the Slovak National Uprising); September 1 (Constitution Day); and December 24, 25, and 26.

Passports and Visas

American and British citizens do not need a visa to enter Slovakia. A valid passport is sufficient for stays of up to 30 days. Questions should be directed to the Slovakian Embassy (⊠ 3900 Linnean Ave. NW, Washington, DC, ☎ 202/363–6315). Canadian citizens must obtain a visa (C$50) before entering the country; for applications and information contact the Slovak Embassy (⊠ 50 Rideau Terrace, Ottawa, Ontario K1M 2A1, ☎ 613/749–4442).

Telephones

INTERNATIONAL CALLS

The country code for Slovakia is 42. Dial ☎ 00–420–00101 (AT&T) or ☎ 00–420–00112 (MCI) to reach an English-speaking operator who can effortlessly connect your direct, collect, or credit-card call to the United States.

Otherwise, you can make a more time-consuming and expensive international call from Bratislava's main post office (⊠ Nám. SNP 36) or for an even larger fee, at major hotels throughout the country.

For international directory inquiries call 0149; call 0139 for information on international services and rates.

LOCAL CALLS

For local directory assistance call 120. Call 121 for directory inquiries in Slovakia that are outside the city from which you're calling. Not all operators speak English so you may have to ask a hotel clerk for help.

Tipping

To reward good service in a restaurant, round up the bill to the nearest multiple of 10 (if the bill comes to 86 Sk., for example, give the waiter 90 Sk.). A tip of 10% is considered appropriate in expensive restaurants or on group tabs. Tip porters 20 Sk. For room service, a 20-Sk. tip is sufficient. In taxis, round up the bill to the nearest multiple of 10. Give tour guides and helpful concierges 20 Sk.–30 Sk.

Visitor Information

Satur Tours and Travel Agency (formerly known as Čedok) has remained the official travel bureau for Slovakia. With offices in almost every city throughout the country, it will supply you with hotel and tour information and book air, rail, and bus tickets, but do not expect much in the way of general information. For Satur addresses and telephone numbers, *see* Visitor Information *in* specific region A to Z sections, *above.*

4 Hungary

Freed from the iron fist of Soviet rule, newly democratic Hungary is in the midst of full-swing revitalization. Budapest offers breathtaking Old World grandeur and thriving cultural life—a must-stop on any trip to Central Europe. In distinctive smaller cities like Pécs, Szeged, Debrecen, and Kecskemét, cobblestone steets wind among lovely baroque buildings. In the countryside, gleaming sunflower fields blanket gently swelling hills, and sleepy villages of thatched-roof cottages cluster around carefully tended vineyards. Hearty meals spiced with rich red paprika, the generosity and warmth of the Magyar soul: These and more sustain visitors to this land of vital spirit and beauty.

By Alan Levy

Updated by
Julie Tomasz

HUNGARY SITS AT THE CROSSROADS of central Europe, having retained its own identity by absorbing countless invasions and foreign occupations. Its industrious, resilient people have a history of brave but unfortunate uprisings: against the Turks in the 17th century, the Hapsburgs in 1848, and the Soviet Union in 1956. Each has resulted in a period of readjustment, a return to politics as the art of the possible.

The 1960s and 1970s saw matters improve politically and materially for the majority of Hungarians. Communist Party leader János Kádár remained relatively popular at home and abroad, allowing Hungary to expand and improve trade and relations with the West. The bubble began to burst during the 1980s, however, when the economy stagnated and inflation escalated. The peaceful transition to democracy began when young reformers in the party shunted aside the aging Kádár in 1988 and began speaking openly about multiparty democracy, a market economy, and a break from Moscow—daring ideas at the time.

Events quickly gathered pace, and by spring 1990, as the Iron Curtain fell, Hungarians went to the polls in the first free elections in 40 years. A center-right government led by Prime Minister József Antal took office, sweeping away the Communists and their renamed successor party, the Socialists, who finished fourth. Ironically, four years later, in the nation's next elections, Hungarians voted out the ailing center-right party in favor of none other than the Hungarian Socialist Party, which now rules in coalition with the Free Democrats. *Plus ça change . . .*

Because Hungary is a small, agriculturally oriented country, visitors are often surprised by its grandeur and Old World charm, especially in the capital, Budapest, which bustles with life as never before. Hungarians like to complain about their economic problems, but they spare visitors bureaucratic hassles at the border and airport. Entry is easy and quick for Westerners, most of whom no longer need visas. Gone are the days when visitors were forced to make daily currency exchanges and register with local police on arrival.

Two rivers cross the country: The famous Duna (Danube) flows from the west through Budapest on its way to the southern frontier, and the smaller Tisza flows from the northeast across the Nagyalföld (Great Plain). What Hungary lacks in size, it makes up for in beauty and charm. Western Hungary is dominated by the largest lake in Central Europe, Lake Balaton. Although some overdevelopment has blighted its splendor, its shores are still lined with baroque villages, relaxing spas, magnificent vineyards, and shaded garden restaurants serving the catch of the day. In eastern Hungary, the Nagyalföld offers visitors a chance to explore the folklore and customs of the Magyars (the Hungarians' name for themselves and their language). It is an area of spicy food, strong wine, and the proud *csikós* (horsemen). The unspoiled towns of the provincial areas are rich in history and culture.

However, it is Budapest, a city of more than 2 million people, that draws travelers from all over the world. The hills of Buda rise from the brackish waters of the Danube, which bisects the city; on the flatlands of Pest is an imposing array of hotels, restaurants, and shopping areas. Throughout Hungary, comfortable accommodations can be found for comparatively modest prices, and there's an impressive network of inexpensive guest houses.

Hungarians are known for their hospitality and love talking to foreigners, although their unusual language, which has no links to other Euro-

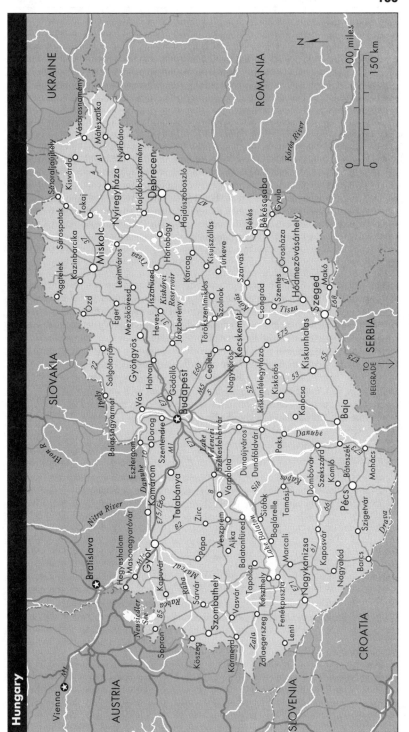

Hungary

pean tongues, can be a problem. Today, however, everyone seems to be learning English, especially young people. Trying out a few words of German will delight the older generation. But what all Hungarians share is a deep love of music, and the calendar is studded with it, from Budapest's famous opera to its annual spring music festival. And everywhere Gypsy violinists are likely to serenade you during your evening meal.

Pleasures and Pastimes

Beaches and Water Sports

Lake Balaton, the largest lake in Central Europe, is the most popular playground of this landlocked nation. If you're looking to relax in the sun and enjoy some water sports, settle in here for several days, basing yourself in either the northern shore's main town, Balatonfüred, or picturesque Tihany. For a break from the beach (and the summer crowds), you can make a few excursions by car or bicycle to explore the towns hugging the shore, especially Badacsony and Tihany, as well as the smaller, less-trodden villages farther inland, such as those in and around the Káli Basin, near Zánka.

Dining

Through the lean postwar years the Hungarian kitchen lost none of its spice and sparkle. Meats, rich sauces, and creamy desserts predominate, but the more health-conscious will also find salads, even out of season. (Strict vegetarians should note, however, that even meatless dishes are usually cooked with lard [*zsír*].) In addition to the ubiquitous dishes with which most foreigners are familiar, such as chunky beef *gulyás* (goulash) and *paprikás csirke* (chicken paprika) served with *galuska* (little pinched dumplings), traditional Hungarian classics include fiery *halászlé* (fish soup), scarlet with hot paprika; *fogas* (pike perch) from Lake Balaton; and goose liver, duck, and veal specialties. Lake Balaton is the major source of fish in Hungary, particularly for *süllő*, a kind of perch. Most restaurants offer it breaded, although some will grill it. Hungarians are also very fond of carp (*ponty*), catfish (*harcsa*), and eel (*angolna*), which are usually stewed in a garlic-and-tomato sauce.

Portions are large, so don't plan to eat more than one main Hungarian meal a day. Desserts are lavish, and every inn seems to have its house *torta* (cake), though *rétes* (strudels), *Somlói galuska* (a steamed sponge cake soaked in chocolate sauce and whipped cream), and *palacsinta* (stuffed crepes) are ubiquitous. Traditional rétes fillings are *mák* (sugary poppy seeds), *meggy* (sour cherry), and *túró* (sweetened cottage cheese); palacsintas always come rolled with *dió* (sweet ground walnut), *túró*, or *lekvár* (jam)—usually *barack* (apricot). Unless you're taking a cure in a spa, don't expect to lose weight in Hungary.

In major cities, there is a good selection of restaurants, from the grander establishments that echo the imperial past of the Hapsburg era to the less expensive, rustic spots favored by locals. In addition to the standard *vendéglő* or *étterem* (restaurants), visitors can eat at an *önkiszolgáló étterem* (self-service restaurant), a *bistró étel bár* (sit-down snack bar), a *büfé* (snack counter), an *eszpresszó* (café), or a *söröző* (pub). And no matter how strict your diet, don't pass up a visit to at least one *cukrászda* (pastry shop). In Budapest, numerous new ethnic restaurants—from Chinese to Mexican to Hare Krishna Indian—are springing up all the time. The selection of restaurants in the dining sections is primarily Hungarian and Continental, but if you get a craving for sushi or tortellini, consult the restaurant listings in the *Budapest Sun* (☞ Budapest A to Z, *below*) for the latest information on what's cooking where.

Although prices are steadily increasing, there are plenty of good, affordable restaurants offering a variety of Hungarian dishes. Even in Budapest, eating out can provide you with some of the best value for the money of any European capital. In almost all restaurants, an inexpensive prix-fixe lunch called a *menü* is available, usually for as little as 300 Ft. It includes soup or salad, an entrée, and a dessert. One caveat: Some of the more touristy restaurants unfortunately sometimes follow the international practice of embellishing tourists' bills; it doesn't hurt to discreetly check the total before paying. Also note that many restaurants have a fine-print policy of charging for each slice of bread consumed from the bread basket.

Hungarians eat early—you risk offhand service and cold food after 9 PM. Lunch, the main meal for many, is served from noon to 2. At most moderately priced and inexpensive restaurants, casual but neat dress is acceptable.

CATEGORY	BUDAPEST*	ALL AREAS*
$$$$	over 3,100 Ft.	over 2,400 Ft.
$$$	2,200 Ft.–3,100 Ft.	1,700 Ft.–2,400 Ft.
$$	1,300 Ft.–2,200 Ft.	1,000 Ft.–1,700 Ft.
$	under 1,300 Ft.	under 1,000 Ft.

*per person for a three-course meal, excluding wine and tip

Folk Art

Hungary's centuries-old traditions of handmade folk art are still beautifully alive, with specific crafts and styles special to various regions around the country. Intricately carved wooden boxes, vibrantly colorful embroidered tablecloths and shirts, matte-black pottery pitchers, delicately woven lace collars, ceramic plates splashed with painted flowers and birds, and decorative heavy leather whips are among the favorite handcrafted pieces a visitor can purchase. You'll find them in folk-art stores around the country, but can purchase them directly from the artisans at crafts fairs and from peddlers on the streets. Dolls dressed in national costume are also popular souvenirs.

Hiking

Northern Hungary offers superlative opportunities for hikers and nature seekers. Base yourself in Eger—for lovely sightseeing, excellent wine, and good lodging—and make day trips north to Szilvásvárad for hiking or biking in the hills of the Bükk range and south for the same in the Mátra range, near Gyöngyös. Moving slightly farther north, you can spend a night or two in the magical palace hotel in Lillafüred, making excursions to the magnificent caves at Aggtelek, near the Slovak border, and to Tokaj, farther east, for some less athletic wine tasting.

Lodging

Outside Budapest there are very few very expensive hotels, so you will improve your chances of having a memorable lodging experience by arranging a stay in one of the options noted below. For specific recommendations or information about how to book lodging in these accommodations, see the lodging and information sections throughout the chapter.

Castles and Mansions: Bought back from the government over the last several years, more and more of Hungary's magnificent, centuries-old castles and mansions are being restored and opened as country resorts; a night or two in one of these majestic old places makes for an unusual and romantic lodging experience. **Guest Houses:** Also called *panziók* (pensions), small guest houses, often found lying just outside the heart of cities or towns, provide simple accommodations—well suited to people on a budget. Like B&Bs, most are run by couples or families, and offer simple breakfast facilities and usually have private bathrooms. Arrangements can be made directly with the panzió or through local tourist offices and travel agents abroad. **Private Rooms:** For those with simple lodging needs and a tight budget, renting a room in a private home is a good option. In the provinces it is safe to accept rooms offered to you directly; they will almost always be clean and in a relatively good neighborhood, and the prospective landlord will probably not cheat you. Look for signs reading SZOBA KIADÓ (or the German ZIMMER FREI). Reservations and referrals can also be made by any tourist office, and if you go that route, you have someone to complain to if things don't work out. **Village Homes:** Village tourism is a growing trend in Hungary, affording visitors a chance to sink into life in tiny, typical villages around the country. The Hungarian Tourist Board's *Village Tourism* publication provides descriptions and color photos of many of the village homes now open to guests. **Apartment and Cottage Rentals:** Apartments in Budapest and cottages at Lake Balaton are available for short- and long-term rental and can make the most economic lodging for families—particularly for those who prefer to cook their own meals. Rates and reservations can be obtained from tourist offices in Hungary and abroad. Also consult the free annual accommodations directory published by the **Hungarian Tourist Board** (☞ Visitor Information *in* Hungary A to Z, *below*); published in five languages, it lists basic information about hotels, pensions, bungalows, and tourist hostels throughout the country. A separate brochure lists the country's campgrounds.

CATEGORY	BUDAPEST*	OTHER AREAS*
$$$$	over 30,000 Ft.	over 11,000 Ft.
$$$	20,000–30,000 Ft.	9,000–11,000 Ft.
$$	10,000–20,000 Ft.	5,000–9,000 Ft.
$	under 10,000 Ft.	under 5,000 Ft.

All prices are for a standard double room with bath and breakfast during peak season (June through August) and are based on the press-time exchange rate of 140 Ft. to the U.S. dollar. For single rooms with bath, count on about 80% of the double-room rate. During the off-season (in Budapest, September through March; at Lake Balaton, May and September), rates can be considerably lower than those given above. Prices at Lake Balaton tend to be significantly higher than those in the rest of the countryside. Note that most large hotels require payment in hard currency.

Porcelain

Among the most sought-after items in Hungary are the exquisite hand-painted Herend and Zsolnay porcelain. Unfortunately, the prices on all makes of porcelain have risen considerably in the last few years. For guaranteed authenticity, make your purchases at the specific Herend and Zsolnay stores in major cities, or at the factories themselves in Herend and Pécs.

Spas and Thermal Baths

Several thousand years ago, the first settlers of the area that is now Budapest chose their home because of its abundance of hot springs. Centuries later, the Romans and the Turks built baths and developed cultures based on medicinal bathing. One tourist brochure claims it is just barely a hyperbole to say that "it is enough to push a stick into the ground and up will come thermal water—and with a bit of luck, it will have a curative effect." Indeed, there are over 1,000 medicinal hot springs bubbling up around the country. Budapest alone has some 14 historic working baths, which attract ailing patients with medical prescriptions for specific water cures as well as "recreational" bathers—locals and tourists alike—wanting to soak in the relaxing waters, try some of the many massages and treatments, and experience the architectural beauty of the bathhouses themselves.

For most, a visit to a bath involves soaking in several thermal pools of varying temperatures and curative contents—perhaps throwing in a game of aquatic chess—relaxing in a steam room or sauna, and getting a brisk, if not brutal, massage (average cost: 200 Ft. for a half hour). Many bath facilities are single-sex, and most people walk around nude or with miniature loincloths, provided at the door, with which one can only attempt to remain decent.

In addition to the ancient beauties there are newer, modern baths open to the public at many spa hotels. They lack the charm and aesthetic appeal of their older peers but provide the latest treatments in sparkling facilities. Of the areas outside Budapest covered in this guidebook, Debrecen, Hévíz, and Eger are famous spa towns with popular bath facilities. For more information, page through the "Hungary: Land of Spas" brochure published by the Hungarian Tourist Board, available free from most tourist offices.

Wine, Beer, and Spirits

Hungary tempts wine connoisseurs with its important wine regions, especially Villány, near Pécs, in the south; Eger and Tokaj in the north; and the northern shore of Lake Balaton. **Tokay,** the best-known and most abundant white wine, can be too heavy, dark, and sweet for many tastes, even Hungarians (which is why red wine is often recommended with poultry, veal, and even fish dishes). However, **Tokaji Aszú,** the best of the breed, makes a good dessert wine. **Badacsony** white wines are lighter and livelier, though not particularly dry.

The gourmet red table wine of Hungary, **Egri Bikavér** (Bull's Blood of Eger, usually with *el toro* himself on the label), is the best buy and the safest bet with all foods. Other good reds and the best rosés come from **Villanyi**; the most adventurous reds—with sometimes successful links to both Austrian and Californian wine making and viticulture—are from the **Sopron** area.

Before- and after-dinner drinks tend toward schnapps, most notably **Barack-pálinka,** an apricot brandy. A plum brandy called **Kosher szilva-pálinka,** bottled under rabbinical supervision, is very chic. **Unicum,** Hungary's national liqueur, is a dark, thick, vaguely minty, and quite potent drink that could be likened to Germany's Jägermeister. Its unique chubby green bottle makes it a good souvenir to take home.

Major Hungarian beers are Kőbányai, Dreher, Aranyhordó, Balaton, Világos, and Aszok. Czech, German, and Austrian beers are widely available on tap.

Exploring Hungary

Hungary's main geographical regions begin with the capital city and thriving urban heart of **Budapest.** Just north of Budapest, the Danube River forms a gentle heart-shaped curve along which lie the romantic and historic towns of the region called the **Danube Bend.** Southwest of Budapest are the vineyards, quaint villages, and popular, developed summer resorts around **Lake Balaton.** The more rural and gently mountainous stretch of **northern Hungary** also includes the handsome, vibrant town of Eger and the famous wine village of Tokaj; the contrastingly flat and dry expanses of the **Great Plain,** in the east, are spiced with legendary traditions of horsemanship and agriculture and anchored by the interesting and lively cities of Kecskemét and Debrecen. The verdant, rolling countryside of **Transdanubia** stretches west of the Danube to the borders of Austria, Slovenia, and Croatia; in the northern hills nestle the gemlike, beautifully restored towns of Sopron and Kőszeg, and in the south, the culturally rich, dynamically beautiful city of Pécs. Given Hungary's relatively small size, most of these points are less than a few hours away from Budapest by car.

Great Itineraries

Numbers in the text correspond to numbers in the margin and on the maps.

IF YOU HAVE 3 DAYS

⛰ **Budapest** ①–㊹ alone offers a full vacation's worth of things to see and experience, but in one day an efficient and motivated visitor can pack in some of the don't-misses: exploration of **Castle Hill** ①–⑮, a stroll on the **Danube korzo,** a glimpse of **Országház** (Parliament) ㉙, a look at **Hősök tere** (Heroes' Square) ㊾, followed by a dip in the **Széchenyi Baths,** a hearty meal—padded by as many pastry-and-espresso stops as your doctor will allow—and a night at the **Operaház** (Opera House) ㊽. After a night's rest in Budapest, hop on an early boat to explore the charming artists' village of **Szentendre** ㊾ and the majestic fortress of **Visegrád** ㉍, upriver in the Danube Bend. You can spend another night in Budapest; the next morning, drive down to **Badacsony** ㉘ on Lake Balaton's northern shore. Here, you can experience the country's famous lake as well as its beloved wines. Follow a refreshing swim with a lunch of fresh Balaton fish and some wine tasting in the cool cellars on Mount Badacsony's vineyard-covered slopes. On your way back to Budapest, stop for a stroll on **Tihany**'s ㉕ cobblestone streets and the views from its lovely hilltop abbey.

IF YOU HAVE 6 DAYS

Spend two full days exploring ⛰ **Budapest** ①–㊹, selecting from the walk below (☞ Budapest, *below*). In the evening, attend a performance at the **Operaház** (Opera House) ㊽ or a folk-dancing show to get a taste of the city's sparkling cultural life. Spend your third day visiting the Danube Bend's crown jewels, the villages of **Szentendre** ㊾ and **Visegrád** ㉍, making the trip by scenic boat or by car. Return to Budapest for the night and head out the next morning for a day on the Great Plain, strolling among the sights of lovely ⛰ **Kecskemét** ㊙ before venturing out to the *puszta* (prairie) in the **Bugac National Park** ㊐ or **Kerekegyháza,** to experience the unique horsemanship stunts and demonstrations of Hungary's legendary cowboys, the *csikós*. Depending on how much you want to drive and how much of Budapest's nightlife you want to take in, you can either go back to Budapest (85 kilometers [53 miles] from Kecskemét) for the night or spend it here in Kecskemét. On day five, drive down to ⛰ **Pécs** ㊕ to see its beautiful town square, cathedral, and excellent museums. After a night's rest, make your way on scenic secondary roads through southern Transdanubia to **Keszthely** ㊉ on the northwestern tip of Lake Balaton, visiting the spectacular Festetics mansion before moving east along the northern shore to ⛰ **Badacsony** ㉘. On the way, make a stop in picturesque **Szigliget** ㉙ and scale its castle hill to gaze at the sweeping Lake Balaton view. In Badacsony, spend the rest of the afternoon hiking up the vineyard-carpeted slopes of Mount Badacsony, rewarded by generous wine tastings in the local cellars and a big fish dinner with live Gypsy music. Depending on your traveling speed (and how much wine you've tasted), instead of sleeping in Badacsony, you may prefer to move on along the northern shore and spend the fifth night in ⛰ **Tihany** ㉕ or ⛰ **Balatonfüred** ㉔, both of which have good lodging possibilities with more facilities and amenities. Either way, you can spend your sixth day exploring Tihany and Balatonfüred, cooling off with a swim in the lake before heading back to Budapest.

When to Tour

The ideal times to visit Hungary are in the spring (May through June) and end of summer and early fall (late August through September). The months of July and August, peak vacation season for Hungarians as well as foreign tourists, can be extremely hot and humid; Budapest is hot and crowded, and the entire Lake Balaton region is overrun with vacationers. Many of Hungary's major fairs and festivals take place during the spring and fall, including the late-March to early April Spring Festival (in many cities and towns) and the myriad wine-harvest festivals in late summer and early fall. Lake Balaton is the only area that really closes down and gets boarded up during the low season, generally from mid- or late September until at least Easter, if not mid-May. Wherever you go, spring in Hungary also brings a spectacular show of cherry and almond blossoms, fragrantly blooming lilac bushes, and brilliant crimson expanses of flowering poppies. Summer holds the unforgettable and quintessentially Hungarian sights of sweeping fields of swaying golden sunflowers and giant white storks summering with their families in their bushy nests built on chimney tops.

BUDAPEST

Situated on both banks of the Danube, Budapest unites the colorful hills of Buda and the wide, businesslike boulevards of Pest. Though it was the site of a Roman outpost during the 1st century, the city was not officially created until 1873, when the towns of Óbuda, Pest, and Buda were joined. Since then, Budapest has been the cultural, political, intellectual, and commercial heart of Hungary; for the 20% of the nation's population who live in the capital, anywhere else is simply "the country."

Budapest has suffered many ravages in the course of its long history. It was totally destroyed by the Mongols in 1241, captured by the Turks in 1541, and nearly destroyed again by Soviet troops in 1945. But this bustling industrial and cultural center survived as the capital of the People's Republic of Hungary after the war—and then, as the 1980s drew to a close, it became one of the Eastern bloc's few thriving bastions of capitalism. Today, judging by the city's flourishing cafés and restaurants, markets and bars, the stagnation wrought by the Communists seems a thing of the very distant past.

Much of the charm of a visit to Budapest lies in unexpected glimpses into shadowy courtyards and in long vistas down sunlit cobbled streets. Although some 30,000 buildings were destroyed during World War II and in 1956, the past lingers on in the often crumbling architectural details of the antique structures that remain and in the memories and lifestyles of Budapest's citizens.

The principal sights of the city fall roughly into three areas, each of which can be comfortably covered on foot. The Budapest hills are best explored by public transportation. Note that street names have been changed in the past few years to purge all reminders of the Communist regime. Underneath the new names, the old ones remain, canceled out by a big red slash. Also note that a Roman-numeral prefix listed before an address refers to one of Budapest's 22 districts.

Exploring Budapest

Castle Hill (Várhegy)

Most of the major sights of Buda are on Várhegy (Castle Hill), a long, narrow plateau laced with cobblestone streets, clustered with beautifully preserved baroque, Gothic, and Renaissance houses, and crowned by the magnificent Royal Palace. The area is theoretically banned to private cars (except for those of neighborhood residents and Hilton Hotel guests), but the streets manage to be lined bumper to bumper with Trabants and Mercedes all the same—sometimes the only visual element to verify you're not in a fairy tale. As in all of Budapest, thriving urban new has taken up residence in historic old; international corporate offices, diplomatic residences, restaurants, and boutiques occupy many of its landmark buildings. But these are still the exceptions, as most flats and homes are lived in by private families. The most striking example, perhaps, is the Hilton Hotel on Hess András tér, which has ingeniously incorporated remains of Castle Hill's oldest church (a tower and one wall), built by Dominican friars in the 13th century.

Numbers in the text correspond to numbers in the margin and on the Castle Hill (Várhegy) map.

A GOOD WALK

Castle Hill's cobblestone streets and numerous museums are made to be explored on foot: Plan to spend about a day here. Most of the transportation options for getting to Castle Hill deposit you on Szent György tér or Dísz tér. (It's impossible to not find Castle Hill, but it is possible to be confused about how to get on top of it. If you're already on the Buda side of the river, you can take the Castle bus—*Várbusz*—from the Moszkva tér metro station, northwest of Castle Hill. If you're starting out from Pest, you can take a taxi or Bus 16 from Erzsébet tér or, the most scenic alternative, cross the Széchenyi Lánchíd (Chain Bridge) on foot to Clark Ádám tér and ride the *Sikló* (funicular rail) up Castle Hill (☞ Clark Ádám tér, *below*).

Begin your exploration by walking slightly farther south to visit the **Királyi Palota** (Royal Palace), at the southern end of the hill. Of the palace's several major museums, the **Magyar Nemzeti Galéria** (Hungarian National Gallery) ③ and the **Budapesti Történeti Múzeum** (Budapest History Museum) ④ are particularly interesting. From here, you can cover the rest of the area by walking north along its handful of charming streets. From Dísz tér, start with Tárnok utca, whose houses and usually open courtyards offer glimpses of how Hungarians have integrated contemporary life into Gothic, Renaissance, and baroque settings; of particular interest are the houses at No. 16, now the Arany Hordo restaurant, and at No. 18, the 15th-century **Arany Sas Patika** (Golden Eagle Pharmacy Museum), with a naïf Madonna and child in an overhead niche. This tiny museum displays instruments, prescriptions, books, and other artifacts from 16th- and 17th-century pharmacies. Modern commerce is also integrated into Tárnok utca's historic homes; you'll encounter numerous folk souvenir shops and tiny boutiques lining the street. Tárnok utca funnels into Szentháromság tér, home of **Mátyás templom** (St. Matthias Church) ⑧ and just behind it, the **Halászbástya** (Fishermen's Bastion) ⑨.

After exploring them, double back to Dísz tér and set out northward again on Úri utca, which runs parallel to Tárnok utca; less commercialized by boutiques and other shops, it is also the longest and oldest street in the castle district, lined with many stately houses, all worth special attention for their delicately carved details. Both gateways of the baroque palace at Nos. 48–50 are articulated by Gothic niches.

Bécsi Kapu tér, **13**

Budapesti Történeti
Múzeum, **4**

Budavári Labirintus, **7**

Hadtörténeti
Múzeum, **15**

Halászbástya, **9**

Kapistrán tér, **14**

Középkori Zsidó
Imaház, **12**

Ludwig Múzeum, **1**

Magyar Kereskedelmi
és Vendéglátóipari
Múzeum, **10**

Magyar Nemzeti
Galéria, **3**

Mátyás templom, **8**

Országos Széchenyi
Könyvtár, **5**

Statue of Prince Eugene
of Savoy, **2**

Várszínház, **6**

Zenetörténeti
Múzeum, **11**

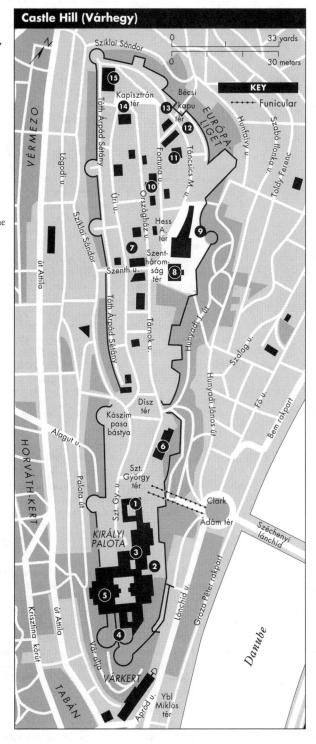

Castle Hill (Várhegy)

KEY

••••••• Funicular

The endearing little **Telefónia Museum** (Telephone Museum), at No. 49, is worth a stop, as is the **Budavári Labirintus** (Labyrinth of Buda Castle) ⑦, at No. 9. At the end of Úri utca you'll reach **Kapisztrán tér** ⑭. From here, you can walk south again on a parallel street, Országház utca (Parliament Street), the main thoroughfare of 18th-century Buda; it takes its name from the building at No. 28, which was the seat of Parliament from 1790 to 1807. Before it was appropriated for secular use, this building was the church and convent of the Order of St. Clare. You'll end up back at Szentháromság tér, with just two streets remaining to explore.

You can stroll down charming little Fortuna utca, named for the 18th-century Fortuna Inn, which now houses the **Magyar Kereskedelmi és Vendéglátóipari Múzeum** (Hungarian Museum of Commerce and Catering) ⑩. At the end of Fortuna utca you'll reach **Bécsi kapu tér** (Vienna Gate Square) ⑬, named for the stone gateway (rebuilt in 1936) marking the northern entrance to Castle Hill, opening toward Vienna—or, closer at hand, Moszkva tér just below. Go back south on the last of the district's streets, Táncsics Mihály utca, stopping at the **Középkori Zsidó Imaház** (Medieval Synagogue) ⑫ and the **Zenetörténeti Múzeum** (Museum of Music History) ⑪. Next door, at No. 9, is the baroque house (formerly the Royal Mint) where rebel writer Tancsics Mihály was imprisoned in the dungeons and freed by the people on the Day of Revolution, March 15, 1848. You'll find yourself in front of the Hilton Hotel, back at Hess András tér, bordering Szentháromság tér. Those whose cobblestone-jostled feet haven't yet protested can finish off their tour of Castle Hill by doubling back to the northern end and strolling south back to Dísz tér on **Tóth Árpád sétány,** the romantic, tree-lined promenade along the Buda side of the hill.

TIMING

Castle Hill is small enough to cover in one day, but perusing its major museums and several tiny exhibits will require more time.

SIGHTS TO SEE

⑬ **Bécsi kapu tér** (Vienna Gate Square). Marking the northern entrance to Castle Hill, the stone gateway (rebuilt in 1936) called "Vienna Gate" opens toward Vienna—or, closer at hand, Moszkva tér just below. The square named after it has some fine baroque and rococo houses, but is dominated by the enormous neo-Romanesque (1913–17) headquarters of the **Országos Levéltár** (Hungarian National Archives), which looks more like a cathedral, as befits a shrine to paperwork.

④ **Budapesti Történeti Múzeum** (Budapest History Museum). The palace's baroque southern wing (E) contains the Budapest History Museum, displaying a fascinating new permanent exhibit of modern Budapest history from Buda's liberation from the Turks in 1686 through the 1970s. Viewing the vintage 19th- and 20th-century photos and videos of the castle, the Chain Bridge, and other Budapest monuments—and seeing them as the backdrop to the horrors of WWII and the 1956 Revolution—helps to put your later sightseeing in context; while you're browsing, peek out one of the windows overlooking the Danube and Pest and let it start seeping in.

Through historical documents, objects, and art, other permanent exhibits depict the medieval history of the Buda fortress and the capital as a whole. This is the best place to view remains of the medieval Royal Palace and other archaeological excavations. Some of the artifacts unearthed during excavations are in the vestibule in the basement; others are still among the remains of medieval structures. Down in the cellars are the original medieval vaults of the palace, portraits of King Matthias and his second wife, Beatrice of Aragon, and many late-14th-century statues that probably adorned the Renaissance palace. ⊠ *Buda Castle (Wing E), Szt. György tér 2,* ☎ *1/175–7533.* 🔲 *100 Ft.* ☉ *Mar.–Nov., Wed.–Mon. 10–6; Dec., Wed.–Mon. 10–4; Jan.–Feb., Wed.–Mon. 10–5.*

❼ Budavári Labirintus (Labyrinth of Buda Castle). Used as a wine cellar and a source of water during the 16th and 17th centuries and as an air-raid shelter during World War II, the labyrinth—entered at Úri utca 9 below a house dating to the beginning of the 18th century—has housed a cave theater since 1984, which presents a multimedia show, known as *Panoptikum,* that recounts early Hungarian history using marionettes and montages. The Labyrinth Cafe (open Tues.–Sun. from 6 PM) has frequent live blues and jazz. *Budavári Labirintus:* ☎ *1/175–6858.* 🔲 Panoptikum *show 350 Ft.* ☉ *Mid-Mar.–mid-Jan., Tues.–Sun. 10–6.*

❿ Hadtörténeti Múzeum (Museum of Military History). At the northwestern corner of Kapisztrán tér is the casern housing the Museum of Military History. The exhibits, which include collections of uniforms and military regalia, trace the military history of Hungary from the original Magyar conquest in the 9th century, through the period of Ottoman rule, to the middle of this century. ⊠ *I, Tóth Árpád sétány 40,* ☎ *1/156–9522.* 🔲 *100 Ft.; Sat. free. English-language tours (arrange in advance) 500 Ft.* ☉ *Mar.–Oct., Tues.–Sat. 10–5, Sun. 10–6; Nov.–Feb., Tues.–Sat. 10–4, Sun. 10–5.*

★ ❾ Halászbástya (Fishermen's Bastion). The wondrous porch overlooking the Danube and Pest is the neo-Romanesque Fishermen's Bastion, a merry cluster of white stone towers and arches and columns above a modern bronze statue of St. Stephen, Hungary's first king. Medieval fishwives once peddled their wares here, but the site is now home to souvenirs, crafts, and music. On a sunny summer morning you might hear a brass band in full uniform as well as a Hungarian zitherist sporting a white handlebar mustache and full folkloric garb, both competing for your ear as you marvel at the exquisite Danube view.

NEED A BREAK? Fishermen's Bastion is crowned by a round tower housing the elegant **Café-Restaurant Halászbástya,** which extends along the upper rampart. It is the perfect place from which to watch both the distant panorama and the bastion's passing parade. Prices are sky-high, so it's best to opt for a small refreshment.

⓮ Kapisztrán tér. Castle Hill's northernmost square was named after St. John of Capistrano, an Italian friar who in 1456 recruited a crusading army to fight the Turks who were threatening Hungary. There's a statue of this honored Franciscan on the northwest corner; also here are the ☞ **Hadtörténeti Múzeum** (Museum of Military History) and the remains of the 12th-century Gothic **Mária Magdolna templom** (Church of St. Mary Magdalene). Its *torony* (tower), completed in 1496, is the only part left standing; the rest of the church was destroyed by air raids during World War II.

★ Királyi Palota (Royal Palace). During a seven-week siege at the end of 1944, the entire Castle Hill district of palaces, mansions, and churches was turned into one vast ruin. The final German stand was in the Royal Palace, which was entirely gutted by fire; by the end of the siege its walls were reduced to rubble, and just a few scarred pillars and blackened statues protruded from the wreckage. The destruction was incalculable, yet it gave archaeologists and art historians an opportunity to discover the medieval buildings that once stood on the site of this baroque and neobaroque palace. Fortunately, details of the edifices of the kings of the Árpád and Anjou dynasties, of the Holy Roman Emperor Sigismund, and of the great 15th-century king Mátthiás Corvinus had been preserved in some 80 medieval reports, travelogues, books, and itineraries that were subsequently used to reconstruct the complex.

The postwar rebuilding was slow and painstaking. In some places debris more than 20 feet deep had to be removed; the remains found on the medieval levels were restored to their original planes. Freed from mounds of rubble, the foundation walls and medieval castle walls were completed, and the ramparts surrounding the medieval royal residence were re-created as close to their original shape and size as possible. Out of this herculean labor emerged the Royal Palace of today, a vast cultural center and museum complex (☞ Budapesti Történeti Múzeum, *above, and* Ludwig Muzeum, Magyar Nemzeti Galéria, *and* Országos Széchenyi Könyvtár, *below*).

⑫ **Középkori Zsidó Imaház** (Medieval Synagogue). The excavated one-room Medieval Synagogue is now used as a museum. On display are objects relating to the Jewish community, including religious inscriptions, frescoes, and tombstones dating to the 15th century. There are a number of Hebrew gravestones in the entranceway. ⊠ *Táncsics Mihály u. 26,* ☎ *1/155–8849.* 🎫 *50 Ft.* ⊙ *May–Oct., Tues.–Fri. 10–2, weekends 10–6.*

❶ **Ludwig Museum.** Boasting a collection of more than 200 pieces of Hungarian and contemporary world art, including works by Picasso and Lichtenstein, the Ludwig Museum occupies the castle's northern wing. ⊠ *Buda Castle (Wing A), Dísz tér 17,* ☎ *1/175–7533.* 🎫 *100 Ft.; free Tues.* ⊙ *Tues.–Sun. 10–6.*

⑩ **Magyar Kereskedelmi és Vendéglátóipari Múzeum** (Hungarian Museum of Commerce and Catering). The 18th-century Fortuna Inn that once welcomed guests now houses the Catering Museum. Once displaying a turn-of-the-century pastry shop, it has a new exhibit, "Vendégváró Budapest" (Guest-welcoming Budapest), about the city as a tourist destination from 1870 to the 1930s. The Commerce Museum, just across the courtyard, chronicles the history of Hungarian commerce from the late 19th century to 1947, when the new Communist regime "liberated" the economy into socialism. The four-room exhibit includes everything from an antique chocolate-and-caramel vending machine to early shoe-polish advertisements. ⊠ *Fortuna utca 4,* ☎ *1/175–6249.* 🎫 *40 Ft.; free Fri.* ⊙ *Mid-Mar.–Oct., Tues.–Sun. 10–6; Nov.–mid-Mar., Tues.–Sun. 10–4.*

❸ **Magyar Nemzeti Galéria.** The immense center block of the palace (made up of Wings B, C, and D) contains the Magyar Nemzeti Galéria (Hungarian National Gallery), which exhibits a wide range of Hungarian fine art, from medieval ecclesiastical paintings, stone carvings, and statues, through Gothic, Renaissance, and baroque art, to works of the 19th and 20th centuries, which are richly represented. Especially notable are the works of the romantic painter Mihály Munkácsy (1844–1900), the impressionist Pál Szinyei Merse, and the surrealist Kosztka Csontváry, whom Picasso much admired. There is also a large collection of modern Hungarian sculpture. ⊠ *Buda Castle (Wing C), Dísz tér 17,* ☎ *1/175–7533.* 🎫 *100 Ft.; free Wed.; tour for up to 5 people with English-speaking guide (book in advance) 1,000 Ft.* ⊙ *Mar.–Nov., Tues.–Sun. 10–6; Dec.–Feb., Tues.–Sun. 10–4.*

★ **❽** **Mátyás templom** (Matthias Church). The Gothic Matthias Church is officially the Buda Church of Our Lady, but better known by the name of the 15th-century's "just king" of Hungary, who was married here twice. It is sometimes called the Coronation Church, because the last two kings of Hungary were crowned here: the Hapsburg emperor Franz Joseph in 1867 and his grandnephew Karl IV in 1916. Originally built for the city's German population in the mid-13th century, the church has endured many alterations and assaults. For almost 150 years it was the main mosque of the Turkish overlords—and the predominant impact of its festive pillars is decidedly Byzantine. Badly damaged during the recapture of Buda in 1686, it was completely rebuilt between 1873 and 1896 by Frigyes Schulek, who gave it an asymmetrical western front, with one high and one low spire, and a fine rose window; the south porch is from the 14th century.

The **Szentháromság Kápolna** (Trinity Chapel) holds an *encolpion*—an enameled casket containing a miniature copy of the Gospel to be worn on the chest; it belonged to the 12th-century king Béla III and his wife, Anne of Chatillon. Their burial crowns and a cross, scepter, and rings found in their excavated graves are also displayed here. The church's **treasury** contains Renaissance and baroque chalices, monstrances, and vestments. High Mass is celebrated every Sunday at 10 AM with full orchestra and choir—and often with major soloists; get here early if you want a seat. During the summer there are usually organ recitals on Friday at 8 PM. Tourists are asked to remain at the back of the church during services (it's least intrusive to come after 10 AM weekdays and after 1 PM Sundays and holidays). ⊠ *I, Szentháromság tér 2,* ☎ *1/155–5657.* ⊙ *Daily 7 AM–8 PM.* ☜ *Church free, except during concerts; treasury 50 Ft.* ⊙ *Treasury daily 9–5:30.*

❺ **Országos Széchenyi Könyvtár** (Széchenyi National Library). The western wing (F) of the Royal Palace is home to the Széchenyi National Library, which houses more than 2 million volumes. Its archives include well-preserved medieval codices, manuscripts, and the correspondence of historic eminences. This is not a lending library, but the reading rooms are open to the public (though you must show a passport), and even the most valuable materials can be viewed on microfilm. Small, temporary exhibits on rare books and documents are usually on display. *To arrange a tour with an English-speaking guide,* ☎ *1/175–7533, ext. 384.* ☜ *30 Ft.* ⊙ *Reading rooms Mon. 1–9, Tues.–Sat. 9–9; exhibits Mon. 1–6, Tues.–Sat. 10–6.*

❷ **Statue of Prince Eugene of Savoy.** In front of the Royal Palace, facing the Danube by the entrance to Wing C, stands an equestrian statue of Prince Eugene of Savoy, a commander of the army that liberated Hungary from the Turks at the end of the 17th century. From the terrace on which the statue stands there is a superb view across the river to Pest.

Szentháromság tér. Meaning "Holy Trinity Square," this square is named for its baroque **Trinity Column,** erected in 1712–13 as a gesture of thanksgiving by survivors of a plague. The column stands in front of the famous Gothic Mátyás templom (☞ *above*), its large pedestal a perfect seat from which to watch the wedding spectacles that take over the church on spring and summer weekends: From morning till night, in a continuous cycle accompanied by organ music, frilly engaged pairs flow in one after the other and, after a brief transformation inside, back out onto the square just as the next couple in line begins.

★ **Tóth Árpád sétány.** This romantic, tree-lined promenade along the Buda side of the hill is often mistakenly overlooked by sightseers. Beginning at the Hadtörténeti Museum, the promenade takes you "behind the scenes" along the back sides of the matte-pastel baroque houses you saw on Úri utca, boasting regal, arched windows and wrought-iron gates. On a late spring afternoon, the fragrance of the cherry trees in full, vivid bloom may be enough to revive even the most wearied feet and spirits.

Úri utca. Running parallel to Tárnok utca, Úri utca has been less commercialized by boutiques and other shops; the longest and oldest street in the castle district, it is lined with many stately houses, all worth special attention for their delicately carved details. Both gateways of the baroque palace at **Nos. 48–50** are articulated by Gothic niches. The **Telefónia Múzeum** (Telephone Museum), at No. 49, is an endearing little museum entered through a peaceful, shady central courtyard shared with the local district police station. Although vintage telephone systems of museum value are still in use all over the country, both the oldest and most recent products of telecommunication—from the 1882 wooden box with hose attachment to the latest, slickest fax machines—can be observed and tested here. *Telefónia Múzeum:* ⊠ *Úri utca 49,* ☎ *1/201–8188.* 🖼 *30 Ft.* ☉ *Nov.–Apr., Tues.–Sun. 10–4; May–Oct., Tues.–Sun. 10–6.*

❻ Várszínház. On Színház utca, a street connecting Szent György tér and Dísz tér, the Várszínház (Castle Theater) was once a Franciscan church but was transformed into a late-baroque-style royal theater in 1787 under the supervision of courtier Farkas Kempelen. The first theatrical performance in Hungarian was held here in 1790. Heavily damaged during World War II, the theater was rebuilt and reopened in 1978. While the building retains its original facade, the interior was renovated with marble and concrete. It is now used as the studio theater of the National Theater and occasionally for classical recitals, and there is usually a historical exhibition in its foyer. ⊠ *Színház utca 1–3,* ☎ *1/175–8011.*

⓫ Zenetörténeti Múzeum (Museum of Music History). This handsome gray-and-pearl-stone 18th-century palace once owned by the Erdődy noble family is where Beethoven allegedly stayed in 1800 when he came to Buda to conduct his works. Now a museum, it displays rare manuscripts and old instruments downstairs in its permanent collection and temporary exhibits upstairs in a small, sunlit hall adorned with marble pillars. The museum also often hosts intimate classical recitals. ⊠ *Táncsics Mihály u. 7,* ☎ *1/175–9011.* 🖼 *60 Ft.* ☉ *Tues.–Sun. 10–6.*

Numbers in the text correspond to numbers in the margin and on the Budapest map.

Tabán and Gellért Hill

Spreading below Castle Hill is the old quarter called the Tabán (from the Turkish word for "armory"). A onetime suburb of Buda, it was known at the end of the 17th century as Little Serbia (*Rác*) because so many Serbian refugees settled here after fleeing from the Turks. It later became a quaint and romantic district of vineyards and small taverns. Though most of the small houses characteristic of this district have been demolished—mainly in the interest of easing traffic—a few picturesque buildings remain.

Gellért-hegy (Gellért Hill), 761 feet high, is the most beautiful natural formation on the Buda bank. It takes its name from St. Gellért (Gerard) of Csanad, a Venetian bishop who came to Hungary in the 11th century and was supposedly flung to his death from the top of the hill by pagans. More misery awaits you as you ascend, but take solace from the cluster of hot springs at the foot of the hill, which soothe and cure bathers at the Rác, Rudas, and Gellért baths.

A GOOD WALK

From the **Semmelweis Orvostörténeti Múzeum** (Semelweis Museum of Medical History) ⑯, walk around the corner to Szarvas tér and a few yards toward the river to the **Tabán plébánia-templom** (Tabán Parish Church) ⑰. Walking south on Attila út and crossing to the other side of Hegyalja út you'll be at the foot of Gellért Hill. From here, take a deep breath and climb the paths and stairs to the **Citadella** ㉑ fortress at the top of the hill (about 30 minutes). After taking in the views and exploring the area, you can descend and treat yourself to a soak or a swim at the **Gellért Hotel and Thermal Baths** ⑳ at the southeastern foot of the hill. On foot, take the paths down the southeastern side of the hill. You can also take Bus 27 down the back of the hill to Móricz Zsigmond körtér and walk back toward the Gellért on busy Bartók Béla út, or take Trams 47, 49, 18, or 19 a couple of stops to Szent Gellért tér.

TIMING

The Citadella and Szabadság Szobor are lit in golden lights every night, but the entire Gellért-hegy is at its scenic best every year on August 20, when it forms the backdrop to the spectacular St. Stephen's Day fireworks display.

SIGHTS TO SEE

★ ㉑ **Citadella.** The Citadella fortress atop the hill was a much-hated sight for Hungarians. They called it the Gellért Bastille, for it was erected, on the site of an earlier wooden observatory, by the Austrian army as a lookout after the 1848–49 War of Independence. But no matter what its history may be, the views here are breathtaking. Renovation as a tourist site during the 1960s improved its image, with the addition of cafés, a beer garden, wine cellars, and a tourist hostel. In its inner wall is a small graphic exhibition (with some relics) of Budapest's 2,000-year history. ⊡ *Free.* ◷ *24 hrs.*

Erzsébethíd. The Erzsébethíd (Elizabeth Bridge) was named for Empress Elizabeth (of whom the Hungarians were particularly fond), the wife of Franz Joseph and a beautiful but unhappy anorexic who was stabbed to death in 1898 by an anarchist while boarding a boat on Lake Geneva. Built between 1897 and 1903, it was the longest single-span suspension bridge in Europe at the time.

★ ⑳ **Gellért Hotel and Thermal Baths.** At the foot of the Gellért Hill at the base of the green wrought-iron Szabadsághíd (Liberty Bridge), are these beautiful art-nouveau establishments (☞ Dining and Lodging, *below*). The Gellért is the oldest spa hotel in Hungary, with hot springs that have supplied curative baths for nearly 2,000 years. It is the most popular among tourists, with a wealth of treatments—including chamomile steam baths, salt-vapor inhalations, and hot mud packs—many of which require a doctor's prescription. Men and women have separate bathing facilities indoors; outside is a popular coed wave pool. (☞ Outdoor Activities and Sports, *below*). ⊠ *XI, Gellért tér 1,* ☎ *1/185–2200 (hotel), 1/185–3555 (baths). ⊡ Indoor baths and steam rooms 300 Ft. per 1½ hrs; indoors and pool 800 Ft. per day. ◷ Baths weekdays 6 AM–6 PM, weekends 6:30 AM–noon (summer until 4 PM). Sat. massage only until 2 PM, no massage on Sun. Wave pool May–early Sept., daily 6 AM–6 PM.*

⑱ **Rác Fürdő** (Rác Baths). The bright-yellow building tucked away at the foot of Gellért Hill near the Elizabeth Bridge houses these baths, built during the reign of King Zsigmond in the early 15th century and rebuilt by Miklós Ybl in the mid-19th century. Its waters contain alkaline salts and other minerals. Women can bathe on Monday, Wednesday, and Friday; men on Tuesday, Thursday, and Saturday. (☞ Outdoor Ac-

198

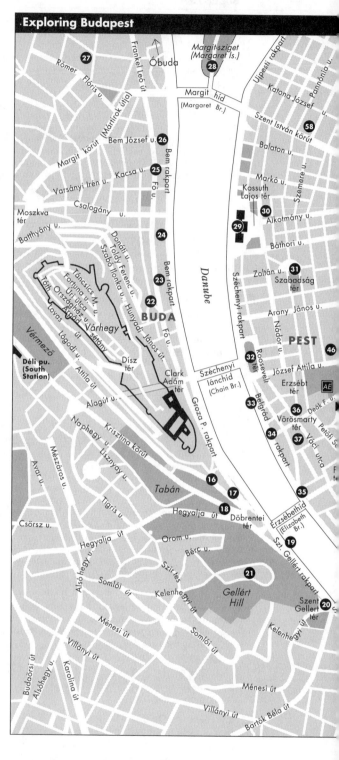

Exploring Budapest

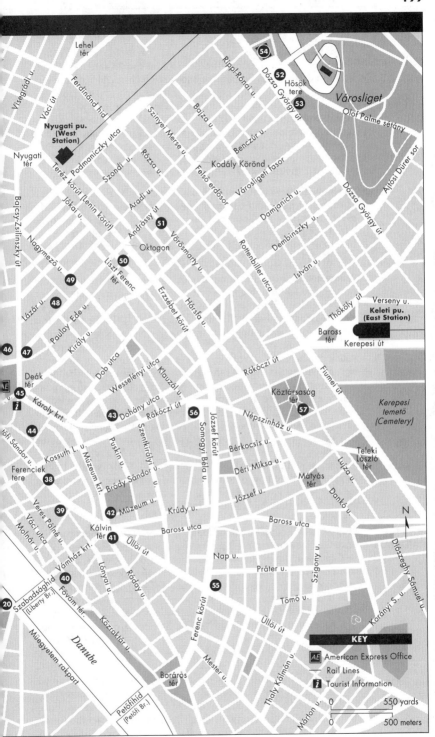

Lehel tér

Viségrádi u.

Váci út

Ferdinánd híd

Rippl-Rónai u.

Dózsa György út

54

52

Hősök tere

53

Városliget

Olof Palme sétány

Nyugati pu.
(West Station)

Nyugati tér

Teréz körút (Lenin körút)

Podmaniczky utca

Szinyei Merse u.

Bajza u.

Benczúr u.

Kodály Körönd

Andrássy út

Ajtósi Dürer sor

Bajcsy-Zsilinszky út

Szondi u.

Rózsa u.

Aradi u.

Felső erdősor

Városligeti fasor

Damjanich u.

Dózsa György út

Jókai u.

51

Vörösmarty u.

Dembinszky u.

Nagymező u.

Oktogon

50

Liszt Ferenc tér

Erzsébet körút

Hársfa u.

Rottenbiller utca

István u.

49

Lázár u.

48

Paulay Ede u.

Király u.

Dob utca

Wesselényi utca

Klauzál u.

Rákóczi út

Köztársaság tér

Thököly út

Verseny u.

Keleti pu.
(East Station)

Baross tér

Kerepesi út

Fiumei út

Kerepesi temető (Cemetery)

46

47

Deák tér

45

AE

i

Károly krt.

44

Kossuth L. u.

Dohány utca

43

Rákóczi út

56

Szentkirályi u.

Puskin u.

József körút

Somogyi Béla u.

Népszínház u.

57

Bérkocsis u.

Déri Miksa u.

Mátyás tér

Teleki László tér

Luzsa u.

Dankó u.

Petőfi Sándor u.

Ferenciek tere

38

Múzeum krt.

Bródy Sándor u.

42

Múzeum u.

Krúdy u.

József u.

Baross utca

N

Veres Pálné u.

39

Váci utca

Molnár u.

Kálvin tér

41

Üllői út

Baross utca

Nap u.

Szigony u.

Diószeghy Sámuel u.

Vámház krt.

40

Lónyai u.

Ráday u.

Práter u.

Korányi S. u.

20

Szabadsághíd
(Liberty Br.)

Fővám tér

Közraktár u.

Ferenc körút

Tömő u.

Üllői út

55

KEY

Danube

Műegyetem rakpart

Boráros tér

Mester u.

Thaly Kálmán u.

Márton u.

AE American Express Office

— Rail Lines

i Tourist Information

Petőfihíd
(Petőfi Br.)

0 _____ 550 yards

0 _____ 500 meters

tivities and Sports, *below*). ⊠ *I, Hadnagy utca 8–10,* ☎ *1/156–1322.* 🎫 *120 Ft.* ⏱ *Mon.–Sat. 6:30 AM–6 PM.*

⑲ Rudas Fürdő (Rudas Baths). On the riverbank at the foot of Gellért-hegy are these baths, its original Turkish pool making its interior possibly the most dramatically beautiful of Budapest's baths. A high, domed roof admits pinpricks of bluish green light into the dark, circular stone hall with its austere columns and arches. Fed by eight springs with a year-round temperature of 44°C (111°F), the Rudas's highly fluoridated waters have been known for 1,000 years. The facility is open to men only; a less interesting outer swimming pool is open to both sexes. (☞ Outdoor Activities and Sports, *below*). ⊠ *I, Döbrentei tér 9,* ☎ *1/156–1322.* 🎫 *250 Ft.* ⏱ *Weekdays 6 AM–6 PM; weekends 6 AM–noon.*

⑯ Semmelweis Orvostörténeti Múzeum (Semelweis Museum of Medical History). The splendid baroque house where Ignác Semmelweis, the great Hungarian physician and discoverer of the cause of puerperal (childbed) fever, was born in 1818 is now a museum that traces the history of healing. Semmelweis's grave is in the garden. ⊠ *Apród utca 1–3,* ☎ *1/175–3533.* 🎫 *60 Ft.* ⏱ *Tues.–Sun. 10:30–5:30.*

Szabadság Szobor (Liberation Memorial). Visible from many parts of the city, this 130-foot-high 1947 memorial, which starts just below the southern edge of the fort and towers above it, honors the 1944–45 siege of Budapest and the Russian soldiers who fell in the battle. It is the work of noted Hungarian sculptor Zsigmond Kisfaludi-Stróbl, and from the distance it looks light, airy, and even liberating. A sturdy young girl, her hair and robe swirling in the wind, holds a palm branch high above her head. Until recently, she was further embellished with sculptures of giants slaying dragons, Red Army soldiers, and peasants rejoicing at the freedom that Soviet liberation promised (but failed) to bring to Hungary. Yet since 1992, her mood has lightened: In the Budapest city government's systematic purging of Communist symbols, the Red Combat infantrymen who had flanked the Liberation statue for decades were hacked off and carted away. The soldier who had stood the highest and the one who was shaking hands with a grateful Hungarian worker are now on display among the other evicted statues in the new Szobor Park (Statue Park) in the city's 22nd district (☞ Off the Beaten Path, *below*). ⊠ *Gellért-hegy.*

OFF THE **SZOBOR PARK –** For a look at Budapest's too-recent Iron Curtain past,
BEATEN PATH make the 30-minute trip out to Szobor Park (Statue Park), where 42 of the Communist statues and memorials that once dominated the city's streets and squares have been exiled and put out to pasture since the political changes in 1989. Here you can wander among mammoth Lenin and Marx statues and buy socialist-nostalgia souvenirs and relics while songs from the Hungarian and Russian workers' movement play bombastically in the background. ⊠ *XXII, Balatoni út, corner of Szabadkai út,* ☎ 𝐅𝐀𝐗 *1/227-7446.* 🎫 *150 Ft.* ⏱ *Mid-Apr.–Oct., daily 10–6; Nov.–mid-Apr., weekends 10–dusk, weather permitting.*

Szarvas-ház. The Louis XVI–style Szarvas-ház (Stag House) is named for the former Szarvas Café or, more accurately, for its extant trade sign, with an emblem of a stag not quite at bay, which can be seen above the triangular arched entryway. Today the structure houses the Arany Szarvas restaurant, which is renowned for its excellent game dishes and preserves some of the mood of the old Tabán. ⊠ *Szarvas tér 1.*

⑰ Tabán plébánia-templom (Tabán Parish Church). In 1736, this church was built on the site of a Turkish mosque and subsequently renovated and reconstructed several times. Its present form—mustard-colored stone with a rotund, green clock tower—could be described as restrained baroque. ⊠ *I, Attila u. 1.*

North Buda

A GOOD WALK

Most of these sights are along Fő utca (Main Street), a long, straight thoroughfare that starts at the Chain Bridge and runs parallel to the Danube. It is lined on both sides with multistory late-18th-century houses—many darkened by soot and showing their age more than those you've seen in sparklingly restored areas like Castle Hill. This north-bound exploration can be done with the help of Bus 86, which covers the waterfront, or on foot, although distances are fairly great.

Beginning at **Batthyány tér** ㉔, with its head-on view of Parliament across the Danube, continue north on Fő utca, passing (or stopping to bathe at) the famous Turkish **Király-fürdő** (King Baths) ㉕. From **Bem József tér** ㉖, one block north, turn left (away from the river) up Fekete Sas utca, crossing busy Margit körút and turning right, one block past, up Mecset utca. This will take you up the hill to **Gül Baba türbéje** (Tomb of Gül Baba) ㉗.

TIMING

In planning your tour, remember that museums are closed Mondays and that the Király Baths are open to men and women on different days of the week.

SIGHTS TO SEE

㉔ **Batthyány tér.** This lovely square, open on its river side, affords a grand view of Parliament, directly across the Danube. The M2 subway, the HÉV electric railway from Szentendre, and various suburban and local buses converge on the square, as do peddlers hawking everything from freshly picked flowers to tattered, mismatched pairs of shoes. At No. 7 Batthyány tér is the beautiful baroque twin-towered **Szent Anna-templom** (Church of St. Anne, dating from 1740–62), its interior inspired by Italian art and its oval cupola adorned with frescoes and statuary.

NEED A BREAK?

The **Angelika** café (⊠ Batthyány tér 7, ☎ 1/212–3784), housed in the Church of St. Anne building, serves swirled meringues, chestnut-filled layer cakes, and a plethora of other heavenly pastries, all baked on the premises from family recipes. You can sit inside on small velvet chairs at marble-topped tables or at one of the umbrella-shaded tables outdoors. It's open daily 10 AM–10 PM.

㉖ **Bem József tér.** This square near the river is not particularly picturesque and can get heavy with traffic, but it houses the statue of its important namesake, Polish general József Bem, who offered his services to the 1848 revolutionaries in Vienna and then Hungary. Reorganizing the rebel forces in Transylvania, he inflicted numerous defeats on the Hapsburgs and was the war's most successful general. It was at this statue on October 23, 1956, that a great student demonstration in sympathy with the Poles' striving for liberal reforms exploded into the brave and tragic Hungarian uprising suppressed by the Red Army.

Capuchin Church. This church was converted from a Turkish mosque at the end of the 17th century. Damaged during the revolution in 1849, it acquired its current romantic-style exterior when it was rebuilt a few years later. ⊠ *Fő utca.*

☾ **Children's Railway.** The 12-kilometer (7-mile) Children's Railway (formerly Pioneer Railway because it was operated in Communist days by the Young Pioneers) runs from Széchenyihegy to Hűvösvölgy. The sweeping views and fresh air make the trip well worthwhile for children and adults alike. Departures are from Széchenyi-hegy, which you can reach by taking the cogwheel railway from the station opposite Hotel Budapest. ⊠ *Szillágyi Erzsébet fasor 47.* 🚇 *One-way tickets 60 Ft.* ☉ *Trains run mid-Jan.–late Mar. and late Sept.–Dec., Wed.–Sun. 8 AM–4 PM; rest of yr, Tues.–Sun. 8 AM–5 PM.*

OFF THE BEATEN PATH **JÁNOSHEGY** (Janos Hill) – A *libegő* (chairlift) will take you to Janos Hill—at 527 meters, the highest point in Budapest—where you can climb a lookout tower for the best view of the city. ⊠ *Take Bus 158 from Moszkva tér to the last stop, Zugligeti út,* ☎ *1/156–7975 or 1/176–3764.* 🚇 *100 Ft. one- way, 150 Ft. round-trip.* ☉ *Mid-May–mid-Sept., daily 9–5; mid-Sept.–mid-May (depending on weather), daily 9:30–4; closed every other Mon.*

㉒ **Corvin tér.** This charming square on Fő utca is the site of the turn-of-the-century Folk Art Institute and Buda Concert Hall, at No. 8.

㉗ **Gül Baba türbéje** (Tomb of Gül Baba). Gül Baba, a 16th-century dervish and poet whose name means "father of roses" in Turkish, was buried in a tomb built of carved stone blocks with four oval windows. He fought in several wars waged by the Turks and fell during the siege of Buda in 1541. The tomb remains a place of pilgrimage; it is considered Europe's northernmost Muslim shrine and marks the spot where he was slain. Set at an elevation on Rózsadomb (Rose Hill), the tomb is near a good lookout for views of Buda and across the river to Pest. ⊠ *Mecset utca 14,* ☎ *1/155–8764.* 🚇 *30 Ft.* ☉ *May 15–Sept. 15, Tues.–Sun. 10–4. Group tours can be arranged during rest of yr.*

㉕ **Király-fürdő** (King Baths). The royal gem of Turkish baths in Budapest was built in the 16th century by the Turkish pasha of Buda. Its stone cupola, crowned by a golden moon and crescent, arches over the steamy, dark pools indoors. It is open to men on Monday, Wednesday, and Friday; to women on Tuesday, Thursday, and Saturday. (☞ Outdoor Activities and Sports, *below.*) ⊠ *II, Fő utca 84,* ☎ *1/202–3688.* 🚇 *220 Ft.* ☉ *Weekdays 6:30 AM–6 PM, Sat. 6:30 AM–noon.*

㉓ **Szilágyi Dezső tér.** This is another of the charming little squares punctuating Fő utca (Main Street); here you'll find Béla Bartók's house, at No. 4.

Margit-sziget (Margaret Island)

More than 2½ kilometers (1½ miles) long and covering nearly 80 hectares (200 acres), **Margit-sziget** (Margaret Island) ㉘ is ideal for strolling, jogging, sunbathing, or just delighting in the fragrances of its lawns and gardens. Like Central Park in New York City, when the weather is fine, the island draws a multitudinous cross section of the city's population out to its gardens and sporting facilities. The outdoor pool complex of the **Palatinus Baths** (toward the Buda side), built in 1921, can attract tens of thousands of people on a summer day. Nearby are a tennis stadium, a youth athletic center, boathouses, sports grounds, and, most impressive of all, the **Nemzeti Sportuszoda** (National Sports Swimming Pool), designed by the architect Alfred Hájos (while still in his teens, Hájos won two gold medals in swimming at the first modern Olympic Games, held in Athens in 1896). In addition, walkers, joggers, bicyclists, and rollerbladers do laps around the island's perimeter and up and down the main road, closed to traffic except for Bus 26 (and a few official vehicles), which travels up and down the island and across the Margaret Bridge to and from Pest.

The island's natural curative hot springs have given rise to the Ramada Grand and Thermal hotels on the northern end of the island (☞ Lodging, *below*) and are piped in to two spa hotels on the mainland, the Aquincum on the Buda bank and the Hélia on the Pest side.

A GOOD WALK

Entering the island from its southern end at the **Margit-híd** (Margaret Bridge), stroll (or rent a bicycle and pedal) north along any of the several tree-shaded paths, including the **Artists Promenade,** pausing for a picnic on an open lawn, and eventually ending up at the **Japanese garden** at the northern end. From here, you can wander back to the southern end or take Bus 26 on the island's only road. A walk around the circumference of the island on the popular jogging path is also pleasant.

TIMING

To fully experience Margaret Island's role in Budapest life, go on a Saturday or Sunday afternoon to join and/or watch the many people picnicking, strolling, kicking a soccer ball, and otherwise whiling away the day. Sunday is a particularly good choice for strategic sightseers, who can utilize the rest of the week to cover those city sights and areas that are closed on Sundays. On weekdays, you'll share the island only with joggers and kids playing hooky from school.

SIGHTS TO SEE

Artists' Promenade. Through the center of the island runs the Artists' Promenade, lined with busts of Hungarian artists, writers, and musicians. Shaded by giant plane trees, it's a perfect place to stroll on a hot summer afternoon. The promenade passes close to the **rose garden** (in the center of the island), a large grassy lawn surrounded by blooming flower beds planted with hundreds of kinds of flowers. It's a great spot for a picnic or to watch a game of soccer or Ultimate Frisbee, both of which are regularly played here on weekend afternoons.

Margit-híd (Margaret Bridge). At the southern end of the island, the Margaret Bridge is the closer of the two entrances for those coming from downtown Buda or Pest. Just north of the Chain Bridge, the bridge walkway provides gorgeous midriver views of Castle Hill and Parliament. Toward the end of 1944, the Margit-híd was blown up by the retreating Nazis while it was crowded with rush-hour traffic. It was rebuilt in the same unusual shape—forming an obtuse angle in midstream, with a short leg leading down to the island. The original bridge was built during the 1840s by French engineer Ernest Gouin in collaboration with Gustave Eiffel.

㉘ Margit-sziget (Margaret Island). The island was first mentioned almost 2,000 years ago as the summer residence of the commander of the Roman garrison at nearby Aquincum. Later known as Rabbit Island (Insula Leporum), it was a royal hunting ground during the Árpád dynasty. King Imre, who reigned from 1196 to 1204, held court here, and several convents and monasteries were built here during the Middle Ages. It takes its current name from St. Margaret, the pious daughter of King Béla IV, who at the ripe old age of 10 retired to a Dominican nunnery here. She died in 1271 at the age of 29.

Marosvásárhely Musical Fountain. At the northern end of the island is a copy of the water-powered Marosvásárhely Musical Fountain, which plays songs and chimes. The original was designed more than 150 years ago by a Transylvanian named Péter Bodor. It stands near a picturesque, artificial **rock garden** with Japanese dwarf trees and lily ponds. The stream coursing through it never freezes, for it comes from a natural hot spring causing it instead to give off thick steam in winter that enshrouds the garden in a mystical cloud.

☺ **Margit-sziget Vadaspark** (Margaret Island Game Park). Just east of the rose garden is a small would-be petting zoo, if the animals were allowed to be petted. A fenced-in compound houses a menagerie of goats, rabbits, donkeys, assorted fowl and ducks, and gargantuan peacocks that sit heavily on straining tree branches and make loud "meow"-ing noises that can be heard around the island.

Downtown Pest and the Small Ring Road

Budapest's urban heart is full of bona fide sights plus innumerable tiny streets and grand avenues where you can wander for hours admiring the city's stately old buildings—some freshly sparkling after their first painting in decades, others silently but still elegantly crumbling.

Dominated by the Parliament building, the district surrounding Kossuth tér is the legislative, diplomatic, and administrative nexus of Budapest; most of the ministries are here, as are the National Bank and Courts of Justice. Downriver, the romantic Danube promenade, the Duna Korzó, extends along the stretch of riverfront across from Castle Hill. With Vörösmarty tér and pedestrian shopping street Váci utca just inland, this area forms Pest's tourist core. Going south, the Korzó ends at Március 15 tér. One block in from the river, Ferenciek tere marks the beginning of the university area, spreading south of Kossuth Lajos utca. Here, the streets are narrower and the echoes of your footsteps louder as they resound off of the elegantly aging stone buildings.

Pest is laid out in broad circular *körúts* ("ring roads" or boulevards). Vámház körút is the first sector of the 2½-kilometer (1½-mile) Kis körút (Little Ring Road), which traces the route of the Old Town wall from the Liberty Bridge to Deák tér. Construction of the inner körút began in 1872 and was completed in 1880. Changing names as it curves, after Kálvin tér it becomes Múzeum körút (passing by the National Museum), and then Károly körút for its final stretch ending at Deák tér. Deák tér, the only place where all three subway lines converge, could be called the dead-center of downtown. East of the körút are the weathered streets of Budapest's former ghetto, where the Great Synagogue presides proudly.

A GOOD WALK

Starting at Kossuth tér to see the **Országház** (Parliament) ㉙ and the **Néprajzi Múzeum** (Museum of Ethnography), it's worth walking a few blocks southeast to take in stately **Szabadság tér** ㉚ before heading back to the Danube and south to the foot of the **Széchenyi Lánchíd** (Chain Bridge) at **Roosevelt tér** ㉜. As this tour involves quite a bit of walking, you may want to take Tram 2 from Kossuth tér a few stops downriver to Roosevelt tér to save your energy. While time and/or energy may not allow it just now, at some point during your visit, a walk across the Chain Bridge is a must. From Roosevelt tér go south, across the street, and join the **korzó** ㉝ along the river, strolling past the **Vigadó** ㉞ at Vigadó tér, all the way to the **Belvárosi plébánia templom** (Inner City Parish Church) ㉟ at Március 15 tér, just under the **Erzsébethíd** (Elizabeth Bridge). Double back up the korzó to Vigadó tér and walk in from the river on Vigadó utca to **Vörösmarty tér** ㊱.

After a refreshment at Gerbeaud (☞ Need a Break? *below*), follow the crowds down pedestrian-only **Váci utca** ㊲. You'll end up across busy Kossuth Lajos utca from Ferenciek tere. Walking in (south) on Károlyi Miháy utca, past **Egyetem tér** ㊳, and continuing on Kecskeméti utca to Kálvin tér, you are going through the darker, narrower streets of the studenty, increasingly trendy area sometimes called SoKo (South of Kossuth). A detour into any of the side streets leading back toward the Danube will give you a good flavor of the area. To save time and energy, you can also take the blue metro from Ferenciek tere one stop to **Kálvin tér** ④. Just north of Kálvin tér on Múzeum körút is the **Nemzeti Múzeum** (National Museum). **The Nagy Zsinagóga** (Great Synagogue) ④ is about ¾ of a kilometer farther north along the Kis körút (Small Ring Road)—a longish walk or a short tram ride. From here, more walking along the körút, or a tram ride to the last stop, brings you to Pest's main hub, Deák tér. The **Szent István Bazilika** (St. Stephen's Basilica) ④ is an extra but rewarding 500-meter walk north on Bajcsy-Zsilinszky út.

SIGHTS TO SEE

③⑤ **Belvárosi plébánia templom** (Inner City Parish Church). Dating to the 12th century, this is the oldest ecclesiastical building in Pest. It's actually built on something even older—the remains of the Contra Aquincum, a 3rd-century Roman fortress and tower, parts of which are visible next to the church. There is hardly any architectural style that cannot be found in some part or another, starting with a single Romanesque arch in its south tower. The single nave still has its original Gothic chancel and some 15th-century Gothic frescoes. Two side chapels contain beautifully carved Renaissance altarpieces and tabernacles of red marble from the early 16th century. During Budapest's years of Turkish occupation, the church served as a mosque—and this is remembered by a *mihrab*, a Muslim prayer niche. During the 18th century, the church was given two baroque towers and its present facade. In 1808 it was enriched with a rococo pulpit, and still later a superb winged triptych was added to the main altar. From 1867 to 1875, Franz Liszt lived only a few steps away from the church, in a town house where he held regular "musical Sundays" at which Richard and Cosima Wagner were frequent guests and participants. Liszt's own musical Sunday mornings often began in this church. An admirer of its acoustics and organ, he conducted many masses here, including the first Budapest performance of his *Missa Choralis* in 1872. ⊠ *V, Március 15 tér 2.*

③⑨ **Egyetem tér** (University Square). Budapest's University of Law sits on University Square in the heart of the city's university neighborhood. On one corner is the cool gray-and-green marble **Egyetemi Templom** (University Church), one of Hungary's best and most beautiful baroque buildings. Built between 1725 and 1742, it boasts an especially splendid pulpit.

④⑤ **Evangélikus Templom and Evangélikus Múzeum** (Lutheran Church and Lutheran Museum). The neoclassical Lutheran Church sits in the center of it all on busy Deák tér. Classical concerts are usually held here on the last Sunday of every month at 6 PM. The church's interior designer, János Krausz, flouted then-traditional church architecture by placing a single large interior beneath the huge vaulted roof structure. The adjoining school, which the revolutionary poet Petőfi attended in 1833–34, is now the Lutheran Museum, which traces the role of Protestantism in Hungarian history and contains Martin Luther's original will. ⊠ *Deák Ferenc tér 4,* ☎ *1/117–4173.* ☞ *Museum 50 Ft.; church free (except during concerts).* ⊙ *Museum Tues.–Sun. 10–6.*

③⑧ **Ferenciek Templom** (Franciscan church). This pale-yellow church was built in 1743. On the wall facing Kossuth Lajos utca is a bronze relief showing a scene from the devastating flood of 1838, which swept away many houses and people; the detail is so vivid that it almost makes you seasick. A faded arrow below the relief indicates the high-water mark of almost 4 feet. Next to it is the **Nereids Fountain,** a popular meeting place for students from the nearby Eötvös Loránd University, which elaborates on the square's nautical motif. ✉ *V, Ferenciek tere.*

Greek Orthodox Church. Built at the end of the 18th century in late-baroque style, the Greek Orthodox Church was remodeled a century later by Miklós Ybl, who designed the Opera House and many other landmarks that give today's Budapest its monumental appearance. The church retains some fine wood carvings and a dazzling array of icons by a late-18th-century Serbian master Miklós Jankovich. ✉ *V, Petőfi tér 2/b.*

④ **Kálvin tér** (Calvin Square). Calvin Square takes its name from the neoclassical Protestant church that tries to dominate this busy traffic hub; more glaringly noticeable, however, is the billboard of a giant bottle of Coca-Cola. The Kecskeméti Kapu, a main gate of Pest, once stood here, as well as a cattle market that was also a den of thieves. At the beginning of the 19th century, this was where Pest ended and the prairie began.

NEED A BREAK?   The Hotel Korona's popular café, **Korona Passage** (✉ Kecskeméti utca 14, ☎ 1/117–4111), has a *palacsinta* (crepe) bar where you can watch the cooks prepare giant Hungarian crepes brimming with such fillings as apple, chocolate, and *túró* (sweetened cottage cheese). The café also serves soups and sandwiches and has a salad bar.

★ ㉝ **Korzó.** The neighborhood to the south of Roosevelt tér has regained much of its past elegance—if not its architectural grandeur—with the erection of the Atrium Hyatt, Forum, and Budapest Marriott luxury hotels. Traversing all three and continuing well beyond them is the riverside Korzó, a pedestrian promenade lined with park benches and appealing outdoor cafés from which one can enjoy postcard-perfect views of Gellért Hill and Castle Hill directly across the Danube. Evening strolls are highly recommended, when the views are lit up in shimmering gold. In summer and during holidays and festivals, you'll often find stalls selling colorful folk crafts and souvenirs, usually next to the Marriott Hotel.

NEED A BREAK?   The **Bécsi Kávéház** (Viennese Café; ✉ V, Apáczai Csere János u. 12–14, ☎ 1/117–8088), in the Fórum Hotel, serves the best *isler* (giant chocolate-covered cookies filled with apricot or raspberry jam) and cream pastries in town.

㊷ **Magyar Nemzeti Múzeum** (Hungarian National Museum). Built between 1837 and 1847, the Hungarian National Museum is a fine example of 19th-century classicism—simple, well proportioned, and surrounded by a large garden. In front of this building on March 15, 1848, Sándor Petőfi recited his revolutionary poem, the "National Song" ("Nemzeti dal"), and the "12 Points," a list of political demands by young Hungarians calling on the people to rise up against the Hapsburgs. Celebrations of the national holiday commemorating the failed revolution are held on these steps every year on March 15.

The museum's most sacred treasure, the **Szent Korona** (Holy Crown), reposes with other royal relics in a domed Hall of Honor off the main lobby. The crown sits like a golden soufflé above a Byzantine band of holy scenes in enamel and pearls and other gems. It seems to date from the 12th century, so it could not be the crown that Pope Sylvester II presented to St. Stephen in the year 1000, when he was crowned the first king of Hungary. Nevertheless, it is known as the Crown of St. Stephen and has been regarded—even by Communist governments—as the legal symbol of Hungarian sovereignty and unbroken statehood for nearly a millennium. In 1945 the fleeing Hungarian army handed over the crown and its accompanying regalia to the Americans rather than have them fall into Soviet hands. They were restored to Hungary in 1978.

Other rarities include a completely furnished Turkish tent; masterworks of cabinet making and wood carving, including pews from churches in Nyírbátor and Transylvania; a piano that belonged to both Beethoven and Liszt; and, in the treasury, masterpieces of goldsmithing, among them the 11th-century Constantions Monomachos crown from Byzantium and the richly pictorial 16th-century chalice of Miklós Pálffy. Looking at it is like reading the "Prince Valiant" comic strip in gold. The museum's epic Hungarian history exhibit reopened in August 1996, updated with exhibits chronicling the end of communism and the much-celebrated exodus of the Russian troops. ⊠ *IX, Múzeum körút 14–16,* ☎ *1/138–2122.* 🖼 *200 Ft.* ☉ *Mid-Mar.–mid-Oct., Tues.–Sun. 10–6; mid-Oct.–mid-Mar., Tues.–Sun. 10–5.*

★ ㊸ **Nagy Zsinagóga** (Great Synagogue). Europe's largest synagogue, the Great Synagogue was designed by Ludwig Förs and built between 1844 and 1859 in a Byzantine-Moorish style described as "consciously archaic Romantic-Eastern." Desecrated by German and Hungarian Nazis, it is being reconstructed with donations from all over the world, with particular help from the Emanuel Foundation, named for actor Tony Curtis's father, the late Emanuel Schwartz, who emigrated from Budapest to the Bronx (restorations are due to be completed by fall of 1996). In the courtyard behind the synagogue, a weeping willow made of metal honors the victims of the Holocaust. Liszt and Saint-Saëns are among the great musicians who have played its grand organ. ⊠ *Dohány u. 2– 8,* ☎ *1/342–1335.* 🖼 *Free.* ☉ *Weekdays 10–3, Sun. 10–1.*

★ ㉚ **Néprajzi Múzeum** (Museum of Ethnography). The 1890s neoclassical temple opposite Parliament formerly housed the Supreme Court. Now a vast, impressive permanent exhibition, "The Folk Culture of the Hungarian People," explains all aspects of peasant life from the end of the 18th century until World War I; explanatory texts are provided in both English and Hungarian. These are the authentic pieces you can't see at touristy folk shops. The central room of the building alone is worth the entrance fee: a majestic, cavernous hall with ornate marble staircases and pillars, and towering stained-glass windows. ⊠ *V, Kossuth tér 12,* ☎ *1/132–6340.* 🖼 *100 Ft.; Tues. free.* ☉ *Tues.–Sun. 10–6.*

★ ㉙ **Országház** (Parliament). The most visible, though not highly accessible, symbol of Budapest's left bank is the huge neo-Gothic Parliament. Mirrored in the Danube much the way Britain's Parliament is reflected by the Thames, it lies midway between the Margaret and Chain bridges and can be reached by the M2 subway (Kossuth tér station) and waterfront Tram 2. A fine example of historicizing, eclectic fin-de-siècle architecture, it was designed by the Hungarian architect Ímre Steindl and built by a thousand workers between 1885 and 1902. Both its exterior and interior reflect the taste of its time—grandiose yet delicate. The grace and dignity of its long facade and 24 slender towers, with spacious arcades and high windows balancing its vast central dome, lend this living landmark a refreshingly baroque spatial effect. The outside is lined with 90 statues of great figures in Hungarian history; the corbels are ornamented by 242 allegorical statues. Inside are 691 rooms, 10 courtyards, and 29 staircases; some 40 kilograms (88 pounds) of gold were used for the staircases and halls. These halls are also a gallery of late-19th-century Hungarian art, with frescoes and canvases depicting Hungarian history, starting with Mihály Munkácsy's large painting of the Magyar Conquest of 896. Unfortunately, because

Parliament is a workplace for legislators, the building is not open to individual visitors and must be toured in groups at certain hours on specific city tours organized by IBUSZ (☎ 1/118–5776 or 1/118–3925) or Budapest Tourist (☎ 1/117–3555). ☒ *V, Kossuth tér.*

③② **Roosevelt tér.** This square opening onto the Danube is less closely connected with a U.S. president than with the progressive Hungarian statesman Count István Széchenyi, dubbed "the greatest Hungarian" even by his adversary, Kossuth. The neo-Renaissance palace of the **Magyar Tudományos Akadémia** (Academy of Sciences) on the north side was built between 1862 and 1864, after Széchenyi's suicide. It is a fitting memorial, for in 1825, the statesman donated a year's income from all his estates to establish the academy. Another Széchenyi project, the ☞ **Chain Bridge** (Széchenyi Lánchíd), leads into the square; there stands a statue of Széchenyi near one of another statesman, Ferenc Deák, whose negotiations led to the establishment of the dual monarchy after Kossuth's 1848–49 revolution failed. Both men lived on this square.

Serbian Orthodox Church. Built in 1688, this lovely burnt-orange church, one of Budapest's oldest buildings, sits in a shaded garden surrounded by thick stone walls of the same color detailed with large-tile mosaics and wrought-iron gates. ☒ *V, Szerb utca.*

★ ③① **Szabadság tér** (Liberty Square). This is the site of a solemn-looking neoclassical shrine, the **National Bank,** and of the **Hungarian Television Headquarters,** a former stock exchange of Disneyland proportions with what look like four temples and two castles on its roof. In the square's center remains one of the few monuments to the Russian "liberation" that was spared the recent cleansing of symbols of the past regime. The decision to retain this obelisk—because it represents liberation from the Nazis during World War II—caused outrage among many groups, prompting some to vow to haul it away themselves (though for the moment it remains). With the Stars and Stripes flying out in front, the **American Embassy** is at Szabadság tér 12. Movie fans may notice that scenes from the film *Evita,* starring Madonna and Antonio Banderas, were filmed on the square.

Széchenyi Lánchíd (Chain Bridge). The oldest and most beautiful of the Danube's eight bridges. Before the lánchíd was built, the river could be crossed only by ferry or by a pontoon bridge that had to be removed when ice blocks began floating downstream in winter. It was constructed at the initiative of the great Hungarian reformer and philanthropist Count István Széchenyi, using an 1839 design by the French civil engineer William Tierney Clark, who had also designed London's Hammersmith Bridge. This classical, almost poetically graceful and symmetrical suspension bridge was finished by his Scottish namesake, Adam Clark, who also built the 383-yard tunnel under Castle Hill, thus connecting the Danube quay with the rest of Buda. After it was destroyed by the Nazis, the bridge was rebuilt in its original form (though slightly widened for traffic) and was reopened in 1949, on the centenary of its inauguration. At the Buda end of the bridge is **Clark Ádám tér** (Adam Clark Square), where you can zip up to Castle Hill on the sometimes crowded Sikló funicular rail. 🎫 *100 Ft.* ⊙ *Funicular runs daily 7:30 AM–10 PM; closed alternate Mon.*

★ ④⑥ **Szent István Bazilika** (St. Stephen's Basilica). Dark and massive, one of the chief landmarks of Pest and the city's largest church (it can hold 8,500) is St. Stephen's Basilica. Its very Holy Roman front porch greets you with a tympanum bustling with statuary. The basilica's dome and the dome of Parliament are by far the most visible in the Pest skyline, and this is no accident: With the Magyar Millennium of 1896 in mind, both domes were consciously planned to be 315 feet high.

The millennium was not yet in sight when architect József Hild began building the basilica in neoclassical style in 1851, two years after the revolution was suppressed. After Hild's death, the project was taken over in 1867 by Miklós Ybl, the architect who did the most to transform modern Pest into a monumental metropolis—in contrast to medieval Buda across the river. Wherever he could, Ybl shifted Hild's motifs toward the neo-Renaissance mode that Ybl favored. When the dome collapsed, partly damaging the walls, he made even more drastic changes with the millennium approaching. Ybl died in 1891, five years before the thousand-year celebration, and the basilica was completed in neo-Renaissance style by József Kauser—but not until 1905.

Below the cupola, the interior is surprisingly cool and restful, a rich collection of late-19th-century Hungarian art: mosaics, altarpieces, and statuary (what heady days the millennium must have meant for local talents!). There are 150 kinds of marble, all from Hungary except for the Carrara in the sanctuary's centerpiece: a white statue of King (St.) Stephen I, Hungary's first king and patron saint. Stephen's mummified right hand is preserved as a relic in the **Szent Jobb Chapel**; the guard will illuminate it for you for two minutes for about 50 Ft. Visitors can also climb the 364 stairs to the top of the cupola for a spectacular view of the city. Extensive restorations have been underway at the aging basilica for years, with a target completion date of 2010, and some part of the structure is likely to be under scaffolding when you visit. ⊠ *V, Szt. István tér,* ☎ *1/117–2859.* ☞ *Church free, cupola 150 Ft.* ☉ *Church Mon.–Sat. 7–7, Sun. 1–5; Szt. Jobb Chapel Apr.–Sept., Mon.–Sat. 9–5, Sun. 1–5; Oct.–Mar., Mon.–Sat. 10–4.*

University of Economics. Just below the Liberty Bridge on the waterfront, the monumental neo-Renaissance building was once the Customs House. Built in 1871–74 by Miklós Ybl, it is now the Közgazdagsági Egyetem (University of Economics), also known as közgáz, after a stint during the Communist era as Karl Marx University.

㊲ Váci utca. Immediately north of Elizabeth Bridge is Budapest's best-known shopping street, Váci utca, a pedestrian precinct with electrified 19th-century lampposts, smart shops with chic window displays and credit-card emblems on ornate doorways. No bargain basement, Váci utca takes its special flavor from the mix of native clothiers, furriers, tailors, dress designers, shoemakers, folk artists, and others who offer alternatives to the internationally known boutique superstars. There are also bookstores—first- and secondhand in addition to foreign-language—and china and crystal shops, as well as gourmet food stores redolent of paprika. With rapid democratization, street commerce on Váci utca has shifted to a freer market: News vendors hawk today's Western press, and Transylvanian women in regional costumes peddle hand-embroidered cloths. Watch your purses and wallets here—against inflated prices *and* active pickpockets.

㊹ Városház. The monumental former city council building, which used to be a hospital for wounded soldiers and then a resort for the elderly ("home" would be too cozy for so vast a hulk), is now Budapest's city hall. It's enormous enough to loom over the row of shops and businesses lining Károly körút in front of it, but can only be entered through courtyards or side streets (Gerlóczy utca is the most accessible). Its 57-window facade, interrupted by five projections, fronts on Városház utca, which parallels the körút. The Tuscan columns at the main entrance and the allegorical statuary of *Atlas, War, and Peace* are especially splendid. There was once a chapel in the center of the main facade, but now only its spire remains. ⊠ *V, Városház u. 9–12,* ☏ *1/118–6066.*

④⓪ Vásárcsarnok. The magnificent Central Market Hall, a 19th-century iron-frame construction, was reopened in late 1994 after years of renovation (and disputes over who would foot the bill). Even during the leanest years of Communist shortages, the abundance of food came as a revelation to visitors from East and West. Today, the cavernous, three-story hall once again teems with shoppers browsing among stalls packed with salamis and red-paprika chains, crusty bread, fresh fish, and other tastes of Hungary. Upstairs you can buy folk embroideries and souvenirs. ⊠ *IX, Vámhaz körút 1–3.* ⊘ *Mon. 6 AM–5 PM, Tues.–Fri. 6 AM–6 PM, Sat. 6 AM–2 PM.*

㉞ Vigadó (Concert Hall). Designed in a striking romantic style by Frigyes Feszl and inaugurated in 1865 with Franz Liszt conducting his own *St. Elizabeth Oratorio,* the concert hall is a curious mixture of Byzantine, Moorish, Romanesque, and Hungarian motifs, punctuated by dancing statues and sturdy pillars. Brahms, Debussy, and Casals are among the other immortals who have graced its stage. Mahler's *Symphony No. 1* and many works by Bartók were first performed here. Severely damaged in World War II, the hall was rebuilt and reopened in 1980. ⊠ *V, Vigadó tér 2.*

★ **㊱ Vörösmarty tér.** This large, handsome square at the northern end of Váci utca is the heart of Pest's tourist life. Street musicians and sidewalk cafés make it one of the liveliest places in Budapest and a good spot to sit and relax—if you can manage to ward off the aggressive caricature sketchers. Grouped around a white-marble statue of the 19th-century poet and dramatist Mihály Vörösmarty are luxury shops, airline offices, and an elegant former pissoir. Now a lovely kiosk, it displays gold-painted historic scenes of the square's golden days, which may be returning since its 1984 restoration.

NEED A BREAK?   The best-known, tastiest, and most tasteful address on Vörösmarty Square belongs to the **Gerbeaud** pastry shop (⊠ Vörösmarty tér 7, ☏ 1/118–1311), founded in 1858 by a French confectioner, Henri Kugler, and later taken over by the Swiss family Gerbeaud. Filling most of a square block, it offers dozens and dozens of kinds of sweets at any time (as well as ice cream, sandwiches, coffee, and other drinks), served in a salon setting of green-marble tables and Regency-style marble fireplaces or at tables outside in summer. A mildly hostile staff is an integral part of the Gerbeaud tradition.

☉ Wizard's. This is a popular video arcade jam-packed with flashing video games, car-racing simulators, virtual-reality machines, and other high-tech toys. The laser tag game attracts a fair share of not-so-youngsters stopping in for a quick laser battle before moving on to a bar or disco. ⊠ *V, Irányi u. at Ferenciek tere,* ☏ *1/266–6433.* ⊘ *Daily 11 AM–1 AM.*

Zsidó Múzeum (Jewish Museum). The four-room Jewish Museum, around the corner from the Great Synagogue, features displays explaining the effect of the Holocaust on Hungarian and Transylvanian Jews. In late 1993, burglars ransacked the museum and got away with approximately 80% of its priceless collection; several months later, the stolen objects were found in Romania and returned to their home. ⊠ *Dohány utca 2,* ☏ *1/342–8949.* ▦ *100 Ft. donation.* ⊘ *Weekdays 10–3, Sun. 10–1.*

Andrássy Út

Behind the basilica, back at the crossroad along Bajcsy-Zsilinszky út, begins Budapest's grandest avenue, **Andrássy út.** For too many years, this broad boulevard of music and mansions bore the tongue-twisting, mind-bending name of Népköztársaság (Avenue of the People's Republic) and for a while before that, Stalin Avenue. In 1990, however, it reverted to its old name honoring Count Gyula Andrássy, a statesman who in 1867 became the first constitutional premier of Hungary. The boulevard that would eventually bear his name was begun in 1872, as Buda and Pest (and Óbuda) were about to be unified. Most of the mansions that line it were completed by 1884. It took another dozen years before the first **underground railway** on the Continent was completed for—you guessed it!—the Magyar Millennium in 1896. Though preceded by London's Underground (1863), Budapest's was the world's first electrified subway. Only slightly modernized but recently refurbished for the 1996 millecentenary, this "Little Metro" is still running a 3.7-kilometer (2.3-mile) stretch from Vörösmarty tér to the far end of City Park. Using tiny yellow trains with tanklike treads, and stopping at antique stations marked FÖLDALATTI (Underground) on their wrought-iron entranceways, Line 1 is a tourist attraction in itself. Six of its 10 stations are along Andrássy út.

A GOOD WALK

A walking tour of Andrássy út's sights is straightforward: Begin at its downtown end, near Deák tér, and stroll its length (about 2 kilometers [1¼ miles] all the way to **Hősök tere** (Heroes' Square) ㉒. The first third of the avenue, from Bajcsy-Zsilinszky út to the eight-sided intersection called Oktogon, boasts a row of eclectic city palaces with balconies held up by stone giants. Pause at the **Operaház** (Opera House) ㊽ and other points along the way. One block past the Opera, Andrássy út intersects Budapest's Broadway: Nagymező utca contains several theaters, cabarets, and nightclubs. Andrássy út alters when it crosses the Nagy körút (Outer Ring Road), at the Oktogon crossing. Four rows of trees and scores of flower beds make the thoroughfare look more like a garden promenade, but its cultural character lingers. Farther up, past **Kodály körönd,** the rest of Andrássy út is dominated by widely spaced mansions surrounded by private gardens. At Hősök tere, browse through the **Műcsarnok** (Palace of Exhibitions) ㊳ and/or the **Szépművészeti Múzeum** (Museum of Fine Arts) ㊾, and finish off with a stroll into the Vajdahunyad Vár (Vajdahunyad Castle) and Városliget (City Park; ☞ A Good Walk *in* Városliget [City Park], *below*). You can return to Deák tér on the subway, the Millenniumi Földalatti (Millennial Underground).

TIMING

As most museums are closed Mondays, it's best to explore Andrássy Út on other days, preferably weekdays or early Saturday, when stores are also open for browsing. During opera season, you can time your exploration to land you at the Opera House stairs just before 7 PM to watch the spectacle of operagoers flowing in for the evening's performance.

SIGHTS TO SEE

Drechsler Kastély (Drechsler Palace). Across the street from the Opera House is the French Renaissance–style Drechsler Palace. An early work by Ödön Lechner, Hungary's master of art nouveau, it is now the home of the National Ballet School. ⊠ *VI, Andrássy út 25.*

Hopp Ferenc Kelet-Ázsiai Művészeti Múzeum (Ferenc Hopp Museum of Eastern Asiatic Arts). For a change of flavor, you can stop in at the Ferenc Hopp Museum of Eastern Asiatic Arts, housing a rich collection of exotica from the Indian subcontinent and Far Eastern ceram-

ics. ✉ *Andrássy út 103*, ☎ *1/132–8476.* 🎫 *40 Ft.; Tues. free.* 🕐
Oct.–mid-Apr., Tues.–Sun. 10–5; mid-Apr.–Sept., Tues.–Sun. 10–6.

★ **52** **Hősök tere** (Heroes' Square). Andrássy út ends in grandeur at Heroes'
Square, with Budapest's answer to Berlin's Brandenburg Gate. Cleaned
and refurbished in 1996 for the millecentenary, the **Millennial Monument** is a semicircular twin colonnade with statues of Hungary's kings
and leaders between its pillars. Set back in its open center, a 118-foot
stone column is crowned by a dynamic statue of the archangel Gabriel,
his outstretched arms bearing the ancient emblems of Hungary. At its
base ride seven bronze horsemen: the Magyar chieftains, led by Árpád,
whose tribes conquered the land in 896. Most of the statues were sculpted
by György Zala, whose rendition of Gabriel won him a Grand Prix in
Paris in 1900. Before the column lies a simple marble slab, the **National
War Memorial,** the nation's altar, at which every visiting foreign dignitary lays a ceremonial wreath. England's Queen Elizabeth upheld the
tradition during her royal visit in May of 1992. In 1991 Pope John
Paul II conducted a mass here. Just a few months earlier, half a million Hungarians had convened to recall the memory of Imre Nagy, the
reform-minded Communist prime minister who partially inspired the
1956 revolution. Heroes' Square is flanked by the ☞ **Műcsarnok** and
the ☞ **Szépművészeti Múzeum.**

Kodály Körönd. A handsome traffic circle with imposing statues of three
Hungarian warriors—leavened by a fourth one of a poet—the Kodály
Körönd is surrounded by plane and chestnut trees. Look carefully at
the towered mansions on the north side of the circle—behind the soot
you'll see the fading colors of ornate frescoes peeking through. The circle takes its name from the composer Zoltán Kodály, who lived just
beyond it at Andrássy út 89.

NEED A
BREAK?
The **Média Club,** (✉ VI, Andrássy út 101, ☎ 1/322–1639) the restaurant in the building housing the National Association of Hungarian Journalists, has a wonderful terrace out front on Andrássy út. Have a quick
bowl of soup or a sweet palacsinta from its admired kitchen, or just rejuvenate with a shot of espresso. It's closed Sunday after lunch.

51 **Liszt Ferenc Emlékmúzeum** (Franz Liszt Memorial Museum). Andrássy
út No. 67 was the original location of the old Academy of Music and
Franz Liszt's last home; entered around the corner, it now houses a museum. Several rooms display the original furniture and instruments from
Liszt's time there; another houses temporary exhibits. The museum hosts
excellent, free classical concerts Saturday mornings at 11 (but none in
August). ✉ *Vörösmarty u. 35*, ☎ *1/342–7320.* 🎫 *50 Ft.* 🕐 *Weekdays 10–6, Sat. 9–5. Free classical concerts Sept.–July, Sat. 11 AM.*

50 **Liszt Ferenc Zeneakadémia** (Franz Liszt Academy of Music). Along with
the **Vigadó** (☞ Downtown Pest and the Small Ring Road, *above*), this
is one of the city's main concert halls. The academy in fact has two auditoriums: a green-and-gold 1,200-seat main hall and a smaller hall for
chamber music and solo recitals. Outside this exuberant art-nouveau
building opened in 1907, Liszt reigns, enthroned on the facade; the statue
is by Strobl, who cast him standing up outside the Opera House. The
academy has been operating as a highly revered teaching institute for
almost 120 years; Liszt was its first chairman and Erkel its first director. The pianist Ernő (formerly Ernst) Dohnányi and composers Béla
Bartók and Zoltán Kodály were teachers here. ✉ *Liszt Ferenc tér 8.*

Magyar Állami Bábszínház. The Hungarian State Puppet Theater,
housed in a templelike eclectic building, produces colorful shows that
both children and adults find enjoyable even if they don't understand

Hungarian. Watch for showings of *Cinderella* (*Hamupipőke*) and *Snow White and the Seven Dwarfs* (*Hófehérke*), part of the theater's regular repertoire. ⌧ *VI, Andrássy út 69,* ☎ *1/122–5051.*

49 Mai Mano Fotógaléria. This weathered old ornate building bedecked in green majolica decorations was built in 1894 as a photography studio, where the wealthy bourgeoisie would come to be photographed by imperial and royal court photographer Mai Manó. Inside, ironwork and frescoes ornament the curving staircase leading up to the tiny photo gallery, the only one in Budapest with a solely photographic focus. Established in late 1995, the gallery displays changing exhibits and sells books and publications, serving as well as an information center on Hungarian photography. Plans are underway to restore the tired old building to its original splendor and to expand the facilities to make it once again the capital's grand photography venue. ⌧ *V, Nagymező u. 20, no phone.* ▣ *Free.* ☉ *Weekdays 2–6.*

53 Műcsarnok (Palace of Exhibitions). The city's largest hall for special exhibitions—a striking 1895 temple of culture with a colorful tympanum. After four years of being boarded up for exhaustive renovations, the Palace of Exhibitions reopened its doors to the public during the 1995 Budapest Spring Festival. Its program of events includes exhibitions of contemporary Hungarian and international art and a rich series of films, plays, and concerts. ⌧ *XIV, Dózsa György út 37,* ☎ *1/343–7401.* ▣ *200 Ft.; Tues. free.* ☉ *Tues.–Sun. 10–6.*

★ **48 Operaház** (Opera House). Miklós Ybl's crowning achievement is the Opera House, built between 1875 and 1884 in neo-Renaissance style. There are those who prefer its architecture to that of the Vienna State Opera, which it resembles but on a smaller scale, or the Paris Opera, which could swallow it up whole. Badly damaged during the siege of 1944–45, Budapest's Opera House was restored to its original splendor for its 1984 centenary. Two buxom marble sphinxes guard the driveway; the main entrance is flanked by Alajos Strobl's "romantic-realist" limestone statues of Liszt and of another 19th-century Hungarian composer, Ferenc Erkel, the father of Hungarian opera (his patriotic opera *Bánk bán* is still performed for national celebrations). On the facade are smaller statues of composers and muses.

Inside, the spectacle begins even before the performance does. You glide up grand staircases and through wood-paneled corridors and gilt lime-green salons into a glittering jewel box of an auditorium. Its four tiers of boxes are held up by helmeted sphinxes beneath a frescoed ceiling that is also the work of Lotz. Lower down there are frescoes everywhere, with intertwined motifs of Apollo and Dionysus. In its early years, the Budapest Opera was conducted by Gustav Mahler (from 1888 to 1891) and after World War II, by Otto Klemperer. The acoustics are good, and the stage is deep. The singing and playing can vary from awful to great, and tickets are relatively cheap and easy to come by, at least by tourist standards. And descending from *La Bohème* into the Földalatti station beneath the Opera House was described by travel writer Stephen Brook in *The Double Eagle* (1988) as stepping "out of one period piece and into another."

The best way to experience the Opera House's interior is to see a ballet or opera, but there are no performances in summer, except for the week-long BudaFest international opera and ballet festival in mid-August. The Opera House is open only to ticket holders, but 50-minute tours are usually conducted daily at 3 PM and 4 PM; meet by the sphinx at the Dálszínház utca entrance. It's a good idea to call ahead to confirm that one is being given (☎ 1/131–2550, ext. 156). The cost is about 500 Ft. ⊠ *VI, Andrássy út 22,* ☎ *1/131–2250.*

㊼ Postamúzeum (Postal Museum). The best of Andrássy út's many marvelous stone mansions happens to be visitable, for the Postal Museum occupies an apartment with frescoes by Károly Lotz (whose work adorned the basilica and the National Museum's grand staircase) and a fine marble fireplace. Among the displays is an exhibition on the history of Hungarian mail, radio, and telecommunications. Even if the exhibits don't thrill you, the venue is worth the visit. ⊠ *Andrássy út 3,* ☎ *1/342–7938.* 🎟 *20 Ft.* ⊙ *Tues.–Sun. 10–6.*

★ ㊴ Szépművészeti Múzeum (Museum of Fine Arts). Across Heroes' Square from the Műcsarnok and built by the same team of Albert Schickedanz and Fülöp Herzog between 1900 and 1906, the Museum of Fine Arts houses Hungary's finest collection, rich in Flemish and Dutch Old Masters. With seven fine El Grecos and five beautiful Goyas as well as paintings by Velázquez and Murillo, the collection of Spanish Old Masters is considered by many to be the best outside Spain. The Italian school is represented by Giorgione, Bellini, Correggio, Tintoretto, and Titian masterpieces and, above all, two superb Raphael paintings: *Eszterházy Madonna* and his immortal *Portrait of a Youth,* rescued after a world-famous art heist. Nineteenth-century French art includes works by Delacroix, Pissarro, Cézanne, Toulouse-Lautrec, Gauguin, Renoir, and Monet. There are also more than 100,000 drawings (including five by Rembrandt and three studies by Leonardo), Egyptian and Greco-Roman exhibitions, late-Gothic winged altars from northern Hungary and Transylvania, and works by all the leading figures of Hungarian art up to the present. A new 20th-century collection was added to the museum's permanent exhibits in spring 1994, comprising a greatly varied but unified series of statues, paintings, and drawings by Chagall, Le Corbusier, and others. ⊠ *XIV, Dózsa György út 41,* ☎ *1/343–9759.* 🎟 *200 Ft.* ⊙ *Tues.–Sun. 10–5:30; usually closed Jan.–Mar.*

Városliget (City Park)

A GOOD WALK

Heroes' Square is the gateway to the **Városliget** (City Park): a square kilometer (almost half a square mile) of recreation, entertainment, beauty, and culture calculated to delight children and adults alike. A bridge behind the Millennial Monument leads across a boating basin that becomes an artificial ice-skating rink in winter; to the south of this lake stands a statue of George Washington, erected in 1906 with donations by Hungarian emigrants to the United States. Next to the lake stands **Vajdahunyad Vár** (Vajdahunyad Castle) built in myriad architectural styles. Visitors can soak or swim at the turn-of-the-century Széchenyi Baths, jog along the park paths, or careen on Vidám Park's roller coaster. There's also the Municipal Grand Circus, the Budapest Zoo, and Petőfi Csarnok, a leisure-time youth center and major concert hall on the site of an old industrial exhibition.

TIMING

Fair-weather weekends, when the children's attractions are teeming with kids and parents and the Széchenyi Baths brimming with bathers, are the best time for people-watchers to visit City Park; for the more solitary, the main sights are rarely crowded on weekdays.

SIGHTS TO SEE

🕭 **Budapesti Állatkert.** Budapest's zoo is a fairly depressing urban zoo brightened—for humans, anyway—by an elephant pavilion decorated with Zsolnay majolica and glazed ceramic animals. It cares for a variety of exotic animals, including hippos, a favorite of local youngsters. ⊠ *XIV,*

Állatkerti körút 6–12, behind Heroes' Sq., ☎ *1/343–6073.* 🎫 *250 Ft.* ☉ *Mar. and Oct., Tues.–Sun. 9–5; Apr. and Sept., daily 9–6; May, daily 9–6:30; June–Aug., daily 9–7; Nov.–Feb., Tues.–Sun. 9–4.*

☾ **Fővárosi Nagycirkusz.** The city's Municipal Grand Circus puts on colorful performances by local acrobats, clowns, and animal trainers, as well as by international guests, in its small ring. ✉ *XIV, Állatkerti körút 7,* ☎ *1/343–8300.*

Széchenyi Fürdő (Széchenyi Baths). Dating from 1876, the vast Széchenyi Baths are in a beautiful neobaroque building in the middle of City Park and comprise one of the biggest spas in Europe. There are several thermal pools indoors as well as two outdoors, which remain open even in winter, when dense steam hangs thick over the hot water's surface—you can just barely make out the figures of elderly men, submerged shoulder deep, crowded around waterproof chess boards. (☞ Outdoor Activities and Sports, *below.*) ✉ *XIV, Állatkerti körút 11,* ☎ *1/121–0310.* 🎫 *220 Ft.* ☉ *May–Sept., daily 6–6; Oct.–Apr., daily 6–5.*

★ **Vajdahunyad Vár** (Vajdahunyad Castle). Beside the lake in Városliget stands this castle, an art historian's Disneyland, named for the Transylvanian home (today in Hunedoara, Romania) of János Hunyadi, a 15th-century Hungarian hero in the struggle against the Turks. This fantastic medley borrows from all of Hungary's historic and architectural past, starting with the Romanesque gateway of the cloister of Jak in western Hungary. A Gothic castle, Transylvanian turrets, Renaissance loggia, baroque portico, and Byzantine decoration are all guarded by a spooky modern (1903) bronze statue of the anonymous medieval chronicler who was the first recorder of Hungarian history. Designed for the millennial celebration in 1896 but not completed until 1908, this hodgepodge houses the surprisingly interesting **Mezőgazdasági Múzeum** (Agricultural Museum), with intriguingly arranged sections on animal husbandry, forestry, horticulture, hunting, and fishing. ✉ *XIV, Városliget, Széchenyi Island,* ☎ *1/343–3198.* 🎫 *Museum 60 Ft.* ☉ *Mar.–Nov., Tues.–Sat. 10–5, Sun. 10–6; Dec.–Feb., Tues.–Fri. 10–4, weekends 10–5.*

☾ **Vidám Park.** Budapest's amusement park is next to the zoo and is crawling with happy children with their parents or grandparents in tow. Rides cost under $1 (some are for preschoolers). There are also game rooms and a scenic railway. Next to the main park is a separate, smaller section for toddlers. In winter, only a few rides operate. ✉ *Városliget, Állatkerti krt. 14–16,* ☎ *1/343–0996.* 🎫 *Mid-Mar.–Aug. 50 Ft.; Sept.–mid-Mar. free.* ☉ *Mid-Mar.–Aug., daily 10–7:30; Sept.–mid-Mar., daily 10–late afternoon.*

Eastern Pest and the Great Ring Road

This section covers primarily Kossuth Lajos–Rákóczi út and the Nagykörút (Great Ring Road)—busy, less-touristy urban thoroughfares full of people, cars, shops, and Budapest's unique urban flavor.

Beginning at the Erzsébet Bridge, Kossuth Lajos utca is Budapest's busiest shopping street. Try to look above and beyond the store windows to the architecture and activity along Kossuth Lajos utca and its continuation, Rákóczi út, which begins when it crosses the Kis körút (Small Ring Road) at the busy intersection called Astoria.

Rákóczi út is so named because it was on the 1906 route of the procession that brought back the remains of Prince Ferenc II Rákóczi of Transylvania, hero of an early 18th-century uprising against the Hapsburgs, nearly two centuries after he died in defeat and exile in Turkey.

Most of Rákóczi út is lined with hotels, shops, and department stores and ends at the grandiose Keleti (Eastern) Railway Station.

Pest's Great Ring Road, the Nagy körút, was laid out at the end of the 19th century in a wide semicircle anchored to the Danube at both ends; an arm of the river was covered over to create this 114-foot-wide thoroughfare. The large apartment buildings on both sides also date from this era. Along with theaters, stores, and cafés, they form a boulevard unique in Europe for its "unified eclecticism," which blends a variety of historic styles into a harmonious whole. Its entire length of almost 4½ kilometers (2¾ miles) from Margaret Bridge to Petőfi Bridge is traversed by Trams 4 and 6, but strolling it in stretches is also a good way to experience the hustle and bustle of downtown Budapest.

Like its smaller counterpart, the Kis Körút (Small Ring Road), the Great Ring Road comprises sectors of various names. Beginning with Ferenc körút at the Petőfi Bridge, it changes to József körút at the intersection marked by the Museum of Applied Arts, then to Erzsébet körút at Blaha Lujza Square. Teréz körút begins at the busy Oktogon crossing with Andrássy út—boasting the biggest Burger King in the world—and ends at the Nyugati (West) Railway Station, where Szent István takes over for the final stretch to the Margaret Bridge.

A GOOD WALK

Beginning with a visit to the **Iparművészeti Múzeum** (Museum of Applied Arts) (55), near the southern end of the boulevard, walk or take Tram 4 or 6 north (away from the Petőfi Bridge) to the New York Kávéház (☞ Need a Break? *below*) on Erzsébet körút, just past Blaha Lujza tér—all in all about 1¾ kilometers (1 mile) from the museum. The neo-Rennaissance **Keleti pályaudvar** (Eastern Railway Station) is a one metro-stop detour away from Blaha Lujza tér. Continuing in the same direction on the körút, go several stops on the tram to **Nyugati pályaudvar** (Western Railway Station) and walk the remaining sector, Szent István körút, past the **Vígszínház** (Comedy Theater) (58) to the Margaret Bridge. From the bridge, views of Margaret Island, to the north, and Parliament, Castle Hill, the Chain Bridge, and Gellért Hill, to the south, are gorgeous.

TIMING

As this area is packed with stores, it's best to explore during store hours—weekdays until around 5 PM, and Saturdays until 1 PM; Saturdays will be most crowded. Keep in mind that the Museum of Applied and Decorative Arts is closed Mondays.

SIGHTS TO SEE

★ (55) **Iparművészeti Múzeum** (Museum of Applied and Decorative Arts). The templelike structure housing this museum is indeed a shrine to Hungarian art nouveau, and in front of it, drawing pen in hand, sits a statue of its creator, Ödön Lechner, Hungary's master of art nouveau. Opened in the millennial year of 1896, it was only the third museum of its kind in Europe. Its dome of tiles is crowned by a majolica lantern from the same source: the Zsolnay ceramic works in Pécs. Inside its central hall are playfully swirling whitewashed, double-decker, Moorish-style galleries and arcades. The museum, which collects and studies objects of interior decoration and use, has five departments: furniture, textiles, goldsmithing, ceramics, and everyday objects. ✉ *Üllői út 33–37,* ☎ *1/217–5222.* 🎫 *80 Ft.* ⏲ *Tues.–Sun. 10–6.*

(56) **Kapel Szent Roch** (St. Roch Chapel). At the corner of Rákóczi út and Gyulai Pál utca stands the charming yellow 18th-century St. Roch Chapel, its impact rendered even more colorful by peasant women peddling lace and embroidery on its small square. The chapel is the old-

est remnant of Pest's former outer district. It was built beside a hospice where doomed victims of the great plague of 1711 were sent to die as far away as possible from residential areas. The former St. Roch Hospital next door at No. 2 Gyulai Pál utca is now the **Semmelweis Hospital.** The section along Rákóczi út was built in 1841 on the site of the old hospice; the wing on Gyulai Pál utca dates to 1798.

NEED A BREAK?	Once the haunt of famous writers and intellectuals, whose caricatures decorate the walls, the **New York Kávéház** (✉ VII, Erzsébet krt. 9–11, ☎ 1/322–1648) is a lavishly decorated, eclectic neobaroque café and restaurant in the ornate 1894 New York Palace building.

Keleti pályaudvar (Eastern Railway Station). The grandiose, imperial-looking Eastern Railway Station was built in 1884 and considered Europe's most modern until well into this century. Its neo-Renaissance facade, which resembles a gateway, is flanked by statues of two British inventors and railway pioneers, James Watt and George Stephenson. ✉ *VII, Rákóczi út.*

Klotild and Matild buildings. Braced on either side of heavily trafficked Kossuth Lajos utca, the imposing Klotild and Matild buildings, with their distinctive twin towers, were built in an interesting combination of art-nouveau and eclectic styles. They house the headquarters of the IBUSZ travel agency, among other tenants.

⑤ **Köztársaság tér** (Square of the Republic). Composed of faceless concrete buildings, this square is not particularly alluring aesthetically but is significant because it was where the Communist Party of Budapest had its headquarters, and it was also the scene of heavy fighting in 1956. Here also is the city's second opera house, the **Ferenc Erkel Theatre.** Budapest's largest, with 3,000 seats, it was built in 1910–11 and offers operas and concerts throughout the year.

Párizsi Udvar (Paris Court). At the corner of Petőfi Sándor utca and Kossuth Lajos utca, on the site of the former Inner City Savings Bank, is the Paris Court, a glass-roofed arcade with touristy boutiques and shops. Built in 1914 in richly ornamental neo-Gothic and eclectic styles, the arcade is among the most attractive and atmospheric meccas of Pest.

Nyugati pályaudvar (Western Railway Station). The iron-laced glass hall of the Western Railway Station is in complete contrast to—and much more modern than—the newer Eastern Railway Station. Built in the 1870s, it was designed by a team of architects from Gustav Eiffel's office in Paris. ✉ *VI, Teréz krt.*

★ ⑤ **Vígszínház** (Comedy Theater). Designed in neobaroque style by the Viennese imperial architectural team of Fellner and Helmer and built in 1895–86, the gemlike Comedy Theater twinkles with just a tiny, playful anticipation of art nouveau and sparkles inside and out since its recent refurbishment. The theater hosts primarily musicals, such as Hungarian adaptations of *Cats* and *West Side Story,* as well as dance performances and classical concerts. ✉ *XIII, Pannónia u. 1,* ☎ *1/111–1650.*

Óbuda

Until its unification with Buda and Pest in 1872 to form the city of Budapest, Óbuda (the name means Old Buda) was a separate town that used to be the main settlement; now it is usually thought of as a suburb. Although the vast new apartment blocks of Budapest's biggest housing project and busy roadways are what first strike the eye, the historic core of Óbuda has been preserved in its entirety as an ancient monument.

A GOOD WALK

Óbuda is easily reached by car, bus, or streetcar via the Árpád Bridge from Pest or by the HÉV suburban railway from Batthyány tér to Árpádhid. Once you're there, covering all the sights on foot involves large but manageable distances along major exhaust-permeated roadways. One way to tackle it is to take Tram 17 from its southern terminus at the Buda side of the Margaret Bridge to Kiscelli utca and walk uphill to the **Kiscelli Múzeum.** Then walk back down the same street all the way past **Flórián tér,** continuing toward the Danube and making a left onto Hídfő utca or Szentlélek tér to enter **Fő tér.** After exploring the square and taking in the museums in the **Zichy Kúria** (Zichy Mansion), walk a block or two southeast to the HÉV suburban railway stop and take the train just north to the museum complex at **Aquincum.**

TIMING

It's best to begin touring Óbuda during the cooler, early hours of the day, as the heat on the area's busy roads can get overbearing. Avoid Mondays, when museums are closed.

SIGHTS TO SEE

Aquincum. This complex comprises the reconstructed remains of a Roman settlement dating from the 1st century AD and the capital of the Roman province of Pannonia. Careful excavations at Aquincum have unearthed a varied selection of artifacts and mosaics, giving a tantalizing inkling of what life was like in the provinces of the Roman Empire. A gymnasium and a central heating system have been unearthed, along with the ruins of two baths and a shrine to Mithras, the Persian god of light, truth, and the sun. The **Aquincum Museum** displays the dig's most notable finds: ceramics signed by the city's best-known potter, Ressatus of Aquincum; a red-marble sarcophagus showing a triton and flying Eros on one side and on the other, Telesphorus, the angel of death, depicted as a hooded dwarf; and jewelry from a Roman lady's tomb. ⊠ *III, Szentendrei út 139,* ☎ *1/250–1650.* 🔜 *100 Ft.* ☼ *Apr. and Oct., Tues.–Sun. 10–5; May–Sept., Tues.–Sun. 10–6. Grounds open at 9.*

Flórián tér. The center of today's Óbuda is Flórián tér, where Roman ruins were first discovered when the foundations of a house were dug in 1778. Two centuries later, careful excavations were carried out during the reconstruction of the square, and today the restored ancient ruins lay in the center of the square in boggling contrast to the racing traffic and cement-block housing projects surrounding it.

Fő tér. Óbuda's charming old main square is the most picturesque part of Óbuda. The square has been spruced up in recent years, and there are now several good restaurants and interesting museums in and around the baroque ☞ **Zichy Kúria** (Zichy Mansion), which has become a neighborhood cultural center. Among the most popular offerings are the summer concerts in the courtyard and the evening jazz concerts.

Hercules Villa. A fine 3rd-century Roman dwelling, it takes its name from the myth depicted on its beautiful mosaic floor. The ruin was unearthed between 1958 and 1967 and has recently reopened after a several-year hiatus. ⊠ *III, Meggyfa u. 19–21, no phone (inquire at Aquincum* ☎ *1/250–1650).* 🔜 *50 Ft.* ☼ *Apr. and Oct., Tues.–Sun. 10–5; May–Sept., Tues.–Sun. 10–6.*

Kiscelli Múzeum. A strenuous climb up the steep, dilapidated sidewalks of Remethegy (Hermit's Hill) will deposit you at the elegant, mustard-yellow baroque mansion that houses the Kiscelli Museum. Built between 1744 and 1760 as a Trinitarian monastery with funds donated by the wealthy Zichy family, today it houses an eclectic mix of paintings, sculptures, engravings, and sundry items related to the history of Budapest. Included here is the printing press on which poet and revolutionary Petőfi Sándor printed his famous "Nemzeti Dal" ("National Song"), in 1848, inciting the Hungarian people to rise up against the Hapsburgs. ⊠ *III, Kiscelli u. 108,* ☎ *1/188–8560.* 🎫 *100 Ft.* ☉ *Nov.–Mar., Tues.–Sun. 10–4; Apr.–Oct., Tues.–Sun. 10–6.*

Roman Amphitheater. Probably dating back to the 2nd century, Óbuda's Roman military amphitheater once held some 16,000 people and, at 144 yards in diameter, was one of Europe's largest. A block of dwellings called the Round House was later built by the Romans above the amphitheater; massive stone walls found in the Round House's cellar were actually parts of the amphitheater. Below the amphitheater are the cells where prisoners and lions were held while awaiting confrontation. ⊠ *Pacsirtamező u. at the junction where it meets Bécsi út.*

Zichy Kúria (Zichy Mansion). One wing of the Zichy Mansion is taken up by the **Óbudai Helytörténeti Múzeum** (Óbuda Local History Museum); permanent exhibitions here include traditional rooms from typical homes in the district of Békásmegyer and a popular exhibit covering the history of toys from 1860 to 1960. Another wing houses the **Kassák Múzeum,** which honors the literary and artistic works of a pioneer of the Hungarian avant-garde, Lajos Kassák. ⊠ *Zichy Mansion, Fő tér 1. Local History Museum:* ☎ *1/250–1020.* 🎫 *50 Ft.* ☉ *Tues.–Fri. 2–6, Sat.–Sun. 10–6. Kassák Museum:* ☎ *1/168–7021.* 🎫 *40 Ft.* ☉ *Mid-Oct.–Feb., Tues.–Sun. 10–5; Mar.–mid-Oct., Tues.–Sun. 10–6.*

Dining

See Dining *in* Pleasures and Pastimes, *above,* for general dining information.

Andrássy Út

$$$$ ✕ **Barokk.** This small and intimate restaurant offers dishes adapted from 17th- and 18th-century recipes, creatively named with references to Pope Innocent XI and "the landed proprietor." A favorite is the thick tenderloin flavored with nuts, garlic, and honey and served with pancakes with grated apple. The 10 or so tables are set with gold-rimmed glasses and porcelain vases filled with fresh flowers. The warm atmosphere is enhanced by striking reproductions of baroque furniture and piped-in baroque music. Waiters, dressed in white, ruffled, Baroque-collared shirts, are friendly and quite expert in explaining the menu. ⊠ *VI, Mozsár u. 12,* ☎ *1/131–8942. No credit cards.*

$$ ✕ **Off-Broadway Kávéház.** This cozy basement eatery in Budapest's "Broadway" district was opened by the well-known thespian wife-husband team, actress Kathleen Gáti and film director Gábor Dettre. The long room, with an old fireplace at one end and only a handful of tables, is tastefully decorated with candles, dried flowers, and changing art exhibits. Unusual in Budapest, the menu features large portions of primarily vegetarian and healthful food, such as cream of carrot soup laced with nutmeg, Algerian rice salad, vegetarian lasagna, and Ms. Gáti's popular *Nusi Nasi*—sweet poppy-seed cakes, banana breads, lemon squares, and the like. ⊠ *VI, Zichy Jenő u. 47,* ☎ *1/131–5920. AE, DC.*

Castle Hill

$$$$ ✕ **Alabárdos.** As medieval as its name, the Halberdier (the wielder of that ancient weapon, the halberd), this vaulted wooden room in a 400-year-old Gothic house across from the Matthias Church and Budapest Hilton is widely regarded as one of Hungary's best restaurants. It has only a handful of tables, set with exquisite Herend and Zsolnay porcelain, though in summer a courtyard garden doubles its capacity. The impeccable service, flowery decor, quiet music, and overriding discretion make this an excellent place for a serious business meal. Specialties are Hungarian meats and steaks with goose-liver trimmings. The room's lights go out every time the flambéed mixed grill is delivered; if you don't like to be the center of attention, try the filet mignon in green-pepper sauce, also flambéed but without the pyrotechnics. ⊠ *I, Országház u. 2,* ☎ *1/156–0851. Reservations essential. Jacket and tie. AE, DC, MC, V. Closed Sun.*

$$ ✕ **Arany Hordó.** True to its name (the Golden Barrel), this 14th-century building in the castle district has a beer house on the ground floor. The cellar has a wine tavern, with candlelit tables tucked into nooks of the mazelike stone passageways; those who need to eat above ground can sit in the small, homey dining room on the second floor. Wherever you sit, the menu offers solid Hungarian fare. Try their Lake Balaton *fogas* (pike perch) specialties, like fogas fillet in rosemary-lemon sauce. There is live Gypsy music in the evenings. ⊠ *I, Tárnok u. 14–16,* ☎ *1/156–1367 or 1/212–3742. No credit cards.*

Downtown Pest and the Small Ring Road

$$$$ ✕ **Légrádi Testvérek.** This tiny, intimate restaurant hidden on a narrow street in the heart of Pest is one of the capital's most prestigious and luxurious offerings. Prompt, unobtrusive service is provided at candlelit, lace-covered tables set with Herend china and sterling silver cutlery. Hors d'oeuvres include Russian caviar and terrines of foie gras. Standard but beautifully presented entrées range from chateaubriand to wild boar. The game dishes are highly recommended. ⊠ *V, Magyar u. 23,* ☎ *1/118–6804. Jacket and tie. AE. Closed weekends. No lunch.*

$$$ ✕ **Múzeum.** Fans swear that this elegant, candlelit salon with mirrors, mosaics, and swift-moving waiters features the best dining in Budapest. The salads are generous, the Hungarian wines excellent, and the chef dares to be creative. ⊠ *VIII, Múzeum körút 12,* ☎ *1/267–0375. Jacket and tie. AE. Closed Sun.*

$$ ✕ **Cyrano.** Sophisticatedly chic but casually friendly, this smooth young
★   bistro just off Vörösmarty tér was a success the moment it opened a few years ago. The decor is artistic-contemporary, with wrought-iron chairs, green-marble floors, and long-stemmed azure glasses. A creative kitchen sends out elegantly presented Hungarian and Continental dishes, from standards such as goulash and chicken *paprikás* to more eclectic tastes like tender fried Camembert cheese with blueberry jam and peaches stuffed with Roquefort cream and dressed with a lightly herbed sauce. ⊠ *V, Kristóf tér 7–8,* ☎ *1/266–3096. Reservations essential. AE, DC, MC.*

$$ ✕ **Duna-Corso.** This stolid, family-oriented institution, which has stood on this riverfront square for nearly two decades, offers good, solid food at reasonable prices right in the center of Pest's luxury-hotel belt. The bean-and-cabbage soup (laced with smoked pork), roast duck with sauerkraut, and goose cracklings with potatoes are as simple and hearty as ever, and the service is still pokey and friendly. This noisy, bustling spot is lively enough to forestall feelings of loneliness if you're by yourself. For views of the castle and Chain Bridge, a table on the vast outdoor terrace is the best seat in town. ⊠ *V, Vigadó tér 3,* ☎ *1/118–6362. No credit cards.*

$ ✕ **Bohémtanya.** Locals have known and loved this place for years for its hearty, reliably tasty fare, heaping portions, and relaxed atmosphere. The prices are equally appealing, and to help out newcomers, the menu is arranged by price. The word is out, however, so be on the safe side and reserve a table. Comfortable dark-wood booths and tables make you want to linger over your last inexpensive beer. ⊠ *VI, Paulay Ede utca 6,* ☎ *1/122–1453. No credit cards.*

$ ✕ **Fészek.** Hidden away inside the nearly 100-year-old Fészek Artists' Club is this local favorite. The large, neoclassical dining room has high ceilings and mustard-color walls trimmed with ornate molding and dark-wood panels. In summer guests dine outdoors at candlelit tables set in a Venetian-style courtyard, originally monks' cloisters, with pillared archways, colorful majolica decorations, and blooming chestnut trees. The extensive, almost daunting menu features all the Hungarian classics, with such specialties as turkey stuffed with goose liver and a variety of game dishes. Guests must pay a 150-Ft. Artists' Club cover charge upon entering the building; if you've reserved a table in advance, it will be charged to your bill instead. ⊠ *VII, Dob u. 55 (corner of Kertész u.),* ☎ *1/322–6043. AE.*

$ ✕ **Kispipa.** Under the same management as Fészek (☞ *above*), this tiny, well-known restaurant with arched yellow-glass windows and piano bar features a similar expansive menu of first-rate Hungarian cuisine. The kitchen has a loyal following of both locals and foreigners (drawn in part by unexpectedly low prices), and critics have named its venison ragout soup seasoned with tarragon the best in town. A singer at the piano entertains from 7 PM. ⊠ *VII, Akácfa u. 38,* ☎ *1/342–2587. Reservations essential. AE, MC. Closed Sun. and holidays.*

$ ✕ **Tüköry Söröző.** Solid, hearty Hungarian fare comes in big portions
★ at this popular spot close to Parliament. Red-check tablecloths, low lighting, and dark-wood booths give it a cozy, rustic atmosphere. Best bets include pork cutlets stuffed with savory liver or apples and cheese, washed down with a big mug of inexpensive beer. Courageous carnivores can sample the beefsteak tartare, topped with a raw egg; many say it's the best in town. ⊠ *V, Hold u. 15,* ☎ *361/269–5027. No credit cards. Closed weekends.*

North Buda

$$$$ ✕ **Vadrózsa.** The Wild Rose always has fresh ones on the table at this restaurant in an old villa perched on a hilltop in the exclusive Rózsadomb district of Buda. It's elegant to the last detail—even the service is white glove—and the garden is delightful in summer. ⊠ *II. Pentelei Molnár u. 15,* ☎ *1/135–1118. Reservations essential. Jacket and tie. AE, DC, MC, V.*

$$$ ✕ **Udvarház.** The views from this Buda hilltop restaurant are unsurpassed. Dining indoors at tables set with white linens and candles or outdoors on the open terrace, your meals are accompanied by vistas of the Danube bridges and Parliament far below. Folklore shows and live Gypsy music frequently enliven the scene. Unless you want to wait for the infrequent bus, car, or taxi is the only way to travel to and from this high point. ⊠ *III, Hármashatárhegyi út 2,* ☎ *1/188–8780. AE, DC, MC, V. Closed Mon. Nov.–Mar. No lunch weekdays.*

$$–$$$ ✕ **Náncsi Néni.** Aunt Nancy's restaurant is a perennial favorite, de-
★ spite its out-of-the-way location. Irresistibly cozy, the dining room feels like Grandma's country kitchen: Chains of paprika and garlic dangle from the low wooden ceiling above tables set with red-and-white gingham tablecloths, candles, and fresh bread tucked into tiny baskets. Shelves along the walls are crammed with jars of home-pickled beets, peppers, and the like, which you can purchase to take home. On the home-style Hungarian menu (large portions!) turkey dishes feature a

222

Dining

Alabárdos, **15**

Arany Hordó, **12**

Bagolyvár, **44**

Barokk, **39**

Bohémtanya, **34**

Cyrano, **29**

Duna-Corso, **26**

Fészek, **37**

Gundel, **42**

Kehli, **2**

Kisbuda Gyöngye, **3**

Kispipa, **36**

Légrádi Testvérek, **31**

Marxim, **8**

Múzeum, **32**

Náncsi Nèni, **9**

Off-Broadway
Kávéház, **38**

Postakocsi, **1**

Robinson
Restaurant, **43**

Tabáni Kakas, **16**

Tüköry Söröző, **23**

Udvarház, **7**

Vadrózsa, **6**

Lodging

Alba Hotel, **11**

Astoria, **33**

Atrium Hyatt, **24**

Budapest Hilton, **13**

Budapest Marriott, **28**

Citadella, **18**

Fórum, **25**

Gellért, **21**

Hotel Centrál, **41**

Hotel Mercure Korona
Budapest, **30**

Kempinski Hotel
Corvinus Budapest, **27**

Kulturinov, **14**

Medosz, **40**

Molnár Panzió, **19**

Nemzeti, **35**

Novotel, **20**

Panorama Hotel &
Bungalows, **17**

Radisson SAS Béke, **22**

Ramada Grand
Hotel, **4**

Thermal Hotel Helia, **5**

Victoria, **10**

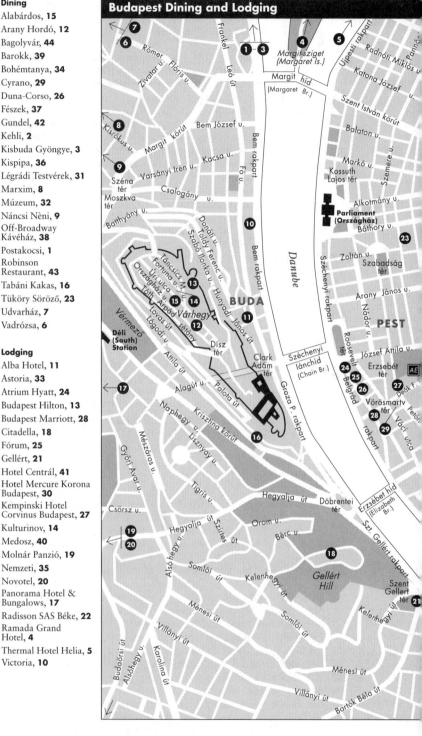

Budapest Dining and Lodging

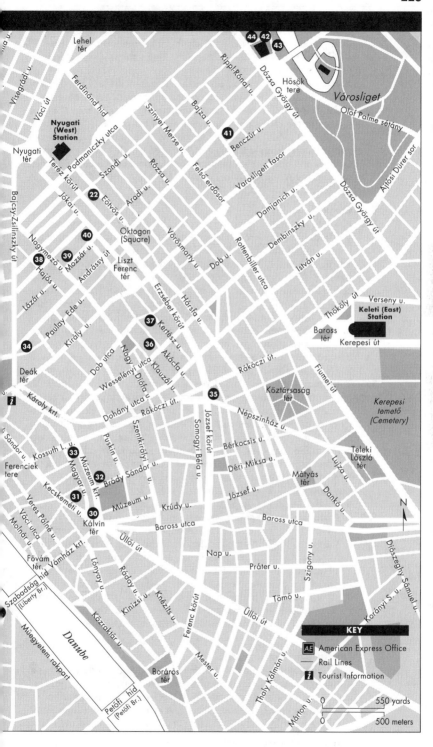

Lehel tér

Rippl-Rónai u.

Dózsa György út

44 42
43

Hősök tere

Városliget

Olof Palme sétány

Visegrádi u.

Váci út

Ferdinánd híd

Szinyei Merse u.

Balzsa u.

41

Benczúr u.

Ajtósi Dürer sor

Nyugati (West) Station

Podmaniczky utca

Rózsa u.

Felső erdősor

Városligeti fasor

Dózsa György út

Nyugati tér

Teréz körút

Szondi u.

Aradi u.

Damjanich u.

Dembinszky u.

Bajcsy-Zsilinszky út

Jókai u.

22 Eötvös u.

Oktogon (Square)

Vörösmarty u.

Dob u.

Rottenbiller utca

István u.

Nagymező u.

40

Mozsár u.

Andrássy út

Liszt Ferenc tér

Verseny u.

38

39

Thököly út

Keleti (East) Station

Lázár u.

Hajós u.

Paulay Ede u.

Király u.

Erzsébet körút

Hársfa u.

Baross tér

Kerepesi út

34

37 Kertész u.

Fiumei út

Deák tér

36 Akácfa u.

Dob utca

Nagy Diófa u.

Wesselényi utca

Klauzál u.

Rákóczi út.

Köztársaság tér

Kerepesi temető (Cemetery)

Károly krt.

Dohány utca u.

Rákóczi út.

35

Népszínház u.

Szentkirályi u.

József körút

Somogyi Béla u.

Teleki László tér

Luzsa u.

Sándor u.

Kossuth L. u.

33

Puskin u.

Bérkocsis u.

Déri Miksa u.

Ferenciek tere

Magyar u.

32 Bródy Sándor u.

Mátyás tér

Dankó u.

Kecskeméti u.

31

Múzeum krt.

Múzeum u.

Krúdy u.

József u.

Veres Pálné u.

30

Kálvin tér

Baross utca

Baross utca

Molnár u.

Váci utca

Szigony u.

Diószeghy Sámuel u.

Fővám tér

Vámház krt.

Üllői út

Nap u.

Práter u.

Korányi S. u.

Szabadság híd (Liberty Br.)

Lónyay u.

Ráday u.

Kinizsi u.

Knézits u.

Tömő u.

Üllői út

Műegyetem rakpart

Danube

Közraktár u.

Ferenc körút

KEY

AE American Express Office

— Rail Lines

i Tourist Information

Boráros tér

Mester u.

Thaly Kálmán u.

0 _____ 550 yards

0 _____ 500 meters

Petőfi híd (Petőfi Br.)

Márton u.

N

creative flair, such as breast fillets stuffed with apples, peaches, mushrooms, cheese, and sour cream. Special touches include a popular outdoor garden in summer and free champagne for all couples in love. ⊠ *II, Ördögárok út 80, ☎ 1/176–5809. Reservations essential in summer. AE, MC, V.*

$ ✕ **Marxim.** Two years after the death of socialism in Hungary, this simple pizza-and-pasta restaurant opened up to mock the old regime—and milk it for all it's worth. From the flashing red star above the door outside to the clever puns on menu items, the theme is "communist nostalgia." Classic black-and-white photos of decorated hard-liners and papier-mâché doves stuck in gnarled barbed-wire fences line the walls. Crowds and blaring rock music make Marxim best suited for a lunch or snack. ⊠ *II, Kisrókus u. 23, ☎ 1/212–4183. AE, DC, MC, V. No lunch Sun.*

Óbuda

$$$ ✕ **Kehli.** Formerly known as Hídvendéglő (Bridge Inn), this pricey but laid-back neighborhood tavern is on a hard-to-find street near the Óbuda end of the Árpád Bridge. The inn is small, paneled, and sepia-toned, with an old wooden wagon out front and a garden (which in summer more than doubles the restaurant's capacity). The food is hearty and heavy, just the way legendary Hungarian writer and voracious eater Gyula Krúdy (to whom the restaurant is dedicated) liked it when he lived (and feasted) in the neighborhood. Select from appetizers, such as fried button mushrooms stuffed with brains or hot bone marrow with garlic toast, before moving on to fried goose livers with mashed potatoes or turkey breast stuffed with cheese and goose liver. ⊠ *III, Mókus utca 22, ☎ 1/250–4241. AE.*

$$$ ✕ **Kisbuda Gyöngye.** Considered one of the city's finest restaurants,
★   this intimate Óbuda restaurant is decorated with antique furniture, and its walls are creatively decorated with an eclectic but elegant patchwork of carved wooden cupboard doors and panels. A violin-piano duo sets a romantic mood, and in warm weather you can dine outdoors in the cozy back garden. Try the chicken Cumberland (grilled boneless breasts marinated in basil and spices) or the fresh trout smothered in a cream sauce nutted with mushrooms and capers. ⊠ *III, Kenyeres u. 34, ☎ 1/168–6402 or 1/168–9246. Reservations essential. AE. Closed Sun. July–Aug. No dinner Sun.*

$$$ ✕ **Postakocsi.** In this cavernous cellar under the main square of Óbuda stands the public stagecoach that set out on the first journey from here to Vienna in 1752. It serves as the bar of this large restaurant, which is decorated with saddles, horseshoes, and other equestrian doodads. The Hungarian menu includes such Transylvanian specialties as stuffed sirloin of beef. Goose liver is everywhere—inside mushrooms, in the dressings and secret stuffings of the steaks, fried with french fries, roasted with apples, and in the Hungarian goose-liver stew. Gypsy musicians wander from room to room, something of a mixed blessing. ⊠ *III, Fő tér 2, ☎ 1/188–9941. Jacket and tie. AE, DC, MC, V.*

Tabán and Gellért Hill

$$ ✕ **Tabáni Kakas.** Just below Castle Hill, this popular restaurant has a distinctly warm and friendly atmosphere and specializes in large helpings of poultry dishes, particularly goose. Try the catfish paprikás or the roast duck with steamed cabbage. A pianist plays and sings every evening except Monday. ⊠ *I, Attila út 27, ☎ 1/175–7165. AE, MC.*

Városliget (City Park)

$$$$ ✕ **Gundel.** Redesigned by world-famous designers Adam Tihany,
★   Emery Roth, and Milton Glaser with dark-wood paneling, navy-blue upholstered chairs and love seats, and tables set with Zsolnay porce-

lain and sterling silver, Gundel occupies a palatial mansion in City Park. It is the shrine where Hungary's famous dessert, *Gundel palacsinta* (Gundel pancakes), was invented around the turn of the century by the restaurant's second owner, Károly Gundel. Filled with walnuts, lemon rind, raisins, and orange peel and coated with chocolate sauce, the crepes are flamed in rum at the table—and they never disappoint. The earlier courses are hardly a mere prelude. Appetizers, such as the wild rice and smoked quail-egg salad, are light and refined. The main dishes are delicious, particularly the duck roast with braised cabbage and the butter-fried lamb scallopini served on cabbage pancakes. England's Queen Elizabeth is among the many distinguished guests who have dined here. ⊠ *XIV, Állatkerti körút 2,* ☎ *1/121–3550. Reservations essential. Jacket and tie. AE, DC, MC, V.*

$$$$ ✕ **Robinson Restaurant.** Many favor this intimate dining room on the lake in City Park as the best restaurant in town. Service is doting and the kitchen first-rate, featuring elegantly prepared Hungarian and Continental cuisine, such as crisp roast sucking pig flavored with champagne or fresh *fogas* (fish) stuffed with spinach. Finish it off with a flourish by ordering a flaming cup of coffee *Diablo*, fueled with Grand Marnier. Padded pastel decor and low lighting wash the room in pleasant, if not Hungarian, elegance. Outdoor lakeside seating in summer is especially popular. ⊠ *Városliget,* ☎ *1/343–0955. Reservations essential. Jacket and tie. AE, DC, MC, V.*

$$ ✕ **Bagolyvár.** George Lang opened this restaurant next door to his gas-
★ tronomic palace, Gundel, in 1993. An immaculate dining room with soaring wooden-beam ceilings has a familial, informal, yet elegantly professional atmosphere, and the kitchen produces first-rate daily menus of home-style Hungarian specialties. Soups, served in shiny silver tureens, are particularly good. Musicians entertain with cimbalom or accordion music nightly from 7 PM. In warm weather there is outdoor dining in a lovely back garden. ⊠ *Állatkerti körút 2,* ☎ *1/121–3550, ext. 222. AE, DC, MC, V.*

Lodging

Budapest is well equipped with hotels and hostels, but the increase in tourism since 1989 has put a strain on the city's often crowded lodgings. Advance reservations are strongly advised, especially at the lower-price hotels. Many of the major luxury and business-class hotel chains are represented in Budapest; however, all of them are Hungarian-run franchise operations with native touches that you won't find in any other Hilton or Ramada.

Some hotels have large numbers of rooms reserved through booking agencies such as IBUSZ, but you can save yourself the commission if you book a room directly. If a hotel receptionist tells you no rooms are available, that means the rooms the hotel books itself are all occupied.

In winter it's not difficult to find a hotel room, even at the last minute, and prices are usually reduced by 20%–30%. By far the cheapest and most accessible beds in the city are rooms (around 1,500 Ft. per person) in private homes. Although most tourist offices book private rooms, the supply is limited, so try to arrive in Budapest early in the morning.

Addresses below are preceded by the district number (in Roman numerals) and include the Hungarian postal code. Districts V, VI, and VII are in downtown Pest; I is the main tourist district of Buda.

$$$$ 🏨 **Budapest Hilton.** Built in 1977 around a 13th-century monastery
★ adjacent to the Matthias Church, this perfectly integrated architectural

wonder overlooks the Danube from the choicest site on Castle Hill. Every contemporary room has a remarkable view; Danube vistas cost more. Children, regardless of age, get free accommodation when sharing a room with their parents. Note: breakfast is not included in room rates. ⊠ *I, Hess András tér 1–3, H-1014 Budapest,* ☎ *1/214–3000; in U.S. and Canada,* ☎ *800/445–8667;* FAX *1/156–0285. 295 rooms with bath, 27 suites. 3 restaurants, 2 bars, café, wine cellar, beauty salon, sauna, exercise room, shops, ballroom, casino, laundry services and dry cleaning, business services, meeting rooms, travel services, parking (free and fee). AE, DC, MC, V.*

$$$$ 🏨 **Fórum Hotel.** This boxy modern riverside hotel consistently wins applause for its gracious appointments, excellent service, and gorgeous views across the Danube to Castle Hill. The rooms, 60% of which have Danube views (more expensive), are done in shades of brown and cream, with welcoming upholstered furniture. Rooms on higher floors ensure the least noise. The Fórum's are among the most modern hotel fitness facilities in the country, and considering how addictive the Viennese Café's pastries are, you might need to use them. The central location and efficient business services makes it popular with businesspeople. Note: breakfast is not included in the room rates. ⊠ *V, Apáczai Csere János u. 12–14, Box 231, H-1368,* ☎ *1/117–9111,* FAX *1/117–9808. 376 rooms with bath, 24 suites. 2 restaurants, bar, café, no-smoking floors, health club, business center, meeting rooms, drugstore, car rental, doctor, parking (fee). AE, DC, MC, V.*

$$$$ 🏨 **Gellért.** The double-deck rotunda of this grand Hungarian hotel leads
★ you to expect a string orchestra, concealed behind massive marble pillars, playing "The Emperor Waltz." Built in 1918, the *Jugendstil* (art nouveau) Gellért was favored by Otto von Habsburg, son of the last emperor. Rooms come in all shapes and sizes—from palatial suites to awkward, tiny rooms—and have either early 20th-century furnishings, including some Jugendstil pieces, or newer, more basic contemporary furnishings. The best views—across the Danube or up Gellért Hill— are more expensive; avoid those that face the building's inner core. Amenities are up to date, and the coffee shop is among the city's best; but the pièce de résistance is the monumental thermal baths, including an outdoor pool with a wave machine. Admission to the spa is free to hotel guests (medical treatments cost extra); corridors and an elevator lead directly to the baths from the second, third, and fourth floors. ⊠ *XI, Gellért tér 1, H-1111,* ☎ *1/185–2200,* FAX *1/166–6631. 233 rooms with bath, 13 suites. Restaurant, bar, brasserie, café, indoor pool, outdoor wave pool, beauty salon, spa, thermal baths, shops, baby-sitting, business services, meeting rooms, parking (fee). AE, DC, MC, V.*

$$$$ 🏨 **Kempinski Hotel Corvinus Budapest.** Opened in August 1992, this
★ sleek luxury hotel is the favored lodging of visiting VIPs—from rock superstars to business moguls and foreign dignitaries—offering a central-city location and superior facilities. From overnight shoe-shine service to afternoon chamber music in the lobby, the Kempinski delivers extra details with class and polish. Unlike those of its local peers, rooms are spacious, with elegant contemporary decor themed around blond and black Swedish geometric inlaid woods and an emphasis on functional touches, such as three phones in every room. Large, sparkling bathrooms, most with tubs and separate shower stalls and stocked with every toiletry, are the best in Budapest. An automatic current in the smallish pool allows you to swim long distances without getting anywhere. Breakfast is not included in the room rates. ⊠ *V, Erzsébet tér 7–8, H-1051,* ☎ *1/266–1000; in the U.S. and Canada,* ☎ *800/426–3135;* FAX *1/266–2000. 339 rooms with bath, 28 suites. 2 restaurants, bar, lobby lounge, pub, indoor pool, barbershop, beauty salon, mas-*

sage, health club, shops, laundry service and dry cleaning, business services, meeting rooms, travel services, parking (fee). AE, DC, MC, V.

$$$$ 🏨 **Radisson SAS Béke.** In 1985 it was a family-oriented inn where a room cost less than $6 a night; a decade later, after a lavish overhaul the well-situated Béke (on a main boulevard near the Nyugati [West] Railroad Station) is a luxury hotel with a glittering turn-of-the-century facade, liveried doormen, a lobby lined with mosaics and statuary, and bellmen bowing before the grand marble staircase. Popular with Italians and Americans, this hotel has all the business amenities plus the efficient services of a helpful staff. Freshly renovated rooms resemble solidly modern living rooms, with two-tone wood furnishings and pastel decor. Inward-facing rooms have the least street noise, but no view. ✉ *VI, Teréz krt. 43, H-1067,* ☎ *1/132-3300,* FAX *1/153–3380. 238 rooms with bath, 8 suites. 2 restaurants, 2 bars, café, pool, sauna, solarium, hairdresser, shops, casino, business center, meeting rooms, travel agency, parking (fee). AE, DC, MC, V.*

$$$ 🏨 **Astoria.** At a busy intersection in downtown Pest stands a revitalized turn-of-the-century hotel that remains an oasis of quiet and serenity in hectic surroundings. Staff members are always—albeit unobtrusively— on hand. Rooms are genteel, spacious, and comfortable, and renovations have remained faithful to the original furnishings and decor: rather like Grandma's sitting room, in Empire style with an occasional antique. The Astoria's opulent café is a popular meeting place. ✉ *V, Kossuth Lajos u. 19–21, H-1053,* ☎ *1/117–3411,* FAX *1/118–6798. 123 rooms with bath or shower, 5 suites. Restaurant, bar, café, nightclub, business services, meeting rooms, free parking. AE, DC, MC, V.*

$$$ 🏨 **Atrium Hyatt.** The spectacular 10-story interior—a mix of glass capsule elevators, cascading tropical greenery, an open bar, and café—is surpassed only by the views across the Danube to the castle (rooms with a river view cost substantially more). Accommodations are modern but homey—cream walls with framed prints and upholsteries in mauves and minty blues. Well situated in the inner city near the Pest waterfront, the Hyatt and its facilities and amenities remain in the vanguard of the downtown hotels. ✉ *V, Roosevelt tér 2, H-1051,* ☎ *1/266–1234,* FAX *1/266– 9101. 328 rooms with bath, 27 suites. 3 restaurants, 2 bars, indoor pool, beauty salon, sauna, solarium, health club, business center, casino, ballroom, conference facilities, valet services, travel services, private underground parking on site (fee). AE, DC, V.*

$$$ 🏨 **Budapest Marriott.** Bought by the Marriott chain in 1993, this so-
★ phisticated yet friendly hotel on the Danube in downtown Pest is still sparkling from its recent $13 million overhaul. Attention to detail is evident from the moment you enter the lobby, from the impeccably presented buffet of colorfully glazed cakes and pastries to the feather-light ring of the front-desk bell. The decor is an elegant blend of contemporary and traditional—marble floors, forest-green leather couches, darkwood panels accented with brass lamps, and fresh flower arrangements in the lobby. Roomy beds, lushly patterned carpets, floral bedspreads, and etched glass create a serene ambience in the guest rooms. The layout takes full advantage of the hotel's prime Danube location, offering breathtaking views of Gellért Hill, the Chain and Elizabeth bridges, and Castle Hill from the lobby, ballroom, every guest room, and even the swimming pool of the impressive health club. In summer you can bask in the sun on the front deck and watch the boats drift past on the Danube. ✉ *V, Apáczai Csere János u. 4, H-1364,* ☎ *1/266–7000; in U.S. and Canada,* ☎ *800/831–4004;* FAX *1/266–5000. 362 rooms with bath, 20 suites. 3 restaurants, bar, no-smoking rooms, indoor pool, health club, squash, shops, ballroom, baby-sitting, laundry service and dry cleaning, business services, meeting rooms, travel services, parking (fee). AE, DC, MC, V.*

$$$ 🏨 **Hotel Mercure Korona Budapest.** Bought by the French Mercure chain in 1995, the Austrian-built Korona is on busy Kálvin tér in the center of the city, near the river and close to the National Museum and other sights. Small, angular rooms are modern and functional, with slightly worn black-painted wood furnishings and pink-and-aqua decor. Higher rooms let in the least street noise; best views look onto the National Museum. ⊠ *V, Kecskeméti u. 14, H-1053,* ☎ *1/117–4111,* FAX *1/118–3867. 421 rooms with bath, 11 suites. 2 restaurants, bar, café, no-smoking floor, pool, massage, sauna, solarium, exercise room, laundry service and dry cleaning, business center, meeting rooms, travel services, parking garage (fee).*

$$$ 🏨 **Novotel.** This member of the French motor-inn chain is on the rim of a large park near the highways to Vienna and Lake Balaton. Connected to the Budapest Convention Center, it is favored by musicians performing here as well as convention delegates. Though the rooms are ordinary, with tiny bathrooms, soft mattresses, and a motel-generic decor, the amenities are more than ample, including closed-circuit TV news in English, French, and German; a complete business center; and, famous around town, the Bowling Brasserie, featuring "fried meats, draft beer," and a bowling alley. There is no charge for children under 16 staying in their parents' room. ⊠ *XII, Alkotás út 63–67, H-1123,* ☎ *1/186–9588; in the U.S., 213/277–6915;* FAX *1/166–5636. 318 rooms with bath, 6 suites. Restaurant, 2 bars, indoor pool, hairdresser, sauna, solarium, bowling, exercise room, shops, concert hall, laundry services and dry cleaning, business center, meeting rooms, travel services, parking. AE, DC, MC, V.*

$$$ 🏨 **Ramada Grand Hotel.** Built in 1873 and long in disrepair, this venerable hotel reopened in 1987 as perhaps the world's stateliest Ramada Inn, on Margaret Island in the middle of the Danube. Room rates may have increased, but at least the high ceilings haven't been lowered. Nor have the old-fashioned room trimmings—down comforters, ornate chandeliers, Old World furniture—been lost in the streamlining. Graham Greene always took the same suite that he had before World War II, and the U.S. Embassy likes to send visitors here. Choose between views across the Danube onto a less attractive, industrial section of Pest or out onto the verdant lawns and trees of a tranquil park. Because it's connected to a bubbling thermal spa next door, and has an island location, the Ramada feels removed from the city but is still only a short taxi or bus ride away. ⊠ *XIII, Margit-sziget, H-1138,* ☎ *1/311–1000, for reservations 1/131–7769; in the U.S. and Canada,* ☎ *800/228–9898;* FAX *1/153–3029. 164 rooms with bath, 10 suites. Restaurant, ice cream parlor, indoor pool, beauty salon, massage, spa, thermal baths, exercise room, bicycles, meeting rooms, travel services, free parking. AE, DC, MC, V.*

$$$ 🏨 **Thermal Hotel Helia.** A sleek Scandinavian design and less hectic location upriver from downtown make this spa hotel on the Danube a change of pace from its Pest peers. Its neighborhood is nondescript, but guests can be in town in minutes or stay and take advantage of the thermal baths and special health packages—including everything from Turkish baths to electrotherapy and fitness tests. The staff is friendly and helpful, and most of the comfortable rooms have Danube views. ⊠ *XIII, Kárpát u. 62–64, H-1133,* ☎ *1/270–3277; in the U.S. and Canada,* ☎ *800/223–5652;* FAX *1/270–2262. 254 rooms with bath; 8 suites, 4 with sauna. 2 restaurants, bar, café, indoor pool, beauty salon, hot tub, massage, sauna, spa, steam room, thermal baths, tennis courts, exercise room, shops, business services, meeting rooms, free parking. AE, DC, MC, V.*

$$ 🏨 **Alba Hotel.** Tucked behind an alleyway at the foot of Castle Hill, this spotless, modern gem of a hotel is a short walk via the Chain Bridge from lively business and shopping districts. Rooms are snug and quiet,

with clean white-and-pale-gray contemporary decor and charmingly typical Budapest views over a kaleidoscope of rooftops and chimneys. Half have bathtubs and air-conditioning. Swiss management ensures efficient service. ⊠ *I, Apor Péter u. 3, H-1011,* ☎ *1/175–9244,* 𝐅𝐀𝐗 *1/175–9899. 95 rooms with bath. Bar, breakfast room, no-smoking rooms, meeting room, parking (fee). AE, DC, MC, V.*

\$\$ 🏨 **Hotel Centrál.** Relive history—stay in this hotel, well situated in a leafy diplomatic quarter just one block from Heroes' Square, as visiting Communist dignitaries once did. The architecture and furnishings are straight out of the 1950s, but rooms are comfortable and most have unusually large bathrooms. Suites are classically elegant, with turn-of-the-century Hungarian eclectic furnishings; ask for the room that was Rudolf Nureyev's favorite. ⊠ *VI, Munkácsy Mihály u. 5–7, H-1063,* ☎ *1/321–2000,* 𝐅𝐀𝐗 *1/322–9445. 36 rooms with bath, 6 suites. Restaurant, free parking. AE, DC, MC, V.*

\$\$ 🏨 **Nemzeti.** With a lovely baby-blue baroque facade, the Nemzeti is another hotel that reflects the grand mood of the turn of the century; it was completely restored in 1987. The high-ceiling lobby and public areas—with pillars, arches, and wrought-iron railings—are elegant, but the guest rooms are small and unexceptional, although they will likely improve with renovations and installation of air-conditioning, targeted for 1997. It's located at bustling Blaha Lujza tér in the center of Pest, which tends toward the seedy after dark; to ensure a quiet night, ask for a room facing the inner courtyard. ⊠ *VIII, József körút 4, H-1088,* ☎ *1/269–9310,* 𝐅𝐀𝐗 *1/114–0019. 76 rooms with bath. Restaurant, brasserie, piano bar, meeting room. AE, DC, MC, V.*

\$\$ 🏨 **Panoráma Hotel & Bungalows.** Perched 1,017 feet above the Danube near the upper terminus of the cogwheel railway and surrounded by giant pine trees, the Panorama resembles a grand hunting lodge. Hotel rooms are modern and comfortable, decorated with cheerful pastel colors and prints. Rooms with views offer spectacular vistas over the hills of Buda and beyond to Pest. The charming bungalows, though a bit close together, are like miniature cabins in the woods, with pinewood floors and walls and a cozy sitting area; some also have kitchens. Unless you have vertigo, you will admire the view of the entire city from the terrace. The restaurant serves international cuisine and features live Gypsy music nightly. ⊠ *XII, Rege u. 21, H-1121,* ☎ *1/175–0522,* 𝐅𝐀𝐗 *1/175–9727. 35 rooms with bath, 53 self-catering bungalows. Restaurant, terrace bar, pool, sauna, solarium. AE, DC, MC, V.*

\$\$ 🏨 **Victoria.** The dark, stately Parliament building and city lights twin-
★ kling over the river can be seen from the picture windows of every room at this young establishment right on the Danube. The tiny Victoria mixes the charm of a small inn with the modern comforts and efficiency of a business hotel. The absence of conventions is a plus, and the location—an easy walk from Castle Hill sights and downtown Pest—couldn't be better. Higher floors have less street noise. ⊠ *I, Bem rakpart 11, H-1011,* ☎ *1/201–8644,* 𝐅𝐀𝐗 *1/201–5816. 24 rooms with bath, 2 with balcony; 1 suite. Bar, sauna, meeting room, parking (fee). AE, DC, MC, V.*

\$ 🏨 **Citadella.** Comparatively basic, with four beds in some rooms and showers down the hall, the Citadella is nevertheless very popular for its price and for its stunning location—right inside the fortress. Half of the rooms comprise a youth hostel, giving the hotel a young and lively communal atmosphere. None of the rooms have bathrooms, and half have showers. Breakfast is not included in the rates. ⊠ *XI, Citadella sétány, Gellérthegy, H-1118,* ☎ *1/166–5794,* 𝐅𝐀𝐗 *1/186–0505. 20 rooms, none with bath. Breakfast room. No credit cards.*

$ ▦ **Kulturinov.** One wing of a magnificent 1902 neobaroque castle now
★ houses basic budget accommodations. Rooms come with two or three
beds and are clean and delightfully peaceful. The neighborhood—one
of Budapest's most famous squares in the luxurious castle district—is
magical. ⊠ *I, Szentháromság tér 6, H-1014,* ☎ *1/155–0122 or 1/175–
1651,* FAX *1/175–1886. 16 rooms with shower. Snack bar, reading
room, meeting rooms. AE, DC, MC, V.*

$ ▦ **Medosz.** The Medosz offers a central Pest location near Oktogon,
a major transportation hub, and lovely Andrássy út. Its modern, socialist-realist concrete appearance wins no points for architecture, but
the surrounding buildings, including the nearby Opera House, more
than compensate. Rooms are neat but very basic—no TVs or telephones—with small, low beds, worn upholstery, and a depressing left-
over-1950s institutional feel. Most rooms face a pleasant park in front,
but if you prefer quiet, request one facing the rear. ⊠ *VI, Jókai tér 9,
H-1061,* ☎ *1/153–1700 or 1/153–1434,* FAX *1/132–4316. 63 rooms
with bath, 7 suites. Restaurant. No credit cards.*

$ ▦ **Molnár Panzió.** Fresh air and peace and quiet await at this immac-
ulate guest house nestled high above Buda on Széchenyi Hill. Rooms
in the octagonal main house are polyhedric, clean, and bright, with pleasant wood paneling and pastel-color modern furnishings; most have distant views of Castle Hill and Gellért Hill, and some have balconies.
Service is at once friendly and professional, and the restaurant is first-
rate. Rooms in a new addition are due to be complete by 1997. ⊠ *XII,
Fodor u. 143, H-1124,* ☎ *1/209–2974,* ☎ FAX *1/209–2973. 25 rooms
with bath. Restaurant, bar, sauna, exercise room, playground, travel
services, free parking. AE, DC, MC, V.*

Nightlife and the Arts

Nightlife

Budapest's nightlife is vibrant and diverse. For basic beer and wine drinking, *sörözős* (beer bars) and *borozős* (wine bars) abound, although the
latter tend to serve the early-morning-spritzer-before-work types rather
than nighttime revelers. For quiet conversation there are *drink-bárs* in
most hotels and all over town, but beware of the inflated prices and
steep cover charges. Cafés are preferable for unescorted women.

Most nightspots and clubs have bars, pool tables, and dance floors.
As is the case in most other cities, the life of a club or disco in Budapest
can be somewhat ephemeral. In one year, several different clubs may
open and close at the same address. Those listed below are quite popular and seem to be here to stay. But for the very latest on the more
transient "in" spots, consult the nightlife sections of the *Budapest Sun*
and *Budapest Week*.

A word of warning to the smoke-sensitive: Budapest is a city of smok-
ers. No matter where you spend your night out, chances are you'll come
home smelling of cigarette smoke.

BARS AND CLUBS

Bahnhof (⊠ VI, Váci út 1, at Nyugati pu.) is, appropriately, in the Nyugati (Western) train station and attracts swarms of young people to dance
on its spacious, crowded dance floor to live bands and DJ'd music.

The most popular of Budapest's Irish pubs and a favorite expat wa-
tering hole is **Becketts** (⊠ V, Bajcsy-Zsilinszky út 72, ☎ 1/111–1035),
where Guinness flows freely and excellent Irish fare is served in authentic polished wood and brass decor.

A hip, low-key crowd mingles at the stylish **Cafe Incognito** (⊠ VI, Liszt
Ferenc tér 3, ☎ 1/267–9428), with low lighting and funky music kept

at a conversation-friendly volume by savvy DJs. Couches and armchairs in the back are comfy and private.

Café Pierrot (⊠ I, Fortuna u. 14, ☎ 1/175–6971), an elegant café and piano bar on a small street on Castle Hill, is well suited to a secret rendezvous.

The look is sophisticated and stylish, but the mood low-key and unpretentious at the new **Fél 10 Jazz Club** (⊠ VIII, Baross u. 30, ☎ 1/133–7721), near Kálvin tér. Three open levels with balconylike sitting areas, a dance floor, and two bars are impeccably decorated with twisting-patterned black wrought-iron tables and chairs with maroon cushions.

The **Jazz Café** (⊠ V, Ballasi Bálint u. 25, ☎ 1/269–5506) hosts local jazz bands several nights a week in a small basement space of blue neon lights and funky papier-mâché statues.

Housed in an old stone mansion near Heroes' Square, the conceptually schizophrenic **Made Inn** (⊠ VI, Andrássy út 112, ☎ 1/111–3437) has an elaborate decor modeled on an underground mine shaft, a kitchen specializing in Mediterranean foods, a large outdoor bar, and a disco dance floor packed with local and international Beautiful People. It's closed Monday and Tuesday November–April.

Picasso Point (⊠ V, Hajós u. 31, ☎ 1/269–5544), a very popular, spacious bar with a hip coffeehouse feel and Pablo-themed decor, hosts local art exhibits upstairs and live jazz and rock bands downstairs.

Fortuna (⊠ I, Hess András tér 4, ☎ 1/155–7177), in a historic medieval house on Castle Hill, is a popular and ultrastylish disco with a large model clientele and a larger dose of "attitude"; how quickly you get in depends on how you measure up to the bouncer's discerning entry criteria. It's open only Wednesday, Friday, and Saturday nights from 10 PM.

CASINOS

Most casinos are open daily from 2 PM until 4 or 5 AM and offer gambling in hard currency—usually dollars—only.

In an 1879 building designed by prolific architect Miklós Ybl, who also designed the State Opera House, the **Várkert Casino** (⊠ I, Miklós Ybl tér 9, ☎ 1/202–4244) is the most attractive of the city's casinos. The **Gresham Casino** (⊠ V, Roosevelt tér 5, ☎ 1/117–2407) is in the famous Gresham Palace at the Pest end of the Chain Bridge. Sylvester Stallone is alleged to be an owner of the popular **Las Vegas Casino** (⊠ V, Roosevelt tér 2, ☎ 1/117–6022), in the Atrium Hyatt Hotel.

The Arts

For the latest on arts events, consult the entertainment listings of the English-language newspapers (☞ Contacts and Resources *in* Budapest A to Z, *below*) Their weekly entertainment calendars map out all that's happening in Budapest's arts and culture world—from thrash bands in wild clubs to performances at the Opera House and traditional Hungarian folk-dancing lessons at local cultural houses. Another option is to stop in at the **National Philharmonic ticket office** (⊠ Vörösmarty tér 1) and browse through the scores of free programs and fliers and scan the walls coated with upcoming concert posters. Hotels and tourist offices will also provide you with a copy of the monthly publication *Programme,* which contains details of all cultural events.

CLASSICAL MUSIC AND OPERA

The **Budapest Kongresszusi Központ** (Budapest Convention Center; ⊠ XII, Jagelló út 1–3, ☎ 1/161–2869) is the city's largest-capacity (but least atmospheric) classical concert venue and usually hosts the largest-selling events of the Spring Festival.

Liszt Ferenc Zeneakadémia (Franz Liszt Academy of Music; ⊠ VI, Liszt Ferenc tér 8, ☎ 1/342–0179), usually referred to as the Music Academy, is Budapest's premier classical concert venue, hosting orchestra and chamber music concerts in its splendid main hall.

The glittering **Magyar Állami Operaház** (Hungarian State Opera House; ⊠ VI, Andrassy út 22, ☎ 1/153–0170), Budapest's main venue for operas and classical ballet, presents an international repertoire of classical and modern works as well as such Hungarian favorites as Kodály's *Háry János*. Except during the one-week BudaFest international opera and ballet festival in mid-August, the Opera House is closed during the summer.

The homely little sister of the Opera House, the **Erkel Színház** (Erkel Theater; ⊠ VII, Köztársaság tér 30, ☎ 1/133–0540) is Budapest's other main opera and ballet venue. There are no regular performances in the summer.

The tiny recital room of the **Bartók Béla Emlékház** (Bartók Béla Memorial House; ⊠ II, Csalán út 29, ☎ 1/176–2100) hosts intimate Friday evening chamber music recitals by well-known ensembles from mid-March to June and September to mid-December.

Colorful operettas like those by Lehár and Kalman are staged at their main Budapest venue, the **Operetta Theater** (⊠ VI, Nagymező u. 19, ☎ 1/132–0535); also look for modern dance productions and Hungarian renditions of popular Broadway classics.

Classical concerts are held regularly at the **Pesti Vigadó** (Pest Concert Hall; ⊠ V, Vigadó tér 2, ☎ 1/117–6222).

ENGLISH-LANGUAGE MOVIES

Many of the English-language movies that come to Budapest are subtitled in Hungarian rather than dubbed. There are more than 30 cinemas that regularly show films in English, and tickets are very inexpensive by Western standards (about 300 Ft.). Consult the movie matrix in the *Budapest Sun* or *Budapest Week* for a weekly list of what's showing.

FOLK DANCING

Many of Budapest's district cultural centers regularly hold traditional regional folk-dancing evenings, or dance houses (*táncház*), often with general instruction at the beginning. In addition to offering good exercise, these sessions provide a less touristy way to taste Hungarian culture. Ask your hotel clerk to find out the latest programs at these more popular cultural centers.

Almássy Recreation Center (⊠ VII, Almássy tér 6, ☎ 1/142–0387) holds numerous folk-dancing evenings, featuring Hungarian as well as Greek and other ethnic cultures. Traditionally the wildest táncház is held Saturday nights at the **Inner City Youth and Cultural Center** (⊠ V, Molnár u. 9, ☎ 1/117–5928), where the stomping and whirling goes on way into the night. Hungary's best-known folk ensemble, Muzsikás, hosts a weekly dance house at the **Marczibányi tér Cultural Center,** (⊠ II, Marczibányi tér 5/a, ☎ 1/212–5789), usually on Thursday nights.

FOLKLORE PERFORMANCES

The **Folklór Centrum** (⊠ XI, Fehérvári út 47, ☎ 1/203–3868) has been a major venue for folklore performances for over 30 years. It hosts regular traditional folk concerts and dance performances from spring through fall.

Budapest has dozens of art galleries showing and selling old works as well as the very latest. The **Csontváry Gallery** (⊠ V, Vörösmarty tér 1, ☎ 1/118–4594), right in the center of town, is a good place to view works by today's Hungarian painters. **Dovin Gallery** (⊠ V, Galamb u. 6, ☎ 1/118–3673) specializes in Hungarian contemporary paintings. New York celebrity Yoko Ono opened **Gallery 56** (⊠ V, Falk Miksa u. 7, ☎ 1/269–2529) in the fall of 1992 to show art by internationally famed artists, such as Keith Haring, as well as her own works. **Mai Mano Fotógaléria** (☞ Andrássy út, *above*).

THEATERS
The **Madách Theater** (⊠ VII, Erzsébet körút 31–33, ☎ 1/322–0677) produces colorful musicals in Hungarian, including a popular adaptation of *Cats*. English-language dramas are not common in Budapest, but when there are any, they are usually staged at the **Merlin Theater** (⊠ V, Gerlóczy utca 4, ☎ 1/117–9338). In the summer, the Merlin usually hosts an English-language theater series. Another musical theater is the **Thália Theater** (⊠ VI, Nagymező u. 22–24, ☎ 1/112–4230). The sparkling **Vígszínház** (Comedy Theater; ⊠ XIII, Szent István körút 14, ☎ 1/111–1650) hosts classical concerts and dance performances, but is primarily a venue for musicals, such as the Hungarian adaptation of *West Side Story*.

TICKET OFFICES
Tickets can be bought at the venues themselves, but many ticket offices sell them without extra charge. Prices are still very low, so markups of even 30% shouldn't dent your wallet if you book through your hotel. Inquire at Tourinform if you're not sure where to go.

Theater and opera tickets are sold at the **Central Theater Booking Office** (Pest: ⊠ VI, Andrassy út 18, ☎ 1/112–0000; Buda: ⊠ II, Moszkva tér 3, ☎ 1/135–9136). For classical concert, ballet, and opera tickets, as well as tickets for major pop and rock shows, go to the **National Philharmonic Ticket Office** (⊠ V, Vörösmarty tér 1, ☎ 1/117–6222). **Music Mix Ticket Service** (⊠ V, Váci utca 33, ☎ 1/138–2237 or 1/117–7736) specializes in popular music, but handles other genres as well.

Outdoor Activities and Sports

Bicycling
Because of constant thefts, bicycle rentals are difficult to find in Hungary. A rental outfit on Margaret Island (⊠ Hajós Alfréd sétány 1, across from Thermal Hotel, ☎ 1/269–2747) offers popular four-wheeled pedaled contraptions called *Bringóhintó*s, as well as traditional two-wheelers; standard bikes cost about 400 Ft. per hour, 1,450 Ft. for 24 hours. For more information about renting in Budapest, contact **Tourinform** (⊠ V, Sütő u. 2, ☎ 1/117–9800). For brochures and general information on bicycling conditions and suggested routes, try Tourinform or contact the **National Society of Bicycle Commuters** (⊠ III, Miklós tér 1, ☎ 1/250–0420 or 1/250–0424, ext. 28 on both) or the **Bicycle Touring Association of Hungary** (⊠ V, Bajcsy-Zsilinszky út 31, 2nd floor, Apt. 3, ☎ 1/111–2467).

Golf
Golf is still a new sport in Hungary, one that many Hungarians can't afford. The closest place to putt is 35 kilometers (22 miles) north of the city at the **Budapest Golfpark** (☎ 1/117–6025, 1/117–2749, or 06/60–321–673) in Kisoroszi. The park has an 18-hole, 72-par course and a driving range. Greens fees range from 4,500 Ft. to 5,000 Ft. Carts

and equipment can be rented. The club also has two tennis courts. The park is closed November–February.

Health and Fitness Clubs

Andi Stúdió (⊠ V, Hold u. 29, ☎ 1/111–0740) is a trendy fitness club with adequate but sometimes overcrowded facilities. For about 400 Ft. you can work out on the weight machines (no real cardiovascular equipment to speak of) or take an aerobics class, held every hour. **Gold's Gym** (⊠ VIII, Szentkirályi u. 26, ☎ 1/267–4334) stands out as being the least cramped of its peers, with good weight-training and cardiovascular equipment and hourly aerobics classes in larger-than-usual spaces. A one-visit pass costs around 650 Ft. The highest-tech facilities are at the Marriott Hotel's **World Class Fitness Center** (⊠ VI, Apáczai Csere János u. 4, ☎ 1/266–4290), offering weight machines, treadmills, StairMasters, and rowing machines, as well as aerobics classes and a squash court. One visit costs around 1,400 Ft.; a game of squash, around $15.

Horseback Riding

The **Nemzeti Lovarda** (National Horse Academy; ⊠ VIII, Kerepesi út 7, ☎ 1/113–5210) offers lessons to equestrians of all levels. The average charge is 600 Ft. per hour. Call ahead to assure yourself a horse. In the verdant outskirts of Buda, the **Petneházy Club** (⊠ 1029 Feketefej út 2, Adyliget, ☎ 1/176–5992) is a fully equipped resort with horseback-riding lessons and trail rides for around 1,500 Ft. per hour.

Jogging

The path around the perimeter of **Margaret Island,** as well as the numerous pathways in the center, are level and inviting for a good run. **Városliget** (City Park) in flat Pest has paths and roads good for jogging. The forests of the area in Buda called **Hűvösvölgy** (Cool Valley) are laced with meandering, hilly trails that are perfect for long, picturesque runs (or walks) above the pollution and bustle of Pest. Trails begin at the top of Törökvész út, off Bimbó út; take Bus 11 from Batthyány tér to the last stop.

Spas and Thermal Baths

☞ Pleasures and Pastimes, *above.* In addition to those listed below, newer, modern baths are open to the public at hotels such as the Ramada Grand Hotel (⊠ XIII, Margitsziget, ☎ 1/311–1000) and the Thermal Hotel Helia (⊠ XIII, Kárpát u. 62, ☎ 1/270–3277). They lack the charm and aesthetic appeal of their older peers but provide the latest treatments in sparkling facilities.

★ **Gellért Thermal Baths.** (☞ Tabán and Gellért Hill, *above*). **Király Baths.** (☞ North Buda, *above*). **Lukács Baths.** Built in the 19th century but modeled on the Turkish originals and fed with waters from a source dating from the Bronze Age and Roman times, the facilities here are coed. ⊠ II, Frankel Leó u. 25–29, ☎ 1/115–4280. ☉ *Weekdays 6:30 AM–7 PM, Sat. 6:30 AM–2 PM, Sun. 6:30 AM–1 PM.* 💳 120
★ Ft. **Rác Baths.** (☞ Tabán and Gellért Hill, *above*). **Rudas Medicinal**
★ **Baths.** (☞ Tabán and Gellért Hill, *above*). **Széchenyi Baths.** (☞ Városliget, *above*).

Tennis and Squash

Városmajor Tennis Academy (⊠ XII, Városmajor u. 63–69, ☎ 1/202–5337) has five outdoor courts (clay and hexapet) available daily 7 AM–9 PM. They are lit for night play and covered by a tent in winter. Court fees run 500 Ft.–700 Ft. per hour. Racket rentals and lessons are also offered. On Margaret Island, **Club-Sziget** (⊠ XIII, Europa House, Margitsziget, ☎ 1/112–9472) charges 500 Ft.–600 Ft. per hour to play on one of its four clay courts; reserve several days in advance. **On-line**

Squash Club (⊠ Budaörs, Forrás u. 8, ☎ 23/416–945), on the near outskirts of town (about 10 minutes by car from the centrum), is a trendy full-facility fitness club with five squash courts. Hourly rates run around 1,500 Ft.–1,900 Ft., depending on when you play. The club offers racket and ball rentals and stays open until midnight. The Marriott Hotel's **World Class Fitness Center** (⊠ V, Apáczai Csere János u. 4, ☎ 1/266–4290) has one excellent squash court available for about $15 an hour.

Shopping

Shopping Districts

You'll find plenty of expensive boutiques, folk-art and souvenir shops, foreign-language bookstores, and classical-record shops on or around touristy **Váci utca**, Budapest's famous, upscale pedestrian-only promenade. While a stroll along Váci utca is integral to a Budapest visit, browsing among some of the smaller, less touristy, more typically Hungarian shops in Pest—on the **Kis körút** (Small Ring Road) and **Nagy körút** (Great Ring Road), and **Kossuth Lajos utca**—may prove more interesting and less pricey. The area just south of Kossuth Lajos utca, sometimes newly referred to as **SoKo** (South of Kossuth), is slowly budding with trendy little clothing shops and bohemian-style cafés.

Department Stores

Skála Metro (⊠ VI, Nyugati tér 1–2, ☎ 1/153–2222), opposite the Nyugati (Western) Railroad Station, is one of the largest and best-known department stores, selling a little bit of not entirely everything. **Divatcsarnok** (⊠ VI, Andrássy út 39, ☎ 1/122–4000) has a good selection of clothes and an ornate hall decorated with frescoes by 19th-century Hungarian painter Károly Lotz. For those willing to splurge on Western goods, there is a **Marks and Spencer** (⊠ V, Váci u. 11/b, ☎ 1/118–5160) store just past Vörösmarty tér. Farther down Váci utca is the **Made In World Center** (⊠ corner of Váci u. and Haris Köz), a tiny, upscale underground shopping arcade of trendy fashion boutiques, a music store, and gift shops. Váci utca's sleekest department store, **Fontana,** has several floors of cosmetics, clothing, and other goods, all with price tags reflecting the store's expensive address.

Markets

For true bargains and possibly an adventure, make an early morning trip to the vast **Ecseri Piac** (⊠ IX, Nagykőrösi út; take Bus 54 from Boráros tér), on the outskirts of the city. A colorful, chaotic market that shoppers have flocked to for decades, it is an arsenal of second-hand goods, where you can find everything from frayed Russian army fatigues to Herend and Zsolnay porcelain vases to 150-year-old handmade silver chalices worthy of being in a museum. Goods are sold at permanent tables set up in rows, from trunks of cars parked on the perimeter, and by lone, shady characters clutching just one or two items. As a foreigner, you may be overcharged, so prepare to haggle—it's part of the flea-market experience. Ecseri is open weekdays 8–4, Saturday 8–3, but the best selection is on Saturday mornings.

A colorful outdoor flea market is held weekend mornings from 7–2 at **Petőfi Csarnok** (⊠ XIV, Városliget, Zichy Mihály út 14, ☎ 1/343–4327), in City Park. The quantity and selection is smaller than at Ecseri Piac, but it offers a fun flea-market experience closer to the city center. Many visitors buy red-star medals, Russian military watches, and other memorabilia from Communist days here. One other option is **Vásárcsarnok** (☞ Market Hall in Downtown Pest, *below*).

Specialty Stores

BÁV (⊠ V, Ferenciek tere 12, ☎ 1/118–3381; V, Kossuth Lajos u. 1, ☎ 1/118–4403), the State Commission Trading House, has antiques of all shapes, sizes, kinds, and prices at its several branches around the city. While they both have a variety of objects, carpets are the specialty at the Ferenciek tere store, furniture and porcelain at the branch on Kossuth Lajos utca. **Qualitás** (⊠ V, Falk Miksa u. 32; V, Kígyó u. 5; ⊠ VII, Dohány u. 1; ⊠ XII, Krisztina körút 73) sells paintings, furniture, and decorative objects at its several branches around town. **Polgár Galéria és Aukciósház** (⊠ V, Kossuth Lajos u. 3, ☎ 1/118–6954) sells everything from jewelry to furniture and also holds several auctions a year. You'll find antiques of all forms and functions at the **Ecseri Piac** market (☞ Markets, *above*).

You'll encounter **bookselling stands** throughout the streets and metro stations of the city, many of which sell English-language souvenir picture books at discount prices. **Váci utca** is lined with bookstores that sell glossy coffee-table books about Budapest and Hungary; **Universum** (V, Váci u. 31–33) has a particularly good selection.

Bestsellers (⊠ V, Október 6 u. 11, ☎ 1/112–1295) sells exclusively English-language books and publications, including best-selling paperbacks and a variety of travel guides about Hungary and beyond. The **Central European University Bookstore** (⊠ V, Nádor u. 9), in the Central European University, is a smaller, more academically focused branch of Bestsellers bookstore. If you're interested in reading up on this part of the world, this is the store for you. **Libri International Bookstore** (⊠ V, Váci u. 32) has a good selection of books in English, including coffee-table and picture books about Budapest and Hungary. Other stores with good selections of books in English are **Idegennyelvű Könyvesbolt** (⊠ V, Petőfi Sándor u. 2), **Longman ELT** (⊠ VIII, Kölcsey u. 2), **Litea Bookshop and Tea Salon** (⊠ I, Hess András tér 4), and **Atlantisz Book Island** (⊠ V, Váci u. 31–33).

Hungary is famous for its age-old Herend china, which is hand-painted in the village of Herend near Lake Balaton. The brand's Budapest store, **Herend Porcelán Márkabolt** (⊠ V, József Nádor tér 11, ☎ 1/117–2622), sells a variety of the delicate (and pricey) pieces, from figurines to dinner sets. For the Herend name and quality without the Herend price tag, visit **Herend Village Pottery** (⊠ II, Bem rakpart 37, ☎ 1/156–7899), where you can choose from Herend's less costly, practical-use-oriented line of more durable ceramic cups, dishes, and table settings. Hungary's famous, exquisite **Zsolnay** porcelain, created and hand-painted in Pécs, is sold at the **Zsolnay Márkabolt** (⊠ V, Kristóf tér 2, ☎ 1/266–6305). Hungarian and Czech crystal is considerably less expensive here than in the United States. **Goda Kristály** (⊠ V, Váci u. 9, ☎ 1/118–4630; ⊠ V, Kígyó u. 5, ☎ 1/118–3324) has beautiful colored and clear pieces. **Haas & Czjzek** (⊠ VI, Bajcsy-Zsilinszky út 23, ☎ 1/111–4094) has been in the business for more than 100 years, selling a variety of porcelain, glass, and ceramic pieces in traditional and contemporary styles. Crystal and porcelain dealers also sell their wares at the **Ecseri Piac** flea market (☞ Markets, *above*), often at discount prices, but those looking for authentic Herend and Zsolnay should beware of imitations.

High-fashion women's outfits created by today's top Hungarian designers are for sale at **Monarchia** (⊠ V, Szabadsajtó út 6, ☎ 1/118–

3146), a tiny boutique with rich burgundy velvet draperies and ceilings higher than its floor space. Six young Hungarian fashion designers sell their imaginative, excellent pieces at their own little boutique, **Orlando** (⊠ V, Haris köz).

FOLK ART

Handmade articles, such as embroidered tablecloths and painted plates, are sold all over the city by Transylvanian women wearing traditional scarves and colorful skirts. You can usually find them standing at **Moszkva tér, Jászai Mari tér,** outside the **Kossuth tér** metro, around **Váci utca,** and in the larger metro stations. All types of folk art—pottery, blouses, jewelry boxes, wood carvings, embroidery—can be purchased at one of the many branches of Népművészet Háziipar, also called **Folkart Centrum** (⊠ V, Váci u. 14, ☎ 1/118–5840), a large cooperative chain that handles the production and sale of folk art by many artisans. Prices are reasonable, and selection and quality are good. A hint on how to check for authenticity: If the fourth to sixth digits of the serial number pasted onto the item are 900, the piece is handmade, usually by a well-known artisan. (Other, smaller branches include those at ⊠ XI, Bartók Béla u. 50, ☎ 1/166–4831; ⊠ V, Kálvin tér 5, ☎ 1/137–3785; and ⊠ XIII, Szent István körút 26, ☎ 1/131–0211.) **Éva Dolls** (⊠ V, Kecskeméti u. 10, ☎ 1/117–4305), a small store near Kálvin tér, has pricey but beautiful crafts.

MUSIC

Recordings of Hungarian folk music or of pieces played by Hungarian artists are increasingly available on compact discs, though cassettes and records are much cheaper and are sold throughout the city.

FOTEX Records (⊠ V, Szervita tér 2, ☎ 118–3395; ⊠ V, Váci u. 13, ☎ 1/118–3128; ⊠ VI, Teréz körút 27, ☎ 1/132–7175; ⊠ XII, Alkotás út 11, ☎ 1/155–6886) is a flashy, Western-style music store with a cross-section of musical types but focused on contemporary pop. It has branches throughout the city. **Hungaroton Hanglemez Szalon** (⊠ V, Vörösmarty tér 1, ☎ 1/138–2810) has a large selection of all types of music and is centrally located, on Vörösmarty tér. The **Rózsavölgyi Zenebolt** (⊠ V, Szervita tér 5, ☎ 1/118–3500) is an old, established music store crowded with sheet music and largely classical recordings, but with other selections as well.

Budapest A to Z

Arriving and Departing

BY BOAT

From mid-July to early September, two swift hydrofoils leave Vienna daily at 8 AM and 1:10 PM (once-a-day trips are scheduled early April–mid-July and early September–early November). After a five-hour journey downriver, with a stop in the Slovak capital, Bratislava, and views of Hungary's largest church, the cathedral in Esztergom, the boats make a grand entrance into Budapest via its main artery, the Danube. The upriver journey takes an hour longer. For reservations and information in Budapest, call **MAHART** (☎ 1/118–1704 or 1/118–1586; in Vienna, 01/72–92–161 or 01/72–92–162). The cost is 750 AS one-way.

BY CAR

The main routes into Budapest are the newly completed M1 from Vienna (via Győr), the M3 from near Gyöngyös, the M5 from Kecskemét, and the M7 from the Balaton; the latter three are being upgraded over the next few years and extended to Hungary's borders with Ukraine, Serbia, and Slovenia.

BY PLANE

Ferihegy (☎ 1/157–9123), Hungary's only commercial airport, is about 22 kilometers (14 miles) southeast of Budapest. All **Lufthansa** and **Malév** flights operate from the newer Terminal 2, 4 kilometers (2½ miles) farther from the city; other airlines use Terminal 1. For same-day flight information, call 1/157–7155; operators theoretically speak some English. **Malév**'s (☎ 1/266–9033, 1/267–2911, or 1/267–4333 [ticketing]) popular nonstop direct flight between New York and Budapest operates out of Ferihegy 2 every day most of the year. Its daily nonstop to and from London flies year-round. Direct service between Atlanta and Budapest, with a 45-minute stop in Vienna, was also recently begun jointly by Malév, Delta, and Austrian airlines.

The most convenient way to fly between Hungary and the United States is with the **Malév Hungarian Airlines** (☎ 1/266–9033, 1/267–2911, or 1/267–4333 [ticketing]) **nonstop direct service** between JFK International Airport in New York and Budapest's Ferihegy Airport—the only direct flight that exists. All are on roomy Boeing 767-200s and take approximately nine hours. The service runs daily most of the year. Tickets can also be purchased through Malév's partner, Delta Airlines (1/266–1400 or 1/266–4637), which buys a limited set of seats on the service. Direct service between Atlanta and Budapest, with a 45-minute stop in Vienna, was also jointly begun by Malév, Delta, and **Austrian Airlines** (☎ 1/117–1676) in May 1996.

Malév and other national airlines fly nonstop from most European capitals. **British Airways** (☎ 1/266–7790 or 1/118–3299) and **Malév** offer daily nonstop service between Budapest and London.

Between the Airport and Downtown: Many hotels offer their guests car or minibus transportation to and from Ferihegy, but all of them charge for the service. You should arrange for a pickup in advance.

By Taxi: Allow 40 minutes during nonpeak hours and at least an hour during rush hours (7 AM–9 AM from the airport, 4 PM–6 PM from the city). Official airport taxis are queued at the exit and overseen by a taxi monitor; rates are fixed according to the zone of your final destination. A taxi ride to the center of Budapest will cost around 3,000 Ft. Avoid taxi drivers who offer their services before you are out of the arrivals lounge.

By Bus: LRI Centrum-Airport-Centrum minibuses run every half hour from 5:30 AM to 9:30 PM to and from the Erzsébet tér bus station (Platform 1) in downtown Budapest. It takes almost the same time as taxis but costs only 400 Ft. from either airport terminal.

The **LRI Airport Shuttle** provides convenient door-to-door service between the airport and any address in the city. To get to the airport, call to arrange a pickup (☎ 1/157–8555); to get to the city, make arrangements at LRI's airport desk. Service to or from either terminal costs around 1,000 Ft. per person.

BY TRAIN

There are three main *pályaudvar* (train stations) in Budapest: **Keleti** (Eastern), **Nyugati** (Western), and **Déli** (Southern). Trains from Vienna usually operate from the Keleti Station, while those to Balaton depart from the Déli.

Getting Around

BY BOAT

During the summer the Budapest Transportation Authority (BKV) runs a not-so-regular boat service that links the north and south of the city, stopping at points on both banks, including Margit-sziget (Margaret Island); at press time, details were uncertain—contact Tourinform for current schedules.

BY BUS AND TRAM

Trams (*villamos*) and buses are abundant and convenient. One fare ticket (50 Ft.; valid on all forms of public transportation) is valid for only one ride in one direction. Tickets cannot be bought on board; they are widely available in metro stations and newsstands and must be canceled on board—watch how other passengers do it—unless you've purchased a *napijegy* (day ticket; 400 Ft., a three-day ticket costs 800 Ft.), which allows unlimited travel on all services within the city limits. Hold onto whatever ticket you have; spot-checks by aggressive undercover checkers (look for the red armbands) are numerous and often targeted at tourists. Most lines run from 5 AM and stop operating at 11 PM, but there is all-night service on certain key lines. Consult the separate night-bus map posted in most metro stations for all-night routes.

BY CAR

Budapest, like any Western city, is plagued by traffic jams during the day, but motorists should have no problem later in the evening. Parking, however, is a problem—prepare to learn new parking techniques such as curb balancing and sidewalk straddling. Motorists not accustomed to sharing the city streets with trams should pay extra attention.

BY METRO

Service on Budapest's subways is cheap, fast, frequent, and comfortable; stations are easily located on maps and streets by the big letter M (for metro). Tickets—50 Ft.; valid on all forms of mass transportation—can be bought at hotels, metro stations, newsstands, and kiosks. They are valid for one ride only; you can't change lines or direction. Tickets must be canceled in the time-clock machines in station entrances and should be kept until the end of the journey, as there are frequent checks by undercover inspectors; a fine for traveling without a validated ticket is about 400 Ft. A napijegy (day ticket) costs 400 Ft. (a three-day ticket, 800 Ft.) and allows unlimited travel on all services within the city limits.

Line 1 (marked FÖLDALATTI), which starts downtown at Vörösmarty tér and follows Andrássy út out past Gundel restaurant and City Park, is an antique tourist attraction in itself, built in the 1890s for the Magyar millennium; its yellow trains with tank treads still work. Lines 2 and 3 were built 90 years later. Line 2 (red) runs from the eastern suburbs, past the Keleti (Eastern) Station, through the Inner City area, and under the Danube to the Déli (Southern) Station. (One of the stations, Moszkva tér, is where the *Várbusz* [Castle Bus] can be boarded.) Line 3 (blue) runs from the southern suburbs to Deák tér, through the Inner City, and northward to the Nyugati (West) Station and the northern suburbs. On all three lines, fare tickets are canceled in machines at the station entrance. All three metro lines meet at the Deák tér station and run from 4:30 AM to 11 PM.

BY TAXI

Taxis are plentiful and a good value, but make sure they have a working meter. The average initial charge is 40 Ft.–60 Ft., plus 80 Ft.–90 Ft. per kilometer plus 16 Ft.–20 Ft. per minute of waiting time. Many drivers try to charge outrageous prices, especially if they sense that their passenger is a tourist. Avoid unmarked "freelance" taxis; stick with those affiliated with an established company. Your safest and most reliable bet is to do what the locals do: Order a taxi by phone; it will arrive in about 5 to 10 minutes. The best rates are with **Fö taxi** (☎

1/222–2222), **Citytaxi** (☎ 1/211–1111), **6 X 6** (☎ 1/266–6666), and **Teletaxi** (☎ 1/155–5555).

Contacts and Resources

APARTMENT RENTALS

Amadeus Apartments (✉ Üllői út 197, H-1091, ☎ 30/422–893, 𝖥𝖠𝖷 1/177–2871) oversees five well-kept apartments in downtown Budapest, each consisting of two rooms plus a fully equipped kitchen and bathroom; sizes vary between 50 and 75 square meters. It's an excellent option for families with children and travelers wanting to save money without sacrificing privacy, central location, and general quality. Free transportation from the train station or airport is included; guarded parking areas (700 Ft.–1,500 Ft. per day) are provided for those with cars. The two-person, high-season rate is approximately $50–$60 a day.

Cooptourist (✉ I, Attila u. 107, ☎ 1/175–2846 or 1/175–2937) and **Charles Apartments** (✉ I, Hegyalja út 23, ☎ 1/201–1796 or 1/212–3830) are two other private agencies dealing specifically with apartment accommodations, which are also available through **IBUSZ**'s main office (✉ V, Ferenciek tere 10, ☎ 1/118–6866).

B&B RESERVATION AGENCIES

IBUSZ Welcome Hotel Service (✉ Apáczai Csere János u. 1, ☎ 1/118–3925 or 1/118–5776, 𝖥𝖠𝖷 1/117–9099), open 24 hours a day, arranges rooms in private homes, reserves rooms in inns and hotels, and books private apartments. Arrangements can also be made through IBUSZ offices in the United States and Great Britain (☞ Visitor Information *in* Important Contacts A to Z). Besides arranging rooms in private apartments, **Cooptourist** (☞ *above*) also makes reservations in its affiliated inns and hotels.

CAR RENTALS

Avis (main office, ✉ V, Szervita tér 8, ☎ 1/118–4240; Terminal 1, ☎ 1/157–6421; Terminal 2, ☎ 1/157–7265), **Budget-Pannonia** (main office, ✉ Hotel Mercure Buda, I, Krisztina körút 41–43, ☎ 1/156–6333; Terminal 1, ☎ 1/157–8197; Terminal 2, ☎ 1/157–8481), and **Hertz** (✉ V, Marriott Hotel, Apáczai Csere János u. 4, ☎ 1/266–4344; airport, ☎ 1/157–7171) are all here for those who prefer companies they know back home. Rates are high: Weekend rates for automatics begin around $70 per day plus 70¢ per kilometer. Rates tend to be significantly lower if you arrange your rental *from home* through the American offices. Ask your travel agent for help.

Local companies offer lower rates. Inquire at **Americana Rent-A-Car** (✉ Ibis Hotel Volga, XIII, Dózsa György út 65, ☎ 1/270–2177) about unlimited mileage weekend specials. **Fötaxi** (main office, ✉ VII, Kertész u. 24–28, ☎ 1/322–1471; Terminal 1, ☎ 1/157–8618; Terminal 2, ☎ 1/157–8606) has special rates on smaller and non-Western makes, including inexpensive Russian Ladas (not a luxury make).

DOCTORS AND DENTISTS

Doctor: Ask your hotel or embassy for recommendations or visit the **R-Clinic** (✉ II, Felsőzöldmáli út 13, ☎ 1/250–3488, 1/250–3489, or 1/250–3490), a private clinic staffed by English-speaking doctors offering 24-hour medical and ambulance service. The clinic accepts major credit cards and prepares full reports for your insurance company. U.S. and Canadian visitors are advised to take out full medical insurance. U.K. visitors are covered for emergencies and essential treatment.

Dentist: In dental emergencies, contact the **Stomatológiai Intézet** (Central Dental Institutes; ✉ VIII, Szentkirályi u. 40, ☎ 1/133–0970), which offers 24-hour dental service. Otherwise, it's best to wait until you return home. **Dr. Pál Gerlóczy** (✉ XII, Zugligeti út 60, ☎ 1/176–3600) has a private English-speaking dental practice and accepts credit cards.

EMBASSIES AND CONSULATES

U.S. (✉ V, Szabadság tér 12, ☎ 1/267–4400). **Canada** (✉ XII, Budakeszi út 32, ☎ 1/275–1200). **U.K.** (✉ V, Harmincad u. 6 (☎ 1/266–2888, FAX 1/266–0907).

EMERGENCIES

Police (☎ 07). **Ambulance** (☎ 04), or call **SOS** (✉ XI, Fraknó u. 32, ☎ 1/204–5500 or 1/204–5501), a 24-hour private ambulance service with English-speaking personnel.

ENGLISH-LANGUAGE BOOKSTORES

☞ Books *in* Shopping, *above.*

ENGLISH-LANGUAGE PERIODICALS

Several English-language weekly newspapers have sprouted up to placate Budapest's large expatriate community. The *Budapest Sun, Budapest Week,* and the *Budapest Business Journal* are sold at major newsstands, hotels, and tourist points.

ENGLISH-LANGUAGE RADIO

Radio Bridge, on 102.1 FM, broadcasts Voice of America news every hour on the hour. A 15-minute program called "Central Europe Today," which features news and business coverage, also plays at 8 AM Monday through Friday.

GUIDED TOURS

Orientation Tours: IBUSZ conducts three-hour bus tours of the city that operate all year and cost about 2,200 Ft. Starting from Erzsébet tér, they take in parts of both Buda and Pest. **Gray Line Cityrama** (✉ V, Báthori u. 22, ☎ 1/132–5344) also offers a three-hour city bus tour (about 2,400 Ft. per person). For a different twist, you can board the **Barbie Bus** (☎ 06/30–433–216) and tour the sights with the wind in your hair and the sun on your face in a bubble-gum-pink cabriolet—topless—bus. Tours last approximately two hours and are given in German or English, covering sights on both sides of the river. Daily departures, from the Café Korona on Dísz tér on Castle Hill, are at 11 AM and 2 PM, weather permitting (the Barbie Bus's top is permanently down).

Special-Interest Tours: IBUSZ, Cityrama, and **Budapest Tourist** organize a number of unusual tours, featuring trips to the Buda Hills, goulash parties, and visits to such traditional sites as the National Gallery and Parliament. These companies will provide personal guides on request. Also check at your hotel.

Boat Tours: From May through October boats leave from the dock at Vigadó tér on 1½-hour cruises between the railroad bridges north and south of the Árpád and Petőfi bridges, respectively. The trip, organized by **MAHART** (☎ 1/118–1704), runs twice a day (at noon and 7 PM) and costs about 500 Ft.; from mid-June through August, the evening cruise features live music and costs about 100 Ft. more. In April, cruises operate on Saturday and Sunday only.

Hour-long evening sightseeing cruises on the ***Danube Legend*** depart nightly at 8:15 from April to November, and twice nightly (at 9 and 10) from May through September. Guests receive headphones and listen to a recorded explanation of the sights in the language of their choice. Drinks are also served. Boats depart from Pier 6–7 at Vigadó tér (☎ 1/117–2203 for reservations and information).

The ***Duna-Bella*** takes guests on one-hour tours on the Danube, including a stop on Margaret Island and shipboard cocktails. Recorded commentary is provided through earphones. The tour is offered July through August, three times a day; May through September, twice daily; and April through October, once a day. Boats depart from Pier 6–7 at Vigadó tér (☎ 1/117–2203 for reservations and information).

Jewish-Heritage Tours: The Chosen Tours (⊠ XII, Zolyomi lépcső 27, ☎ 1/319–3427, ☎ FAX 1/319–6800) offers a three-hour bus tour ($17) called "Budapest Through Jewish Eyes" and a two-hour walking tour ($11) highlighting the sights and cultural life of the city's important Jewish history. Bus tours run three times a week; walking tours, two, from April (after Passover) through October. Arrangements can also be made, however, for unscheduled and off-season tours for groups of four or more.

Personal Guides: The major travel agencies—**IBUSZ** and **Budapest Tourist**—will arrange for guides. The weekly English-language newspapers, the *Budapest Sun* and *Budapest Week,* sometimes carry advertisements for guides.

LATE-NIGHT PHARMACIES
The state-run pharmacies close between 6 and 8 PM, but several pharmacies stay open at night and on the weekend, offering 24-hour service, with a small surcharge for items that aren't officially stamped as urgent by a physician. You must ring the buzzer next to the night window and someone will respond over the intercom. Central ones include those at **Teréz körút 41** (☎ 1/111–4439) in the sixth district, near the Nyugati Train Station; and the one at **Rákóczi út 39** (☎ 1/114–3695) in the eighth district, near the Keleti Train Station.

TRAVEL AGENCIES
American Express (⊠ V, Déak Ferenc u. 10, ☎ 1/266–8680, FAX 1/267–2028). **Getz International** (⊠ V, Falk Miksa u. 5, ☎ 1/312–0645 or 1/312–0649, FAX 1/112–1014). **Vista** (⊠ VII, Károly körút 21, ☎ 1/269–6032, 1/342–9316, or 1/342–1534; FAX 1/269–6031).

VISITOR INFORMATION
Tourinform (⊠ V, Sütő u. 2, ☎ 1/117–9800), open April–October, daily 8–8, and November–March, weekdays 8–8, weekends 8–3. **IBUSZ Welcome Hotel Service** (⊠ Apáczai Csere János u. 1, ☎ 1/118–3925 or 1/118–5776, FAX 1/117–9099), open 24 hours. **IBUSZ** (central branch: ⊠ V, Ferenciek tere 10, ☎ 118–6866). **American Express Travel Related Services** (⊠ V, Deák Ferenc u. 10, ☎ 1/266–8680, FAX 1/267–2028). **Budapest Tourist** (⊠ V, Roosevelt tér 5, ☎ 1/117–3555).

THE DANUBE BEND

About 40 kilometers (25 miles) north of Budapest, the Danube abandons its eastward course and turns abruptly south toward the capital, cutting through the Börzsöny and Visegrád hills. This area is called the Danube Bend and includes the baroque town of Szentendre, the hilltop castle ruins and town of Visegrád, and the cathedral town of Esztergom. The attractive combination of hillside and river should dispel any notion that Hungary is one vast, boring plain. The most scenically varied part of Hungary, the region is home to a chain of riverside spas and beaches, bare volcanic mountains, and limestone hills. Here, in the heartland, are the traces of the country's history—the remains of the Roman Empire's frontier, the battlefields of the Middle Ages, and the relics of the Hungarian Renaissance.

The west bank of the Danube is the more interesting side, with three charming and picturesque towns—Szentendre, Visegrád, and Esztergom—all of which richly repay to visit them. The district can be covered by car in one day, the total round-trip no more than 112 kilometers (70 miles), although this affords only a cursory look. A day trip to Szentendre while based in Budapest plus two days for Visegrád and Esztergom, with a night in either (both have charming small hotels), would suffice for a more thorough and leisurely experience of this delightful part of Hungary.

On the Danube's eastern bank, Vác is the only larger town of any real interest. The Danube is not crossed by any bridges, but there are numerous ferries (between Visegrád and Nagymaros, Basaharc and Szob, Szentendre Island and Vác), making it possible to combine a visit to both sides of the Danube on the same excursion.

Though the Danube Bend's west bank contains the bulk of historical sights, the less-traveled east bank has the excellent hiking trails of the Börzsöny mountain range, which extends along the Danube from Vác to Zebegény before curving toward the Slovak border.

Work had started on a hydroelectric dam near Nagymaros, across from Visegrád, in the mid-1980s. The project was proposed by Austria and Czechoslovakia and reluctantly agreed to by Hungary, but protests from the Blues (Hungary's equivalent of Germany's Greens), coupled with rapid democratization, seem to have aborted the project and rescued a region of great natural beauty. The Pilis and Visegrád hills on the Danube's western side and the Börzsöny Hills on the east are popular nature escapes for many Budapest dwellers, who make day trips to hike in the clean, verdant forests of the region.

Numbers in the margin correspond to numbers on the Danube Bend map.

Szentendre

★ ⑤⑨ *21 km (13 mi) north of Budapest.*

A romantic little town with a lively atmosphere and a flourishing artists' colony, this is the highlight of the Danube Bend. With its profusion of enchanting church steeples, colorful baroque houses, and winding, narrow cobblestone streets, as well as its close proximity to Budapest, it's no wonder Szentendre attracts swarms of visitors, tripling its population in peak season. Yet the town's charm and appeal still rise far above the occasionally overbearing summer crowds and touristy shops.

Szentendre was first settled by Serbs and Greeks fleeing the advancing Turks in the 16th and 17th centuries. They built houses and churches in their own style—rich in reds and blues seldom seen elsewhere in Hungary. The local cuisine, too, has a tangible Mediterranean influence. To truly savor Szentendre, duck into any and every cobblestone side street that appeals to you. Baroque houses with shingle roofs (often with an arched eye-of-God upstairs window) and colorful stone walls will enchant your eye and pique your curiosity.

Fö tér is Szentendre's picturesque main square, the centerpiece of which is an ornate **Memorial Cross** erected by Serbs in gratitude because the town was spared from a plague. The cross has a crucifixion painted on it and stands atop a triangular pillar adorned with a dozen icon paintings. During the Szentendre Spring and Summer Days cultural festivals (☞ Nightlife and the Arts, *below*), you are likely to witness a Cimarosa or Mozart opera performed in the square by an ensemble from Budapest with full chamber orchestra.

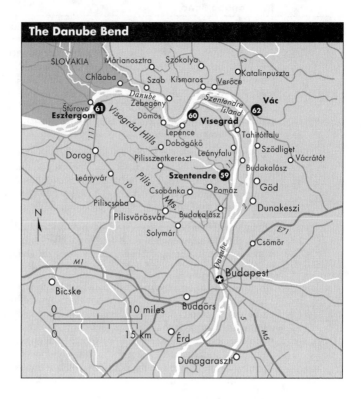

The Danube Bend

Every house on Fő tér is a designated landmark, and three of them are open to the public: the **Ferenczy Museum** at No. 6, with paintings of Szentendre landscapes and statues and tapestries by a distinguished family of artists; the **Kmetty Museum** at No. 21, with works by János Kmetty, a pioneer of Hungarian avant-garde painting; and the **Szentendrei Képtár** (Municipal Gallery) at Nos. 2–5, with an excellent collection of local contemporary art and international changing exhibits. ☜ *Each museum 60 Ft. ⊙ Mid-Mar.–Oct., Tues.–Sun. 10–4; Nov.–mid-Mar., Fri.–Sun. 10–4.*

Gracing the corner of Görög utca (Greek Street) and Szentendre's main square, Fő tér, the so-called **Greek Church** (also known as Blagovestenska Church) is actually a Serbian Orthodox church that takes its name from the Greek inscription on a red-marble gravestone set in its wall. This elegant edifice was built between 1752 and 1754 by a rococo master, Andreas Mayerhoffer, on the site of a wooden church dating to the Great Serbian Migration (around 690). Its greatest glory—a symmetrical floor-to-ceiling panoply of stunning icons—was painted between 1802 and 1804 by Mihailo Zivkovic, a Serbian painter from Buda. ⊠ *Görög u. at Fő tér.* ☜ *50 Ft. ⊙ Apr.–Oct., Tues.–Sun. 10–5; Nov.–Dec. and Mar., Fri.–Sun. 10–4.*

★ If you have time for only one of Szentendre's myriad museums, don't miss the **Margit Kovács Museum,** which displays the collected works of Budapest ceramics artist Margit Kovács, who died in 1977. She left behind a wealth of richly textured work that ranges from ceramics to life-size sculptures. Admission to the museum is limited to 15 persons at a time, so it is wise to line up early or at lunchtime, when the herds of tour groups are occupied elsewhere. ⊠ *Vastagh György u. 1 (off Görög u.),* ☏ *26/310–244.* ☜ *200 Ft. ⊙ Mid-Mar.–Oct., Tues.–Sun. 10–6; Nov.–mid-Mar., Tues.–Sun. 10–4.*

Perched atop Vár-domb (Castle Hill) is Szentendre's oldest surviving monument, the **Catholic Parish Church,** dating to the 13th century. After many reconstructions, its oldest visible part is a 15th-century sundial in the doorway. The church's small cobblestone yard hosts an arts-and-crafts market and, often on weekends in summer, street entertainment. From here, views over Szentendre's angular tile rooftops and steeples and of the Danube beyond are superb. ⊠ *Vár-domb.* 🎫 *Free.* ☉ *Erratically; check with Tourinform.*

★ The **Serbian Orthodox Collection of Religious Art** displays exquisite artifacts relating to the history of the Serbian Orthodox Church in Hungary from the 15th to 19th centuries. Icons, altars, robes, 16th-century prayer books, and a 17th-century cross with—legend has it—a bullet hole through it were collected from all over the country, after being sold or stolen from Serbian churches that were abandoned when most Serbs returned to their homeland at the turn of the century and following World War I. The museum shares a tranquil yard with the imposing Serbian Orthodox Cathedral. ⊠ *Pátriárka u. 5,* ☎ *26/312–399.* 🎫 *30 Ft.* ☉ *May–Sept., Wed.–Sun. 10–6; Oct.–Dec. and Mar.–Apr., Wed.–Sun. 10–4; Jan.–Feb., Fri.–Sun. 10–4.*

The crimson steeple of the handsome **Serbian Orthodox Cathedral** presides over a restful tree-shaded yard crowning the hill just north of Vár-domb (Castle Hill). Built in the 1740s with a much more lavish but arguably less beautiful iconostasis than is found in the Greek Church below it, the cathedral is newly shining after a recent interior renovation. ⊠ *Pátriárka u.,* ☎ *26/312–399.* ☉ *Erratically; check with Tourinform or Serbian Orthodox Collection of Religious Art museum officials.*

Szentendre's farthest-flung museum is the **Szabadtéri Néprajzi Múzeum** (Open-Air Ethnographic Museum), the largest open-air museum in the country. It is a living re-creation of 18th- and 19th-century village life from different regions of Hungary—the sort of place where blacksmith shops and a horse-powered mill compete with wooden houses and folk handicrafts for your attention. During regular crafts demonstrations, visitors can sit back and watch or give it a try themselves. Five kilometers (3 miles) to the northwest, the museum is reachable by bus from the Szentendre terminus of the HÉV suburban railway. ⊠ *Szabadságforrás út,* ☎ *26/312–304.* 🎫 *200 Ft.* ☉ *Apr.–Oct., Tues.–Sun. 10–6.*

NEED A BREAK?   For a quick cholesterol boost, grab a floppy, freshly fried *lángos* (flat, salty fried dough) drizzled with sour cream or brushed with garlic at **Piknik Büfé** (⊠ Dumtsa Jenő u. 22), just next door to the Tourinform office.

Dining and Lodging

$$$ ✕ **Görög Kancsó.** Named after its location on "Greek Street," the Greek Pitcher serves Greek specialties and Hungarian pork livers with equal care and flavor. White-lace linens, mismatched antique chairs and tables, a baby grand piano, and a collection of antique vases and pictures wash the dining room in handsome elegance. In summer, however, most of the dining and socializing take place on the sidewalk café across the road from the Danube, where simpler, less expensive fare is offered. The help is young, charming, and very efficient. ⊠ *Görög u. 1,* ☎ *26/315–528. AE, DC, MC, V accepted May–Sept. only.*

$$ ✕ **Aranysárkány.** On the road up to the Serbian Orthodox Cathedral,
★ the Golden Dragon lies in wait with seven large tables, which you share with strangers on a busy night. The delicious food is prepared before your eyes in a turbulent open kitchen where dishes break and exuberance is rampant. All the activity is justified by the cold cherry soup with white

wine and whipped cream or the hot Dragon Soup with quail eggs and vegetables. Try the grilled goose liver *Orosházi* style, wrapped in bacon and accompanied by a layered potato-and-cheese cake, broccoli, and a grilled tomato. The cheese dumplings with strawberry whipped cream are also recommended. ✉ *Alkotmány u. 1/a,* ☎ *26/311–670. AE.*

$$ ✕ **Korona.** This revamped traditional-style restaurant is on the main square in an 18th-century baroque house. The menu is based on fish and various Hungarian specialties. Try the *bableves* (bean soup). The view of local comings and goings from its sidewalk café is unmatched, but some pass it up for a chance to cook up their own goulash (with the cook's guidance) in a big kettle in the back garden. ✉ *Fő tér 18– 19,* ☎ *26/311–516. No credit cards.*

$$ ✕ **Rab Ráby.** Fish soup and fresh grilled trout are the specialties in this
★ extremely popular, friendly restaurant with rustic wood beams and myriad old instruments, lanterns, cowbells and other eclectic antiques. In summer guests can also dine in the tiny inner cobblestone yard. ✉ *Péter Pál u. 1,* ☎ *26/310–819. No credit cards.*

$$ ✕ **Régi Módi.** This attractive upstairs restaurant featuring fine wines and game specialties is approached through a courtyard across from the Margit Kovács Múzeum. Lace curtains and antique knickknacks give the small dining room an intimate, homey elegance. The summer terrace is a delightful place to dine alfresco and look out over the red-tile rooftops. ✉ *Futó u. 3,* ☎ *26/311–105. AE, DC, MC, V.*

$$ ✕ **Vidám Szerzetesek.** The Happy Monks opened as a family restaurant in 1982, though in recent years it has become something of a tourist haunt; the reasonably priced menu, after all, is in 19 languages—including English, Arab, Chinese, Turkish, Serbian, and Japanese. The atmosphere is casual and decidedly cheerful; the food is typically Hungarian: heavy, hearty, and delicious. Try the Suhajda hat soup, topped with a tasty dough cap baked over the bowl. ✉ *Bogdányi út 3–5,* ☎ *26/310–544. No credit cards. Closed Mon.*

$$ ▣ **Bükkös Panzió.** Just west of the main square and across the bridge over tiny Bükkös Brook, this neat, well-run inn is one of the most conveniently located hotels in the village. The narrow staircase and small rooms give it a homey feel. It books up well in advance during July and August, so plan ahead. ✉ *Bükkös part 16, H-2000 Szentendre,* ☎ *26/312–021 or* ▣ 𝔽𝔸𝕏 *26/310–782. 16 rooms with bath. Restaurant, laundry services. MC, V.*

$$ ▣ **Kentaur Ház.** This handsome, modern, chalet-style hotel is a two-minute walk from Fő tér, as well as on what may be Hungary's last surviving square still to bear Marx's name (it has been somehow overlooked in the wave of purging street names of their Communist-era nomenclatures). Rooms are clean and simple, with pale-gray carpeting, blond unfinished-wood paneling, and pastel-pink walls hung with original paintings by local artists. Upstairs rooms are sunniest and most spacious. ✉ *Marx tér 3–5, H-2000 Szentendre,* ☎ *26/312–125. 16 rooms with bath. Bar, breakfast room. No credit cards.*

$$ ▣ **St. Andrea Panzió.** This remodeled *panzió* atop a grassy incline has all the makings of a Swiss chalet. Attic space has been converted into modernized rooms with television sets and sparkling tile showers. On a warm day you can eat breakfast on the outside patio. ✉ *Egressy út 22, H-2000 Szentendre,* ☎ *26/311–989,* 𝔽𝔸𝕏 *26/311–928. 8 rooms with bath. Restaurant. No credit cards.*

$ ▣ **Átrium Panzió.** Built in 1992, this lovely and quiet pension is opposite the famous Serbian Orthodox Museum, a short walk from the main square. The building is rustic, with raw-wood interiors and slanted alpine-style ceilings. The hosts are friendly and welcoming and will organize sightseeing tours. Breakfast is included. ✉ *Pátriarka u. 6, H-2000 Szentendre,* ☎ *26/314–006,* FAX *26/313–998. 7 rooms with shower. Restaurant, bar. No credit cards.*

Outdoor Activities and Sports

BICYCLING

The waterfront and streets beyond Szentendre's main square are perfect for a bike ride—free of jostling cobblestones and relatively calm and quiet. Check with Tourinform for local rental outfits. Rentals are available in Budapest (☞ Outdoor Activities and Sports *in* Budapest A to Z, *above*); bicycles are permitted on the HÉV suburban railway. Many people make the trip between Budapest and Szentendre on bicycle along the designated bike path, which runs on busy roads in some places, but is pleasant and separate from the road for the stretch between Békásmegyer and Szentendre.

BOATING AND WATER SPORTS

The **Viking Motor Yacht Club** (✉ Duna korzó 3, ☎ 26/319–707), a short walk north along the Danube from the center of town, offers expensive rental rates for water skis, Jet Skis, and motorboats—all about 10,000 Ft. per hour. Rentals are available from May through October on the dock, daily 9–8. The club's main office is on a ship.

HORSEBACK RIDING

Pomáz, just 15 minutes from Szentendre by HÉV, is known for its well-respected riding school, at the **Udvaros Csárda és Lovarda** (Garden Tavern and Riding Center; ✉ Mártírok u. 3, ☎ 26/325–560 or 26/325-287). Reasonably experienced riders can enjoy one-hour excursions (400 Ft.) through a 3-acre range near Kőhegy, at the foot of the Pilis mountain range. Schiffer Sándor, the owner of the school, takes good care of his team of 10 Hungarian half-bloods and gives riding lessons for 300 Ft. per half hour. Reservations are preferred; if you call the school after 4 PM, you have a good chance of reaching someone who speaks English.

Nightlife and the Arts

Most of Szentendre's concerts and entertainment events occur during the spring and summer. For current schedules and ticket information, contact **Tourinform** (✉ Dumtsa Jenő u. 22, ☎ 26/317–965 or 26/317–966).

The annual **Spring Festival,** usually held from mid-March through early April, offers classical concerts in some of Szentendre's churches, as well as jazz, folk, and rock performances in the cultural center and other venues about town. The **Arts Schools Festival,** held around the same time as the Spring Festival (mid-March through early April) every year, shows off Szentendre's thriving young local talent in concerts and special exhibits throughout the town. In July, the **Szentendre Summer Days** festival brings open-air theater performances and jazz and classical concerts to Fő tér and the cobblestone courtyard fronting the town hall. Although the plays are usually in Hungarian, the setting alone can make it an enjoyable experience.

Shopping

Flooded with tourists in summer, Szentendre is saturated with the requisite **souvenir shops.** Among the attractive but overpriced goods sold in every store are dolls dressed in traditional folk costumes, wooden trinkets, pottery, and colorful hand-embroidered tablecloths, doilies, and blouses. The best bargains are the hand-embroidered blankets and bags sold by dozens of elderly women in traditional folk attire, who stand for hours on the town's crowded streets. (Because of high weekend traffic, most Szentendre stores stay open all day Saturday and Sunday. Galleries are closed Monday and accept major credit cards, although other stores may not.)

Renowned master confectioner Károly Szabó's **Marcipán Museum and Sweet Shop** (⊠ Dumtsa Jenő u. 14, ☎ 26/311–484) offers mouthfuls of colorful handmade marzipan creations—from frogs to flowers to souvenir medallions. A makeshift companion museum displays an intricate marzipan model of Budapest's Parliament building, a life-size (80-kilogram) chocolate Michael Jackson, and other unusual candied feats. A second branch is nearby at Fő tér 16, ☎ 26/311–165.

Topped with an abstract-statue trio of topless, pale-pink, and baby-blue women in polka-dot bikini panties, it's hard to miss the **Christoff Galéria** (⊠ Bartók Béla u. 8, ☎ 26/317–031) as you climb the steep hill to its door. The gallery sells works by local and Hungarian contemporary artists, including those of ef Zambo, creator of its crowning females.

The **Erdész Galéria** (⊠ Bercsényi u. 4, ☎ 26/317–925) displays an impressive selection of contemporary Hungarian paintings and sculptures, as well as applied-arts works such as leather bags, colored glass vases, and handmade paper. The unique, curvaceous silver pieces handcrafted by a famous local jeweler make exquisite gifts.

The one tiny room of **art-éria galéria** (⊠ Városház tér 1, ☎ 26/310–111) is crammed with paintings, graphics, and sculptures by 21 of Szentendre's best contemporary artists.

The sophisticated **Műhely Galéria** (⊠ Fő tér 20, ☎ 26/310–139), on Szentendre's main square, displays oil and watercolor paintings, marble and bronze statues, and other fine artworks by approximately 30 local artists.

Beautiful stationery, booklets, and other handmade paper products are displayed and sold at the **László Vincze Paper Mill** (⊠ Angyal u. 5, ☎ 26/318–501). In this small workshop at the top of a broken cobblestone street, Mr. Vincze lovingly creates his thick, watermarked paper, using traditional, 2,000-year old bleaching methods.

Péter-Pál Galéria (⊠ Péter-Pál u. 1, ☎ 26/311–182) offers textiles, wrought-iron work, and glass and ceramic pieces handcrafted by Szentendre's best artisans, many of whom have works displayed throughout Hungary and abroad.

Visegrád

60 *23 km (14 mi) north of Szentendre.*

Visegrád was the seat of the Hungarian kings during the 14th century, when a fortress built here by the Angevin kings became the royal residence. Today, the imposing fortress at the top of the hill towers over the peaceful little town of quiet, tree-lined streets and solid old houses. The forested hills rising just behind the town offer popular hiking possibilities. For a taste of Visegrád's best, climb to the Citadel, and wander and take in the views of the Danube curving through the countryside; but make time to stroll around the village center a bit—on Fő utca and other streets that pique your interest. Easy half-day hikes into the hills begin in the center of town and round out the Visegrád sampling.

★ Crowning the top of a 350-meter hill, the dramatic **Fellegvár** (Citadel) was built in the 13th century and served as the seat of Hungarian kings in the early 14th century. In the Middle Ages, the Citadel was where the Holy Crown and other royal regalia were kept, until they were stolen by a dishonorable maid of honor in 1440; twenty-three years later, King

In case you want to be welcomed there.

We're here to see that you're always welcomed at establishments everywhere. That's why millions of people carry the American Express® Card – for peace of mind, confidence, and security, around the world or just around the corner.

do more

Cards

In case you're running low.

We're here to help with more than 118,000 Express Cash locations around the world. In order to enroll, just call American Express before you start your vacation.

do more

Express Cash

And just in case.

We're here with American Express® Travelers Cheques
and Cheques *for Two*.® They're the safest way to carry
money on your vacation and the surest way to get a
refund, practically anywhere, anytime.
Another way we help you...

do more ®

AMERICAN EXPRESS

**Travelers
Cheques**

Matthias had to pay 80,000 Ft. to retrieve them from Austria. (Now the crown is safe in the Hungarian National Museum in Budapest, after the United States returned it from Fort Knox in 1978.) At press time, a *panoptikum* show portraying the era of the kings was being planned for regular showing, to be included free with admission. The breathtaking, panoramic views of the Danube Bend below are ample reward for the strenuous, 40-minute hike up. ☎ *26/398–101.* ⌨ *150 Ft.* ☉ *Mid-Mar.–mid-Nov., daily 9–5 or 6.*

In the 13th–14th centuries, King Matthias Corvinus had a separate palace built on the banks of the Danube below the Fellegvár. It was eventually razed by the Turks, and not until 1934 were the ruins finally excavated. Nowadays you can see the disheveled remnants of the palace, known as the **Mátyás Király Múzeum,** via the entrance on Fő utca. Especially worth seeing is the red-marble well built by a 15th-century Italian architect and later decorated with the arms of King Matthias. It is situated in a ceremonial courtyard restored in accordance with designs found in ancient documents. Above the courtyard rise the palace's various halls; on the left you can still see a few fine original carvings, which give an idea of how magnificent the palace must once have been. The nearby lookout tower on Nagy Villám Hill offers spectacular views of the Danube Bend. Thursdays in May, the museum hosts medieval-crafts demonstrations, and the second weekend in July, the colorful festivities of the Visegrád International Palace Games, where performers sport costumes and play medieval music. ✉ *Fő u. 23,* ☎ *26/398–026.* ⌨ *100 Ft.* ☉ *Apr.–Oct., Tues.–Sun. 9–4:30; Nov.–Mar., Tues.–Sun. 8–3:30.*

OFF THE BEATEN PATH
MILLENNIAL CHAPEL – Like a tiny precious gem, the miniature chapel sits in a small clearing, tucked away on a corner down Fő utca, Visegrád's main street. The bite-size, powder-yellow church was built in 1896 to celebrate the Hungarian millennium and is open only on Pentecost and a few other holidays. ✉ *Fő u. 113.*

Dining and Lodging

$$ ✕ **Gulás Csárda.** This cozy little restaurant, decorated with antique folk
★ art and memorabilia, has only five tables inside, but additional tables are added outside during the summer. The cuisine is typical home-style Hungarian, with a limited selection of top-rate traditional dishes. Try the *halászlé* (fish stew) served in a pot and kept warm on a small spirit burner. ✉ *Nagy Lajos király u., no phone. No credit cards.*

$$ ✕ **Sirály Restaurant.** Right across from the ferry station, the airy Seagull Restaurant is justifiably well regarded for its rolled fillet of venison and its many vegetarian dishes, including fried soy steak with vegetables. In summer, when cooking is often done on the terrace overlooking the Danube, expect barbecued meats and stews, soups, and *gulyas* served in old-fashioned pots. Music is provided by a Gypsy band during lunch and by a cheesy synthesizer player on most evenings. ✉ *Rév u. 15,* ☎ *26/398–376. AE, MC, V.*

$ ✕ **Fekete Holló.** The popular Black Raven restaurant has an elegant yet comfortable atmosphere—a great place for a full meal or just a beer. Try the chef's creative specialties, such as coconut chicken leg with pineapples, or stick to regional staples like simple, fresh fried or grilled fish; either way save room for the palacsinta (sweet pancakes with nuts and chocolate). ✉ *Rév út 12,* ☎ *26/397–289. No credit cards. Closed Nov.–Mar.*

$$$ 🏨 **Silvanus.** Set high up on Fekete Hill, this hotel is renowned for its spectacular views. Rooms are bright and clean, with simple basic furnishings, and offer a choice of forest or Danube (2,300 Ft. more ex-

pensive) views. At the end of a steep, narrow road, the Silvanus is recommended for motorists (although a bus does stop nearby) and hikers or bikers—there are linking trails in the forest behind. Rooms must be paid for in hard currency. ⊠ *Fekete-hegy, H-2025 Visegrád,* ☎ *26/398–311,* FAX *26/398–170. 74 rooms, 60 with bath; 4 suites. Restaurant, bar, pub, terrace café, bowling, mountain bikes, gift shop. AE, DC, MC, V.*

$ ☎ **ELTE Vendégház.** On a quiet residential street just north of the town center, this four-story cement-block hotel has clean, comfortable, minimally furnished rooms. Breakfast is included. ⊠ *Fő út 117, H-2025 Visegrád,* ☎ *26/398–165. 33 rooms with bath. Restaurant. No credit cards. Closed Jan.–Feb.*

$ ☎ **Haus Honti.** This intimate alpine-style pension, named after its friendly young owner, József Honti, is in a quiet residential area, a three-minute walk from the town center. Apple trees and a stream running close to the house create a peaceful, rustic ambience. Tiny, clean rooms are tucked under sloping ceilings and have balconies, some with lovely Danube views. Breakfast, served outdoors in nice weather, costs a couple of dollars more. ⊠ *Fő u. 66, H-2025 Visegrád,* ☎ *26/398–120. 7 rooms with bath. No credit cards.*

Nightlife and the Arts

The **Visegrád International Palace Games,** held annually on the second weekend in July, take the castle complex back to its medieval heyday, with horseback jousting tournaments, archery games, a medieval music and crafts fair, and other festivities. Contact Hungaro-Reisen or Visegrád Tours (☞ Visitor Information *in* Danube Bend A to Z, *below*) for specifics.

Outdoor Activities and Sports

HIKING

Visegrád makes a great base for exploring the trails of the Visegrád and Pilis hills. A hiking map is posted on the corner of Fő utca and Rév utca, just above the pale-green Roman Catholic Parish Church. A well-trodden, well-marked hiking trail (posted with red signs) leads from the edge of Visegrád to the town of Pilisszentlászló, a wonderful 8.7-kilometer (about three-hour) journey through the oak and beech forests of the Visegrád Hills into the Pilis conservation region. Bears, bison, deer, and wild boar roam freely here; less menacing flora include fields of yellow-blooming spring pheasant's eye and black pulsatilla.

SWIMMING

The Danube at Visegrád is out of bounds for swimmers, although at press time two artificial lakes built just next to the river bank were filling up with Danube water to serve as swimming and boating venues. Because of the Danube's unfortunate state of pollution, swimming may not be recommended. For current status, inquire at Visegrád Tours (☞ Visitor Information *in* Danube Bend A to Z, *below*). The outdoor thermal pools at **Lepence,** 3 kilometers (2 miles) southwest of Visegrád on Route 11, combine good soaking with excellent Danube Bend views. ⊠ *Lepence-völgyi Termál és Strandfürdő, Lepence,* ☎ *26/398–208.* 🎫 *300 Ft.* ☉ *Daily May–Sept.*

TOBOGGAN SLIDE

☾ Winding through the trees on Nagy-Villám Hill is the **Wiegand Toboggan Run,** one of the longest slides you've ever seen. You ride on a small cart that is pulled uphill by trolley, then careen down the slope in a small, steel trough that resembles a bobsled run. For adults, runs cost 150 Ft., 800 Ft. for six runs; children under 14 ride for 120 Ft. per run, 600 Ft. for six runs. ⊠ *Panoráma út, ½ km from Fellegvár,* ☎ *26/397–*

397. ◯ Apr.–Oct., daily 10–5; Mar. and Nov., weekends and holidays 10–4; Dec.–Feb. (weather permitting), weekends 11–3 or 4.

Esztergom

61 *21 km (13 mi) north of Visegrád.*

The pride of the region, Esztergom stands on the site of a Roman fortress, at the westernmost curve of the heart-shaped Danube Bend, where the Danube marks the border between Hungary and Slovakia. (The bridge that once joined these two countries was destroyed by the Nazis near the end of World War II, though parts of the span can still be seen.) St. Stephen, the first Christian king of Hungary and founder of the nation, was crowned here in the year 1000, establishing Esztergom as Hungary's first capital, which it remained for the next 250 years. The majestic basilica, Hungary's largest, is Esztergom's main draw, followed by the fine art collection of the Christian Museum housed in the Primate's Palace. If you like strolling, leave yourself a little time to explore the narrow streets of Viziváros (Watertown) below the basilica, lined with brightly painted baroque buildings.

★ Esztergom's **Bazilika** (cathedral), the largest in Hungary, stands on a hill overlooking the town; it is now the seat of the cardinal primate of Hungary. It was here, in the center of Hungarian Catholicism, that the famous anticommunist cleric, Cardinal József Mindszenty, was finally reburied in 1991, ending an era of religious intolerance and prosecution and a sorrowful chapter in Hungarian history. Its most interesting features are the Bakócz Chapel (1506), named for a primate of Hungary who only narrowly missed becoming pope; and the sacristy, which contains a valuable collection of medieval ecclesiastical art. If your timing is lucky, you may be blessed with a chance to attend a concert during one of the various classical music festivals held here in summer (☞ Nightlife and the Arts, *below*). ⊠ *Szent István tér,* ☎ *33/311–895.* 🎫 *Free. ◯ Apr.–late Oct., daily 6–6; late Oct.–Mar., daily 6–4.*

Considered by many to be Hungary's finest art gallery, the **Keresztény Múzeum** (Museum of Christian Art), in the Primate's Palace, houses a large collection of early Hungarian and Italian paintings (the 14th- and 15th-century Italian collection is unusually large for a museum outside Italy). Unique holdings include the so-called *Coffin of Our Lord* from Garamszentbenedek, now in the Czech Republic; the wooden statues of the Apostles and of the Roman soldiers guarding the coffin are masterpieces of Hungarian baroque sculpture. The building also houses the Primate's Archives, which contain 20,000 volumes, including several medieval codices. Permission to visit the archives must be obtained in advance. *Primate's Palace,* ⊠ *Mindszenty tér 2,* ☎ *33/313–880.* 🎫 *100 Ft. ◯ Mid-Mar.–Sept., Tues.–Sun. 10–6; Oct.–Nov. and Mar.–mid-Mar., Tues.–Sun. 10–5.*

To the south of the cathedral, on **Szent Tamás Hill,** is a small church dedicated to St. Thomas à Becket of Canterbury. From here you can look down on the town and see how the Danube temporarily splits, forming an island (Prímás-sziget) that locals use as a base for water-skiing and swimming, in spite of the pollution.

Dining and Lodging

$$ ✕ **Kispipa.** Lively and popular with Hungarians, the Kispipa, not far from the town center, is especially memorable for its good choice of wines. The food menu includes soups, stews, and traditional Hungarian dishes such as fried goose with heavy cream. ⊠ *Kossuth Lajos utca 19, no phone. Reservations not accepted. No credit cards.*

\$\$ ✕ **Primáspince.** Arched ceilings and exposed brick walls make a charming setting for refined Hungarian fare at this touristy but good restaurant just below the cathedral. Try the tournedos Budapest style (tender beef with sautéed vegetables and paprika) or the thick turkey breast Fiaker style (stuffed with ham and melted cheese). ⊠ *Szent István tér 4,* ☎ *33/313–495. AE, DC, MC, V. No dinner Jan.–Feb.*

\$ ✕ **Halászcsárda.** The specialty at this friendly, informal restaurant is fish (the fish soup is especially good). The casual outdoor patio, shielded by a thatched roof, gives the place a backyard-barbecue feel. After dinner explore the island it's on, formed by the branching of the Danube. ⊠ *Primás-ziget, Gesztenye fasor 14,* ☎ *33/311–052. No credit cards.*

\$\$ ▣ **Hotel Esztergom.** On Primás-sziget (Primate's Island), a popular park and recreation area just across the Kossuth Bridge from the Parish Church, this is a comfortable, sports-oriented hotel. All rooms have balconies. ⊠ *Primás szíget, Nagy Duna Sétány, H-2500 Esztergom,* ☎ *33/312–883,* ℻ *33/312–853. 34 rooms with bath, 2 suites. Restaurant, bar, roof terrace café, meeting room. AE, DC, MC, V.*

\$–\$\$ ▣ **Ria Panzio.** In this small, friendly guest house near the cathedral, all rooms face a garden courtyard. ⊠ *Batthyányi u. 11, H-2500 Esztergom,* ☎ *33/313–115. 13 rooms with bath. Breakfast room. No credit cards.*

\$ ▣ **Alabárdos Panzió.** Conveniently located downhill from the basilica, this cozy, remodeled home provides an excellent view of Castle Hill from upstairs. A 1995 expansion has increased the capacity, and all rooms (doubles and quads) are less cramped than at other small pensions. ⊠ *Pázmány Péter u. 49, H-2500 Esztergom,* ☎ ℻ *33/312–640. 21 rooms with bath. Breakfast room. No credit cards.*

Nightlife and the Arts

Every two years Esztergom hosts the **Nemzetközi Gitár Fesztivál** (International Guitar Festival) during which renowned classical guitarists from around the world hold master classes and workshops for participants. Recitals are held nearly every night in Esztergom's **Zöldház Művelődési Központ** (Green House Cultural Center) or the **Tanítóképző Főiskola** (Teaching University), where the festival is based, or elsewhere in Budapest and neighboring towns. The climax of it all is the glorious closing concert, held in the basilica, in which the hundreds of participants join together and perform as a guitar orchestra. The festival runs for two weeks, usually beginning in early August; the next one will be held in 1997. Tickets and information are available at the tourist offices.

Vác

62 *34 km (21 mi) north of Budapest; 20 km (12 mi) south of Nagymaros, which is accessed by ferry from Visegrád.*

With its lovely riverfront promenade, its cathedral, and less delightful Triumphal Arch, the small city of Vác, on the Danube's east bank, is well worth a short visit if only to watch the sun slowly set from the promenade. Vác's historic town center is full of pretty baroque buildings in matte yellows and reds and offers many visual rewards and photo opportunities for those who wander onto a few of its narrow cobblestone side streets heading in toward the river.

Along the Danube north of Vác lies a string of pleasant summer resorts, nestling below the picturesque Börzsöny Hills and stretching as far as Szob, just east of the Slovakian border.

Vác's 18th-century **cathedral** (Székesegyház) on Konstantin tér is the pride of the town. Built in 1763–77 by Archbishop Kristóf Migazzi to the designs of the Italian architect Isidor Carnevale, the structure is considered an outstanding example of Hungarian neoclassicism. The most interesting features are the murals by the Austrian Franz Anton Maulbertsch, both on the dome and behind the altar. Exquisite frescoes decorate the walls inside. To find it, head south down Köztársaság út from Március 15 tér—it's definitely hard to miss. ⊠ *Konstantin tér,* ☎ *27/317–010.* ⊙ *For groups with advance notice.*

<table>
<tr><td>NEED A
BREAK?</td><td>It's hard to resist the sweet aromas of fresh-baked breads and sweets wafting out onto the cobblestone street from Vuk Pék bakery (⊠ Kossuth u. 16, no phone). Nor is it easy to miss its aquamarine facade. Pick a pastry to go or take a break at one of the three tiny tables inside.</td></tr>
</table>

In 1764, when Archbishop Migazzi heard that Queen Maria Theresa planned to visit his humble town, he hurriedly arranged the construction of a **triumphal arch.** The queen came and left, but the awkward arch remains, at the edge of the city's historic core next to a cement-and-barbed-wire prison complex (the country's biggest) for Hungary's hardened criminals. ⊠ *Köztársaság út, just past Barabás utca.*

The **promenade** along the Danube is a wonderful place to stroll or picnic, looking out at the flashing river or back toward the pretty historic town. The main entrance to the riverfront area is from Petróczy utca, which begins at the cathedral on Konstantin tér and feeds straight into the promenade.

Vácrátóti Arborétum, 4 kilometers (2¼ miles) from Vác, is Hungary's biggest and best botanical garden, with over 12,000 plant species. The arboretum's top priority is botanical research and collection under the auspices of the Hungarian Academy of Sciences, but visitors are welcome to stroll along the paths and sit on benches in the leafy shade. ⊠ *Alkotmány u. 4–6,* ☎ *27/360–122 or 27/360–147.* ☎ *60 Ft.* ⊙ *Apr.–Sept., daily 8–6; Oct.–Mar. daily 8–4.*

Dining

$ ✕ **Halászkert Étterem.** The large terrace of this riverfront restaurant next to the ferry landing is a popular place for a hearty lunch or dinner of Hungarian fish specialties. ⊠ *Liszt Ferenc sétány 9,* ☎ *27/315–985. AE, MC.*

Nightlife and the Arts

In July and August, a series of outdoor classical concerts is held in the verdant **Vácrátóti Arborétum,** a short drive from Vác. In Vác, the last weekend in July brings the **Váci Világi Vígalom** (Vác World Jamboree) festival, with folk dancing, music, crafts fairs, and other festivities throughout town.

Outdoor Activities and Sports

Vác is the gateway to hiking in the forests of the **Börzsöny Hills,** rich in natural springs, castle ruins, and splendid Danube Bend vistas. Consult the Börzsöny hiking map, available at Tourinform, for planning a walk on the well-marked trails. The **Börzsöny Természetjáró Kör** (Börzsöny Nature Walk Group) organizes free guided nature walks every other Sunday all year round. Naturally, Hungarian is the official language, but chances are good that younger group members will speak English. Yet even without understanding what is spoken, the trips afford a nice opportunity to be guided through the area by knowledgeable people. Contact Tourinform for details.

Danube Bend A to Z

Arriving and Departing

BY BOAT

If you have enough time, you can travel to the west-bank towns by boat from Budapest, a leisurely and pleasant journey, especially in summer and spring. Boating from Budapest to Esztergom takes about five hours, to Visegrád about three hours. Boats leave from the main Pest dock at Vigadó tér. The disadvantage of boat travel is that a round-trip by slow boat doesn't allow much time for sightseeing; the Esztergom route, for example, allows only under two hours before it's time to head back. Many people combine boat travel with trains and buses, heading upriver by boat in the morning and back down by bus or train as it's getting dark. There is daily service from Budapest to Visegrád, stopping in Szentendre. Less frequent boats go to Vác, on the east bank, as well. Contact **MAHART** in Budapest for complete schedule information (☎ 1/118–1704).

For faster river travel, on summer Saturdays and public holidays (generally from late May to early September) a **hydrofoil** service brings Visegrád within an hour and Esztergom within just over an hour of Budapest; from late June the hydrofoils also run on Fridays. One-way fares are 650 Ft.–700 Ft. Timetables are also on display at the docks, in major hotels, and at most travel agencies in Budapest, or contact **MAHART.**

BY BUS

Buses run regularly between Budapest's Árpád híd bus station and most towns along both sides of the Danube.

BY CAR

Route 12 runs along the western shore of the Danube, connecting Budapest to Szentendre, Visegrád, and Esztergom. Route 11 runs along the eastern shore for driving between Budapest and Vác.

BY TRAIN

Vác and Esztergom have frequent daily express and local train service to and from Budapest's Nyugati (Western) Station. Trains do not run to Visegrád. The HÉV suburban railway runs between Batthyány tér (or Margaret Island, one stop north) in Budapest and Szentendre about every 10 to 20 minutes every day; the trip tales 40 minutes and costs around 130 Ft.

Getting Around

BY BICYCLE

Many activity-minded travelers take advantage of the Danube Bend's clean air and relatively close distances between sights and navigate the region by bicycle. Some routes have separate bike paths, others run along the roads. Consult the "Danube Bend Cyclists' Map" (available at tourist offices) and Tourinform for exact information.

BY BOAT

Boat travel along the river is slow and scenic and popular with tourists. **MAHART**'s boats ply the river between Budapest and Esztergom, Szentendre, and Visegrád. You can plan your sightseeing to catch a boat connection from one town to the other (☞ Arriving and Departing, *above*).

BY BUS

Buses link all major towns along both banks.

BY FERRY

As there are no bridges across the Danube in this region, there is regular daily passenger and car **ferry service** between several points on opposite sides of the Danube (except in winter when the river is too icy). The crossing generally takes about ten minutes and costs roughly 250–300 Ft. per car and under 100 Ft. per passenger. The crossing between Nagymaros and Visegrád is recommended, as it affords gorgeous views of Visegrád's citadel and includes a beautiful drive through rolling hills on route 12 south of Nagymaros. Contact the relevant tourist office for schedule details.

BY TRAIN

There are no trains to Visegrád, so train travel between the towns covered here is difficult.

Contacts and Resources

EMERGENCIES

Police (☎ 07). **Ambulance** (☎ 04). **Fire** (☎ 05).

GUIDED TOURS

IBUSZ (☎ 1/118–1139 or 1/118–1043) organizes day-long bus trips from Budapest along the Danube stopping in Esztergom, Visegrád, and Szentendre on Tuesdays and Fridays from May through October, and Saturdays only from November through April; the cost, including lunch, is about 6,500 Ft. Full-day boat tours of Szentendre and Visegrád run May through October on Wednesdays and Saturdays and cost about 7,000 Ft., including lunch and a cocktail.

VISITOR INFORMATION

Budapest: Dunatours (⊠ VI, Bajcsy-Zsilinszky út 17, ☎ 1/131–4533 or 1/111–4555, ℻ 1/111–6827). **Tourinform** (⊠ V, Sütő u. 2, ☎ 1/117–9800). **Esztergom: Grantours** (⊠ Széchenyi tér 25, ☎ ℻ 33/313–756); **IBUSZ** (⊠ Lőrinc u. 1, ☎ 33/312–552); **Komtourist** (⊠ Lőrinc u. 6, ☎ 33/312–082). **Szentendre: Tourinform** (⊠ Dumsta J. u. 22, ☎ ℻ 26/317–965); **Dunatours** (⊠ Bogdányi út 1, on the quay, ☎ 26/311–311). **Vác: Tourinform** (⊠ Dr. Csányi krt. 45, ☎ 27/316–160). **Visegrád: Visegrád Tours** (⊠ Sirály Restaurant, Rév u. 13, ☎ ℻ 26/398–160). **Hungaro-Reisen** (⊠ Fő u. 68, ☎ ℻ 26/398–112).

LAKE BALATON

Lake Balaton, the largest lake in Central Europe, stretches 80 kilometers (50 miles) across Hungary. Its vast surface area is drastically contrasted with its modest depths—only three meters at the center, and just 16 meters at its deepest point at the Tihany Peninsula. The Balaton—regarded as the most popular playground of this landlocked nation—is just 90 kilometers (56 miles) to the southwest of Budapest, so it is within easy reach of the capital by car, train, bus, and even bicycle. On a hot day in July or August, it'll seem the entire country and half of Germany are packed towel to towel on the lake's grassy public beaches, paddling about in the warm water and consuming fried meats and beer at the omnipresent snack bars.

On the lake's hilly northern shore, ideal for growing grapes, is **Balatonfüred,** Hungary's oldest spa town, famed for its natural springs that bubble out curative waters drunk for medicinal purposes. The national park on the **Tihany Peninsula** is just to the south, and regular boat service links Tihany and Balatonfüred with Siófok on the southern shore. Flatter and more crowded with resorts, cottages, and trade-union rest houses, the southern shore (beginning with Balatonszentgyörgy; ☞ *below*) is not as attractive as the northern one (north shore locals say the only redeeming quality of the southern shore is its views back across the lake to the north), nor are there as many sights. Families with small children prefer the southern shore for its shallower, warmer

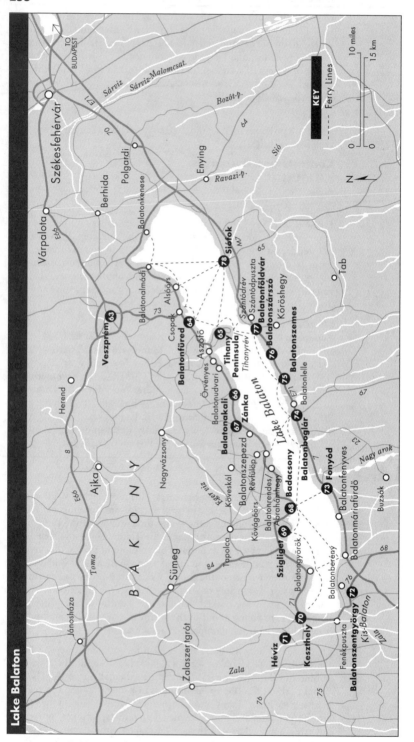

waters (you can walk for almost 2 kilometers [1¼ miles] before it deepens), which are ideal for youngsters and those who like to wallow—just ask one of the thousands of portly Hungarian grandmothers splashing themselves on a hot summer day. The water warms up to 25°C (77°F) in summer.

Every town along both shores has at least one *strand* (beach). The typical Balaton *strand* is a complex of blocky wooden changing cabanas and snack bars, fronted by a grassy flat stretch along the water for sitting and sunbathing. Most have paddleboat and other simple boat rentals. A small entrance fee is usually charged.

Those interested in exploring beyond the beach can set out by car, bicycle, or foot, on beautiful village-to-village tours—stopping to view lovely old baroque churches, photograph a stork family perched high in its chimney-top nest, or climb a vineyard-covered hill for sweeping vistas. Since most vacationers keep close to the shore, a small amount of exploring into the roads and countryside heading away from the lake will reward you with a break from the summer crowds and picturesque scenery.

Numbers in the margin correspond to numbers on the Lake Balaton map.

Veszprém

63 *116 km (72 mi) southwest of Budapest, 18 km (11 mi) north of Balatonfüred.*

Hilly **Veszprém** is the center of cultural life in the Balaton region. ★ **Várhegy** (Castle Hill) is the most attractive part of town, north of Szabadság tér. **Hősök Kapuja** (Heroes' Gate), at the entrance to the Castle, houses a small exhibit on Hungary's history. Just past the gate and down a little alley to the left is the **Tűztorony** (Fire Tower); note that the lower level is medieval while the upper stories are baroque. There is a good view of the town and surrounding area from the balcony. ☺ *May–Oct., Tues.–Sun. 10–6.*

Vár utca, the only street in the castle area, leads to a small square in front of the **Bishop's Palace** and the **cathedral;** outdoor concerts are held here in the summer. Vár utca continues past the square up to a terrace erected on the north staircase of the castle. Stand beside the modern statues of St. Stephen and his queen, Gizella, for a far-reaching view of the old quarter of town.

OFF THE BEATEN PATH **HEREND** – Sixteen kilometers (10 miles) northwest of Veszprém on Road 8, Herend is the home of Hungary's renowned hand-painted porcelain. The factory, founded in 1839, displays many valuable pieces in its **museum.** ☎ *88/361-144.* ◻ *150 Ft.* ☺ *May–Oct., daily 8:30–4; Nov.–Dec. and Mar., weekdays 10–3; Apr., Mon.–Sat. 8:30–4.*

Dining and Lodging

$ ✕ **Club Skorpio.** This city-center eatery might look like an alpine hut, but the menu is top class and features grilled meats and specialties such as pheasant soup and steamed wild duck. ◻ *Virág Benedek út 1,* ☎ *88/420–319. No credit cards.*

$ ✕ **Diana.** The Diana is just a little southwest of the town center, but ★ worth the trip if you want to experience the old-fashioned charm of a small provincial Hungarian restaurant. The decor is "cozy traditional," with wooden booths and tables, and the fish and game specialties are perennial favorites. There is also a 10-room pension on the premises. ◻ *József Attila u. 22,* ☎ *88/421–061. No credit cards.*

$ ☷ **Veszprém.** This modern, comfortable hotel in the center of town is in one of the less attractive buildings in Veszprém, but is convenient to all the major sights and to the bus station. ☒ *Budapest u. 6, H-8200 Veszprém,* ☎ *88/424–677,* ℻ *88/424–076. 52 rooms with bath, 10 with shower, and 10 with sink. Restaurant, bar, beauty salon. No credit cards.*

Balatonfüred

64   *115 km (71 mi) southwest of Budapest.*

Fed by 11 medicinal springs, Balatonfüred first gained popularity as a health resort (the lake's oldest) where ailing people with heart conditions and fatigue would come to take or, more accurately, to drink a cure. The waters, said to have stimulating and beneficial effects on the heart and nerves, are still an integral part of the town's identity and consumed voraciously, but only the internationally renowned cardiac hospital has actual bathing facilities. Today Balatonfüred, also known simply as Füred, is probably the Balaton's most popular destination, with every amenity to match. Above its busy boat landing, beaches, and promenade lined with great plane and poplar trees, the twisting streets of the Old Town climb hillsides thickly planted with vines. The climate and landscape also make this one of the best wine-growing districts in Hungary. Every year in July, the most elaborate of Lake Balaton's debutante cotillions, the Anna Balls, is held here.

The center of town is **Gyógy tér** (Spa Square), where the bubbling waters from five volcanic springs rise beneath a slim, colonnaded pavilion. In the square's centerpiece, the neoclassical **Well House** of the Kossuth Spring, you can sample the water, which has a pleasant, surprisingly cool, refreshing taste despite the sulfurous aroma; for those who can't get enough, a sign indicating a 30-liter-per-person limit is posted. All the buildings on the square are pillared like Greek temples. At No. 3 is the **Horváth Ház** (Horváth House), where the Szentgyörgyi-Horváth family arranged the first ball in 1825 in honor of their daughter Anna. It was there that she fell in love with Eriö Kiss, who became a general in the 1848–49 War of Independence and died a hero.

The Anna Balls, the event in Lake Balaton that most approximates a debutante cotillion, is now held every July in another colonnaded building on the square, the **Trade Unions' Sanatorium** (1802). Under its arcades is the **Balaton Pantheon**: aesthetically interesting tablets and reliefs honoring Hungarian and foreign notables who either worked for Lake Balaton or spread the word about it. Among them is Jaroslav Hašek, the Czech author of the *Good Soldier Schweik,* who also wrote tales about Balaton. On the eastern side of the square is the **Cardiac Hospital,** where hundreds of patients from all over the world are treated. Here, too, Rabindranath Tagore, the Indian author and Nobel Prize winner, recovered from a heart attack in 1926. The tree that he planted to commemorate his stay still stands in a little grove at the western end of the paths leading from the square down to the lakeside. Tagore also wrote a poem for the planting, which is memorialized beneath the tree on a strikingly animated bust of Tagore: WHEN I AM NO LONGER ON EARTH, MY TREE,/LET THE EVER-RENEWED LEAVES OF THY SPRING/MURMUR TO THE WAYFARER:/THE POET DID LOVE WHILE HE LIVED. In the same grove are trees honoring visits by another Nobel laureate, the Italian poet Salvatore Quasimodo, in 1961; and Indian prime minister Indira Gandhi, in 1972. An adjoining grove honors Soviet cosmonauts and their Hungarian partner-in-space, Bertalan Farkas.

Beginning near the boat landing, the **Tagore sétány** (Tagore Promenade) runs for nearly a kilometer (almost ½ mile) and is lined by trees, restaurants, and shops. From here, you can gaze across the water at the picturesque abbey perched high on a hill on the Tihany Peninsula.

A stroll up **Blaha Lujza utca** from Gyógy tér will take you past several landmarks, such as the **Blaha Lujza Ház** (Lujza Blaha House), a neoclassical villa built in 1867 and, later, the summer home of this famous turn-of-the-century actress, humanist, and singer (today it's a hotel); and the charming little **Kerek templom** (Round Church), consecrated in 1846, built in a classical style and with a truly rounded interior.

NEED A BREAK?

The plush **Kedves Café** (⌧ Blaha Lujza u. 7, ☎ 87/343–229), built in 1795, is today one of Lake Balaton's most popular and famous pastry shops. It is frequented in summer by actors and writers, who give periodic readings on the premises. The Kedves also boasts a summer garden and a first-class restaurant.

Dining and Lodging

$$$ ✕ **Tölgyfa Csárda.** Perched high on a hilltop, the Oak Tree Tavern has breathtaking views over the steeples and rooftops of Balatonfüred and the Tihany Peninsula. Its decor and menu are worthy of a first-class Budapest restaurant, and nightly live Gypsy music keeps the atmosphere festive. ⌧ *Meleghegy (walk north on Jókai Mór út and turn right on Mérleg út),* ☎ *87/343–036. AE. Closed late Oct.–mid-Apr.*

$$
★ ✕ **Baricska Csárda.** Perched on a hill overlooking wine and water— its own vineyard and Lake Balaton (and from some vantage points, a gas station)—this rambling, reed-thatched rustic inn, crawling with vines, has many wood-rafter rooms, vaulted cellars, and terraces. The food is hearty yet ambitious: spicy soups in kettles, roasted trout and fogas, fish paprikash with gnocchi to soak up the rich, creamy sauce, and desserts that mix pumpkin and poppy seed with a flair known nowhere else. In summer, colorful Gypsy wedding shows are held nightly under the grape arbors. ⌧ *Baricska dülő, off Rd. 71 (Széchenyi út) behind Shell station,* ☎ *87/343–105. Reservations essential. AE, V. Closed mid-Nov.–mid-Mar.*

$ ✕ **Halászkert Étterem.** The Fisherman's Garden is on busy Highway 71. It features some 40 fish dishes and is famous for its Balaton pike perch, at its best when grilled over an open flame. Meals are served until 1 AM during the summer, and for all-night revelers, pizza is served until 6 AM. In between courses you can twirl on the restaurant's outdoor dance floor. ⌧ *Széchenyi 2, off Jókai Mór út, near dock,* ☎ *86/343– 039. AE, DC, MC, V. Closed Dec.–Feb.*

$$$ ⌂ **Annabella.** The cool, spacious guest quarters in this large, Miami-style high-rise are especially pleasant in summer heat. Overlooking the lake and Tagore Promenade, it has access to excellent swimming and water-sports facilities and is just around the corner from the main square in town. ⌧ *Deák Ferenc u. 25, H-8231 Balatonfüred,* ☎ *87/342–222,* FAX *87/343–084. 390 rooms with bath. Restaurant, bar, brasserie, café, indoor and outdoor pools, barbershop, sauna, nightclub, laundry service. AE, DC, MC, V. Closed mid-Oct.–mid-Apr.*

$$$ ⌂ **Füred.** This 12-story lakefront hotel caters to small conventions and groups but is a pleasant place for individual guests, too. The hotel lies close to the lake and has a beach of its own. ⌧ *Széchenyi út 20, H-8230 Balatonfüred,* ☎ *87/343–033,* FAX *87/343–034. 125 rooms with bath, 27 suites. 2 restaurants, bar, coffee shop, tennis court, bowling, beach, water-sports equipment, parking. AE, DC, MC, V.*

$$$ ⊞ **Margaréta.** This attractive apartment hotel stands across the street from the lakefront Hotel Marina and, unfortunately, behind a large gas station. It is smaller and more intimate than most of its neighbors, and its restaurant is popular locally. Each room has a minifridge, a balcony, a phone, a TV, and a radio. ⊠ *Széchenyi út 29, H-8230 Balatonfüred,* ☎ ℻ *87/343–824. 51 rooms with bath, 1 suite. Restaurant, bar, laundry service. AE, DC, MC, V. Closed mid-Nov.–mid-Mar.*

$$$ ⊞ **Marina.** This spiffy 12-story beachfront skyscraper from the mid-
★   1980s has much less character than the refurbished and more pricey Lido wing, dating to 1970, which opens directly onto the water and where all rooms have balconies. Lido guests can, of course, use the highrise facilities, too, which include a large indoor swimming pool and a rooftop restaurant. ⊠ *Széchenyi út 26, H-8239 Balatonfüred,* ☎ *87/343–644, ℻ 87/343–052. 291 rooms with bath, 58 suites. Restaurant, bar, beer tavern, indoor pool, beauty salon, massage, sauna, solarium, bowling, beach, boating, water sports, nightclub. AE, DC, MC, V. Closed Oct.–late Apr.*

$ ⊞ **Blaha Lujza.** In the old section of town, this sober summer house, built in a classic Roman style, was formerly owned by legendary Hungarian actress Blaha Lujza. Nowadays it's a friendly, unassuming inn within short walking distance of the lake. Rooms and facilities are simple, clean, and functional. ⊠ *Blaha Lujza u. 4, H-8230 Balatonfüred,* ☎ ℻ *87/343–094. 17 rooms with bath, 2 with shared bath. Restaurant. No credit cards.*

Outdoor Activities and Sports

Most hotels have their own private beaches, with water-sports facilities and equipment or special access to these nearby. Besides these, Balatonfüred has three public beaches, where you can rent sailboards, paddle boats, and other water toys; these are also available at Hungary's largest campground, **Füred Camping** (⊠ Széchenyi u. 24, next to the Hotel Marina, ☎ 87/343–823). Although motorboats are banned from the lake, those desperate to waterski can try the campground's electric waterski machine, which tows enthusiasts around a 1-kilometer circle. A two-tow ticket runs around 600 Ft.

In season you can rent **bicycles** from temporary, private outfits set up in central locations around town and near the beaches; one is usually working at the entrance to Füred Camping. Inquire at the tourist office for other current locations. Average prices for mountain-bike rentals are 400 Ft.–500 Ft. per hour or 2,500 Ft. per day. You can also usually rent **mopeds** in front of the Halászkert restaurant (⊠ Széchenyi út 2) for around 700 Ft. per hour and 3,500 Ft. per day.

Trail rides and horseback-riding lessons are available at the **Csikós Lovasudvar** (⊠ Klára-puszta, Pécshely, ☎ 87/445–308), about 10 kilometers (6 miles) away in Pécshely. Half-hour lessons cost around 800 Ft., hour-long trail rides about 1,000 Ft. More passive horse enthusiasts can go on a carriage ride for about 900 Ft. per hour.

Tihany and the Tihany Peninsula

65 *11 km (7 mi) southwest of Balatonfüred.*

The quaint town of Tihany, with its twisting, narrow cobblestone streets and famous hilltop abbey, is on the Tihany Félsziget (Tihany Peninsula), joined to the mainland by a narrow neck and jutting 5 kilometers (3 miles) into the lake. Only 12 square kilometers (less than 5 square miles), the peninsula is not only a major tourist resort but perhaps the most historic part of the Balaton area. In 1952 the entire peninsula was declared a national park, and because of its geological rarities, it became Hungary's first nature-conservation zone. On it are more than 110 geyser craters, remains of former hot springs, reminiscent of those found in Iceland, Siberia, and Wyoming's Yellowstone Park.

The smooth Belső Tó (Inner Lake), 82 feet higher than Lake Balaton, is one of the peninsula's own two lakes; around it are barren yellowish-white rocks and volcanic cones rising against the sky. Standing atop any hill in the area, you can see water in every direction. Though the hills surrounding the lake are known for their white wines, the peculiarities of this peninsula give rise to a notable Hungarian red, Tihany cabernet.

★ Tihany's crowning glory is the **Bencés Apátság** (Benedictine Abbey) with foundations laid by King Andras I in 1055. The abbey's charter—containing some 100 Hungarian words in its Latin text, thus making it the oldest written source of the Hungarian language—is kept in Pannonhalma. Rebuilt in baroque style between 1719 and 1784, the abbey's church towers above the village in feudal splendor. Its gilt-silver high altar, abbot's throne, pulpit, organ case, choir parapet, and swirling crowd of saintly and angelic faces are all the work (between 1753 and 1765) of Sebestyén Stuhlhoff. A joiner from Augsburg, Stuhlhoff lived and worked in the monastery as a lay brother for 25 years after the death of his Hungarian sweetheart. Local tradition says he immortalized her features as the angel who is kneeling on the right-hand side of the altar to the Virgin Mary. The magnificent baroque organ, adorned by stucco cherubs, can be heard during evening concerts in summer.

In a baroque house adjoining and entered through the abbey is the **Bencés Apátsági Múzeum** (Benedictine Abbey Museum), visited by more than 100,000 tourists annually. The best exhibits are in the basement lapidarium: relics from Roman colonization, including mosaic floors; a relief of David from the 2nd or 3rd century; and 1,200-year-old carved stones—all labeled in English as well as Hungarian. Three of the upstairs rooms were lived in for five days in 1921 by the last emperor of the dissolved Austro-Hungarian monarchy, Karl IV, in a futile foray to regain the throne of Hungary. Banished to Madeira, he died of pneumonia there a year later. The rooms are preserved with nostalgic relish for Franz Joseph's doomed successor and his empress, Zita. ⊠ *Első András tér 1,* ☎ *87/448–405 (abbey), 87/448–650 (museum).* 🖃 *100 Ft.* ⊘ *May–Sept., daily 9–5:30; Nov.–Mar., daily 10–3; Apr. and Oct., daily 10–4:30; Sun. and holidays yr-round, from 11 (after mass).*

Just outside the abbey complex, a pair of contemporary **statues** offer a startling contrast. Imre Varga's reverent 1972 statue of King Andras I is called *The Founder;* Amerigo Tot's strikingly modern 1970 abstraction is irreverently titled *His Majesty the Kilowatt.*

NEED A BREAK?   **Rege Cukrászda,** the café and pastry shop at ⊠ Első András tér 2, just below the abbey, offers not only fresh and creamy desserts but also a panoramic view of Lake Balaton from its terrace. It's closed November–March.

The **Skanzen,** Tihany's open-air museum of ethnography, presents an unlikely ensemble of old houses that include a potter's shed (with a local artist-in-residence); a wine-growing exhibition; a display of agricultural implements; a farmhouse with exquisitely carved peasant furniture; and the former house of the Fishermen's Guild, with an ancient boat (used until 1934) parked inside. ⊠ *Szabad tér 1, no phone.* ☎ *80 Ft.* ⊙ *May–Sept., Tues.–Sun. 10–6.*

Visszhang domb (Echo Hill), at the end of Piski István sétány, is where as many as 16 syllables can be bounced off the abbey wall. Nowadays, with the inroads of traffic and construction, you'll have to settle for a two-second echo.

NEED A BREAK?	You can practice projecting from the terraces of the **Echo Restaurant** (⊠ Visszhang út 23, ☎ 87/448-460), an inn atop Echo Hill. Whet your whistle with anything from a cup of coffee to fogas (young pike perch), carp, and catfish specialties.

Dining and Lodging

$$$ ✕ **Sport.** Beautifully situated near the Tihany boat landing, this first-class garden restaurant faces south to afford a panoramic view of Lake Balaton. Large bay windows allow similar views from inside the 1920s main house, where the back wall is richly painted by women folk artists from Kalocsa. Fish soup is a main-course specialty. There is disco dancing in the evening. ⊠ *Fürdőtelep 34,* ☎ *87/448-251. AE, DC, MC, V. Closed Oct.–Easter.*

$$ ✕ **Halásztánya.** The relaxed atmosphere and Gypsy music in the evening contribute to the popularity of the Halásztánya, which specializes in fish. ⊠ *Visszhang u. 11,* ☎ *87/448-771. Reservations not accepted. No credit cards. Closed Nov.–Mar.*

$$–$$$ ✕⊞ **Kolostor söröző és Panzió.** At the foot of the abbey steps, this beer restaurant and moderately priced pension hotel offers striking views of the church complex above, shimmeringly illuminated through the trees at night. There is an outdoor grill in the garden, along with terrace seating. Inside this spacious chalet is a glass-enclosed working brewery producing four kinds of beer, and during the day you can watch men in blue smocks seriously sipping and puckering for quality control. It is all very thirst provoking, as are the fish specialties, which include eel paprikash; trout with almonds; the Balaton's ubiquitous pike perch, fogas; and its young, *süllő,* served in fillets with tiny crayfish and dill sauce. Cozy, wood-paneled rooms are built into the attic space above the restaurant. ⊠ *Kossuth utca 14, H-8237 Tihany,* ☎ FAX *87/448-408; hotel* ☎ *87/448-009. 7 rooms with bath. Breakfast room. No credit cards.*

$$$$ ⊞ **Club Tihany.** This 32-acre holiday village calls itself an "island of opportunities" for sports and recreation; essentially, it is a year-round resort complex of Club Med proportions at the tip of the Tihany Peninsula. The list of activities is staggering—from fishing to massage therapy. More recently, a spa was added, offering thermal bathing and massage therapies. Housing is provided in 161 luxury bungalows that offer a choice of architecture—suburban A-frame, modern atrium, or sloped-roof minifarmhouse, all with kitchen facilities; or you can stay in the bland main building, the Hotel Tihany. Note: Prices include breakfast and dinner. ⊠ *Rév u. 3, H-8237,* ☎ *87/448-088,* FAX *87/448-110. 330 rooms with bath, 161 bungalows. 3 restaurants, 2 bars, wine bar, pool, hairdresser, spa, tennis, exercise room, beach, water sports, meeting rooms. AE, DC, MC, V.*

$$$–$$$$ ⊞ **Kastély Hotel.** Lush landscaped gardens surround this stately mansion on the water's edge, built at the turn of the century for József Hapsburg. Inside, it's all understated elegance; rooms have balconies, views, and crisp sheets. A newer, less attractive building houses the Kastely's sister, the Park Hotel, with 60 less expensive rooms. ⊠ *Fürdötelepi út*
★

1, H-8237 Tihany, ☎ *87/448–611,* FAX *87/448–409. 25 rooms with bath, 1 suite. Restaurant, bar, café, sauna, miniature golf, tennis courts, beach, water sports, laundry services. AE, DC, MC, V. Closed mid-Oct.–mid-Apr.*

Nightlife and the Arts

The Benedictine Abbey's popular summer organ-concert series runs from around mid-June through mid-September and features well-known musicians performing on the abbey's magnificent organ. Concerts are generally held every other week, sometimes more frequently. Contact the abbey (⊠ Első András tér 1, ☎ 87/448–405) for information and tickets.

Outdoor Activities and Sports

BICYCLING

Bicycle rentals are available from **Tihany Tourist** (☞ Visitor Information *in* Lake Balaton A to Z, *below*); a mountain bike costs about 300 Ft.–400 Ft. per hour.

FISHING

Belső-tó (Inner Lake) is a popular angling spot in which you can try your luck at hooking ponty, catfish, and other local fish. Fishing permits can be bought on site at the nearby hotel.

HIKING

Footpaths crisscross the entire peninsula, allowing visitors to climb the small hills on its west side for splendid views of the area or hike down Belső-tó (Inner Lake). If in midsummer you climb its highest hill, the **Csúcshegy** (761 feet—approximately a two-hour hike), you will find the land below carpeted with purple lavender and the air filled with its fragrance. Introduced from France into Hungary, lavender thrives on the lime-rich soil and strong sunshine of Tihany. (The State Lavender and Medicinal Herb Farm here supplies the Hungarian pharmaceutical and cosmetics industries.)

HORSEBACK RIDING

Aszófő Lovasudvar (Aszófő Riding Center; ⊠ Aszófői út 1, ☎ 87/445–078) offers horseback-riding lessons, riding in the ring, and trail rides through the peninsula's lovely scenery; longer tours include a stop at a local wine cellar for some vintage refreshment. A two-hour trail ride costs around 1,200 Ft. The center has showers and changing rooms, as well as a snack bar.

En Route The miniature town of Örvényes, about 7 kilometers (4 miles) west of Tihany has the only working **vizi malom** (water mill) in the Balaton region. Built in the 18th century, it still grinds grain into flour while also serving as a museum. In the miller's room is a collection of folk art, wood carvings, pottery, furniture, and pipes. Near the water mill, a statue of St. John of Nepomuk stands on a **baroque stone bridge,** also from the 18th century. On a nearby hill are the ruins of a Romanesque church; only its chancel has survived. On Templom utca, a few steps from the bridge, is the baroque **St. Imre templom** (St. Imre Church), built in the late 18th century. *Water mill:* ⊠ *Szent Imre u. 1,* ☎ *87/449–360.* 🎫 *50 Ft.* ☉ *May, daily 9–4; June–Sept., daily 9–5.*

Another 1 kilometer (½ mile) west of Örvényes, **Balatonudvari** is a pleasant beach resort famous for its cemetery, which was declared a national shrine because of its beautiful, unique heart-shaped tombstones carved from white limestone at the turn of the 18th century. The cemetery is just off of the highway, at the eastern end of town; it is easily visible from the highway. Balatonudvari's beach itself is at **Kiliántelep,** 2 kilometers (1 mile) to the west.

Balatonakali

66   *3 km (2 mi) west of Kiliántelep.*

The thriving beach resort of Balatonakali has ferry service and three large camping grounds. On the slopes of Fenye-hegy, above the town, are vineyards (muscatel is the local specialty) lined with whitewashed winepress houses with thatched roofs and stone cellars, similar to those at Örvényes, if not as ornate. A 4-kilometer (2½-mile) excursion into the volcanic hills north of Balatonakali leads to **Dörgicse**, a sleepy, less-trafficked little village where elderly ladies will stop their yard work to watch your car go by. Here you can view ruins of a medieval double church dating from the 11th century or take a 10-minute walk to the strange rock formations of **Kő-völgy** (Stone Valley), beyond which are fine mountain views.

Dining

$$ ✕ **Mandula Csárda.** Named for its almond trees, this 19th-century vintner's house is now an elegantly rustic and totally romantic thatched-roof roadside inn with a shady vineyard terrace where Gypsy musicians serenade you as you sip delicious Balaton and Badacsony wines. It also has a playground for children. The management is fond of—and good at—organizing such activities as Gypsy, outlaw, and goulash parties, as well as horseback riding and carriage outings to interesting nearby sights. ⊠ *On Hwy. 71, halfway between Balatonudvari and Balatonakali, H-8243,* ☎ *87/444–511. No credit cards. Closed late Sept.–early May.*

Zánka

67   *5 km (3 mi) west of Balatonakali.*

Zánka is a popular, relatively low-key beach resort with a large, pleasant beach, as well as a small, older village section up the hill from the water. The iron-rich Vérkút (Blood Spring), named after the bright stains it left on the rocks near which it flowed, put Zánka on the map as a spa late in the 19th century but has since dried up. The town's **Református templom** (Reformed Church; ⊠ Petőfi Sándor u. 3) is of medieval origin, but it was rebuilt in 1786 and again a century later with various elements preserved—leaving a pulpit supported by Roman foundations and Romanesque columns. The steeple's and church's mismatched coloring (gray-beige and white, respectively) is not due to oversight, but occurred because the present steeple was added later (late 1800s) to the much older body of the church. The church is open during services, Sundays at 11 AM; someone is usually around to let you in an hour or so before.

The town of Zánka is not to be confused with the neighboring Zánka Gyermeküdülő (Zánka Children's Resort), the monstrous—in size and appearance—former Communist Pioneer Camp capable of housing 2,500 youngsters.

Lodging

$$ 🏨 **Kővirág Panzió.** A 10-minute drive inland from Zánka's beach, this family-run pension is in the peaceful village of nearby Köveskál. Six two-story suites are in a lovely, restored turn-of-the-century building (converted from a bull stable) typical of the Balaton region, with whitewashed walls and arched eye-of-God windows peeking out from under a reed-thatched roof. Each unit has a rustic-village feel, furnished with original hand-painted peasant furniture and mix-and-match antique carved-wood pieces, and scattered with folk handicrafts and knickknacks. On cool nights you can build a fire in typical stone beehive fireplaces, with animal skins (wild boar, woolly sheep, or spotted cow) sprawled on the stone floors before them. Those who don't miss TVs, telephones, and other amenities may enjoy the Kővirág as an escape from the Balaton shore's myriad standard, faceless hotels. With large downstairs living rooms and two bedrooms upstairs sleeping four, the apartments offer good value and comfort for families or couples traveling together. ⊠ *Fő út 9/A, H-8274 Köveskál,* ☎ *87/478–569. 6 suites with bath. Restaurant. No credit cards. Closed early Oct.–Easter.*

Outdoor Activities and Sports

Zánka is well situated for inland exploring in the beautiful hilly countryside of the Káli-medence (Káli Basin). You can hike, bike, drive, or use a combination of these to get to the peak of Hegyestő, a volcanic protrusion that is the area's highest hill (336 meters) and is fabled to possess mysterious "positive energy." It's a marvelous spot for lake gazing or a picnic. (Access to Hegyestő is via the road to Monszló after leaving Zánka.)

The road between Zánka and Köveskál and beyond toward Tapolca takes you into beautiful rural scenery: fruitful vineyards spreading up the slopes of the protruding volcanic hills, tiny village clusters punctuated by centuries-old church steeples.

Three kilometers (2 miles) inland, to the northwest, is **Kővágóörs,** one of the prettiest villages of the Balaton, with a fine array of cottages in the local peasant style. It makes a wonderful place to pedal or stroll.

Badacsony

★ ❻❽ *20 km (12 mi) southwest of Zánka.*

One of the northern shore's most treasured images is the slopes of Mt. Badacsony (1,437 feet high), simply called the Badacsony, rising from the lake. The mysterious, coffinlike basalt peak of the Balaton Highlands is actually an extinct volcano flanked by smaller cone-shaped hills. The masses of lava that coagulated here created bizarre and beautiful rock formations. At the upper edge, salt columns tower 180–200 feet like organ pipes in a huge semicircle. In 1965 Hungarian conservationists won a major victory that ended the quarrying of basalt from Mt. Badacsony, which is now a protected nature-preservation area.

The land below has been tilled painfully and lovingly for centuries. There are vineyards everywhere and splendid wine in every inn and tavern. In descending order of dryness, the best-loved Badacsony white wines are **Rizlingszilváni, Kéknyelű,** and **Szürkebarát.** Their proud producers claim that "no vine will produce good wine unless it can see its own reflection in the Balaton." They believe it is not enough for the sun simply to shine on a vine; the undersides of the leaves also need light, which is reflected from the lake's mirrorlike surface. Others claim the wine draws its strength from the fire of old volcanoes.

Badacsony is really an administrative name for the entire area and includes not just the mountain but also five settlements at its foot. Boats and trains deliver you to Badacsony-Üdülőtelep (Badacsony Resort). July and August draw hoards of visitors to the wine cellars and beaches, especially on weekends, making it at times unpleasantly crowded. Spring or fall are ideal.

A good starting point for Badacsony sightseeing is the **Egry József Memorial Museum,** formerly the home and studio of a famous painter of Balaton landscapes. His evocative paintings smoothly blend pastel colors beautifully depicting the lake's constantly changing hues, from its angry bright green during storms to its tranquil deep blues. ⊠ *Egry*

sétány 12, Badacsony-Űdülőtelep, ☎ *87/431–140.* 🎫 *80 Ft.* 🕐
May–Oct., Tues.–Sun. 10–6.

Szegedy Róza út, the steep main street climbing the mountain, is paved
with basalt stones and is flanked by vineyards and villas; water from
the Kisfaludy Spring flows downhill along the side of the road. This
is the place to get acquainted with the writer Sándor Kisfaludy and his
beloved bride from Badacsony, Róza Szegedy, to whom he dedicated
his love poems. At the summit of her street is **Szegedy Róza Ház** (Róza
Szegedy House), a baroque winepress house built in 1790 on a grand
scale—with thatched roof, gabled wall, six semicircular arcades, and
an arched and pillared balcony running the length of the four raftered
upstairs rooms (it was here that the hometown girl met the visiting bard
from Budapest). The house is now a memorial museum to both of them,
furnished much the way it was when he was doing his best work im-
mortalizing his two true loves, the Badacsony and his wife. ⊠ *Szegedy
Róza út, no phone.* 🎫 *50 Ft.* 🕐 *Mar.–Oct., Tues.–Sun. 10–5.*

The steep climb to the **Kisfaludy kilátó** (Kisfaludy Lookout Tower) on
Mt. Badacsony's summit is an integral part of the Badacsony experience and a rewarding bit of exercise. Serious summitry begins behind
the Kisfaludy House at the **Rózsakő** (Rose Stone), a flat, smooth basalt
slab with many carved inscriptions. Local legend has it that if a boy
and a girl sit on it with their backs to Lake Balaton, they will marry
within a year. From here, a trail marked in yellow leads upstairs to the
foot of the columns that stretch to the top. Steep flights of stone steps
take you through a narrow gap between rocks and basalt walls until
you reach a tree-lined plateau. You are now at the 1,391-foot level.
Follow the blue triangular markings along a path to the Kisfaludy kilátó.
When you have climbed its 46-foot height, you have scaled Mt. Badacsony. Even with time out for rests and views, the ascent from Rózsakő
should take less than an hour.

Wine-tasting opportunities abound in Badacsony. Many restaurants and
inns have their own tastings, as do the numerous smaller, private cellars dotting the hill. Look for signs saying *bor* or *Wein* (wine, in Hungarian and German) to point the way. Most places are open mid-May
to mid-September daily from around noon until 9 or 10. Two well-
known cellars with regular tastings are **Rizapuzta** (⊠ Badacsonytomaj,
☎ 87/431–243) and **Imre Borozó** (⊠ Szegedy Róza u. 87, no phone).

Dining and Lodging

$$ ✕ **Halászkert.** The festive Fish Garden has won numerous international
awards for its tasty Hungarian cuisine. Inside are wooden rafters and
tables draped with cheerful traditional blue-and-white *kékfestő* table-
cloths; outside is a large terrace with umbrella-shaded tables. Ample
wine selections and live Gypsy music in the evenings make for a lively
atmosphere. ⊠ *Park u. 5,* ☎ *87/431–054. MC, V. Closed Nov.–Mar.*

$$ ✕ **Kisfaludy-ház.** Perched above the Szegedy Róza Hacz is this Badacsony institution, once a winepress house owned by the poet's family.
Its wine cellar lies directly over the Kisfaludy Spring, the waters of which
accompanied your upward hike, but the stellar attraction is a vast two-
tiered terrace that affords a breathtaking panoramic view of virtually
the entire lake. Naturally, the wines are excellent and are incorporated
into some of the cooking, such as creamy wine soup. The grilled meats
and palacsinta desserts are excellent, as are the wines. ⊠ *Szegedy
Róza u. 87,* ☎ *87/431–016. AE, DC, MC, V. Closed Nov.–Easter.*

$$ 🏨 **Club Tomaj.** On the shore of Lake Balaton in the Badacsonytomaj
neighborhood, this is the largest hotel in the area. It's just a step away
from the hotel to the Club's private beach. Breakfast is served for an

additional fee. ⊠ *Balatoni út 14, H-8258 Badacsonytomaj,* ☎ *87/471–040,* ℻ *87/471–059. 46 rooms with bath, 4 suites. Restaurant, café, sauna, tennis court, bowling, beach. No credit cards. Closed Nov.–Mar.*

$$ ☷ **Óbester Fogadó.** This charming pension occupies a 350-year old house surrounded by vineyards, on the lower slopes of Mt. Badacsony. Rooms are comfortably rustic, with white-tile floors, unfinished wood furnishings, and views down onto the lake or into the vineyards. Operated by a friendly husband-wife team, the Óbester is decidedly informal and homey, with several cats and the family dog usually napping in the sun outside. Guests have ample opportunity to taste the house wines from the deep, cool cellar, whose foundations are suspected to date back to Roman times. At the end of the day you can sit in the garden under the walnut tree, a glass of your favorite wine in hand, and watch the lake change colors as the sun sets. ⊠ *Római út 177, H-8261 Badacsony,* ☎ *87/431–648,* ℻ *87/431–644, ext. 15. 8 rooms with bath, 2 suites. Breakfast room, wine cellar. MC.*

Outdoor Activities and Sports

The upper paths and roads along the slopes of Mt. Badacsony are excellent for scenic walking—or swerving, if after a particularly inspiring round of wine tasting. Well-marked trails lead up to the summit of Mt. Badacsony.

For beach activities, you can go to one of Badacsony's several beaches or head 6 kilometers (3 miles) northeast, to those at Balatonrendes and Ábrahámhegy, combined communities forming one of Lake Balaton's quieter resorts.

Szigliget

★ ⑥⑨ *11 km (7 mi) from Badacsony.*

The village of Szigliget was formerly an island in the Balaton. It's a tranquil, picturesque town with a fine array of thatched-roof winepress houses and a small, attractive beach. Towering over the town is the ruin of the 13th-century **Óvár** (Old Castle), a fortress so well protected that it was never taken by the Turks; it was demolished in the early 18th century by Hapsburgs fearful of rebellions. A steep path starting from Kisfaludy utca brings you to the top of the hill, where you can explore the ruins, under ongoing archaeological restoration (a sign maps out the restoration plan), and take in the breathtaking views of Lake Balaton and Badacsony's verdant hill.

Down in the village on Iharos út, at the intersection with the road to Badacsony, the Romanesque remains of the **Avas templon** (Avas Church), from the Arpad dynasty, still contain a 12th-century basalt tower with stone spire. The **Eszterházy Summer Mansion** in the main square, Fő tér, was built in the 18th century and rebuilt in neoclassical style in the 19th. Lately a holiday retreat for writers (and closed to the public), it has a 25-acre park with yews, willows, walnuts, pines, and more than 500 kinds of ornamental trees and shrubs.

Keszthely

⑦⓪ *18 km (10 mi) from Szigliget.*

Keszthely, the largest town on the northern shore, lies at the westernmost end of Lake Balaton. Founded in 1404, Keszthely today offers a rare combination of historic cultural center and restful summer resort. With a beautifully preserved pedestrians-only avenue (Kossuth Lajos utca) in the historic center of town, the spectacular baroque Festetics Palace, and a relative absence of honky-tonk, Keszthely is far more classically attractive and sophisticated than other large Balaton towns. Continuing the cultural and arts tradition begun by Count György Festetics two centuries ago, Keszthely hosts numerous cultural events, including an annual summer arts festival. Just south of town is the vast swamp called Kis-Balaton (Little Balaton), formerly part of Lake Balaton and now a protected nature area filled with birds. Water flowing into Lake Balaton from its little sibling frequently churns up sediment, making the water around Keszthely's beaches disconcertingly cloudy.

The **Pethő Ház,** a striking town house of medieval origins, was rebuilt in baroque style with a handsome arcaded gallery above its courtyard. In 1830 the house became the birthplace of Karl Goldmark, composer of the opera *Queen of Sheba*. Hidden through its courtyard you'll find the recently restored 18th-century **synagogue,** in front of which stands a small memorial honoring the 829 Jewish people from the neighborhood, turned into a ghetto in 1944, who were killed during the Holocaust. ⊠ *Kossuth Lajos u. 22.*

The **Georgikon Farm Museum** shows the history and development of the Georgikon School, established some 200 years ago by Count Festetics as the first agricultural school in Europe. ⊠ *Bercsényi Miklós u. 67,* ☎ *82/311–563.* 🎫 *60 Ft.* ☯ *Apr.–Oct., Tues.–Sat. 10–5, Sun. 10–6.*

Near the railroad station, housed in an imposing neobaroque building (1928), the **Balaton Museum** has exhibits on regional history, ethnography, folk art, and painting. ⊠ *Múzeum u. 2,* ☎ *83/312–351.* 🎫 *60 Ft.* ☯ *Mid-May–mid-Oct., Tues.–Sun. 10–6; mid-Oct.–mid-May, Tues.–Sat. 9–5.*

★   The jewel of Keszthely is the magnificent **Festetics Kastély** (Festetics Palace), one of the finest baroque complexes in Hungary. Begun around 1745, it was the seat of the enlightened and philanthropic Festetics dynasty, which had acquired Keszthely six years earlier. The palace's distinctive churchlike tower and more than 100 rooms were added between 1883 and 1887, and the interior is exceedingly lush. The **Helikon Könyvtár** (Helikon Library) in the south wing contains some 52,000 volumes and precious codices and documents of Festetics family history, but it can also be admired for its carved-oak furniture and collection of etchings and paintings. Chamber and orchestral concerts are held in the **Mirror Gallery** ballroom or, in summer, in the courtyard. The palace opens onto a splendid park lined with rare plants and fine sculptures. ⊠ *Kastély u. 1,* ☎ *83/312–191.* 🎫 *350 Ft.* ☯ *Tues.–Sun. 9–5.*

Dining and Lodging

$–$$ ✕ **Gösser Söröző.** This centrally located beer garden keeps long hours and plenty of beer on tap for its clientele. The food is better than you might guess judging just from the touristy atmosphere. Aside from barroom snacks, the menu features Hungarian specialties, such as *gulyásleves, gombás rostélyos,* and *töltöttpaprika*. In summer, guests can dine in an outdoor garden, and live music starts after 6 PM. ⊠ *Kossuth Lajos u. 35, just north of Fő tér,* ☎ *83/312–265. AE, DC, V.*

$$$$ 🏨 **Béta Hotel Hullám.** This attractive turn-of-the-century mansion with an elegant tower sits right on the Balaton shore. Rooms are clean and simply furnished with functional brown furniture and have TVs and minibars but no telephones. Guests can use the pool and other recreational facilities at the Helikon Hotel nearby. ⊠ *Balatonpart 1, H-8360 Keszthely,* ☎ *83/312–644,* 📠 *83/315–950. 42 rooms with bath, 6 suites. Restaurant, bar, beach. AE, DC, MC, V. Closed Nov.–Mar.*

$$$$ 🖫 **Helikon Hotel.** This large and comfortable lakeside hotel is convenient and popular with groups. Guests can choose from numerous sports facilities, such as an indoor swimming pool, an indoor tennis court, bowling, a sauna, a solarium, sailing, surfing, rowing, fishing, and, in winter, skating. The hotel also offers slimming treatments and beauty care. ⊠ *Balaton part 5, H-8360 Keszthely,* ☎ *83/315–330,* ͞FAX *83/315–403. 224 rooms with bath, 8 suites. Restaurant, bar, indoor pool, beauty salon, sauna, bowling, health club, beach, water sports. AE, DC, MC, V.*

Nightlife and the Arts

The **Balaton Festival** held annually in May features high-caliber classical concerts and other festivities held in venues around town and outdoors on Kossuth Lajos utca. In summer, classical concerts and master classes are held almost daily in the Festetics Palace's Mirror Hall.

Outdoor Activities and Sports

BALLOONING

Hot-air balloon rides in the Keszthely region have become popular with those tourists who can afford it (29,500 Ft. per person). Dr. Bóka György (a practicing M.D. and balloon pilot) and his friendly team will take you up in his blue-and-yellow balloon for an hour-long tour of the Balaton sky. The trip includes a postlanding champagne ritual to celebrate solid ground. Flights depend strongly on wind and air-pressure conditions; in summer, they can usually fly only in early morning and early evening. Transportation to and from the sight is included. (Contact address: ⊠ Móricz Zsigmond u. 7, ☎ 83/312–421.)

BIRD-WATCHING

The largest river feeding Balaton, the Zala, enters the lake at its southwestern corner. On either side there is a vast swamp, formerly part of the lake. Known as **Kis-Balaton** (Little Balaton), its almost 3,500 acres of marshland were put under nature preservation in 1949. In 1953 a bird-watching station was opened nearby, and ornithologists have found some 80 species nesting among the reeds, many of them rare for this region. The white egret is the most treasured of them. Most of the area can be visited only by special permission. Contact Horváth Jenő at the **Kutató-ház** (Research Station; ⊠ Fenékpuszta, ☎ 83/315–341) of the Közép Dunántúl Természetvédelmi Igazgatóság (Central Transdanubian Environmanetal Protection Directorate) to arrange a bird-watching tour (around 2,500 Ft.) The Kis-Balaton is entered near where Highway 71 ends its trip around the lake and yields to Highway 76 continuing south.

HORSEBACK RIDING

Mustang riding center (☎ 83/312–289) offers lessons (800 Ft. per hour), riding in the ring (600 Ft. per hour), and carriage rides (1,000 Ft.).

WATER SPORTS

You can rent paddleboats and other water toys at the public beach (next to the Hotel Hullám) or from the Helikon Hotel (☞ Dining and Lodging, *above*).

Shopping

Pedestrian-only **Kossuth Lajos utca** is lined with stores selling folk crafts and souvenirs.

Hévíz

71 *6 km (4 mi) inland (northwest) from Keszthely.*

Hévíz is one Hungary's biggest and most famous spa resorts, with the largest natural curative thermal lake in Europe. Lake Hévíz covers nearly 60,000 square yards, with warm water that never grows cooler than 33°–35°C (91.4°–95°F) in summer and 30°–32°C (86°–89.6°F) in winter, thus allowing year-round bathing, particularly where the lake is covered by a roof and looks like a racetrack grandstand. Richly endowed with sulfur, alkali, calcium salts, and other curative components, the Hévíz water is recommended for spinal, rheumatic, gynecological, and articular disorders, and is drunk to help digestive problems and receding gums. Fed by a spring producing 86 million liters of water a day, the lake cycles through a complete water change every 28 hours. Squeamish bathers, however, should be forewarned that along with its photogenic lily pads, the lake naturally contains assorted sludgy mud and plant material. It's all good for you, though—even the mud, which is 50% organic and full of iodine and estrogen.

The vast spa park is home to hospitals, sanatoriums, expensive hotels, and a casino. The public bath facilities are in the **Állami Gyógyfürdő Kórház** (State Medicinal Bath Hospital), a large turreted complex on the lakeshore. Bathing for more than three hours at a time is not recommended. ✉ *Dr. Schüller Vilmos sétány 1,* ☎ *83/340-455.* 💲 *250 Ft. (valid for 3 hrs).* ⊙ *May–Sept., daily 9–6; Oct.–Apr., daily 9–4:30.*

Lodging

$$$$ 🏨 **Aqua Thermal Hotel.** This large, luxurious spa-hotel has its own thermal baths and physiotherapy unit (plus a full dental service!). It has a convenient city-center location, but the rooms are smaller than average and therefore not suited to families who intend to share a single room. Numerous cure packages are available. ✉ *Kossuth Lajos u. 13–15, H-8380 Hévíz,* ☎ *83/341-090,* 📠 *83/340-970. 230 rooms with bath. Restaurant, bar, hairdresser, sauna, solarium, thermal bath, medical services. AE, DC, MC, V.*

$$ 🏨 **Thermal Hotel Hévíz.** Very similar in its offerings to those of its neighbor the Aqua Thermal, this large spa-hotel has the additional attraction of a casino. ✉ *Kossuth Lajos u. 9–11, H-8380 Hévíz,* ☎ *83/341-180,* 📠 *83/340-660. 203 rooms with bath. Restaurant, indoor and outdoor pools, sauna, solarium, thermal baths, casino, medical services. AE, DC, MC, V.*

Balatonszentgyörgy

🕢 *14 km (9 mi) east of Keszthely, 70 km (43 mi) west of Siófok.*

It's worth stopping in Balatonszentgyörgy to see **Csillagvár** (Star Castle), hidden away at the end of a dirt road past the gaping chasms of the Balaton Brick factory quarry. The house was built in the 1820s as a hunting lodge for László, the Festetics family's eccentric. Though it is not star-shaped inside, wedge-shaped projections on the ground floor give the outside this effect. Today it is a museum of 16th- and 17th-century life in the border fortresses of the Balaton and is worth exploring for its fine cut-stone stairs and deep well, from which drinking water is still drawn; refreshments are available in the adjoining former stable. ✉ *Irtási dűlő,* ☎ *85/377-532.* 💲 *100 Ft.* ⊙ *May–Aug., daily 9–6.*

Downtown, almost 3 kilometers (2 miles) away, is another architecturally interesting museum, the beautifully furnished **Talpasház** (House on Soles), so named because its upright beams are encased in thick foundation boards. The house is filled not only with exquisite antique peasant furniture, textiles, and pottery but also with the work of contemporary local folk artists; some of their work is for sale on the premises, and visitors can also try to create their own works on a pottery wheel. ⊠ *Csillagvár u. 68, no phone.* 📞 *70 Ft.* ⊙ *Late May–Sept., daily 9–7.*

Fonyód

🕖 *20 km (12 mi) east of Balatonszentgyörgy, 45 km (28 mi) west of Siófok.*

With seven beaches stretching 7 kilometers (almost 4½ miles) along the shore, Fonyód is second only to Siófok among the most-developed resorts on the southern shore of the lake. Vacationers from Pécs, 90 kilometers (56 miles) to the southeast, particularly favor Fonyód for their summer homes. An ancient settlement, where late Stone Age and Bronze Age tools as well as Roman ruins have been excavated, Fonyód sits at the base of a twin-peaked hill rising directly from the shore. Atop one of the peaks, **Vár-hegy** (Castle Hill; 764 feet), stood an important fortress during Turkish times. Only its trenches and the foundation walls of a Romanesque church still stand; the peak is worth climbing for the views of its crowning ruin from the disheveled courtyard: You look across the lake almost directly at Badacsony and, off in the distance to the left, Keszthely. You can drive up or walk: Beginning at the train station, red markers indicate the path up the hill; allow a little over an hour for the uphill walk.

Dining

$$ ✕ **Présház Csárda.** Above the remains of Fonyód Castle, the driveway leading to a four-pillar veranda is so imposing that you may expect to be greeted by Scarlett O'Hara. But behind the noble facade of the 150-year-old Winepress-House Inn is a thatched-roof structure typical of the region and a wine cellar 24 yards long, all with cozy rustic furnishings. The Hungarian dishes and local wines are excellent. ⊠ *Lenke u. 22, no phone. No credit cards. Closed Sept.–mid-May.*

OFF THE
BEATEN PATH

BUZSÁK – An interesting excursion from Fonyód is to the village of Buzsák, 16 kilometers (10 miles) to the south. Buzsák is famous for its colorful folk art, unique peasant needlework, and fine carving, mostly by shepherds. Today's products can be bought in local shops, but earlier masterworks are displayed in the museum of the **Buzsáki Tájház** (Buzsák Regional House), three venerable, well-decorated rustic buildings, which in addition to the museum house a restaurant and a folk-art shop. Inquire about the village Saints' Festival, known as the Buzsáki Búcsú, held for two or three days around August 20. ⊠ *Tanács tér 7,* ☎ *85/330–342.* 📞 *50 Ft.* ⊙ *May and Sept., daily 9–5; June–mid-Oct., daily 9–7. At other times visits can be made by prior arrangement.*

Balatonboglár

🕖 *12 km (7 mi) east of Fonyód.*

At the rate the resorts of Balatonboglár and Balatonlelle, its neighbor immediately to the east, are mushrooming, they may soon merge into a minimegalopolis with Fonyód. Balatonboglár, mentioned as a community as early as 1211, is along with Fonyód the only other place on the southern shore that has hills by the lake. Eruptions of basalt tuff (stratified volcanic detritus) created these hills: At 541 feet, Balatonboglár's highest, **Vár-hegy,** is 223 feet lower than Fonyód's peak of the same name. Near its summit are the double ramparts of early Iron Age defensive earthworks as well as the foundation walls of a Roman watchtower. There is a good view from the spherical **Xantus Lookout Tower.** Atop the smaller **Sándor-hegy,** the crater of the tuff volcano is

still visible. There are many fine houses in the village; one neoclassical (1834) mansion is headquarters of a huge State Wine Farm and Research Station that supplies much of Hungary and Europe with Balaton
wines. The village is separated from the beach resort by railroad tracks
and Highway 7. Frequent ferries to Révfülöp offer quick transport to
the northern shore.

Balatonszemes

73 *7 km (4 mi) east of Balatonlelle.*

Balatonszemes is an older, established lakeside resort with a town history dating to the 14th century. Now a school, the former **Hunyady Mansion** on Gárdonyi Géza utca was built in baroque style in the second
half of the 18th century, as was the former granary opposite it. The **parish
church** at Fő utca 23 was built in Gothic style in the 15th century, and
some of its ornamented windows and the buttressed walls of the chancel still survive. Its richly decorated pastorium is from 1517.

Another of Balatonszemes's attractions is **Bagolyvár** (Owl Castle), an
eccentric stronghold with many turrets. It was built by an Italian architect at the beginning of this century on the site of an old Turkish fort
known as Fool's Castle (Bolondvár). The two southern round bastions
of the old Fool's Castle are incorporated in the more recent structure.

Balatonszárszó

76 *5 km (3 mi) east of Balatonszemes.*

Balatonszárszó is where the Hungarian poet Attila József—one of the
few Hungarian poets whose genius survives translation—committed
suicide in 1937 by throwing himself under a train. The boardinghouse
where he spent his last weeks is now the **József Attila Memorial Museum,** with extensive documentation of his life, his work, and his
death. ⊠ *József Attila u. 7, no phone.* 🖃 *60 Ft.* ☉ *Tues.–Sun. 10–6;
Nov.–Mar., Tues.–Sun. 10–2.*

Balatonföldvár

77 *5 km (3 mi) east of Balatonszárszó.*

The second part of Balatonföldvár's name means "earthwork," and,
indeed, this popular resort village, developed as one of the aristocratic
Széchenyi family's estates, was built beside an old Celtic fortification.
The fortification has largely been damaged and obscured by posh villas along Petőfi Sándor utca and József Attila utca. The destruction of
the past can perhaps be justified, if not excused, by the result: Balatonföldvár is the southern shore's most attractively laid-out resort. Its
harbor is alive with sailboats in summer, while on the shore, weeping
willows droop to the water. An alley of plane trees is crowned by a superb view of the hills of Tihany across the water. Flower beds and spacious, symmetrical promenades all contribute to the impression that
the entire town is one big park, a rare impression indeed on the over-
developed southern shore.

OFF THE   **SZÁNTÓDPUSZTA –** Continue a few kilometers to Szántódpuszta, just op-
BEATEN PATH posite the Tihany Peninsula on the southern shore of Lake Balaton, where
the narrow neck of water separates Szántód from the peninsula (a ferry
takes passengers across). Szántódpuszta itself is a living museum and
entertainment center; the group of buildings erected there in the 18th
and 19th centuries and recently reconstructed features several exhibits,
including relics of local history, works of fine and folk art, and a display

of industrial history. Between May and September the museum hosts a variety of programs, including horse and dog shows, folk-art displays, and fairs. ☎ *84/348–947.* 🖂 *60 Ft.* ☉ *May–mid-June, daily 9–6; mid-June–late Aug., daily 9–7; late Aug.–Sept., daily 9–6.*

Siófok

78 *18 km (11 mi) east of Balatonföldvár, 105 km (65 mi) southwest of Budapest.*

Siófok is the largest city on the southern shore and one of Hungary's major tourist and holiday centers. It is also arguably the ugliest. It has a resident population of some 23,000, but in the high season the number swells to more than 100,000. In 1863 a railway station was built for the city, paving the way for its "golden age," at the turn of the century, when a horse-racing course was built with stands to accommodate 1,500 spectators. During the closing stages of World War II the city sustained heavy damage; to boost tourism during the 1960s, the Pannonia Hotel Company built four of what many consider to be the ugliest hotels in the area. If, however, these were Siófok's *only* ugly buildings, there would still be hope for a ray of aesthetic redemption. But the sad truth is, the city is overrun by unsightly modern structures. Its shoreline has been ruined by a long, honky-tonk strip crammed with concrete-bunker hotels, discos, go-go bars, and tacky restaurants. So while Siófok is not for those seeking a peaceful lakeside getaway, it is exactly what hoards of action-seeking young people want—an all-in-one playground.

One worthwhile attraction is the **Kálmán Imre Múzeum** (Imre Kálmán Museum), housed in the birthplace of composer Kálmán (1882–1953), known internationally as the Prince of Operetta. Inside this small house-cum-museum are his first piano, original scores, his smoking jacket, and lots of old pictures. 🖂 *Kálmán Imre sétány 5,* ☎ *84/311–287.* 🖂 *70 Ft.* ☉ *May–Oct., Tues.–Sun. 9–5; Nov.–Apr., Tues.–Sun. 9–4.*

Dining and Lodging

$$ ✕ **Csárdás Étterem.** The oldest and one of the best restaurants in Siófok, ★ Csárdás has consistently won awards for its hearty, never-bland Hungarian cuisine as well as its service and ambience. House specialties include a breaded and fried pork fillet stuffed with cheese, ham, and smoked bacon. In summer you can sit on the terrace pondering your English-language menu. 🖂 *Fő u. 105,* ☎ *84/310–642. AE, MC, V. Closed Nov.–Mar. 15.*

$$ ✕ **Janus Étterem.** This elegant restaurant, once an old villa, was renovated in 1992 under the guidance of Imre Makovecz, one of Hungary's preeminent architects (Makovecz also designed the church across the street). The menu features fresh fish and excellent Hungarian specialties. 🖂 *Fő u. 93–95,* ☎ *84/312–546. AE, DC, MC, V.*

$$$$ 🏨 **Janus.** Every room in this bright luxury hotel, opened in 1993, is clean and comfortably contemporary and contains a minibar and a safe. The "relaxation center" downstairs features a swimming pool, sauna, and whirlpool. 🖂 *Fő u. 93–95, H-8600 Siófok,* ☎ *84/312–546,* **FAX** *84/312–432. 17 rooms and 7 suites, all with bath. Restaurant, bar, indoor pool, sauna, whirlpool, exercise room, meeting rooms. AE, DC, MC, V.*

$$ 🏨 **Hotel Korona.** This three-story rectangular block has the advantage of being somewhat removed from the multilane traffic of the city's main street and about 100 meters from the lakeshore. All rooms have balconies and are clean and simple. A small garden and a tennis court out back are a plus. ✉ *Erkel Ferenc u. 53, H-8600 Siófok,* ☎ *84/310–471. 34 rooms with bath. Restaurant, tennis court, garden.*

Nightlife and the Arts

Loyal to Siófok-born operetta composer Imre Kálmán, popular operetta concerts are held regularly in the summer at the **Kulturális Központ** (Cultural Center; ✉ Fő tér 2, ☎ 84/311–855).

Outdoor Activities and Sports

GO-CARTS

Speed demons can whiz around at the Go Cart Track (✉ On Hwy. 70, by the railroad crossing, ☎ 06/20–229–984); a 10-minute drive is around 1,500 Ft.

HORSEBACK RIDING

The **Lovas Centrum** (✉ Somlai Arthur u. 1, ☎ 84/315–048) offers horseback-riding lessons and trail rides. A one-hour ride costs approximately 1,200 Ft., as does a 25-minute lesson.

MOPEDS

No resort is a bona fide tourist town without moped rentals, and in Siófok they're available from the rental outfit set up in the parking lot on Kinizsi utca, in front of the main stand of hotels. Bicycles are also for rent here.

WATER SPORTS

Boating and other water-sports equipment is available for hire at the **Water Sports Center,** on the waterfront on Vitorlás utca 10 (☎ 84/311–161). Kayaks and canoes cost about 200 Ft. per hour, sailboats around 2,000 Ft.–4,500 Ft. per hour.

TENNIS

The **Sport Centrum** (✉ Küszhegyi út, ☎ 84/314–523) has eight tennis courts as well as a handball court, sauna, and lest things are getting too athletic, a bar.

Lake Balaton A to Z

Arriving and Departing

BY BUS

Buses headed for the Lake Balaton region depart from Budapest's Erzsebét tér station daily; contact **Volánbusz** (☎ 1/117–2318) for current schedules.

BY CAR

Highway E71 /M7 is the main artery between Budapest and Lake Balaton. M7 continues down the lake's southern shore to Siófok and towns farther west. E71 goes along the northern shore to Balatonfüred and lakeside towns southwest. The drive from Budapest to Siófok, for example, takes about an hour and a half, except on weekends, when traffic can be severe. From Budapest to Balatonfüred is about the same.

BY TRAIN

Daily express trains run from Budapest's Déli (South) Station to Siófok and Balatonfüred. The two-hour trips cost about $10 each way.

Getting Around

BY BOAT

The slowest but most scenic way to travel between Lake Balaton's major resorts is by ferry. Schedules for **MAHART** (☎ 1/118–1704), the national ferry company, are available from most of the tourist offices listed below.

Buses frequently link Lake Balaton's major resorts, but book ahead to avoid long waits. Buses leave from Erzsébet tér in Budapest and go to most towns along Balaton's northern and southern shores. Reservations can be made through the tourist offices IBUSZ (☞ Guided Tours, *below*) or Volánbusz (☎ 1/117–2318).

BY CAR
Road 71 runs along the northern shore; M7 covers the southern shore. Traffic can be heavy during summer weekends, and driving around the lake can be slow.

BY TRAIN
Trains from Budapest serve all the resorts on the northern shore; a separate line links resorts on the southern shore. An express train from Budapest takes just over two hours to reach Siófok or Balatonfüred. Be sure to book tickets well in advance in high season.

Contacts and Resources

EMERGENCIES
Police (☎ 07). **Ambulance** (☎ 04). **Fire** (☎ 05).

GUIDED TOURS
IBUSZ has several tours to Balaton from Budapest; inquire at the head office in Budapest (✉ V, Ferenciek tere 10, ☎ 118–6866). **Balatontourist and Siotours** (☞ Visitor Information, *below*) offer myriad packages. Tours more easily organized directly with the hotels in the Balaton area include boat trips to vineyards, folk-music evenings, and overnight trips to local inns.

MAHART (☎ 84/310–050) offers several boating tours and cruises on Lake Balaton. The **"Panorama Tour"** leaves Siófok Tuesday and Thursday at 9:30 AM and stops for guided sightseeing in Balatonfüred and Tihany. The total trip takes seven hours and is offered early July through August. The **"Sunset Tour"** is a 1½-hour cruise on the lake during which guests can sip a glass of champagne and nibble snacks while watching the sun sink. Departures are from Siófok early July through August, daily at 7:15 PM, except Monday. From Balatonfüred, you can board a ship for an all-day tour of the wine-growing area of Badacsony, including wine tastings, snacks, sightseeing, and lunch with live Gypsy music. This **"Wine Tasting Tour"** runs early July through August, Thursday at 9:30 AM. The **"Badacsony Tour"** is also a trip to Badacsony but it departs at 10:30 AM from Keszthely, on the same days as the tour from Balatonfüred, and returns at 4:30 PM.

OUTDOOR ACTIVITIES AND SPORTS
Fishing in Lake Balaton requires a permit; permits cost approximately 1,000 Ft. per day, 3,000 Ft. for a week. Most tourist offices sell them.

VISITOR INFORMATION
Two separate agencies provide information about the Balaton region: **Balatontourist** covers the northern shore; **Siótour,** the southern shore.

North Shore: Balatonfüred (✉ Blaha Lujza u. 5, ☎ 86/342–822 or 86/343–471). **Budapest** (✉ V, Váci u. 7, ☎ 1/267–2726, FAX 1/267–2727). **Héviz: Héviz Tourist** (✉ Rákóczi u. 4, ☎ 83/341–348). **Keszthely: Tourinform** (✉ Kossuth u. 28, ☎ FAX 83/314–144). **Tihany: Balatontourist** (✉ Kossuth u. 20, ☎ 87/448–519); **Tihany Tourist** (✉ Kossuth u. 11, ☎ 87/448–481). **Veszprém: Balatontourist** (✉ Kossuth Lajos u. 21, ☎ 88/429–630).

South Shore: Balatonboglár: Siótours (✉ Dózsa György u. 1, ☎ 85/350–665). **Balatonföldvár: Siótours** (✉ Széchenyi u. 9–11, ☎ 84/340–

099). **Balatonlelle: Siótours** (⊠ Szövetség u. 1, ☎ 85/451-145). **Balatonszemes: Siótours** (⊠ Vasútállomás [train station], ☎ FAX 84/360-057).
Balatonszárszó: Siótours (⊠ Vasútállomás [train station], ☎ FAX 84/362–
956). **Budapest: Siótours** (⊠ Klauzál tér 2–3, ☎ 1/312–6080). **Fonyód:
Siótours** (⊠ Ady Endre u. 2, ☎ 85/361–850 or 85/361–852). **Siófok:
Tourinform** (⊠ Fő u., at the Water Tower, ☎ 84/315–355, FAX 84/310–
117); **IBUSZ** (⊠ Fő u. 174, ☎ 84/311–066); **Siótours** (⊠ Szabadság
tér 6, ☎ 84/310–900, FAX 84/310–307).

NORTHERN HUNGARY

Northern Hungary stretches from the Danube Bend, north of Budapest, along the northeastern frontier with Slovakia as far west as Sá-
toraljaújhely. It is a clearly defined area, marked by several mountain
ranges of no great height but of considerable scenic beauty. Most of
the peaks reach 3,000 feet and are thickly wooded almost to their summit. Oak, beech, and ash are the main forest trees, with comparatively
few patches of pine and fir. Naturalists, botanists, geologists, ethnog-
raphers, and folklorists find much of interest in the hills. Grottoes and
caves abound, as well as thermal baths. In the state game reserves, herds
of deer and wild boar roam freely, and eagles and the very rare red-
footed falcon are not uncommon sights.

Historically, the valleys of northern Hungary have always been of
considerable strategic importance, as they provided the only access to
the Carpathian Mountains. **Eger,** renowned throughout Hungarian history as one of the guardians of these strategic routes, retains its splendor, with many ruins picturesquely dotting the surrounding hilltops.
The **Mátra Mountains,** less than 90 kilometers (55 miles) from Budapest,
provide opportunities for year-round recreation and are the center for
winter sports. Last but not least, this is one of the great wine-growing
districts of Hungary, with Gyöngyös and Eger contributing the "Magyar nectar" and Tokaj producing the "wine of kings."

*Numbers in the margin correspond to numbers on the Northern Hun-
gary and the Great Plain map.*

Hollókő

★   *100 km (62 mi) northeast of Budapest.*

This tiny mountain village close to the Slovakian border was added to
the UNESCO list of World Cultural Heritage Sites in 1988 to help preserve its unique medieval structure and age-old *Palóc* (ethnographic
group indigenous to northern Hungary) cultural and handcrafting traditions still practiced today by the village's 400 inhabitants. The most
famous of these traditions are those practiced during Easter, when the
villagers dress in colorful embroidered costumes. UNESCO's distinction has brought arguably positive and negative elements to Hollókő.
The small village has become a popular day-trip tourist destination and
has adapted somewhat to that role; for example, the villagers agree to
dress in traditional costume on days when bus tours come through.

But Hollókő is authentically enchanting: Old whitewashed houses with
hand-carved wooden verandas and awnings cluster together on narrow
cobblestone pathways; directly above them loom the hilltop ruins (now
being restored) of a 13th-century castle, behind which blackberry bushes
are laden with sweet fruit in summer. It's a wonderful place to spend a
few hours strolling, peeking in at artisans carving wooden objects or
embroidering, and breathing in the mountain air.

277

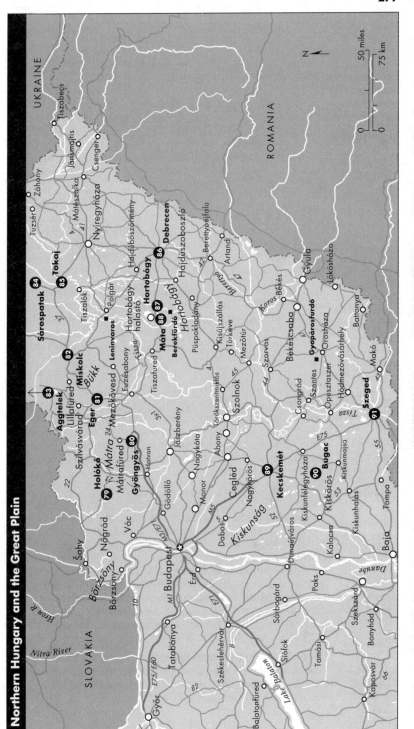

Northern Hungary and the Great Plain

Dining

$ ✕ **Muskátli Vendéglő.** Named for the bright red and pink flowers lining its windowsills, the Geranium Restaurant is a cozy little eatery on Hollókő's main street, with indoor and garden seating. Specialties include *Palócgulyás,* a rich local goulash thick with chunks of pork and beans, and *Nógrádi palócpecsenye,* pork cutlets smothered in mustard-garlic sauce. On a hot summer day, a cold fruit soup is deliciously refreshing. ⊠ *Kossuth út 61,* ☎ *32/378–062. No credit cards.*

Gyöngyös

⑧⓪ *40 km (25 mi) southeast of Hollókő, 75 km (46 mi) northeast of Budapest.*

The city of Gyöngyös, famous for its excellent wines (don't pass up the chance to sample the *Debrői hárslevelű,* a magnificent white wine produced in a nearby village), lies at the base of the volcanic Mátra mountain range, Hungary's best-developed mountain vacation area. Early in the 1960s huge lignite deposits were discovered, and the large-scale mines and power stations established since then have changed the character of the entire region.

Although it doesn't have an abundance of sights and reasons to linger in it's own right, Gyöngyös serves as the gateway to the Mátras and is a good starting point for visiting the many beautiful resorts that lie just north of it, popular in summer for their invigorating mountain air and in winter for their ski trails. The best known is Mátrafüred, at 1,300 feet, which can be reached by narrow-gauge railway from Gyöngyös. Just a few kilometers from Mátrafüred is Kékestető, the highest point in Hungary (1,014 meters).

Among the chief sights of the town is the 14th-century Church of **Szent Bertalan** (St. Bartholomew), on Fő tér. It is Hungary's largest Gothic church; unfortunately, because of ongoing restoration, it is often closed during hours it is designated to be open (the best times for a visit, it seems, are in the morning and for Sunday services). ⊠ *Fő tér.* 🎟 *Free.* ☉ *Daily 7–noon and 1:30–5.*

The **Mátra Múzeum** (Mátra Museum), housed in a handsome neoclassical mansion built in 1723, provides naturalistic preparation for excursions into the Mátras with its extensive exhibits on the flora and fauna of the region, as well as geological and historical displays. Amid recorded sounds of indigenous birdsongs, you can examine deer, eagles, and other fauna you may encounter, as well as those you'll be luckier to avoid, like the sharp-tusked wild boar. Also on display is "Bruno," the hulking 1- to 2-million-year-old skeleton of a young mammoth found in the northern Mátra. Unless you're a fan of dank cellars filled with snakes and bugs and their accompanying odors, avoid the "Mikro-varium" exhibit downstairs. ⊠ *Kossuth Lajos u. 40,* ☎ *37/311–447.* 🎟 *100 Ft.* ☉ *Mar.–Oct., Tues.–Sun. 9–5; Nov.–Feb., Tues.–Sun. 10–2.*

Outdoor Activities and Sports

Make a stop at the Eger Tourist office (☞ Visitor Information *in* Northern Hungary A to Z, *below*) for maps, books, and advice about the area's rich outdoor offerings.

BICYCLING

Avar Komplex (⊠ Béke út 4, Mátrafüred, ☎ 06–20/410–102) is a good source for information and equipment and organizes custom-designed bicycle tours for all abilities and cardiovascular states. From mid-May through the end of the summer they also hold regular Saturday afternoon trips (meeting at 3 PM) open to all; call ahead to confirm details.

Mountain bike rentals run approximately 150 Ft. per hour, and are available for longer-term rentals (at lower rates) as well.

HIKING

Mátrafüred and Mátraháza are popular starting points for hikes up Kékestető (1,014 meters), Hungary's highest peak. Views from the TV and lookout tower are phenomenal. Don't expect to find yourself alone with only the rushing wind at the top of the peak; it's actually somewhat developed, with a couple of hotels where you can spend a night dozing in the highest bed in Hungary.

HORSEBACK RIDING

The **Horus Riding Center** (✉ Kazinczy út 1, ☎ 37/315–523) offers guided trail rides for groups of six or more (1,500 Ft. per person), riding in outdoor and indoor rings (800 Ft.–1,200 Ft. per hour), riding lessons (1,600 Ft. per hour), and carriage rides (5,000 Ft. per hour). It is open Tuesday–Sunday 8–4.

En Route Route 24 is the scenic route between Gyöngyös and Eger, climbing and twisting through the Mátras, with several good lookout points with lovely views. You can pause in Sirok to snap a photo of its castle ruins, piled high on a hill looming over the village.

Eger

★ ⑧ *40 km (25 mi) east of Gyöngyös.*

With vineyard surroundings and more than 175 of Hungary's historic monuments—a figure surpassed only by Budapest and Sopron—the picture-book baroque city of Eger is ripe for exploration. Lying in a fertile valley between the Mátra Mountains and their eastern neighbor, the Bükk range, Eger bears witness to much history, heartbreak, and glory. It was settled quite early in the Hungarian conquest of the land, and it was one of five bishoprics created by King Stephen I when he Christianized the country almost a millennium ago.

In 1552 the city was attacked by the Turks, but the commander, István Dobó, and fewer than 2,000 men and women held out for 38 days against 80,000 Turkish soldiers and drove them away. One of Hungary's great legends tells of the women of Eger pouring hot pitch onto the heads of the Turks as they attempted to scale the castle walls (the event is depicted in a famous painting now in the National Gallery in Budapest). Despite such heroism, however, Eger fell to the Turks in 1596 and became one of the most important northern outposts of Muslim power until its reconquest in 1687.

Today, Eger's cobblestone streets are ripe for strolling and sightseeing, lined with restored baroque and rococo buildings. Wherever you wander, make a point of peeking into open courtyards, where you're likely to happen upon a pretty wrought-iron gate and other otherwise hidden architectural gems.

The grand neoclassical **Bazilika** (basilica), the second-largest cathedral in Hungary, was built in the center of town early in the 19th century. It is approached by a stunning stairway flanked by statues of saints Stephen, László, Peter, and Paul—the work of the 19th-century Italian sculptor Marco Casagrande, who also carved 22 biblical reliefs inside and outside the building. From June through August, organ recitals are given Monday through Saturday at 11:30 AM and Sunday at 12:45 PM. ✉ *Eszterházy tér,* ☎ *36/316–592.* 🎟 *Free.* ☉ *Daily 6 AM–7 PM (during masses, wait until the service is over before looking around).*

The square block of a baroque building opposite the basilica is a former **lyceum,** now the Eszterházy Teacher Training College. The lyceum boasts a handsome library with a fine trompe-l'oeil ceiling fresco that presents an intoxicating illusion of depth. High up in the structure's six-story observatory, built in 1776 and now a museum, are a horizontal sundial with a tiny gold cannon, which, when filled with gunpowder, used to explode at exactly high noon. Also, the noonday sun, shining through a tiny aperture, makes a palm-size silvery spot on the meridian line on the marble floor. Climb higher to the "Specula Periscope" grand finale: being shut in a darkened room with a man who manipulates three rods of a periscope—in operation since 1776—to project panoramic views of Eger onto a round table. Children squeal with delight as real people and cars hurry and scurry across the table like hyperactive Legos. ⊠ *Eszterházy tér 1,* ☎ *36/410–466, ext. 71.* 🎟 *120 Ft.* ☉ *Mid-Mar.–mid-Dec., Tues.–Fri. 9–1:30, weekends 9:30–12:30.*

Eger's rococo **Cistercian Church,** closed for many years, has been reclaimed by the order and can be visited during mass on Sundays (held at 7, 8, and 10 AM and 7 PM); other times it can be viewed through a locked gate. The church was built during the first half of the 18th century. Its main altar (1770) is dominated by a splendid statue of St. Francis Borgia kneeling beneath Christ on the cross; surrounding stuccowork depicts sacrifices by Abraham and Moses. ⊠ *Széchenyi u. 15,* ☎ *36/316–592.* 🎟 *Free.* ☉ *Tues.–Sat. 9:30–12:30 and 2:30–5:30, Sun. 7–7 (during masses, it's best to wait until the service is over before looking around).*

NEED A BREAK?	On Eger's central pedestrian street, the **Dobos Cukrászda** (⊠ Széchenyi u. 6, ☎ 36/413–335) is a great spot to revive wearied sightseers with the house specialty, *Dobos Bomba* (chocolate-covered cake), or another fresh confection.

On a hilltop almost a kilometer away from the end of Széchenyi utca, is the light and lovely, dove-grey **Ráctemplom** (Serbian Orthodox Church), which contains more than 100 icon paintings on wood that look as if they were fashioned from gold and marble. From the graveyard you can enjoy a fine view of Eger. ⊠ *Vitkovits u. 30, no phone.* 🎟 *50 Ft.* ☉ *Tues.–Sun. 10–noon and 2–4.*

The **Provost's House,** on picturesque Kossuth Lajos utca, is a small rococo palace still considered one of Hungary's finest mansions despite abuse by the Red Army (soldiers ruined several frescoes by heating the building with oil). Those in the octagonal hall upstairs, as well as the hall's stuccowork, have been restored at great cost. The wrought-iron balcony outside is the work of German artist Henrik Fazola. The Provost's House now serves as European headquarters of the International Committee of Historic Towns (ICOMOS) and is, alas, not open regularly to the public. ⊠ *Kossuth Lajos u. 4.*

During a brief stay in Eger (1758–61), German artist Henrik Fazola graced many buildings with his work, but none so exquisitely as the multilevel, mirror-image twin gates to the **Megye Ház** (County Council Hall). Sent to Paris in 1889 for the international exposition, the gates won a gold medal 130 years after their creation. On the wall to the right of the entrance, note the sign that indicates the level of floodwaters during the flooding of the Eger stream on August 31, 1878. In fact, if you stay alert, you will see similar signs throughout this area of the city. Inside the Megye Ház is a museum with exhibits about Eger and Heves County in the 18th and 19th centuries. ⊠ *Kossuth Lajos u. 9,* ☎ *36/312–744.* 🎟 *50 Ft. (grounds entrance), 160 Ft. (including museum).* ☉ *Apr.–Oct., Tues.–Sun. 9–5.*

Your passport around the world.

- Worldwide access
- Operators who speak your language
- Monthly itemized billing

Use your MCI Card® and these access numbers for an easy way to call when traveling worldwide.

MCI ★ Calling Card

415 555 1234 2244
J.D. SMITH

Austria (CC)♦†	022-903-012
Belarus	
From Gomel and Mogilev regions	8-10-800-103
From all other localities	8-800-103
Belgium (CC)♦†	0800-10012
Bulgaria	00800-0001
Croatia (CC)★	99-385-0112
Czech Republic (CC)♦	00-42-000112
Denmark (CC)♦†	8001-0022
Finland (CC)♦†	9800-102-80
France (CC)♦†	0800-99-0019
Germany (CC)†	0130-0012
Greece (CC)♦†	00-800-1211
Hungary (CC)♦	00▼800-01411
Iceland (CC)♦†	800-9002
Ireland (CC)†	1-800-55-1001
Italy (CC)♦†	172-1022
Kazakhstan (CC)	1-800-131-4321
Liechtenstein (CC)♦	155-0222
Luxembourg†	0800-0112
Monaco (CC)♦	800-90-19

Netherlands (CC)♦†	06-022-91-22
Norway (CC)♦†	800-19912
Poland (CC)✛†	00-800-111-21-22
Portugal (CC)✛†	05-017-1234
Romania (CC)✛	01-800-1800
Russia (CC)✛♦	747-3322
For a Russian-speaking operator	747-3320
San Marino (CC)♦	172-1022
Slovak Republic (CC)	00-42-000112
Slovenia	080-8808
Spain (CC)†	900-99-0014
Sweden (CC)♦†	020-795-922
Switzerland (CC)♦†	155-0222
Turkey (CC)♦†	00-8001-1177
Ukraine (CC)✛	8▼10-013
United Kingdom (CC)†	
To call to the U.S. using BT■	0800-89-0222
To call to the U.S. using Mercury■	0500-89-0222
Vatican City (CC)†	172-1022

To sign up for the MCI Card, dial the access number of the country you are in and ask to speak with a customer service representative.

http://www.mci.com

(CC) Country-to-country calling available. May not be available to/from all international locations. (Canada, Puerto Rico, and U.S. Virgin Islands are considered Domestic Access locations.) ♦ Public phones may require deposit of coin or phone card for dial tone. † Automation available from most locations. ★ Not available from public pay phones. ▼ Wait for second dial tone. ✛ Limited availability. ■ International communications carrier.

It helps to be pushy in airports.

Introducing the revolutionary new TransPorter™ from American Tourister®. It's the first suitcase you can push around without a fight. TransPorter's™ exclusive four-wheel design lets you push it in front of you with almost no effort–the wheels take the weight. Or pull it on two wheels if you choose. You can even stack on other bags and use it like a luggage cart.

Stable 4-wheel design.

TransPorter™ is designed like a dresser, with built-in shelves to organize your belongings. Or collapse the shelves and pack it like a traditional suitcase. Inside, there's a suiter feature to help keep suits and dresses from wrinkling. When push comes to shove, you can't beat a TransPorter™. For more information on how you can be this pushy, call 1-800-542-1300.

Shelves collapse on command.

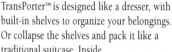

Making travel less primitive.®

©1996 American Tourister®

Eger Vár (Eger Castle), now a haunting ruin, was built after the devastating Tartar invasion of 1241–42; when Béla IV returned from exile in Italy, he ordered the erection of mighty fortresses like those he had seen in the west. Within the castle walls, an imposing Romanesque cathedral was built and then during the 15th century, rebuilt in Gothic style; today only its foundations remain. Inside the foundation area, a statue of Szent István (St. Stephen), erected in 1900, looks out benignly over the city. Nearby are catacombs—which you sometimes can tour with an English-speaking guide, so be sure to ask for one—that were built in the second half of the 16th century by Italian engineers. By racing back and forth through this labyrinth of underground tunnels and appearing at various ends of the castle, the hundreds of defenders tricked the attacking Turks into thinking there were thousands of them. The Gothic-style **Püspök Ház** (Bishop's House) contains the castle history museum and, in the basement, a numismatic museum where coins can be minted and certified (in English). The coins are of various exotic types, including Turkish. A prison museum is near the main entrance. English-speaking guides are usually available at the castle ticket booth; tours cost roughly 100 Ft. ⊠ *Dózsa György tér,* ☎ *36/312–744.* ◩ *Castle 50 Ft., museums (including general castle admission) 160 Ft.* ⊙ *Castle grounds daily 8–8; museums Apr.–Sept., Tues.–Sun. 9–5 (catacombs and prison museum remain open on Mon. 9–5).*

Downtown, picturesque **Dobó tér** is marked by two intensely animated statues produced early in this century by a father-and-son team. *Dobó the Defender* is by Alajos Stróbl; the sculpture of a Magyar battling two Turks, by Stróbl's son, Zsigmond Kisfaludi-Stróbl. Their works flank the Minorite church, which with its twin spires and finely carved pulpit, pews, and organ loft, is considered one of the best baroque churches in Central Europe. *Church:* ◩ *Free.* ⊙ *Daily 10–5.*

A bridge over the Eger stream—it's too small to be classified as a river— leads to an early 17th-century Turkish **minaret,** from the top of which Muslims were called to prayer; this is the northernmost surviving Turkish building in Europe. The minaret is 40 yards high and has 97 steps that lead to an observation platform. ⊠ *Torony u.,* ☎ *36/410–233 (Hotel Minaret).* ◩ *30 Ft.* ⊙ *Apr.–Sept. (or later, weather permitting), daily 9–5 or 6.*

Eger wine is renowned beyond Hungary. The best-known variety is *Egri Bikavér* (Bull's Blood of Eger), a full-bodied red wine. Other outstanding vintages are the *Medoc Noir,* a dark red dessert wine; *Leányka,* a delightful dry white; and the sweeter white *Muskotály.* The place to sample them is the **Szépasszony-völgy,** a vineyard area within Eger's city limits. Some 250 small wine cellars (some of them literally holes-in-the-wall and most of them now private) stand open and inviting in the warm weather, and a few are there in winter, too. You may be given a tour of the cellar, and wines will be tapped from the barrel into your glass by the vintner himself at the tiniest cost (but it's prudent to inquire politely how much it will cost before imbibing). For a huge meal lubricated by wine tastings, try **Ködmön Csárda** (⊠ Szépasszony-völgy u., ☎ 36/313–172), a touristy but atmospheric cellar restaurant at the main entrance to the valley.

Dining and Lodging

$$ ✕ **Fehér Szarvas.** The name of this sleekly paneled rustic cellar adjoining the Park Hotel means "white stag," and game is the uncontested specialty of the house: sliced fillet of venison in a mustard-cream sauce with potato croquettes; venison fillet served in a pan sizzling with chicken liver, sausage, and herb butter; leg of wild boar in a red-wine sauce of mushrooms and bacon. The food is rich and often delicately seasoned.

The skulls and skins hanging from rafters and walls make the inn look like Archduke Franz Ferdinand's trophy room. Live music is sometimes featured in the evenings. ⊠ *Klapka György u. 8,* ☎ *36/411–129. AE, DC, MC, V. No lunch.*

$$ **✕ Talizmán.** In a rustic arched basement room a few doors away from ★ Eger's castle gate, this is one of the most popular restaurants in the region (many people make the trip from Budapest just to eat here). Service is excellent and the menu, in English and German, features *legényfogó leves* (wedding soup or, literally, "catcher of young men"). Made with meat, vegetables, cream, and liver, this stew is one of the lures that young Hungarian girls have used for centuries to attract potential husbands. A less poetic but equally exotic offering is the cabbage with goose legs. ⊠ *Kossuth Lajos u. 19,* ☎ *36/410–883. Reservations essential. AE, V. Closed 1st wk in Jan.*

$ **✕ HBH Bajor Sörház.** Although designed to look like a Bavarian beer tavern, this place does not reek of hops or smoke. It is, rather, an elegant family restaurant decorated with sepia photos of old Eger. Speciálties include a tart oxtail soup, served family style in a silver tureen; and the Beer Drinker's Delight—a pork cutlet stuffed with brains and baked in a pastry crust. Both go well with the Munich Hofbräuhaus beer, brewed on the premises, that gives the house its initials. ⊠ *Bajcsy Zsilinszky u. 19 (on Dobó tér),* ☎ *36/316–312. AE, MC, V.*

$$$ **🏨 Hotel Eger-Park.** Two very different hotels share the same phone num- ★ ber and a connecting passageway but have separate addresses around the corner from each other and seem a century apart. The Park is an old-fashioned grand hotel, very genteel and with spacious rooms, though it usually closes from November through March. The Eger, built in 1982, looks like a monstrous honeycomb from the outside, but is more tastefully and imaginatively modern inside and fully equipped year-round. Guests are free to use the facilities of both hotels. ⊠ *Park: Klapka György u. 8, H-3300 Eger,* ☎ *36/413–233,* 📠 *36/413–213. Eger: Szálloda u. 1–3, H-3300 Eger,* ☎ *36/413–114. 159 rooms with bath, 6 suites. 3 restaurants, 2 bars (1 with beer, bowling, and billiards), pool, sauna, solarium, 2 tennis courts, health club, laundry services, meeting rooms. AE, DC, MC, V.*

$$ **🏨 Hotel Senator Ház.** This quaint little inn sits on Eger's main square ★ in a lovely 18th-century town house. Rooms are bright and clean, decorated in pale tans and whites, and come equipped with large-hotel amenities, such as hair dryers, bathtubs, and minibars. The elegant miniature lobby, furnished with leather chairs, an antique writing desk, and various wooden antiques, feels like a cozy, elegant study. ⊠ *Dobó tér 11, H-3300 Eger,* ☎ *36/320–466. 11 rooms with bath. Restaurant. AE, DC, MC, V.*

$$ **🏨 Minaret.** This quaint hotel built in 1989 stands opposite the 17th-century Turkish tower in an old quarter of town, where it blends in as though it's been here forever. Rooms are nothing special, with dark-brown basic furnishings and brown-and-gray industrial carpeting, but the location and price (at the low end of this category) are excellent and the atmosphere, friendly and informal. The addition of an outdoor pool is planned to be completed in 1997. ⊠ *Harangöntő u. 3–5, H-3300 Eger,* ☎ *36/410–233, 36/410–473, or 36/410–020;* 📠 *36/410– 713. 38 rooms with shower. Restaurant. AE, DC, MC, V.*

$ **🏨 Garten Panzió.** Named after the profusion of blooming lilacs, geraniums, acacias, and other flora thriving here, this informal, family-run pension sits at the top of a quiet, rural hill, a 10-minute walk from Eger's main square. Rooms here are clean and cozy and brightened with fresh flowers and live plants; all have minifridges but no TVs or telephones. The suite, with a cozy eat-in kitchen, is great for families. The smiling owners, Olga and Sanyi, are happy to help plan visits to nearby wine cellars or walks in the surrounding countryside. They can also arrange tennis at the neighboring courts. ⊠ *Legányi u. 6, H-3300 Eger,* ☎ *36/320–371. 6 rooms with bath, 1 suite. Breakfast room. No credit cards.*

Nightlife and the Arts
Old Jack's Pub (⊠ Rákóczi út 28, ☎ 36/425–050) is a popular English-style pub just outside the center of town.

From mid-May to mid-September, 30-minute **organ concerts** are held in Eger's grand basilica Monday through Saturday at 11:30 AM and Sunday at 12:45 PM. Admission is 150 Ft. and is paid at the door. For more information, contact the main parish (☎ 36/316–592) or Tourinform (☎ 36/321–807). All summer long (June to mid-September), live **bands** warm up the summer evenings and play for free out on Kis Dobó tér, part of Eger's main square, nightly from 7–10 PM. The **Agria Art Festival** spans the end of June through mid-August, featuring theater performances and concerts of musical genres from Renaissance to jazz to laser karaoke. Performances are held several times a week, usually in the lovely inner courtyard of the Franciscan Church. Every summer during the first two weeks of July, **Celebration Weeks in Baroque Eger** is held, a cultural festival offering classical concerts, dance programs, and more in Eger's picturesque venues and streets and squares. In early September, the three- to four-day **Eger Harvest Festival** celebrates the grape harvest with a traditional harvest parade through the town center, ample wine tastings in the main squares, appearances by the crowned Wine Queen, an outdoor Harvest Ball on Dobó tér, and more.

Outdoor Activities and Sports
BICYCLING
The forested hills of the Bükk National Park around the village of Szilvásvárad, north of Eger, comprise some of the country's most popular mountain-biking terrain. Rentals, maps, route advice, and tour guides are available at Csaba Tarnai's **Mountain Bike Kölcsönző** (⊠ Szalajkavölgy út, at entrance to Bükk National Park in Szilvásvárad–Szalajka Valley, ☎ 60/352–695).

HIKING
Bükk National Park, just north of Eger, has plenty of well-marked, frequently trodden trails. The most popular excursions begin in the village of Szilvásvárad. Tourinform (☞ Visitor Information *in* Northern Hungary A to Z, *below*) can give you a hiking map and suggest routes according to your level of energy and how much time you have.

HORSEBACK RIDING
A famous breeding center of the prized white Lipizzaner horses since the late 15th century, the village of Szilvásvárad (☞ Off the Beaten Path, *below*) is the center of the region's horse culture. If you'd like to do some riding, contact **Kovács Péter Lovardája** (Peter Kovács's Stable; ⊠ Egri út 62, Szilvásvárad, ☎ 36/355–343). In Eger, the stables at the **Mátyus Udvarház** (⊠ Off Noszvaji út, ☎ 36/312–804) can accommodate your every equestrian need. Hourly rates in the area run around 1,000 Ft. for riding with a lunge line, 1,500 Ft. for taking the reins into your own hands.

SWIMMING
Eger's **Strandfürdő** (open-air baths; ⊠ Petőfi Sándor tér 2, ☎ 36/412–202) are set in a vast park in the center of town. You can pick where to plunge from among six pools of varying sizes, temperatures, and curative powers.

OFF THE
BEATEN PATH

SZILVÁSVÁRAD – About 25 kilometers (16 miles) from Eger up into the Bükk Mountains brings you to this picturesque village, one of Hungary's most important equestrian centers. For over 500 years, the famous elegant white Lipizzaner breed of horses has been bred here, and every year on a weekend in early September they prance and pose in the **Lipicai Lovasfesztivál,** an international carriage-driving competition held in the equestrian stadium. At other times, you can admire them grazing in the village fields and also familiarize yourself with their proud history at the **Lipicai Múzeum** (Lipizzaner Museum). Szilvásvárad is also a popular base from which to take advantage of the excellent hiking and biking opportunities through the surrounding gentle green hills of Bükk National Park (☞ Outdoor Activities and Sports, *above*). *Lipicai Múzeum:* ⊠ Park u. 8, ☎ 36/355–155. ☜ 40 Ft. ☉ *Tues.–Sun. 9–noon and 1–5.*

Miskolc

⊗ *63 km (39 mi) northeast of Eger.*

East of the Bükk Mountains lies industrial Miskolc, the third-largest city (pop. 200,000) in Hungary. A sprawling, dirty city cluttered with factories and industrial plants (many of them now idle), Miskolc is often maligned as one of the country's least desirable places to visit. Yet it contains some interesting baroque buildings, as well as the medieval castle of Diósgyőr, clashing yet coexisting with the housing projects and traffic that surround it. And one of Miskolc's prime, unexpected assets is the beautiful countryside around the village. Traveling west toward Lillafüred (☞ Dining and Lodging, *below*), past behemoth factories and plants, it's hard not to be wary of just what sort of countryside lies ahead; but almost immediately after passing the LEAVING MISKOLC sign and just before despair settles in, the scenery changes dramatically: The tree-covered hills of the Bükk range rise and crowd together as the road curves up and around them.

The regal, ruined stone body of **Diósgyőr Castle** stands exposed in the midst of Miskolc's urban clamor, surrounded by congested traffic and cement-block housing projects, as if trapped in a land that was long taken over by an entirely new reality. It embodies the stark contrast between Hungary's ancient and modern industrial elements. Boasting four mighty towers, Diósgyőr is considered one of Hungary's most beautiful medieval castles. Built between the mid-13th and late 14th centuries, it was originally a retreat for King Louis I, of the Angevin dynasty, but was later adopted by the queens (the castle is also known as Queen's Castle). ⊠ *Vár u. 24,* ☎ *46/370–735.* ☜ *100 Ft.* ☉ *Call for hrs; closed Mon.*

Dining and Lodging

$$–$$$ ✕ 🏨 **Hotel Palota.** As you round the bend on the road from Miskolc, ★ the fairy-tale spire of this baroque palace's tower rises majestically from a fold in the hills. Built in 1930, the Palota was operated as a luxury hotel until World War II. In the 1940s, it was taken over by a trade union and in classic Communist style, was stripped of many of those elements deemed overly bourgeois: Fireplaces were sealed up and the swimming pool filled in. Still state-owned today, the Palota is again a popular hotel retreat and is slowly undergoing renovations to restore some of the elements that the trade union did away with. The lobby and numerous public rooms have a dark, venerable majesty, with soaring, ornately sculpted ceilings, rich woodwork, and epic frescoes. Some original decorations and furnishings are still here, including burgundy-velvet wallpaper, crystal chandeliers, and heavily carved wooden chairs.

Guest rooms are fairly simple, with low-key wood furnishings and lovely large windows with sheer curtains, most looking out onto the surrounding greenery. Rooms without private bathrooms are less recently renovated. The striking Mátthiás Restaurant is in a round, Gothic room with vaulted ceilings, heavy wood furnishings, and original colorful stained-glass windows depicting what were pre-Trianon Hungary's most important cities. It specializes in game from the Bükk Mountains and trout from the nearby stocked lake and has live traditional Hungarian music every evening. ✉ *Erzsébet sétány 1, H-3517 Miskolc Lillafüred,* ☎ *46/331–411,* FAX *46/379–273. 45 rooms with bath, 90 rooms with shared bath, 4 suites. Restaurant, bar, meeting rooms. AE, DC, MC, V.*

Aggtelek

83 *55 km (35 mi) north of Miskolc.*

One of the most extensive cave systems in Europe lies at Aggtelek, right on the Slovak border. Containing the largest stalactite system in Europe, the largest of the caves, the Baradla, is 24 kilometers (15 miles) long, extending under Slovakia; its stalactite and stalagmite formations are of extraordinary size—some more than 49 feet high. In one of the chambers of the cave is a 400-seat concert hall, where classical music is performed in mid-August. Here, you are treated to a light show accompanied by Bach's booming organ masterpiece, the Toccata in D Minor. When the lights are left off for a brief period, you experience the purest darkness there is, totally devoid of light; try holding your hand up to your face—no matter how hard you strain, you won't see it.

Additional caves are being discovered and opened to the public. There are three entrances: in Aggtelek, at Vörös-tó (Red Lake), and in the village of Jósvafő. Guided tours vary in length and difficulty, from the short, one-hour walks beginning at Aggtelek or Jósvafő, to the five- to eight-hour, 7-kilometer (4-mile) exploration for subterranean enthusiasts. Of the shorter tours, the medium-length (1½- to 2-hour) tour beginning at Vörös-tó is considered the best; the group congregates at Jósvafő and then takes a public bus (about 45 Ft.) en masse to the Vörös-tó entrance, then makes its way back to Jósvafő underground. Although tours are conducted in Hungarian, written English translations are available at the ticket offices. Requests for the long tour must be sent in writing to the National Park headquarters at least one month ahead of time so the unmaintained sections can be rigged with proper lighting.

The caves are open year-round—they maintain a constant temperature, regardless of the weather. Keep in mind that it's chilly and damp underground—bring a sweater or light jacket and wear shoes with good traction. ✉ *Directorate of Aggtelek National Park, Tengerszem oldal 1, H-3758 Jósvafő,* ☎ FAX *48/350–006,* FAX *48/343–073. 1-hr tours beginning at Aggtelek: mid-Mar.–Sept., daily at 10, 1, 3, and 5 (Oct.–mid-Mar., last tour is at 3);* 🎟 *270 Ft. 1-hr tours from Jósvafő: mid-Mar.–Sept., daily at noon and 5 (Oct.–mid-Mar last tour is at 1);* 🎟 *230 Ft. 1½- to 2-hr tours from Jósvafő: mid-Mar.–Sept., daily at 9, 1:30, and 2:45 (Oct.–mid-Sept., last tour is at 2:30);* 🎟 *320 Ft. Long tour (with 1-month prior written request) from Aggtelek: 1700 Ft. (minimum 5 adults or equivalent admission cost).*

Sárospatak

84 *80 km (50 mi) northeast of Miskolc.*

For hundreds of years, this northern town at the foot of the Zemplén Mountains thrived as the region's elite cultural and intellectual center, its numerous progressive schools and universities educating such famous national thinkers as statesman Lajos Kossuth and writer Zsigmond Móricz. Its former Calvinist College (currently a state-run school) was founded in 1531 and for many years had close links with Britain. In the 18th century, George II of England took a personal interest in the college, and for about 50 years education was conducted in both English and Hungarian. In 1616, Sárospatak's golden age began when its gorgeous castle became home to the famous Hungarian noble family, the Rákóczi, and was the scene of their unsuccessful plot to free Hungary from the Hapsburgs. Today, however, Sárospatak's reality is more that of an economically struggling eastern town, and it has noticeably fewer and lower-standard tourist facilities than its more western neighbors. Its rich, historic aura, however, remains in its picturesque castle and many fine medieval houses.

★ Poised on the bank of the Bodrog River, the part-Gothic, part-Renaissance, part-baroque **Sárospatak vár** (Sárospatak Castle) is one of Hungary's most beautiful castles—now excellently restored. Begun in the 11th century, it was constructed and added to over several centuries in various architectural styles. A six-lanced rose emblem, which signifies silence, marks the spot in the castle's northeast corner where the Rákóczi family conspired to incite a revolution against the Hapsburgs. The first, though unsuccessful, uprising was led by Ferenc Rákóczi I on April 9, 1670; in 1703, after his father's death, Ferenc Rákóczi II took up the sword against the Imperial army in a nine-year rebellion that was ultimately fruitless. You can spend a couple of hours exploring the grounds and visiting the castle museum, which houses an excellent collection of antique furniture from the 16th to 19th centuries, portraits of the Rákóczi family, and various weapons and antique clothing. ⊠ *Kádár Kata u. 21,* ☎ *47/311–083.* 🎫 *100 Ft.* ☻ *Tues.–Sun. 10–6.*

Dining and Lodging

$$ ✗🆃 **Hotel Bodrog.** Sárospatak's main hotel and restaurant is centrally located and adequately comfortable and clean, but is trapped in its charmless, 1980s Communist institutionality. Inside the drab cement-block exterior are rooms with simple, basic furnishings; green-gray carpeting and upholsteries; and televisions and minibars. The restaurant features an extensive selection of wines from nearby Tokaj and serves standard Hungarian fare. Fresh grilled trout from the Bodrog River is a good bet. Breakfast is not included in the rates. ⊠ *Rákóczi u. 58, H-3950 Sárospatak,* ☎ *47/311–744,* 📠 *47/311–527. 50 rooms with bath. Restaurant, massage, sauna, meeting rooms. AE, MC, V.*

$ ✗🆃 **Hotel Borostyán.** This small hotel housed in a medieval building just steps from the castle was a monastery established by Ferenc Rákóczi II in the late 17th century. With recently renovated rooms and far more personality than the Hotel Bodrog, the Borostyán is the better lodging option, but is often fully booked. In classic monastic style, rooms are on the small side, many with a small set of steps splitting them into two levels; furnishings are simple, with small beds and wood floors. The restaurant features grilled fish and standard Hungarian fare. Specialties include *Sárospataki cigánypecsenye,* garlicky pork cutlets topped with a sunny-side-up egg. ⊠ *Kádár Kata u. 28, H-3950 Sáropatak,* ☎ *47/312–611,* 📠 *47/311–551. 5 rooms with bath, 4 with shared toilet. Restaurant, sauna, solarium, exercise room. No credit cards.*

Nightlife and the Arts

In late July, the Sárospatak Cultural Center (⊠ Eötvös u. 6, ☎ 47/311–811) hosts a Dixieland and blues festival, featuring performances by bands from around the country. During the annual **Zempléni Művészeti**

Napok (Zemplén County Arts Days) in mid- to late August, well-known musicians perform classical concerts in the castle's courtyard. For information, contact the Sárospatak Cultural Center (✉ Eötvös u. 6, ☎ 47/311–811) or the IBUSZ office (☞ Visitor Information *in* Northern Hungary A to Z, *below*).

Tokaj

85 *54 km (33 mi) east of Miskolc.*

This enchanting little village is the center of one of Hungary's most famous wine regions. It is home of the legendary Aszú wine, a dessert wine made from grapes allowed to shrivel on the vine. Aszú is produced to varying degrees of sweetness, based on how many bushels of sweet grape paste made from these grapes are added to the wine essence, the already highly sweet juice first pressed from them; the scale goes from two *puttonyos* (bushels) to nectar-rich six puttonyos.

The region's famed wines, dubbed (allegedly by Louis XV) the "wine of kings and king of wines," are typically golden yellow with slightly brownish tints and an almost oily texture and have been admired outside Hungary since Polish merchants first became hooked in the Middle Ages. Swedish and French kings, Russian czars, and even popes have been regular imbibers over the centuries. In 1562, after a few sips of wine from the nearby village of Tállya, Pope Pius IV is said to have declared, "*Summum pontificem talia vina decent*" ("These wines are fit for a pope"). Other countries—France, Germany, and Russia included—have tried without success to produce the wine from Tokaj grapes; the secret apparently lies in the combination of volcanic soil and climate.

The surrounding countryside is beautiful, especially in October, when the grapes hang from the vines in thick clusters. Before or after descending into the wine cellars for some epic tasting, be sure to pause while the bells toll at the lovely baroque Roman Catholic church (1770) on the main square and wend your way along some of the narrow side streets winding up into the vineyard-covered hills: Views of the red-tile roofs and sloping vineyards are like sweet Aszú for the eyes.

If your eyes can still focus after a round of wine tasting, be sure to look up at the top of lampposts and chimneys, where giant white storks preside over the village from their big bushy nests. They usually return to their nests in late April or May after wintering in warmer climes.

The third floor of **Tokaj Museum,** housed in a late-18th-century house that was formerly the home of a Greek merchant, displays objects connected with the history of the wine's production. The first and second floors contain exhibits of ecclesiastical art and the history of the county, respectively. ✉ *Bethlen Gábor u. 7,* ☎ *47/352–636.* 💳 *100 Ft.* ☉ *Apr.–Oct., daily 10–5; Nov.–Mar., Wed.–Sun. 9–3.*

Tokaj's most famous wine cellar, the nearly 700-year-old **Rákóczi-pince** (Rákóczi Cellar), is also Europe's largest, comprising some 1½ kilometers (1 mile) of branching tunnels extending into the hills (today, about 400 meters are in use). Here you can sample Tokaj's famed wines and purchase bottles of your favorites for the road (all major credit cards are accepted). A standard cellar tour with a tasting of six different wines and some *pogácsa* (salty biscuits) costs around 650 Ft. ✉ *Kossuth tér 13,* ☎ *47/352–408.* ☉ *Mar.–Oct., daily 10–7 (July–Aug. until 8).*

The Várhelyi family offers wine tastings in the cool, damp cellar of their 16th-century house, called **Himesudvar.** Upon ascending from below, you can purchase attractively labeled bottles of your favorite wines and continue imbibing in their pleasant garden. A standard sampling of five different wines costs around 250 Ft. or 500 Ft., depending on how large a taste of each you want. ✉ *Bem út 2,* ☎ *47/352–416.* ☉ *Daily 9–9 (ring the bell if you can't find anyone).*

Dining and Lodging

$　✕ **Róna Étterem.** From goose liver to fresh carp, the kitchen of this popular restaurant serves up excellent hearty Hungarian specialties. The simple dining room is clean and pleasantly decorated with wood paneling, upholstered chairs, and original paintings by local artists. ✉ *Bethlen Gábor u. 19,* ☎ *47/352–116. No credit cards.*

$　✕🖩 **Hotel Tokaj.** What is possibly the weirdest looking building in the country houses Tokaj's main hotel. Giant red balls that look like clown's noses protrude from each boxy cement balcony under a rainbow-striped facade. Recently renovated rooms are simply furnished and adequately comfortable, and most have balconies. The large, popular restaurant features excellent fish specialties, including spicy *halászlé* (fish soup) served with a swirl of sour cream. ✉ *Rákóczi u. 5, H-3910 Tokaj,* ☎ *47/352–344,* ℻ *47/352–759. 30 rooms with bath, 12 with shared toilet. Restaurant, meeting rooms. MC, V.*

$　🖩 **Makk Marci Panzió.** Rooms in this family-run pension in the center of town are clean and cozy. Reserve well ahead of time—the seven rooms fill up quickly. Breakfast is served in the pizzeria downstairs. ✉ *Liget köz 1, H-3910 Tokaj,* ☎ ℻ *47/352–226. 7 rooms with bath. Restaurant. AE, MC.*

Nightlife and the Arts

Classical concerts by well-known artists are performed here during the **Zemplén Művészeti Napok** (Zemplén Art Days), a countywide classical music festival held annually in mid-August. For information, contact Tokaj Tours (☞ Visitor Information *in* Northern Hungary A to Z, *below*).

Naturally, Tokaj's best festival is the annual **Szüreti Hetek** (Harvest Weeks) from early September to early October, celebrating the autumn grape harvest with a parade, a street ball, folk-art markets, and a plethora of wine-tasting opportunities from the local vintners' stands set up on and around the main square. For information, contact Tokaj Tours (☞ Visitor Information *in* Northern Hungary A to Z, *below*).

Northern Hungary A to Z

Arriving and Departing

BY BUS
Most buses to northern Hungary depart from Budapest's Népstadion station.

BY CAR
Highway M3 is the main link between Budapest and northern Hungary.

BY TRAIN
Trains between Eger and Budapest run several times daily from Keleti Station. Trains run frequently all day between Budapest and Miskolc.

Getting Around

BY CAR
The M3 is the main highway cutting north to Slovakia. Secondary roads through the Mátra and Bükk mountains are windy but in good shape and wonderfully scenic.

Several daily trains connect Miskolc with Sacrospatak and Miskolc with Tokaj. Szilvásvárad and Eger are easily accessible from each other by frequent trains.

Contacts and Resources

VISITOR INFORMATION

Eger: Tourinform (⊠ Dobó tér 2, ☎ 36/321−807, FAX 36/321−304). **Gyöngyös: Egertourist/Mátratourist** (⊠ Hanisz tér 2, ☎ 37/311−565). **Sárospatak: IBUSZ** (⊠ Rákóczi u. 15, ☎ FAX 47/311−244). **Tokaj: Tokaj Tours** (⊠ Serház u. 1, ☎ FAX 47/352−259).

THE GREAT PLAIN

Hungary's Great Plain—the **Nagyalföld**—stretches south from Budapest to the borders of Croatia and Serbia and as far east as Ukraine and Romania. It covers an area of 51,800 square kilometers (20,000 square miles) and is what most people think of as the typical Hungarian landscape. Almost completely flat, it is the home of shepherds and their flocks and, above all, of splendid horses and the *csikós,* their riders. The plain has a wild, almost alien air; its sprawling villages consist mostly of one-story houses, though there are many large farms and up-to-date market gardens. The plain, which is divided into two almost equal parts by the Tisza River, also contains several of Hungary's most historic cities. However, even though the Great Plain preserves much from medieval times (largely because it was never occupied by the Turks), today it remains the least developed area of Hungary.

As you near the region, you will soon find yourself driving in a hypnotically straight line through the dream landscape of the Hortobágy, a grassy *puszta,* or prairie. Here, the land flattens out like a *palacsinta* (pancake), opening into vast stretches of dusty grassland interrupted only by stands of trees and distant thatched-roof *tanyák* (ranches), the only detectable movement the herds of *racka* sheep or cattle drifting lazily across the horizon guided by shepherds and their trusty *puli* herd dogs. Covering more than 250,000 acres, the Hortobágy became the first of Hungary's four national parks in 1973; its flora and fauna—including primeval breeds of longhorn cattle and *racka* sheep, prairie dogs, and *nóniusz* horses—are all under strict protection.

No matter how little time you have, you should make a point of taking in a traditional horse show, like the one offered by the Epona Riding Center in Máta. As touristy as the shows are, they are integral to the Great Plain experience, not to mention a lot of fun.

The region is not only grass and sand. Debrecen, Kecskemét, and Szeged are vibrant cities with beautiful sights of historic and architectural interest and exciting local culture.

Debrecen

86 *226 km (140 mi) east of Budapest.*

With a population approaching a quarter of a million, Debrecen is Hungary's second-largest city. Though it has considerably less clout than Budapest, Debrecen was Hungary's capital twice, albeit only briefly. In 1849 Lajos Kossuth declared Hungarian independence from the Hapsburgs; in 1944, the Red Army liberated Debrecen from the Nazis and made the city the provisional capital until Budapest was taken.

Debrecen has been inhabited since the Stone Age. It was already a sizable village by the end of the 12th century and, by the 14th, a privileged and important market town. It takes its name from a Slavonic term for "good earth," and indeed, much of the country's wheat, fruit, and vegetables, as well as meat, pork, and poultry, have been produced in this area for centuries.

Today, Debrecen is a vibrant, friendly city, with a sizable population of young people attending its several esteemed universities. Debrecen has only one trolley line (appropriately numbered 1), but it runs fast and frequently in a nearly straight line from the railroad station along Piac utca and out to the Nagyerdő (Great Forest), a giant city park. All in all, it's a good place to spend a day exploring the sights before heading out for a puszta experience.

For almost 500 years, Debrecen has been the stronghold of Hungarian Protestantism—its inhabitants have called it "the Calvinist Rome." In 1536 Calvinism began to replace Roman Catholicism in Debrecen, and two years later the **Református Kollégium** (Reformed College) was founded on what is now Kálvin tér (Calvin Square). Early in the 19th century the college's medieval building was replaced by a pillared structure that offers a vivid lesson in Hungarian religious and political history: The facade's busts honor prominent students and educators as well as Calvin and Zwingli. Inside, the main staircase is lined with frescoes of student life and significant moments in the college's history (all painted during the 1930s in honor of the school's 400th anniversary). At the top of the stairs is the **Oratory**, which has twice been the setting for provisional parliaments. In 1849 Kossuth first proclaimed Hungarian sovereignty here, and the new National Assembly's Chamber of Deputies met here during the last stages of the doomed revolution. Again in 1944, the Provisional National Assembly met in this somber room of dark, carved wood and whitewashed walls. Kossuth's pulpit and pew are marked, and two rare surviving flags of his revolution hang on the front wall. Some relics from 1944 line the back wall. Also worth seeing at the Reformed College are its **library,** which rotates exhibitions of illuminated manuscripts and rare Bibles; and two **museums**—one of the school's history, the other of religious art. ⊠ *Kálvin tér 16,* ☎ *52/414–744.* 🔲 *40 Ft.* ⏱ *Tues.–Sat. 9–5, Sun. 10–1.*

A **memorial garden** connects the Reformed College and the adjoining Great Church. Statues honor the local poet Mihály Csokonai Vitéz (1773–1805) and Prince István Bocskai of Transylvania. A column with a bronze ship commemorates 41 Hungarian Protestant pastors condemned because of their faith to be galley slaves in 1675, and the Dutch admiral, Michael de Ruyter, who rescued them near Naples.

Because the Oratory in the Reformed College was too small, Kossuth reread his declaration of independence by popular demand to a cheering public in 1849 in the twin-turreted **Nagytemplom** (Great Church), which holds 5,000 people. The church was built at the start of the 19th century in neoclassical style. As befits the austerity of Calvinism, the Great Church is devoid of decoration, but, with all the baroque throughout Hungary, you may welcome the contrast. ⊠ *Kálvin tér 16,* ☎ *52/327–017.* 🔲 *30 Ft.* ⏱ *Mid-Mar.–mid-Oct., daily 9–4; mid-Oct.–mid-Mar., daily 9–noon.*

NEED A
BREAK?
The café in the majestic **Grand Hotel Arany Bika** (⊠ Piac u. 11–15, ☎ 52/416–777) serves delicious, if somewhat expensive, coffees and pastries, daily 8 AM–10 PM. Its intimate wood-paneled nooks are ideal for a private or romantic snack.

The **Déri Múzeum,** behind the Reformed Church, was founded in the 1920s to house the art and antiquities of a wealthy Hungarian silk manufacturer living in Vienna. Its two exhibition floors are devoted to local history, archaeology, and weapons, as well as to Egyptian, Greek, Roman, Etruscan, and Far Eastern art. On the top floor are Hungarian and foreign fine art from the 15th to the 20th centuries, including the striking *Ecce Homo* by Mihály Munkácsy. The four statues in front of the museum were sculpted by Ferenc Medgyessy and won a Grand Prix at the international exposition in Paris seven years later. ⊠ *Déri tér 1,* ☎ *52/417–560, 577.* 🎫 *80 Ft. (100 Ft. for Munkácsy exhibit).* ⊙ *Apr.–Oct., Tues.–Sun. 10–6; Nov.–Mar., Tues.–Sun. 10–4.*

Debrecen's main artery, **Piac utca** (Market Street), which has reverted to its old name after decades as Red Army Way, runs from the Great Church to the railroad station. Passing its rows of shops and businesses and watching the people stream by on the sidewalk, you'll get a feel for Debrecen's calm urban feel, as well as pass several interesting sights. At the corner of Széchenyi utca, the **Kistemplom** (Small Church)—Debrecen's oldest surviving church, built in 1720—looks like a rococo chesspiece castle. It is known to the locals as the "truncated church" because, early in this century, its onion dome was blown down in a gale. Across the street from the Kistemplom is the **Megyeház** (county hall), built in 1911–12 in Transylvanian art nouveau, a darker and heavier version of the Paris, Munich, and Vienna versions. The ceramic sculptures and ornaments on the facade are of Zsolnay majolica. Inside, stairs and halls are illuminated by brass chandeliers that also spotlight the elegant symmetry and restraint of the decor. In the Council Hall upstairs, stained-glass windows by Károly Kernstock depict seven leaders of the tribes that conquered Hungary in 896. Note: If the church is locked, ask for the key from the caretakers. *Kistemplom:* ⊠ *Révész tér 2,* ☎ *52/343–872.* 🎫 *Free.* ⊙ *Daily 9 AM–11:30 AM. Megyeház:* ⊠ *Piac utca 54,* ☎ *52/417–777.* ⊙ *Mon.–Thurs. 8–3:30, Fri. 8–1.*

★ The **Tímárház** (Tanner House) opened in a restored 19th-century building in November 1995 as the center for preserving and maintaining the ancient folk-arts-and-crafts traditions of Hajdú-Bihár county. In its delightful, small complex you can wander into the artisans' workshops and watch them creating exquisite, prize-winning pieces—from impossibly fine, intricately handmade lacework to colorful hand-loomed wool rugs to straw and wicker baskets. The artisans—lauded as among the best in the country—are friendly and encourage visitors of all ages to try their hand at the crafts. The complex's showroom displays magnificent leather whips, heavy wool shepherd robes, and other examples of the county's traditional folk art created by the workshop artisans and others from the region. The embroidered textiles are some of the best you'll see anywhere. Although the displayed pieces are not for sale, the staff can help visitors contact the artists to custom-order something. A tiny gift shop, however, does sell a small selection of representative goods at great prices. ⊠ *Gál István u. 6, no phone.* 🎫 *50 Ft.* ⊙ *Tues.–Sun. 10–5.*

A 10-minute walk from the Megyeháza along Kossuth Lajos utca will take you to the **Vörös templom** (Red Church), as remarkable a Calvinist church as you'll find anywhere in Europe. Outwardly an undistinguished redbrick house of worship, built with the usual unadorned interior in 1886 and consecrated in 1888, the church celebrated its 50th anniversary at the zenith of the applied-arts movement in Hungary. Its worshipers commissioned artist Jenő Haranghy to paint the walls with biblical allegories using no human bodies or faces (just an occasional limb), but rather plenty of grapes, trees, and symbols. Giant, gaudy frescoes covering the walls, ceilings, niches, and crannies represent, among other subjects, a stag in fresh water, the Martin Luther anthem "A Mighty

Fortress Is Our God," and the 23rd Psalm (with a dozen sheep representing the Twelve Tribes of Israel and the Twelve Apostles). The Red
Church is open only during religious services (10 AM on Sunday and
religious holidays), but you might try for a private church visit from
the deaconage (☎ 52/325–736) on Kossuth Lajos utca. ⊠ *Méliusz tér.*

A restored 18th-century house, which has served variously as barracks,
city jail, and tenement, has been transformed into the **Ferenc Medgyessy
Memorial Museum.** Vibrant, confrontational, and comprehensive, the
exhibit juxtaposes sculptor Medgyessy's works with photomontages
showing where they originally stood or where copies of them now stand.
You may already be familiar with his work *Szoptató Anya* (Breast-feed-
ing Mother)—its design is featured on the 1,000-Ft. bill. ⊠ *Péterfia u.
28,* ☎ *52/413–572.* 🖾 *60 Ft.* ☉ *Apr.–Oct., Tues.–Sun. 10–6;
Nov.–Mar., Tues.–Sun. 10–4.*

Debrecen's one trolley line runs out to the **Nagyerdő** (Great Forest),
a huge city park with a zoo, sports stadium, swimming pools, artificial rowing lake, a 20-acre thermal spa, cemetery, crematorium, amusement park, restaurants, open-air theater, and the photogenic Kossuth
Lajos University, with a handsome neobaroque facade fronted by a large
pool and fountain around which six bronze nudes pose in the sun. The
university is one of the few in central Europe with a real campus, and
every summer, from mid-July to mid-August, it is the setting for a world-
renowned Hungarian-language program.

Dining and Lodging

$$ ✕ **Csokonai.** Across the street from the Asian-style Csokonai Theater,
★   in a cozy, candlelit brick cellar, is Debrecen's best restaurant (as evi-
dence, most of the guests are local residents). It is a consistent winner
of the gastronomic award *védnöki tábla,* a much-coveted honor. The
restaurant has a reputation among gourmands for its shellfish, roasted-
at-the-table skewered meats, frogs' legs, paprika crab, and many kinds
of fish. One of the owner's innovations is to let guests cook their own
meat *à la Willa-franca* (a hot old-fashioned iron that you press on the
meat to cook it). ⊠ *Kossuth u. 21,* ☎ *52/410–802. No credit cards.
No lunch Sun.*

$ ✕ **Sörpince a Flaskához.** When you walk into this completely unpre-
tentious and very popular neighborhood pub (literally, Beer Cellar at
the Flask), you may be surprised when you're presented with a nicely
bound menu in four languages. The English section proclaims the
virtues of "salty Hungarian pancake dishes," which include pancakes
stuffed with fish and "Beer Cellar pancakes baked from salty batter
stuffed with pork liver." They taste even better than they read, and so
do the pigs' feet, a house specialty; the sour-cream-based soups; and
delicate desserts. ⊠ *Miklós u. 2,* ☎ *52/314–582. AE, MC, V.*

$$$ ✕🏨 **Grand Hotel Arany Bika.** The Golden Bull is an art-nouveau clas-
★   sic erected in 1915 by a Renaissance man named Alfréd Hajós, who
won two Olympic gold medals for swimming in Athens in 1896 and
another gold medal for architecture in Paris in 1924. A new wing added
to this downtown landmark in 1966 serves to enhance the light and
spacious feeling of the original building, in which panels of stained glass
illuminate a solidly, but not stolidly, elegant foundation. The spacious
guest rooms in the old ("grand") section are simple and attractive, with
high ceilings, wood floors, and Oriental-style rugs; those in the newer,
less-expensive "tourist" wing are clean but a bit worn and institutional.
If the young staff at the front desk can sometimes be a little distracted,
the service and food, provided beneath the murals of the wide-open
puszta in the Hortobágy dining room, are impeccable. Try the local

specialty, *töltöttkáposzta* (stuffed cabbage). ⊠ *Piac u. 11–15, H-4025 Debrecen,* ☎ *52/416–777,* FAX *52/421–834. 246 rooms with bath, 4 suites. 2 restaurants, bar, café, sauna, solarium, casino, business services, meeting rooms. AE, DC, MC, V.*

$$ 🏨 **Hotel Cívis.** Fronting on Debrecen's main square and backing onto a stylish shopping center of which it is a part, this hotel was built in 1989 as an apartment house composed of studio apartments and only later converted to a hotel (thus every suite contains a well-equipped kitchen). Many of the rooms are quiet, except for those facing the main street. The decor—inside and out—is uniformly brown; as if to reinforce the color scheme, sepia-toned photos of Debrecen in earlier times hang on many of the walls. ⊠ *Kávin tér 4, H-4026 Debrecen,* ☎ FAX *52/418–522. 60 rooms with bath, 4 suites. Restaurant, 2 bars, business services, meeting room. AE, DC, MC, V.*

$ ★ 🏨 **Centrum Panzió.** This cheery little inn is just down the street from the Great Church. Its smiling, friendly owners, Csilla and István, keep the entire place sparkling and running smoothly all year round for their mostly foreign guests. Guest rooms are in separate small buildings in the flowering back garden. Most are in a charming, two-story yellow villa with a red-tile roof; slightly less elegant smaller rooms are in cozy, shellacked log cabins. All rooms are immaculately neat, with contemporary furnishings and well-stocked kitchenettes. Smoking is not permitted inside, only in the garden. ⊠ *Péterfia u. 37/A, H-4026 Debrecen,* ☎ FAX *52/416–193. 8 rooms with bath, 4 suites. Breakfast room. No credit cards.*

Nightlife and the Arts

Casino Debrecen (⊠ Piac u. 11–13, ☎ 52/416–777) in the Grand Hotel Aranybika can keep gamblers entertained with French and American roulette, blackjack, poker, and various slot machines. It's open every evening from 6 PM until 2 AM.

Debrecen's main cultural venues are the **Csokonai Theater** (⊠ Kossuth u. 10, ☎ 52/417–811) and **Kölcsey Cultural Center** (Hunyadi u. 1–3, ☎ 52/419–647).

Debrecen summers are filled with annual cultural festivals. Preceding the season, in mid to late March, the **Debrecen Tavaszi Fesztivál** (Debrecen Spring Festival) packs two weeks full of concerts, dance and theater performances, and special art exhibits. Main events are held at the Csokonai Theater, the Bartók Hall, and the Kölcsey Cultural Center. Contact the Kölcsey Cultural Center (⊠ Hunyadi u. 1–3, ☎ 52/419–647) or Tourinform for information. The biannual **Béla Bartók International Choral Festival,** held in 1996 and scheduled next for early July, 1998, is a competition for choirs from around the world, and provides choral-music aficionados with numerous full-scale concerts in the Bartók Hall. Jazz fans can hear local ensembles as well as groups from around Hungary and abroad during the **Debrecen Jazz Festival** in mid-July. One of city's favorite occasions is the **Flower Carnival** on St. Stephen's Day (August 20), the main event of which is a big, festive parade of flower-encrusted floats and carriages that make their way down Debrecen's main street along the tram line all the way to the Nagyerdő Stadium.

Outdoor Activities and Sports

The Nagyerdő (Great Forest) is bubbling with thermal baths and pools. One complex, the **Nagyerdei Lido** (⊠ Nagyerdei Strand; ☎ 52/346–000) boasts 5,000 square meters of water surface comprising eight pools, including a large pool for active swimming (most people soak idly in Hungary's public pools) and a wave pool.

A visit to the Great Plain is hardly complete without at least some contact with horses. There are myriad horseback-riding outfits outside Debrecen on the puszta. The **Epona Rider Village** in Máta (☞ Máta, *below*) is excellent, but Tourinform can recommend and help arrange other possibilities as well.

Hortobágy

87 *39 km (24 mi) west of Debrecen.*

The main visitor center for and gateway to the prairie is the little village of Hortobágy. Traveling from Debrecen, you'll reach this town just before you would cross the Hortobágy River. Before heading out to the prairie itself, you can take in Hortobágy's own sights: a prairie museum, its famous stone bridge, and the historic Hortobágyi Csárda (Hortobágy Inn).

Crossing the Hortobágy River is one of the puszta's famous symbols: the curving, white-stone **Nine-Arch Bridge.** It was built in the early 19th century and is the longest (548 feet) stone bridge in Hungary. A festival is held here every August, with folk-art markets, traditional horse shows, and other festivities. ☒ *On Route 33, at Petőfi tér.*

Built in 1699, the **Hortobágyi Csárda** (Hortobágy Inn) has been a regional institution for most of the last three centuries. Its construction is typical of the Great Plain: a long, white stone structure with arching windows, brown-wood details, and a stork nest—and occasionally storks—on its chimney. Though it no longer has guest rooms, its restaurant and service facilities have expanded vastly in recent years (☞ Dining and Lodging, *below*). ☒ *Petőfi tér 2,* ☎ *52/369–139. Closed Jan.*

For a glimpse into traditional Hortobágy pastoral life, visit the **Pásztormúzeum** (Shepherd Museum), across the street from the Hortobágyi Csárda. The lot in front of the museum is the tourism center for the area, bustling with visitors and local touristic enterprises. ☒ *Petőfi tér 1,* ☎ *52/369–119.* ☒ *80 Ft.* ☉ *May–Sept., Tues.–Sun. 9–5; Oct. and Apr., Tues.–Sun. 9–4; Nov.–Mar., Tues.–Sun. 9–4 (with prior notice only).*

OFF THE BEATEN PATH | **HORTOBÁGYHALASTÓ** – About 5 kilometers (3 miles) west of Hortobágy, Hortobágyhalastó (Great Plain Fish Pond) is a tiny, sleepy hamlet at the end of a dirt road where chickens strut about in small yards and the center of town is essentially an old phone booth. However, it's not the village but the 5,000-acre-pond nature reserve of the same name at its edge that draws dedicated bird-watchers from far and wide to look for some of the 150 species in residence. A nature walk around the entire reserve will take most of a day and requires advance permission from the Hortobágyi Nemzeti Park Igazgatóság (National Park's headquarters; ☒ Sumen u. 2, H-4024 Debrecen, ☎ 52/319–472 or 52/319–206, ☒ 52/310–645); contact Tourinform in Debrecen (☞ Visitor Information *in* the Great Plains A to Z, *below*) for assistance.

Dining

$ ✕ **Hortobágyi Csárda.** This historic roadside inn could get by on fame
★ and trappings alone—dried corn-and-paprika wreaths, flasks, saddles, and antlers hang from its rafters and walls—but its kitchen concentrates on food that rewards the wayfarer's palate. This is the place to order the regional specialty: *Hortobágyi húsospalacsinta* (Hortobágy pancakes), which are filled with beef and braised with a tomato-and-sour-cream sauce. The portions are small, so follow the pancakes with

bográcsgulyás—goulash soup puszta style, with meat and dumplings and the spicier components of the kitchen cabinet simmering in a copper pot. Veal *paprikash* and solid beef and lamb *pörkölt* (thick stews with paprika and sour cream) are also recommended, as are the cheese-curd or apricot-jam dessert pancakes. All this comes with Gypsy music at night (except in November and December). ⊠ *Petöfi tér 1,* ☎ *52/ 369–139. Reservations essential during annual horse show and bridge fair. AE, DC, MC, V. Closed Jan.*

Nightlife and the Arts

The **Hortobágyi Lovas Napok** (Hortobágy Horseman Days) is held every year on the first weekend in July next to the Nine-Arch Bridge, offering three days of traditional horse stunts and demonstrations, colorful folklore shows, riding contests, and other horsey festivities. The festivities also take place in neighboring Máta.

The three-day **Hortobágyi híd vásár** (Hortobágy Bridge Fair), held annually around August 20, brings horse shows, a folk-art fair, ox roasts, and festive crowds to the plot beneath the famous Nine-Arch Bridge.

Máta

88 *About 2 km (1 mi) from Hortobágy.*

The hamlet of **Máta** is home to the Epona Rider Village, with some 500 champion horses and award-winning riders, which over the last few years have made it one the region's most important equestrian centers. From around May through September there is a daily two-hour "Rangeman's Show." Groups of 16 can ride the prairie in covered wagons pulled by horses of the prize-winning nóniusz breed and driven by herders in blue shirts and skirts. You'll see herds of racka sheep with twisted horns, gray cattle, water buffalo, and wild boars, all tended by shepherds, cowherds, and swineherds dressed in distinctive costumes and aided by shaggy puli herd dogs and Komondor sheepdogs. At various stops along the route of this perambulatory minirodeo, csikós do stunts with the animals; the best involves five horses piloted by one man who stands straddling the last two. Inspired guests can even try a little (less risky) riding themselves with help from the csikós. The safari returns to Máta, where you can order an apricot brandy at the Nyerges Presszó (Saddled Espresso) and let it all soak in. In winter and in bad weather, indoor shows are organized. ⊠ *Hortobágy-Máta,* ☎ *52/369–020. Departures at 10, 2, and 4 (more frequently if demand warrants).* ▣ *Riding shows and wagon tours 1,300 Ft. Call ahead to inquire about arranging for an English-speaking guide.*

Dining and Lodging

$$$$ ✕▣ **Epona Rider Village.** This vast, luxury equestrian complex out on
★ the Great Plain opened in 1992 and has rapidly become one of Hungary's best and most imaginative resorts. The contemporary, puszta-style buildings house stables, family cottages, and special "rider houses," complete with private three-horse stables. The main building contains the standard rooms, all with balconies and attractive contemporary furnishings. Tennis courts, a swimming pool, and myriad horse-related activities provide ample entertainment in an area otherwise considered to be the middle of nowhere. Two restaurants serve regional specialties as well as standard Hungarian dishes. ⊠ *H-4071 Hortobágy-Máta,* ☎ *52/369–020 or 52/369–092,* 𝔽𝔸𝕏 *52/369–027. 54 rooms with bath. 2 restaurants, 2 bars, café, pool, massage, sauna, solarium, 2 tennis courts, exercise room, horseback riding, business services, meeting rooms. AE, DC, MC, V.*

Nightlife and the Arts

Equestrian fans will not want to miss the **Hortobágy International Horse Festival,** held here (and in neighboring Hortobágy) annually the first week of July, during which exciting show-jumping and carriage-driving competitions are held, as well as traditional horseback stunts by the csikós, folk-music and dance performances, and a folk-art fair.

Outdoor Activities and Sports

The **Epona Rider Village** (☞ *above*; ⊠ Hortobágy-Máta, ☎ 52/369–020) offers horseback riding lessons (800 Ft. beginner, 1,200 Ft. intermediate and advanced dressage) and guided rides out on the puszta (about 1,000 Ft. per hour) on their excellent horses.

Kecskemét

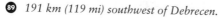 *191 km (119 mi) southwest of Debrecen.*

With a name roughly translating as "Goat Walk," this sprawling town smack in the middle of the country never fails to surprise unsuspecting first-time visitors with its elegant landmark buildings, interesting museums, and friendly, welcoming people. Its main square, Szabadság tér (Liberty Square) is marvelous, marred only by two faceless cement-block buildings, one of which houses the city's very own McDonald's (a true sign the city is not just a dusty prairie town anymore). Home of the elite Kodály Institute, where famous composer and pedagogue Zoltán Kodály's methods are taught, the city also maintains a fairly active cultural life.

The Kecskemét area, fruit center of the Great Plain, produces 25% of Hungary's fruit exports (apples, pears, sour cherries, apricots, and more), 30% of its wine output, and best known of all, *barackpálinka,* a smooth yet tangy apricot brandy that can warm the heart and blur the mind in just one shot. Ask for home-brewed *házi pálinka,* which is much better than the commercial brews.

A short drive from town takes you into the expansive sandy grasslands of the Kiskunság National Park, the smaller of the two protected areas (the other is the Hortobágy National Park) of the Great Plain. A trip to the Kecskemét region is incomplete without at least driving through some of this prairie land. Better yet, you can watch a traditional horse show, do some riding, or immerse yourself in the experience by spending a night or two at one of the inns out on the prairie.

Until a small affiliated gallery opened recently in Budapest, the **Magyar Fotográfia Múzeum** (Hungarian Photography Museum) was the only museum in Hungary dedicated solely to photography. With a growing collection of over 275,000 photos, documents, and equipment pieces, it continues to be the most important photography center in the country. The main exhibits are fine works by such pioneers of Hungarian photography as André Kertész, Brassaï, and Martin Munkácsi, all of whom moved and gained fame abroad. ⊠ *Katona József tér 12,* ☎ *76/483–221.* ⊠ *100 Ft.* ☉ *Wed.–Sun. 10–5.*

The handsome Moorish-romantic **zsinagóga** (synagogue) anchoring one end of Szabadság tér is beautifully restored, but stripped of its original purpose. Today it is the headquarters of the House of Science and Technology and houses a small collection of reproductions from Budapest's Museum of Fine Arts. ⊠ *Rákóczi u. 2,* ☎ *76/487–611.* ⊠ *Free.* ☉ *Weekdays 8–4, weekends during special events or exhibits.*

Kecskemét's most famous building is the **Cifrapalota** (Ornamental Palace), a unique and remarkable Hungarian-style art-nouveau building, built in 1902. A three-story cream-colored structure studded with folksy lilac, blue, red, and yellow Zsolnay majolica flowers and hearts, it stands on Szabadság tér's corner like a cheerful cream pastry. Once a residential building, today it houses the Kecskeméti képtár (Kecskemét Gallery), displaying artwork by Hungarian fine artists as well as occasional international exhibits. ⊠ *Rákóczi u. 1,* ☎ *76/480–776.* 🖼 *50 Ft.* ☺ *Tues.–Sun. 10–5.*

NEED A
BREAK?

You can treat yourself to fresh pastries or ice cream at the café that shares this book's name, the **Fodor Cukrászda** (Fodor Confectionary; ⊠ Szabadság tér 2, ☎ 76/497-545). It's right on the main square and is closed December 25–January 25.

★ Built in 1893–96 by Ödön Lechner in the Hungarian art-nouveau style that he created, the **Városház** (town hall) is one of the style's finest examples. Window frames are here arched, there pointed, and the roof, covered with tiny copper- and gold-colored tiles, looks as if it has been rained on by coins from heaven. In typical Lechner style, the outlines of the central facade make a curvy line to a pointed top, under which 37 little bells add the finishing visual and auditory touch: Every hour from 7 AM to 8 PM, they flood the main square with ringing melodies from Kodaly, Beethoven, Mozart, and other major composers as well as traditional Hungarian folk songs. The building's **Dísz Terem** (Ceremonial Hall) is a spectacular palace of glimmering gold-painted vaulted ceilings, exquisitely carved wooden pews, colorful frescoes by Bertalan Székely (who also frescoed Budapest's Matthiás Church), and a gorgeously ornate chandelier that floats above the room like an ethereal bouquet of lights and shining brass. The hall can be viewed with advance notice only and on Saturdays is often booked with back-to-back weddings; plan ahead. ⊠ *Kossuth tér 1,* ☎ *76/483–683.* 🖼 *Main building 50 Ft.* ☺ *Weekdays 8–6, weekends 9–1; Dísz Terem on advance notice.*

The oldest building on Kossuth tér is the **Szent Miklós templom** (Church of St. Nicholas), also known as the Barátság templom (Friendship Church) because of St. Nick's role as the saint of friendship. Built in Gothic style in either the 13th or the 15th century (a subject of debate) but rebuilt in baroque style during the 18th century, the church sits in a tiny yard entered through pretty wrought-iron gates. ⊠ *Kossuth tér 5.* 🖼 *Free.*

The unusual **Szórakoténusz Játékmúzeum és Műhely** (Szórakoténusz Toy Museum and Workshop) is the only institution in Central Europe that collects, preserves, and studies the traditions and cultures of toys and toy making in Hungary and its neighboring countries. Two rooms contain permanent exhibits chronicling the history of Hungarian toys, beginning with archaeological pieces like stone figures and clay toys from medieval guilds; there are also changing international exhibits. In the workshop, artisans prepare traditional toys and invite visitors to try it themselves. Next door to the toy museum is the small **Magyar Naív Művészek Múzeuma** (Hungarian Naive Art Museum), where you can see a collection of this simple style of painting and sculpting created by Hungarian artists. ⊠ *Gáspár András u. 11,* ☎ *76/481–469.* 🖼 *100 Ft.* ☺ *Museums mid-Mar.–Oct., Tues.–Sun. 10–6, Nov.–mid-Mar., Tues.–Sun. 10–5; toy workshop Sat. 10–noon and 2:30–5, Sun. 10–noon.*

OFF THE
BEATEN PATH

PIAC – As Kecskemét is Hungary's fruit capital, why not experience it firsthand by visiting the bustling *piac* (market), where—depending on the season—you can indulge in freshly plucked apples, cherries, and the famous Kecskemét apricots, as well as heaps of fresh veggies and meats. Provided there is no sudden spring freeze, apricot season is around June through August. ⊠ *Budai u., near corner of Nagykörösi út.* ⊙ *Daily 6–1.*

Dining and Lodging

$–$$ ✕ **Kisbugaci Csárda.** Tucked away on a dark side street, this cozy eatery is warm and bright. The inner area has wood paneling and upholstered booths; the outer section has simple wooden tables covered with locally embroidered tablecloths and matching curtains. Food is heavy, ample, and tasty. Try the *király rétes,* a meat strudel drenched in paprika sauce, or the kitchen's goose specialties, like the *Bugaci libakóstoló*—a sampling of goose liver, thigh, and breast. Request a plate of dried paprikas if you really want to spice things up. ⊠ *Munkácsy u. 10,* ☎ *76/486–782. MC. No dinner Sun.*

$ ✕ **Liberté Kávéház.** This popular restaurant's location, right on Szabadság tér, can't be beat. Casually and classically elegant, the expansive dining room has wood paneling, upholstered chairs, and soaring ceilings. The *Alföldi babgulyás,* a Great Plain–region bean goulash, is anything but vegetarian, with chunks of beef, as well as meaty red beans and home-style pinched noodles; with a basket of crusty bread, it's a meal in itself. An unusual and rich menu item is the turkey breast stuffed with chestnut purée. ⊠ *Szabadság tér 2,* ☎ *76/480–350. MC.*

$$ ✕⊡ **Pongrácz Manor.** For total puszta immersion, spend a night or two
★ at this traditional Great Plain ranch, about 25 kilometers (16 miles) from Kecskemét and 7 kilometers (4 miles) from the nearest little village. An attractive complex of whitewashed buildings with reed roofs, the manor's rooms are small, simple, and comfortable, offering views onto the prairie. Those who dislike horses may not want to stay here, but horse lovers will be well occupied with riding opportunities (the stable houses some 60 horses and donkeys), as well as with chances to watch the resident, champion *csikósok* (cowboys) do their stunts. An unusual such resident cowboy is Erika, one of only two women in the world who do the daredevil stunt of driving five galloping horses at full speed while standing on the backs of the two in the rear. At press time, she was training to beat the world record by using eight horses. Anglers can try their luck in the nearby lake; the restaurant's kitchen will cook to order whatever you catch (there's a limit of one fish per person, per day on what you can keep). Those without luck at the lake will not go hungry: The restaurant serves hearty regional dishes indoors or outside, many of which are baked in a traditional puszta wood-burning oven. The Pongráz Manor is often booked up with tour groups, so reserve ahead. ⊠ *Kunpuszta 76, H-6041 Kerekegyháza,* ☎ FAX *76/371–240. 26 rooms with bath, 5 rooms with shared bath, 5 suites. Restaurant, wine cellar, pool, sauna, 2 tennis courts, bowling, horseback riding, squash, fishing, billiards, prairie tours. No credit cards. Closed Jan.–Mar.*

$$$ ⊡ **Arany Homok Hotel.** Kecskemét's biggest and best-known hotel has a prime location right on the picturesque main square—a delight for guests with windows facing the square, but a shame for the square itself, which is marred by the hotel's heinous concrete-bunker design. Newly renovated rooms (third through fifth floors) have new, simple blonde-wood furnishings, generic gray wall-to-wall carpeting, and small bathrooms with aqua-blue tiles. All doubles have balconies. For quieter nights, avoid the rooms overlooking the bus station behind the hotel. ⊠ *Kossuth tér 3, H-6000 Kecskemét,* ☎ *76/486–286,* FAX *76/481–195. 111 rooms with bath, 2 suites. Restaurant/bar, breakfast* room, casino, laundry service, meeting room, travel services. AE, DC, MC, V.

$ 📺 **Fábián Panzió.** It's hard to miss this very pink villa just off the main square. Inside, the contemporary decor brings pink (now muted) plus white, turquoise, and lavender, all carefully coordinated down to the tiniest detail. The owners, Fábián and his wife, keep their pension immaculate: Floors in the tiny entranceway are polished until they look wet; paint and carpeting in guest rooms and hallways are fresh. Even the paths through the blooming back garden are spotless. Rooms—some in the main house and some in additional cottages in the garden—feature similar white-and-pastel contemporary decor and furnishings, as well as extra amenities like remote-controlled climate control and 22-channel satellite TV. Roomiest and most quiet rooms are in the back cottages. ✉ *Kápolna u. 14, H-6000 Kecskemét,* ☎ *76/477–677,* 📠 *76/477–175. 10 rooms with bath. Breakfast area, garden, laundry service. No credit cards.*

Nightlife and the Arts

You won't see many locals here, but you'll find the latest nightlife at **Casino Kecskemét** (✉ Széchenyi tér 2, ☎ 76/486–286) in the Arany Homok Hotel, open every night from 6 PM until 2 AM.

The beautiful **Katona József Theater** (✉ Katona József tér 5, ☎ 76/483–283) is known for its excellent dramatic productions (in Hungarian) and also hosts classical concerts, operas, and dance performances during the Spring Festival and other celebrations. The **Kodály Zoltán Zenepedagógiai Intézet** (Zoltán Kodály Music Pedagogy Institute; ✉ Kéttemplom köz 1, ☎ 76/481–518) often holds student and faculty recitals, particularly during its annual international music seminar in mid- to late July.

Kecskemét's one- to two-week **Spring Festival** is held annually in mid-March and features concerts, dance performances, theater productions, art exhibits, and other cultural happenings by local and special guest artists from around the country and abroad. Every two years in early July, the city hosts a giant children's festival, **Európa Jövője Gyermektalálkozó** (Future of Europe Children's Convention), during which children's groups from some 25 countries put on colorful folk-dance and singing performances outside on the main square.

For schedule and ticket information on all cultural events, contact Tourinform.

Outdoor Activities and Sports

The nearby puszta (prairie) is the setting for myriad traditional horse-stunt shows, carriage rides, and guided horseback rides, and other active and passive **horsey activities.** Full-length shows and day-long excursions are bus tour–centric (because of the costs involved), although essentially anything can be arranged if a smaller group or individuals are willing to pay for it. **Nyakvágó Kft.** (✉ Kunszentmiklós, Bösztörpuszta-Nagyállás, ☎📠 76/351–198 or ☎ 76/351–201) sometimes offers full- and half-day "Puszta Programs" for smaller groups of individuals who want to take part in the program on the same day. The program includes carriage rides, horse shows, a visit to a working farm, and folk dancing, all lubricated with wine and *pálinka* (brandy) and including typical puszta snacks and meals. A full-day program costs roughly 10,700 Ft., a half-day costs about 8,400 Ft. Contact Tourinform (☞ Visitor Information *in* The Great Plain A to Z, *below*) or Bugac Tours for other possibilities and for help making necessary arrangements.

Bugac

⑨⓪ *46 km (29 mi) south of Kecskemét.*

The Bugac puszta (Bugac Prairie) is the central and most visited section of the 35,000-hectare Kiskunsági National Park—the smaller sister of Hortobágy National Park (farther northeast); together they comprise the entire Great Plain. Bugac puszta's expansive, sandy, impossibly flat grassland scenery has provided Hungarian poets and artists with inexhaustible material over the centuries. Although the dry, open stretches may seem numbingly uniform to the casual eye, the Bugac's fragile ecosystem is the most varied of the entire park; its primeval juniper trees, extremely rare in the region, are the area's most protected and treasured flora. Today, Bugac continues to inspire visitors with its strong equestrian traditions—Prince Charles did some riding here in 1990—and the myriad fun but touristy horse shows and tours offered in its boundaries. The park's half-hour traditional horse show is held daily at around 1 PM; its price is included in the entrance fee. You can also wander around the area and peek into the Kiskunság National Park Museum, which has exhibits about pastoral life on the prairie. *Park: ⊠ Bugac puszta. ⊠ 650 Ft. ☉ Mid-Apr.–Oct., daily 9:30–5. Information: ⊠ Karikás Csárda, ☎ 76/372–688; in Kecskemét, Bugac Tours, Szabadság tér 1/a, ☎ 76/ 481–643 or 482–500.*

Dining

$$ ✕ **Bugaci Csárda.** Bugac's most famous and popular restaurant is a bus-tour magnet but is still considered a mandatory part of a puszta visit. At the end of a dirt road just past the park's main entrance, the restaurant is in a traditional whitewashed, thatched-roof house decorated inside with cheerful red-and-white folk embroideries. Here you can feast on all the Hungarian standards along with live Gypsy music. *⊠ Hwy. 54, next to park entrance, ☎ 76/372–522. No credit cards. Closed Nov.–Mar.*

Outdoor Activities and Sports

The region specializes in equestrian sports. Possibilities for horseback-riding lessons, trail rides, and horse carriage rides abound. Contact **Bugaci Ménes** (☎ FAX 76/372–617) in Bugac or **Bugac Tours** (⊠ Szabadság tér 1/a, Kecskemét, ☎ 76/482–500 or ☎ FAX 76/481–643; ⊠ Karikás Csárda, Bugac, ☎ 76/372–688).

Szeged

⑨① *87 km (54 mi) south of Kecskemét.*

The largest city in southern Hungary and the nation's fifth largest was almost completely rebuilt after a disastrous flood in 1879, using a concentric plan not unlike that of the Pest side of Budapest, with avenues connecting two boulevards like the spokes of a wheel.

Szeged is famous for two things: its open-air festival, held each year in July or August; and its paprika, an important ingredient of Hungarian cuisine. But Szeged's paprikas are useful not only in goulash kettles but in test tubes as well: Local biochemist Albert Szentgyörgyi won the Nobel Prize in 1937 for his discoveries about Vitamin C, extracted from his hometown vegetable. In late summer and early autumn, Szeged offers a rich array of rack after rack of red peppers drying in the open air.

Although it lacks a large number of traditional sights, Szeged is a favorite place for young, budget travelers who enjoy the dynamic atmosphere at its peak during the school year, when students from the city's schools and universities liven up the streets, cafés, and bars.

The heart of the inner city is the large **Széchenyi tér,** lined with trees and surrounded by imposing buildings. Most notable is the eclectic neobaroque **Városház** (town hall; ☒ Széchenyi tér 10), built at the turn of the 19th century and after suffering major damage during the Great Flood, reconstructed by well-known eclectic art-nouveau architect, Ödön Lechner. At the square's opposite end is the pale-green **Hotel Tisza** (☒ Wesselényi u. 4), its guest rooms and lobby looking tired and worn, but whose lovely and still active concert hall has been blessed with multiple performances by legendary composer Béla Bartók, as well as cellist Pablo Casals and conductor Ernő Dohnányi. Its restaurant was a favorite haunt of famous writer Mihály Babits.

NEED A BREAK?	Grab a hot strudel stuffed with apple, poppy seed, or peppery cabbage at the counter of **Hatos Rétes bakery** (☒ Klauzal tér 6), a popular spot not only for a quick strudel, but also palacsinta—salty (ham, cheese) or sweet (plum, raspberry, chestnut)—and other fresh pastries, hot from the oven.

★ Szeged's most striking building is the **Fogadalmi Templom** (Votive Church, really a cathedral), an imposing neo-Romanesque brick edifice built between 1912 and 1929 in fulfillment of a municipal promise made after the Great Flood. One of Hungary's largest churches, it seats 6,000 and has a splendid organ with 12,000 pipes. The church forms the backdrop to the annual Szegedi Szabadtéri Játékok (Szeged Open-air Festival), held in vast Dóm tér (Cathedral Square). Outstanding performances of Hungary's great national drama, Imre Madách's *Tragedy of Man,* are given each summer at the festival, as well as a rich variety of other theatrical pieces, operas, and concerts. ☒ *Dóm tér,* ☏ *62/312–157 or 62/323–955. Church:* ☐ *Free.* ☉ *Mon.–Wed. and Fri.–Sat. 9–6, Thurs. 12:30–6, Sun. 9:30–10, 11–11:30, and 12:30–6. Crypt:* ☐ *30 Ft.* ☉ *Apr.–Sept., Mon.–Sat. 10–2.*

Szeged's **Régi Zsinagóga** (Old Synagogue) was built in 1839 in neoclassical style. On its outside wall a marker written in Hungarian and Hebrew shows the height of the floodwaters in 1879. It is open only rarely for special events. ☒ *Hajnóczi u. 12.*

Near the Old Synagogue, at the corner of Gutenberg utca and Jósika utca, is the larger **Új Zsinagóga** (New Synagogue), finished in 1905; it is Szeged's purest and finest representation of art nouveau. Its wood and stone carvings, wrought iron, and furnishings are all the work of local craftsmen. A memorial to Szeged's victims of Nazism is in the entrance hall. ☒ *Gutenberg u. 20,* ☏ *62/311–402.* ☐ *60 Ft.* ☉ *Daily except Jewish holidays 9–2.*

OFF THE BEATEN PATH	**NATIONAL HISTORIC MEMORIAL PARK –** The ultimate in monuments to Hungarian history and pride is this enormous park in Ópusztaszer, 29 kilometers (18 miles) north of Szeged. It was built on the site of the first parliamentary congregation of the nomadic Magyar tribes, held in AD 895, in which they agreed to be ruled by mighty Árpád. Paths meander among an open-air musuem of traditional village buildings. The main reason to come is the **Feszty Körkép** (Feszty Panorama), an astounding 1600-square meter (15-meter high, 113-meter long), 360-degree panoramic oil painting depicting the arrival of the Magyar tribes to the Carpathian Basin 1,100 years ago—effectively, the birth of Hungary. It was painted in 1892–94 by Árpád Feszti and exhibited in Budapest to celebrate the Magyar millennium. Sixty percent of it was destroyed dur-

ing a World War II bombing, and it wasn't until 1991 that a group of art restorers brought it here and started a painstaking project to resurrect it in time for Hungary's millecentennial celebrations in 1996. Today, housed in its own giant rotunda, the painting is viewable as part of a multimedia experience: Groups of up to 100 at a time are let in every half hour for a 25-minute viewing of the painting, accompanied by a recorded explanation and, at the end, a special sound show in which different recordings are played near different parts of the painting to add sound—galloping horses, trumpeting horns, screaming virgins, rushing water—to the scene depicted. The attraction is so popular that it's a good idea to call ahead and reserve a spot in the slot of your choice (tickets are for a set showing). The explanation is in Hungarian, but English-language versions on CD, available at the entrance, can be listened to on headphones before or after the viewing. ⊠ *Nemzeti Történeti Emlkpark, Szoborkert 68, Ópusztaszer,* ☎ *62/375-357 or 62/375-133.* 🎟 *Park 100 Ft., Feszty körkép 500 Ft.* ☺ *Apr.–Oct., Tues.–Sun. 9–7; Nov.–Mar., Tues.–Sun. 9–5.*

Dining and Lodging

$$ ✗ **Alabárdos Étterem.** This elegant eatery is housed in an 1810 landmark and serves well-presented traditional Hungarian cuisine. The Alabárdos specialty is not just a meal, but an experience: the lights are dimmed as waiters rush to your table with a flaming spear of skewered meats, which they then prepare in a special spicy ragout at your table; the ritual is accompanied by a special serenade played by the Gypsy band. Also sample some of the many different house pálinkas brought out on a cart. ⊠ *Oskola u. 13,* ☎ *62/312–914. Jacket required. AE, MC.*

$$ ✗ **Botond Restaurant.** An 1810 neoclassical building that formerly housed Szeged's first printing press is now this popular restaurant. Set on Széchenyi tér, its outdoor terrace is a prime dining spot in good weather. ⊠ *Széchenyi tér 13,* ☎ *62/312–435. AE, D, MC, V.*

$$ ✗ **Öreg Kőrössy Halászkert Vendéglő.** This traditional thatched-roof fisherman's inn on the Tisza River was first opened in 1930 by József Kőrössy (the restaurant's name is Old Kőrössy) and his son. Decades and various owners (including the state) later, the atmosphere is still rustic and festive, and the menu still features the original house staples like rich-red *Öreg Kőrössy halászlé* (fish soup), *Kőrössy* fish *paprikás,* and whole roast fish—all fresh from the Tisza. To further appreciate the river's role, take a look at the line on the wall marking the water's level during a flood in 1970. ⊠ *Felső-Tiszapart 1,* ☎ *62/327–410. No credit cards.*

$ 🏠 **Marika Panzió.** This friendly inn sits on a historic street in the Alsóváros (Lower Town), a five-minute drive from the city center. Cozy rooms have light-wood paneling and larger-hotel amenities like color TVs and minibars. The back garden has a small swimming pool. ⊠ *Nyíl u. 45, H-6725 Szeged,* ☎ FAX *62/313–861. 9 rooms with bath. Breakfast room, pool, free parking. No credit cards.*

Nightlife and the Arts

Szeged's own symphony orchestra, theater company, and famous contemporary dance troupe form the solid foundation for a rich cultural life. The **Szeged Nemzeti Színház** (Szeged National Theater; ⊠ Kárász u. 15, ☎ 62/476–555) stages Hungarian dramas, as well as classical concerts, operas, and ballets. Chamber-music concerts are often held in the conservatory and in the historic recital hall of the Hotel Tisza (⊠ Wesselényi u. 1). Szeged's most important event, drawing crowds from around the country, is the annual **Szegedi Szabadtéri Napok** (Szeged

Open-Air Festival), a tradition established in the 1930s, held early July through August. The gala series of dramas, operas, operettas, classical concerts, and folk-dance performances by Hungarian and international artists is held outdoors on the vast cobblestone Dóm tér (Cathedral Square), with the magnificent Votive Church looming as the backdrop to the stage. Tickets are always hot commodities; plan far ahead. For tickets and information, contact the ticket office (⊠ Deák u. 28–30, ☎ 62/471–466).

Outdoor Activities and Sports

Contact Tourinform or **MOHOSZ** (Csongrád County Committee of the National Anglers Association; ⊠ Bocskai u. 2, ☎ 62/310–196) for information on fishing in the Tisza River. The **Gold Lovasklub** (Gold Horse Club; ⊠ Honfoglalás u. 65, Szeged-Tápé, ☎ 62/324–937) offers horseback riding and carriage rides.

Shopping

You'll have no trouble finding packages of authentic **Szegedi paprika** in all sizes and degrees of spiciness in most of the city's shops. Szeged's other famous product is its excellent **salami** made by the local Pick Salami factory, which has been producing Hungary's most famous, most exported salamis since 1869. You'll find an extensive selection at the factory outlet stores (⊠ Jókai u. 1, in Nagyáruház Passage; ⊠ Maros u. 1, next to factory).

The Great Plain A to Z

Arriving and Departing

BY BUS

Volánbusz operates service from Budapest's Népstadion and Erzsébet tér terminals to towns throughout the Great Plain.

BY CAR

From Budapest, the M4 goes straight to Debrecen, the M5 to Kecskemét and Szeged.

BY TRAIN

Service to the Great Plain from Budapest is quite good; daily service is available from the capital's Nyugati (West) and Keleti (East) stations. Express trains run between Budapest and Debrecen, Kecskemét, and Szeged.

Getting Around

BY BUS

Buses connect most towns in the region.

BY CAR

The flat expanses of this region make for easy, if eventually numbing, driving. Secondary-route 47 runs along the eastern edge of the country, connecting Debrecen and Szeged. Debrecen and Kecskemét are easily driven between as well via the M4 through Szolnok, then dropping south in Cegléd. The puszta regions of Bugac and Hortobágy are accessible from Kecskemét and Debrecen by well-marked roads.

BY TRAIN

The eastern and western parts of the region are best connected via the rail junction in Szolnok, in the geometric center of the Great Plain.

Contacts and Resources

VISITOR INFORMATION

Bugac: Bugac Tours (⊠ Karikás Csárda, Bugac, ☎ 76/372–688; ⊠ Szabadság tér 1/a, Kecskemét, ☎ 76/482–500, ℻ 76/481–643).
Debrecen: Tourinform (⊠ Piac u. 20, ☎ 52/412–250, ℻ 52/314–139).

Kecskemét: Tourinform (✉ Kossuth tér 1, ☎ ℻ 76/481−065). **Szeged: Tourinform** (✉ Victor Hugo u. 1, ☎ 62/311−711, ℻ 62/312−509).

TRANSDANUBIA

Western Hungary, often referred to as Transdanubia (Dunántúl in Hungarian) is the area south and west of the Danube, stretching to the Slovak and Austrian borders in the west and north and to Slovenia and Croatia in the south. It presents a highly picturesque landscape, including several ranges of hills and small mountains. Most of its surface is covered with farmland, vineyards, and orchards—all nurtured and made verdant by a climate that is noticeably more humid than in the rest of the country.

The Romans called the region Pannonia (for centuries it was a frontier province; today it is far richer in Roman ruins than the rest of Hungary). Centuries later, the 150-year Turkish occupation left its mark on the region, particularly in the south, where it's not uncommon to see a former mosque serving as a Christian church. As in much of the rest of Hungary, Austrian influence is clearly visible in the region's baroque buildings, particularly in the magnificent Eszterházy Palace in Fertőd.

The varied terrain of Transdanubia offers much to explore, from the vineyards of Villány to the dense forest around Sopron, where a wide swath cut through the trees serves as a reminder of the recent past—when Transdanubia's western perimeter formed part of the now-defunct Iron Curtain. These days, however, the area is blooming as Hungary's gateway to Western Europe; Vienna, after all, is rarely more than a few hours' drive away.

En Route Perched proudly above the countryside on top of a high hill on the way to Sopron—135 kilometers (84 miles) west of Budapest, 100 kilometers (62 miles) east of Sopron—the vast, 1,000-year old Benedictine ★ **Pannonhalma Abbey** gleams like a gift from heaven. During the Middle Ages, it was an important ecclesiastical center and wielded considerable political influence. The abbey housed Hungary's first school and was allegedly the first place the Holy Scriptures were read on Hungarian soil. Still a working monastery and school, 68 monks and 360 students live in Pannonhalma. A late-Gothic cloister and a 55-meter neoclassical tower are the two stylistic exceptions to the predominantly baroque architecture. The library of over 300,000 volumes houses some priceless medieval documents, including the first to contain a large number of Hungarian words: the 11th-century deed to the abbey of Tihany. Visits are permitted only with a guide, which is included in the admission price. Occasional organ recitals are held in the basilica in summer. ✉ *Pannonhalma, off Route 82 south of Győr,* ☎ *96/470−191,* ℻ *96/470−162.* ◉ *300 Ft. (500 Ft. for foreign-language guide).* ☉ *Late Mar.−May and Oct.−mid-Nov., daily 9−4; June−Sept., daily 9−5; mid-Nov.−late Mar., Tues.−Sun. 10−3; closed Sun. mornings and holidays during mass.*

Numbers in the margin correspond to numbers on the Transdanubia map.

Sopron

★ ❷ *211 km (131 mi) northwest of Budapest, 100 km (62 mi) west of Pannonhalma.*

Lying on the Austrian frontier, between Lake Fertő (in German, Neusiedlersee) and the Sopron Hills, Sopron is one of Hungary's most

Transdanubia

picturesque towns. Barely an hour away from Vienna by car, it is a shopping center for many Austrians, who flock here for the day to buy goose liver, salami, apricot brandy, and eyeglasses—all considerably less expensive here than in Austria. The joke in Sopron is that every day at noon, "We play the Austrian national hymn so that the Austrians have to stand still for two minutes while we Hungarians shop." Dental work is also a bargain by Austrian standards; the town is chock-full of dentist advertisements in German, and nearly every hotel boasts an in-house dentist.

There is much more to Sopron, however, than conspicuous consumption by foreigners. Behind the narrow storefronts along the City Ring Várkerület (called Lenin Boulevard until 1989) and within the city walls (one set built by Romans, the other by medieval Magyars) lies a horseshoe-shaped inner city that is a wondrous eclectic mix of Gothic, baroque, and Renaissance, centered around Fő tér, the charming main square of perfectly proportioned Italianate architecture. Sopron's faithful and inspired restoration won a 1975 Europe Prize Gold Medal for Protection of Monuments, and the work continues slowly but carefully.

Today's city of 60,000 was a small Celtic settlement more than 2,300 years ago. During Roman times, under the name of Scarabantia, it stood on the main European north–south trade route, the Amber Road; it also happened to be near the junction with the east–west route used by Byzantine merchants. In 896 the Magyars conquered the Carpathian basin and later named the city Suprun for a medieval Hungarian warrior. After the Hapsburgs took over the territory during the Turkish wars of the 16th and 17th centuries, they renamed the city Ödenburg (Castle on the Ruins) and made it the capital of the rich and fertile Austrian Burgenland. Ferdinand III, later Holy Roman Emperor, was crowned king of Hungary here in 1625, and at a special session of the

Hungarian Parliament in 1681, Prince Paul Esterházy was elected palatine (ruling deputy) of Hungary. And always, under any name or regime, Sopron was a fine and prosperous place in which to live.

A sightseeing note: For those who plan to visit as many museums as they can, one collective ticket covering most of Sopron's museums is available for 400 Ft.

The symbol of today's and yesterday's and surely tomorrow's Sopron—and entranceway to the Old City—is the 200-foot-high **Tűztorony** (Fire Tower), with foundations dating to the days of the Árpád dynasty (9th–13th centuries) and perhaps farther back, if Roman archaeological finds in its cellar signify more than treasure. Remarkable for its uniquely harmonious blend of architectural styles, the tower has a Romanesque base rising to a circular balcony of Renaissance loggias topped by an octagonal clock tower that is itself capped by a brass baroque onion dome and belfry from more recent times. The upper portions were rebuilt in baroque style after most of the earlier Fire Tower was, appropriately, destroyed by the Great Fire of 1676, started by students roasting chestnuts in a high wind. Throughout the centuries the tower bell tolled the alarm for fire or the death of a prominent citizen, and from the loggias live musicians trumpeted the approach of an enemy or serenaded the citizenry. Both warning concerts were accompanied by flags (red for fire, blue for enemy) pointing in the direction of danger. ⊠ Fő tér, ☎ 99/311–463. 🎟 100 Ft. ☉ Apr., Tues.–Sun. 10–4; May–Sept., Tues.–Sun. 10–6.

★ At No. 8 on Fő tér, Sopron's main square, is the city's finest Renaissance building: the turreted **Storno Ház** (Storno House). Inside its two-story loggia, a popular upstairs museum houses a remarkable and surprising family collection of furniture, porcelain, sculptures, and paintings. The Stornos were a rags-to-riches dynasty of chimney sweeps who over several generations bought or just relieved grateful owners of unwanted treasures and evolved into a family of painters and sculptors themselves. The dynasty died out in Switzerland and Germany a few years ago, but its heirs and the Hungarian state have agreed nothing will be removed from the Storno House. On an exterior wall of the house hangs a plaque commemorating visits by King Matthias Corvinus (1482–83) and Franz Liszt (1840 and 1881). Downstairs is a small collection about Sopron's history. ⊠ Fő tér 8, ☎ 99/311–327. 🎟 100 Ft. ☉ May–Sept., Tues.–Sun. 10–6; Jan.–Apr. and Oct.–Dec., Tues.–Sun. 10–2. Upstairs museum can be visited by guided tour only, given every ½ hr (last one begins ½ hr before closing); tape-recorded tours on cassette are available in English.

At Fő tér 6, the fine Renaissance courtyard of the Fabricius House leads to the **Rómaikori Kőtár** (Roman Archaeology Museum) in the church-like vaulted medieval cellar, a perfect setting for the gigantic statues of Jupiter, Juno, and Minerva unearthed beneath the square during the digging of foundations for the city hall a century ago. On the second floor a separate museum (with identical hours and admission prices) re-creates the living environment of 17th- and 18th-century apartments. ⊠ Fő tér 6, ☎ 99/311–327. 🎟 40 Ft. ☉ May–Aug., Tues.–Sun. 10–6; Sept., Tues.–Sun. 10–2.

The 19th-century Angels' Drugstore is now the **Angyal Patika Múzeum** (Angel Pharmacy Museum), with old Viennese porcelain vessels and papers pertaining to Ignaz Philipp Semmelweis (1815–65), the Hungarian physician whose pioneering work in antiseptics, while in Vienna, made childbirth safer. ⊠ Fő tér 2, ☎ 99/311–327. 🎟 40 Ft. ☉ Tues.–Sun. 9:30–noon and 12:30–2.

The centerpiece of Fő tér, Sopron's exquisite main square, is a sparkling, spiraling three-tiered **Holy Trinity Column,** aswirl with gilded angels— the earliest (1701) and loveliest baroque monument to a plague in all of Hungary.

Standing before Fő tér's Holy Trinity Column is the early Gothic (1280–1300) **Goat Church,** named, legend has it, for a medieval billy goat that scratched up a treasure, enabling early-day Franciscans to build a church on the site (the Benedictines took over in 1802). More likely, however, the name comes from the figures of goats carved into its crests: the coat of arms of the Gutsch family, who financed the church. The Goat Church is built of limestone and has a soaring, pointed, 141-foot-high 14th-century steeple, three naves, its original Gothic choir (betraying French influence), and, after several rebuildings, a Hungarian Gothic–baroque red-marble pulpit, a rococo main altar, baroque altars by Croatian craftsmen, and a painting of St. Stephen by one of the Stornos. ⊠ *Fő tér at Templom utca.* ⊠ *Free.* ☉ *Daily 10–noon and 2–5.*

In the Gothic **Chapter House** of the Goat Church, monks meditated, contemplating on the curved pillars the Seven Deadly Sins in sculptures similar to those atop Notre Dame Cathedral in Paris. Avarice is a monkey; Lewdness, a bear; Incredulity, a griffin; Inconstancy, a crab crawling backward; and Vanity, a woman with a mirror in hand. ⊠ *Templom u. 1.* ⊠ *Free (donations accepted).* ☉ *Apr.–mid-Oct., daily 10–noon and 2–5.*

The antique-blue former **Eszterházy Kastély** (Eszterházy Palace)—part medieval, part baroque—has many musical memories buried within. Here, in 1773, the Eszterházy's music master, Franz Joseph Haydn, met Empress Maria Theresa. ⊠ *Templom u. 2. Not open to the public.*

Two doors down from the Eszterházy Palace is the red medieval and baroque **Bezerédy Palace,** where Franz Liszt gave a piano recital in 1840; during intermission, one young woman filched one of the maestro's white gloves, then cut it up into 29 pieces, and finally shared it with the other ladies present. ☉ *Templom u. 2. Not open to the public.*

The medieval **zsinagóga** (synagogue), complete with a stone *mikva,* a ritual bath for women, is now a religious museum, with a plaque honoring the 1,587 Jews of Sopron who were murdered by the Nazis; only 274 survived, and today there are scarcely enough Jews to muster a minyan (quorum of 10), let alone a congregation. The synagogue stands on Új utca (New Street), which despite its name is Sopron's oldest. ⊠ *Új u. 22,* ☎ *99/311–327.* ⊠ *80 Ft.* ☉ *May–Aug., Wed.–Mon. 9–5; Sept., Wed.–Mon. 10–2.*

The **Cézár Ház** (Cézár House) boasts a popular wine cellar downstairs, but upstairs, in rooms where the Hungarian Parliament met in 1681, is a private **museum** created by the widow of József Soproni-Horváth (1891–1961), a remarkable artist who prefixed his hometown's name to his own so he wouldn't be just another Joe Croat. This Horváth nevertheless stands out in the world of art for the wonders he worked with watercolors. He used that fragile medium to bring large surfaces alive in a density usually associated with oil paintings, while depicting realistic scenes, such as a girl grieving over her drowned sister's body. ⊠ *Hátsókapú u. 2,* ☎ *99/312–326.* ⊠ *60 Ft.* ☉ *Thurs.–Sun. 10–1 (Sat. also 3–6).*

Along **St. George Street** (Szent György utca), numerous dragons of religion and architecture coexist in sightly harmony. The **Erdődy Vár** (Erdődy Palace) at No. 16 is Sopron's richest rococo building. Two doors down, at No. 12, is the **Eggenberg House,** where the widow of Prince Johann Eggenberg held Protestant services during the harshest days of the Counter-Reformation and beyond. A stone pulpit in the courtyard bears the Hohenzollern coat of arms. But the street takes its name from **St. George's Church,** a 14th-century Catholic church so sensitively "baroqued" some 300 years later that its interior is still as soft as whipped cream. The church is generally open daily 9–5; the other buildings are not open to the public.

St. Mary's Column (1745), with its finely sculpted biblical reliefs, is a superb baroque specimen. It was built to mark the former site of the medieval Church of Our Lady, destroyed by Sopron citizens in 1632 because they feared the Turks would use it as a strategic firing tower. ⊠ *At the Előkapu (Outer Gate).*

NEED A BREAK?	Tiny glass chandeliers and marble-topped tables round out the elegant baroque decor of the spacious **Várkapu Kávéház** (⊠ Hátsókapu u. 3, ☎ 99/311–523). Pick a fresh pastry from the glass display counter to complement a potent espresso.

Strolling along **Várkerület,** the circular boulevard embracing Sopron's inner core, you'll experience a vibrant harmony of beautifully preserved baroque and rococo architecture and the fashionable shops and cafés of Sopron's thriving downtown business district.

Dining and Lodging

$$ ✕ **Barokk Étterem.** The Baroque Restaurant opened in 1992, supplanting authentic baroque designs with pastel colors and modern fixtures. Still, the entrance is through a lovely courtyard (though during the day it is crammed with racks of clothing from the neighboring boutiques), and the dining room has a soothing arched ceiling. Specialties of the house include meat fondue for two, trout, and beef Wellington with goose-liver stuffing. ⊠ *Várkerület 25,* ☎ *99/312–227. AE, MC, V. Closed Sun.*

$$ ✕ **Corvinus.** The location, in the 700-year old Storno House on Sopron's delightful cobblestoned main square, couldn't be better. Sitting at the outdoor tables, you can practically do your sightseeing during lunch. Inside, the informal dining room has vaulted ceilings painted black with gold stars; downstairs is a cozy brick cellar lit by candles. The menu features an array of pizzas as well as Hungarian standards, such as roast goose liver. The special Hungarian soup comes in a small ceramic pot sealed with a baked-on pastry cap. ⊠ *Fő tér 7–8,* ☎ *99/314–841. AE, DC, MC, V.*

$$ ✕ **Palatinus Étterem.** In this popular, informal restaurant, everything is prepared fresh daily—even the sauerkraut. The cordial chefs are often willing to cook up something not on the menu; otherwise, stick with the traditional Hungarian offerings. English menus are available. Lunch and dinner guests are entertained by a pianist. ⊠ *Új u. 23,* ☎ *99/311–395. AE, DC, MC, V.*

$$$$ 🏨 **Hotel Sopron.** On a hill just above the city core, this classy, mod-
  ★ ern hotel built in the early 1980s is blessed with gorgeous views of Sopron's steeples and rooftops. Rooms have contemporary furnishings in blonde- and dark-wood geometric patterns; those on the first two floors have balconies. Unless you prefer looking at the cemetery behind the hotel, request a room with a city view. ⊠ *Fövényverem u. 7, H-9400 Sopron,* ☎ 🖷 *99/314–254. 112 rooms with bath. Restaurant, bar, pool, sauna, solarium, 2 tennis courts, exercise room, bicycles, playground, meeting room. AE, MC, V.*

$$$$ 🏨 **Pannonia Med Hotel.** In the 17th century, the Golden Hind Inn stood here, welcoming stagecoach travelers on their journeys between Vienna and Budapest. Leveled by a fire, the inn was rebuilt in elegant neoclassical style in 1893 to become the Pannonia Hotel. A century later, it shines from a recent complete overhaul, retaining the original architectural style inside and out, with beautifully restored public areas with soaring ceilings and delicate chandeliers. Decor in standard guest rooms is disappointingly less inspiring (as is the staff service), with comfortable but simple furnishings. Several more expensive suites, however, are decorated with more fitting antique-style furnishings. ⊠ *Várkerület 75, H-9400 Sopron,* ☎ *99/312–180,* FAX *99/340–766. 25 rooms with bath, 12 suites. Restaurant, bar, beauty salon, sauna, solarium, meeting rooms. AE, DC, MC, V.*

$$$ 🏨 **Palatinus Hotel.** The small rooms at this hotel, built in 1981, are simply furnished with low wooden beds and generic carpeting. The location, in the city center within reach of every important sight, is perfect for day and night sightseeing. The staff is friendly and multilingual. ⊠ *Új u. 23, H-9400 Sopron,* ☎ FAX *99/311–395. 25 rooms with shower, 4 suites. Restaurant, bar. AE, DC, MC, V.*

Nightlife and the Arts

From mid- to late March, Sopron's cultural life warms up during the annual **Spring Festival,** offering classical concerts, folk-dance performances, and other events. Peak season for cultural events is from late June through late July, when the **Sopron Festival Weeks** brings music, dance, and theater performances and art exhibits to churches and venues around town. Contact Locomotiv Tourist (☞ Visitor Information *in* Transdanubia A to Z, *below*) or the Theater and Festival Office (⊠ Széchenyi tér 17–18, ☎ 99/338–673) for details.

Casino Sopron (⊠ Liszt Ferenc u. 1) is open every day until 3 AM for those who want to try their luck into the wee hours.

Outdoor Activities and Sports

The forested hills of the Fertő-Hanság National Park around Sopron have many well-marked hiking trails. Ask for a map and advice at the tourist office or contact the **Sopron Erdészeti és Faipari Egyetem** (Forestry University; ⊠ Bajcsy-Zsilinszky u. 4, ☎ 99/311–100).

Shopping

Várkerület is Sopron's main shopping street.

Herend Village Pottery (Új u. 5, ☎ 99/338–668) sells high-quality Herend ceramics hand-painted with tiny blue flowers and other cheerful, colorful patterns.

If you can't wait to shop at the less expensive factory outlet in Pécs (☞ *below*), you can purchase exquisite Zsolnay porcelain at the **Zsolnay Márkabolt** (⊠ Előkapu 11, ☎ 99/311–367), a tiny room lined with glass cabinets displaying the delicate, hand-painted wares.

En Route 27 kilometers (17 miles) southeast of Sopron in Fertőd, the magnifi-
★   cent yellow baroque **Eszterházy Palace,** built in 1720–60 as a residence for the Hungarian noble family, is prized as one of the country's most exquisite palaces. Though badly damaged in World War II, it has been painstakingly restored, making it clear why in its day it was referred to as the Hungarian Versailles. Swirling rococo wrought-iron gates mark the entrance to the orderly, manicured park fronting the palace. Its 126 rooms include a lavish Hall of Mirrors and a three-story-high concert hall, where classical concerts are held in summer. Joseph Haydn, court conductor to the Eszterházy family here for 30 years, is the subject of a small museum inside. Slippers—mandatory, to preserve the palace

floors—are provided at the entrance. ⊠ *Bartók Béla u. 2, Fertőd (just off Rte. 85),* ☎ *99/370–971.* 🎫 *150 Ft.* ☉ *Mid-Apr.–mid-Oct., Tues.–Sun. 9–5.*

Kőszeg

❾❸ *45 km (28 mi) south of Sopron.*

Clustered at an altitude of 886 feet in the forested hills near the Austrian border, Kőszeg is Hungary's highest and also one of its most enchanting little cities. Justly called the "jewel box of Hungary," Kőszeg is a living postcard of quiet cobblestone streets winding among Gothic and baroque houses, with picturesque church steeples and a castle tower rising up in between.

Continually quarreled over by the Austrians and Hungarians, Kőszeg was designed with an eye for defensibility—a moat, a drawbridge, thick ramparts, and a 14th-century fortified castle were essential to its survival. It was from this castle in 1532 that a few hundred Hungarian peasant soldiers beat back a Turkish army of nearly 200,000 and forced Sultan Suleiman I to abandon his attempt to conquer Vienna. To celebrate Christianity's narrow escape, the bells of Kőszeg's churches and castle toll every day at 11 AM, the hour the Turks turned tail.

Music, too, reigned in Kőszeg: Haydn spent many of his creative years in Kőszeg as court composer to the Eszterházys; Franz Liszt gave a concert in 1846 in what is now just the shabby shell of Kőszeg's grandiose but beloved Ballhouse.

Jézus Szíve Plébánia Templom (Sacred Heart Church) is a creamy neo-Gothic concoction by Viennese architect Ludwig Schöne. Erected between 1892 and 1894 on the site of a onetime coffeehouse, it is reminiscent both of Vienna's St. Stephen's Cathedral (for its mosaic roof and spires) and, inside, of Venice's San Marco (for the candy-stripe pillars supporting its three naves). If after inspecting the church, you stand outside admiring its facade from Chernel utca at the right rear, you will see a wholly different church, with flying buttresses and wriggly little pinecone spires. ⊠ *Fő tér at Várkör.* 🎫 *Free.*

The **Szent Jakab templom** (St. James Church) is the treasure of the city. St. James dates much farther back than its 18th-century baroque facade and even beyond its Gothic interior; in fact, St. James is the oldest church in Kőszeg. Inside are astonishingly well-preserved 15th-century wall paintings, one of the Virgin Mary with mantle (painted, in fresco technique, on wet plaster) and one of a giant St. Christopher (painted *al secco,* on dry wall). The baroque main altar, commissioned in 1693 by Prince Paul Eszterházy, boasts a Gothic wooden Madonna and child from the late 15th or early 16th century. ⊠ *Jurisics tér at Rajnis u.* 🎫 *Free.* ☉ *Daily 9–5.*

Right next to St. James Church is the smaller **Szent Imre templom** (St. Emerich's Church). If you're wondering why two landmarks serving the same purpose were planted side by side, they symbolize Kőszeg's ethnic mix, formed over the centuries by Hungarian tribes moving west and by Germans expanding to the east. Not long after the Counter-Reformation, St. Emerich's Church converted to Catholicism and replaced many of its Protestant trappings with baroque furnishings, most notably a high altar flanked by gilt and vivid statues of St. Stephen inviting and St. Ladislas defending the Virgin Mary. ⊠ *Jurisics tér at Chernel u.* 🎫 *Free.* ☉ *Daily 9–5.*

Jurisics tér was named after the Croatian captain, Miklós Jurisics, who commanded Kőszeg's dramatic defense against the Turks in 1532.

Like other fine squares in this part of Hungary, Jurisics Square is not square but triangular.

On one side of Jurisics tér is a sprightly Gothic dowager of a **Városház** (city hall), dressed for a midsummer ball with red-and-yellow stripes skirting the ground floor; the upper level is decorated with fresco medallions of the Kőszeg, Hungarian, and Jurisics crests, painted in 1712. Inside the front door is a surprising courtyard with walls painted cool white and brown, reminiscent of a Hungarian *csárda* (inn). Without question, this is one of Hungary's most beautiful city halls. ⊠ *Jurisics tér 8,* ☎ *94/360–046. Not open for visits.*

Jurisics Square converges on the handsome **Hősi kapu** (Heroes' Gate), whose imposing tower's Renaissance-Gothic facade belies its fairly recent construction, in 1932, to celebrate the 400th anniversary of the Turkish siege. This historic victory is commemorated in relief inside the portal, where another relief mourns Kőszeg's loss of life in World War I, a defeat that also cost the city two-thirds of its market for textiles and agriculture after the breakup of the Austro-Hungarian Empire. The observation tower affords fine views; within the tower you can climb through a small natural-history museum up to a loggia and survey the city's charms. ⊠ *Jurisics tér 6,* ☎ *94/360–240.* 🗐 *80 Ft.* ◷ *Tues.–Sun. 10–5.*

The **Sgraffitóház** on Jurisics tér dates to the Renaissance, when sgraffito was still a respectable art form. It now houses a pizzeria. ⊠ *Jurisics tér 7.*

Beneath a loft for drying medicinal herbs, the **Apotéka az Arany Egyszarvúhoz** (Golden Unicorn Pharmacy) is now a pharmacy museum (Patika Múzeum) with enough antique furniture and paintings to stock a small museum of Austrian baroque art. ⊠ *Jurisics tér 11,* ☎ *94/36–0337.* 🗐 *30 Ft.* ◷ *Tues.–Sun. 10–5.*

On the corner of Rájnis József utca and Várkör (City Ring), the street that girdles the inner town, you are welcomed into the old quarter by **statues of Sts. Leonard and Donatus.** The former carries a chain, for he is patron saint of prisoners and blacksmiths (as well as shepherds, animals, and sick people). The latter, the patron saint of wine, should hang his holy head a little. Kőszeg wine growers thrived until the turn of the 20th century, when a plague of lice called phylloxera wiped out their industry. Now Kőszeg "imports" its wine from nearby Sopron. Rájnis utca nevertheless still has a few wine cellars, where the stuff is happily drunk with gusto.

NEED A BREAK?
While you're in the town's historic wine district, it's only fitting to raise a glass or two at the **Kőszeg Szöllő Termelői Szövetkezete Borozója** (Kőszeg Vintners Association Winery; ⊠ Rajnis u. 16), in the cellar of a 15th-century Gothic house. It's closed on Mondays.

The **Jurisics Vár** (Jurisics Castle), which you enter by crossing two former moats, is named not for the nobility who have inhabited it over the years but for the Croatian captain Miklós Jurisics, who commanded its victorious defense against the Turks in 1532. In the first enclosure are a youth hostel, a bathhouse where the local brass band rehearses, and a modern (1963) statue of the heroic Jurisics. One of the most interesting exhibits in the **Jurisics Miklós Vármúzeum** (comprising exhibits on the city's and the castle's histories) is the "Book of the Vine's Growth," a chronicle kept for more than a century and a half, starting in 1740, by a succession of town clerks whose duty was to trace the sizes and shapes of vine buds drawn in their true dimensions on April 24 of each year. The tradition is still played out the same time every year amid festive pomp and circumstance. ⊠ *Rájnis József u. 9,* ☎ *94/360–240.* ▣ *100 Ft.* ☉ *Tues.–Sun. 10–5.*

Dining and Lodging

$$ ✕ **Bécsikapu Sörözö.** This brasserie near the castle cooks tasty Hungarian standards with a flair for game. Save lots of room for the yogurt and cottage cheese palacsinta, puffed up like a soufflé and stuffed with sweet curd and raisin filling. ⊠ *Rájnis József u. 5,* ☎ *94/360– 297. MC, V.*

$$ ✕ **Kulacs Vendéglö.** This simple informal eatery is popular for its central location near Fő tér, its home-style fare, and its low prices. If your arteries can handle it, try the *Kulacs pecsenye*: spare ribs covered with fried onions and bacon and topped with a sunny-side-up egg. Typical Hungarian red-and-white embroidered tablecloths and curtains add a cheerful touch to the small dining room. In summer, you can eat outdoors in the courtyard. ⊠ *Várkör 12,* ☎ *94/362–318. MC, V.*

$ ✕ **Ibrahim Kávézó.** Named after a Turkish pasha, this small, new café sports a strong Turkish theme, with a red canopy hanging above the tiny bar and bright-blue painted ceilings peppered with bronze studs. The larger back room features a kitschy fountain with a bronze cobra spitting water into a heart-shaped marble basin. Try the deer-steak bourguignonne with potato dumplings, whose recipe the owner brought with him when he left the nearby Bécsikapu Sörözö to open this restaurant. ⊠ *Fő tér 17,* ☎ *94/360–854. No credit cards.*

$$ ▦ **Írottkő.** Centrally located on the town's main square, this modern but not unsightly hotel harmonizes nicely with the fine ensemble of old houses above the storefronts. Its four-story atrium is sleek, and the guest rooms are functional, but not so luxurious that you'd want to stay indoors when there's so much to see outside. The staff is friendly and multilingual. ⊠ *Fő tér 4, H-9730 Kőszeg,* ☎ *94/360–373. 52 rooms with bath or shower. Bar. No credit cards.*

$ ▦ **Alpokalja Pánzio.** On the western edge of town along the highway to Austria, this cheerful, clean chalet-style pension is convenient for travelers with cars. Small, sunny rooms are tucked under wood-paneled sloping ceilings. If views are important, be sure to avoid rooms that face the auto yard and train tracks out back. A TV in your room costs a few extra dollars. ⊠ *Szombathelyi u. 8, H-9730 Kőszeg,* ☎ ⅨX *94/360–056, 13 rooms with shower. Restaurant. DC, MC, V.*

$ ▦ **Szálloda az Arany Strucchoz.** This former baroque inn was built in 1718 and is now one of the oldest hotels in Hungary. Although it is definitely showing its age, it holds the best location in town: on the main square next to the Sacred Heart Church (which accompanies your dreams with its punctual chimes). Much of the ground floor is given over to a dingy, smoky café with, fortunately, a separate entrance around the corner. Within the hotel portion are wide arches and spacious rooms with wilting, bare-bones furnishings adequate for a decent night's sleep. Just slightly more expensive, a corner room with 19th-century Biedermeier furnishings and a balcony looking onto the main square is the prize of the hotel. ⊠ *Várkör 124, H-9730 Kőszeg,* ☎ *94/360–323. 18 rooms with bath or shower. Café. No credit cards.*

Nightlife and the Arts

Kőszeg is anything but a night town. An evening's activity can usually center around dinner and a prebedtime cobblestone stroll. For exact schedule and ticket information on cultural events, contact Savaria Tourist.

Every April 21–24, music and dance festivities are organized to celebrate the **szöllő rajzolás** (grape drawing), a tradition since 1740 in which the town clerks record the sizes and shapes of the year's vine buds in a special book on April 24. The town's biggest cultural event is the annual **East West Folk Festival** in mid-June—a weekend of open-air international folk music and dance performances on Fő tér, in the castle courtyard, and throughout the inner town. In summer, **organ concerts** are occasionally held in the Sacred Heart Church. The grape **harvest** is usually celebrated in late September with a series of woodwind ensemble concerts and a harvest parade.

Szombathely

🌀 *20 km (13 mi) south of Kőszeg.*

Szombathely (pronounced *some*-baht-hay) was founded as Savaria by the Roman emperor Claudius in AD 43 and was an important settlement along the Amber Road from the Baltic to Rome. Ancient remains dating back to the 2nd century are visible today, in clashing contrast to the baroque, Secessionist, and cement-block Socialist architecture around it.

Today, Szombathely is a busy city of 80,000, with bustling streets crammed with boutiques and department stores flocked to by bargain-hunting Austrians. Somewhat jolting after the picturesque peace permeating its Transdanubian peers Sopron and Kőszeg, the city rewards those interested in ancient Roman ruins and/or shopping sprees.

Some of the Amber Road from the Baltic to Rome can be seen in the **Járdányi Paulovits István Romkert** (Garden of Ruins), which also boasts a collection of ancient ceramics and tools and the well-preserved remains of a 4th-century mosaic floor. ⊠ *Szily János tér 1,* ☎ *94/313–369.* 🎟 *80 Ft.* ☉ *Apr.–Oct., daily 10–6; Nov.–Mar., daily 10–3.*

The city's **Katedrál** (cathedral) is a soaring baroque masterpiece designed by the 18th-century Tyrolean architect Melchior Hefele, who also built the Bishop's Palace and girls' boarding school that flank it. Except for its Madonna Chapel, the entire cathedral was reduced to a heap of rubble on March 4, 1945, when bombs dropped by American planes exploded in the nave and sanctuary. It was admirably rebuilt in 1947, and work continues today on finer touches. When there is no mass in progress, the interior can be viewed only through a locked gate at the church entrance; during Sunday morning services, however, the entire church is open (to avoid disturbing the service, it's best to do a full exploration immediately before or after). ⊠ *Templom tér.* 🎟 *Cathedral and palace 30 Ft.* ☉ *Tues.–Sun. 9–4.*

Sala Terrena, the ground-floor museum in the Bishop's Palace, is an amusing attempt by Dorfmeister, Sr., to extend the impression of the Roman garden with frescoes of portals and ruins, gods and goddesses. A treasury also displays ecclesiastical items. ⊠ *Berzsenyi Daniel tér 3,* ☎ *94/312–056.* 🎟 *40 Ft.* ☉ *Weekdays 9:30–3:30, Sat. 9:30–11:30.*

In a baroque house at one end of splendid Berszenyi Daniel tér, the eccentric **Dr. Lajos Smidt Museum** displays the treasures of a surgeon who was an incorrigible collector of everything—from high straw shoes to Empire furniture, from form-letter military mail sent by combat infantrymen during World War I to concentration-camp currency from World War II. ⊠ *Hollán Ernő u. 2,* ☎ *94/311–038.* 🎟 *80 Ft.* ☉ *Tues.–Sun. 10–5.*

NEED A
BREAK?

At one corner of Fő tér, **Café Claudia** (Savária tér 1, ☎ 94/313–375) bakes pastries worthy of Vienna's best *Konditoreien*—all cream and sugar, sweetness and light.

Another grand square that isn't a square but rather a vast triangular funnel is **Fő tér** (recently renamed from Köztársaság tér—Republic Square), the business center of the city. Sealed off to traffic, it is a vast plaza of baroque and Secessionist facades containing myriad boutiques and knick-knack shops—and two Julius Meinl Austrian food markets.

Off the south side of Fő tér, where Rákóczi utca begins, is a curious conglomeration. On one side is the **Iseum**—the remnants (dating to the 2nd century AD) of a temple of Isis, shrine of a Roman cult that made animal sacrifices to the Egyptian goddess on this spot; these relics are separated from the modern, cement-bunker **Municipal Art Gallery** by some old gravestones. Across the street the culture shock is even more severe: The acoustically modern Béla Bartók Concert Hall has been built into the back side of a huge, redbrick, onion-dome, Byzantine-style former **synagogue,** created in 1881 by Ludwig Schöne (the Viennese architect who gave Kőszeg its Heart of Jesus Parish Church). At the locked front end of the former synagogue, a monument honors the 4,228 Jews of Szombathely exterminated in the Holocaust.

Dining and Lodging

$$ ✗ **Kispityer Halászcsárda.** From huge kettles, this large, noisy inn on
★ the south side of town dishes out the best and widest selection of fish yet encountered in this land of lakes and rivers. Begin your meal with the spicy, almost boneless fish soup, or its bonier big brother, carp soup, the "pride of the Hungarian kitchen." Move on to the Rába-style sheet fish served with sauerkraut and sour cream; or to any of the two dozen other fish specialties, described quite comically in English (translation may not be the chef's strong point). Strolling musicians will play for you at table-side. ⊠ *Rumi út 18,* ☎ *94/311–227. AE, MC, V. Closed Mon.*

$ ✗ **Gyöngyös Étterem.** This centrally located restaurant, a stone's throw from the Savaria Hotel, is the cheapest sit-down place in town. The food on the multilingual menu is wholesome; *Eszterházy pecsenye* (Eszterházy-style pork loin) and *gombás rostélyos* (mushroom steak) are worth a try if they're available. ⊠ *Széll Kálmán u. 8,* ☎ *94/312– 665. No credit cards. Closed Mon.*

$$ ▥ **Claudius.** Named for the Roman emperor who colonized Szombathely, this large lakeside hotel occupies a green setting about a 15-minute walk from downtown. Though its amenities are not quite luxurious, the balcony views from most rooms are rewarding and relaxing. Your hotel registration card grants you free admission to a large indoor public swimming and thermal bath complex next door. ⊠ *Bartók Béla krt. 39, H-9700 Szombathely,* ☎ *94/313–760,* 🆇 *94/313–545. 97 rooms with bath, 5 suites. Restaurant, bar, sauna, exercise room, nightclub. AE, DC, MC, V.*

$$ ▥ **Savaria.** From the rear, its glittering winter garden–ballroom gives the impression of a theater; from the front terrace, its palatial café-restaurant—with cluster chandeliers and tapering mirrors of copper and marble, and a wooden balcony above the bar—suggest a five-star grand hotel. It is neither: just a two-star downtown hostelry that happens to be a severe Secessionist classic from the turn of the century, recently and perfectly renewed. The personnel is young and obliging. The very reasonable room rate includes breakfast in the glorious café. ⊠ *Mártírok tere 4, H-9700 Szombathely,* ☎ *94/311–440,* 🆇 *94/324–*

532, telex 94/337–200. 93 rooms, 60 with bath or shower, 33 with sink. Restaurant, coffeehouse, meeting rooms. AE, DC, MC, V.

Nightlife and the Arts

The Szombathely Symphony Orchestra (☎ 94/314–472) performs at the Béla Bartók Concert Hall (✉ Rákóczi Ferenc u. 3, ☎ 94/313–747). During the annual Spring Festival held from late March into early April, classical concerts, folk-music and -dance performances, and other cultural events are held almost every night around town. Contact Savaria Tourist (☞ Visitor Information *in* Transdanubia A to Z, *below*). The gala **Savaria International Dance Competition** is held annually on one day in early June, featuring a full day of elegant ballroom dancing by competing pairs from around the world.

Shopping

The small showroom of **Folk Art Centrum** (✉ Király u. 1, ☎ 94/312–292) offers a selection of traditional folk crafts from various regions of Hungary.

Tekla Üveg-Porceln Üzlet (✉ Fő tér 10, ☎ 94/318–034), in the heart of the city's shopping core, is a wide, open room lined with shelves displaying a broad variety of crystal, glassware, Zsolnay and Hollóháza porcelain, and other decorative breakables.

If you want to go where the shopaholic Austrians go, head to the **Röltex Borostyánkő Árúház** (✉ Szent Márton u. 21, ☎ 94/312–597), a multistory department store selling a little bit of just about everything.

Pécs

⑨⑤ *238 km (148 mi) southeast of Szombathely, 197 km (122 mi) southwest of Budapest.*

The southwest's premier city and the fifth largest in Hungary, Pécs (pronounced *paytch*) is a vibrant, cultured, beautiful city that will leave you aesthetically and intellectually satiated. Pécs went through various incarnations in the course of its long history. The Franks called it Quinque Ecclesiae; the Slavs, Pet Cerkve; and the Hapsburgs, Fünfkirchen; all three names mean "five churches." Today there are many more churches, plus two mosques, and a handsome synagogue. Pécs is also the seat of Europe's sixth-oldest university (1367). In any language, however, Pécs could just as well be renamed City of Many Museums, for on one square block alone there are seven. Three of them—the Zsolnay, Vasarely, and Csontváry—justify a two- or three-day stay in this sparkling, eclectic city in the Mecsek Hills, just 30 kilometers (19 miles) north of the Slovenian border.

At the foot of Széchenyi tér, the grand sloping monumental thoroughfare that is the pride of the city, stands the dainty **Zsolnay Fountain,** a petite art-nouveau majolica temple guarded by shiny ox-headed gargoyles made of fly green eosin porcelain that gush pure drinking water piped into Pécs via Roman aqueducts. The fountain was built in the early 19th century by the famous Zsolnay family, who pioneered and developed their unique porcelain art here in Pécs.

NEED A BREAK? | A short walk down pedestrians-only Kiŕly utca, opening from Széchenyi tér, is the **Caflisch Cukrászda** (✉ Király u. 32, ☎ 72/310–391), a small, informal café established in 1789 with tiny round tables and small chandeliers. Open until 9 PM, it is especially cozy in candlelight.

★ **Belvárosi plébánia templom** (Inner City Parish Church). Széchenyi tér is crowned by a Turkish oddity that is a tourist's delight: a 16th-century mosque. Dating from the years of Turkish occupation (1543–1686), the mosque is now a Catholic church, which you might infer from the cross surmounting a gilded crescent atop the dome. Despite the fierce religious war raging on its walls—Christian statuary and frescoes beneath Turkish arcades and mihrabs (prayer niches)—this church, also referred to as the Gazi Khassim Pasha Jammi, remains the largest and finest relic of Turkish architecture in Hungary. ⊠ *Széchenyi tér.* 🖾 *Free.* ⊙ *Mid-Apr.–mid-Oct., weekdays 10–4, weekends 11:30–4; mid-Oct.–mid-Apr., weekdays 11–noon.*

★ **Zsolnay Múzeum.** Occupying the upper floor of the oldest surviving building in Pécs, this museum dates from 1324 and was built and rebuilt in Romanesque, Renaissance, and baroque styles over its checkered history. A stroll through its rooms is a merry show-and-tell waltz through a revolution in pottery that started in 1851, when Miklós Zsolnay, a local merchant, bought the site of an old kiln and set up a stoneware factory for his son Ignác to run. Ignác's brother, Vilmos, a shopkeeper with an artistic bent, bought the factory from him in 1863, imported experts from Germany, and with the help of a Pécs pharmacist for chemical experiments and his daughters for hand painting, created the distinctive porcelain with which the name Zsolnay has since been associated.

Among the museums's exhibits are Vilmos's early efforts at Delft blue handmade vases, cups, and saucers; his two-layer ceramics; examples of the gold-brocade rims that became a Zsolnay trademark; table settings for royal families; Madonnas and baptismal fonts; and landscapes and portraits made of china. Be sure to look up and notice the unusual Zsolnay chandeliers lighting your way. A new exhibit in the rooms across the hall re-creates a room in the family's home, with pieces from their collection of antique furniture and art objects, to evoke a sense of the milieu in which they lived and worked. The inner room exhibits oil paintings by Vilmos and his daughter Julia. There is a Zsolnay store in the center of Pécs at Jokai tér 2 (☞ Shopping, *below*), where you can purchase a wide selection of ceramics. ⊠ *Káptalan u. 2,* 🕾 *72/310–172.* 🖾 *120 Ft.* ⊙ *Tues.–Sun. 10–6.*

Zsolnay Porcelain Factory. If you haven't had enough Zsolnay after visiting the Zsolnay Museum, join the groups of tourists (usually German or Hungarian) braving heavily trafficked Zsolnay Vilmos utca to visit here, where gleaming monumental towers and statuary of seemingly pollution-proof porcelain hold their own among giant smokestacks. The factory can be visited by guided tour only with groups of 10–30. Call the factory or ask Tourinform to help find out when the next group is coming so that you can tag along.

On a hill behind the factory is the ultimate monument to the dynasty's founder, who died in 1900: the **Zsolnay Mausoleum,** similar to Napoléon's Tomb in Paris, with the bones of Vilmos and his wife in a blue ceramic well and, over the doorway, a relief of Vilmos, with disciples wearing the faces of his wife, daughters, and son kneeling before him. The mausoleum is open Tuesday–Sunday 10–4 and can be seen on approximately one-hour tours with a guide, provided on-site. For a tour in English, call ahead (🕾 72/450–291) to make sure it's available. Admission and tour fee is 100 Ft. ⊠ *Zsolnay Vilmos u. 69, factory tour information* 🕾 *72/325–266.* 🖾 *Free.*

The pioneer of Op Art (who later settled in France) was born Győző Vásárhelyi in 1908 in the merry fun house that is the **Vasarely Múzeum** (Vasarely Museum). The first hall is a corridor of visual tricks devised by his disciples, at the end of which hangs a hypnotic canvas of shifting cubes by Jean-Pierre Yvaral. Upstairs, the illusions grow profound: A zebra gallops by while chess pieces and blood cells seem to come at you. At one point it seems as if you are inside a prison looking out, and then suddenly you are outside looking in. Without a doubt, you leave the Vasarely with all your certainties overturned. ⊠ *Káptalan u. 3,* ☎ *72/310–172.* 🎫 *120 Ft.* ⏱ *Tues.–Sun. 10–6.*

Another museum on Káptalan Street is the **Endre Nemes Múzeum,** with displays (accompanied by English texts) of the ceramics of Vilmos Zsolnay and his followers. Another section of the museum contains a street scene titled *Utca* (street), constructed entirely of white foam plastic by the sculptor Erzsébet Schaár. The people on the street are constructed of gypsum, simple in body structure but with finely drawn heads and faces (the heads of Marx and Sándor Petőfi, the famous Hungarian poet, also are visible). ⊠ *Káptalan u. 5,* ☎ *72/310–172.* 🎫 *120 Ft.* ⏱ *May–Sept., Tues.–Sun. noon–4.*

★ One of the three major galleries in Pécs, the **Csontváry Múzeum** is just around the corner from its peers; but if you've just left the Vasarely and you have the time, it's probably best to wait a day and bring a fresh eye to this next museum. Mihály Tivadar Csontváry Kosztka (1853–1919) was a pharmacist in the Tatra Mountains who, in his late twenties, sketched a scene of an ox cart outside his drugstore on a prescription pad. Told he had artistic talent, he worked and studied and saved money for 24 years to achieve enough financial and artistic independence to, as he put it, "catch up with, let alone surpass, the great masters." An early expressionist and forerunner of surrealism, Csontváry influenced Picasso; his work is to be found almost exclusively here and in a room of the Hungarian National Gallery in Budapest.

The paintings in the five rooms of the museum in Pécs are arranged to show Csontváry's progression from soulful portraits to seemingly conventional landscapes executed with decidedly unconventional colors to his 1904 *Temple of Zeus in Athens* (about which Csontváry said, "This is the first painting in which the canvas can no longer be seen.") A few months later, with an even greater intensification of unexpected colors, *The Ruins of Baalbek* and *The Wailing Wall in Jerusalem* filled giant canvases. After a 1905 tryout in Budapest, Csontváry was ready for a 1907 exhibition in Paris, which turned out to be a huge critical success. Not long after finishing his last great epic painting, *Mary at the Well in Nazareth* (1908), megalomania gripped him. Though his canvases grew ever larger, Csontváry finished nothing that he started after 1909 except a patriotic drawing of Emperor Franz Joseph, completed at the start of World War I in 1914. The last room of the exhibit is filled only with sketches.

After he died in Budapest in 1919, Csontváry's canvases were about to be reused as furniture covers when a collector from Pécs named Gedeon Gerlóczy rescued them with a ransom of 10,000 forints. The collection in Pécs is now valued at more than $10 million. ⊠ *Janus Pannonius u. 11,* ☎ *72/310–172.* 🎫 *120 Ft.* ⏱ *Apr.–Oct., Tues.–Sun. 10–6; Nov.–Mar., Tues.–Sun. 10–4.*

★ One of Europe's most magnificent cathedrals is the famous **Pécs Bazilica** (Pécs Basilica), promoted from cathedral to basilica rank after Pope John Paul II's visit in 1991. At the beginning of the 19th century, Mihály Pollack directed the transformation of the exterior, changing it from baroque to neoclassical; its interior remained Gothic. Near the end of the century, Bishop Nándor Dulánszky decided to restore the cathedral to its original Árpád-period style—the result is a four-spired monument that dominates the Pécs skyline and boasts an utterly breathtaking interior profusely frescoed in shimmering golds, silvers, and blues. The caretaker must be paid an extra fee to turn on all the lights for optimal viewing. ⊠ *Szent István tér.* ▣ *130 Ft. (including treasury and crypt); full-lighting fee 300 Ft.; tape-recorded tour in foreign language 200 Ft.* ⊙ *Apr.–Oct., weekdays 10–1 and 2–5, Sat. 9–1, Sun. 1–5; Nov.–Mar., weekdays 10–1 and 2–4, Sat. 10–1, Sun. 1–4.*

In front of Pécs Basilica is a small park, just beyond which is the 4th-century **Ókeresztény mauzóleum,** Hungary's largest and most important early Christian mausoleum. Some of the subterranean crypts and chapels date to its earliest days; the murals on the walls (Adam and Eve, Daniel in the lion's den, the Resurrection) are in remarkably good condition. In 1987, the mausoleum–museum won a World Biennial Prize for architecture. ⊠ *Szent István tér,* ☎ *72/311–526.* ▣ *120 Ft.* ⊙ *Apr.–Oct., Tues.–Sun. 10–6; Nov.–Mar., Tues.–Sun. 10–4.*

OFF THE
BEATEN PATH   **VILLÁNY** – Thirty kilometers (19 miles) south of Pécs, nestled in the low, verdant Villányi Hills, is the town of Villány, center of one of Hungary's most famous wine regions. Villány's exceptional and unique red wines are heralded here and abroad; its burgundies, cabernets, and ports are said to give the best of their French and Italian peers a run for the money. Visiting a few of Villány's and neighboring town Villánykövesd's historic wine cellars makes a great day trip from Pécs. Many offer regular wine tastings and sales. Tourinform in Pécs has an informative brochure and listing of cellars. Those who wish to educate themselves before imbibing can stop in the **Wine Museum** (⊠ Bem u. 8, ☎ 72/ 492–130) for a look at the history of the region's viticulture, which dates back some 2,000 years. The museum is open Tuesday through Sunday 9–5; admission is free.

Dining and Lodging

$$ ✕ **Cellárium.** Deep in an ancient cellar dating to Turkish times, this delightful restaurant has a cheerful, youthful atmosphere. The owner's creative touches include dressing the waiters in prison uniforms and putting the extensive, very reasonably priced menu into the form of a small newspaper titled *Cella News,* which guests can take home with them. Tiny reading lamps or oil lamps on the tables provide cozy lighting in the long tunnel-shaped rooms with brick and stucco walls. Adventurous palates may try the "Hungarian stew with the comb and balls of cockerel," a rustic village dish rarely offered in restaurants. ⊠ *Hunyadi u. 2,* ☎ *72/314–453. MC, V.*

$$ ✕ **Dóm.** This small restaurant centrally located on Pécs's pedestrian shopping street is dominated by a giant wood-frame structure designed after the city's basilica. Dark wood pewlike booths and high frescoed ceilings further the theme. The menu includes Hungarian classics as well as more interactive platters, in which guests cook their own choice of meat on sizzling lava stones. ⊠ *Király u. 3,* ☎ *72/310– 732. No credit cards.*

$$ ✕ **Iparos Kisvendéglő.** The very popular, informal Craftsman restaurant has a wide selection of pork, turkey, chicken, veal, and game dishes, as well as a small selection of fresh salads. ⊠ *Rákóczi út 24–26,* ☎ *72/333–400. AE, DC, MC, V.*

$$$ ▥ **Palatinus.** In the pedestrians-only center of Pécs, the Palatinus main-
★ tains a good balance between old and new: The outside of the renovated building has fully preserved its traditional look, while the rooms are modern in most every respect (equipped with TVs and telephones), though unexceptional in decor. Best views are from the fifth floor. The hotel's stunning ballroom, built in the Hungarian Secessionist style, is

well suited for parties, balls, and conferences; in fact, the Hungarian composer Béla Bartók held a concert of his own here in 1923. ⊠ *Király u. 5, H-7621 Pécs,* ☎ *72/233–022,* FAX *72/232–261. 88 rooms with bath, 6 suites. Restaurant, brasserie, massage, sauna, solarium, bowling. AE, DC, MC, V.*

$$ 🏠 **Toboz Panzió.** Nestled among the pines high up in the Mecsek Hills, the delightful Pinecone Pension offers forest tranquillity just a short drive or bus ride from downtown or 20–30 minutes by foot. Hiking trails into the hills begin just behind the house. Rooms are clean and bright, especially those with skylight windows. Room sizes vary, and some of the shower stalls in those without private bathrooms are awkwardly built right into the bedroom; for optimal comfort, request a large room with a private bath on the top floor. ⊠ *Fenyves sor 5, H-7635 Pécs,* ☎ FAX *72/325–232. 4 rooms with bath, 8 rooms with shower (no bath), 1 suite. Breakfast room. No credit cards.*

Nightlife and the Arts

NIGHTLIFE

British-style pubs are all the rage in Hungarian city nightlife, and the **John Bull Pub** (⊠ Széchenyi tér 1, ☎ 72/325–439), part of a successful chain around the country, plays the part well, elegantly done up with dark woods and polished brass and amply stocked with Guinness on tap. Its dead-center location on Pécs's main square lures in lots of visitors as well as locals. The **Fregatt Arizona Pub** (⊠ Király u. 21, ☎ 72/210–486), with pub-type decor and low vaulted ceilings, is another popular English-style bar with Guinness on tap.

THE ARTS

The **Pécsi Nemzeti Színház** (Pécs National Theater; ⊠ Színház tér 1, ☎ 72/211–965) is the main venue for regular performances by the Pécs Symphony Orchestra and the theater's opera and modern ballet companies. The theater is closed from late May until September, except for the **Nemzetközi Zenei Fesztivál** (International Music Festival), held from late June into early July, with concerts by the Pécs Symphony Orchestra and international guests. The **International English Center** (⊠ Mária u. 9, ☎ 72/312–010) sometimes hosts English-language readings and lectures, as well as jazz and folk concerts. **September** brings harvest-related festivities such as classical concerts, folk-music and -dance performances, and a parade or two to venues in and around Pécs. Inquire at Tourinform for specifics. Tourinform publishes a monthly arts and events calendar in English and can help with further schedule and ticket information.

Outdoor Activities and Sports

The **Mecsek Hills** rise up just behind Pécs, with abundant well-marked hiking trails through its forests and fresh air. Guided walks are often organized on Saturday or Sunday by local naturalist groups; contact Tourinform for dates and times.

Shopping

Kiraly utca, a vibrant, pedestrians-only street lined with beautifully preserved romantic and baroque facades, is Pécs's main shopping zone, full of colorful boutiques and outdoor cafés, where you can take a shopping break and watch the town stream by.

In all of Hungary, the best place to buy exquisite Zsolnay porcelain is at the **Zsolnay Márkabolt** (⊠ Jókai tér 2, ☎ 72/310–220), here in downtown Pécs, birthplace and center of the Zsolnay craft. As the Zsolnay factory's own outlet, the store offers guaranteed authenticity and the best prices on the full spectrum of pieces—from tea sets profusely painted with colorful, gold-winged butterflies to simply elegant white-and-night-blue dinner services.

Bookpoint (✉ Mária u. 9, ☎ 72/312–010), in the International English Center, sells a variety of new and used English-language books and periodicals, as well as postcards and posters. It's closed Saturdays.

Pécs's **kirakodóvásár** (flea market; ✉ Vásártér, ☎ 72/224–313) offers great browsing and bargain hunting among its eclectic mix of goods—from used clothing to handcrafted folk art to fresh vegetables. It's held every weekend (from 8 until noon or 1), but the first weekend of every month is always the best in quantity and variety.

Transdanubia A to Z

Arriving and Departing

BY CAR

From Budapest, you can get to Pannonhalma, Fertőd, and Sopron via the M1 through Győr, switching onto the appropriate secondary route there. Pécs and Budapest are directly connected by the M6.

BY TRAIN

There are good rail connections from Budapest to Sopron, Szombathely, and Pécs. Trains to Sopron and Fertőd go north through Győr.

Getting Around

BY BUS

If you're without a car, you'll need to rely on buses to get you to smaller towns like Pannonhalma, which are not on the rail lines. Regular buses link all of the towns in our coverage. Inquire at tourist offices.

BY CAR

Traveling around Transdanubia is done best by car: It offers the greatest freedom to take a side road to sleepy old villages or stop to wonder at the scenic, verdant hills. Except for Pécs, all the towns covered here are fairly short driving distances from one another. Significantly farther south and east, Pécs can be reached from Szombathely along connecting major secondary roads past the southern tip of the Balaton and through Kaposvár. It's a beautiful drive.

BY TRAIN

Trains connect most of the areas covered.

Contacts and Resources

VISITOR INFORMATION

Kőszeg: Savaria Tourist (✉ Várkör 69, ☎ FAX 94/360–238). **Pécs: Tourinform** (✉ Széchenyi tér 9, ☎ 72/213–315, FAX 72/212–632). **Sopron: Locomotiv Tourist** (✉ Új u. 1, at Fő tér, ☎ 99/312–077); **IBUSZ** (✉ Ógabona té 1, ☎ 99/338–695). **Szombathely: IBUSZ** (✉ Fő tér 44, ☎ 94/314–141, FAX 94/325–189); **Savaria Tourist** (✉ Mártirok tere 1, ☎ 94/312–348, FAX 94/311–314; ✉ Berzsenyi tér 2, ☎ 94/324–341).

HUNGARY A TO Z

Arriving and Departing

By Bus

There is regular bus service between Budapest and selected major cities in the region. From Budapest, buses to Bratislava and Prague depart from the Erzsébet tér station (☎ 1/117–2318). Buses to Krakow, Sofia, and Brasso operate from the Népstadion station (☎ 1/252–1896).

By Car

At press time, Hungary was continuing a massive upgrading and reconstruction of many of its motorways, gearing up for its role as the main bridge for trade between the Balkan countries and the former Soviet Union and Western Europe. Work is scheduled to continue beyond 1997. To help fund the project, tolls on major highways were introduced for the first time in January 1996. Charging 940 Ft. per car, the much-heralded, recently completed M1 from Budapest to Vienna immediately became the most expensive road to travel in Europe. (The price has since gone up; count on about $10.) M1 tolls can be paid in dollars and with major credit cards, as well. Other toll roads include the M5, from Budapest to Serbia, and the M3 (incomplete at press time), from Budapest to Ukraine.

By Plane
See Arriving by Plane *in* Budapest A to Z, *above*.

By Train
Keleti pályaudvar (Eastern Station) receives most international rail traffic coming in from the west. Nyugati pályaudvar (Western Station) handles a combination of international and domestic trains. Déli pályaudvar (Southern Station) is primarily for domestic travel in southern Hungary.

Getting Around

By Boat
Hungary is well equipped with nautical transport, and Budapest is situated on a major international waterway, the Danube. Vienna is five hours away by hydrofoil or boat. For information about excursions or pleasure cruises, contact **MAHART Tours** (⊠ Belgrád rakpart, Budapest V, ☎ 1/118−1704, 1/118−1586, or 1/118−1743).

By Bus
Long-distance buses link Budapest with most cities in Hungary as well as with much of Eastern and Western Europe. Services to the eastern part of the country leave from the Nepstadion station (☎ 1/252−4496). Buses to the west and south, to Austria and the former Yugoslavia, leave from the main Volán bus station at Erzsébet tér in downtown Pest (☎ 1/117−2318 or 1/117−2966). Though inexpensive, these buses tend to be crowded, so reserve your seat. For the Danube Bend, buses leave from the bus terminal at Árpád Bridge (☎ 1/129−1450).

By Car
Getting around by car is the best way to see Hungary. It's a small country, and even country-spanning distances are manageable. Speed traps are numerous, so it's best to keep at the speed limit; fines run around the equivalent of $20. Spot checks are frequent, as well, and police can occasionally try to take advantage of foreigners, so always have your papers at hand.

Gas stations have become plentiful in Hungary, and many on the main highways stay open all night, even on holidays. Major chains, such as MOL, Shell, and OMV, now have Western-style full-facility stations with rest rooms, brightly lit convenience stores, and 24-hour service. Lines are rarely long, and supplies are essentially stable. Unleaded gasoline (*bleifrei* or *ólommentes*) is generally available at most stations, and is usually the 95 octane level choice. If your car requires unleaded gasoline, be sure to double check for leaded gas before you pump.

DOCUMENTATION
To drive in Hungary, U.S. and Canadian visitors need an International Driver's License—although their domestic licenses are usually accepted anyway—and U.K. visitors may use their own domestic licenses.

ROAD CONDITIONS

There are three classes of roads: highways (designated by the letter M and a single digit), secondary roads (designated by a two-digit number), and minor roads (designated by a three-digit number). Highways and secondary roads are generally good. The conditions of minor roads vary considerably; keep in mind that tractors and horse-drawn carts may slow your route down in rural areas. In planning your driving route with a map, opt for the larger roadways whenever possible; you'll generally end up saving time even if there is a shorter but smaller road. It's not so much the condition of the smaller roads, but the kind of traffic on them and the number of towns (where the speed limit is 50 kph) they pass through, that will slow you down. If you're in no hurry, however, explore the smaller roads!

At press time, Hungary was continuing a massive upgrading and reconstruction of many of its motorways, gearing up for its role as the main bridge for trade between the Balkan countries and the former Soviet Union, and western Europe. Work is scheduled to continue beyond 1997. To help fund the project, tolls on major highways were introduced for the first time in January 1996. Charging 940 Ft. per car, the much-heralded, recently completed M1 from Budapest to Vienna immediately became the most expensive road to travel in Europe. M1 tolls can be paid in dollars with major credit cards, as well. Other toll roads include the M5, from Budapest to Serbia, and the M3 (incomplete at press time), from Budapest to the Ukraine.

RULES OF THE ROAD

Hungarians drive on the right and observe the usual Continental rules of the road. Unless otherwise noted, the speed limit in developed areas is 50 kph (30 mph), on main roads 90 kph (55 mph), and on highways 120 kph (75 mph). Seat belts are compulsory, and drinking alcohol is totally prohibited—the penalties are very severe.

By Train

Travel by train from Budapest to other large cities or to Lake Balaton is cheap and efficient. Remember to take *gyorsvonat* (express trains) and not *személyvonat* (locals), which are extremely slow. A *helyjegy* (seat reservation), which costs about 55 Ft. (200 Ft. for Inter-City trains) and is sold up to 60 days in advance, is advisable for all express trains, especially during weekend travel in summer. It is also worth paying a little extra for first-class tickets. The Hungarian Railroad Inter-City express—which links the country's major cities—is comfortable, clean, and almost always on time; the service costs only an extra 200 Ft.

FARES

Only Hungarian citizens are entitled to student discounts; non-Hungarian senior citizens (men over 60, women over 55), however, are eligible for a 20% discount. InterRail cards are available for those under 26, and the Rail Europe Senior Travel Pass entitles senior citizens to a 30% reduction on all train fares. Snacks and drinks can be purchased on most express trains, but pack a lunch just in case. For more information about rail travel, contact or visit **MAV Passenger Service** (✉ Andrassy út 35, Budapest VI, ☎ 1/322–8275).

Contacts and Resources

B&B Reservation Agencies

See Apartment Rentals and B&B Reservation Agencies *in* Budapest A to Z, *above*.

Camping
Hungarian Camping and Caravanning Club (⊠ VIII, Üllői út 6, ☎ 1/133–6536).

Car Rentals
There are no special requirements for renting a car in Hungary, but be sure to shop around, as prices can differ greatly. **Avis** and **Hertz** offer Western makes for as much as $400–$900 per week. Smaller local companies, on the other hand, can rent Hungarian cars for as low as $130 per week. *See* Car Rentals *in* Budapest A to Z, *above,* for a list of agencies.

Foreign driver's licenses are generally acceptable by car rental agencies, but are technically not valid legally; they are almost always accepted by the police, but it can get messy and expensive if you are stopped by a police officer who insists you need an International Driver's License (which, legally, you do).

Customs and Duties
ON DEPARTURE
Take care when you leave Hungary that you have the right documentation for exporting goods. Keep receipts of any items bought from Konsumtourist, Intertourist, or Képcsarnok Vállalat. A special permit is needed for works of art, antiques, or objects of museum value. Upon leaving, you are entitled to a VAT refund on new goods (i.e., not works of art, antiques, or objects of museum value) valued at more than 25,000 Ft. (VAT inclusive). But applying for the refund may rack up more frustration than money: Cash refunds are given only in forints and you may find yourself in the airport minutes before boarding with a handful of soft currency, of which no more than 10,000 forints may be taken out of the country. If you made your purchases by credit card you can file for a credit to your card or to your bank account (again in forints), but just don't expect it to come through in a hurry. If you intend to apply for the credit, make sure you get customs to stamp the original purchase invoice before you leave the country. For more information, pick up a tax refund brochure from any tourist office or hotel, or contact the **APEH Budapest Directorate Foreigners' Refund Office** (⊠ V, Sas u. 2, ☎ 1/118–1910) or **Intel Trade Rt.** (⊠ I, Csalogány u. 6-10, ☎ 1/201–8120 or 1/156–9800). For further Hungarian customs information, inquire at the National Customs and Revenue Office (⊠ VI, Rózsa u. 89, ☎ 1/131–3536). If you have trouble communicating, ask Tourinform (☎ 1/117–9800) for help.

Emergencies
Police (☎ 07). **Ambulance** (☎ 04). **Fire** (☎ 05).

Hungarian Automobile Club's Yellow Angels breakdown service (⊠ XIV, Francia út 38/B, ☎ 1/252–8000; when outside Budapest, ☎ 088).

Guided Tours
ACTIVE TOURS
IBUSZ Travel Riding and Hobbies department (☞ *below*) offers good tennis and golf packages, spa treatment packages (including those specializing in dental treatments!), equestrian holiday packages at stud farms, and angling packages on the Tisza River. They also run excellent horseback riding tours from late April to mid-October. Participants ride 20 to 30 miles a day through lovely countryside, avoiding roads and populated areas as much as possible. In addition to the riding, tours include picnic lunches, hearty dinners, wine tastings, overnight stays in country inns, and usually one day of area sightseeing on the horses' day off. Choose among several six-, eight-, and nine-day tours in Hortobágy or Bugac prairies, a long weekend trip in Balaton region, as well as traditional hunting rides and coach-driving training programs for

more advanced riders. Guided **bicycle tours** (for people in good shape!) include an 11-day trip from Vienna to Lake Balaton, a 10-day tour around the Bugac puszta region, a 15-day trip through southern Hungary, and an eight-day Lake Balaton tour. In addition to meals and lodging, tours may include stops at interesting sights along the way, city sightseeing, short boat trips, bicycle rental, and gear transport. These tours are generally run June through August. Other guided tours include **"wandering" trips** with coach transport between walking areas, and special **bird-watching tours** for ornithologists.

BALATON

Gray Line Cityrama takes groups twice a week (no tours in winter) to the Herend porcelain factory and museum, in Herend, and then over to lovely vineyard-rich Badacsony. Well lubricated after a three-course meal with Gypsy music and wine tasting, the group moves on to Veszprém to visit its medieval castle hill and then heads back to Budapest.

BOAT TOURS

Contact **MAHART Tours** (✉ Belgrád rakpart, Budapest V, ☎ 1/118–1704) for information about their roster of boat tours on Lake Balaton and on the Danube in and beyond Budapest.

BUDAPEST ORIENTATION

IBUSZ (☞ Visitor Information, *below*) conducts three-hour bus tours of Budapest year-round (cost about 2,200 Ft.) . **Gray Line Cityrama** (✉ V, Báthori u. 22, ☎ 1/132–5344) also offers a three-hour Budapest bus tour (about 2,400 Ft. per person).

DANUBE BEND DAY TRIPS

IBUSZ runs its popular "Danube Bend by Boat" tour (approx. 10,000 Ft.) tours twice a week from May until September. The full day begins with sightseeing in Szentendre, then lunch on the boat, followed by a visit to Visegrád. Back on the boat passengers sip a cocktail and watch the scenery on the way home.

DAY TRIPS TO THE GREAT PLAIN

Gray Line Cityrama (☞ *above*) runs day trips several times a week to the Great Plain from Budapest. They begin with a sightseeing walk through Kecskemet, then head out to the prairie town of Lajosmizse, where drinking, dining, Gypsy music, carriage rides, and a traditional csikós horse show take over. The cost is approximately 10,000 Ft.

IBUSZ (☞ *below*) also operates full-day tours out to the Great Plain, to Lajosmizse as well as to Bugac, both first taking in Keckemét's sights. Costs run 9,000 Ft.–11,000 Ft.

GENERAL

IBUSZ (☞ *below*) offers a variety of changing bus tours to places around the country, from cave visits in the Mátra Mountains to wine tasting in the Tokaj region to traditional pig roasts on the Great Plain.

Language

Hungarian (*Magyar*) tends to look and sound intimidating at first because it is not an Indo-European language. Generally, older people speak some German, and many younger people speak at least rudimentary English, which has become the most popular language to learn. It's a safe bet that anyone in the tourist trade will speak at least one of the two languages.

Lodging

Hungary's three big hotel chains are **Danubius Hotels** (✉ H–1138 Budapest, Margit-sziget, ☎ 1/112–1000, FAX 1/153–1883), **HungarHotels** (✉ H–1052 Budapest, Petőfi Sándor u. 16, ☎ 1/118–3393, FAX 1/118–

0894), and **Pannonia Hotels** (✉ H–1088 Budapest, Rákóczi út 9, ☎ 1/266–8281). All three are represented in the United States by **Hungarian Hotels Sales Office Inc.** (✉ 6033 W. Century Blvd., Suite 670, Los Angeles, CA 90045, ☎ 310/649–5960 or 800/833–3402).

Mail

Airmail letters and postcards generally take seven days to travel between Hungary and the United States, sometimes more than twice as long, however, during the Christmas season.

In Hungary, go to Budapest's main downtown post office branch (✉ Magyar Posta 4. sz., H-1052 Budapest, Városház utca 18). The post offices near Budapest's Keleti (Eastern) (✉ VII, Baross tér 11c) and Nyugati (Western) (✉ VI, Teréz körút 51) train stations are open 24 hours. The American Express office in Hungary is in Budapest (✉ H-1052 Budapest, Deák Ferenc u. 10, ☎ 1/266–8680).

POSTAL RATES

From Hungary, all airmail postcards and letters to the United States, the United Kingdom, and the rest of Western Europe cost 10 Ft. per 10 grams; an airmail postcard will cost about 70 Ft., a letter from 100 Ft. Surface-mail postcards to the United Kingdom and the rest of Western Europe cost 60 Ft., letters from 75 Ft.

RECEIVING MAIL

Although it's not recommended for urgent or valuable correspondences, a poste restante service, for general delivery, is available through any post office in Budapest. The envelope should have your name written on it, as well as "Posta Maradó" (poste restante) in big letters.

Money and Expenses

Eurocheque holders can cash personal checks in all banks and in most hotels. Many banks now also cash American Express and Visa traveler's checks. American Express has a full-service office in Budapest (✉ V, Deák Ferenc u. 10, ☎ 1/267–2020, 1/267–2313, or 1/266–8680; FAX 1/267–2029), which also dispenses cash to its cardholders. Hungary's first Citibank (✉ V, Vörösmarty tér 4) opened in 1995, offering full services to account holders, including a 24-hour cash machine.

CURRENCY

Hungary's unit of currency is the forint (Ft.), divided into 100 fillérs (f.). There are bills of 50, 100, 500, 1,000, and 5,000 forints; coins of 1, 2, 5, 10, 20, 50, 100, and 200 forints; and coins of 10, 20, and 50 fillérs. The exchange rate was approximately 145 Ft. to the U.S. dollar, 105 Ft. to the Canadian dollar, and 217 Ft. to the pound sterling at press time. Note that official exchange rates are adjusted at frequent intervals. Although cash card and Eurocheque facilities are becoming easier to find in big cities, it is probably still wise to bring traveler's checks, which can be cashed all over the country in banks and hotels. There is still a black market in hard currency, but changing money on the street is risky and illegal, and the bank rate almost always comes close. Stick with banks and official exchange offices.

CREDIT CARDS

Plastic has recently entered Hungary's financial scene: Most credit cards are accepted, though don't rely on them in smaller towns or less expensive accommodations and restaurants, while hundreds of 24-hour cash machines have sprung up throughout Budapest and in major towns around the country. Some accept Plus network bank cards and Visa credit cards, others Cirrus and MasterCard; American Express is accepted at the automat outside the American Express office building. You can withdraw forints only (automatically converted at the bank's official exchange rate) directly from your account. Most levy a 1% or $3 service charge. Instructions are in English. For those without plastic, many cash-exchange machines, into which you feed paper currency for forints, have also sprung up. Most bank automats and cash-exchange machines are clustered around their respective bank branches throughout downtown Pest.

WHAT IT WILL COST

The forint, which is expected to be convertible by 1997, was significantly devalued over the last two years, and inflation rages on at an annual rate of more than 25%. Tourists receive more forints for their dollar, but will find that prices have risen to keep up with inflation. More and more hotels now set their rates in hard currency to avoid the forint's instability. Although first-class hotel chains in Budapest charge standard international prices, quality hotels are still modest by Western standards. And even with inflation and the 25% value-added tax (VAT) in the service industry, enjoyable vacations with all the trimmings still remain less expensive than in nearby Western cities like Vienna.

SAMPLE COSTS

Cup of coffee, 80 Ft.; bottle of beer, 150 Ft.–200 Ft.; soft drinks, 80 Ft.; ham sandwich, 100 Ft.; 1-mile taxi ride, 130 Ft.; museum admission, 80 Ft.–200 Ft.

National Holidays

Most businesses remain closed on the following national holidays: January 1; March 15 (Anniversary of 1848 Revolution); March 30–31 (Easter and Easter Monday); May 1 (Labor Day); May 18–19 (Pentecost); August 20 (St. Stephen's and Constitution Day); October 23 (1956 Revolution Day); December 24–26.

Opening and Closing Times

Banks are generally open weekdays 8–3, often with a one-hour lunch break at around noon; most close at noon on Fridays. Museums are generally open Tuesday through Sunday from 10 to 6, and are closed on Mondays; most stop admitting people 30 minutes before closing time. Many have a free-admission day; see individual listings in tours below, but double-check, as the days tend to change. Department stores are open weekdays 10 to 5 or 6, Saturdays until 1. Grocery stores are generally open weekdays from 7 AM to 6 or 7 PM, Saturdays until 1 PM; "non-stops" or *éjjeli-nappali* are (theoretically) open 24 hours.

Outdoor Activities and Sports

BICYCLING

Tourinform (☞ Visitor Information, *below*) in Budapest can provide you with the "Hungary by Bike" brochure and general information on current rental outfits. For specifics on bicycling conditions and suggested routes, try contacting the **National Society of Bicycle Commuters** (⊠ III, Miklós tér 1, ☎ 1/250–0420 or 1/250–0424, ext. 28 on both) or the **Bicycle Touring Association of Hungary** (⊠ V, Bajcsy-Zsilinszky út 31, 2nd floor, Apt. 3, ☎ 1/111–2467).

CAMPING

Most of the over 100 campsites in Hungary are open from May through September. Since rates are no longer state-regulated, prices vary. An average rate is 700 Ft. a day per site in Budapest, slightly less elsewhere. There's usually a small charge for hot water, electricity, and parking, plus an accommodations fee—about 250 Ft. per person per night. Children under 14 frequently get a 50% reduction. Camping is forbidden except in appointed areas. Information, reservations, and an informative English-language campsite listing can be obtained from travel agencies, the **Hungarian Camping and Caravanning Club** (⊠ VIII, Üllői út 6, ☎ 1/133–6536), and **Tourinform** (☞ *below*).

GOLF

The **Hungarian Professional Golf Association** is based at Budapest Golfpark (☎ 1/117–6025, 1/117–2749, or 06/60–321–673) in Kisoroszi.

Student and Youth Travel

In Hungary, as a general rule, only Hungarian citizens and students at Hungarian institutions qualify for student discounts on domestic travel fares and admission fees. Travelers under 25, however, qualify for excellent youth rates on international airfares; those under 26 are eligible for youth rates on international train fares. The International Student Identity Card (ISIC) is accepted in Budapest and other large Hungarian cities, but not as widely as it is in Western countries. If you buy your student identity card in Budapest at the **Express Youth and Travel Office,** which specializes in providing information on all aspects of student and youth travel throughout the country and abroad, it will cost about one-third the price of buying the card in the United States. Main branches include ⊠ V, Zoltán utca 10, ☎ 1/111–6418; V, Szabadság tér 16, ☎ 1/111–7679; and ⊠ VII, Keleti train station, ☎ 1/342–5337.

Telephones

The country code for Hungary is 36. Within Hungary, most towns can be dialed directly—dial 06 and wait for the buzzing tone, then dial the local number. It is unnecessary to use the city code, 1, when dialing within Budapest.

Though continuously improving, the Hungarian telephone system is still antiquated, especially in the countryside. Be patient. With the slow improving of Hungary's telephone system comes the problem of numbers changing—sometimes without forewarning. Tens of thousands of phone numbers in Budapest alone will be changed over the next few years; if you're having trouble getting through, ask your concierge to check the number for you (or if the number begins with a 1, try dialing it starting with a 3 instead—many changes will be of this type).

DIRECTORY ASSISTANCE AND OPERATOR INFORMATION

Dial 1/117–0170 for Budapest directory assistance, 1/267–3333 for countryside. Some operators speak English and, depending on their mood, may assist you in English. A safer bet is to consult *The Phone Book,* an English-language Yellow Pages–style telephone directory full of important Budapest numbers as well as cultural and tourist information; it's provided in guest rooms of most major hotels and is sold at many English-language bookstores.

PAY PHONES

Hungarian pay phones use 10 Ft. coins—the cost of a three-minute local call—and also accept 20 Ft. and 50 Ft. coins. Gray card-operated telephones outnumber coin-operated phones in Budapest and the Balaton region. The cards—available at post offices and most newsstands and kiosks—come in units of 50 (500 Ft.) and 120 (1,100 Ft.) calls. Don't be surprised if a flock of kids gathers around your pay phone while you talk—collecting and trading used phone cards is a raging fad.

Tipping

Four decades of socialism have not restrained the extended palm in Hungary—so tip when in doubt. Coatroom and gas-pump attendants, hairdressers, waiters, and taxi drivers all expect tips. At least an extra 10% should be added to a restaurant bill or taxi fare. If a Gypsy band plays exclusively for your table, you can leave 100 Ft. in a plate discreetly provided for that purpose.

Travel Agencies

American Express (⊠ V, Déak Ferenc u. 10, ☎ 1/266–8680, FAX 1/267–2028). **Getz International** (⊠ V, Falk Miksa u. 5, ☎ 1/312–0645 or 1/312–0649, FAX 1/112–1014). **Vista** (⊠ VII, Károly körút 21, ☎ 1/269–6032, 1/342–9316, or 1/342–1534; FAX 1/269–6031).

Visitor Information

American Express Travel Related Services (⊠ V, Deák Ferenc u. 10, ☎ 1/266–8680, FAX 1/267–2028). **Budapest Tourist** (⊠ V, Roosevelt tér 5, ☎ 1/117–3555). The **IBUSZ** (⊠ Central branch: V, Ferenciek tere 10, ☎ 118–6866). **IBUSZ Travel Riding and Hobbies** department (⊠ V, Ferenciek tere 10, ☎ 1/118–2967) arranges lodging in Hungary's historic castles and mansions. Ask for their colorful brochure listing the latest properties. **IBUSZ Welcome Hotel Service** (⊠ V, Apáczai Csere János u. 1, ☎ 1/118–3925 or 1/118–5776); open 24 hours. **Tourinform** (⊠ V, Sütő u. 2, ☎ 1/117–9800), open April–October, daily 8–8, and November–March, weekdays 8–8, weekends 8–3.

5 Poland

A country of flowers and trees and sunshine, of outdoor cafés and Old World charm, Poland is at its best in spring and summer. Not-to-be-missed locales include historic Kraków, a uniquely preserved Renaissance city where one of Poland's most famous sons, Copernicus, studied; the wild, flat lakelands of Mazuria, with nesting storks and other wildlife; the grand landscapes of the Tatra Mountains, with their local wooden-building styles, brown bears, and mountain pastures covered with wildflowers in spring and snow-covered slopes that entice skiers in winter. The birthplace of Chopin, Poland also delights visitors with its musical and theatrical traditions.

By Emma
Harris, with
contributions
from Witold
Orzechowski

POLES ARE FOND OF QUOTING, with a wry grimace, the old Chinese valediction, "May you live in interesting times." The times are certainly interesting in 1990s Poland—the home of the Solidarity trade union movement that sent shock waves through the Soviet bloc in 1980 and the first of the Eastern European states to shake off Communist rule. But as the grimace implies, being on the firing line of history—something the Poles are very used to—can be an uncomfortable experience. You will be constantly reminded that the current return to free-market capitalism after 45 years of state socialism is an experiment on an unprecedented scale that brings inconveniences and surprises as well as benefits.

With 38 million inhabitants living in a territory of 315,000 square kilometers (121,000 square miles), Poland in the 1990s is suspended between the old world and the new, and the images can be confusing. You will see bright, new, privately owned shops in shabby buildings that have not been renovated for decades. Glowing new billboards advertise goods that most Poles cannot afford. Buildings change function overnight as they are handed back to their prewar owners. Public services, such as transportation, are underfunded, and water supplies and central heating can be erratic, as local authorities attempt with insufficient funds to keep the show on the road. Blatantly neon-lighted sex shops in city centers coexist awkwardly with the church-backed campaign to strengthen family life by banning abortion and making divorce more difficult.

The official trappings of the Communist state were quickly dismantled after the Solidarity victory in the 1989 elections. The nation's name was changed back to the Republic of Poland (although you will notice many documents still bearing the old legend of the Polish People's Republic); the state emblem is now, as before the war, a crowned eagle. Statues of Communist leaders have largely disappeared from public places (a suggestion, made by one town planner, that as an economy measure only the heads should be removed and replaced by the heads of Polish artists or patriots was not followed up); many street names have been changed, and Communist Party buildings have been turned into schools, universities, or banks.

Communism never sat easily with the Poles. It represented yet another stage in their age-old struggle to retain their identity in the face of pressure from neighbors to the west and east. Converted to Christianity and founded as a unified state during the 10th century on the great north European plain, which affords no easily demarcated or defended frontiers, Poland lay for a thousand years at the heart of Europe, precisely at the halfway point on a line drawn from the Atlantic coast of Spain to the Ural Mountains. This has never been an enviable position. During the Middle Ages, Poland fought against German advance, uniting with its eastern neighbors in 1410 to inflict a crushing defeat on the Teutonic Knights in the Battle of Grunwald. In the golden age of Polish history during the 16th and 17th centuries—of which you will be reminded by splendid Renaissance buildings in many parts of the country—Poland pushed eastward against its Slavic neighbors, taking Kiev and dreaming of a kingdom that stretched from the Baltic to the Black Sea. It saw itself now as the bastion of Christendom against the hordes from the east, a role best symbolized when Polish king John III Sobieski led the allied Christian forces to defeat the Turks at Vienna in 1683. This role is often referred to in the context of more recent Polish history.

By the end of the 18th century, powerful neighbors had united to obliterate Poland—with its outmoded tendency to practice democracy at the highest levels of state and elect foreigners to the throne—from the map of Europe; its territories were to remain divided among the Austrian, Prussian, and Russian empires until World War I. This period of partition, which has left marked traces on the Polish psyche, is often used to explain patterns of character or public behavior—the Polish tendency to subvert all forms of organized authority, for example, or Polish devotion to the Roman Catholic church as a marker of national identity, a devotion that would later survive the disapproval of the Communist state.

The period of partition has also left physical traces on the map of Poland, despite the tendency of the postwar years to impose uniformity. The formerly Prussian-ruled regions of western Poland, centered in Poznań, are still regarded as cleaner and better organized than the Russian-ruled central areas around the capital, Warsaw; the former Austrian zone in the south, particularly the city of Kraków, retains a reputation for stuffiness and dignified behavior along the lines of the Hapsburg model. The architecture of the three regions also bears traces of distinct 19th-century imperial styles.

During the 20th century, after a brief period of revived independence in the interwar years, Poland fell victim to peculiarly vicious forms of the old struggle between east and west. It was first crushed by Hitler's *Drang nach Osten* (drive toward the east), which killed 6 million Polish citizens, including 3 million of the Jews who had played such a major role in the nation's history. In 1945 Poland's borders were shifted 322 kilometers (200 miles) farther west (via the annexation of German territory), and the country was placed behind the Iron Curtain in Stalin's postwar settlement. These mid-century experiences are embedded deep in the Polish soul. The 19th-century insurrectionary tradition was revived in resistance to the Nazi occupation and is still honored throughout Poland in the candles and flowers placed in front of memorials to its victims. These are now being joined by monuments to those who died fighting against Soviet power during the 1940s and '50s.

Poland's historic cities—Kraków, Warsaw, Gdańsk—tell much of the tale of European history and culture. Its countryside offers unrivaled possibilities of escape from the 20th century. Paradoxically, communism—which after 1956 dropped attempts to collectivize agriculture and left the Polish peasant on his small, uneconomic plot—has preserved rural Poland in a romantic, preindustrial state. Despite appalling pollution—which has attracted public attention but mercifully is largely confined to the industrial southwest—cornflowers still bloom, storks hunt for frogs in marshland or perch atop untidy nests by cottage chimneys, and horse carts make their way lazily along field tracks.

And, despite a certain wary reserve in public behavior that can verge on rudeness in some contexts, the Poles will win you over wherever you go with their strong individualism—expressed in flair in dress and style—their well-developed sense of humor, and their capacity for enjoyment and conviviality.

Pleasures and Pastimes

Dining

While even Poland's most ardent fans will admit that it does not have one of the world's great cuisines, the traditions of old Polish cuisine are currently being revived. Butter and cream, as well as honey-based sauces for sweet-and-sour dishes can be widely found. Soups are in-

Poland

*Baltic
Sea*

*Zatoka
Gdańsko*

Wejherowo

Gdynia

Gdańsk

Słupsk

Sławno

Kołobrzeg

Koszalin

Miastko

Kościerzyna

Tczew

Malbo

Świnoujście

Karlin

Starogard
Gdański

Sztum

*Zalew
Szczeciński*

Nowogard

Szczecinek

Chojnice

Kwidzyn

Szczecin

Goleniów

Stargard
Szczeciński

Jastrowie

Grudziądz

Pyrzyce

Kalisz
Pom.

Piła

Bydgoszcz

Toruń

Wisła R.

Notec R.

Chodzież

Gorzów
Wielkopolski

Rogoźno

Inowrocław

Włoc

Odra R.

GERMANY

Skwierzyna

Pnjewy

Gniezno

Poznań

Września

Krośniewice

Świebodzin

Środa
Wielkopolski

Zielona
Góra

Leszno

Jarocin

Kalisz

Zgierz

Kożuchów

Krotoszyn

Zduńska

Szprotawa

Rawicz

Ostrów
Wielkopolski

Sieradz

Warta R.

Lubin

Bolesławiec

Odra R.

Kępno

Wieluń

Zgorzelec

Legnica

Wrocław

Oleśnica

Neisse R.

Jelenia
Góra

Kluczbork

Cz

Brzeg

Wałbrzych

Opole

Lubliniec

Nysa

Bytom

Kudowa Zdroj

Kłodzko

Gliwice

Chorzów

Katowice

Wodzisław

CZECH
REPUBLIC

Bielsi
Biało

variably excellent, often thick and nourishing, with lots of peas and
beans. Clear beet soup, *barszcz,* is regarded as the most traditional,
but soured barley soup, *żurek,* should be tried at least once. Pickled
or soused herring is also a favorite Polish entrée and usually very good.
The Polish chef's greatest love affair is with pork in all its varieties,
including suckling pig and wild boar. Traditional sausages, *kiełbasy,*
usually dried and smoked, are delicious; *myśliwska* (hunter's sausage)
is regarded as the greatest delicacy. Another popular hunter's dish, *bigos,*
is made from soured and fresh cabbage, cooked (for several days or
weeks) together with many different kinds of meat and sausage. There
is not a major tradition in Poland of serving desserts to follow meals.
Kompot (stewed fruit) is customarily served at an early stage in the
meal, and you sip the juice rather than eat the fruit. Expensive restaurants in cities now offer a selection of desserts as well as cakes and
pastries; you can also go on to a café for coffee and one of Poland's
excellent cakes.

The traditional, waiter-service restaurant is still the main feature of
the dining scene in Poland, across all price ranges. But if you are in a
hurry there is more variety than ever. The old low-cost, self-service
milk bars (*bar mleczny*) and cheap cafeterias are fast disappearing,
replaced by pizza parlors and other fast-food outlets. Many cafés serve
hot snacks alongside the traditional tea, coffee, and cakes. And if you
are really pressed for time, you will nearly always be able to find a
street stall (usually housed in a small white caravan) that serves *za-
piekanki:* French bread toasted with cheese and mushrooms. Increasing numbers of Vietnamese street stalls selling spicy dishes are
to be found in all Polish cities.

A somewhat random selection of French, German, and Eastern European wines can usually be found in restaurants; the last often represent the best value for the money, especially the Hungarian reds such
as *Egri Bikavér* (Bull's Blood of Eger) or one of the Bulgarian *Sofia*
varieties. Note, however, that expensive imported wines and spirits are
very highly taxed as luxury items, and the prices charged for them in
restaurants can therefore be astronomical.

Although upscale city restaurants have adapted to Western mealtimes,
and some offer lunch starting at noon, Poles traditionally eat their main
meal of the day (*obiad,* dinner) between 3 and 5. Many restaurants
therefore open at 1 and do not get into full swing until mid-afternoon.
Although in cities, there is a growing trend to stay open later ("to the
last customer" is a popular new slogan), many restaurants still close
relatively early, and it may be difficult to order a meal after 9. A few
restaurants offer fixed-price meals between about 1 and 5; these do
not always represent a savings over à la carte prices.

Like so much else in today's Poland, official ratings of restaurants (from
Category Lux down through S and 1 to 4) have long been out of date
and are currently in flux. Certainly the top categories (L, S, and 1) do
not tell you a great deal, and many new restaurants remain uncatego-
rized, regardless of their quality.

CATEGORY	WARSAW*	OTHER AREAS*
$$$$	over $30	over $25
$$$	$20–$30	$15–$25
$$	$10–$20	$7–$15
$	under $10	under $7

*per person for a three-course meal, including service but not drinks

Hiking, Walking, and Cycling

There are nearly endless possibilities for hiking in Poland. All national parks have well-marked trails that cover some of the most beautiful countryside. The most spectacular terrain is in the south in the Tatra Mountains and in the Podhale region, and in the wild and deserted Bieszczady region in the southeast (on the Slovak and Ukrainian borders). The national parks have the additional advantage of providing overnight accommodations at regular intervals in walkers' huts and hostels, which can, however, be fairly primitive. Elsewhere in the country, it is more difficult to guarantee you'll find a bed at the right point on your route. The flat areas of the north are perhaps best for biking, but there are many parts of the country where you can enjoy touring tracks and byroads, for the Poles themselves are great cycling enthusiasts.

Lodging

Lodging options in most parts of Poland are still fairly restricted. State control of lodging facilities was virtually absolute until 1990, and private investment has not yet had time to make a real mark in this sector. Cheap and comfortable bed-and-breakfast accommodations in private homes or pensions are widely available only in the mountains or on the coast; look for signs in windows with the words POKOJE GOŚCINNE (guest rooms) or inquire at tourist information offices in resorts. In cities, private bed-and-breakfast accommodations are to be used only as a last resort; they are often run by disreputable proprietors who charge exorbitant prices.

Some privately owned hotels and wayside inns began to appear in the 1980s, and their number has increased rapidly since 1989. But often in the cities, your choice will be limited to hotels in, or just emerging from, the state sector. Only a small number of hotels—for example, the Marriott in Warsaw—are owned and managed by international chains; all other hotels bearing familiar names (Holiday Inn, Novotel) are run by Orbis, the state travel conglomerate, which at press time was in the process of privatization. Orbis hotels throughout the country offer a good international standard of accommodation, usually at international prices. Standards at municipally owned hotels vary enormously; ask to see your room before checking in. Gromada, the peasant cooperative, runs excellent, inexpensive hotels. The Polish Tourist Association, PTTK, also has a network of relatively inexpensive hotels throughout Poland, but single and double rooms are limited in number, and most of the accommodations are in dormitories.

Prices have fluctuated greatly since 1990, when state controls on hotel prices were abandoned. If you check rooms and price lists carefully, you may find real bargains outside the major cities. Service charges are included in the room price, but value-added tax (VAT)—introduced in 1993—is usually quoted as an additional percentage, ranging from 20% in the case of top-category hotels, down to 7%. Breakfast is also usually included in the price quoted by hotels for overnight accommodation, but this is not universal and is worth checking. Government star ratings (from five down to one) are outdated and refer to ownership category and size as much as to standards; they do, however, give an indication of price, which by no means always reflects the quality of the accommodations offered. Bathrooms may be fitted with either tubs or showers, and this is not necessarily reflected in the price. High-season prices on the coast (May to September) and in the southern mountain region (December to March and July through August) are up to 50% higher than off-season prices. Seasonal variations elsewhere in the country are less marked, apart from brief high-season rates for special occasions, as in Poznań during the trade fair.

CATEGORY	COST*
$$$$	over $200
$$$	$100–$200
$$	$50–$100
$	under $50

All prices are for two people in a double room, with bath or shower and breakfast.

Nightlife and the Arts

Poland has a strong musical tradition, and in the big cities in season (which unfortunately does not cover the main summer holiday period, but runs from October to May), you will have opportunities to hear outstanding musicians and orchestras—still at very moderate prices. Café musical performances in the evenings are frequent, and many up-market cafés have daytime pianists. Jazz is also popular; jazz clubs can be found for all tastes in most medium-size towns. Nightclubs with discos and floor shows are springing up everywhere, and at least in larger cities you will always have a range of entertainment to choose from into the small hours.

Shopping

Although the range of shops is increasing, Poland is not yet a shopper's paradise. Many local products have disappeared entirely—thanks to the manufacturing slump that followed the economic reforms. But Polish leather products are well designed, of high quality, and cheaper than their Western counterparts. The best region for leather is the south, Kraków for more sophisticated products, the mountains for folk equivalents. Amber and silver jewelry are on sale all over Poland, but it is on the Baltic coast that amber is found, and this is the best place to search for unusual pieces. Wood, woven, and embroidered folk arts and crafts are often intriguing to Western visitors and are to be found in Cepelia stores all over Poland; if possible, try to visit local folk artists' workshops. Glassware, including cut glass, is beautifully designed and relatively cheap. And, of course, anywhere in the country, you will find Polish vodka (*wódka*): **Polonez** or **Żytnia** are clear rye vodkas; **Żubrówka** is pale green and flavored with bison grass from the Białowieska forest; **Jarzębiak** is flavored with rowan berries.

Skiing

Southern Poland is the main region for winter sports, with skiing facilities both in the Tatras and the Podhale region and farther west in the Beskid Mountains. Here, Szczyrk has recently become a very popular center. The facilities in these resorts can be overcrowded, and you should not expect very sophisticated après-ski. For cross-country skiing, there is also good terrain in the northeast, particularly around Mrągowo.

Water Sports, Boating, and Sailing

The Mazury region provides the best opportunities for water sports, especially waterskiing. The main centers are Giżycko, Mrągowo, and Wilkasy. Local tourist enterprises there rent boats; consult the tourist offices for details.

Exploring Poland

Poland is a large country and has a great variety of scenery and architecture to offer the first-time visitor. The silvery Baltic Sea coast and Mazurian Lakes of the north lie 650 kilometers (400 miles) from the towering Tatra Mountains of the south—and between are historic cities and castles that call for your attention. If you are using public transportation, Warsaw is the hub from which all fast trains radiate: it is usually smart to begin and end your travels through Poland here.

Great Itineraries

Numbers in the text correspond to numbers in the margin and on the maps.

IF YOU HAVE 3 DAYS

Begin in **Warsaw** ①–㊼, where you should take in Warsaw's Old Town—destroyed during the Second World War and reconstructed during the 1950s—as well as the baroque palace in Wilanów and the neoclassical palace on the water in the Łazienki Park. On your second day, rent a car so that en route to Kraków, you can visit **Kazimierz Dolny** (81), a charming Renaissance village on the Vistula River, and catch at least a glimpse of Poland's lush countryside. Alternatively, you can go to Kraków by public transportation via **Częstochowa** (69), where the 14th-century Pauline monastery contains Poland's holiest relic: the icon of the Black Madonna. No matter how you get there, leave at least a whole day for **Kraków** ㊽–(68). Seat of Poland's oldest university and once the nation's capital (before finally relinquishing the honor to Warsaw in 1611), its uniquely intact Renaissance Old Town—listed by UNESCO as one of the 12 great historic cities of the world—contains a wealth of works of art and is home to the university where Nicholas Copernicus studied.

IF YOU HAVE 5 DAYS

Begin your stay in **Gdańsk** (84) and explore the historic Old City, which was originally one of the main Hanseatic ports on the Baltic. By car, take the E16 and T83 to Malbork and see the vast castle that was the headquarters of the Teutonic Knights (to do this properly, you need at least half a day). From Malbork, rejoin the E16 to head for **Toruń** (95), a small walled town on the Vistula River and Copernicus's birthplace. This is a good place for a stopover, as you have a number of restaurants and hotels to choose from. From Toruń, the T81 and E81 will take you to **Warsaw** ①–㊼. This route can also be done easily by train, but if you wish instead to explore the Mazurian Lakes on your way to Warsaw, a car is essential. From **Malbork** (86), take the cross-country route via Dzierzgon to Ostróda, and then the A170 to Olsztyn, before taking the E81 to Warsaw.

After a day exploring Warsaw, make your way to **Kraków** ㊽–(68). From here take a day trip to **Zakopane** (75), two hours away by bus, on the way admiring the foothills of the Podhale region and the High Tatra range in the distance. A day in Zakopane will allow you to try regional cooking and get a feel for life in the mountains.

When to Tour Poland

Spring, though sometimes late, is usually mild and sunny and is a good time for intense, energetic sightseeing. Summers can be hot and humid, especially in southern Poland, but this is still the busiest tourist season. If you are interested in the arts, remember that theaters and concert halls close completely in the summer for at least two months (July and August) and often do not get going with the new season's programs until October. The fabled Polish Golden Autumn, when landscapes are at their best, lasts until November and can be a good time for touring. The winter sports season is from December to March, when high-season rates are once again in effect in the mountains. In general, central heating is universal and efficient in Poland, but air-conditioning is a rarity.

WARSAW

Your first view of Warsaw (Warszawa) is likely to produce an impression of monotony and gray concrete, broken suddenly by a curious wedding-cake edifice rising majestically in the center of the city: Stalin's 1950s gift of the Palace of Culture and Science. In the early 1990s, an American entrepreneur wanted to purchase it in order to cut off the elaborate pinnacle and crenelated outbuildings and turn it into a skyscraper that would house a business center. Varsovians, after decades of mocking this symbol of Russian imperialism, shyly admitted to a certain sentimental attachment to it. The scheme fell through, and the Palace of Culture will still be there in 1997 to act as a useful orientation point to visitors.

Central Warsaw's predominating bleakness is a heritage of the city's 20th-century history: seventy-five percent destroyed by Hitler's armies in 1944, it was rebuilt in the "functional" styles of the 1950s and '60s and then, as economic times grew harder, largely left to decay. The local topography does not help: Warsaw is entirely flat, apart from the drop down the Vistula (Wisła) embankment, which runs through the city north to south.

But as you explore, you will forget your initial reservations. Fragments of the old Warsaw that survived the war acquire a special poignancy in their isolation: odd rows of art-nouveau tenements, like those on the south side of the great square around the Palace of Culture and Science or on ulica Wilcza; the elegant aleje Ujazdowskie, now the diplomatic quarter, leading to the Belvedere Palace and the Łazienki Palace and Park. The reconstructed areas of the city—the historic Old Town area, rebuilt brick by brick in the 1950s; the Royal Castle; the Ujazdowski Palace—are moving tributes to the Poles' ability to survive and preserve their history and traditions.

Moreover, Warsaw is at last getting a face-lift, and the pace of change is so fast that even locals can't keep up. The butcher shop where customers have faithfully lined up for meat over the past 25 years closes down one evening and is replaced the next day by a smart, white-tiled computer store. The local grocery turns overnight into a well-lighted boutique selling imported fashions at prices that seem like a king's ransom. All this is brightening the face of the city; gleaming paint and tiles in strong primary colors, clean windows, and fierce strip lighting are all still a novelty in Warsaw. While some may live to regret the disappearance of the local shoemaker or tailor—those picturesque survivors whom communism froze in a time warp—the new arrivals undoubtedly create a more cheerful and vibrant image. Visitors in search of Old World charm may be disappointed, but they can console themselves with the thought that the range of facilities available in many areas—notably dining out—is markedly improved.

Exploring Warsaw

The geographical core and political center of Poland since 1611, when King Zygmunt III moved the capital here from Kraków, Warsaw will doubtless shock the first-time visitor with its bleak postwar architecture. When one learns, however, of the history of this city, dismay is sure to turn first to amazement and then to deep appreciation for the surviving one-third of its inhabitants who so energetically rebuilt their city—literally from the ashes—starting in 1945. Warsaw was in the worst location possible during World War II, and perhaps nowhere else in Europe are there so many reminders of that time; plaques can be found all over describing the multiple massacres of Polish citizens by the Nazis.

(The city's darkest hours came in April 1943, when the inhabitants of the Jewish ghetto rose up in arms against the Nazis and were viciously and brutally put down, and in the summer of 1944, when the Warsaw Uprising was ultimately defeated.)

Amid the drabness of modern Warsaw you will find a few architectural attractions. Although most of the buildings in central Warsaw were built in an austere, quasi-Gothic Stalinist style, a large number of prewar buildings were carefully restored or, in many cases, completely reconstructed from old prints and paintings. A case in point is the beautiful **Rynek Starego Miasta** (Old Town Square), while the Royal Palace, which houses a museum, is the greatest of the rebuilt monuments.

Apart from the embankment carved out by the Vistula, which runs through the city north to south, Warsaw is entirely flat. Most sights, attractions, and hotels lie to the west of the river. Major thoroughfares include **aleje Jerozolimskie,** which runs east–west, and **Nowy Świat,** which runs north–south through a main shopping district, passes the university, and ends at the entrance to the **Stare Miasto** (Old Town). Be careful about Nowy Świat: Its name changes six times between its starting point in Wilanów (where it's called aleja Wilanowska) and its terminus (where it's named Krakowskie Przezdmieście). To orient yourself, start at the central train station, the Marriott Hotel, or the Palace of Culture, all of which sit within a block of one another on aleje Jerozolimskie (the Marriott, a glass skyscraper, and the Palace of Culture, the enormous brick monstrosity that looks like a wedding cake, are the two most visible buildings in town). Walk west toward the river on aleje Jerozolimskie two blocks to Nowy Świat. Heading north, this street is a main shopping district, closed to all traffic except buses; in about 20 minutes the street (now called **Krakowskie Przedmieście**) will terminate at **plac Zamkowy,** the plaza that marks the entrance to the Old Town. North of here is **Nowe Miasto** (New Town), primarily a residential area, and to the west lie **Muranów** and **Mirów,** former Jewish districts. **Praga,** a poorer quarter of workers and artisans that emerged from the war fairly intact, and the enormous **Zoological Park,** are situated east of the Wisła.

Numbers in the text correspond to numbers in the margin and on the Warsaw map.

The Old Town

The Old Town is for those who enjoy museums, art, and historic architecture away from the bustle of everyday city life. It is closed to traffic, and in its narrow streets you can relax and leave the 20th century behind for a while. Everything here is within easy walking distance.

A GOOD WALK

Begin at **plac Zamkowy** (Castle Square) ①, first visiting the **Zamek Królewski** (Royal Castle) ②. Make your way next along the narrow ulica Kanonia, where you'll find the great cracked **Zygmunt bell** in the middle of a quiet, cobbled square—just where it fell from the cathedral tower during the bombardment of 1939. Continue along ulica Jezuicka, where you might turn through one of the archways and admire the view over the Vistula from the terrace that runs at the back of the houses. The **Rynek Starego Miasta** (Old Town Square) ③ is a place to relax and to take in buildings like the Klucznikowska Mansion at Rynek Starego Miasta 21. Now housing an elegant restaurant, this fine structure has a Gothic brick portal and cellars, which are remnants of the first 15th-century building on this site. Also be sure to visit the **Warsaw Historical Museum** ④ or the **Adam Mickiewicz Museum of**

Literature ⑤. Continue north from the Rynek along Krzywe Koło and the ramparts of the Old Town's walls to reach the **Barbakan** ⑥, marking the boundary between the Old and New towns.

On ulica Freta, you will find the **Kościół Dominkanów** (Dominican Church) ⑦ and the house where Marie Skłodowska-Curie was born, now the **Muzeum Marii Skłodowskiej-Curie** (Marie Curie Museum) ⑧. Ulica Freta takes you to the **Rynek Nowego Miasta** (New Town Square) ⑩, near which there are fine churches from different periods, built from the 15th to 17th centuries, including **Kościół Najświętszej Marii Panny** (St. Mary's Church) ⑪ and **Kościół Sakramentek** (Church of the Sisters of the Blessed Sacrament) ⑫. Returning from the New Town, take ulica Świętojerska to plac Krasińskich, with its **Pomnik Bohaterów Warszawy 1939–1945** (Monument to the Heroes of Warsaw) ⑬, and go back along ulica Długa to the Barbakan. Ulica Nowomiejska will take you back to the Rynek—always worth a second visit—and then go by ulica Świętojańska, with **Archikatedralna Bazylika świętego Jana** (Cathedral Church of St. John) ⑮ on your left, to return to plac Zamkowy.

TIMING

The Old Town is not large in area. If you are content admiring the outsides of buildings, you can see it in half a day. But to take it in fully, you will need a whole day to explore. Remember that most museums do not open until 10 AM and that most shops do not open until 11 AM. Museums also often close relatively early, around 4. At the Royal Castle, give yourself about three hours if you want to explore all of its exhibits fully. The Old Town Square, with its cafés and restaurants, is a good place to relax in the evening.

SIGHTS TO SEE

⑤ **Adam Mickiewicz Museum of Literature.** If you are interested in Polish writers, you might visit the Adam Mickiewicz Museum of Literature, which contains manuscripts, mementos, and portraits, particularly from the romantic period. ⊠ *Rynek Starego Miasta 20,* ☎ *022/31–40–61.* ⊇ *Zł 2.5.* ☉ *Tues.–Sat. 10–2:30.*

⑮ **Archikatedralna Bazylika świętego Jana** (Cathedral Church of St. John). Ulica Świętojańska, leading from the Old Town Square to the Royal Castle, takes its name from Warsaw's Cathedral of St. John, which was built at the turn of the 14th century; coronations of the Polish kings took place here from the 16th to the 18th centuries. The crypts contain the tombs of the last two princes of Mazovia, the archbishops of Warsaw, and such famous Poles as the 19th-century, Nobel Prize–winning novelist Henryk Sienkiewicz, the author of *Quo Vadis?* ⊠ *On the north side of ul. Świętojańska, 1 block up from pl. Zamkowy.*

⑥ **Barbakan.** The pinnacled, redbrick Barbakan, the mid-16th-century stronghold in the old city wall on ulica Freta, now marks the boundary between the Old Town and the New Town. It houses a tiny art gallery at the top of a narrow staircase; less successful artists festoon the outside walls with their wares.

OFF THE
BEATEN PATH

KOŚCIÓŁ ŚW. STANISŁAWA KOSTKI – In October 1984, parish priest Jerzy Popiełuszko was brutally murdered by the Polish secret service because he spoke out against the regime. Once his murder was discovered, Father Popiełuszko's church became the site of frequent Solidarity demonstrations. You can visit the grave of this martyr on the grounds of this church in the district of Żoliborz, north of the New Town. Take Bus A or J from ulica Bonifraterska to plac Komuny Paryskiej, then walk two blocks west along ulica Zygmunta Krasinskiego. ⊠ *Ul. Stanisława Hozjusza 2.*

❼ Kościół Dominkanów (Dominican Church). The baroque Dominican Church in Warsaw's New Town was badly damaged in the aftermath of the 1943 uprising, when the adjoining monastery served as a field hospital for wounded insurrectionists. It was reconstructed in the 1950s. ⊠ *Ul. Freta 8–10.*

⓰ Kościół Jezuitów (Jesuit Church). On the left-hand side of the entrance to St. John's Cathedral is the early 17th-century Jesuit Church, founded by King John Sobieski, the victor at Vienna. Throughout the postwar years, a visit to this church at Eastertime was considered a must by Varsovians: Its Gethsemane decorations always contained a hidden political message (in 1985, for example, the risen Christ had the face of Father Jerzy Popiełuszko, the Warsaw priest who was murdered the previous year by members of the Polish security service. ⊠ *On the north side of ul. Świętojańska, 1 block up from pl. Zamkowy.*

⓫ Kościół Najświętszej Marii Panny (St. Mary's Church). The oldest church in the New Town, St. Mary's was built as a parish church by the princes of Mazovia in the early 15th century. It has been destroyed and rebuilt many times throughout its history. The Gothic bell tower dates from the early 16th century. ⊠ *Przyrynek 2.*

⓬ Kościół Sakramentek (Church of the Sisters of the Blessed Sacrament). Built as a thanksgiving offering by King John Sobieski's queen, Marysieńka, after his victory against the Turks at Vienna in 1683, the cool, white Kościół Sakramentek stands on the east side of New Town Square. ⊠ *Rynek Nowego Miasta 2.*

❽ Muzeum Marii Skłodowskiej-Curie (Marie Curie Museum). The house in which Marie Curie was born is on ulica Freta; a small museum inside is dedicated to the great physicist, chemist, winner of two Nobel Prizes, and discoverer of radium. ⊠ *Ul. Freta 16,* ☎ *022/31–80–92.* 🎟 *Zł 2.* ⊙ *Tues.–Sat. 10–4:30, Sun. 10–2:30.*

⓮ Pałac Krasińskich (Krasinski Palace). The late-17th-century, baroque Krasinski Palace currently houses the historic prints collection of Poland's National Library. ⊠ *Pl. Krasińskich 5.*

❶ Plac Zamkowy (Castle Square). This is a popular rendezvous; take care to avoid the skateboarders who have made the gently sloping square their province. Marking the entrance to the Old Town from the southeast is the **Zygmunt Column,** which honors King Zygmunt III Wasa, king of Poland and Sweden, who in the early 17th century transferred the capital of the country from Kraków to Warsaw.

⓭ Pomnik Bohaterów Warszawy 1939–1945 (Monument to the Heroes of Warsaw). Unveiled in 1989, this monument constitutes a poignant reminder of what World War II meant for the citizens of Warsaw. Massive bronze figures raise defiant fists above the opening to sewers used in 1944 by Polish resistance fighters in Warsaw's Old Town to escape from the Nazis. ⊠ *Corner of pl. Krasińskich and ul. Długa.*

⓰ Rynek Nowego Miasta (New Town Square). The leafy New Town Square is slightly more irregular and relaxed than its Old Town counterpart. The houses on the square, and in nearby streets like ulica Kościelna, have curiously stark and formalized wall paintings.

★ ❸ Rynek Starego Miasta (Old Town Square). This is the hub of life in Warsaw's Old Town. The earliest settlers came to this spot during the 10th and 11th centuries. Legend has it that a peasant named Wars was

342

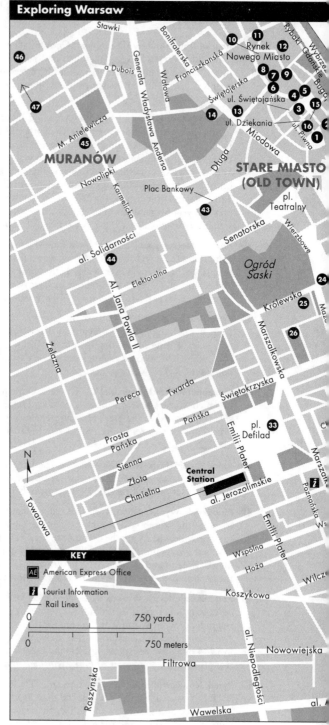

Exploring Warsaw

KEY

AE American Express Office

i Tourist Information

— Rail Lines

0 — 750 yards

0 — 750 meters

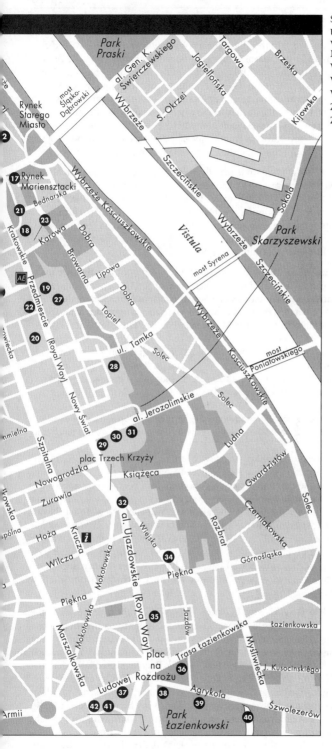

directed to the site by a mermaid named Sawa—hence the name of the city in Polish, **Warszawa** (Sawa has been immortalized in Warsaw's official emblem). In the 14th century Warsaw was already a walled city, and in 1413 its citizens obtained a borough charter from the princes of Mazovia. The present layout of the Old Town dates from this time, and traces of the original Gothic buildings still surround the Old Town Square. The appearance of today's square, however, largely dates from the late 16th and 17th centuries, when Warsaw's wealth and importance grew rapidly as a result of the 1569 Polish-Lithuanian union and Warsaw's new status as capital city. The great merchant families of the city set about rebuilding their properties in contemporary style.

The Old Town Square is usually very busy, even though no traffic is allowed and there is no longer a formal market. Artists and craftspeople of all kinds still sell their wares here in the summer, but don't expect many bargains—tourists are their prime targets. Musical performances are often held here on weekends on a stage erected at the north end. Horse-drawn cabs await visitors; for zł 50 you can be driven around the Old Town in traditional style.

❹ Warsaw Historical Museum. Four fine examples of **Renaissance mansions** can be found on the northern side of the Old Town Square: the **Talenti Mansion** at No. 38, the **Negro House** at No. 36 (note the sculpture of a black slave on the facade), the **Szlichtyngowska Mansion** at No. 34, and the **Baryczka Mansion** at No. 32. These historical homes, some of which contain Renaissance ceiling paintings, now house this museum, which offers daily screenings of a short documentary film made in 1945 about the destruction of Warsaw. ⊠ *Rynek Starego Miasta 28–42,* ☎ *022/635–16–25.* 🎫 *Zł 3.5.* ⊘ *Tues. and Thurs. noon–7; Wed., Fri., and Sat. 10–3:30; Sun. 10:30–4:30.*

NEED A BREAK? **Hortex** (⊠ Rynek Starego Miasta 3–9) has a large open-air café in summer; at the same address on the ground floor is a quick-service lunch bar.

---

❾ Warszawska Syrenka (Warsaw Mermaid). Krzywe Koło (Crooked Wheel Street) runs from the Old Town Square to the reconstructed ramparts of the city wall. From this corner, which is graced by a towering stone mermaid known as the Warszawska Syrenka, you can again look out over the Vistula and also over Warsaw's New Town (Nowe Miasto), stretching to the north beyond the city walls. As you look out over the town walls and down the Vistula embankment, you will see the **Stara Prochownia** (Old Powder Tower) on ulica Boleść, just past the intersection with ulica Bugaj; this has now been turned into an interesting theater, a popular venue for poetry readings, music, and drama.

★ ❷ Zamek Królewski (Royal Castle). Warsaw's Royal Castle stands on the East side of ☞ **Castle Square.** The princes of Mazovia first built a residence on this spot overlooking the Vistula in the 14th century; its present Renaissance form dates from the reign of King Sigismund III, who needed a magnificent palace for his new capital. Reconstructed later than the Old Town, in the 1970s, it now gleams as it did in its earliest years, with gilt, marble, and wall paintings; it houses impressive art collections—including the famous views of Warsaw by Bernardo Bellotto (also known as Canaletto)—and period furniture. Tours with an English-speaking guide begin from the side entrance every hour or by previous appointment. ⊠ *Pl. Zamkowy 4,* ☎ *022/635–39–95.* 🎫 *Zł 10; Sun. zł 3. Tours start hourly from side entrance.* ⊘ *Tues.–Sat. 10–2:30, Sun. 9–2:30.*

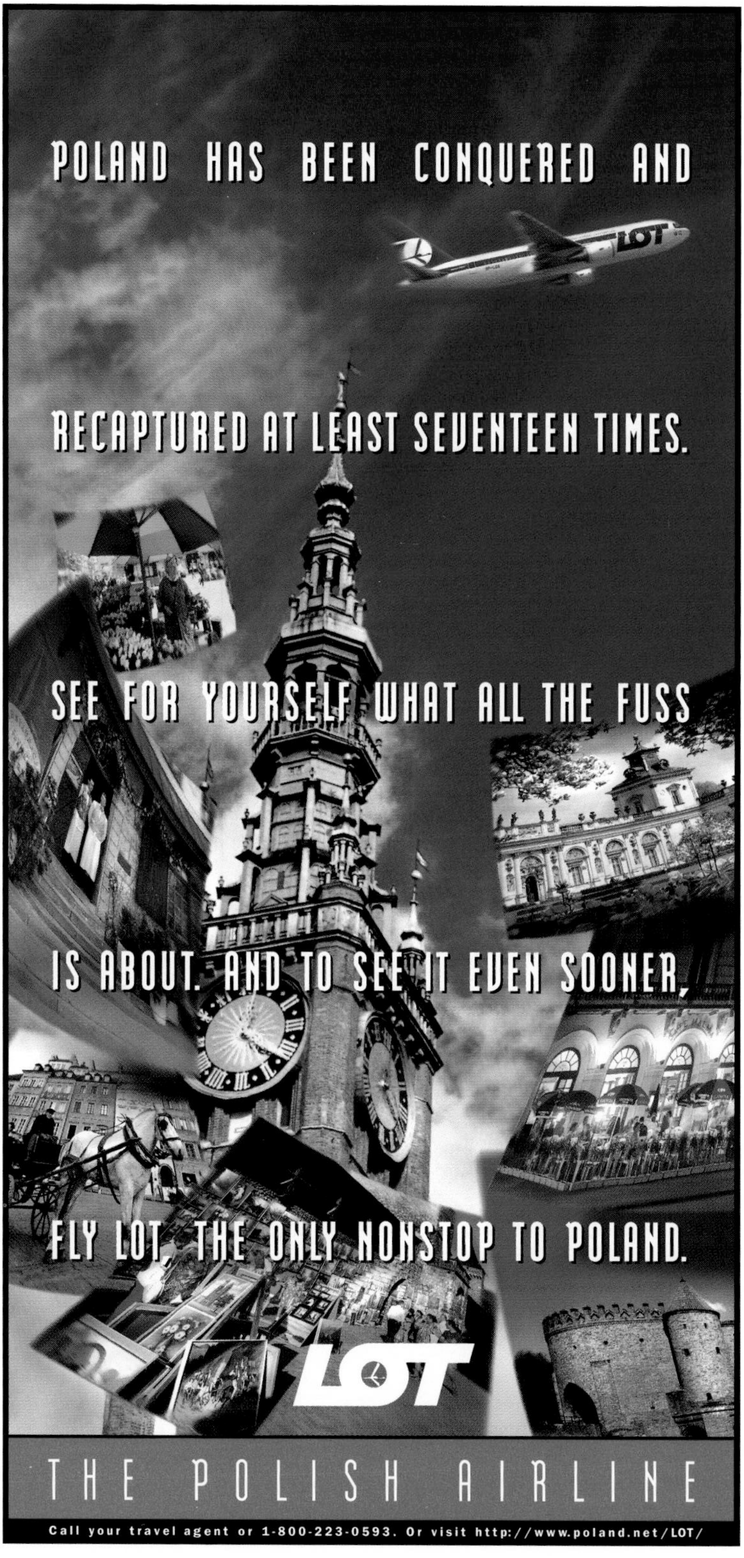

POLAND HAS BEEN CONQUERED AND
RECAPTURED AT LEAST SEVENTEEN TIMES.
SEE FOR YOURSELF WHAT ALL THE FUSS
IS ABOUT. AND TO SEE IT EVEN SOONER,
FLY LOT, THE ONLY NONSTOP TO POLAND.
LOT
THE POLISH AIRLINE
Call your travel agent or 1-800-223-0593. Or visit http://www.poland.net/LOT/

It helps to be pushy in airports.

Stable 4-wheel design.

Introducing the revolutionary new TransPorter™ from American Tourister® It's the first suitcase you can push around without a fight. TransPorter's™ exclusive four-wheel design lets you push it in front of you with almost no effort—the wheels take the weight. Or pull it on two wheels if you choose. You can even stack on other bags and use it like a luggage cart.

TransPorter™ is designed like a dresser, with built-in shelves to organize your belongings. Or collapse the shelves and pack it like a traditional suitcase. Inside, there's a suiter feature to help keep suits and dresses from wrinkling. When push comes to shove, you can't beat a TransPorter™ For more information on how you can be this pushy, call 1-800-542-1300.

Shelves collapse on command.

American Tourister®

Making travel less primitive.®

©1996 American Tourister®

Kawiarnia Literacka (✉ Krakowskie Przedmieście 87–89, ☎ 022/635-
89–95), on the ground floor of the PEN club premises, is an airy café
with classic jazz in the evenings on weekends.

The Royal Route

A GOOD WALK

Krakowskie Przedmieście and **Nowy Świat** form the first part of the
Royal Route, or King's Road, which led from the Royal Castle to the
summer palace at Wilanów, a distance of about 7½ kilometers (4½ miles).
The first stage of the route, from plac Zamkowy to aleje Jerozolimski,
is about 3 kilometers (2 miles). Krakowskie Przedmieście is a wide thor-
oughfare lined with fine churches—**Kościół św. Anny** (St. Anne's
Church) ⑰, **Kościół Karmelitów** (Church of the Discalced [barefoot]
Carmelites) ⑱, **Kościół Wizytek** (Church of the Visitation Sisters) ⑲,
Kościół Świętego Krzyża (Holy Cross Church) ⑳—and elegant mansions and palaces, including **Pałac Kazanowskich** (Kazanowski Palace) ㉑,
Pałac Czapskich (Czapski Palace) ㉒, **Pałac Namiestnikowski** (Governor's Palace) ㉓, and **Pałac Potockich** (Potocki Palace).

You can detour from the route down the hill via ulica Bednarska to the
leafy **Rynek Mariensztacki** (Mariensztat Square), a 10-minute walk. Another detour—this one to the west along Bagińskiego—will bring you
in two minutes to the wide-open spaces of the plac Piłsudskiego, site of
the **Grób Nieznanego Żołnierza** (Tomb of the Unknown Soldier) ㉔ and
the **Teatr Wielki** (Opera House). Take ulica Mazowiecka from the southwest corner, passing the **Galeria Zachęta** (Zachęta Gallery) ㉕ on your
right, and turn west into ulica Kredytowa. On your right is the 18th-
century neoclassical **Kościół Ewangelicko-Augsburski** (Augsburg Evangelical Church), which like St. Alexander's Church in plac Trzech Krzyży,
was modeled on the Pantheon. Go a block farther to find the **Muzeum
Etnograficzne** (Ethnographic Museum) ㉖; return to Krakowskie Przedmieście via ulica Traugutta. Beyond the campus of **Warsaw University** ㉗,
beside the **statue of Nicholas Copernicus,** the road narrows and becomes
ulica Nowy Świat, a pedestrian precinct with elegant shops and cafés
housed in 18th-century houses. From here, you can detour down the hill
to the east—a 10 minutes' walk—to the **Pałac Ostrogskich** (Ostrogski
Palace) ㉘. At the south end of ulica Nowy Świat you will find the massive **former headquarters of the Communist Party** ㉙ and immediately
east of this building, the **Muzeum Narodowe** (National Museum of
Warsaw) ㉚—in which you can easily spend half a day—and the **Muzeum
Wojska Polskiego** (Polish Army Museum) ㉛. At the south end of **plac
Trzech Krzyży** (Three Crosses Square) is **Kościół św. Aleksandra** (St. Alexan-
der's Church) ㉜, built in the early 19th century as a copy of the Roman
Pantheon. If you have time, from the tram stop at the corner of Nowy
Świat make the two-stop trip west along aleje Jerozolimski to the **Pałac
Kultury i Nauki** (Palace of Culture and Science) ㉝.

TIMING

At a brisk walking pace you can cover this route in less than an hour,
but to soak in the sights along the way, allow a whole morning or afternoon.

SIGHTS TO SEE

Deaf and Blind Institute. An early 19th–century building now somewhat dwarfed by the Sheraton Hotel houses the Deaf and Blind Institute, established in 1817 and one of the first in Europe. ✉ *Pl. Trzech
Krzyży 4–6.*

㉙ **Former Headquarters of the Polish Communist Party.** At the south end
of New World Street, at its intersection with Aleje Jerozolimskie, is the
former headquarters of the Polish Communist Party. This despised, solid

white symbol of oppression has been converted into a banking center and stock exchange. ⊠ *Nowy Świat 6.*

BAZAR RÓŻYCKIEGO – On the east side of the Vistula River is one of the largest open markets in Eastern Europe and a haven of free enterprise that survived 45 years of Communist rule. Here you can find traders from all over the former Eastern bloc and farther afield selling an amazing variety of goods, from computers to Russian vodka. Beware of pickpockets. ⊠ *Ul. Targowa 55. Take Tram 7 east from al. Jerozolimskie.*

㉕ **Galeria Zachęta** (Zachęta Gallery). Built in the last years of the 19th century by the Society for the Encouragement of the Fine Arts, this art gallery stands on the corner of ulica Królewska and plac Piłsudskiego. It was in this building that the first president of the post–World War I Polish Republic, Gabriel Narutowicz, was assassinated by a right-wing fanatic in 1922. It has no permanent collection but organizes thought-provoking special exhibitions (primarily modern art) in high-ceiling, well-lighted halls. ⊠ *Pl. Małachowskiego 3,* ☎ *022/27–69–09.* 🎫 *Varies.* ☉ *Tues.–Sun. 10–6.*

㉔ **Grób Nieznanego Żołnierza** (Tomb of the Unknown Soldier). Built as a memorial after World War I, the Tomb of the Unknown Soldier contains the body of a Polish soldier brought from the eastern battlefields of the Polish-Soviet war of 1919–1920—a fact not much mentioned in the 45 years of Communist rule after World War II. Ceremonial changes of the guard take place at 10 AM on Sunday; many visitors may be faintly surprised to see the Polish Army still using the goose step on occasions of this kind. The memorial is a surviving fragment of the early 18th-century ☞ **Saxon Palace,** which used to stand here on the west side of plac Piłsudskiego.

⑱ **Kościół Karmelitów** (Church of the Discalced Carmelites). The late-17th-century baroque Church of the Discalced Carmelites stands back across a square from the main line of the street. ⊠ *Krakowskie Przedmieście 52.*

㉜ **Kościół świętego Aleksandra** (St. Alexander's Church). Built in the early 19th century as a copy of the Roman Pantheon, St. Alexander's stands on an island in the middle of **plac Trzech Krzyży,** a name which is notoriously difficult for foreigners to pronounce and means "Three Crosses Square." One of the crosses in question is on the church itself.

⑳ **Kościół świętego Krzyża** (Holy Cross Church). With a massive sculpted crucifix atop the steps, this baroque church contains, immured in a pillar, the heart of Poland's most famous composer, Fryderyk Chopin. ⊠ *Krakowskie Przedmieście 3.*

⑰ **Kościół świętej Anny** (St. Anne's Church). Built in 1454 by Anne, princess of Mazovia, St. Anne's Church stands on the south corner of plac Zamkowy. It was rebuilt in high-Baroque style after destruction during the Swedish invasions in the 17th century; thanks to 1990s redecoration and regilding it once again glows in its original splendor. A plaque on the wall outside marks the spot where Pope John Paul II celebrated Mass in 1980, during his first visit to Poland after his election to the papacy. ⊠ *Krakowskie Przedmieście 68.*

⑲ **Kościół Wizytek** (Church of the Visitation Sisters). The late-baroque Kościół Wizytek adjoins ☞ **Warsaw University.** In front of it stands a statue of Cardinal Stefan Wyszyński, primate of Poland from 1948 to 1981. Wyszyński was imprisoned during the 1950s but lived to see a Polish pope and the birth of Solidarity; the fresh flowers always lying at the foot of the statue are evidence of the warmth with which he is remembered. ⌧ *Krakowskie Przedmieście 30.*

㉖ Muzeum Etnograficzne (Ethnographic Museum). A fascinating collection of Polish folk art, crafts, and costumes from all parts of the country reside on permanent display here. ⌧ *Ul. Kredytowa 1,* ☎ *022/27–76–41.* ⌹ *Zł 3.* ☉ *Tues., Thurs., and Fri. 9–4; Wed. 11–6; weekends and holidays 10–5.*

★ **㉚ Muzeum Narodowe** (National Museum of Warsaw). In a functional 1930s building, the National Museum has an impressive collection of contemporary Polish and European paintings, Gothic icons, and works from antiquity. The famous Canaletto paintings that were used to facilitate the rebuilding of Warsaw after the war are also on display here. ⌧ *Al. Jerozolimskie 3,* ☎ *022/621–10–31.* ⌹ *Zł 3.5, Wed. free.* ☉ *Wed., Fri., and Sat. 10–4; Thurs. noon–6; Sun. and holidays 10–5; closed day after holidays.*

㉛ Muzeum Wojska Polskiego (Polish Army Museum). If you're interested in military matters, you might want to visit this museum's exhibits of weaponry, armor, and uniforms, which trace Polish military history for the past 10 centuries. Heavy armaments are displayed outside. ⌧ *Al. Jerozolimskie 3,* ☎ *022/629–52–71.* ⌹ *Zł 2, Wed. free.* ☉ *Wed. noon–6, Thurs.–Sat. 11–4, Sun. and holidays 10:30–5; closed day after holidays.*

Ogród Saski (Saxon Gardens). The Saxon Gardens were once the park of the Saxon Palace, of which nothing now remains but a fragment which was used to make the Tomb of the Unknown Soldier. The park was designed by French and Saxon landscape gardeners; visitors can still admire the 18th-century sculptures, artificial lake, and sundial. ⌧ *Between pl. Piłsudskiego and ul. Marszałkowska.*

㉒ Pałac Czapskich (Czapski Palace). Now the home of the Academy of Fine Arts, the Czapski Palace dates from the late 17th century but was rebuilt in 1740 in rococo style. Zygmunt Krasiński, the Polish romantic poet, was born here in 1812, and Chopin once lived in the palace mews. ⌧ *Krakowskie Przedmieście 5.*

㉑ Pałac Kazanowskich (Kazanowski Palace). On the corner of Krakowskie Przedmieście and ulica Bednarska is the Pałac Kazanowskich. Built in the mid-17th century, it was given a neoclassical front elevation in the 19th century. The courtyard at the rear still contains massive late-Renaissance buttresses and is worth a visit because of its plaque commemorating Zagloba's fight with the monkeys from Sienkiewicz's historical novel *The Deluge.* In a small garden in front of the palace stands the **monument to Adam Mickiewicz,** the great Polish romantic poet. It was here that Warsaw University students gathered in March 1968, after a performance of Mickiewicz's hitherto banned play *Fore-fathers' Eve,* and set in motion the events that led to the toppling of Poland's long-serving Communist leader Władysław Gomułka. ⌧ *Krakowskie Przedmieście 62.*

㉝ Pałac Kultury i Nauki (Palace of Culture and Science). This massive wedding-cake structure is the main landmark in the city, and from the 30th floor you can get a panoramic view. The old joke runs that this is Warsaw's best view because it is the only place where you can't see the palace. You ride up by elevator (tickets are zł 5, available from the cash desk behind the coatroom at the east entrance), and on a clear day you can see for miles in all directions. The palace houses a number of institutions and recreational facilities, including a swimming pool and the museum of science and technology. It has a good puppet theater—an art form at which the Poles excel and that is not only for children—called **Teatr Lalek** and nicknamed Lalka (entrance on north side, ☎ 022/620–49–50). ⊠ *Pl. defilad,* ☎ *022/620–02–11.*

㉓ Pałac Namiestnikowski (Governor's Palace). This palace was built in the 17th century by the Radziwiłł family (into which Jackie Kennedy's sister Lee later married). In the 19th century it functioned as the administrative office of the czarist occupiers—hence its present name. In 1955 the Warsaw Pact was signed here, later the palace served as the headquarters for the Presidium of the Council of Ministers, and since 1995 it has been the official residence of Poland's president. In the forecourt is an **equestrian statue of Prince Józef Poniatowski,** a nephew of the last king of Poland and one of Napoléon's marshals. He was wounded and drowned in the Elster River during the Battle of the Nations at Leipzig in 1813, following the disastrous retreat of Napoléon's Grande Armée from Russia. ⊠ *Krakowskie Przedmieście 46–48.*

NEED A BREAK? The café of the **Hotel Europejski** (⊠ Krakowskie Przedmieście 13, 00–071) still has palm trees and a grand piano despite the recently introduced yellow-plastic furniture. It serves sandwiches as well as the usual cakes and drinks.

㉘ Pałac Ostrogskich (Ostrogski Palace). The headquarters of the **Chopin Society** is in the 17th-century Ostrogski Palace, which towers impressively above ulica Tamka. The best approach is via the steps from ulica Tamka. In the 19th century the Warsaw Conservatory was housed here (Paderewski was one of its students); now a venue for Chopin concerts, it has a small museum with mementos of the composer. ⊠ *Ul. Okólnik 1,* ☎ *022/27–54–71.* 🎟 *Free.* ☉ *Mon.–Wed., Fri., and Sat. 10–2; Thurs. noon–6; closed holidays.*

NEED A BREAK? **Blikle** (⊠ Nowy Świat 35), Warsaw's oldest cake shop, has a black-and-white tiled café that offers savory snacks as well as Blikle's famous doughnuts.

Pałac Potockich (Potocki Palace). The charming semirococo 18th-century Pałac Potockich now houses the Ministry of Arts and is accessible from the street through a narrow wrought-iron gate. ⊠ *Krakowskie Przedmieście 15.*

Rynek Mariensztacki (Marisensztat Square). The steeply sloping, cobbled ulica Bednarska leads from Krakowskie Przedmieście down to Rynek Mariensztacki, a quiet, leafy 18th-century square surrounded in summer by café tables.

Statue of Nicholas Copernicus. A sedate seated statue of Nicholas Copernicus holding a globe stands in front of the headquarters of the Polish Academy of Sciences, in the early 19th-century neoclassical **Staszic Palace** (⊠ Nowy Świat 72). This statue, like many other notable Warsaw monuments, is the work of the 19th-century Danish sculptor Bertel Thorvaldsen.

NEED A BREAK? **Nowy Świat** (⊠ Nowy Świat 63), on the corner of Nowy Świat and ulica Świętokrzyska, is a spacious, traditional café, with plenty of foreign-language newspapers for those who want to linger over coffee.

Teatr Wielki (Opera House). The massive, neoclassical Opera House, built in the 1820s and reconstructed after the war, has an auditorium with over 2,000 seats and occupies the whole south side of plac Teatralny and the north side of plac Piłsudskiego. There is also a **Mu-**

seum of Theater on the first floor of the building. ⊠ *Pl. Teatralny. Muzeum Teatralny,* ☎ *022/26–52–13.* ⊙ *Tues.–Sun. 10–2.*

㉗ **Warsaw University.** The high wrought-iron gates of Warsaw University lead into a leafy campus; the **Pałac Kazimierzowski,** which currently houses the university administration, was in the 18th century the Military Cadet School where Tadeusz Kościuszko studied. ⊠ *Krakowskie Przedmieście 26–28.*

The Łazienki Park and Diplomatic Quarter

A GOOD WALK

The Łazienki Park and the diplomatic quarter lie along the Royal Route leading from the Old Town to Wilanów, at the point beyond plac Trzech Krzyży. From here it is about two miles to the southern edge of the Łazienki Park. Enter aleje Ujazdowskie, a fashionable avenue where the rich built residences during the 19th century. Many of their mansions now hold foreign embassies. Five minutes' walk down ulica Wiejska, on your left, is the **Sejm** (Polish parliament) ㉞. Parallel to aleje Ujazdowskie after ulica Piękna you may choose to stroll under the trees of the **Park Ujazdowski** ㉟, keeping farther away from the traffic. At plac Na Rozdrożu you'll leave the diplomatic quarter and enter Warsaw's "Whitehall." If you are interested in modern art, the **Zamek Ujazdowski** ㊱, the home of the Center for Contemporary Art, is 200 yards east from plac na Rozdrożu, down a path through the park parallel to the Trasa Łazienkowska. The wartime **Gestapo headquarters** ㊲ is 200 yards in the opposite direction from the square, on aleje Szucha. The rest of this part of the Royal Route is lined with government buildings, among them the office of the Council of Ministers. On your left are the **Botanical Gardens** ㊳ and **Park Łazienkowski** (Łazienki Park) ㊴. To reach the **Pałac Łazienkowski** (Palace on the Lake) ㊵, enter by the gates opposite ulica Bagatela, beside the **Pałac Belweder** (Belvedere Palace) ㊶.

At the top of the hill of the Vistula embankment, you enter ulica Belwederska. It is at this point that you must board Bus 122 for **Wilanów Palace** ㊷, since the rest of the Royal Route, which until the 1980s ran through open countryside, is now lined on both sides by high-rise housing developments.

TIMING

Take a morning or afternoon to explore this route. If, however, you wish to linger at some of the sights, make it a whole day: The Łazienki Park and Palace on the Lake deserve three or four hours at the least. Tree-lined and shady, this is a good walk for a hot summer day.

SIGHTS TO SEE

㊳ **Botanical Gardens.** These gardens, covering an area of roughly 3 acres, were laid out in 1818, and at the entrance stands the neoclassical **observatory,** now part of ☞ **Warsaw University.** ⊠ *Al. Ujazdowskie 4.*

㊲ **Gestapo headquarters.** The building that currently houses the Polish Ministry of National Education was the Gestapo headquarters during World War II; a small museum commemorates the horrors that took place behind its peaceful facade. ⊠ *Al. Szucha,* ☎ *022/629–49–19.* ▧ *Free.* ⊙ *Tues.–Sat. 10–2.*

㊶ **Pałac Belweder** (Belvedere Palace). Built in the early 18th century, the palace was reconstructed in 1818 in neoclassical style by the Russian governor of Poland, the Grand Duke Constantine. Until 1994 it was the official residence of Poland's president. The Pałac Belweder stands just south of the main gates to the Łazienki Park. ⊠ *Ul. Belwederska 2.*

★ ㊵ **Pałac Łazienkowski** (Palace on the Lake). The neoclassical Palace on the Lake is the focal point of the Łazienki Park. This magnificent summer residence was so faithfully reconstructed after the war that there is still no electricity—be sure to visit when it's sunny, or you won't see anything inside. The palace holds some splendid 18th-century furniture as well as part of Stanisław August's art collection. ⊠ *Ul. Agrykola 1,* ☎ *022/621–82–12.* 🎫 *Zł 3.5.* ☉ *Tues.–Sun. 9:30–3.*

㊴ Park Łazienkowski (Łazienki Park). The 180 acres of the Łazienki Park, commissioned during the late 18th century by King Słanisław August Poniatowski, run along the Vistula escarpment, parallel to and east of the Royal Route. The **Museum of Hunting** in the old coach houses on the east side of the park contains a fascinating collection of stuffed birds and animals found in Poland. If you prefer live fauna, look out for the peacocks that wander through the park and the delicate red squirrels that in Poland answer to the name Basia, a diminutive of Barbara. One of the most beloved sights in the Park is the **Chopin Memorial,** a sculpture under a streaming willow tree that shows the composer in a typical romantic pose, with flowing hair. The surrounding rose beds are lined with benches, and in the summer outdoor concerts of Chopin's piano music are held here every Sunday. ⊠ *Between pl. na Rozdrożu and ul. Bagatela.*

㉟ Park Ujazdowski (Ujazdów Park). At the entrance to the formal gardens of the Park Ujazdowski on the corner of aleje Ujazdowskie and ulica Piękna, there is a **19th-century weighing booth** just inside the gate, still in operation. On aleje Ujazdowskie (entrance on ul. Piękna), there is a good **playground** for small children, with sand, swings, and slides.

Russian Embassy. A reminder of Poland's long and tangled relationship with Russia can be found in the massive, Colonial-style former Soviet Embassy—now the embassy of the Commonwealth of Independent States—which for 45 years after World War II channeled directives from Moscow to a more or less compliant Polish Communist government. ⊠ *Belwederska 49.*

㉞ Sejm. The Polish Houses of the Sejm (parliament) are housed in a round, white debating chamber that was built during the 1920s, after the rebirth of an independent Polish state. ⊠ *Ul. Wiejska 6.*

NEED A BREAK? **Ambasador** (⊠ Ul. Matejki 4) is a large, bright café decorated with brocade. It's at its best in the summer, when it offers seating on a tree-lined garden terrace.

★ ㊷ Wilanów Palace. A baroque gateway and false moat lead to the wide courtyard that stretches in front of Wilanów Palace, built between 1681 and 1696 by King John III Sobieski. After his death, the palace passed through various hands before being bought at the end of the 18th century by Stanisław Kostka Potocki, who was responsible for amassing a major collection of art and for the layout of the gardens and who opened the first public museum here in 1805. Potocki's neo-Gothic tomb can be seen to the left of the driveway as you approach the palace. The palace interiors still hold much of the original furniture; there's also a striking display of 16th- to 18th-century Polish portraits on the first floor. English-speaking guides are available.

Outside, to the left of the main entrance, is a romantic park with pagodas, summerhouses, and bridges overlooking a lake. Behind the palace is a formal Italian garden from which you can admire the magnificent gilt decoration on the palace walls and the large sundial. There's also a **gallery** of contemporary Polish art in the grounds, and stables to the right of the entrance now house a **poster gallery.** The latter is well worth visiting, for this is a branch of art in which Poland excels. ⊠ *Ul. Wiertnicza 1,* ☎ *022/42–81–01.* 🎟 *Palace and gallery zł 4; park and gallery zł 2.* ⊙ *Wed.–Sun. 9:30–2:30.*

❸❻ Zamek Ujazdowski. If you are interested in modern art, you will find it in the somewhat unlikely setting of the 18th-century Zamek Ujazdowski, reconstructed in the 1980s. This is now the home of the Center for Contemporary Art and hosts a variety of exhibitions by Polish, European, and North American artists. It has a terrace at the back looking over formal gardens laid out down to the Vistula River. ⊠ *Al. Ujazdowskie 6 (walk down through the park from pl. na Rozdrożu),* ☎ *022/628–12–71.* 🎟 *Zł 2.5.* ⊙ *Tues.–Sun. 11–5.*

Jewish Warsaw

Not a great deal of Jewish Warsaw survives. About 395,000 Jews lived in Warsaw in 1939, roughly one-third of the city's population. By the end of World War II they had disappeared, sent to their deaths in the gas chambers of Treblinka as part of Hitler's "final solution." The history of this city is closely interwoven with the history of its Jewish community, and although this tour of a ghost world is continually overshadowed by the specter of the Holocaust, it is one that many still wish to make.

A GOOD WALK

The wartime ghetto area is northwest of Warsaw's Old Town. Begin at plac Bankowy with the **Jewish Historical Institute and Museum** ㊸. From there, walk west along aleje Solidarności toward ulica Jana Pawła II, passing the **Femina cinema** ㊹ on your left. Turn north along ulica Jana Pawła II to ulica Mordechaja Anielewicza; here turn east to reach the **Pomnik Bohaterów Getta** (Monument to the Heroes of the Warsaw Ghetto) ㊺. From the monument, take ulica Karmelicka north to ulica Stawki, where you will find the **Umschlagplatz** ㊻. Trams run along ulica Jana Pawła II to help you on your route; from the corner of ulica Dzika and ulica Okopowa you can take any tram south along ulica Okopowa to reach the **Jewish Cemetery** ㊼.

TIMING

It is possible to see all the sights listed in a morning or afternoon, although this would involve some energetic walking. Allow a whole day, to give time for reflection and to explore the cemetery fully.

SIGHTS TO SEE

㊹ Femina cinema (Aleje Solidarności No. 115). Before the war this area was the heart of Warsaw's Jewish quarter, which was walled off by the Nazis in November 1940 to isolate the Jewish community from "Aryan" Warsaw. The cinema is one of the few buildings in this district that survived the war. It was here that the ghetto orchestra organized concerts in 1941 and 1942; many outstanding musicians found themselves behind the ghetto walls and continued to make music despite the odds.

㊼ Jewish Cemetery. Behind a high brick wall on ulica Okopowa you will find Warsaw's Jewish Cemetery, an island of continuity amid so much destruction of the city's Jewish heritage. The cemetery survived the war, and although badly overgrown and neglected during the postwar period, in the 1990s it is gradually being restored. Here you will find fine 19th-century headstones and much that testifies to the Jewish community's role in Polish history and culture. Ludwik Zamenhof, the creator of Esperanto, is buried here, as are Henryk Wohl, minister of the treasury in the national government during the 1864 uprising against Russian rule; Szymon Askenazy, the historian and diplomat; Hipolit Wawelberg, the cofounder of Warsaw Polytechnic; and poet Bolesław Leśmian. ⊠ *Okopowa 49–51 (take Bus 170 from pl. Bankowy).*

OFF THE
BEATEN PATH
    POWĄZKI CEMETERY – Dating from 1790, Warsaw's oldest cemetery is well worth a visit if you are in the mood for a reflective stroll. Many well-known Polish names appear on the often elaborate headstones and tombs; there is a recent memorial to the victims of the Katyn massacre. Enter from ulica Powązkowska. ⊠ *Ul. Powązkowska 43–45.*

㊸ Jewish Historical Institute and Museum. You will find the Jewish Historical Institute and Museum behind a glittering new office block on the southeast corner of plac Bankowy—the site of what had been the largest temple in Warsaw, the Tłomackie Synagogue. It displays a permanent collection of mementos and artifacts and periodically organizes special exhibitions. ⊠ *Al. Solidarności 79,* ☎ *022/27–18–43.* 🎫 *Free.* ⊙ *Weekdays 9–3.*

NEED A
BREAK?
    Al Capone (⊠ Pl. Bankowy 1) is a large and comfortable bar—with motorbikes suspended on the walls and a billiard room—where you can have coffee, or something stronger, at any time of day.

㊺ Pomnik Bohaterów Getta (Monument to the Heroes of the Warsaw Ghetto). On April 19, 1943, the Jewish Fighting Organization began an uprising in a desperate attempt to resist the mass transports to Treblinka that had been taking place since the beginning of the year. Though doomed from the start despite their reckless bravery, the ghetto fighters managed to keep up resistance for a month. But by May 16, General Jürgen Stroop could report to his superior officer that "the former Jewish district in Warsaw had ceased to exist." The ghetto was a smoldering ruin, razed by Nazi flamethrowers. The monument marks the site of the house at **ulica Miła 18,** the site of the uprising's command bunker and where its leader, Mordechai Anielewicz, was killed. ⊠ *Ul Zamenhofa, between ul. Anielewicza and ul. Lewartowskiego.*

★ **㊻ Umschlagplatz.** This was the rail terminus from which tens of thousands of the Warsaw ghetto's inhabitants were shipped in cattle cars to the extermination camp of Treblinka, about 100 kilometers (60 miles) northeast of Warsaw. The low building to the left of the square was used to detain those who had to wait overnight for transport; the beginning of the rail tracks survives on the right. At the entrance to the square is a memorial gateway, erected in 1988 on the 45th anniversary of the uprising. ⊠ *Corner of ul. Stawki and ul. Dzika.*

OFF THE
BEATEN PATH
    KAMPINOSKI NATIONAL PARK – Ten kilometers (6½ miles) west of Warsaw's city boundaries, the **Puszcza Kampinoska** stretches more than 230 square kilometers (89 square miles) to the west of the city. The park has forest, marshes, sand dunes, and farmland as well as nature reserves. It is home to a wide variety of wildlife, including elk, deer, and wild boars, as well as many species of birds; if you are lucky, you'll see a stork's nest perched atop a cottage. Walking routes through the forest are marked by colored bands on trees (maps of the park are available in Warsaw bookstores). Take a packed lunch or other refreshments as there are almost no facilities. At the western corner of the park is Żelazowa Wola, the small 19th-century manor house where Frederic Chopin was born. The house contains a museum devoted to Chopin; on summer Sundays, concerts are held on the terrace. *To walk in the eastern part of the park, take Bus 708 (🚌 Zł 2.5) from Warsaw's Dworzec PKS Marymont to the village of Truskaw, or get off at Laski or Izabelin en route. At all of these places marked paths begin at the bus stop, and a large map of the forest is displayed. The trip to Truskaw from Warsaw takes roughly half an hour. To reach Żelazowa Wola—58 kilometers (36 miles) from Warsaw—take a bus from Warsaw's Dworzec PKS in aleje*

Jerozolimskie (three daily). If driving, 30 kilometers (18½ miles) north of Warsaw turn southwest from the E81 to Palmiry, where there is a large parking area. Information on concerts from the Chopin Society: ⊠ *Ul. Okólnik 1,* ☎ *022/27-95-99.*

Dining

Like everything else in Warsaw, the dining scene is changing rapidly. Some of the better-known state-controlled restaurants have gone swiftly downhill; others have been privatized and have improved substantially. Privately owned restaurants are opening every day, many offering ethnic cuisine (Korean, Japanese, Chinese, and Italian are particularly popular). Gone are the old and seedy bars, replaced by clean and brightly tiled pizza parlors. Prices have also risen spectacularly, and eating out in Warsaw is now much more expensive than in other Polish towns.

$$$$ ✕ **Belvedere.** You could not find a more romantic setting for dinner
★ than this elegant restaurant in the New Orangery at Łazienki Park. The lamp-lighted park spreads out beyond the windows, and candles glitter below the high ceilings. Polish cuisine is a specialty, and many dishes are prepared with a variety of fresh mushrooms; try the mushroom soup. Also recommended is the roast boar, served with an assortment of vegetables. ⊠ *Park Łazienki, enter from Agrykola or ul. Gargarina,* ☎ *022/41-48-06. Jacket and tie. AE, DC, MC, V. Closed public holidays.*

$$$$ ✕ **Dom Restauracyjny Gessler.** You come here partly for the setting: a warren of candlelit bare-brick cellars and ground-floor rooms in one of the historic houses on the Old Town Square. This was the Krokodyl restaurant, an old fixture of the Warsaw dining scene, which has been taken over by the Gessler brothers, sons of a prewar restaurateur. The quality of the cooking has improved. Start with salmon Polish princes–style (*łosoś książąt polskich*), cooked in cream, or broth with dumplings (*bulion z kołdunami*); this could be followed by duck in a marjoram-based sauce, served with noodles. The service is smooth— efficient waiters in long white aprons constitute a novelty in Warsaw. This is one of the restaurants that stay open until the wee hours—to 3 A.M. ⊠ *Rynek Starego Miasta 19–21,* ☎ *022/31-44-27. AE, DC, MC, V. Closed public holidays.*

$$$$ ✕ **Fukier.** This long-established wine bar on the Old Town Square has now become a fascinating network of elaborately decorated dining rooms: There is a talking parrot in a cage, and candles adorn all available shelf space (sometimes dangerously close to clients' elbows). There are solid oak tables, discreetly attentive waiters, and in summer you can dine under the stars on a courtyard patio. The food is "light Old Polish": Steak, served on a grill, is a specialty and might be followed by one of a range of rich cream gâteaux. ⊠ *Rynek Starego Miasta 27,* ☎ *022/31-10-13. Reservations essential. Jacket and tie. AE, DC, MC, V.*

$$$$ ✕ **Marconi.** This Italian restaurant in the Hotel Bristol is often said
★ to have the best chef in town. The walls are green, with engravings of Italy, and one side looks onto a closed inner courtyard. The service is highly attentive. The tables are very discreetly spaced: Try to pick one by the windows, otherwise you can feel marooned in the middle of the floor. The antipasti buffet is excellent and has wonderful sauces. ⊠ *Krakowskie Przedmieście 42–44,* ☎ *022/625-25-25. Jacket and tie. AE, DC, MC, V.*

$$$ ✕ **Bazyliszek.** Under new management since 1990, this second-floor restaurant in a 17th-century merchant's house on the Old Town Square gets top marks for atmosphere. Dine here under high ceilings of carved

Dining
Ambasador, **20**
Bazyliszek, **4**
Belvedere, **30**
Delfin, **13**
Dom Restauracyjny
Gessler, **2**
Flik, **26**
Fukier, **3**
Ha Long, **10**
Kamienne Schodki, **1**
Marconi, **7**
Menora, **9**
Polonia, **16**
U Hopfera, **5**
Wilanów, **29**
Zajazd Napoleoński, **21**

Lodging
Belfer, **12**
Bristol, **7**
Dom Chłopa, **11**
Europejski, **6**
Forum, **18**
Gromada, **23**
Gromada Campsite, **25**
Holiday Inn, **14**
Jan III Sobieski, **22**
Marriott, **15**
Metropol, **17**
Novotel, **24**
Parkowa, **31**
Pensjonat Biała
Dalia, **28**
Polonia, **13**
Sheraton, **19**
Uniwersytecki, **27**
Victoria
InterContinental, **8**
Zajazd Napoleoński, **20**

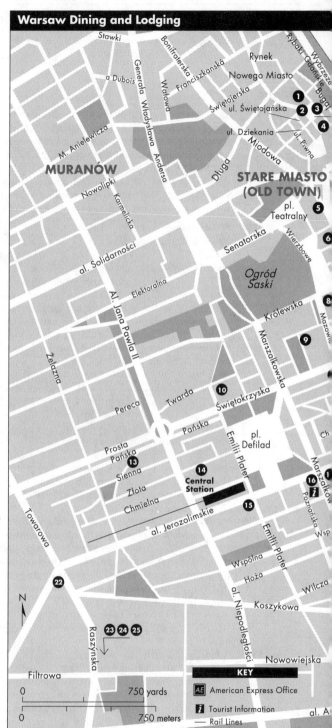

Warsaw Dining and Lodging

MURANÓW

**STARE MIASTO
(OLD TOWN)**

Rynek
Nowego Miasto

pl.
Teatralny

Ogród
Saski

Central
Station

pl.
Defilad

Nowowiejska

KEY
AE American Express Office
i Tourist Information
— Rail Lines

0   750 yards
0   750 meters

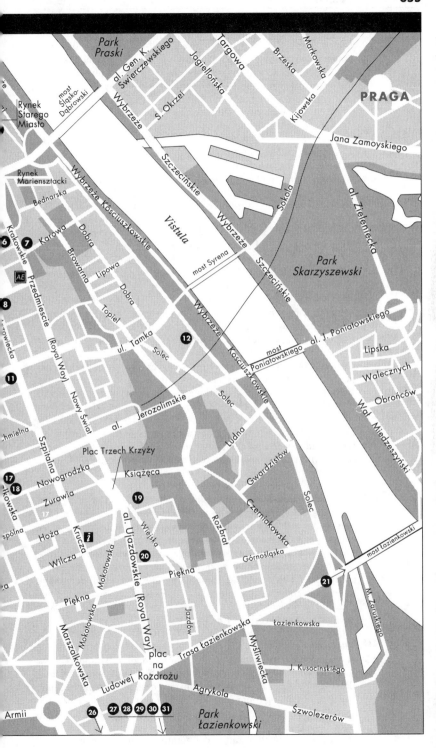

Park
Praski

al. Gen. K.
Świerczewskiego

Jagiellońska

Targowa

Brzeska

Markowska

most
Śląsko-
Dąbrowski

Wybrzeże

S. Okrzei

Kijowska

PRAGA

Rynek
Starego
Miasto

Jana Zamoyskiego

Rynek
Mariensztacki

Wybrzeże Kościuszkowskie

Szczecińskie

al. Zieleniecka

Bednarska

Karowa

Dobra

6 **7**

Krakowskie

Browarna

Lipowa

Wybrzeże

Szczecińskie

Sokola

Vistula

Park
Skarzyszewski

AE

Przedmieście

Dobra

Topiel

most Syrena

8

(Royal Way)

ul. Tamka

Solec

al. J. Poniatowskiego

Lipska

rowiecka

Wybrzeże Kościuszkowskie

12

most
Poniatowskiego

Waleczných

11

Nowy Świat

Solec

Obrońców

hmielna

al. Jerozolimskie

Solec

Ludna

Wał Miedzeszyński

Plac Trzech Krzyży

Szpitalna

Gwardzistów

Nowogrodzka

Książęca

17

Żurawia

19

Czerniakowska

18

kowska

Ho

Hoża

Krucza

i

al. Ujazdowskie

Wiejska

Rozbrat

most Łazienkowski

spólna

Wilcza

Mokotowska

20

Górnośląska

21

M. Zaruskiego

Piękna

Piękna

(Royal Way)

Jazdów

Łazienkowska

Marszałkowska

Mokotowska

Trasa Łazienkowska

Myśliwiecka

J. Kusocińskiego

plac
na
Ludowej Rozdrożu

Agrykola

Szwolezerów

Armii

26 **27** **28** **29** **30** **31**

Park
Łazienkowski

wood, if possible in the Knight's Room, where suits of armor and crossed swords decorate the walls. Waitresses in period dress, who can be relied on to speak English, glide between well-spaced tables. Bazyliszek is a favorite gathering place for special celebrations, and there will usually be a few toasts and songs. The mainstay of the menu is traditional Polish fare, with an emphasis on game dishes. Begin your meal with a platter of home-cured cold cuts and then try the stewed hare in cream sauce, served with beets and noodles. There is a wide selection of desserts, and the wine list is good. ⊠ *Rynek Starego Miasta 3–9,* ☎ *022/31–18–41. Reservations essential. Jacket and tie. AE, DC, MC, V. Closed public holidays.*

$$$ ✕ **Delfin.** In the basement of the Anglers' Association Building, with
★ stuffed fish and trophies on the walls here and there, this restaurant is well known for its excellent freshwater-fish dishes. The waiters are very willing to advise on your order: pike in aspic is a favorite starter, followed by bream or perch in a cream sauce; the accompanying vegetables are always cooked perfectly. The restaurant also has a wide selection of meat dishes and one of the longest wine lists in town. ⊠ *Ul. Twarda 42,* ☎ *022/620–50–80. AE, DC, MC, V. Closed public holidays.*

$$$ ✕ **Wilanów.** Part of the Forum hotel group, this restaurant is housed in an old stable building opposite the Wilanów Palace, the summer residence of King John III Sobieski, 13 kilometers (8 miles) from the city center. The dimly lighted main dining room on the ground floor, known as Hunters' Hall, is decorated with stuffed trophies. The tables are set in wood-paneled half-booths of an odd kidney shape, which can make conversation rather difficult for small parties. The historic setting and period decor are not the restaurant's only asset; the service is polite and efficient, with English-speaking waiters supervised by a maître d' of the old school. The chef has a fine reputation, and the restaurant offers a unique variety of Polish and Continental dishes. Among the former are *Wawelska* steak, larded with prunes and cooked in a bacon wrap, and the *Sobieski* pork cutlet in a sweetish fruit-base sauce, served with rice and apples. A reasonable wine list is now available. ⊠ *Ul. Wiertnicza 27,* ☎ *022/42–13–63. AE, DC, MC, V. Closed Easter, Dec. 25.*

$$$ ✕ **Zajazd Napoleoński.** Thirteen kilometers (8 miles) from downtown,
★ this ground-floor restaurant opens onto the walled garden of an 18th-century inn with Napoleonic associations. We are not told whether the emperor enjoyed the cooking when he stayed here in 1812, but busts and portraits of the inn's most famous visitor are everywhere in the cool, arched dining rooms, while overhead are bare oak beams. Sample some traditional Polish dishes like *barszcz* (borscht) with small dumplings, followed by roast suckling pig, which comes elaborately garnished and glazed. The restaurant is on the main bus route into downtown Warsaw, and taxis are on call. ⊠ *Ul. Płowiecka 83,* ☎ *022/15–30–68. Reservations essential. Jacket required. AE, DC, MC, V. Closed public holidays.*

$$ ✕ **Ambasador.** This brightly lighted, white-and-gilt restaurant is on the ground floor of a 1960s apartment block on Warsaw's diplomatic mile, aleje Ujazdowskie, a stone's throw from the Polish parliament (the Sejm). The spacious dining room is broken up by ranks of potted plants, and noise levels are muted; the restaurant is popular for lunch. The basically Polish cuisine has some international additions: The *kotlet królewski* (pork with a traditional potato stuffing) is recommended. This is also a good place to sample the Polish version of shashlik, made with pork loin. Special orders for wines or dishes are accepted with a few days' notice. Since his departure from the presidency of the country in December 1995, this is reputed to be Lech Wałęsa's favorite restaurant when he is in town. ⊠ *Ul. Matejki 4,* ☎ *022/25–99–61. AE, DC, MC, V. Closed public holidays.*

$$ ✕ **Flik.** Set on a corner overlooking the Morskie Oko Park, this restau-
★ rant in Mokotów, opened in 1992, has a geranium-lined white terrace that makes a fine setting for outdoor summer dining. Inside, the dining room is spacious, with well-spaced tables, light cane furniture, and lots of greenery. The fresh salmon starter is delicious and could be followed—for local flavor—by *zrazy* (rolled beef fillet stuffed with mushrooms). There is a self-service salad bar, and downstairs are a small café and an art gallery. ⊠ *Ul. Puławska 43,* ☎ *022/49–44–06. AE, DC, MC, V. Closed public holidays.*

$$ ✕ **Ha Long.** Opened in 1995 in a side street off Świętokrzyska, this small, traditionally decorated (fringes, lanterns, and flocked wallpaper) Vietnamese/Chinese restaurant has quickly collected a devoted clientele. The portions are very large, so be careful not to order too many items. The sweet-and-sour Pekin soup is a must to start with, and traditional Chinese duck is regarded as a specialty. Draft beer is available. ⊠ *Ul. Emilii Plater 36,* ☎ *022/620–15–23. AE, DC, MC, V.*

$$ ✕ **Kamienne Schodki.** This vaulted restaurant, on the ground floor of
★ a 16th-century house on the corner of the Old Town Square, is famed for its roast duck served with apples (for a long time, the only dish offered). Redecoration has brought back the big crystal mirrors to reflect the candlelit tables, and more items have been added to the menu. Do not miss the duck; chicken or pork *à la polonaise* with garlic stuffing is also quite good. Save room for the light and creamy pastries. In warm weather there is outdoor dining. ⊠ *Rynek Starego Miasta 26,* ☎ *022/31–08–22. AE, DC, MC, V. Closed public holidays.*

$$ ✕ **Polonia.** This restaurant in the Polonia Hotel has a splendidly preserved fin-de-siècle interior, with galleries (in which a small private dining room can be booked), original marble fireplaces, and brass chandeliers. The tables are well spaced in three split-level dining areas; in the evenings there is a small orchestra, and couples waltz on the parquet dance floor. The clientele is varied, while the service is polite if sometimes slow. The cuisine is mainly Polish: The *kotlet myśliwski* (hunter's pork cutlet with mushrooms) is recommended, as is the traditional mainstay *bigos* (cabbage cooked with sausages, various meats, prunes, and red wine). ⊠ *Al. Jerozolimskie 45,* ☎ *022/628–72–41. AE, DC, MC, V. Closed public holidays.*

$ ✕ **Menora.** On the poignantly dilapidated, surviving prewar side of plac Grzybowski, opposite the Jewish Theater and synagogue, this kosher restaurant opened in 1994. It has brought a cozy décor and homely atmosphere into a once-typical plate-glass restaurant of the 1960s. Carp Jewish style (*karp po żydowsku*) is a favorite starter. ⊠ *Plac Grzybowski 2,* ☎ *022/620–37–54. AE, DC, MC, V. Smoking not permitted on the sabbath.*

$ ✕ **U Hopfera.** This small and busy restaurant on the Royal Way has brightly checked tablecloths, fresh flowers, and a friendly and efficient staff. It specializes in Polish dishes, ranging from *schab ze śliwkami* (pork baked with plums) to homemade pierogi with beef stuffing. Open midday to 3 AM, it is probably the only inexpensive restaurant where you can find a meal late at night. ⊠ *Ul. Krakowskie Przedmieście 53,* ☎ *022/635–73–52. AE, DC, MC, V.*

Lodging

Warsaw's overall shortage of hotel beds is likely to continue well into the 1990s. Since the opening of the Marriott Hotel and Holiday Inn (1989), the Sobieski (1991), and the Bristol (1992), the situation at the top end of the price range has improved steadily. But lower down the price scale, options are very restricted. Bed-and-breakfast accommodation is difficult to find and is often exorbitant. In summer there are generally more options: student hostels rent out space, and chalets are available at campsites. Demand is high, so book well in advance. Breakfast is included in hotel rates unless otherwise noted.

Warsaw is a small city, and the location of your hotel is not of crucial importance in terms of travel time to major sights or nightspots. Many hotels are clustered in the downtown area near the intersection of ulica Marszałkowska and aleje Jerozolimskie. This is not an especially scenic area, with very little green space; nevertheless, the neighborhood doesn't turn into a "concrete desert" after business hours, since there are still many residential properties as well as restaurants and nightspots. Despite a rising crime rate throughout Poland, it is still safe to stroll at night through downtown Warsaw; the greatest hazards are likely to be uneven pavements and inadequate lighting.

The hotels on plac Piłsudskiego (formerly plac Zwycięstwa), which is close to parks and within easy walking distance of the Old Town, offer more relaxing surroundings. Most of the suburban hotels have no particular scenic advantage, though they do provide immediate access to larger tracts of open space and fresh air. *See* B&B Reservation Agencies *in* Warsaw A to Z, *below,* for agencies that provide lodging information and reservations.

$$$$ ☷ **Bristol.** Built in 1901 by a consortium headed by Ignacy Paderewski, ★ the concert pianist who served as Poland's prime minister in 1919–20, the Bristol was long at the center of Warsaw's social life. Impressively situated on the Royal Way, next to the Radziwiłł Palace, the Bristol survived World War II more or less intact. Now, after a decade of extensive renovations—practically everything except the original facade has been rebuilt—the Bristol has finally reopened as a Trust House–Forte hotel. The Forte organization aims to revive the hotel's long tradition of luxury and elegance. Breakfast is not included in rates. ✉ *Krakowskie Przedmieście 42–44, 00–325,* ☎ *022/625–25–25,* FAX *022/625–25–77. 163 rooms, 43 suites, all with bath. 2 restaurants, 2 bars, café, pool, sauna, solarium. AE, DC, MC, V.*

$$$$ ☷ **Holiday Inn.** Designed, and later franchised, by Holiday Inn, this gleaming six-story complex opposite Warsaw's Central Station avoids some of the standard chain-hotel impersonality. Softly carpeted and furnished throughout in shades of gray and blue, the public areas are full of light provided by the tree-filled steel-and-glass conservatory that fronts the building up to the third floor. The generously proportioned guest rooms have projecting bay windows that overlook the very center of the city, but unfortunately there's no air-conditioning on the residential floors, so the rooms can become stuffy in hot weather. ✉ *Ul. Złota 2, 00–120,* ☎ *022/620–03–41,* FAX *022/31–05–69. 338 rooms, 10 suites. 3 restaurants, 2 bars, café. AE, DC, MC, V.*

$$$$ ☷ **Jan III Sobieski.** This massive hotel is Austrian-owned and appropriately named for the Polish king who in 1683 saved Vienna from the Turks. Since it opened in 1991, its bright pink, blue, and yellow illusionist facade has startled more than a few Varsovians. Inside, however, the decor is more conventional, and service is impeccable. The rooms are reasonably sized and warmly furnished in soft rosewood and flowered prints. ✉ *Pl. Zawiszy 1, 00–973,* ☎ *022/658–34–44,* FAX *022/659–8828. 436 rooms. 2 restaurants, bar, café. AE, DC, MC, V.*

$$$$ ☷ **Marriott.** In the high-rise Lim Center opposite the Central Station, ★ the Marriott currently offers the city's most prestigious accommodations; it's the only hotel in Poland that's under direct American management. The staff is well trained and helpful; everyone speaks some

English. The views from every room—of central Warsaw and far beyond—are spectacular on a clear day. The health facilities are the best in town. The Lila Veneda restaurant on the second floor runs a special Sunday brunch, complete with Dixieland band. ⊠ *Al. Jerozolimskie 65–79, 00–697,* ☎ *022/630–63–06,* FAX *022/621–12–90. 481 rooms, 24 suites. 5 restaurants, 3 bars, pool, health club, shops, casino, nightclub, business center, parking. AE, DC, MC, V.*

$$$$ 🏨 **Sheraton.** Warsaw's latest luxury hotel, opened in 1996, is halfway along the Royal Route from the Old Town to the Łazienki Palace. The six-story, curved neoclassical building overlooks plac Trzech Krzyży, and behind it are the parks that run along the Vistula embankment. Plac Trzech Krzyży is currently receiving a face-lift: Alongside the Sheraton, a major banking center is to be constructed over the next four years—but building work in the close vicinity could make this hotel less attractive for a time. The interiors are light and bright, rooms are generously sized, and staff are striving to make the Sheraton the friendliest hotel in Warsaw. ⊠ *Ul. Bolesława Prusa 2, 00–504,* ☎ *022/ 657–61–00,* FAX *022/657–62–00. 333 rooms, 13 suites. 3 restaurants, cafés, sauna. AE, DC, MC, V.*

$$$$ 🏨 **Victoria InterContinental.** Overlooking plac Piłsudskiego, the Victoria, opened in the late 1970s, was until 1989 Warsaw's only luxury hotel, hosting innumerable official visitors and state delegations. The large and comfortably furnished guest rooms are decorated in tones of brown and gold, which continues the white-and-bronze theme of the exterior. Health facilities include an attractive basement swimming pool and three exercise rooms, and the hotel is just across the street from the jogging (or walking) paths of the Saxon Gardens. A 10-minute walk from the Old Town, the hotel is near many of Warsaw's main sights; the Teatr Wielki, for example, is on the opposite side of the square. ⊠ *Ul. Królewska 11, 00–065,* ☎ *022/27–92–71,* FAX *022/27–98–56. 328 rooms, 32 suites. 3 restaurants, bar, pool, health clubs, shops, casino, nightclub, parking. AE, DC, MC, V.*

$$$ 🏨 **Europejski.** Although it retains traces of its earlier grandeur, this hotel is now clearly struggling to keep up its traditional standards of service. Built in the late 19th century, the Europejski was opened in 1962 after postwar reconstruction; the renovators managed to retain some original features, including two grand marble staircases. The rooms are very diverse in size and shape but are comfortably furnished, and almost all have views overlooking historic Warsaw—on one side the Royal Route, on the other plac Piłsudskiego. The nearby Saxon Gardens provide terrain suitable for morning jogging; there are no health-club facilities as such (nor is the hotel air-conditioned), though guests can sometimes obtain access to the facilities at the nearby Victoria Hotel, which is under the same management. ⊠ *Krakowskie Przedmieście 13, 00–071,* ☎ *022/26–50–51,* FAX *022/26–11–11. 226 rooms, 13 suites. Restaurant, bar, shops, nightclub. AE, DC, MC, V.*

$$$ 🏨 **Forum.** This dun-colored, 30-story, Swedish-designed metal cube has been a fixture on the Warsaw skyline since 1974. Guest rooms are of average size, and those on the east side of the building offer good views—but don't choose the Forum if you want cheerful surroundings. Depressing tones of brown and green predominate, and the furnishings seem to have been chosen with an eye for function rather than comfort. The staff, used to dealing with rapid-turnover group tours, can be offhand. There are no health or exercise facilities (nor is the hotel air-conditioned), and the Forum is in the middle of a heavily built-up district. On the plus side, the hotel does have two restaurants and is within easy reach of the entertainment districts. ⊠ *Ul. Nowogrodzka 24, 00–511,* ☎ *022/621–02–71,* FAX *022/25–81–57. 750 rooms, 13 suites. 2 restaurants, bar, casino, parking. AE, DC, MC, V.*

$$$ 🏨 **Zajazd Napoleoński.** Napoléon is believed to have stayed here on
★   his way to Moscow with the Grande Armée in 1812. Lovingly restored
and opened as a small family-run hotel in 1984, the Napoleoński
stresses the Empire theme throughout; most of the furnishings, for ex-
ample, are period reproductions. Although the inn is on the main road
out of Warsaw to the east, it stands in its own walled garden, and the
thick stone structure keeps the sound of traffic at bay. The rooms are
spacious, and the fixtures are of unusually high quality. Senator Ed-
ward Kennedy has stayed here, and the hotel is generally popular with
foreign visitors, who find that the distance from downtown (13 kilo-
meters, 8 miles) is more than compensated for by the unique atmosphere
and high standards of personal service. The hotel has no air-conditioning.
⊠ *Ul. Płowiecka 83, 04–501,* ☎ *022/15–30–68,* 🆅🆇 *022/15–22–16.
22 rooms, 3 suites, all with bath. Restaurant. AE, DC, MC, V.*

$$ 🏨 **Dom Chłopa.** This white five-story hotel in the center of Warsaw
was built during the late 1950s by the Gromada peasants' cooperative
and originally had a horticultural and agricultural bookstore and
plant-and-seed store on the ground floor. Times have changed: The store
now sells TVs. The hotel still offers clean and reasonably priced accommodations; rooms are rather small and spartan, but the colors are
cheerful, the bathrooms have been given a face-lift and the downtown
location is excellent. There is no air-conditioning. ⊠ *Pl. Powstańców
Warszawy 2, 00–030,* ☎ *022/27–49–43,* 🆅🆇 *022/26–14–54. 160 rooms
with bath. Restaurant. AE, DC, MC, V.*

$$ 🏨 **Gromada.** Opened in 1995 and just under 1 kilometer (⅔ mile) to
★   Warsaw's airport and about 7 kilometers (4½ miles) from the city cen-
ter, the Gromada is run by a peasants' cooperative of the same name;
the dining room is one of its attractions, and the breakfasts are par-
ticularly recommended. The rooms are comfortable, if standardized.
The hotel stands well back from the busy main road to the airport and
has wooded grounds. There is a good bus service into town. ⊠ *Ul. 17
Stycznia 32, 02–148,* ☎ *022/46–58–22,* 🆅🆇 *022/46–15–80. 140
rooms, including 40 singles, all with bath. Sauna, airport shuttle. AE,
DC, MC, V.*

$$ 🏨 **Metropol.** A major renovation carried out in 1989–90 has vastly
improved the standards at this glass-front seven-story hotel, built in
1965 at Warsaw's main downtown intersection; accommodations are
now better than many expensive hotels. The furnishings are impressively solid and comfortable; bathrooms, though small, are attractively tiled and fitted. The single rooms (which form the majority) are
large enough to contain a bed, armchairs, and desk without feeling
crowded. Each, however, has a balcony overlooking busy ulica
Marszałkowska, and traffic noise can be very intrusive when the windows are open. There is no air-conditioning. TVs can be rented from
reception. ⊠ *Al. Jerozolimskie 45, 00–024,* ☎ *022/621–43–54,* 🆅🆇
*022/628–66–22. 175 rooms, 16 suites, all with bath. Restaurant. AE,
DC, MC, V.*

$$ 🏨 **Novotel.** This small, three-story hotel, built in 1976 around a paved
and shrub-filled courtyard, is only five minutes from Okęcie Airport
(fortunately, *not* under any flight paths). Its situation is almost rural:
Surrounded by trees, the Novotel lies across the road from a major area
of gardens and parkland. Though removed from the heart of the city,
the Novotel is on the main bus routes; Bus 175 will take you down-
town in 10–15 minutes. The atmosphere is friendly, and the rooms light,
clean, and comfortable in a stripped-down style. There are no health
or entertainment facilities and no air-conditioning, and the Novotel is
to be recommended mainly if you like to retire from the hustle and bus-
tle of the city center for a good night's sleep. ⊠ *Ul. 1 Sierpnia 1, 02–*

134, ☎ *022/46–40–51,* ⅀ *022/46–36–86. 150 rooms with bath. Restaurant, bar, parking. AE, DC, MC, V.*

$$ ⊞ **Parkowa.** This 1970s hotel, formerly reserved for official govern-
★ ment delegations, has now gone commercial. It is just south of the
Belvedere Palace in a landscaped area adjacent to the Łazienki Park and
is ideal if you like a peaceful holiday in the midst of the city. The rooms
are well fitted, with good lighting and large desks. ⊠ *Ul. Belwederska
46/50, 00–594,* ☎ *022/694–80–80,* ⅀ *022/41–60–29. 52 rooms, in-
cluding 20 singles, all with bath. In-room satellite TVs, sauna. AE, DC,
MC, V.*

$$ ⊞ **Polonia.** The art-nouveau Polonia, completed in 1913, was the only
Warsaw hotel to survive World War II intact. General Eisenhower
stayed here in 1945, and the U.S. Embassy was housed here in the period immediately after the war. Much of the hotel's splendor was lost
in a major renovation completed in 1974, when the rooms were standardized. The high-ceiling rooms are, however, still reasonably spacious
and comfortable; many of the doubles and suites still have stylish bay
windows and balconies, and many of the bathrooms are large and well
appointed. The restaurant (☞ Dining, *above*) is a marvelous set piece
of fin-de-siècle elegance. The hotel was re-renovated in the early to mid-
1990s. There is no air-conditioning. TVs can be rented from reception.
⊠ *Al. Jerozolimskie 45, 00–024,* ☎ *022/28–51–06,* ⅀ *022/28–66–
32. 206 rooms, 28 suites, all with bath. Restaurant. AE, DC, MC, V.*

$ ⊞ **Belfer.** This hotel is conveniently situated in Powiśle, across the road
from the Vistula River and only 10 minutes by foot (admittedly all uphill) from the Royal Route. Traffic noise can be a problem in summer
in front-facing rooms, but courtyard-facing rooms are peaceful. The
decor throughout is dull, with plenty of dark-wood paneling and
chocolate-brown paint, and there is no air-conditioning, though the
rooms are spacious and comfortable, and everything is spotlessly clean.
⊠ *Wybrzeże Kościuszkowskie 31/33, 00–379,* ☎ *022/625–05–71,*
⅀ *022/625–26–00. 360 rooms, 56 singles, and 10 doubles with bath.
Restaurant, café. AE, DC, MC, V.*

$ ⚠ **Gromada Campsite.** This large campsite on the edge of the Piłsud-
ski Park is open May 1–October 30. It's only five minutes by bus from
the center of town; despite the screen of trees that separates the chalets
from the main road and bus routes, staying here can be noisy. The bathrooms are rudimentary and very cramped, though there is hot water.
A face-lift is scheduled for late 1996. ⊠ *Al. Żwirki i Wigury 3–5, 02–
092,* ☎ *022/25–43–91. 120 beds in 2-person chalets (bedding provided). Cafeteria. No credit cards.*

$ ⊞ **Pensjonat Biała Dalia.** This very small, privately owned pension in
Konstancin Jeziorna, 24 kilometers (15 miles) from the center of Warsaw, stands in a beautifully kept garden and is elegantly furnished in
blue and white. The rooms are fairly large, clean, and comfortable, with
large, solid beds and heavy, upholstered armchairs; flower patterns predominate on the carpets and wallpaper. ⊠ *Ul. Sobieskiego 24, Konstancin Jeziorna, 06–727,* ☎ *022/56–33–70. 5 rooms, 4 with bath.
No credit cards.*

$ ⊞ **Uniwersytecki.** This three-story socialist-realist building on the edge
of Łazienki Park was taken over from the Communist Central Committee in 1990 by Warsaw University. It is used mainly for university
guests, but remaining rooms are rented throughout the year. The spar-
tanly decorated rooms are of good size, with high ceilings. It is probably the best-located hotel in the price range. ⊠ *Ul. Belwederska
26/30, 00–594,* ☎ *022/41–02–54. 90 rooms. Restaurant, bar. No credit
cards.*

Nightlife and the Arts

Warsaw has much to offer those interested in the arts. Find out what's on from **WiK,** the daily **Gazeta Wyborcza, Życie Warszawy,** or the English-language weekly **Warsaw Voice**—or go to Warsaw's only major ticket agency, **ZASP,** at aleje Jerozolimskie 25 (☎ 022/621–94–54), which has listings of most events two weeks ahead. If you know Polish, you can call **Telefoniczny Informator Kulturalny** (☎ 022/629-84-89); it's open weekdays 10 AM–9 PM and weekends 10 AM–6 PM. The tickets for most performances are still relatively inexpensive, but if you want to spend even less, remember that most theaters and concert halls sell general-admission entrance tickets—*wejściówki*—for only about zł 1–zł 2 immediately before the performance. These do not entitle you to a seat, but you can usually find one that is not taken. Wejściówki are often available for performances for which all standard tickets have been sold.

Though Warsaw's range of options has widened recently, it is still—on the whole—a sedate city that goes to bed early. As throughout Central Europe, people tend to meet for a drink in the evenings in *kawiarnie* (cafés)—where you can linger for as long as you like over one cup of coffee or glass of brandy—rather than in bars (most cafés are open until 10). But Western-style bars have become more popular, and apart from those in the big hotels, new ones constantly appear; there is also a growing fashion for pubs. Discos and rock clubs are also mushrooming; jazz clubs have a wide audience. Casinos are mainly the haunt of foreign visitors and a small group of the new, rich business class of Poles.

Nightlife

BARS AND LOUNGES

The dimly lighted and superficially sedate **Zielony Barek** on the ground floor of the Victoria InterContinental Hotel (⊠ Ul. Królewska 11) used to be the nearest thing to an upscale bar that Warsaw had to offer until it was upstaged in the 1990s. The upholstered luxury of the ground-floor **Lounge Bar** of the Hotel Bristol (⊠ Krakowskie Przedmieście 42–44) provides a good setting for a quiet—if very expensive—drink. The **John Bull Pub** (⊠ Zielna 37, ☎ 022/620–06–56) is open to midnight and serves English draught beers. The **Irish Pub** (⊠ Miodowa 3) has become intensely popular since its opening in 1992. Although pints of Guinness are expensive, there is a varied program of folk music until 3 AM most nights. **Harenda** (⊠ Krakowskie Przedmieście 4–6, entrance from ul. Obożna, ☎ 022/26–29–00) is open all night and has a crowded outdoor terrace in summer. The **Empik Pub** (⊠ Nowy Świat 15–17, ☎ 022/26–12–18) is popular with all age groups; there is music on weekends.

CABARET

Orpheus, on the top floor of the Marriott (⊠ Al. Jerozolimskie 65–79, ☎ 022/630–54–16), is elegant and very expensive; hotel guests have priority on admission. **Arena** (⊠ Marszałkowska 104, ☎ 022/27–50–91) has boisterous floor shows, including female wrestling. **Piwnica u Pana Michała** (⊠ Freta 4/6, ☎ 022/31–60–44) offers sedate ballet to guitar music.

CASINOS

The **Casino Warsaw** (⊠ Al. Jerozolimskie 65–79), on the first floor of the Marriott hotel, is Warsaw's plushest and most sedate casino; the clients are often Western businessmen and visitors or Polish jet-setters. It's open daily 1 PM–3 AM. The **Victoria Casino** (⊠ Ul. Królewska 11) is popular with Middle Eastern visitors and Polish businesspeople. It's open daily 1 PM–3 AM. The **Queen's Casino** (⊠ Pałac Kultury i Nauki, entrance from ul. Emilii Plater) is in the basement under the Congress Hall of the Palace of Culture and has a spacious bar.

There is a well-established disco at the student club, **Stodoła** (✉ Batorego 10, ☎ 022/25–86–25). **Hades** (✉ Al. Niepodległośi 162, ☎ 022/49–12–51) is a popular disco in the cellars of the Central School of Economics, with plenty of seating space. **Tango** is an upmarket disco, where high entrance charges—zł 85 at press time—include a buffet supper (✉ Ul. Smolna 15, ☎ 022/27–86–39). **Ground Zero** (✉ Ul. Wspólna 62, ☎ 022/625–43–80) is a large and crowded disco on two levels, with a floor show upstairs.

Akwarium (✉ Ul. Emilii Plater 49, ☎ 022/620–50–72), the Polish Jazz Association's club, runs a regular evening program of modern jazz in crowded, smoky surroundings; top Polish players and foreign groups perform here. **Piwnica Wandy Warskiej** (✉ Ul. Wałowa 7, ☎ 022/31–17–39), in the Old Town, is very popular; you'll need to book ahead. Hotels also often have jazz sessions, as do student clubs. **Kawiarnia Literacka** (✉ Krakowskie Przedmieście 87–89, ☎ 022/26–89–95) has classic jazz on weekends. **Blue Velvet** (✉ Krakowskie Przedmieście 5, ☎ 022/26–62–51, ext. 295) has regular modern jazz evenings.

The Arts

Since 1989 it seems every cinema in Warsaw has been showing foreign films—mainly U.S. box-office hits—nonstop. These are generally shown in their original version with subtitles, allowing you to catch up on what you've missed back home. **Relax** (✉ Ul. Złota 8, ☎ 022/27–77–62) is a popular large cinema in the center of town; it's full for almost all showings. **Skarpa** (✉ Ul. Kopernika 7–9, ☎ 022/26–48–96), off ulica Nowy Świat, is large and modern and offers buffet facilities.

Don't count on seeing many Polish films while visiting Warsaw; only one cinema specializes in Polish features, **Iluzjon Filmoteki Narodowej** (✉ Ul. Żurawia 3–5–7, ☎ 022/628–7431). **Wars** (✉ Rynek Starego Miasta 5–7, ☎ 022/31–44–88), a cinema on the New Town Square, occasionally forgets about box-office success and shows an old Polish classic; it has a good program of foreign films.

The **Filharmonia Narodowa** (National Philharmonic; ✉ Ul. Jasna 5, ☎ 022/26–57–12) offers an excellent season of concerts, with visits from world-renowned performers and orchestras as well as Polish musicians. Very popular **concerts of classical music for children**—run for years by Jadwiga Mackiewicz, who is herself almost a national institution—are held here on Thursday and Sunday at 3; Admission is from zł 2. **Studio Koncertowe Polskiego Radia** (Polish Radio Concert Studio; ✉ Ul. Woronicza 17, ☎ 022/44–32–50), open since 1992, has excellent acoustics and popular programs. **Towarzystwo im. Fryderyka Chopina** (Chopin Society; ✉ Ul. Okólnik 1, ☎ 022/27–95–99) organizes recitals and chamber concerts in the Pałac Ostrogskich.

Teatr Wielki (✉ Pl. Teatralny, ☎ 022/26–32–87), Warsaw's grand opera, stages spectacular productions of the classic international opera and ballet repertoire, as well as Polish operas and ballets. Stanisław Moniuszko's 1865 opera *Straszny Dwór* (*Haunted Manor*), a lively piece with folk costumes and dancing, is a good starting point if you want to explore Polish music: The visual aspects will entertain you, even if the music is unfamiliar. English plot summaries are available at most performances. **Warszawska Opera Kameralna** (✉ Al. Solidarności 76, ☎ 022/31–22–40), the Warsaw chamber opera, which is housed in a beautifully restored 19th-century theater building in the Muranów district, has a very ambitious program and a growing reputation. **Operetka** (✉ Ul. Nowogrodzka 49, ☎ 022/628–0360) offers a range of musicals and light opera, including Polish versions of such old favorites as *My Fair Lady*. Try to get a seat in one of the boxes upstairs.

THEATER

Teatr Narodowy (✉ Pl. Teatralny, ☎ 022/26–32–87), adjoining the opera house and under the same general management, was reopened in 1996 following extensive reconstruction after a fire; its repertoire includes Polish classics. **Teatr Powszechny** (✉ Ul. Zamoyskiego 20, ☎ 022/18–25–16), on the east bank of the Vistula, has a good reputation for modern drama and performs many American and British plays in translation. **Teatr Studio** (✉ Pałac Kultury i Nauki [Palace of Culture and Science], east entrance, ☎ 022/620–21–02) stages a great deal of experimental drama, which may be a good choice for those who don't understand Polish. **Teatr Współczesny** (✉ Ul. Mokotowska 14, ☎ 022/25–59–79) concentrates on Polish classics and those of other nations, though it also occasionally ventures into modern drama. **Teatr Żydowski** (✉ Ul. Grzybowska 12–15, ☎ 022/620–70–25), Warsaw's Jewish theater, performs in Yiddish, but most of its productions are colorful costume dramas in which the action speaks as loudly as the words. Translation—into Polish—is provided through headphones. **Scena Prezentacja** (✉ Ul. Żelazna 51/53, ☎ 022/620–82–88), a small theater opened in the 1980s in an old factory to the west of the city center, has concentrated on modern, mainly small-cast drama. **"Gulliver" Teatr Lalek** (✉ Ul. Różana 16, ☎ 022/45–16–76) is one of Warsaw's excellent puppet theaters, which are as entertaining to adults to kids.

Outdoor Activities and Sports

Health Clubs

The very expensive hotels in Warsaw all have good health-club facilities, but they don't admit nonmembers. The next best thing is the **Stegny Sports Center** (✉ Ul. Idzikowskiego 4, ☎ 022/42–27–00), which has a sauna and exercise rooms.

Hiking and Biking

In Warsaw the local branch of **PTTK** (ramblers' association) organizes daylong hikes on weekends in the nearby countryside: Watch the local papers for advertisements of meeting points and routes. To rent bicycles to explore the flat countryside surrounding Warsaw, contact the **Polski Związek Kolarski,** the cyclists' association (✉ Pl. Żelaznej Bramy 1, ☎ 022/620–28–71), for advice.

Horse Racing

You can reach Warsaw's racecourse by taking Tram 14 or 36 or one of the special buses marked WYŚCIGI, which run from the east side of the Palace of Culture and Science on Saturday in season (May–October). Betting is on a tote system. ✉ *Ul. Puławska 266*, ☎ *022/43–14–41.* 🎫 *Stands zł 10.*

Jogging

Along with dogs and bicycles, joggers are banned from Warsaw's largest and most beautiful park, the Łazienki (although an exception was made for George Bush). Indeed, Varsovians still find joggers faintly ridiculous. The 9½-kilometer (6-mile) trail through parkland and over footbridges from the **Ujazdowski Park** to Mariensztat (parallel to the Royal Route) is a good route. The **Vistula embankment** (the paved surface runs for about 12 kilometers [8 miles]) makes a good straight route. The **Pilsudski Park,** has a circular route of about 4½ kilometers (3 miles). The somewhat restricted pathways of the **Ogród Saski** offer the possibility of jogging in the center of town.

Soccer
Warsaw's soccer team, **Legia,** plays at the field at ulica Łazienkowska 3. ☎ *022/621–08–96.* 🎟 *From zł 3.*

Swimming
Warsaw's indoor pools tend to be overcrowded, and some restrict admission to only those with a season ticket; it's best to check first. Try **Inflancka** (✉ Ul. Inflancka 8, ☎ 022/31–36–83), which was built in the 1970s. The cost is zł 2.5–zł 5 per hour. **Szczęśliwice** (✉ Ul. Bitwy Warszawskiej 1920 r. 15–17, ☎ 022/22–42–96) is a small indoor pool; cost is zł 2.5–zł 5 per hour. **Wisła** (✉ Wał Miedzeszyński 407, ☎ 02/617–24–94) is a good pool, but at some distance from the center of town. Cost is zł 2.5–zł 5 per hour.

Shopping

At press time Warsaw's shopping scene is in some confusion. The old state-controlled cooperative trading outlets have largely closed down, but it is hard to tell which of the many new shops will survive. Because economic reforms have also brought with them a manufacturing slump, locally produced items are often harder to find than the ridiculously expensive imported items. Such Polish specialties as leather goods, amber and silver jewelry, or crystal and glass are in relatively short supply, although it's still possible to find bargains. Shopping hours have been deregulated to some extent. Although many have kept to the old system of opening from 11 AM to 7 PM, an increasing number of privately owned shops are establishing new hours. **RUCH** kiosks, which sell bus and train tickets, newspapers, and cosmetics, are usually open from 7 to 7 (most of these outlets have also recently been privatized).

Shopping Districts
Warsaw's four main shopping streets are **ulica Marszałkowska** (from ul. Królewska to pl. Zbawiciela), **aleje Jerozolimskie** (from the Central Station to pl. Generala de Gaulle), **ulica Nowy Świat,** and **ulica Chmielna** (formerly ul. Rutkowskiego). Ulica Marszałkowska and aleje Jerozolimskie offer mainly larger stores, including, at press time, a small number of international chains. Nowy Świat and ulica Chmielna have smaller stores and more specialized boutiques.

Department Stores
Warsaw's old **Central Department Stores** (✉ Ul. Marszałkowska 104–122), divided into the **Wars, Sawa,** and **Junior** sections, have changed their image. The old empty halls, through which people hurried searching for a rare special delivery, are gone; instead, the stores have now rented out space to small private boutiques that sell mainly imported fashion items. A major refurbishment of these stores took place in the early 1990s, and in 1996 the chain is due for privatization. Warsaw's oldest department store, **Braci Jabłkowskich,** at the corner of ulica Krucza and ulica Chmielna, with a monumental staircase and art-nouveau stained-glass windows, has been expensively renovated and now houses a range of separate stores selling clothing, jewelry, and household items.

Specialty Stores
ANTIQUES
Desa stores (✉ Ul. Marszałkowska 34–50, ☎ 022/621–66–15; ✉ Ul. Nowy Świat 51, ☎ 022/27–47–60) have a fine range of antique fur-

niture, art, and china. Remember, however, that many antiques cannot be exported; they are marked in Desa stores with a pink label.

Desa galleries (⊠ Rynek Starego Miasta 4–6, ☎ 022/31–16–81; ul. Koszykowa 60–62, ☎ 022/621–96–56) offer an interesting selection of paintings and work in pottery and glass. **Galeria Nowy Świat** (⊠ Nowy Świat 23, ☎ 022/26–35–01) combines the sale of modern designer jewelry, antiques, and modern art. **Galeria Zapiecek** (⊠ Ul. Zapiecek 1, ☎ 022/31–99–18) has painting, ceramics and designer furniture.

Cepelia stores (⊠ Pl. Konstytucji 5, ☎ 022/621–26–18; ⊠ Rynek Starego Miasta 8–10, ☎ 022/31–18–05) sell a variety of folk art, including traditional wooden household utensils, wood carvings, silver and amber jewelry, and tapestries. **Artis** (⊠ Emilii Plater 47, ☎ 022/620–59–30), just round the corner from the Holiday Inn, has a very varied offer of wood carvings, silver and amber jewelry, and glass and ceramics. Interesting glassware, pottery, and wickerwork can be found at the shop and gallery run by **Instytut Wzornictwa Przemysłowego** (Institute of Industrial Design; ⊠ Świętojerska 7, ☎ 022/31–04–53), which is open Sunday 10 to 4.

Banasik (⊠ Ul. Piękna 26–34, ☎ 022/62–04–89) is a large store on two floors, with a range of glassware and crystal. **Bolesław Kościański i Syn** (⊠ Ul. Chmielna 98, ☎ 022/24–34–18) has traditional glass and crystal as well as colored artistic glass pieces. **Majolika** (⊠ Ul. Puławska 12a, ☎ 022/49–45–18) is a small store crowded with good, simple glass.

Herbapol stores (⊠ Krakowskie Przedmieście 1, ☎ 022/26–65–95; ⊠ Ul. Złota 3, ☎ 022/26–29–72) stock herbs for every ailment or beauty need. Many customers come just for the herbal toothpaste or exotic herbal teas.

Beekeeping is a popular hobby among Poles, and **Pszczelarski** (⊠ Ul. Piękna 45–45a, ☎ 022/628–61–37) offers a large selection of honey, mead, queen's jelly, and granulated pollen dust (for the health conscious).

All kinds of fishing tackle, waders, gun cases, and shooting sticks (collapsible triangular stools on a spiked base) are available at the **Sklep Myśliwski** (⊠ Ul. Krucza 41–43, ☎ 022/628–26–86).

Orno shops (⊠ Ul. Nowy Świat 52, ☎ 022/26–42–81; ⊠ Ul. Wspólna 63, ☎ 022/629–34–68) sell handcrafted silver and amber pieces; they will also do customized designs. **Metal Galeria** (⊠ Chmielna 32–34, ☎ 022/27–45–09) has a large range of modern silver and gold jewelry, well displayed in austere glass cases. **Silver Line** (⊠ Nowy Świat 59, ☎ 022/26–63–55) specializes in amber jewelry.

JKM (⊠ Krakowskie Przedmieście 65, ☎ 022/27–22–62) is a small shop, crammed with well-designed bags, suitcases, and gloves from the best Polish producers. **Pekar** (⊠ Al. Jerozolimskie 29, ☎ 022/621–90–82) carries a wide range of bags, gloves, and jackets. **Andrzej Kłoda** (⊠ Krakowskie Przedmieście 81, ☎ 022/27–07–40) has his own interesting range of bags, belts, and other accessories.

VODKA

The greatest of all Polish specialties, *wódka* is available in several varieties all over town. **Bum Buss** (✉ Krucza 47a, ☎ 022/625–48–32) has attractive displays, and the staff is helpful. **Delikatesy Porto** (✉ Ul. Świętokrzyska 30, ☎ 022/620–19–30) has a good stock of Polish liquors as well as imports.

Street Markets

Street markets have been brought under control by the city authorities. The market in the great square on the east side of the Palace of Culture and Science has been tamed and forced into standardized wooden stalls, where you can find every imaginable Polish and imported product, from fox coats to stereo equipment. On the steps leading up to the palace, individual dealers sell goods imported from as far afield as China or Thailand. The largest Warsaw market, composed largely of private sellers hawking everything from antiques to blue jeans, is at the **Tysiąclecie Sports Stadium,** on the other side of the river at Rondo Waszyngtona.

Warsaw A to Z

Arriving and Departing

BY BUS

Warsaw's main bus station, **Dworzec PKS** (✉ North of al. Jerozolimskie in Czyste, next to the Warszawa Zachodnia Railway Station, ☎ 022/23–63–94) serves most long-distance express routes and most tourist destinations west of the city (such as Chopin's birthplace, at Żelazowa Wola; ☞ *above*). Local services for points north of the city (such as the Puszcza Kampinoska) run from **Dworzec PKS Marymont** in the northern district of Żoliborz (✉ Corner of ul. Marymoncka and ul. Żeromskiego, ☎ 022/34–74–44); buses headed east leave from **Dworzec PKS Stadion** (✉ Intersection of ul. Targowa, ul. Jana Zamoyskiego, and al. Zieleniecka, on the east bank of the Vistula, ☎ 022/18–54–73). Tickets for all destinations can be purchased at the main bus station, which is often very crowded.

International and long-distance bus services operated by private companies usually arrive and depart from the east side of the central railway station on aleje Jerozolimskie. **Polski Express** (information and reservations ☎ 022/630–29–67) long-distance services pick up from this point.

BY CAR

Within the city, a car can be more of a problem than a convenience. Warsaw currently has too many cars for its road network, and there can be major snarls. Parking, though largely unregulated, causes difficulties. There is a real threat of theft—of contents, parts, or the entire car—if you leave a Western model unattended, and it is not easy to get quick service or repairs. If you do bring your car, leave it overnight in a guarded parking garage.

BY PLANE

Warsaw's **Okęcie Airport** (☎ 022/650–46–28) is 7 kilometers (4 miles) south of the city center. Terminal 1 serves European and transatlantic flights, while Terminal 2 serves domestic traffic. **LOT,** the Polish airline (✉ Al. Jerozolimskie 65–79, ☎ 022/630–50–07; for reservations ☎ 952), takes the lion's share of flights to and from Warsaw. Other airlines flying to Warsaw include **British Airways** (☎ 022/628–94–31; at Okęcie, ☎ 022/46–05–72); **Air France** (☎ 022/628–12–81; at Okęcie, ☎ 022/46–03–03); and **Lufthansa** (☎ 022/27–54–36; at Okęcie, ☎ 022/46–25–27).

Between the Airport and Downtown: The direct route to downtown, where almost all the hotels are, is along aleje Żwirki i Wigury and ulica Raszyńska. Traffic can be heavy here in peak afternoon rush hours (3–5), and taxis may divert along aleje Lotników or ulica Wawelska and aleje Niepodległości. **By Bus:** City buses, which depart from Terminal 1 and take the direct route are cheap but can be very crowded by the time they reach the city center; Terminal 2 is less well served by city bus lines. Some hotels operate a minibus service from the airport. Warsaw city transport Bus 175 leaves Okęcie every 10 minutes during peak hours and every 14 minutes at other times. It runs past almost all major downtown hotels and is reliable and cheap. Purchase tickets for zł 1 at the airport RUCH kiosks or from the automatic vending machine outside the arrivals hall and cancel one ticket per person and item of luggage; the ride downtown takes 20 to 30 minutes in off-peak periods. A bus marked AIRPORT–CITY leaves Terminal 1 every 20 minutes, beginning on the hour, and stops at all the major hotels and Central Station. Tickets cost zł 3.5, and the trip takes 15 to 20 minutes. If your immediate destination is not Warsaw, **Polski Express** now runs direct services from Okęcie to seven other major Polish cities (information and reservations ☎ 022/630–29–67). **By Taxi:** The Okęcie Airport authority has a licensed fleet of marked taxis that stand directly outside the exits from the terminals. You can prepurchase a voucher for your trip at an office inside the airport, directly beside the main exit; the charge is around zł 25 for the trip into town, which takes 10 to 15 minutes in off-peak periods. You would be wise to ignore taxi hawkers and unmarked vehicles. The Marriott Hotel operates its own fleet of marked taxis that shuttle guests between the airport and hotel. If none of these services is available, try calling the **Radio Taxi** service (☎ 919).

BY TRAIN

Warsaw's **Dworzec Centralny** (Central Station; ☎ 022/25–50–00; international rail information, ☎ 022/620–45–12; domestic rail information ☎ 022/620–03–61), as the name implies, is right in the heart of the city, at aleje Jerozolimskie 54, between the Marriott and Holiday Inn hotels. The station is very conveniently situated but has been plagued periodically by teams of pickpockets and muggers who prey on passengers as they board or leave trains. Since Central Station is only a transit station, you might therefore be wise to join or leave your train at its terminus station. For trains running to the south and west (Poznań, Kraków, Wrocław, Łódź), use the eastern station, **Warszawa Wschodnia** (✉ Ul. Kijowska, ☎ 022/19–06–79); for trains running east, go to the western station, **Warszawa Zachodnia** (✉ In the western district of Czyste, just north of al. Jerozolimskie, ☎ 022/36–59–34).

Local trains run from **Warszawa Śródmieście,** next to Central Station, on aleje Jerozolimskie (☎ 022/628–47–41) or from **Dworzec Wileński** (✉ Ul. Targowa, ☎ 022/18–35–21).

Even though computers have been introduced at most of the mainline stations, purchasing tickets can still be a time-consuming business. You can prepurchase tickets up to a month in advance at most stations, and the Central Station offers a telephone order and home delivery service (☎ 022/25–60–33). Orbis offices and other travel agents also sell rail tickets.

Getting Around

Although Warsaw stretches more than 32 kilometers (20 miles) in each direction, the sights of greatest interest to most tourists are concentrated primarily in two areas: Śródmieście, Warsaw's downtown, along ulica Marszałkowska; and Stare Miasto, the Old Town, just over 2 kilometers (1½ miles) away and centered on Rynek Starego Miasta. Both areas are best explored on foot; public transportation, though cheap and efficient, can be uncomfortably crowded. Taxis are readily available and are often the most convenient option for covering longer distances.

BY BUS

A trip on a Warsaw city bus costs zł 1; you have to purchase tickets in advance at a RUCH kiosk and cancel one in the machine on the bus for each ride. Buses, which halt at all stops along their route, are numbered 100 and up. Express buses are numbered from E-1 upward: Buses numbered 500–599 stop at selected stops. Check carefully on the information board at the bus stop before boarding. Night buses (numbered 600 and up) operate between 11 PM and 5 AM; the fare is zł 2.5, and for these buses you can buy tickets directly from the driver if you have not prepurchased the right denominations.

BY TAXI

Since drivers are not allowed by law to pick up fares when flagged down in the street, the best place to pick up a taxi is at a standard city cab stand (marked TAXI). Avoid taxi stands outside hotels (apart from chartered hotel fleets), as you are likely to be charged far more than the going rate. The standard charge for 1½ kilometers (1 mile) is about zł 4—zł 3 for the first kilometer and gr. 80 for each kilometer thereafter. It is not customary to tip taxi drivers, although you can round up the fare to the nearest złoty.

The **Radio Taxi** service (☎ 919) is reliable and efficient, but you will usually need a Polish speaker to place your order.

BY TRAM

Trams are the fastest means of public transport since they are not affected by traffic hold-ups. Purchase tickets from RUCH kiosks or other outlets designated SPRZEDAŻ BILETÓW MZK for zł 1 and cancel one ticket in the machine on the tram for each ride. Trams run on a north–south and east–west grid system along most of the main city routes, pulling up automatically at all stops. Each tram has a diagram of the system.

BY UNDERGROUND

Warsaw's new underground opened in spring 1995. Although as yet it has only one line, running from the southern suburbs to the city center (Natolin to Pl. Politechniki), it is clean, fast, and costs the same as tram and bus—use the same tickets, canceling them at the entrance to the station.

Contacts and Resources

B&B RESERVATION AGENCIES

Ogólnopolska Informacja Noclegowa (☎ 022/643–95–92, weekdays 9–5; ☎ 022/671–58–25, weekdays 5 PM–9 PM and weekends 10 AM–5 PM) has information on all types of accommodations countrywide, from hotels and guest houses to B&Bs. **Romeo i Julia** bureau (⊠ Ul. Emilii Plater 30, m. 15, ☎ 022/629–29–93) has a wide selection of B&B accommodations in a range of prices. **Polonaise** bureau (⊠ Ul. Świętojerska 4/10, ☎ 022/635–07–65) deals with B&B-type accommodations in Warsaw; the staff is helpful and speaks English.

DOCTORS AND DENTISTS

You can schedule same-day appointments at the following centrally located clinics: **Alfa, Lecznica Profesorsko-Ordynatorska** (⊠ Nowy Świat 58a, ☎ 022/26–23–10), open daily 6 AM–9 PM; **Centrum Medyczne** (⊠ Hotel Marriott, al. Jerozolimskie 67/79, ☎ 022/630–51–15), open daily 8 AM–9 PM.

For dental care: **Całodobowa Klinika Stomatologiczna** (✉ Ul. Ludna 10, ☎ 022/625–01–02), open daily 24 hours; **Multident** (✉ Al. Jerozolimskie 25 m. 14, ☎ 022/628–96–95), open daily 9 AM–9 PM.

EMBASSIES AND CONSULATE

All three embassies listed below are on or just off of aleje Jerozolimskie; the British Consulate is closer to the center of town.

U.S. Embassy (✉ Al. Ujazdowskie 29–31, ☎ 022/628–30–41). **Canadian Embassy** (✉ Ul. Matejki 1–5, ☎ 022/629–80–51). **British Embassy** (✉ Al. Róż 1, ☎ 022/628–10–01). **British Consulate** (✉ Ul. Emilii Plater 28, ☎ 022/625–30–30).

EMERGENCIES

Police (☎ 997). **Ambulance** (☎ 999). This will link you with the central emergency station on the corner of ulica Hoża and ulica Poznańska; hospitals do not have emergency rooms.

ENGLISH-LANGUAGE BOOKSTORES

Prus (✉ Krakowskie Przedmieście 7, ☎ 022/26–18–35) has a range of fiction and nonfiction titles. **Batax** (✉ Al. Jerozolimskie 61, ☎ 022/25–41–46) has a reasonable selection of English-language fiction. The secondhand bookstore **Logos** (✉ Al. Ujazdowskie 16, ☎ 02/621–38–67) usually offers quite a wide range of fiction and nonfiction. **Bookland-Longman** (✉ Ul. Solec 22, ☎ 022/625–41–46) concentrates on language textbooks, but also carries some fiction.

GUIDED TOURS

Orbis. It's still the only reliable, established agency to offer guided tours by bus, minibus, or limousine. Most tours start out from one of the major Orbis hotels and can be booked either there or at one of the Orbis offices listed above (☞ Visitor Information, *below*). Orbis's standard half-day tour covers the Old Town, Central Warsaw, and Łazienki Park. The all-day tour also takes in Wilanów. Orbis can arrange to have a qualified guide, registered with the Polish Tourist Association (PTTK), give you a customized tour of the city. Rates start at $50 a day for individual tourists with their own means of transportation.

LATE-NIGHT PHARMACIES

The following pharmacies (*apteka*) are open 24 hours a day: **Apteka Grabowskiego,** on the first floor in ✉ Dworzec Centralny, al. Jerozolimskie 54, ☎ 022/25–69–84; ✉ Ul. Freta 13/15, ☎ 022/31–50–91; ✉ Ul. Widok 19, ☎ 022/27–35–93. The **Swiss Pharmacy** (✉ Al. Róż 2, ☎ 022/628–94–71), open Monday–Saturday 10–6, carries a wide variety of Western medications.

MONEY AND CURRENCY

Where to Change Money: The **Kantor Wymiany Walut** at ulica Marszałkowska 66, on the corner of ulica Wilcza, has swift, friendly service and usually offers slightly better rates than hotels and banks. It's open weekdays 11–7 and Saturday 9–2. Another option is the **Kantor** in the General Post Office at ulica Święto krzyska 31, open 24 hours a day. **TEBOS,** at the Central Railway Station on aleje Jerozolimskie, at the foot of the staircase leading from the main hall to the access passage to platforms is also open 24 hours a day; exercise caution, however—the Central Station is a haunt of pickpockets.

OPENING AND CLOSING TIMES

Although standard Polish opening hours still apply for most Warsaw institutions, a number of food stores are now open late at night, and most shops are open Saturday 9–2.

TRAVEL AGENCIES
American Express (✉ Ul. Bagińskiego 1, ☎ 022/635–20–02, 24-hr
☎ 022/625–40–30). **Getz International Travel Ltd.** (✉ Ul. Warecka 9,
☎ 022/27–73–35) is an efficient agency with friendly service. **Thomas
Cook** (✉ Ul. Nowy Świat 64, ☎ 022/26–47–29) is a centrally located
travel agency.

VISITOR INFORMATION
COIT (✉ Pl. Zamkowy 1/13, ☎ 022/635–18–81), on Castle Square
on the edge of the Old Town, is open 9–6 weekdays, 11–6 weekends.
Orbis has many offices in the city, but not all specialize in helping foreign visitors. Go to the Orbis desk at any major hotel or one of the
following offices: ✉ Ulica Marszałkowska 142, corner of ulica
Królewska, ☎ 022/27–36–73; ✉ Krakowskie Przedmieście 13, ☎ 022/
26–16–67.

KRAKÓW

Kraków (Cracow), seat of Poland's oldest university and once the nation's capital (before finally relinquishing the honor to Warsaw in
1611), is one of the few Polish cities that escaped devastation during
World War II; Hitler's armies were driven out before they had a chance
to destroy it. Today Kraków's fine towers, facades, and churches, il-
lustrating seven centuries of Polish architecture, make it a major attraction for visitors. Its location, about 270 kilometers (170 miles) south
of Warsaw, also makes it a good starting point for hiking and skiing
trips in the mountains of southern Poland.

North of Kraków, the industrial town of **Częstochowa,** where Poland's
holiest icon, the Black Madonna, is housed in the Pauline monastery,
can be reached—with an early start—as a day trip from Kraków.

Exploring Kraków

*290 km (180 mi) south of Warsaw, 270 km (170 mi) southwest of Lublin,
260 km (161 mi) east of Wrocław.*

Listed by UNESCO in 1978 as one of the 12 great historic cities of
the world, Kraków should be a priority in the region if you are interested in art, architecture, or Polish history. Despite problems caused
by pollution from nearby industrial Śląsk (Silesia), it is a uniquely preserved medieval city. A thriving market town in the 10th century
Kraków became Poland's capital in 1037. The original walls are gone,
pulled down according to the fashion of the early 19th century and
replaced by a ring of parkland known as the **Planty,** which encloses
the Old Town.

To the southeast of the Old Town is a neighborhood—Kazimierz—that
was once a town in its own right, chartered in 1335 and named for its
founder, Kazimierz the Great. After 1495, when they were expelled from
Kraków by King John Albert, this was the home of Kraków's Jewish
community. The Jewish community of Kazimierz came to an abrupt
and tragic end during World War II: A ghetto was established here in
March 1941, and its inhabitants were transported to their deaths in
the concentration camp of Auschwitz-Birkenau (☞ Małopolska,
below).

*Numbers in the text correspond to numbers in the margin and on the
Kraków map.*

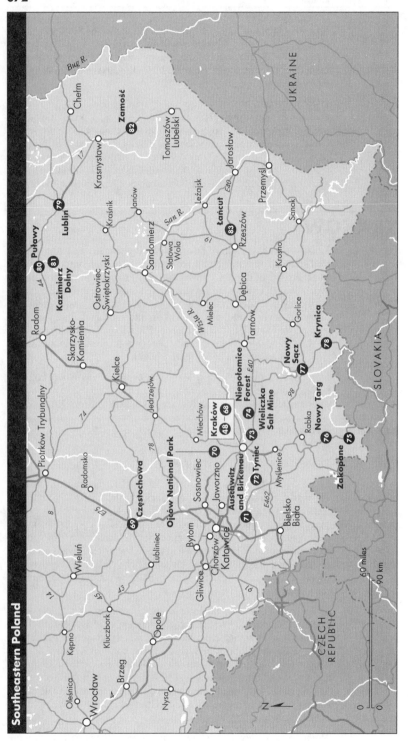

Southeastern Poland

The Old Town

A GOOD WALK

The Old Town is best explored on foot, beginning at the **Barbakan** ④⑧ and city gate on **ulica Floriańska** ④⑨: here, if you have any interest in art, you should visit the Czartoryski Collection in the **Municipal Arsenal** ⑤⓪ and **Dom Jana Matejki** (Jan Matejko's House) ⑤①, and admire the medieval mansions, as well. Ulica Floriańska will take you to the **Rynek Główny** (Main Market Square) ⑤② at the center of the town, where you will find the **Kościół Mariacki** (Church of Our Lady) ⑤③, the Renaissance **Sukiennice** (Cloth Hall) ⑤④, and a collection of magnificent Renaissance town houses.

The historic early buildings of the Jagiellonian University, the **Collegium Maïus** ⑤⑤ and **Collegium Juridicum** ⑤⑥, lie in streets leading off to the southwest and south of the square: Take ulica świelej. Anny to reach ulica Jagiellońska, and then go via ulica Gołębia (where you might visit **Robert Jahoda's Printing Press** ⑤⑦) to Plac Wszystkich Świętych, with the 13th-century **Franciscan church and monastery** ⑤⑧. From here take ulica Grodzka south to the 11th-century **Kościół świelej Andrzeja** (Church of St. Andrew) ⑤⑨, before cutting through to Kraków's oldest street, ulica Kanonicza, where the canons of the cathedral once lived; their **Chapter House** now houses the Archdiocesan Museum. **Ulica Kanonicza** ⑥⓪ leads to the Wawel hill, with its **cathedral** ⑥① and Renaissance **Zamek Królewski** (Royal Castle) ⑥②, which can easily take a day to explore, if you have time. From the Wawel, you can stroll south down the Vistula embankment to visit the **Kościół na Skałce** (Church on the Rock) ⑥③ and the fine 14th-century redbrick Gothic **Kościół świętej Katarzyny** (Church of St. Catherine), at Ulica Skałeczna at the corner of ulica Augustyniańka.

TIMING

In summer Kraków can become very sultry; on hot days try to begin early in the morning, although most museums will not be open until 9:30 or 10. The Wawel Cathedral requires a whole morning or afternoon to itself; the rest of the Old City, at least a day.

SIGHTS TO SEE

④⑧ **Barbakan.** Only one small section of Kraków's city wall still stands, centered on the 15th-century Barbakan, one of the largest of its kind in Europe. It is now being renovated so that visitors will again be able to climb its turrets. ⊠ *Ul. Basztowa, opposite ul. Floriańska.*

★ ⑤⑤ **Collegium Maïus.** The earliest existing building of the Jagiellonian University, the Collegium Maïus, stands on ulica Jagiellońska. The university was founded by Kazimierz the Great in 1364 as the first university in Poland. By 1400 the original buildings had become overcrowded and were replaced with the Collegium Maïus, which has an arcaded courtyard with lecture rooms on the ground floor; the rooms on the upper level were originally for the fellows of the college. The Jagiellonian's most famous student, Nicolaus Copernicus, studied here from 1491 to 1495. To the left of the entrance is the **Stuba Communis** of the early scholars, which has a fine collection of pewter pots, a reminder of the hall's original function. The room is now used only for major university functions. Above the portal is the university's motto: *Plus ratio quam vis* (Better reason than force). Two other Jagiellonian university buildings worth noting, constructed later, are on ulica Gołębia: the **Collegium Physicum** at No. 13 and the **Collegium Slavisticum** at No. 20. ⊠ *Collegium Maius, ul. Jagiellońska 15.* 🖼 *Courtyard free, museum zł 2.* ⊙ *Courtyard weekdays 11–2:30, Sat. 11–1:30; museum weekends 11–2.*

Exploring Kraków

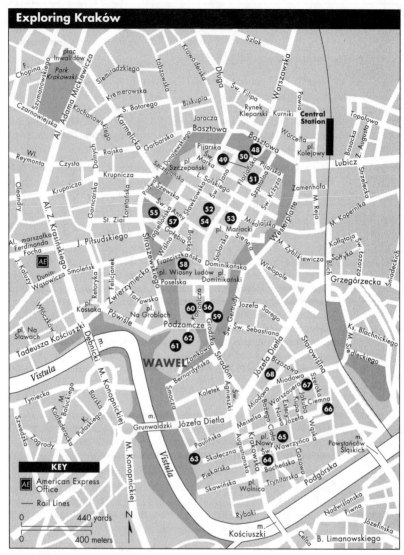

Barbakan, **48**

Collegium
Juridicum, **56**

Collegium Maïus, **55**

Dom Jana Matejki, **51**

Franciscan Church
and Monastery, **58**

Kościół Bożego
Ciała, **65**

Kościół Mariacki, **53**

Kościół na Skałce, **63**

Kościół
św. Andrzeja, **59**

Municipal Arsenal, **50**

Robert Jahoda's
Printing Press, **57**

Rynek Główny, **52**

Stara Synagoga, **66**

Sukiennice, **54**

Synagoga R'emuh, **67**

Synagoga Tempel, **68**

Town Hall of
Kazimierz, **64**

Ulica Floriańska, **49**

Ulica Kanonicza, **60**

Wawel Cathedral, **61**

Zamek Królewski, **62**

56 Collegium Juridicum. On ulica Grodzka, one of Kraków's oldest streets, is the magnificent Gothic Collegium Juridicum, built in the early 15th century to house the university's law students. ✉ *Ul. Grodzka 53.*

51 Dom Jana Matejki. The family house of 19th-century painter Jan Matejko is now a museum of his work. While you examine his romantic paintings, you can also admire the well-preserved interior of this 16th-century building. ✉ *Ul. Floriańska 41,* ☏ *012/22–59–26.* 🖅 *Zł 2.5, Fri. free.* ☉ *Tues.–Thurs. and weekends 10–3:30, Fri. noon–6.*

58 Franciscan church and monastery. The mid-13th-century Franciscan church and monastery are among the earliest brick buildings in Kraków. It also has art-nouveau stained glass windows by Stanisław Wyspiański. ✉ *Pl. Wszystkich Świętych 1.*

OFF THE **KOPIEC KOŚCIUSZKI –** This mound on the outskirts of Kraków was built in
BEATEN PATH tribute to the memory of Tadeusz Kościuszko in 1820, three years after his death. The earth came from battlefields on which he fought; soil from the United States was added in 1926. This is the best place from which to get a panoramic view of the city. Take Tram 1, 2, or 6 from plac Dominikański to the terminus at Salwator and then walk up aleje Waszyngtona to the mound. ☉ *Daily 10–dusk.*

★ **53 Kościół Mariacki** (Church of Our Lady). Dominating the northeast corner of Kraków's Rynek Główny is the twin-towered Church of Our Lady. The first church was built on this site before the town plan of 1257, which is why it stands slightly askew from the main square; the present church, completed in 1397, was built on the foundations of its predecessor. You'll note that the two towers, added in the early 15th century, are of different heights. Legend has it that they were built by two brothers, one of whom grew jealous of the other's work and slew him with the "bloody sword," a symbol of Magdeburg law, which still hangs in the ☞ **Sukiennice.** From the higher tower, a strange bugle call rings out to mark the passing of each hour. It breaks off on an abrupt sobbing note to commemorate an unknown bugler struck in the throat by a Tartar arrow as he was playing his call to warn the city of imminent attack. The main showpiece of the Mariacki church is the magnificent wooden altarpiece with more than 200 carved figures, the work of the 15th-century artist Wit Stwosz (Veit Stoss). The panels offer a detailed picture of medieval life, and Stwosz himself is believed to be represented in the figure in the bottom right-hand corner of the Crucifixion panel. ✉ *Rynek Główny at the corner of ul. Mikołajska.*

63 Kościół na Skałce (Church on the Rock). Standing on the Vistula embankment to the south of the Wawel Hill is the Pauline Church on the Rock. This is the center of the cult of St. Stanisław, bishop and martyr, who is believed to have been beheaded on the orders of the king in the church that stood on this spot in 1079—a tale of rivalry similar to that of Henry II and Thomas à Becket. Starting in the 19th century, this also became the last resting place for well-known Polish writers and artists; among those buried here are the composer Karol Szymanowski and the poet and painter Stanisław Wyspiański. ✉ *Between ul. Paulińska and ul. Skałeczna on the Vistula embankment.*

59 Kościół św. Andrzeja (Church of St. Andrew).The 11th-century fortified Church of St. Andrew is one of Kraków's few well-preserved Romanesque structures (the interior, however, is baroque); it was here that the inhabitants of the district took refuge during Tartar raids. ✉ *At the midpoint on the east side of ul. Grodzka.*

★ ⓸ **Municipal Arsenal.** The surviving fragment of Kraków's city wall op-posite the Barbakan, where students and amateur artists like to hang their paintings for sale in the summer, contains the Renaissance Mu-nicipal Arsenal, which now houses part of the National Museum's **Czartoryski Collection,** one of the best art exhibits in Poland. High-lights include Leonardo da Vinci's *Lady with an Ermine,* Raphael's *Por-trait of a Young Man,* and Rembrandt's *Landscape with the Good Samaritan.* ✉ *Ul. św. Jana 19,* ☎ *012/22–55–66.* 🎫 *Zł 5, Fri. free.* ⊙ *Fri. noon–5:30, Sat.–Tues. 10–3:30.*

Pałac pod Baranami (Palace at the Sign of the Rams). On the corner of ulica świętej Anny, opposite the Town Hall Tower, several Gothic houses were converted into a Renaissance palace by Jost Decjusz, sec-retary to King Sigismund the Old. Confiscated during World War II from the Potocki family, which had owned it since the 19th century, it was home after the war to the famed satirical cabaret *Piwnica pod Baranami.* Returned to the Potocki family in 1990, today the build-ing contains shops, a café, and galleries.

⓹ **Robert Jahoda's Printing Press.** A small museum in a quiet back street that shows the history of printing and bookbinding in Kraków. ✉ *Ul. Gołębia 4,* ☎ *012/22–99–22.* 🎫 *Zł 1.* ⊙ *Daily 10–2; closed 1st week-end of month.*

★ ⓹ **Rynek Główny** (Main Market Square). Europe's largest medieval mar-ketplace, Kraków's magnificent Main Market Square measures 220 square yards and is on a par with St. Mark's Square in Venice in size and grandeur. It even has the same plague of pigeons—although leg-end tells us the ones here are no ordinary birds. They are allegedly the spirits of the knights of Duke Henry IV Probus, who in the 13th cen-tury were cursed and turned into birds.

The great square was not always so spacious. In an earlier period it also contained—in addition to the present buildings—a Gothic town hall, a Renaissance granary, a large weighing house, a foundry, a pil-lory, and hundreds of traders' stalls. A few flower sellers under color-ful umbrellas are all that remain of this bustling commercial activity. A pageant of history has passed through this square. From 1320 on, Polish kings came here on the day after their coronation to meet the city's burghers and receive homage and tribute in the name of all the towns of Poland. Albert Hohenzollern, the grand master of the Teu-tonic Knights, came here in 1525 to pay homage to Sigismund the Old, king of Poland. And in 1794 Tadeusz Kościuszko took his solemn vow to fight against czarist Russia in a national Polish insurrection.

The **Dom pod Jeleniami** (House at the Sign of the Stag) at No. 36 was once an inn where both Goethe (1790) and Czar Nicholas I (1849) found shelter. At No. 45 is the **Dom pod Orłem** (House at the Sign of the Eagle), where Tadeusz Kościuszko lived as a young officer in 1777; a little far-ther down the square, at No. 6, is the **Szary Dom** (Gray House), where he made his staff headquarters in 1794. In 1605, in the house at No. 9, the young Polish noblewoman Maryna Mniszchówna married the False Dymitri, the pretender to the Russian throne (these events are portrayed in Pushkin's play *Boris Godunov* and in Mussorgsky's op-eratic adaptation of it). At No. 16, in a **14th-century house** that be-longed to the Wierzynek merchant family, is a famous restaurant named for them. In 1364, during a "summit" meeting attended by the Holy Roman Emperor, one of the Wierzyneks gave an elaborate feast for the visiting royal dignitaries; this was the beginning of the house's reputation for haute cuisine.

★ **54** **Sukiennice** (Cloth Hall). A **statue of Adam Mickiewicz** stands in front of the eastern entrance to the Renaissance Cloth Hall, which now stands in splendid near-isolation in the middle of Kraków's Main Market Square. The Gothic arches date from the 14th century; but after a fire in 1555 the upper part was rebuilt in Renaissance style. The inner arcades on the ground floor still hold traders' booths, now mainly selling local crafts. On the first floor, in a branch of the **National Museum,** you can view a collection of 19th-century Polish paintings. ⊠ *Rynek Glóny 1–3,* ☎ *012/34–33–37.* ☞ *Zł 5, Thurs. free.* ☉ *Tues., Wed., and Fri.–Sun. 10–3:30, Thurs. noon–6.*

NEED A BREAK? The **Sukiennice Café** (⊠ Rynek Główny 15), on the east side of the Cloth Hall, is the most traditional of Kraków's cafés. Its art-nouveau decor includes fitted mirrors and wall lamps, marble-topped tables, and a no-smoking room with elaborate ceiling paintings.

49 **Ulica Floriańska.** The beautiful **Brama Floriańska** (Florian Gate) was built around 1300 and leads through Kraków's old city walls into ulica Floriańska, one of the streets laid out according to the town plan of 1257. The Gothic houses of the 13th-century burghers still remain, although they were rebuilt and given Renaissance or neoclassical facades. The **house at ulica Floriańska 24,** decorated with an emblem of three bells, was once the workshop of a bell founder, who no doubt had plenty of employment in medieval Kraków, given the number of churches. The chains hanging on the walls of the **house at No. 17** barred the streets to invaders when the city was under siege. At No. 14 you will find the **Hotel pod Różą,** one of the city's oldest, where both Franz Liszt and Russian czar Alexander I stayed. And finally, at the left-hand corner where ulica Floriańska enters the market square, stands the **Dom pod Murzynami** (Negroes' House), a 16th-century tenement decorated with two black faces—testimony to the fascination with Africa entertained by citizens of the Age of Discovery.

NEED A BREAK? **Jama Michalikowa** (⊠ Ul. Floriańska 45, ☎ 012/22–15–61) is a café with a perfectly preserved art-nouveau interior; the walls are hung with drawings by late-19th-century customers, who sometimes had to pay their bills in kind. There is no smoking in the main room.

★ **60** **Ulica Kanonicza,** named for the canons of the cathedral who once lived here, is one of Kraków's oldest streets and leads from the center of town to the foot of the Wawel Hill. Most of the houses date from the 14th and 15th centuries, although they were "modernized" in Renaissance or later styles. Pope John Paul II lived here in the **Chapter House** at No. 19 and later in the late 16th-century **Dean's House,** at No. 21. The Chapter House now houses the Archdiocesan Museum, with a small collection of manuscripts. ⊠ *Ul. Kanonicza 19.* ☞ *Zł 1.* ☉ *Wed.–Sun. 10–3.*

NEED A BREAK? **U Literatów** (⊠ Ul. Kanonicza 7, ☎ 012/21–86–66), behind the 14th-century stone walls of the writers' association house, is a good place for a cool drink or light meal; there are tables in the garden in summer.

★ **61** **Wawel Cathedral.** The **Wawel Hill** is a raised area of about 15 acres that from earliest times formed a natural point for fortification on the flat Vistula Plain. During the 8th century a tribal stronghold had already been constructed here, and from the 10th century the elevation held a royal residence and the seat of the bishops of Kraków. Construction on Wawel Cathedral was begun in 1320, and the structure was consecrated in 1364. Lack of space for expansion on the hill has meant the preservation of the original austere structure, although a few Renaissance and baroque chapels have been crowded around it. The most notable of these is the **Kaplica Zygmuntowska** (Sigismund Chapel), built in the 1520s by the Florentine architect Bartolomeo Bertecci and widely considered to be the finest Renaissance chapel north of the Alps.

From 1037, when Kraków became the capital of Poland, Polish kings were crowned and buried in the Wawel Cathedral. This tradition continued up to the time of the partitions, even after the capital had been moved to Warsaw. During the 19th century, only great national heroes were honored by a Wawel entombment: Tadeusz Kościuszko was buried here in 1817; Adam Mickiewicz and Juliusz Słowacki, the great romantic poets, were also brought back from exile to the Wawel after their deaths; Marshal Józef Piłsudski, the hero of independent interwar Poland, was interred in the cathedral crypt in 1935.

You may also visit the cathedral treasury, archives, library, and museum. Among the showpieces in the library, one of the earliest in Poland, is the 12th-century *Emmeram Gospel* from Regensburg. After touring at ground level, you can climb the wooden staircase of the **Sigismund Tower,** entered through the sacristy. The tower holds the famous **Sigismund Bell,** which was commissioned in 1520 by King Sigismund the Old and is still tolled on all solemn state and church occasions. *Cathedral museum:* ⊠ Zł 2. ⊙ *Tues.–Sun. 10–3.*

Wieża Ratuszowa (Town Hall Tower). This tower at the southwest corner of the Rynek Główny is all that remains of the 16th-century town hall, which was demolished in the early 19th century. The tower now houses a branch of the **Kraków History Museum** and offers a panoramic view of the old city. ⊠ Zł 3. ⊙ *June–Sept., Fri.–Wed. 9–3, Thurs. noon–5.*

··

NEED A   **Wierzynek** (⊠ Rynek Główny 16), the famous restaurant, now has a
BREAK?   ground-floor café that serves delicious cakes.

··

★ ⑥②   **Zamek Królewski** (Royal Castle). The castle that now stands on Kraków's Wawel Hill dates from the early 16th century, when the Romanesque residence that stood on this site was destroyed by fire. King Sigismund the Old brought artists and craftsmen from all over Europe to create his castle, and despite baroque reconstruction after another fire in the late 16th century, the fine Renaissance courtyard remains. After the transfer of the capital to Warsaw at the beginning of the 17th century, Wawel was stripped of its fine furnishings, and later in the century it was devastated by the Swedish wars. Under the Austrians in the 19th century, Wawel was turned into an army barracks. In 1911, a voluntary Polish society purchased the castle from the Austrian authorities and began restoration. Today you can visit the royal chambers on the first floor, furnished in the style of the 16th and 17th centuries and hung with the 16th-century Belgian arras that during World War II was kept in Canada. The Royal Treasury on the ground floor contains a somewhat depleted collection of Polish crown jewels; the most fascinating item displayed here is the *Szczerbiec,* the jagged sword used from the early 14th century onward at the coronation of Polish kings. The Royal Armory houses a collection of Polish and Eastern arms and armor; in the west wing is an imposing collection of Turkish embroidered tents.

On your way out of the castle, note the smoke and flames rising every 10 minutes from the bottom of the hill. Every Polish child knows the legend of the fire-breathing dragon that once terrorized local residents ☾ from his **Smocza Jama** (Dragon's Den), a cave at the foot of Wawel Hill. The dragon threatened to destroy the town unless he was fed a damsel a week. In desperation the king promised half his kingdom and his daughter's hand in marriage to any man who could slay the dragon. The usual quota of knights tried and failed. But finally a crafty cobbler named Krak tricked the dragon into eating a lambskin filled with salt and sulfur. The dragon went wild with thirst, rushed into the Wisła River, and drank until it exploded. Krak the cobbler was made a prince, and the town was named (or renamed) for him. The Dragon's Den is still there, however, and every 15 minutes smoke and flame belch out of it to thrill young visitors. A bronze statue of the dragon itself stands guard at the entrance. ⊠ *Ul. Grodzka,* ☎ *012/22–51–55. Castle:* 🔲 *Zł 8.5.* ⊙ *Tues., Thurs., and weekends 10–3; Wed. and Fri. noon–6; closed Mon. and day after holidays. Follow signs to Smocza Jama, below Thief's Tower on Wawel Hill near Vistula River.* 🔲 *Zł 2.* ⊙ *May–Sept., Mon.–Thurs. and weekends 10–3.*

Kazimierz

A GOOD WALK
Southeast of the Wawel, you can take a tram from the corner of Bernadyńska and Starowiślna streets to the Kazimierz district. (The second tram stop on ulica Krakowska will take you to plac Wolnica, site of the **Kazimierz Town Hall** ⑥④, now the Ethnographic Museum.) To visit the synagogues of Kazimierz, make your way from plac Wolnica along ulica Bożego Ciała, passing the **Kościół Bożego Ciała** ⑥⑤ from which the street takes its name, to ulica Józefa, where you will pass the **Synagoga Wysoka** (High Synagogue), turning left into ulica Jakuba to see the **Ajzyk Synagogue,** which dates from 1638 and is no longer used for worship. Then continue down ulica Józefa to ulica Szeroka, on the corner of which is the **Stara Synagoga** (Old Synagogue) ⑥⑥, now the Jewish Historical Museum. Farther north along ulica Szeroka are the **Synagoga R'emuh** ⑥⑦ and **Jewish cemetery.** Across the street, at Ulica Dajwór 26, is the **Poper or Bocian Synagogue,** dating from 1620.

Take ulica Warschauera, noting the **Kupa Synagogue,** built by subscription in 1590, to ulica Estery, where you must turn north to reach ulica Miodowa. Here walk west to see the **Tempel Synagogue** ⑥⑧ on the corner of ulica Podbrzezie. From here you can continue west along ulica Miodowa until you rejoin the tram route.

TIMING
The main sights of Kazimierz can be visited in a morning or afternoon, since there are only two museums that may be time-consuming.

SIGHTS TO SEE
⑥⑤ **Kościół Bożego Ciała** (Corpus Christi Church). The 15th-century Corpus Christi Church was used by King Charles Gustavus of Sweden as his headquarters during the Siege of Kraków in 1655. ⊠ *Northeast corner of pl. Wolnica.*

⑥⑥ **Stara Synagoga** (Old Synagogue). Standing at the corner of ulica Józefa and ulica Szeroka, this synagogue was built in the 15th century and reconstructed in Renaissance style following a fire in 1557. It was here in 1775 that Tadeusz Kościuszko successfully appealed to the Jewish community to join in the national insurrection. Looted and partly destroyed during the Nazi occupation, it has now been rebuilt and houses the **Museum of the History and Culture of Kraków Jews.** ⊠ *Ul. Szeroka 24,* ☎ *012/22–09–62.* 🔲 *Free.* ⊙ *Wed., Thurs., and weekends 9–3:30, Fri. 11–6; closed 1st weekend of month.*

NEED A
BREAK?
Ariel Café (⊠ Ul. Szeroka 17, ☎ 012/21-38-70) This "Jewish artistic café" is always full; musical or other performances are often given.

67 **Synagoga R'emuh.** The 16th-century Synagoga R'emuh (✉ ul. Szeroka 40) is still used for worship and is associated with the name of the son of its founder, Rabbi Moses Isserles, who is buried in the cemetery attached to the synagogue. Used by the Jewish community from 1533 to 1799, this is the only well-preserved Renaissance Jewish cemetery in Europe. (The so-called new cemetery on ulica Miodowa, which contains many old headstones, was established in the 19th century.)

68 **Tempel Synagogue.** The 19th-century Reformed Tempel Synagogue is one of only two synagogues in Kraków still used for worship. ✉ *Corner of ul. Miodowa and ul. Podbrzezie.*

64 **Town Hall of Kazimierz.** The 15th-century Kazimierz Town Hall, which stands in the middle of plac Wolnica, is now the Ethnographic Museum, displaying a well-mounted collection of regional folk art. ✉ *Pl. Wolnica 1,* ☎ *012/66–28–63.* 🎫 *Zł 5, Mon. free.* ⊙ *Mon. 10–6, Wed.–Fri. 10–3, weekends 10–2.*

Dining

$$$$ ✕ **Cracovia.** The enormous dining room of this 1960s hotel conveys a sense of mass production that fortunately is not apparent in the excellent, internationalized Polish cuisine. Try the *krem z pieczarek* (thick and creamy mushroom soup) followed by chateaubriand, one of the chef's specialties. The side salads are fresh and delicious: Recent selections included sweetened grated carrots, cucumbers in cream, and beets mixed with horseradish. ✉ *Al. Marszałka Ferdinanda Focha 1,* ☎ *012/66–88–00. AE, DC, MC, V.*

$$$$ ✕ **Hawełka.** Recently privatized and upgraded, this first-floor restau-
★   rant sparkles with crystal and silver cutlery. Attentive waiters will advise in English on a range of traditional Polish dishes—the Hawełka's specialty. Try the fried eel in cream-and-dill sauce or one of the excellent veal dishes. There is also an expansive wine list. The Hawełka also has a less pricey restaurant on the ground floor, where mushroom soup served in a bread loaf is a great local favorite. ✉ *Rynek Główny 34,* ☎ *012/22–47–53. Jacket and tie. AE, DC, MC, V.*

$$$$ ✕ **Wierzynek.** Poland's most famous restaurant is in a fine 18th-cen-
★   tury upper room on the Rynek, glittering with chandeliers and silver. It was here after a historic meeting in 1364 that the king of Poland wined and dined the Holy Roman Emperor Charles IV, five kings, and a score of princes. Wierzynek is perhaps resting a little on its laurels these days, and the food may not really be any better than in other restaurants of its class, but the traditional Polish dishes—impressively served by armies of red-jacketed waiters—are very good. The kitchen excels in soups and game: Try the *żurek* (sour barley soup) followed by *zrazy,* small beef rolls filled with mushrooms and served with buckwheat. ✉ *Rynek Główny 15,* ☎ *012/22–98–96. Reservations essential. Jacket and tie. AE, DC, MC, V. Closed public holidays.*

$$$ ✕ **Gambrinus.** Opened in 1995 in a carefully restored 16th-century house in the Mały Rynek, behind the Mariacki Church, Gambrinus offers the longest menu in town, with over 20 kinds of soup alone. Local dishes, such as white herb sausage cooked in sour cabbage with mushrooms or pork roasted with garlic and caraway seeds, are delicious. The decor is simple: The thick stone walls have been left bare and white. ✉ *Mały Rynek 1,* ☎ *012/21–86–81. AE, DC, MC, V.*

$$$ ✕ **Pałac Pugetów.** Eat traditional Polish food by candlelight in Baron
★   Konstanty de Puget's dining room, just outside the walls of the old city. There is both a restaurant and a café; concerts are occasionally given. No smoking is allowed. ✉ *Ul. Starowiślna 13, no phone. AE, DC, MC, V.*

Kraków Dining and Lodging

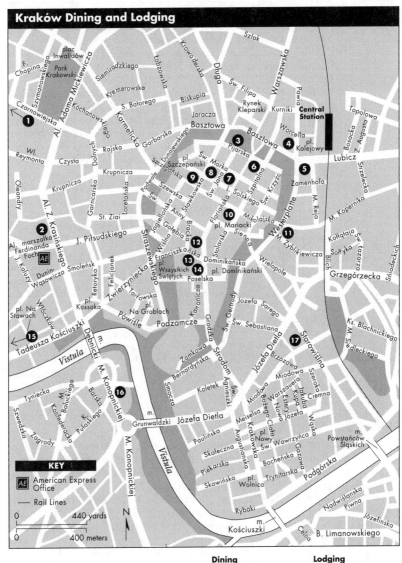

Dining
Balaton, **14**
Cracovia, **2**
Gambrinus, **10**
Hawełka, **9**
Kurza Stopka, **13**
Pałac Pugetów, **17**
Pod Kopcem, **15**
U Pollera, **6**
Wierzynek, **12**

Lodging
Cracovia, **2**
Dom Turysty
PTTK, **11**
Europejski, **5**
Forum, **16**
Francuski, **3**
Grand Hotel, **8**
Holiday Inn, **1**
Hotel Pollera, **6**
Pod Różą, **7**
Warszawski, **4**

$$$ ✕ **Pod Kopcem.** This hotel dining room, in the old Austrian barracks building on St. Bronisława's Hill, has bare brick walls and brightly checked tablecloths. Alcoves and corners offer privacy. The cuisine is internationalized Polish, with a good selection of pork dishes. Try the *golonka* (knuckle of pork) with bread and a side salad. ⊠ *Al. Waszyngtona*, ☎ *012/22–03–57. AE, DC, MC, V.*

$$ ✕ **Balaton.** Kraków's Hungarian restaurant has dark-wood paneling and trestle tables with benches, relieved by bright folk-weave rugs and embroideries on the walls. It is usually crowded, but the waitresses cope cheerfully. *Zupa gulaszowa* (hot spiced fish soup) is good for starters; follow it up with *placek ziemniaczany* (potato pancakes with pork stuffing). Good Hungarian wine is regularly available. ⊠ *Ul. Grodzka 37*, ☎ *012/22–04–69. AE, DC, MC, V.*

$$ ✕ **U Pollera.** The large, balconied fin-de-siècle dining room has a look of decayed grandeur. Recently repossessed by its prewar owner, however, it is on the way up. The chef from the newest Orbis hotel, the Forum, was lured here; the enormous crystal mirrors on the walls have been polished; and a complete redecoration is planned. The cuisine is eclectic but has enough traditional Polish items to satisfy anyone who wants to stick to native specialties. Chicken roasted with garlic and served with crispy potatoes is an excellent main course, and the chocolate gâteau for dessert is wonderfully light and creamy. ⊠ *Ul. Szpitalna 30*, ☎ *012/22–16–21. Jacket required. AE, DC, MC, V.*

$ ✕ **Kurza Stopka.** This small and rather dark restaurant specializes in chicken dishes, as its name (Chicken's Claw) suggests. An unusual crisp and spicy risotto *paprykarz* (paprika) served with a cool cucumber salad is one of the kitchen's specialties. This is the place for an informal and friendly dining experience, despite the din of sometimes large throngs of diners. ⊠ *Pl. Wszystkich Świętych 9*, ☎ *021/22–91–96. No reservations. AE, DC, MC, V.*

Lodging

$$$$ 🏨 **Grand.** This early 19th-century hotel on the corner of ulica Solskiego
★ in the Old Town was completely renovated—the work took 12 years— before reopening in 1990. An air of Regency elegance predominates, though some fine art-nouveau stained-glass windows have been preserved on the first floor. The bedrooms, still reasonably sized despite some alterations, are decorated with Regency striped wallpaper and bedspreads; most of the furniture is period reproduction. The corridors are agreeably unpredictable, with alcoves and potted plants. ⊠ *Ul. Sławkowska 5–7, 31–016*, ☎ *012/21–72–55*, 𝙁𝘼𝙓 *012/21–83– 60, telex 0326498. 50 rooms, 5 suites, all with bath. Restaurant. AE, DC, MC, V.*

$$$ 🏨 **Forum.** Opened in 1988, this modern hotel has proven to be something of a disappointment. Although it commands spectacular views over the Wawel Castle, it is on the right bank of the Vistula, adding 10 minutes travel time to the Old City, while its immediate surroundings are slightly squalid. A four-story, bow-shaped structure on stilts, the Forum has good-size rooms with light and solidly comfortable furnishings; the bathrooms are particularly well appointed. The hotel has the city's best health and sports facilities. ⊠ *Ul. Marii Konopnickiej 28, 30–302*, ☎ *012/66–95–00*, 𝙁𝘼𝙓 *012/66–58–27. 265 rooms, 15 suites, all with bath. Restaurant, 2 bars, indoor pool, sauna, tennis courts. AE, DC, MC, V.*

$$$ 🏨 **Francuski.** This turn-of-the-century hotel is just inside the only remaining fragment of the town walls, within five minutes' walk of the main square. The Francuski reopened in 1991 after a comprehensive renovation that upgraded the bathrooms and fixtures without altering the hotel's basic character. The rooms are comfortable and furnished in updated period style; the entrance hall features a wide mahogany staircase and lush stained-glass windows. ⊠ *Ul. Pijarska 13, 31–015,* ☎ *012/22–51–22,* FAX *012/22–52–70. 36 rooms, 6 suites, all with bath or shower. Restaurant, café. AE, DC, MC, V.*

$$ 🏨 **Cracovia.** Opened in 1964, this mammoth five-story hotel opposite the Błonie (Kraków Common) long provided the city's only luxury accommodations. Now, after 30 years of catering to tourist groups, it is beginning to show signs of strain and has become somewhat downscale. But the rooms, although rather small and standardized, are well appointed with dark, heavy furniture, and the staff members do their best to make you feel at home. It's one of the few hotels to consistently have space during the summer season. ⊠ *Al. Marszałka Ferdinanda Focha 1, 30–111,* ☎ *012/22–86–66,* FAX *012/21–95–86. 415 rooms, 10 suites, all with bath. Restaurant, bar. AE, DC, MC, V.*

$$ 🏨 **Holiday Inn.** This high-rise hotel, the first Holiday Inn built in Central Europe, is 3 kilometers (2 miles) to the west of the city center in pleasant suburban surroundings on the far side of the Kraków Common. It provides standardized but comfortable and cheerfully decorated accommodations and has good parking facilities. Its clients are mainly tourists (including a good number of travelers on packaged tours). This hotel's proximity to open parkland and sports facilities makes it a good choice for those who want to combine sightseeing with a little exercise. ⊠ *Ul. Koniewa 7, 30–150,* ☎ *012/37–50–44,* FAX *012/37–59–38. 310 rooms with bath. Restaurant, sauna, solarium, indoor pool. AE, DC, MC, V.*

$$ 🏨 **Hotel Pollera.** In 1990 Pollera was returned to the Kraków lawyer who was forced to sell it to the state in 1950. He is a descendant of the Poller for whom the hotel is named: an Austrian army officer who married a local girl and settled in Kraków in the early 19th century. The new owner and his eight children—all apparently involved in the business—are very eager to restore the hotel's reputation. The building's exterior has already had a face-lift; and the guest rooms, which had deteriorated greatly over the past 45 years, are also gradually being renovated and upgraded with private bathrooms. The fine art-nouveau entrance hall, dominated by an imposing grand staircase and stained-glass window, is as elegant as ever. ⊠ *Ul. Szpitalna 30, 31–024,* ☎ *012/22–10–44,* FAX *012/22–13–89. 107 rooms, most with bath. Restaurant, some singles have in-room TVs. AE, DC, MC, V.*

$$ 🏨 **Pod Różą.** One of Kraków's oldest hotels, the Pod Różą has seen ★ many distinguished guests, including Czar Alexander I. After renovations in the mid-1990s, the large, high-ceiling guest rooms have bright, soft furnishings, and the bathrooms gleam with white tiles. There is no elevator, though the hotel has only four stories. The Pod Różą has many advantages: It stands on the beautiful ulica Floriańska, and the staff is very helpful. ⊠ *Ul. Floriańska 14, 31–021,* ☎ *012/22–93–99,* FAX *012/21–75–13, telex 0325340. 30 rooms, 1 suite, all with bath. Restaurant, casino. AE, DC, MC, V.*

$ 🏨 **Dom Turysty PTTK.** This six-story 1960s building stands opposite Planty Park, facing the outer walls of the Bernadine convent in the Old Town. Its upper floors contain large, multiple-occupancy rooms that often house groups of students, who can be noisy. The rooms on the lower floors are comfortable though long, narrow, and fairly spartan (the double rooms have two beds head-to-foot along the wall). Nevertheless, the hotel is clean and conveniently located, with parking facilities for guests. ⊠ *Westerplatte 15, 31–033,* ☎ *012/22–95–66,* FAX *012/21–27–26. 51 doubles, 16 with bath; 78 singles, 9 with bath. Restaurant. AE, DC, MC, V.*

$ ☷ Europejski. Although this late-19th-century hotel opposite the main railway station has been undergoing renovation for some time, the standard of accommodation is high in rooms where work has already been completed. All the rooms, even the older and somewhat shabby ones, are reasonably sized and comfortable; rooms facing the busy main street are noisy. ⊠ *Ul. Lubicz 5, 31–034,* ☎ *012/22–09–11,* FAX *012/22–89–25. 30 rooms, most with bath. Restaurant. AE, DC, MC, V.*

$ ☷ Warszawski. This was a busy railway hotel when it was built in the late 19th century on a corner opposite Kraków's main station. Since then it has deteriorated, despite attempts in the 1990s to put on new paint and smarten it up a little. A lot of the original fixtures and furniture remain, and many of the rooms are enormous, but tend to be dark and gloomy and have few amenities.Traffic noise can keep you awake in summer, when the windows are open. There is no restaurant, though a café next door offers breakfast. ⊠ *Ul. Pawia 6, 31–157,* ☎ *012/22–06–22. No credit cards.*

Nightlife and the Arts

Kraków has a lively tradition in theater and music, although during the past few years the arts in Poland have fallen on hard times. You will still find interesting performances, however; check with the tourist office or the daily *Gazeta Krakowska* for details about what's on. The café and cabaret nightlife for which Kraków was renowned has taken on different forms in the 1990s: There is more on offer, and it goes on later.

Bars

The **"Bacchus" Drinks Bar** (⊠ Ul. Solskiego 21), a refurbished and very expensive bar in the Old Town, is popular with a younger crowd. **Pod Ratuszem** (⊠ Rynek Główny 1), underneath the Town Hall Tower, is a large bar in a labyrinth of small cellar rooms and is usually crowded. The **Grand Hotel Café** (⊠ Ul. Sławkowska 5–7, entrance from ul. Solskiego) is a good place for a quiet evening drink.

Cabaret

The cabaret at **Jama Michalika** (⊠ Ul. Floriańska 45) is currently Kraków's best satirical and musical show. Like all the big hotels, the **Hotel Cracovia** has a nightclub with floor shows, including strippers. Regular jazz sessions are held at the **Piwnica pod Hubą** (⊠ Rynek Glóny 12). The **Jazz Club "U Muniaka"** (⊠ Ul. Floriańska 3) is a large cellar club with daily sessions from 8 PM. The journalists' club, **Pod Gruszką** (⊠ Ul. Szczepańska 1) has a programs of light musical floor shows.

Casinos

Kraków's longest–established casino is on the first floor of the **Pod Róża** Hotel (⊠ Ul. Floriańska 14). The casino is open daily 1 PM–3 AM.

Film

Kino pod Baranami (⊠ Rynek Glóny 27, ☎ 012/22–32–65) has a varied program and occasionally shows Polish films.

Music

In Kraków the local philharmonic—**Filharmonia im. Karola Szymanowskiego** (⊠ Ul. Zwierzyniecka 1, ☎ 012/22–94–77)—performs Friday and Saturday. Badly damaged by fire in 1991, the Philharmonic Hall was given a face-lift while being rebuilt. Special Saturday-matinée concerts for children are offered. Chamber-music concerts, occasionally given in the great hall in **Wawel Castle** (☞ Sights to See, *above*), are well worth looking out for.

Opera and Dance

The **Teatr im. Juliusza Słowackiego** (⊠ Pl. św. Ducha 1, ☎ 012/22–43–64) provides a regular program of old opera and ballet favorites as well as dramatic performances.

Theater

Scena pod Ratuszem (⊠ Wieża Ratuszowa, ☎ 012/21–50–16), a tiny theater in the cellar of the old Town Hall Tower, stages small-scale dramas against a bare-brick backdrop. The **Stary Teatr im. Heleny Modrzejewskiej** (⊠ Pl. Szczepański 1, ☎ 012/22–85–66), a 19th-century theater named after Kraków's most famous actress—who ended her career in the United States as Helena Modjeska—stages some of the best productions in Poland; Andrzej Wajda still directs here when his political career permits.

Outdoor Activities and Sports

Hiking

The **Niepołomice Forest** (☞ Side Trips from Kraków, *below*) has extensive flat marked routes over sandy terrain. **Ojców National Park** (☞ Side Trips from Kraków, *below*) has marked trails for hikers, some of which are steeply uphill and fairly rough.

Jogging

If you want to jog in Kraków, the **Planty,** a ring of gardens around the Old Town, makes an excellent 5-kilometer (3-mile) route and is easily accessible from most hotels. The **pathways along the Vistula** provide a good jogging route: West of the Dębiński Bridge, take the path on the right bank; east of the bridge, the one on the left bank.

Shopping

Kraków has always been an interesting place for shopping, but here, as everywhere else in Poland, things are changing rapidly. Many of the craftsmen whose tiny shops made the Old Town such a fascinating place in which to hunt for original purchases have now been driven out of business by high rents and taxes. But the streets off the Rynek have a few new shops selling the leather products that are a specialty of this region. Most shops in Kraków are open weekdays 10–6, Saturday 9–2.

In Kraków the **Sukiennice booths** on the main square are still a good place to look for tooled leatherwork (slippers, bags, and belts) or for the embroidered felt slippers made in the Podhale region. Rabbit-skin slippers are also a local specialty. **Cepelia** on the west side of the Sukiennice (⊠ Rynek Główny 1–3) has a selection of regional specialties. **Craft boutiques** in the reconstructed arcade at ulica Stolarska 3–9 have more exciting (and expensive) handmade products; there is often a selection of beautiful leather, jewelry, and brasswork. **Galeria Res** (⊠ Ul. św. Tomasza 17) has an excellent collection of antique and contemporary folk art. **Fistek Glass** (⊠ Ul. Stolarska 8–10) has original handblown glass in rainbow colors, made by local artists.

Kraków A to Z

Arriving and Departing

BY BUS

Express bus service to Kraków runs regularly from most Polish cities. From the PKS bus station in Warsaw (⊠ Al. Jerozolimskie), the journey takes three hours. Buses arrive at the main PKS station on plac Kolejowy (☎ 012/936), where you can change for buses to other destinations in the region.

BY CAR

A car will not be of much use to you in Kraków, since most of the Old Town is closed to traffic and distances between major sights are short. A car will be invaluable, however, if you set out to explore the rest of the region. You can approach Kraków either by the E77 highway (from Warsaw and north), or via the E40 (from the area around Katowice). There is a high incidence of car theft in most cities, so make sure your car is locked securely before you set out to explore. Use the parking facilities at your hotel or one of the attended municipal garage parking lots (try ⊠ Pl. Szczepański or ⊠ Pl. św. Ducha).

BY PLANE

Kraków's **Balice Airport** (☎ 012/11–19–55), 11 kilometers (7 miles) west of the city, is the region's only airport. It is small, and in spring and fall problems with fog can cause long delays. Take Bus 208 from the Central Railway Station or Bus 152 from the Cracovia Hotel.

There are LOT flights daily to Balice Airport from Warsaw (flying time: 40 minutes) and, during the summer, weekly LOT flights from London. LOT's office in Kraków is at ulice Basztowa 15 (☎ 012/22–50–76); it's open weekdays 8–6.

BY TRAIN

Nonstop express trains from Warsaw take 2¾ hours and arrive at **Kraków Główny** station on the edge of the Old Town (⊠ Pl. Kolejowy, ☎ 012/933); they run early in the morning and in the late afternoon. The bus station is just across the square from Kraków Główny station.

Getting Around

BY BUS

Almost all villages in the region, however isolated, can be reached by PKS bus. The buses themselves are unfailingly ancient, rickety, and over-packed with standees—reason enough to take an express service if it operates to your destination. An express bus—for which seats can be reserved in advance—runs from Kraków to Zakopane and back every two hours. In Zakopane information is available from the bus station on ulica Kościuszki (☎ 0165/146–03).

BY CAR

It is not strictly necessary to have a car to explore the southern region. Public transport will take you to even the most remote and inaccessible places. But it will take time and can be uncomfortably crowded. On the other hand, the narrow mountain roads can be trying for drivers. Although the Kraków–Zakopane highway has recently been much improved, some stretches are still single-lane, and horse-drawn carts can cause major delays.

BY TRAIN

Trains move slowly in the hilly region south of Kraków, but most towns are accessible by train, and the routes can be very picturesque. In Zakopane you can get more information from the station on ulica Chramcówki (☎ 0165/145–04).

Contacts and Resources

EMERGENCIES

Police (☎ 997). **Ambulance** (☎ 999).

GUIDED TOURS

Orbis (⊠ Hotel Cracovia, al. Marszałka Ferdinanda Focha 1, ☎ 012/21–98–80) is still the main tour operator; all its tours are either by bus, minibus, or limousine, at prices ranging from $15 for a half-day coach tour to $140 for a full-day tour in a chauffeur-driven car. A one-day visit to the Nazi concentration camp at **Oświęcim** (Auschwitz) is offered throughout the year, and they offer a standard half-day tour of Kraków, as well as junkets to Pieskowa Skała and Ojców. A day trip to the Dunajec River gorge (including a journey down the river by raft) is also available in the summer. Orbis also organizes day trips to the pope's birthplace at **Wadowice,** to the Bernadine Monastery at **Kalwaria Zebrzydowska,** and to the Pauline Monastery at **Częstochowa.**

LATE-NIGHT PHARMACIES
Individual chemists stay open for 24 hours on a rotating basis; and newspapers carry listings of when the various *apteki* are open. For information dial 012/22–05–11.

VISITOR INFORMATION
Sports Tourist, Tourist Information Center (⊠ Ul. Pawia 8, ☎ 012/22–95–10), open weekdays 9–5, Saturday 9–2. **Orbis** (⊠ Hotel Cracovia, al. Marszałka Ferdinanda Focha 1, ☎ 012/21–98–80), open weekdays 9–5, Saturday 9–2. **Wawel Tour** (⊠ Ul. Swięętego Tomasza 26, ☎ 012/22–08–52), open weekdays 10–6, Saturday 9–2.

MAŁOPOLSKA

Just to the south of Kraków, Poland's great plains give way to the gently folding foothills of the Carpathians, building to the High Tatras on the Slovak border. The climate ranges from harsh, snowbound winters to hot summers. The fine medieval architecture of many towns in Małopolska (Little Poland) comes from a period when the area prospered as the intersection of thriving trade routes. In the countryside, wood homesteads and strip farming tell another story: of the hardships and poverty the peasantry endured before the 20th century brought tourists to the mountains. During the 19th century, when this part of Poland was under Austrian rule as the province of Western Galicia, hundreds of thousands of peasants escaped from grinding toil on poor soil to seek their fortune in the United States; it sometimes seems as if every family here has a cousin in America.

A visit to Kraków and Małopolska is incomplete without trips to at least two nearby destinations: the **Wieliczka Salt Mine,** declared one of the 12 wonders of the world by the United Nations, and **Auschwitz** and **Birkenau,** sites of the Nazi's most gruesome and brutal concentration camps. Farther afield are **Ojców National Park** and **Zakopane,** both of which offer first-rate hiking in unadulterated nature. If you've been looking for insight into the devout Catholicism of the Poles, head to **Częstochowa,** where 5 million people a year come to pray before a painting of the Virgin Mary and baby Jesus known as the *Black Madonna.*

Małopolska remains intensely Catholic and conservative (it is no accident that Lech Wałesa found his strongest support here during the presidential elections of 1990 and 1995), and the traditional way of life in the countryside is relatively untouched. Folk crafts and customs are still very much alive, both in mountainous and foothill (*podhale*) areas: You may see carved-wood beehives in mountain gardens or worshipers setting out for church on Sunday in white-felt embroidered trousers.

This is Poland's main winter sports area: **Zakopane** currently aspires to host the Winter Olympics in 2002. The spa towns of **Szczawnica, Krościenko,** and **Krynica** are good bases for cross-country skiing; the market town of **Nowy Sącz** is also a good base for exploring the Podhale region.

This is one of the few regions in Poland that offers extensive options for inexpensive bed-and-breakfast accommodations in private pensions. Pensions usually offer full board and hearty meals.

Numbers in the margin correspond to numbers on the Southeastern Poland map.

Częstochowa

⑥⑨   *120 km (74 mi) northwest of Kraków, 220 km (136 mi) southwest of Warsaw.*

The pilgrims' town of Częstochowa has only one attraction for tourists:
★ the 14th-century **Pauline Monastery** at Jasna Góra (Hill of Light); the remainder of the town is now grimly industrial. Inside the monastery, however, is Poland's holiest shrine, the famous *Black Madonna of Częstochowa*, an early 15th-century painting of a dark-skinned Madonna and child, the origins of which are uncertain (legend attributes the work to St. Luke). Pilgrims from all over Poland, many on foot, make their way to the shrine each August to participate in Marian devotions. The church and monastery were fortified in the 16th century, and 100 years later Jasna Góra held out against a Swedish siege for 40 days. It was here that the invading Swedish army was halted and finally driven out of the country. The Black Madonna's designation as savior of Poland dates from those turbulent days. The monastery was rebuilt in baroque style during the 17th and 18th centuries, as was the interior of the Gothic church. The **Monastery Treasury** holds an important collection of manuscripts and works of art. ⊠ *Al. Najświętszej Marii Panny 1.* ☉ *Treasury daily 11–1 and 3–5.*

Dining and Lodging

$$ ✕ **Polonia.** The dining room of the Polonia Hotel, although unexciting, probably still offers the best meal in town, with traditional Polish cooking. Almost all main courses feature pork, but the *żurek* (sour rye flour soup) here is a good starter, and the mixed salads are excellent all year round. ⊠ *Ul. Piłsudskiego 9,* ☎ *034/24–40–67, AE, DC, MC, V.*

$$ ✕ **Stacherczak.** Claiming to have the best Chinese chef in Poland, this small restaurant has gathered a popular following since it opened in 1994. Try the soups, especially clear mushroom with soya noodles. ⊠ *Ul. Dąbrowskiego 5,* ☎ *034/24–45–46. AE, DC, MC, V.*

$ ✕ **Astoria.** This old-fashioned and crowded restaurant will provide you with a touch of local color. Try the herrings in cream as a starter, followed by stewed chicken with dumplings. ⊠ *Al. Najświętszej Marii Panny 46,* ☎ *034/24–13–11. No credit cards.*

$$ ▦ **Orbis Patria Hotel.** This six-story 1980s hotel provides a predictable Orbis standard of cuisine and accommodations. Rooms are brightly furnished and comfortable, the staff cheerful and friendly. ⊠ *Ul. Popiełuszki 2, 42–200,* ☎ *034/24–53–59,* ℻ *034/24–63–32. 109 rooms. AE, DC, MC, V.*

$ ▦ **Hotel Polonia.** This was a comfortable hotel for wealthy business travelers when it opened at the turn of the century. The mahogany double doors to the bedrooms remain, along with potted palms in the windows and velvet curtains. The high ceilings and windows make for drafts, but the hotel is clean and the beds comfortable, and after recent renovations, almost all the rooms now have bathrooms. ⊠ *Ul. Piłsudskiego 9, 42–200,* ☎ *034/24–40–67,* ℻ *034/65–11–05. 62 rooms, most with bath or shower. AE, DC, MC, V.*

Ojców National Park

➐ *48 km (30 mi) northwest of Kraków.*

This national park covers the limestone gorge of the Prudnik River. The ridge above the gorge is topped by a series of ruined castles—the "eagles' nests"—that once guarded the trade route from Kraków to Silesia. The best-preserved of these is at **Pieskowa Skała**, which now houses a branch of the Wawel Museum Art Collection. There are also caves in the limestone rock with which many stories and legends are connected; Władysław the Short, a medieval Polish king, is supposed to have escaped his German pursuers here with the help of a spider that spun its web over the mouth of the cave in which he was hiding. The gorge is at its best in autumn, when shades of gold and red stand out against the white limestone. A buffet is served on the terrace of Pieskowa Skała. ⊠ *Take the E22 northwest and turn off at Jerzmanowice for Pieskowa Skała. PKS buses leave regularly from the bus station on pl. Kolejowy in Kraków. Władysław the Short's cave:* 🎟 *Zł 2.5.* ☉ *May–Sept., daily 8–7. Pieskowa Skała Museum:* 🎟 *Zł 2.* ☉ *Tues. noon–5:30, Wed.–Sun. 10–3:30.*

Auschwitz and Birkenau

★ **➐** *50 km (31 mi) southwest of Ojców National Park, 55 km (35 mi) west of Kraków.*

Between 1940 and 1945, more than 1.5 million people, 90% of them Jews from Poland and throughout Europe, died here in the Nazis' largest death-camp complex. In the small town of **Oświęcim** (better known by its German name, Auschwitz), the camp has come to be seen as the epicenter of the moral collapse of the West, proof of the human capacity for tremendous evil. The gas chambers at nearby **Brzezinka** (Birkenau) could kill thousands in a single day, if they weren't killed first by hanging, shooting, injection, malnutrition, slave labor, or disease. The first inmates were Polish political prisoners, and the first gassing victims were Russian POWs; the dead eventually included Jews, Romani (Gypsies), homosexuals, Jehovah's Witnesses, and so-called criminals.

The *Konzentrationslager* (concentration camp) had three parts: Auschwitz, Birkenau, and Monowitz (where a chemical plant was run by prison labor). The barracks at Auschwitz have been completely restored and made into a museum that one survivor, author Primo Levi, described as "something static, rearranged, contrived." With that in mind, begin with the heart-rending **movie** (🎟 zł 1) shot by Soviet troops on January 27, 1945, the day they liberated the few prisoners left behind by the retreating Germans. The English version runs a few times a day, although narration isn't really necessary. Purchase a guidebook in English (most exhibits are in Polish or German) and walk through the notorious gate marked ARBEIT MACHT FREI (Work will make you free). The most provocative exhibits are the huge piles of belongings confiscated from victims, as well as the two tons of human hair intended for use in the German textile industry. The execution wall, prison block, and the reconstructed crematorium at the end of the tour are particularly sobering. Although most of the victims were sent here simply for being Jewish, exhibits on Jewish prisoners have been allotted only one barrack (just like other nationalities). ⊠ *Ul. Więźniów Oświęcimia 20 (you can reach Oświęcim by train or bus from pl. Kolejowy in Kraków or by car on the E22a),* ☎ *0381/321–33.* 🎟 *Free.* ☉*Museum June–Aug., daily 8–7; Sept.–May, daily 8–3.*

Far more affecting than Auschwitz are the unaltered barracks, electric fences, and blown-up gas chambers at the enormous **Birkenau** camp

3 kilometers (2 miles) away. The mass of prisoners lived and died here, including hundreds of thousands who went directly to the gas chambers from boxcars where they had been locked up for days. The camp has been preserved to look much the way it did after the Nazis abandoned it. A walk to the back brings you to the **Monument to the Glory of the Victims,** designed by Polish and Italian artists and erected in 1967. Behind the trees to the right of the monument lies a farm pond, its banks still murky with human ashes and bone fragments. If you want to hear the tape on the camp's history in English, ask the staff at the reception office in the main guardhouse. ✉ *Free.*

Lodging

$$ 🏨 **Hotel Olimpijski.** After a recent face-lift, this 19th-century city-center hotel is bright and comfortable, with a young staff, some of whom speak English. ✉ *Ul. Chemików 2a, 32–600 Oświęcim,* ☎ *033/42– 38–41. 35 rooms, all with bath. Restaurant. AE, DC, MC, V.*

Tyniec

72 *43 km (27 mi) east of Oświęcim, 12 km (8 mi) southwest of Kraków.*

The **Benedictine Abbey** at Tyniec is perched high on a cliff above the Vistula River. From this fortified cloister, the Confederates of Bar set off to raid Kraków in 1772; as a result, later that year the abbey was destroyed by the Russian army. In 1817 the Benedictine order was banned, and the monks disbanded. It was not until 1939 that the order recovered the land, and not until the late 1960s that it again became an abbey and the work of reconstruction began in earnest. From May to September recitals of organ music are held in the abbey church. ✉ *By car, turn south at Liszki from the B–road to Babice and Libiąż. By bus, take Bus 112 from Kraków's Dębniki PKS bus station.* ☉ *Daily 9–4.*

Wieliczka Salt Mine

★ **73** *12 km (7½ mi) southeast of Kraków on the E22.*

Salt has been mined at Wieliczka for a thousand years, and during the 11th century Wieliczka was owned by the Benedictines of Tyniec abbey, who drew a large part of their income from its revenues. By the 14th century the salt was so prized that King Kazimierz the Great built city walls with 11 defense towers at Wieliczka to protect the mines from Tartar raids. There are historic galleries and chambers 150 yards below ground level, including underground lakes and underground chapels carved by medieval miners, the most magnificent of which is the **Chapel of the Blessed Kinga** (Queen Kinga was a 14th-century Polish queen, later beatified). Serious flooding in 1992 brought commercial salt production to a halt after a millennium, but the historic part of the mine, now a museum, is open to visitors. ✉ *Ul. Daniłowicza 10 (take a PKS bus or train from pl. Kolejowy in Kraków or city Bus 103 from al. Krasińskiego, changing to Bus 133 at Nowy Prokocim),* ☎ *012/78–26–53.* ✉ *Zł 10.* ☉ *Daily 8–4.*

Niepołomice

74 *12 km (7½ mi) east of Wieliczka, 25 km (15 mi) east of Kraków.*

The town of Niepołomice is on the western edge of the **forest** and has a 14th-century **hunting lodge** and **church** built by Kazimierz the Great, who, like many other Polish kings of the period, liked to hunt in the forest. The animals—including bison—remain, and you may be lucky enough to see some of them as you stroll under the ancient oak trees.

✉ *By car, take the E22 east from Kraków and turn north at Wieliczka, or take a PKS bus or train from pl. Kolejowy in Kraków; on summer weekends Kraków city transport also runs special buses to Niepołomice from pl. Kolejowy.* ☉ *Church dawn–dusk.*

Zakopane

★ **75** *100 km (62 mi) south of Kraków.*

Nestled at the foot of the Tatra Mountains, 3,281 feet above sea level, Zakopane is the highest town in Poland (and the southernmost, as well). Until the 19th-century romantic movement started a fashion for mountain scenery, Zakopane was a poor and remote village. During the 1870s, when the Tatra Association was founded, people began coming to the mountains for their health and recreation, and Zakopane developed into Poland's leading mountain resort. At the turn of the century it was home to many writers, painters, and musicians. Stanisław Wyspiański based his best-known drama, *Wesele* (Wedding, 1901), on his experiences here. Stanisław Witkiewicz (Witkacy), the artist and playwright, lived here and was responsible for creating the elaborate carved-wood architecture that he called the Zakopane style.

The town of Zakopane is small, it is difficult to get lost, and the sights can be covered easily on foot. Ulica Krupówki, Zakopane's main thoroughfare, runs downhill through the town from northwest to southeast; if you begin at the northwest end, you will pass many fine examples of the Zakopane style of wooden building as well as the town's museum, just beyond ulica Kościuszki, which links the town with the railway and bus stations and runs east to west across Krupówki. At the bottom of the hill, at the southeast end of ulica Krupówki is ulica Kościeliska, with an open-air museum of reconstructed farmsteads built in the traditional folk style, wooden St. Clement's Church, and Witkiewicz's Willa Koliba; the Atma Villa is just round the corner. And at this point, you can take a cable car from the foot of ulica Krupówki to the Gubałówka ridge. You can return to town by the same route or take the path along the ridge to Palkówka and from there back down into town, about 9 kilometers (5 miles).

The hills and valleys around Zakopane contain villages, castles, and vantage points for viewing vividly picturesque scenery, all of which can be reached as day trips from the town by PKS bus. The town of Nowy Targ is well worth a visit, especially on market day, as is the village of Bukowina Tatrzańska; the castles at Czorstyn and Niedzica are perhaps best viewed from the Dunajec River, and the tiny wooden church at Dębno is a unique feature of the region. The Morskie Oko Lake and Kościelisko Valley are possible day trips for more active visitors.

A cable railway can take you from the center of town up to the high ridge of **Gubałówka,** where on a clear day you will have a fine view of the Tatras and of the town. Polish children who visit Zakopane have
⚅ their photograph taken on the **terrace** at Gubałówka in a carriage drawn by four white mountain sheepdogs and driven by a man dressed in a white bearskin. The cable railway station is down from the corner of ulica Krupówki and ulica Kościeliska.

NEED A BREAK?	The **Terrace Café** on Gubałówka, open daily from 10–6 has fine views and good cakes and is an excellent place for sitting and watching life mosey by in the valley below.

At the foot of the hill in Zakopane is the wooden church of **Kościół świelej Klemensa** (Church of St. Clement), the first church built in the town, dating from the mid-19th century. The adjoining cemetery has a number of striking carved-wood memorials; Witkiewicz is buried here, as is Tytus Chałubiński, the founder of the Tatra Association. ⊠ *Ul. Kościeliska opposite ul. Kasprusie.*

The **Muzeum Tatrzańskie** (Tatra Museum) on Zakopane's main street is worth a visit; it has splendid collections of the flora and fauna of the Tatras and a section with mountain crafts. ⊠ *Ul. Krupówki 10,* ☎ *0165/152–05.* ▣ *Zł 2.5.* ☼ *Tues.–Sun. 9–4.*

The **Willa Atma,** a wooden villa in Zakopane style, was home to the Polish composer Karol Szymanowski in the 1920s; it is now a museum with mementos of his life and work. ⊠ *Ul. Kasprusie 19,* ☎ *0165/145– 54.* ▣ *Zł1.* ☼ *Wed., Thurs., and weekends 10–4, Fri. 2–6.*

Stanisław Witkiewicz designed several villas in the Zakopane style. The elaborate **Willa pod Jedlami** (⊠ Ul. Koziniec 1) is considered one of his most ambitious works. Witkiewicz's very first project in the Zakopane style was the **Willa Koliba** at ulica Kościeliska 18. ⊠ *Muzeum Stylu Zakopańskiego im. Stanisława Witkiewicza,* ☎ *0165/136–02.* ▣ *Zł 1.* ☼ *Wed.–Sun. 10–2.*

An open-air museum with examples of local folk buildings is being developed in Zakopane. A dozen or more 19th-century, elaborately carved **wooden farmsteads** have been moved to an urban site and are being restored. ⊠ *Ul. Kościeliska.*

Dining and Lodging

$$$ ✕ **Giewont.** The dining room in the Giewont Hotel is high and galleried, decorated with crystal chandeliers and crisp white tablecloths on well-spaced tables. Service is elegant and discreet. The game dishes are the best items on the menu; try the roast pheasant when it's in season. ⊠ *Ul. Kościuszki 1,* ☎ *0165/120–11. AE, DC, MC, V.*

$$ ✕ **Gazda.** As befits a hotel run by the peasants' cooperative Gromada,
★ the Gazda has the best food for miles around. The large, light dining room, outfitted with linen tablecloths and napkins, is usually full; the service is friendly and prompt. The menu always offers a wide choice, and portions are large. Recommended dishes include roast lamb, and, in season, the bilberry dessert pancakes. ⊠ *Gromada, ul. Zaruskiego 2,* ☎ *0165/150–11. AE, DC, MC, V.*

$$ ✕ **U Wnuka.** This is the best-known and longest-established regional
★ restaurant in Zakopane, with a great variety of local dishes: mountain robber's roast (*pieczeń po zbójnicku*), Zakopane pancakes, shepherd's soup (*zupa juhaska*). It is usually crowded, service is slow, and portions are enormous. On weekends there is regional folk music. ⊠ *Ul. Kościeliska 1,* ☎ *0165/154–68. AE, DC, MC, V.*

$$$ ▥ **Kasprowy.** On the side of Gubałówka, this is convenient only if you have your own means of transportation: It's several kilometers outside town and a 15-minute walk from bus routes. However, the Kasprowy is a good option for skiers: The lift to Butory Wierch is nearby, as are beginners' slopes. The four-story hotel fits snugly into the hillside and has panoramic views of Mt. Giewont and beyond. The rooms are comfortable and well furnished (those overlooking Giewont have a 25% markup), but the public areas have become a little shabby since the hotel opened in 1974. The large, light restaurant has fine views. ⊠ *Ul. Powstańców Śląskich, 34–500,* ☎ *0165/140–11,* ☒ *0165/157– 00. 243 rooms, 12 suites, all with bath. Restaurant, shops, sports-equipment rental. AE, DC, MC, V.*

$$ 🏨 **Gazda.** Opened in 1975 opposite the post office in the center of town,
★ this hotel is in a pleasantly solid, low-rise building. Outside, the stone
figure of a farmer in full folk costume reinforces the local theme (*gazda*
means farmer). The rooms are comfortably furnished in stripped pine
and decorated in light, bright colors. The Gazda has won the Golden
Key award of the Polish Tourist Hotels' Association three times, most
recently in 1994. ⊠ *Gromada, ul. Zaruskiego 2, 34–500,* ☎ *0165/150–
11,* ☒ *0165/153–30. 64 rooms, 54 with bath. Restaurant. AE, DC,
MC, V.*

$$ 🏨 **Giewont.** If you can, pick a room in this late-19th-century hotel with
a view of the peak after which it is named, Mt. Giewont. The rooms
are reasonably well furnished in traditional style but vary greatly in
size; it's a good idea to see the room before moving in. This hotel is
right in the center of town, which can be an advantage if you are not
planning too much energetic sporting activity. ⊠ *Ul. Kościuszki 1,* ☎
0165/120–11, 34–500, ☒ *0165/120–13 (reservations through the
Kasprowy). 48 rooms, 37 with bath. Restaurant. AE, DC, MC, V.*

Nightlife and the Arts

Zakopane offers theatrical and musical performances mainly connected with the artists and writers who made the town their home, particularly Witkacy and Karol Szymanowski; watch for posters on kiosks
for announcements. There are also plenty of opportunities to hear traditional local folk orchestras. As for nightlife, Zakopane still goes to
bed relatively early, but new nightspots are appearing all the time.

BARS
Drink Bar, in the cellars of Morskie Oko (⊠ Ul. Krupówki 30), has
stone walls, a huge fireplace with a fire in winter, and an unobtrusive
traditional folk ensemble playing in the background. **U Ratowników**
(⊠ TOPR, ul. Piłsudskiego 63a) is in the headquarters of the mountain rescue organization: You can sit in a smoky throng on wooden
benches, surrounded by portraits of past heroes of the association, and
listen to the tales of its current members.

CASINOS
In Zakopane, the most popular casino is at **Hotel Kasprowy** (⊠ Polana
Szymoszkowa 1, ☎ 0165/140–10).

FILM
Sokół (⊠ Ul. Orkana 2, ☎ 0165/140–40) in Zakopane shows a variety of films, mainly the latest international hits, as is typical elsewhere.

MUSIC
Occasional concerts are given in Zakopane at the **Willa Atma** (⊠ Ul.
Kasprusie 19, ☎ 0165/145–54). There is a festival of Szymanowski's
music in July, when concerts are held at various points in the town,
and an autumn music festival (September–October). The **Kulczycki
Gallery** (⊠ Ul. Koziniec 8, ☎ 0165/129–36) has occasional concerts
and other events.

THEATER
In Zakopane, the **Teatr im. Stanisława Ignacego Witkiewicza** (⊠ Ul.
Chramcówki 15, ☎ 0165/682–97) has two stages, and often brings
in well-known actors for the season.

Outdoor Activities and Sports
BIKING
Mountain biking has become increasingly popular with tourists in the
1990s. You can hire a bike at **Sport & Fun Company Ltd** (⊠ Rondo 1,
☎ 0165/156–03) for zł 25 per day. **Rent a bike** (⊠ Ul. Sienkiewicza

37, ☎ 0165/142–66) has a small selection of mountain bikes, but is relatively cheap at zł 15–zł 20 per day.

HIKING

The **Gorczański, Pieniński,** and **Tatrzański national parks** all offer excellent hiking territory. The routes are well marked, and all national parks have maps at entrance points explaining distances, times, and degrees of difficulty of the trails. On the lower reaches of trails out of major tourist points (for example, Zakopane, Szczawnica, Krynica), walkers crowd the paths, but they soon thin out higher up.

JOGGING

In Zakopane, the **Droga pod Reglami,** which runs along the foot of the Tatra National Park, makes an excellent, relatively flat jogging route; it can be approached from various points in the town.

SKIING

Zakopane acquired snow-making facilities in 1990, and is still the region's major center for downhill skiing, although **Krynica** and **Krościenko** also have facilities. You'll find the most advanced runs at **Kasprowy Wierch** Mountain, accessed via a cable lift from Łozienice (lower station, ☎ 0165/145–10; upper station, ☎ 0165/144–05). **Chairlifts** also bring skiers to the peaks of **Butory Wierch** (⊠ Lift at ul. Powstańców Śląskich, ☎ 0165/139–41) and **Nosal** (⊠ Ul. Balzera, ☎ 0165/131–81). Tickets can be hard to come by in the season; it may be easier to get them in Orbis (⊠ Ul. Krupówki 22), although you pay a surcharge of 30%.

Shopping

In Zakopane, leather and sheepskin products are local specialties, and you'll find them all over, along with hand-knit socks, sweaters, and caps in white, gray, and black patterns from rough undyed wool. The best places to look are the at **Zakopane market,** held at the foot of ulica Krupówki, on the way to the Gubałówka cable railway. Wednesday is the main market day, but stalls will be found here daily. Street vendors, who work here daily, as they do throughout the region, charge higher prices. **Limba** (⊠ Ul. Kościeliska 1) has a fine assortment of handmade local costumes; these are expensive, but there are also smaller items like belts and walking sticks.

OFF THE BEATEN PATH

DOLINA KOŚCIELISKA (KOŚCIELISKA VALLEY) – Nine kilometers (5 miles) southwest of Zakopane on the road to Kiry and Witów, this valley falls within the **Tatra National Park,** which covers the entire mountain range in both Poland and Slovakia. Remember that you are not allowed to pick flowers here—which may be a temptation in spring when the lower valley is covered with crocuses. The first part of the valley runs for roughly a mile through flat, open pasture, before the stream that gave the Kościeliska its name begins to come down through steep, rocky gorges. You finally emerge at Ornak, 5½ kilometers (3½ miles) from the road, where there are splendid views. Horse-drawn carriages (sleighs in winter) wait at the entrance to take visitors halfway up the valley (for about zł 30), but if you want to reach Ornak, you must make the last stage on foot. **Harnaś** is a bar at the entrance to the valley, where locals come to drink beer and where dishes like *fasolka po bretońsku* (Breton baked beans) or bigos are available from 8 AM to 10 PM. ⊠ *Take a bus from the PKS bus station in Zakopane on ul. Kościuszki to Kiry.*

BUKOWINA TATRZAŃSKA – Thirteen kilometers (8 miles) northeast of Zakopane, Bukowina Tatrzańska is an attractive, largely wood-built village set high on a ridge, once famed for its number of beekeepers and its honey. The path at the top of the ridge, parallel to the main road to Łysa

Polana, affords spectacular views of the Tatra range and is a favored spot for winter sunbathing. ⊠ *Bukowina can easily be reached by PKS bus from the Zakopane bus station on ul. Kościuszki. By car, take Hwy. 15 (the main road to Kraków) north from Zakopane, and 5 km (3 mi) out of town turn east onto Hwy. 67, which leads to the border crossing point at Polana. The left-hand turn into the village of Bukowina is clearly signposted.*

Morskie Oko

30 km (20 mi) southeast of Zakopane. Orbis in Zakopane runs a regular bus service to within 10 minutes' walk of the lake. If you feel more energetic, you can take a PKS bus from the bus station to Łysa Polana and follow the marked trail for 8 km (5 mi).

Morskie Oko is the largest and loveliest of the lakes in the High Tatras, 4,570 feet above sea level. The name means "Eye of the Sea," and an old legend claims it has a secret underground passage connecting it to the ocean. The **Mięguszowiecki** and **Mnich** peaks appear to rise straight up from the water, and the depth of the lake makes it permanently deep blue. A small chalet beside the lake offers tea and light refreshment.

Dining and Lodging

$ ✕⛻ **Schronisko im. Stanisława Staszica.** A climbers' and hikers' hostel, this establishment has a restaurant that serves large portions of basic fare like buckwheat with mushrooms, fasolka po bretońsku, or pancakes with whipped cream. You can also obtain a bed in a clean and spartan three-, four-, five-, or six-person room for as little as $5. ⊠ *Box 201, Zakopane, 34–500,* ☎ *0165/77–609. No credit cards.*

Nowy Targ

🖲 *24 km (15 mi) north of Zakopane, 90 km (56 mi) south of Kraków. Nowy Targ is on the main road from Zakopane to Kraków; buses run from Zakopane every hour.*

The unofficial capital of the Podhale region, Nowy Targ has been a chartered borough since the 14th century, when it stood at an intersection of international trade routes, and it remains an important market center for the entire mountain region. It is worth visiting on Thursday, market day, when farmers bring their livestock in for sale in the streets and a range of local products, including rough wool sweaters and sheepskin coats, are on sale. The White and Black Dunajec streams meet in Nowy Targ to form the Dunajec River, which then runs on through steep limestone gorges to Nowy Sącz.

En Route   12 kilometers (8 miles) east of Nowy Targ on the road to Szczawnica,
★   **Dębno,** a village in the valley of the Dunajec River, has a tiny wooden church dating from the 15th century (it's believed to be the oldest wooden building in the Pohdale region); inside are medieval wall paintings and wooden sculptures. *Buses run from the marketplace in Nowy Targ.*

En Route   **Krościenko,** 25 kilometers (15 miles) east of Nowy Targ and 35 kilometers (22 miles) southwest of Nowy Sącz, is one of the villages that became a holiday resort during the late 19th century and is still popular today as a center for walking vacations. It has many interesting Zakopane-style wooden structures. *Best access by PKS bus from the train station in Nowy Sącz.*

En Route   The small spa of **Szczawnica,** 28 kilometers (17½ miles) east of Nowy Targ, 35 kilometers (22 miles) southwest of Nowy Sącz, like many towns in the region dates from the late 19th century; you can stroll around in the high-vaulted pump rooms and sip the foul-tasting mineral waters. *Best access by PKS bus from the marketplace in Nowy Targ or outside the train station in Nowy Sącz.*

Nowy Sącz

㊡ *100 km (64 mi) southeast of Kraków, 80 km (50 mi) northeast of Zakopane.*

Nowy Sącz has existed as a market town since the 13th century; a ruined 14th-century castle remains from this early period, as do the church on the northeast side of the market square (founded by King Władysław Jagiełło) and the 15th-century church and chapter house on the east side.

Dining and lodging

\$\$ ✕ **Zajazd Sądecki.** This restaurant emphasizes traditional Polish cuisine and has regional specialties on the menu, including pancakes highland style, stuffed with pork and onions. The dining room is cozy, with pine furniture and crisp, white tablecloths. ⊠ *Ul. Królowej Jadwigi 67,* ☎ *018/42–67–17. No credit cards.*

\$\$ 🏨 **Beskid.** This standard, cube-shape Orbis hotel is a typical product of the mid-1960s. It commands good views while being conveniently located near the rail and bus stations in the town center. The rooms are rather small and drab but comfortable, brightened with Podhale folk elements. Breakfasts are delicious, featuring fresh-baked rolls, white cheese mixed with chives, scrambled eggs cooked with chopped bacon, and a variety of jams and honey. ⊠ *Ul. Limanowskiego 1, 33–330 Nowy Sącz,* ☎ *018/207–70,* FAX *018/221–44. 97 rooms, 34 with bath; 25 suites. Restaurant. AE, DC, MC, V.*

Krynica

㊢ *32 km (20 mi) south of Nowy Sącz on Highway 212.*

Krynica is a spa and winter-sports center in a high valley. The salutary properties of the mineral waters were recognized during the 18th century, and the first bathhouse (⊠ Ul. Kraszewskiego 9) was built in 1807. Krynica was developed further in classic spa style in the late 19th century: It has a tree-lined promenade through gardens, a pump room, and concert halls. The waters here are not appetizing to the unaccustomed palate; console yourself with the thought that they are the most concentrated mineral waters in Europe.

Lodging

\$ 🏨 **Hotel Meran.** A small, friendly, three-story hotel, it has wooden balconies and good parking facilities. ⊠ *Ul. Kościelna 9, 33–380,* ☎ *0135/22–50. 30 rooms, all with bath.*

Consult **Pensjonat Wisła** (⊠ Bulwary Dietla 1, ☎ 0135/23–86), a pension which also runs an information service on vacancies elsewhere. You can also look for signs in windows advertising POKOJE (rooms).

Małopolska A to Z

Arriving and Departing

BY BUS

Zakopane is most easily accessible by bus from Kraków, which takes two hours. There are also through services from Warsaw to Zakopane (travel time: five hours). Zakopane's PKS bus station is at the corner of ulica Kościuszki and ulica Chramcówki (☎ 0165/145–03).

The E7 highway—which takes you roughly halfway to Zakopane from Kraków—is now entirely four-lane, while Highway 15 has been substantially improved and widened. Side roads in the region can be very narrow and badly surfaced. In Zakopane and other towns in the region, you should leave your car at a guarded parking lot.

BY TRAIN
Zakopane's train station is on ulica Chramcówki (☎ 0165/145–04). From Kraków, the trip to Zakopane takes six hours because of the rugged nature of the terrain. Unless you take the overnight sleeper from Warsaw, which arrives in Zakopane at 6 AM, it's better to change to a bus in Kraków.

Contacts and Resources

EMERGENCIES
Krynica (☎ 999). **Nowy Sącz** (☎ 999); hospital (⊠ Ul. Młyńska 5, ☎ 018/43–88–77). **Nowy Targ** (☎ 999).

LATE-NIGHT PHARMACIES
Krynica: Vita (⊠ Ul. Kraszewskiego 61, ☎ 0135/39–47). **Nowy Sącz** (⊠ Rynek 27, ☎ 018/43–82–92). **Nowy Targ** (⊠ Ul. Szaflarska 76, ☎ 0187/698–41). **Zakopane: Apteka Pharbita** (⊠ Ul. Chramcówki 34, ☎ 0165/682–21).

PRIVATE ACCOMMODATIONS
For information in Zakopane contact **BIT** (⊠ Ul. Kościuszki 23, ☎ 0165/122–11) for a full range of options, or **Centralne Biuro Zakwaterowania FWP** (⊠ Ul. Kościuszki 19, ☎ 0165/127–63) for places in a large number of pensions where prices range from zł 10 to zł 15 a day.

VISITOR INFORMATION
Częstochowa: IT (⊠ Al. Najświętejszej Marii Panny 37–39, ☎ 034/24–67–55). **Zakopane: BIT** (⊠ Ul. Kościuszki 23, ☎ 0165/122–11), open daily 24 hours; **Orbis** (⊠ Ul. Krupówki 22, ☎ 0165/148–12).

LUBLIN AND EASTERN POLAND

The location of Lublin, the largest town in eastern Poland, protects it to some extent from Western commercial influences and gives the visitor an opportunity to peek at the old Poland—less prosperous and more traditional. Historically, Lublin lay in the heart of Poland and served as a crossroads for east and west. It was in Lublin in 1569 that the eastern duchy of Lithuania joined the kingdom of Poland by signing the Union of Lublin, thus creating the largest empire in Europe at the time. Following World War II, Poland's borders shifted west and Lublin found itself sitting near the Soviet border. Today's Eastern influence comes predominantly from the flood of Russian traders peddling everything from old auto parts to champagne and caviar in the city's marketplace.

But this is not to imply that the changes sweeping across Poland have passed Lublin by. One of the most important current projects is the restoration of Lublin's chief monument, its walled Stare Miasto (Old Town). At the western end of Krakowskie Przedmieście, the quaint cobblestone streets of this district have to date been filled with more rubble and debris from crumbling facades than tourists, but already some of the buildings have been beautifully restored, and the area is looking up. And despite its graying exterior and mild urban decay, Lublin is rich in parks, offering wild, lush greens in summer and golden yellows in autumn.

Lublin is also a good hub for exploring the villages and countryside of the eastern parts of the country. Less than one hour away from the city, visitors can enjoy a picnic in the palace grounds in **Puławy** or a walk along the banks of the Vistula River in the picturesque village of **Kazimierz Dolny.** Like Kazimierz, **Zamość** and **Łańcut** are also accessible as a day trip from Lublin, but all these centers are attractive places for stopovers if you have time.

Numbers in the margin correspond to numbers on the Southeastern Poland map.

Lublin

㊲ *160 km (100 mi) southeast of Warsaw, 270 km (170 mi) northeast of Kraków.*

The tourist attractions of Lublin are in three distinct regions of the city. **Stare Miasto** (Old Town), a medieval walled city of cobblestone streets and crumbling architecture, is at the eastern end of Krakowskie Przedmieście, the main street. The castle and nearby Jewish cemetery are just outside the old city wall, to the northeast. The Catholic and Marie Skłodowska-Curie **universities** and the adjacent Saxon Gardens are on the western edge of Lublin, off Aleja Racławickie; take a bus west from Krakowskie Przedmieście. **Majdanek,** the second-largest Nazi concentration camp in Europe, lies 5 kilometers (3 miles) southeast of central Lublin and can be reached by Bus 153 or 156 from Krakowskie Przedmieście.

At the eastern end of Lublin's main shopping street, Krakowskie Przedmieście, is the **Brama Krakowska** (Kraków Gate), a Gothic and baroque structure that served as the main entrance to the medieval city. Today it separates modern Lublin from the Stare Miasto. It houses the **Muzeum Lubelskie** (Lublin History Museum), which offers an overview of the area's history. ⊠ *Pl. Łokietka 2,* ☎ *081/26–001.* 🎫 *Zł 1.* ⊙ *Wed.–Sat. 9–4, Sun. 9–5.*

Part of Lublin's tremendous success as a medieval trading center stemmed from a royal decree exempting the city from all customs duties. As a result, huge fortunes were made, and the town's merchants were able to build the beautiful 14th- and 15th-century houses—complete with colorful frescoed facades and decorative moldings—that surround the **Rynek** (market square). The Rynek's trapezoidal shape, unusual for a market square, is the result of medieval builders adapting the construction of the town to the shape of the protective walls surrounding Lublin.

★

Filling the center of Lublin's Rynek is the reconstructed **Stary Ratusz** (Old Town Hall), built in the 16th century and rebuilt in neoclassical style in the 1780s by the Italian architect Domenico Merlini. Here a royal tribunal served as the seat of the Crown Court of Justice for Małopolska beginning in 1578; records of its activities can be seen in the museum. On Saturday the hall fills with young couples waiting to be married. ⊠ *Muzeum Trybunału Koronnego:* ⊠ *Rynek 1,* ☎ *081/268– 66.* 🎫 *Zł 1.* ⊙ *Tues.–Sun. 10–3.*

NEED A
BREAK?

At ulica Grodzka 5A, in one of the recently reconstructed medieval tenements, you can visit the small ground-floor **Apteka–Muzeum** (Museum of Pharmacy), which is a reconstruction of an early chemist's shop, and then drink a cup of coffee in the café behind. Open 11–4.

★ The **Dominican Church and Monastery,** dating from 1342, is the jewel of Lublin's Old Town; the interior was renovated in rococo style in the 17th century. Two of its 11 chapels are particularly noteworthy: the **Firlej Chapel,** with its late-Renaissance architecture, and the **Tyszkiewski Chapel,** with its early baroque decoration. Circling the walls above the chapels are paintings depicting the bringing of a piece of the True Cross on which Jesus was crucified to Lublin and the protection the relic has given the city through the ages. Unfortunately, this protection did not extend to the relic itself, which was stolen from the Dominican Church in 1991. The church is often closed now, but try knocking on the monastery door to the right of the entrance to get someone to let you in. ⊠ *Ul. Złota.* 🖾 *Free.* ⊙ *Weekdays 9–noon and 3–6, weekends 3–6.*

Outside the old city wall, just around the corner from Kraków Gate, stands **Lublin Cathedral,** begun in 1625. The exterior of this Jesuit church is an example of Lublin Renaissance style—steep-pitched roofs, highly decorated gables, and elaborate patterned vaulting. Inside to the left of the baroque high altar, a reproduction of the *Black Madonna of Częstochowa* is on display. You can reach the **Kaplica Akustyczna** (Whispering Chapel) by a passage to the right of the high altar. Watch what you say here—the acoustics are so astounding that a whisper in one corner can be heard perfectly in another. Next to the chapel is the **treasury,** the only place to view what remains of the original illusionistic frescoes that decorated the church interior: The images were painted so skillfully that they appear almost three-dimensional. ⊠ *Ul. Królewska.* 🖾 *Whispering Chapel and treasury zł 1.*

During the late 14th century King Kazimierz the Great ordered the construction of **Lublin Castle,** as well as the defensive walls surrounding the city, to protect the wealthy trading center from foreign invasion. Most of the castle was rebuilt during the 19th century, when it was converted to a prison. Run at various times by the Russian czar, the Polish government, and the German Gestapo, the castle prison witnessed the largest number of deaths during World War II, when more than 10,000 political prisoners were murdered by the Nazis. The **Castle Museum** houses historical and ethnographic exhibits and an art **gallery** known for Jan Matejko's *Unia Lubelska* (1869), which depicts the signing of the Lublin Union by the king of Poland and Grand Duke of Lithuania exactly three centuries earlier. ⊠ *Ul. Zamkowa 9,* ☎ *081/25–001.* 🖾 *Zł 1.5.* ⊙ *Wed.–Sat. 9–4, Sun. 9–5.*

Lublin was a center of Jewish culture in the 16th century; the hill behind Lublin Castle is the site of the **Old Jewish Cemetery,** destroyed during World War II by the German SS, which used the rubble from the headstones to pave the entranceway to Majdanek concentration camp. The park at the base of the castle hill was the site of the Jewish ghetto, in which Nazis imprisoned the Jewish population of Lublin until April 1943, when they sent them to Majdanek.

OFF THE
BEATEN PATH

MAJDANEK CONCENTRATION CAMP – Reminders of World War II are never far away in Poland, and several kilometers southeast of Lublin's city center lie the remnants of the Majdanek concentration camp, second in size only to Auschwitz. Established in July 1941, it grew to 1,235 acres, although the plan was to make it five times as large. Majdanek originally housed 5,000 Polish, Russian, and Ukrainian prisoners of war, who were later followed by citizens of 29 other countries, most of them Jewish. From 1941 to 1944, more than 360,000 people lost their lives here, either by direct extermination or through disease.

Standing at the camp entrance is one of two monuments designed for the 25th anniversary of the liberation of Majdanek. The **Monument** of **Struggle and Martyrdom** symbolizes the inmates' faith and hope; the **mausoleum** at the rear of the camp marks the death of that hope. Of the five fields constituting the original camp, only the gas chambers, watchtowers, and crematoria, as well as some barracks on Field Three, remain. The visitor center, to the left of the entrance monument, sells guidebooks in English. ⊠ *Droga Męczenników Majdanka 67,* ☎ *081/42–647.* ⊐ *Free.* ☉ *May–Sept. 15, Tues.–Sun. 8–6; Sept. 16–Apr., Tues.–Sun. 8–3; closed day after holidays.*

Dining and Lodging

$$ ✕ **Karczma Słupska.** Part of a chain of traditional Polish taverns, this local favorite near the Catholic University is a good choice for casual dining. Settle into a rustic, carved-wood booth and feast on such Polish specialties as sautéed carp and pork chop Lublin style. The food is delicious, though the service is slow even by Polish standards. ⊠ *Al. Racławickie 22,* ☎ *081/388–13. No credit cards.*

$$ ✕ **Unia.** Though it is decorated in a bland 1960s style, this hotel
★   restaurant is the best in town. The menu features Polish and international cuisine, and the service is good (but don't expect the waiters to speak English). The mushroom soup makes an excellent appetizer; recommended main courses include beefsteak with french fries, roast duck, or the *de volaille* cutlet (rolled chicken stuffed with cheese). ⊠ *Al. Racławickie 12,* ☎ *081/320–61. AE, DC, MC, V.*

$ ✕ **Victoria.** The ground-floor restaurant offers such traditional Polish specialties as *zupa ogórkowa* (cucumber soup) and cherry soup, in addition to fairly typical meat entrées such as roast pork, veal cutlet, and beef medallions with mashed potatoes. ⊠ *Ul. Narutowicza 58–60,* ☎ *081/270–11. AE, DC, MC, V.*

$$$ ⊞ **Unia Hotel.** The six-story hotel is just off the main road, outside the
★   Old Town. Most of the public spaces are fairly cramped, but the rooms are reasonably spacious and comfortably furnished, each with its own bathroom and television (not a given for this part of Poland). ⊠ *Al. Racławickie 12, 20–037,* ☎ *081/320–61,* ⃞ᴬˣ *081/330–21. Restaurant, meeting room. AE, DC, MC, V.*

$$ ⊞ **PZMot Motel.** A utilitarian concrete block situated near the center of town, the PZMot is efficiently run and offers clean and bright accommodations at a very fair price. Admittedly, singles here are no bigger than the bed, but many of the doubles come with their own bath or shower, and the public bathrooms are clean. The management speaks a little English. The small restaurant serves simple Polish dishes. ⊠ *Ul. Prusa 8, 20–401,* ☎ *081/342–32 or 081/343–72. 64 rooms, some with bath. AE, DC, MC, V.*

$$ ⊞ **Victoria Hotel.** This old hotel is large and well situated, within walking distance of all the Old Town's landmarks. The rooms are on the small side, but the service is efficient and friendly. Rooms over the street, which is on a hill, can be noisy. ⊠ *Ul. Narutowicza 58–60, 20–401,* ☎ *081/270–11,* ⃞ᴬˣ *081/290–26. 190 rooms, most with bath. Restaurant. AE, DC, MC, V.*

$ ⊞ **Dom Nauczyciela.** This hotel, which was formerly reserved for members of the teaching profession, is clean, comfortable, and efficiently run, if a little lacking in elegance. The rooms are small, but adequate. It is well placed, in the university district. ⊠ *Ul. Akademicka 4, 20–033,* ☎ *081/303–66,* ⃞ᴬˣ *081/385–92. 80 rooms, about half with bath. No credit cards.*

Nightlife and the Arts

For up-to-date information about movies, theater, and concerts in Lublin, consult the local papers, **Kurier Lubelski** and **Dziennik Lubelski.** Philharmonic tickets can be purchased at ulica Kapucyńska 7, Tuesday–Sunday noon–7. Theater tickets are available at **Centrum Kultury** (⊠ Ul. Peowiaków 12), the home of all theater groups in Lublin. The **Teatr Muzyczny** is at ul. Kunickiego 35 (☎ 081/276–13) and has a repertoire of light musicals and operetta. Student nightlife centers around Marie Skłodowska-Curie University's **Chatka Żaka Club** (⊠ Ul. I. Radziszewskiego 16, ☎ 081/332–01). The club offers a cafeteria, a bar, a popular disco, and a cinema that often shows American movies.

Outdoor Activities and Sports

On hot summer days the residents of Lublin head for **Zalew Zemborzycki,** a man-made lake about 4 kilometers (2½ miles) south of central Lublin. Set in Las Dąbrowa (Oak Woods), the lake offers sailing and canoe rentals, as well as a great place to take a walk. *To get there, take Bus 25 or 42 from Lublin Cathedral.*

Puławy

★ 🟤 *40 km (25 mi) northwest of Lublin, 120 km (75 mi) southeast of Warsaw.*

The 18th-century **Puławy Palace** in the town of Puławy is a wonderful place to spend an afternoon strolling through parks and gardens or enjoying a picnic lunch. The palace was originally the residence of the Czartoryski family, a patriotic, politically powerful clan. Prince Adam Czartoryski was one of the most educated men of his day and a great patron of art and culture. He attracted so many prominent Poles to Puławy that by the late 18th century it was said to rival Warsaw as a cultural and political capital. Today the yellow-and-white neoclassical building has become the home of an agricultural institute; the site is best known for the beautiful English-style gardens and pavilions.

Set in a building modeled on the Vesta Temple in Tivoli, **Świątynia Sybilli** (Sybil's Temple) is Poland's first museum. Completed in 1809, it houses a collection of national relics that was started after the first partitioning of Poland in an effort to preserve reminders of the country's glorious past and traditions. The museum also contains a rotating selection from the Czartoryski Collection in Kraków. The **Palace Chapel,** built in 1803, is based on the Pantheon in Rome. It's at ulica Piłsudskiego 10, outside the palace grounds (from the palace front, walk two blocks north on ulica Czartoryskich to ulica Piłsudskiego, and then left two blocks). ⊠ *Ul. Czartoryskich 6A,* ☎ *0831/87–86–74.* ✉ *Palace grounds free; Sybil's Temple zł 2.* ☉ *May–Nov., Tues.–Sun. 9–5.*

Kazimierz Dolny

★ 🟤 *12 km (7 mi) south of Puławy, 40 km (25 mi) west of Lublin, 130 km (80 mi) southeast of Warsaw.*

The small town of Kazimierz Dolny, perched on a steep, hilly bank of the placid Vistula River, is like an illustration for the word *quaint.* Its assortment of whitewashed facades and steeply pitched red-tile roofs peeking out over the treetops strikes a harmonious balance with the surrounding forests and sandstone hillsides. The effect is so pleasing that Kazimierz Dolny has thrived for over a century as an artists' colony and vacation spot for city-weary tourists. Often referred to as the Pearl of the Polish Renaissance, Kazimierz Dolny prospered as a port town during the 16th and 17th centuries, but the partitioning of Poland left it cut off from the grain markets of Gdańsk. Thereafter the town fell into decline until it was rediscovered by painters and writers during the 19th century. Today nonartistic visitors can still enjoy the Renaissance architecture along the village's dusty cobblestone streets or commune with nature on a hike through the nearby hills and gorges.

One of the most powerful families in Kazimierz Dolny, the Przybyłas, left behind an ornate house that stands out gaudily amid the surrounding whitewash. Adorning the facades of the **Przybyła Brothers' House,** on the southeast corner of the town's compact **Rynek** (market square), are the two-story bas-relief figures of St. Nicholas (left) and St. Christopher (right), the brothers' patron saints. The **Celej House,** home of another powerful Kazimierz clan, stands one block toward the river from the market square. Embellished with griffins, dragons, and salamanders, it outdoes most of the other houses in town, at least in terms of gaudy decoration. The Celej family departed long ago, and their former residence now houses the **Town Museum of Kazimierz Dolny,** which has many paintings depicting local Jewish life in the past. ⊠ *Ul. Senatorska 11–13,* ☎ *081/81–02–88.* 🎟 *Zł 1.40.* ☉ *May–Oct., Tues.–Sun. 10–2.*

A covered passageway off ulica Senatorska in Kazimierz Dolny leads up to the walled courtyard of the **Church and Monastery of the Reformati Order,** which stands on the southern hill overlooking the town's market square. In the late 18th century an encircling wall was built to protect the monastery's buildings. A plaque inside the passageway memorializes the Nazis' use of the site as a house of torture during the occupation of Poland. The climb up to the courtyard is worthwhile just for the spectacular view of the town. The ruins of the 14th-century **Kazimierz Castle,** which served as a watchtower to protect the Vistula trade route, stand on a steep hill to the northeast of the town's market square; from here there is a view over the town and the Vistula Valley. The **Góra Trzech Krzyży** (Three Crosses Hill) lies to the east of the Kazimierz Dolny market square; the crosses were constructed in 1708 to commemorate the victims of a plague that ravaged the town.

Lodging

$ 🏨 **SARP.** This hotel on the corner of the picturesque square belongs to the Architects' Association, but will now take guests on a commercial basis. The rooms are large and irregular in shape, with simple but adequate furnishings. The public rooms on the ground floor are low and spacious. ⊠ *Rynek 20, 24–120,* ☎ *0831/103–80. 90 rooms, some with bath. Dining room. No credit cards.*

Outdoor Activities and Sports

BOATING

Boat rides on the Vistula leave from ulica Puławska 6. The half-hour ride takes you south to **Janowiec** with its Firlej Castle ruins.

HIKING

Take one of the numerous marked trails, ranging in length from 2 to 6 kilometers (1 to 4 miles), and explore the rich, hilly landscape around Kazimierz. All trails converge in the market square. Tourist tracks lead north (marked red) and south (marked green) along the river from the Rynek, down streets and cart paths, through orchards and quarries, by castles and granaries.

Zamość

㉒ *87 km (54 mi) to the southeast of Lublin, 318 km (198 mi) northeast of Kraków.*

The fortified town of Zamość has been kept marvelously intact since the Renaissance, with a grand central square, wide boulevards, neat rows of colorful houses, arcaded passages, and brightly painted facades. Physically, though, it could use a little updating; hundreds of houses still have no running water or sanitation, although a modernization program is now under way.

Zamość was conceived in the late 16th century by Hetman Jan Zamoyski as an outpost on the thriving trade route between Lublin and Lwów and was largely designed by the Italian architect Bernardo Morando, working in Zamoyski's service. The town thrived, and its strong fortifications spared it from destruction during the Swedish on-slaught of the 17th century. The Polish victory over Lenin's Red Army near Zamość in 1920 kept the way clear for the country's restored independence. World War II saw the town renamed Himmlerstadt and thousands of its residents deported or exterminated to make way for German settlers. The buildings are unscathed, but you may see some-thing else in the eyes of older villagers.

★ Zamość's **Rynek** (market square) is a breathtaking arcaded plaza sur-rounded by the decorative facades of homes built by local merchants. Dominating the square is the impressive baroque **town hall,** topped by a 164-foot spire. It's easy to imagine characters in period costumes mak-ing a grand entrance from its double staircase. In the **Zamość Regional Museum,** which is next door to the town hall, you can see regional ar-tifacts, paintings of the Zamoyski clan, the town's founding family, and a scale model of Zamość. ⊠ *Ul. Ormiańska 24,* ☎ *084/38–64–94.* 🎫 *Zł 1.* ۞ *Daily 10–5.*

St. Thomas Collegiate Church, one of Poland's most beautiful Renais-sance churches, stands near the southwest corner of the Rynek. In the presbytery are four 17th-century paintings ascribed to Domenico Ro-busti, Tintoretto's son. The church is also the final resting place of Jan Zamoyski, buried in the **Zamoyski Chapel** to the right of the high altar.

The **Zamoyski Palace,** home of the founding family of Zamość, lies near the market square, beyond St. Thomas Collegiate Church. The palace lost much of its decorative detail in renovation and restoration and now serves as a courthouse. The Zamość **Arsenal Museum,** behind the Zamoyski Palace, houses a collection of Turkish armaments and rugs, as well as a model of the original town plan. ⊠ *Ul. Zamkowa 2,* ☎ *084/38–40–76.* 🎫 *Zł 1.* ۞ *Daily 10–3:30.*

Near the northwest corner of the Rynek, behind the town hall, is the **Old Academy,** a distinguished center of learning during the 17th and 18th centuries and the third-largest university after those in Kraków and Vilnius (it's now a high school). The oldest entrance to Zamość, the **Lublin Gate,** is to the northwest of the marketplace, across the road from the Old Academy. In 1588, Jan Zamoyski triumphantly led the Austrian archduke Maximilian into town through this gate after de-feating him in his attempt to seize the Polish throne from Sigismund III. He then bricked up the gate to commemorate his victory.

What's left of Zamość's **fortifications** are found at the bottom of ulica Staszica: the **Lwów Gate and Bastion,** designed, like the rest of the Re-naissance town, by Bernardo Morando. With defenses like these, three stories high and 20 feet thick, it's easy to understand why Zamość was one of the few places to escape ruin in the Swedish attack. *Gate and bastion:* 🎫 *Zł 1.* ۞ *Daily 10–4.*

South of the town's marketplace, on ulica Moranda, is the **rotunda,** a monument to a tragic era in Zamość's history. From 1939 to 1944 this fortified emplacement served as an extermination camp where thou-sands of Poles, Jews, and Russians were brutally killed, some even burned alive. Now it serves as a memorial to the victims of Nazi terror in the region, and its museum details the town's suffering in the war. ☉ *Apr. 15–Sept., daily 9–6; Nov.–Apr. 14, daily 10–5.*

Dining and Lodging

$ ✕ **Restauracja Ratuszowa.** This restaurant on the magnificent main market square is housed in a redecorated Renaissance tenement. In the summer, the menu can be quite extensive and includes an excellent *chłodnik* (cold beet soup). ⊠ *Rynek Wielki 13,* ☎ *084/715–57. No credit cards.*

$$ ☷ **Hotel Jubilat.** Built in the 1970s, this hotel offers comfortable rooms on the edge of the Old Town. The decor is dark, but everything is clean, and the bathrooms, after a renovation, are gleaming. ⊠ *Ul. Wyszyń-skiego 52, 22–400,* ☎ *084/64–00. 62 rooms, all with bath. Restaurant. AE, DC, MC, V.*

Łańcut

★ ⑧③ *17 km (10½ mi) northeast of Rzeszów, 130 km (81 mi) southwest of Zamość.*

The neobaroque **Łańcut Palace,** situated within an elegant and serene 76-acre natural reserve, is the main attraction in the town of Łańcut. Built during the 16th century, the palace is one of the most grandiose aristocratic residences in Eastern Europe. In the 19th century it was willed to the Potocki family, who amassed an impressive art collection here. Count Alfred Potocki, the last owner, emigrated to Liechtenstein in 1944 as Russian troops approached, absconding with 11 train cars full of art objects and paintings. Much was left behind, however, and after the war a museum was established in the palace (which had survived intact). Today you can see the family collection of art and interior decorations, including Biedermeier, neoclassical, and rococo furnishings. Of particular interest are the intricate wood-inlay floors, the tiny theater off the dining hall, and the hall of sculpture painted to resemble a trellis of grapevines. More than 40 rooms are open to the public, including the Turkish and Chinese apartments, which reflect the 18th-century fascination with the Near and Far East. Outside, a moat and a system of bastions laid out like a five-pointed star separate the inner Italian and rose gardens from the rest of the park. The **Carriage Museum,** in the old coach house outside the main gates, contains more than 50 vehicles and is one of the largest museums of its kind in Europe. ☎ *017/25–20–08.* ☷ *Both museums zł 5.* ☉ *Park daily until sunset; museums Tues.–Sat. 8–2:30, Sun. 9–4.*

Dining and Lodging

$$ ✕ **Storczyk.** A large restaurant that caters mainly to parties of tourists visiting the palace and museums. The cuisine has been updated in the 1990s, with less fat and more vegetables. There is pleasant waitress service. ⊠ *Ul. Rzeźnicza 8,* ☎ *017/25–25–70. AE, DC, MC, V.*

$$ ☷ **Hotel Zamkowy.** The simple, cozy accommodations within this
★   18th-century palace are somewhat anomalous for their 1970s decor. However, the comfortable rooms overlook the palace courtyard and allow you to peer into the museum beyond. Take a peaceful walk in the palace gardens at sunset and wake up to the sound of birds and crickets. There are only 50 beds, so reservations are imperative. ⊠ *Ul. Zamkowa 1, 37–100,* ☎ *017/25–26–71. 23 rooms, some with bath. Restaurant. AE.*

Lublin and Eastern Poland A to Z

Arriving and Departing

BY BUS

Lublin is the gateway to the region. **Dworzec PKS Główny** (✉ Al. Tysiąclecia 4, ☎ 081/77–66–49), just north of Stare Miasto near the castle, connects Lublin with cities to the west and south. Buses run regularly to Puławy (one hour), Kazimierz Dolny (1½ hours), Rzeszów (three hours), and Warsaw (three hours). Buses 5, 10, 35, 38, 154, and 161 connect the station with ulica Krakowskie Przedmieście. Luggage storage is available daily 6 AM–7 PM for zł 2 per day per bag. To find it, go outside the station and look for the PRZECHOWALNIA BAGAŻU sign. The Russian market just outside the station sells food and every other item imaginable but lures a somewhat seedy element that loiters in and around the terminal.

Located about 4 kilometers (2½ miles) southeast of the town center, **Dworzec PKS Północny** (✉ Ul. Gospodarcza) connects Lublin with points east. Buses run frequently to Zamość (1¾ hours). You can reach the town center on Bus 155 or 159.

BY TRAIN

Lublin Główny (✉ Pl. Dworcowy, ☎ 081/31–56–42), the town's main station, is about 4 kilometers (2½ miles) south of the city center. Frequent train service connects Lublin with Warsaw (2½ hours), Kraków (4½ hours), and Zamość (three hours). Buses 13 and 158 connect the train station with the town center. Luggage storage is available for zł 2 a day per bag. The RUCH newsstand outside the station sells a great city map as well as local bus tickets.

Getting Around

Most of Lublin's restaurants and hotels lie on or around ulica Krakowskie Przedmieście and its continuation to the west, aleja Racławickie. This route is anchored by the Stare Miasto in the east and the Catholic University in the west. The Majdanek concentration camp is a few kilometers southeast. You can easily explore the entire city on foot.

BY BUS

Lublin's bus system is convenient for traveling in from the train station and out to Majdanek, but it's often crowded, and service has been reduced to just three main routes after midnight. Avoid traveling before 9 AM and between 3 PM and 5 PM to escape a crush of passengers. Plainclothes officers frequently patrol the bus system during rush hours, and fare shirkers are fined. You can buy a ticket at the RUCH kiosks or anywhere you see a SPRZEDAŻ BILETÓW MZK sign. Passengers are responsible for canceling their tickets on the bus; look for ticket punchers at the door.

BY TAXI

Taxi stands can be found near the bus and train stations, outside the Stare Miasto near Lublin Cathedral, and up and down ulica Krakowskie Przedmieście. The fares are reasonable: a trip from the train station to the outskirts of town should cost no more than $3.50, including a 5% tip. Radio taxis (☎ 919) are also available.

Contacts and Resources

EMERGENCIES

Police (☎ 997). **Medical emergencies** (☎ 999). There are 24-hour emergency rooms in **Lublin**, at ulice Weteranó 46A (☎ 081/330–92), and in **Zamość**, at ulica Kilińskiego 32 (☎ 084/39–22–00).

LATE-NIGHT PHARMACIES

Two pharmacies (*apteki*) in Lublin (⊠ Ul. Bramowa 8, ☎ 081/205–21; ⊠ Krakowskie Przedmieście 49, ☎ 081/224–25) are open 24 hours.

VISITOR INFORMATION

Lublin's main source of tourist information—**Centrum Informacji Turystycznej**—is in the Old Town (⊠ Krakowskie Przedmieście 78, ☎ 081/244–12). **Orbis** (⊠ Ul. Narutowicza 31/33, ☎ 081/222–56 or 081/222–59) books train tickets and exchanges money. **Turysta Travel** (⊠ Ul. Chopina 14, ☎ 081/291–17) sells city maps and train tickets.

In **Zamość** tourist information is provided by **Zamojski Ośrodek Informacji Turystycznej** (⊠ Rynek Wielki 13, ☎ 084/22–92). **Orbis Travel** has a small office in Zamość (⊠ Ul. Grodzka 18, ☎ 084/30–01).

GDAŃSK AND THE NORTHEAST

Until the Second World War, northern Poland was known as East Prussia. The region was once referred to as "the sand box of the Holy Roman Empire." It is indeed sandy, but it contains some startling landscapes and historic sites, like the fortress of the Teutonic Knights at **Malbork** (easily accessible by train from Gdańsk). And in the northeast lies a land of 1,000 lakes and 1,000-year-old forests (and the attendant mosquitoes): the Mazurian and Augustów-Suwałki lakes form an intriguing labyrinth of interconnecting rivers and canals, set in ancient forests teeming with birds and wild animals. **Olsztyn** or **Giżycko** are good centers for exploring the lakes, but if you want to penetrate this area, you do need a car.

Gdańsk, the third-largest city in Poland and the capital of this region—the northern province of Pomorze Gdańskie (East Pomerania)—is linked with two smaller neighboring towns, **Gdynia** and **Sopot**, in an urban conglomerate called the **Trójmiasto (Tri-City)**, on the southwest bank of the Bay of Gdańsk; these cities operate as one organism and constitute one of Poland's most exciting and vibrant places.

Numbers in the margin correspond to numbers on the Gdańsk and the Northeast map.

Gdańsk

84 *340 km (215 mi) north of Warsaw, 340 km (215 mi) east of Szczecin.*

Maybe it's the sea air, maybe it's the city's history of political tumult. Whatever the reason, Gdańsk is one of Poland's most exciting and vibrant cities. Between 1308 and 1945 under the name Danzig, this Baltic port was an independent city-state populated by a majority of ethnic Germans. When the Nazis fired the first shots of World War II here on September 1, 1939, they began a process of systematic destruction of Poland that would last for six years and leave millions dead. In 1997 Gdańsk celebrates its thousand years of existence as a Baltic city, with nonstop festivals of music and theater, exhibitions, and sailing events.

Street demonstrations in the early 1970s led to the first workers' strikes at the Lenin Shipyards. The government attempted to stifle the agitation by threatening to fire all the strikers and by bringing in soldiers (at least 40 people were killed in riots in the 1970s). But by 1980 the workers had organized enough to form Solidarność (Solidarity), which gained independent trade-union status the same year. Although it lost official government recognition a year later, after the government declared martial law, its members continued to meet secretly. After the

Communist government fell, in 1989 Solidarity leader Lech Wałęsa became president of Poland in the nation's first free elections since World
War II.

Today the carefully restored city streets hum with activity; economic
privatization has brought new cultural events and the opening of galleries and shops. Gdańsk University's presence keeps the city young
and on its toes.

Gdańsk was almost entirely destroyed during World War II, but the
streets of its **Główne Miasto** (Main Town) have been lovingly restored
and still retain their historical and cultural richness. Like most medieval
cities, the historic main town of Gdańsk can readily be explored on
foot. North of Main Town, **Stare Miasto** (Old Town) actually contains
many new hotels and shops, but several churches and the preserved
Old Town Hall earn it its name. At the north end of the Old Town sit
the Gdańsk Shipyards, St. Brigid's Church (Kościół świelej Brygidy),
and the monument to Solidarity; this site, which saw numerous workers' riots and much violence during the 1970s and 1980s, has now settled back into its daily grind. The National Museum is just south of
the old walls of the Main Town.

★ Built in the 15th through the 17th centuries, the **Dwór Artusa** (Artus
Mansion), behind Neptune's Fountain on Gdańsk's Długi Targ, was
named for King Arthur, who otherwise has no affiliation with the
place (alas, there are no signs of Excalibur or Merlin). This and the
other stately mansions on the Długi Targ are reminders of the wealthy
traders and aristocrats who once resided in this posh district. Opened
to the public in 1995 after lengthy restoration work that is still only
partly completed, the mansion's collection includes Renaissance furnishings, paintings, holy figures, and the world's largest Renaissance
stove. ⊠ *Długi Targ 43,* ☎ *058/31–97–22.* 🎫 *Zł 2.* ☉ *Tues.–Thurs.
and weekends 10–4.*

The largest brick church in the world and the largest church in Poland,
★ the **Kościół Najświętszej Marii Panny** (Church of Our Lady), on the
north side of ulica Piwna in Gdańsk's Main Town, holds 25,000 people. Also referred to in abbreviated form as Kościół Mariacki, this enormous 14th-century church underwent major restoration after World
War II, and 15 of its 22 altars have been relocated to museums in Gdańsk
and Warsaw. The highlight of a visit is climbing the hundreds of steps
up the church tower. It costs zł 3 to make the climb, but it's cheaper
and more inspirational than an aerobics class—and the view is sensa-
tional. The church also contains a 500-year-old, 25-foot-high astronomical clock that has only recently been restored to working order
after years of neglect. It keeps track of the solar and lunar phases and
features all of the signs of the zodiac—something of an anomaly in a
Catholic church.

Two blocks west of the Kościół Mariacki on ulica Piwna, the **Wielka
Zbrojownia** (Great Armory) is a good example of 17th-century Dutch
Renaissance architecture. The ground floor is now a trade center, and
the upper floors house an art school.

Three huge and somber crosses perpetually draped with flowers stand
outside the gates of the **Stocznia Gdańska** (Gdansk Shipyards; ⊠ Ul.
Jana z Kolna). Formerly called the Lenin Shipyards, this place gave birth
to the Solidarity movement, which later became the first independent
trade union under a Communist government. The shipyards and the
entire city also witnessed the long, violent struggle for autonomy that
began as a series of impromptu street demonstrations in the early
1970s and blossomed into a nationwide political party that swept the

408

Gdańsk and the Northeast

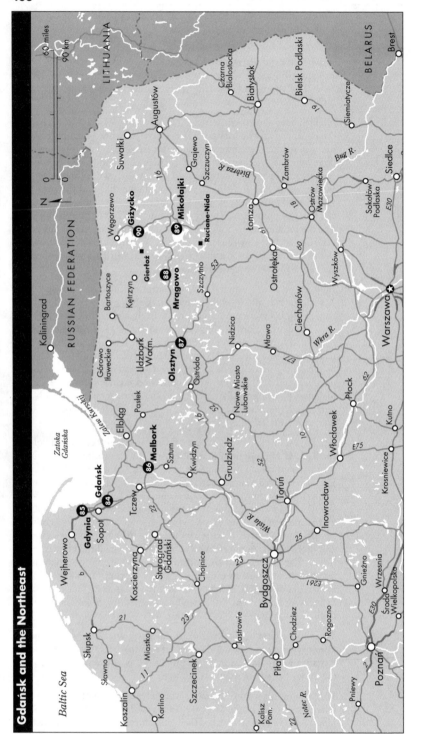

country's first free elections in 1989. The crosses are only one part of the monument to Solidarity; other parts include plaques commemorating the struggle and a moving quotation by Pope John Paul II upon visiting the monument in 1987: "The Grace of God could not have created anything better; in this place, silence is a scream."

The shipyard monument clearly symbolizes the fundamental link in the Polish consciousness between Catholicism and political dissent; another example is the **kościół świelej Brygidy** (St. Brigid's Church), a few blocks north of the shipyard monument on ulica Profesorka near Old Town Hall. After the government declared martial law in 1981 in an attempt to force Solidarity to disband, members began meeting secretly here during masses. There is a statue of Pope John Paul II in the front. More recently, in 1995, the parish priest attracted hostile comment for his anti-Semitic pronouncements.

The **Harbor Crane** is another item on Gdańsk's long list of superlatives. Built in 1444, it was medieval Europe's largest and oldest crane. Today it houses the **Maritime Museum,** with a collection of models of the ships constructed in the Gdańsk Shipyards since 1945. At the museum ticket office, you can also buy tickets for tours of the **Sołdek,** a World War II battleship moored nearby on the canal. ⊠ *Ul. Szeroka 67–68,* ☎ *058/31–86–11.* 🎫 *Zł 5.* ⊘ *Tues. and Fri. 10–5, Wed. and Thurs. 10–6, weekends 10–4; closed day after holidays.*

The worthwhile **Muzeum Narodowe w Gdańsku** (National Museum in Gdańsk) is housed in the former Franciscan Monastery. Exhibits include 14th- to 20th-century art and ethnographic collections. Look for the changing exhibitions; the permanent displays of Gdańsk art and artifacts can hold your interest for only so long. ⊠ *Ul. Toruńska 1, off ul. Okopowa,* ☎ *058/31–70–61.* 🎫 *Zł 3.* ⊘ *Thurs. 10–6; Tues., Wed., Fri.–Sun. 10–4; closed day after holidays.*

The small **Museum Archeologiczne Gdańska** (Gdańsk Archaeological Museum) features displays of Slavic tribal artifacts, including jewelry, pottery, boats, and bones. ⊠ *Ul. Mariacka 25–26,* ☎ *058/31–50–31.* 🎫 *Zł 1.5.* ⊘ *Tues.–Sun. 10:30–4.*

★ The historic entrance to the Old City of Gadańsk is marked by the **Brama Wyżynna** (High Gate), off ulica Wały Jagiellońskie at the entrance to ulica Długa. This magnificent Renaissance gate, built in 1576, is adorned with the flags of Poland, Gdańsk, and the Prussian kingdom. As the king entered the city on his annual visit, he'd pass this gate first, then the **Brama Złota** (Golden Gate), which is just behind it and dates from 1614, combining characteristics of the Italian and Dutch Renaissance. Continuing east along ulica Długa reveals one of the city's most distinctive landmarks, the elaborately gilded **Fontanna Neptuna,** at the western end of Długi Targ. Every day after dusk, this 17th-century fountain is illuminated, adding a romantic glow to the entire area. Around the fountain, vendors selling amber jewelry and souvenirs maintain a centuries-old tradition of trading at this point. At the water's edge is the eastern entrance to the medieval city of Gdańsk: the **Brama Zielona** (Green Gate). If you're a king and you're going to visit a city once a year, you might as well build a place to stay. So up went this gate (which doubled as a royal residence) in 1568. Unfortunately, the name no longer fits: The gate is now painted brown. ⊠ *At the eastern end Długi Targ.*

The former parish church of Gdańsk's Old Town, **Kościół świelej Katarzyny** (St. Catherine's Church), at the corner of ulica Podmłyńska and ulica Katarzynki, is supposedly the oldest church in the city. Parts of it date to the 12th century, the tower was constructed in the 1480s, and the carillon of 37 bells was added in 1634. The 17th-century astronomer Jan Hevelius was buried in the presbytery of the church, below which lies what's left of the town's oldest Christian cemetery (10th century). On a small island in the canal, just north of the church, stands the **Wielki Młyn** (Great Mill). The largest mill in medieval Europe, it operated from the time of its completion in 1350 until 1945. ⊠ *Corner of ul. Podmłyńska and Na Piaskach.*

★ Although Gdańsk's original **Ratusz Główny** (town hall) was completely destroyed during World War II, a careful reconstruction of the exterior and interior now re-creates the glory of Gdańsk's medieval past. Inside the town hall, the **Muzeum Historii Miasta Gdańska** (Gdańsk Historical Museum) covers more than five centuries of Gdańsk's history in exhibits that include paintings, sculptures, and weapons. The tower provides a great view of the city. ⊠ *Ul. Długa 47,* ☎ *058/31–97–22.* 🎫 *Free.* ☺ *Tues.–Thurs. and weekends 10–4.*

The district of Oliwa, north of the city center, is worth visiting for its beautiful **cathedral.** Originally part of a Cistercian monastery, the church was erected during the 13th century. Like most other structures in Poland, it has been rebuilt many times, resulting in a hodgepodge of styles from Gothic to Renaissance and rococo. An amazing 18th-century organ graces the interior. The life's work of a Cistercian monk, the 6,300-pipe organ is decorated with angelic figures that move in time to the music. Demonstrations of the organ and a brief narrated church history are given almost hourly on weekdays in summer, less frequently on weekends and the rest of the year. ⊠ *Ul. Cystersów.*

In a beautiful park surrounding the cathedral in Oliwa are the **Muzeum Sztuki Współczesnej** (Modern Art Museum), with a large collection by Polish artists, from the interwar period onward, and the **Ethnographic Museum,** which has fine examples of local crafts from the 19th century and an interesting display of amber folk jewelry. The cathedral and museums are best approached by train; get off at Gdańsk-Oliwa and walk west up ulica Piastowska to ulica Opacka; or take Tram 2 or 6 toward Sopot. *Muzeum Etnograficzne:* ⊠ *Ul. Opacka 12,* ☎ *058/52–12–71.* 🎫 *Zł 2.5.* ☺ *Tues.–Sun. 10–3. Muzeum Sztuki Współczesnej:* ⊠ *Cysterśw 15A, Pałac Opatów,* ☎ *058/52–12–71.* 🎫 *Zł 2.5.* ☺ *Tues.–Sun. 10–3.*

OFF THE
BEATEN PATH   **WESTERPLATTE –** Ten kilometers (6½ miles) north of the Old Town, Westerplatte is home to a branch of the **National Museum.** World War II broke out here, at the entrance to the northern port. On September 1, 1939, a German warship, the *Schleswig Hostein,* began a bombardment of the Polish army positions here. A monument to the men who defended the Westerplatte for seven days against impossible odds was erected in the 1960s. The Westerplatte can be reached by Bus 106 or 158 from ulica Okopowa, just outside the main town wall, or by water bus from the Dworzec Wodny at the end of ulica Długi Targ. ⊠ *Ul. Majora Sucharskiego 1,* ☎ *058/43–69–72.* 🎫 *Free.* ☺ *Daily 9–4.*

Dining and Lodging

$$$ ✕ **Major.** An Old Town restaurant, the Major has good-size tables, secluded booths, decor of glowing colors, plants and fresh flowers on
★   the tables, and attractive and extremely large dinner plates. Try the game soup, followed by duck roasted with apples and buckwheat grits (*kasza gryczana*). ⊠ *Ul. Długa 18,* ☎ *058/31–10–69. AE, DC, MC, V.*

$$$ ✕ **Pod Łososiem.** The Salmon, a historic Old Town inn that dates to
★   1598, is considered one of the best restaurants in Gdańsk. As the name suggests, fish is the specialty here: Salmon or smoked eel makes a fine

appetizer, and flounder and grilled trout are highly recommended entrées. The menu also features wild fowl such as roast duck, pheasant,
and goose. The dining area is warmly decorated with antique furniture, dark-wood paneling, and huge brass chandeliers; paintings of old
Gdańsk adorn the walls. The service is also top-rate. ⊠ *Ul. Szeroka
53–54,* ☎ *058/31–76–52. AE, DC, MC, V.*

$$$ ✕ **Pod Wieżą.** This elegant restaurant has a reputation for good meat
dishes and generous portions. If they're on the menu when you visit,
try the *zupa rybna* (fish soup), veal steak with mushroom sauce, or roast
duck with apples and brown rice. The waiters generally speak English
and German. ⊠ *Ul. Piwna 51,* ☎ *058/31–39–24. AE, DC, MC, V.*

$$ ✕ **Retman.** This small, quaint restaurant offers good Polish and Continental cuisine. A clientele of mostly Germans and Danes lingers over
plates of schnitzel and chateaubriand in a candlelit wood-paneled
room on the water. The menu features a wide range of freshwater fish
dishes. ⊠ *Ul. Stagiewna 1,* ☎ *058/31–41–14. AE, DC, MC, V.*

$$ ✕ **Tawerna.** This well-established (and well-touristed) restaurant over-
★ looking the river serves traditional Polish and German dishes such as
pork cutlets and pork knuckles with large portions of sauerkraut,
boiled beets, and potatoes. It also specializes in seafood, particularly
fresh and pickled herring. ⊠ *Ul. Powroźnicza 19–20, off Długi Targ,*
☎ *58/31–92–48. AE, DC, MC, V.*

$ ✕ **Pod Żurawiem.** This is a traditional restaurant, serving such Gdańsk
favorites as *golonka* (pig's knuckle) or *gołąbki* (cabbage leaf stuffed
with meat and rice in tomato sauce). It can be smoky. ⊠ *Ul. Wawrzy-
nicza 10,* ☎ *058/31–34–17. Reservations not accepted. No credit
cards.*

$$ 🏨 **Hewelius.** This large, modern high-rise hotel is within walking distance of the Old Town. The rooms are spacious and blandly furnished,
with all modern conveniences. ⊠ *Ul. Heweliusza 22, 80–890,* ☎ *058/
31–56–31,* 🅵🅰🆇 *058/31–19–22. 250 rooms, most with bath. Restaurant, nightclub. AE, DC, MC, V.*

$$ 🏨 **Hotel Mesa.** This superb hotel near the train station was once part
★ of the Communist Party headquarters. Now it's a small hotel run by
a friendly Christian staff (don't worry, you don't have to say grace to
stay here). The rooms are clean, well furnished, and each has a phone,
color TV, and functioning shower. Finding a hotel of Mesa's quality
in Poland seems too good to be true. The catch? With only eight
rooms, it requires advance planning and reservations to book a room
here in summer. ⊠ *Wały Jagiellońskie 36, 80–853,* ☎ *058/31–80–
52,* 🅵🅰🆇 *058/31–80–52. 8 rooms, 4 with bath. Restaurant. AE, MC.*

$$ 🏨 **Marina.** Built in 1982, this large high-rise, popular with Western
businesspeople, is one of Poland's newer hotels and probably Gdańsk's
best. Upper floors have splendid views. ⊠ *Ul. Jelitkowska 20, 80–341,*
☎ *058/53–20–79,* 🅵🅰🆇 *058/53–04–60. 193 rooms with bath or shower.
Restaurant, indoor pool, tennis courts, bowling alley, nightclub. AE,
DC, MC, V.*

Nightlife and the Arts

As elsewhere in Poland, the nightlife in Gdańsk is expanding. Discos
and nightclubs are popping up all over; many of them optimistically
advertise that they stay open until 4 AM or 6 AM, although a lot of them
seem to lack the clientele to make it happen. **Bar Vinifera** (⊠ Ul.
Wodopój 7, south of Hotel Hewelius) is a really small, really intimate
wine bar with red lights and a smoky atmosphere that serves a variety of drinks to a mostly young crowd. **U Szkota** (⊠ Chlebnicka 9–
10), opposite the Kościół Mariacki, is hard to miss, with brightly

colored tartans hanging from the second story. The Highland atmosphere is complemented by waiters clad in Scottish kilts.

Check with Orbis for details on opera and orchestral performances at Gdańsk's **National Opera and Philharmonic** (✉ Ul. Świętego Ducha 2, ☎ 058/31–70–21). Gdańsk has a well-known theater company, **Teatr Wybrzeże** (✉ Ul. Bohateró Monte Cassino, ☎ 58/513–936), where tickets run about zł 20.

Sopot

12 km (7½ mi) north of Gdańsk, 12 km (7½ mi) south of Gdynia.

Sopot is Poland's leading seaside holiday resort, with miles of sandy beaches, which in the mid-1990s have again been cleared as safe for bathing, as the Baltic's chronic pollution problems improve. Sopot enjoyed its heyday in the 1920 and 1930s, when the wealthy flocked here to gamble at the town's large casino. (The original casino was destroyed in a fire during World War II but a new casino has recently opened on the same location.) There is a 19th-century pier (the longest on the Baltic) and a flock of seagoing swans around it.

Lodging

$$$$ 🏨 **Grand Hotel.** This legendary late-19th-century hotel reopened in the
★ mid-1990s after major renovations. Though some of the charm of the original building has been lost, the increase in comfort has been considerable. And the unique location remains: The hotel fronts directly onto the Sopot Beach, with its flock of resident swans, and stands in its own gardens. The dining room offers an uninterrupted view of the Baltic. ✉ *Ul. Powstańców Warszawy 8–12, 81–718,* ☎ *058/51–00–41,* 📠 *058/51–61–24. 140 rooms, all with bath. Restaurant, nightclub. AE, DC, MC, V.*

$$$ 🏨 **Villa Hestia.** In a villa built at the end of the 19th century by a shipping magnate, this small hotel was extensively renovated in the mid-1990s. Set in a landscaped garden with palms, it is in the center of Sopot, 10 minutes' walk from the beach. ✉ *Ul. Władysława IV 3–5, 81–703,* ☎ *058/51–21–00,* 📠 *058/51–02–55. 30 rooms and suites, all with bath. AE, DC, MC, V.*

Nightlife and the Arts

In Sopot, the **Café Sopot** (✉ Ul. Haffnera 81/85) is a fashionable place for a quiet drink. The **Grand Hotel Bar** is an upmarket, quiet bar with views over the beach.

Sopot is home to a branch of Gdańsk's Teatr Wybrzeże (☞ Nightlife and the Arts *in* Gdańsk, *above*), the **Scena Kameralna** (Chamber Theater; ✉ Ul. Bohatcrów Monte Cassino 55/57, ☎ 058/51–58–12). **Opera Leśna** (Forest Opera; ✉ Ul. Moniuszki 12, ☎ 058/51–18–12) puts on performances during the summer at its open-air summer opera house, in the woods to the west of town. The **International Song Festival** is held in August in the open-air concert hall (Muszla Koncertowa) in Skwer Kuracjyny in the center of town by the pier; check Orbis (☞ Visitor Information *in* Gdańsk and the Northeast A to Z, *below*) for schedules and ticket information.

Gdynia

㉟ *24 km (14 mi) north of Gdańsk, 12 km (7½ mi) north of Gdynia.*

The northernmost of the three cities that make up the tricity area, Gdynia has less to offer the visitor than its southern neighbors. In 1922 it was only a tiny fishing village, but by 1939 it had grown into one of the Baltic's biggest ports. In addition to the shipyards and docks that dominate this industrial area, Gdynia boasts a beautifully landscaped promenade.

The **Muzeum Oceanograficzne-Akwarium Morskie** (Oceanographic Museum and Aquarium), near the harbor in Gdynia, has tanks holding more than a thousand species of fish and is worth a visit. ⊠ *Al. Zjednoczenia 1,* ☎ *058/21–70–21.* ⌨ *Zł 2.5.* ☉ *Tues.–Sun. 10–5.*

Opposite the aquarium, a **ship museum** is housed in a World War II battleship, the *Błyskawica*; the museum is open May–mid-October, Tuesday–Sunday 10–1 and 2–4. In keeping with the nautical tradition of the town, Gdynia's **Naval Museum,** south of the pier on Bulwar Nadmorski, traces the history of Polish sea life from Slavic times to the present. ⊠ *Skwer Kościuszki 15,* ☎ *058/26–35–26.* ⌨ *Zł 3.* ☉ *Tues.–Sun. 10–4.*

Malbork

🅰 *45 km (28 mi) southeast of Gdańsk, on the T83 highway.*

★ The monstrous **Malbork Castle** is the central feature of the quiet town of Malbork (the former German city of Marienburg). In 1230 the Teutonic Knights arrived on the banks of the Vistula River and settled here, aiming to establish their own state on these conquered Prussian lands. The castle passed into Polish hands after the second Toruń Treaty in 1466 concluded the 13-year war between the Poles and the Order of Teutonic Knights. For the next three centuries, Malbork served as the royal residence for Polish kings during their annual visit to Pomerania. The castle was half destroyed during World War II, after which the building underwent a major renovation. Visitors can now view the wonderfully restored castle on a two-hour tour. Expect to pay about zł 10 per person for a tour in English or German; or pick up the English guidebook (sold outside the main entrance) and join one of the tours in Polish, which cost about 10% those for foreigners. Displays within the castle include an amber museum, 17th- and 18th-century china, glass, coins, paintings, and a large display of antique weapons and armor. ☎ *055/72–33–64.* ⌨ *Zł 7.* ☉ *May–Sept., Tues.–Sun. 9–4:30; Oct.–Apr., Tues.–Sun. 9–3.*

Olsztyn

🅱 *130 km (81 mi) southeast of Malbork, 150 km (93 mi) southeast of Gdańsk, 215 km (133 mi) north of Warsaw.*

Since World War II, Olsztyn has served as the Warmia and Mazury region's primary industrial center. The city is large and has a good number of hotels and restaurants ready to handle a large influx of summer tourists. Even so, you probably won't want to spend too much time here; Olsztyn is simply too gray and industrialized to offer much to the visitor. In just a few hours you can take in all its main sights, which are clustered near the Rynek.

The Gothic **Brama Wysoka** (High Gate) marks the entrance to the old town of Olsztyn and the main square. Southeast of the Olsztyn town square, **St. James Cathedral** dates from the 15th century. Olsztyn's **castle,** with its ethnographic and historical **museum**, stands just to the west of the town's square. Once again, Copernicus, that Renaissance man who really got around in northern Poland, is featured in a museum exhibit. He successfully directed the defense of the castle from 1516 to 1521 against the Teutonic Knights while serving as an administrator of Warmia province. *Muzeum Warmii i Mazur:* ⊠ *Ul. Zamkowa 1,* ☎ *089/27–95–96.* ⌨ *Zł 2, Wed. free.* ☉ *Tues.–Sun. 9–3.*

Lodging

$$ 🏨 **Orbis Novotel.** This standard 1970s hotel is the most comfortable lodging in the area, in beautiful surroundings on the shores of Lake Ukiel. ✉ *Ul. Sielska 4A, 10–802,* ☎ *089/27–60–81,* 📠 *089/27–54–03. 98 rooms. Restaurant, pool.*

OFF THE
BEATEN PATH   **LIDZBARK WARMIŃSKI –** The well-preserved 14th-century castle in Lidzbark Warmiński (46 kilometers [28½ miles] north of Olsztyn) is yet another former fortress of the Teutonic Knights. It survived World War II only because the local population refused to help the Germans demolish it. Inside the Gothic castle a regional museum features a strange mix of Gothic sculpture, icons, and modern Polish art. Buses run to Lidzbark from Olsztyn. ✉ *Pl. Zamkowy,* ☎ *08983/21–11.* 🎫 *Zł 1.* ☉ *Tues.–Sun. 9–2.*

Mrągowo

88   *60 km (40 mi) east of Olsztyn.*

Normally one of the quieter spots in the Mazurian lakes, Mrągowo fills every July with aspiring country-and-western performers from around the world who attend the **Country Pikniky** (Country Picnic Festival) at the amphitheater on Lake Mamry. For information and tickets contact Activ Holiday (✉ Ul. Ratuszowa 8, ☎ 08984/20–51), open weekdays 8–8. It's about a three-hour bus trip from Olsztyn to Mrągowo.

Lodging

$$$ 🏨 **Mrongovia.** This Orbis luxury hotel was opened in the 1980s, with fine views and large balconies from which they can be admired. The hotel offers many sports facilities and extensive grounds. ✉ *Ul. Giżycka 6, 11–700,* ☎ *08984/32–21,* 📠 *08984/32–20. 130 rooms with bath. Pool, tennis courts. AE, DC, MC, V.*

Mikołajki

89   *85 km (53 mi) east of Olsztyn, 22 km (13½ mi) east of Mrągowo.*

One of the more attractive Mazury resorts, Mikołajki is a quaint fishing village on the shores of Lake Tałty and Lake Mikołajskie. Boating is a popular activity at **Lake Śniardwy,** a large lake just a few minutes' walk from the Mikołajki train station. The incredible nature preserve of **Lake Łukajno,** 4 kilometers (2½ miles) east of Mikołajki, is home to one of the last remaining colonies of wild swans.

OFF THE
BEATEN PATH   **RUCIANE-NIDA –** Between lakes Beldany and Nidzkie, Ruciane-Nida is in the heart of the Pisz Forest. It's especially popular among nature enthusiasts, who come to hike through its pine forests. You can get here from Mikołajki on foot: There is a 22-kilometer (13½-mile) hiking trail, or you can make the trip on horseback or by ferry. Ruciane-Nida is also served by trains from Olsztyn, 70 kilometers (43½ miles) east. The PTTK tent campground is a 15-minute walk from the train station.

Giżycko

90   *95 km (60 mi) northeast of Olsztyn, 35 km (22 mi) northeast of Mrągowo.*

Because its historic buildings were destroyed in 1945, Giżycko lacks character. Nonetheless, this town at the intersection of Lake Niegocin and Lake Kisajno is one of the main Mazurian lake resorts, with a beach (of sorts) and some water-sports possibilities. Its tourist offices provide invaluable information for exploring the entire region.

Lodging

$ ▥ **Hotel Mazury.** This small hotel has recently had a face-lift and offers clean and quiet rooms with balconies and views over Lake Niegocin. ✉ *Ul. Wojska Polskiego 56, 11–500,* ☎ *0878/59–56. 60 rooms, 20 with bath. Restaurant. AE, DC, MC, V.*

Gdańsk and the Northeast A to Z

Arriving and Departing

BY BUS

Gdańsk is the gateway for all of northeastern Poland. Right next to the train station, Gdańsk's **PKS** bus station (✉ Ul. 3 maja, ☎ 058/32–15–32) may prove useful to those who want to venture to small towns off the tracks; otherwise train service is more frequent and comprehensive.

BY CAR

From Warsaw, the E81, a well-kept two-lane road for the whole of its length, offers a smooth trip to Gdańsk. From the west, the quickest route to the coast from the border crossing at Frankfurt an der Oder is to take the E8 to Poznań, and then the E83 via Gniezno and Bydgoszcz to Świecie, where it becomes the E16 and continues via Tczew to the coast.

BY FERRY

Ferries travel daily from Gdańsk to Helsinki and to Oxelösund, Sweden. Fares range from about $30 to $60, depending on the season. You can book a ticket at the **Orbis** office in the Hotel Hevelius (✉ Ul. Heweliusa 22, ☎ 058/31–34–56) or at **Polish Baltic Shipping Company** (✉ Ul. Przemysłowa 1, Gdańsk, ☎ 058/43–18–87 or 058/43–69–78).

BY PLANE

Gdańsk's airport is at Rębiechwo (☎ 058/41–52–51). Bus 162 will take you to the center of town, or take the LOT bus, which runs between the airport and the LOT Office (✉ Wały Jagielońskie 2/4).

BY TRAIN

The main rail station, **Gdańsk Główny** (✉ Podwale Grodzkie 1, ☎ 058/31–00–51), has a 24-hour baggage check, a snack bar, and a traveler's lounge. Trains leave here for Hel (two trains a day, 2½ hours traveling time), Warsaw (five trains a day, four hours), Kraków (five trains a day, eight hours), Poznań (five trains a day, four hours), and Malbork (15 trains a day, one hour).

Getting Around

BY CAR

The road network in this part of Poland is relatively well developed, and there are plenty of gas and service stations. Although Gdańsk's Old Town and Main Town areas are easily walkable, a car will be useful if you wish to visit other parts of the Trójmiasto (the Sopot Beach, the museums and cathedral at Oliwa), as well as sights farther afield.

BY BUS, TRAM, AND TROLLEY

A service runs through the Trójmiasto, taking you from Gdańsk through Oliwa and Sopot to Gdynia. There is a regular service, although some buses can be crowded. The whole trip takes about 1¾ hours. The buses run from 5 AM to 11 PM; after 11 PM there is an hourly night-bus service. PKS buses link all the small towns and villages of the region.

Trams are useful within Gdańsk when you wish to visit the cathedral or museums at Oliwa, or to visit the shipyards and Solidarity memorial.

BY TRAIN
The towns of the region can all be reached by train. Within the Trójmiasto area, a fast electric-train service runs every 15 minutes from Gdańsk Główny via Oliwa, Sopot, and Gdynia to Wejherowo. The service operates from 4 AM to 1 AM.

BY WATER BUS
In summer, an hourly service links Gdańsk with Sopot and Gdynia, via Westerplatte and Hel. In Gdańsk, the station is on the Długie Pobrzeże by the Zielona Brama (☎ 058/31–49–26); in Sopot, at the pier; in Gdynia at Aleje Zjednoczenia 2 (☎ 058/20–21–54).

Contacts and Resources

EMERGENCIES
Gdańsk: police (☎ 997); **ambulance** (☎ 999). The emergency room in Gdańsk is at aleje Zwycięstwa 49 (☎ 058/41–10–00). **Sopot: police** (☎ 997); **medical emergencies** (☎ 999). The emergency room in Sopot is at ulica Chrobrego 6–8 (☎ 058/51–24–55).

LATE-NIGHT PHARMACIES
Gdańsk: The **Apteka Dworcowa** at the main rail station (⊠ Ul. Podwale Grodzkie 1, ☎ 058/31–28–41) provides 24-hour service. **Gdynia: Pod Gryfem** (⊠ Ul. Starowiejska 34, ☎ 058/20–19–82). **Sopot:** There is 24-hour service at **Apteka Kuracyjna** (⊠ Al. Niepodległości 715, ☎ 058/51–22–76).

VISITOR INFORMATION
Gdańsk: Centralny Ośrodek Informacji Turystycznaj (⊠ Heweliusza 27, ☎ 058/31–43–55) is the city's main travel office; **Orbis** (⊠ Heweliusza 22, ☎ 058/41–00–00) has a good selection of maps and brochures. **Gdynia: Orbis** (⊠ Ul. Świętojańska 36, ☎ 058/20–00–70) provides information on travel and accommodation and will book tickets; **Sports Tourist** (⊠ Ul. Starowiejska 35, ☎ 058/21–91–64) has maps and sells train tickets. **Giżycko: Centrum Mazur** (☎ 0878/33–83). **Malbork: Orbis Malbork** (⊠ Ul. Przedzamcze, ☎ 055/32–59). **Sopot: Orbis** Sopot (⊠ Ul. Bohaterów Monte Cassino 49, ☎ 058/51–26–15).

WESTERN POLAND

Comprised of the provinces of **Wielkopolska** (Great Poland) and **Dolny Śląsk** (Lower Silesia), western Poland has always been the traditional heartland of the Polish state—despite spending much of the past half-millennium under German, Prussian, and Austro-Hungarian control. Great Poland is part of the flat, vast plain that extends north through Europe and is typified by smooth farmland, splotches of forest, and many lakes. There are many opportunities here for walking, swimming, fishing, and hunting. The hills of Lower Silesia rise gently to the Karkonosze Mountains, where you'll find more energetic walking trails and resorts that lure skiers during winter. Wrocław and Poznań, two of western Poland's primary cities, attract crowds year-round for theater, music, and other cultural diversions.

Although the early Polish state had its origins in the west, the region has fallen (more than once) under German influence. The Poles of Greater Poland are affectionately mocked by their countrymen for having absorbed the archetypal German habits of cleanliness, order, and—to put the matter politely—thrift. Lower Silesia and Pomerania were integrated with Poland only as recently as 1945, so don't be surprised if the west feels sober, restrained, and altogether more Germanic than anything else you'll find in modern Poland.

Gniezno, the first capital of Poland, is worth visiting for its cathedral, and, together with a visit to the nearby early lake settlement at Biskupin, could be a day trip from Poznań. Toruń, the birthplace of Nicholas Copernicus, is also a good base from which to explore the northern part of this region: It is attractively situated on the banks of the Vistula, has a good range of hotels, and has good rail and bus connections.

Numbers in the margin correspond to numbers on the Western Poland map.

Wrocław

91 *350 km (220 mi) southwest of Warsaw, 260 km (165 mi) northwest of Kraków, 170 km (105 mi) south of Poznań.*

Midway between Kraków and Poznań on the Odra River, Wrocław, the capital of **Dolny Śląsk** (Lower Silesia), dates to the 10th century, when the Ostrów Tumski islet on the Odra became a fortified Slav settlement. There are now some 100 bridges spanning the city's 90-kilometer (56-mile) network of slow-moving canals and tributaries, giving Wrocław its particular charm. Indeed, after Venice and St. Petersburg, Wrocław is the city with the third-largest number of bridges in Europe. Wrocław's population is also notable: Almost half the residents of Poland's fourth-largest city are less than 30 years old—most of them are students at one of the city's many institutions of higher learning.

Following the destruction that ravaged Wrocław during World War II, many of the city's historic buildings were restored. Wrocław's greatest architectural attractions are its many brick Gothic churches, the majority of which lie in or around **Stare Miasto** (Old Town) and **Ostrów Tumski**. This area is small enough to explore easily on foot.

The **Rynek** (market square) together with the adjoining **plac Solny** (Salt Square) form the heart of Stare Miasto, which stretches between the Fosa Miejska moat and the Odra River. Wrocław's Rynek is almost as grand as Kraków's and bustles with activity. The grandest of the colorful mansions that sit on Wrocław's Rynek are on the western side. Among these is the **Pod Gryfami** (Griffin House; ⊠ Rynek 2), which dates from the 15th century. Its steep gable is decorated with reliefs of eagles, lions, and griffins. Of the many old houses in the area, the two little **Jaś i Małgosia** (Hansel and Gretel) houses, just off the square to the northwest, are particularly appealing. They are linked by a **baroque arcade.** ⊠ *Intersection of ul. Odrzańska and ul. Wita Stwosza.*

★ The magnificently ornate **Ratusz** (town hall) is the highlight of the Rynek. Mostly Gothic in style, with a dash of Renaissance and baroque, the Ratusz was under continuous construction from the 13th to 16th centuries as Wrocław grew and prospered. In the center of the spired, pinnacled, and gabled **east facade** is a Renaissance **astronomical clock** from 1580. The **Gothic portal** was the main entrance of the Ratusz until 1616. The lavish **south facade,** dating from the 15th to 16th centuries, will leave you awestruck with its delicately wrought sculptures, friezes, reliefs, and oriels. The simple **west facade** is worth a peek just to see the flat oriel dated 1504. Today the Ratusz houses the **Historical Museum of Wrocław.** ⊠ *Rynek–Ratusz,* ☎ *071/44–36–38.* 🖃 *Zł 3, Wed. free.* 🕓 *Wed.–Fri. 10–4, Sat. 11–5, Sun. 10–6.*

★ The massive Gothic, 14th-century **Kościół świelej Marii Magdaleny** (St. Mary Magdalene's Church) has a 12th-century **Romanesque portal** on the south wall that is considered the finest example of Romanesque architecture in Poland. ⊠ *1 block east of the Rynek at the corner of ul. Szewska and ul. św. Marii Kaznodziejska.*

The 14th-century brick **Kościół świelej Elżbiety** (Church of St. Elizabeth) has been under reconstruction since fires ravaged it in 1975 and 1976. If the church is open, you can brave the 302-step climb to the top of the **tower** and look inside at its magnificent organ. ⊠ *Ul. Kiełbaśnicza; it can also be reached through the baroque arcade linking the Jaś and Małgosia houses at the intersection of ul. Odrzańska and ul. Wita Stwosza.*

Wrocław's university district lies between ulica Uniwersytecka and the river. The vast 18th-century **Wrocław University** was built between 1728 and 1741 by Emperor Leopold I on the site of the west wing of the former prince's castle. Behind the fountain and up the frescoed staircase is the magnificent assembly hall, **Aula Leopoldina.** The Aula is decorated with illusionist frescoes and life-size sculptures of great philosophers and patrons of learning. ⊠ *Aula, pl. Universytecki 1.* 🖂 *Zł 2 suggested.* ☉ *Daily 9–3:30.*

NEED A
BREAK?
Café Uni (⊠ Pl. Uniwersytecki 11) is a great place to sip coffee and admire the 565-foot facade of the university. The café has an outdoor patio and often hosts recitals.

★ **Ostrów Tumski** (Cathedral Island), to the north of the river—although no longer an island—is the cradle of Wrocław and one of its oldest and most charming quarters. Its winding streets, beautiful bridges, and wonderful churches are nine blocks northwest of the Rynek. The **Most Piaskowy** (Sand Bridge), which connects the left bank of the Odra with the Wyspa Piasek (Sand Island), halfway to Ostrów Tumski, was once part of the amber route, an ancient trade route that led from the Baltic down to the Adriatic. On the other side of Wyspa Piaskowa, the **Most Tumski** (Cathedral Bridge) and **Most Młyński** (Mill Bridge), two gracefully designed and painted bridges, lead to Ostrów Tumski.

On the **Wyspa Piasek,** directly opposite the Most Piaskowy, is a former Augustinian monastery used as Nazi headquarters during the war; the building is now the **University Library.** The 14th-century **Kościół Najświętszej Marii Panny** (St. Mary's Church) is in the middle of the island. The church's interior was restored after World War II to its original Gothic appearance, with a lofty vaulted ceiling and brilliantly colored stained-glass windows.

NEED A
BREAK?
The **vegetable market,** in the market hall next to the church, is a great place to buy picnic supplies for lunching on the banks of Cathedral Island. ☉ *Weekdays 8–6, Sat. 9–3.*

A cluster of churches stand on Ostrów Tumski including the **Kościół świelej Piotra i świelej Pawła** (Sts. Peter and Paul Church), which has no aisles. The early 14th-century Kościół świelej Krzyża (Holy Cross Church), just beyond the **statue of Pope John XXIII** (1968) on Ostrów Tumski, is housed on the upper level of a rigid and forbidding building erected by Duke Henryk as his own mausoleum (the duke's Gothic sarcophagus has been moved to the Wrocław Historical Museum). On the lower level of Duke Henryk's mausoleum lies the 13th-century Kościół świelej Bartłomieja (St. Bartholomew's Church).

The 13th-century **Katedra świelej Jana Chrzciciela** (Cathedral of St. John the Baptist; ⊠ Pl. Katedralny), with its two truncated towers, is the focal point of Ostrów Tumski. Its chancel is the earliest example of Gothic architecture in Poland. The cathedral houses the largest

Western Poland

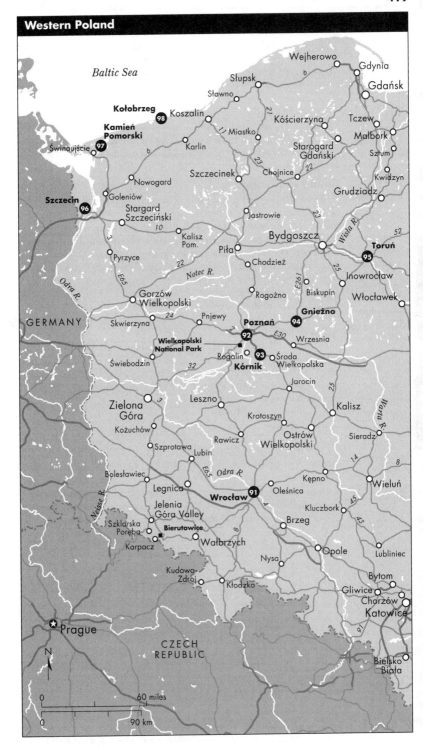

Baltic Sea

Wejherowo
Gdynia
Gdańsk

Słupsk
Sławno
Kołobrzeg
Koszalin
Kamień
Pomorski
Świnoujście
Karlin
Miastko
Kościerzyna
Tczew
Malbork
Starogard
Gdański
Sztum
Kwidzyn

Nowogard
Szczecinek
Chojnice
Grudziadz

Szczecin
Goleniów
Stargard
Szczeciński
Jastrowie

Pyrzyce
Kalisz
Pom.
Piła
Bydgoszcz
Toruń

Chodzież
Inowrocław
Włocławek

Notec R.
Rogożno
Biskupin

Gorzów
Wielkopolski
Pnjewy
Poznań
Gniezno

Skwierzyna
Wrzesnia

Wielkopolski
National Park
Rogalin
Środa
Wielkopolska
Kórnik

Świebodzin
Jarocin

Zielona
Góra
Leszno
Kalisz

Kożuchów
Krotoszyn
Sieradz

Szprotawa
Rawicz
Ostrów
Wielkopolski

Lubin
Bolesławiec
Odra R.
Kępno
Wieluń

Legnica
Oleśnica
Kluczbork

Jelenia
Góra Valley
Wrocław
Brzeg

Szklarska
Poręba
Bierutowice
Wałbrzych
Opole
Lubliniec

Karpacz
Nysa
Bytom

Kudowa-
Zdrój
Kłodzko
Gliwice
Chorzów
Katowice

GERMANY

Prague

N

CZECH
REPUBLIC
Bielsko
Biała

0   60 miles
0   90 km

organ in the country, featuring 163 stops and 10,000 pipes. On the southern side of the cathedral is **St. Elizabeth's Chapel,** with a notable fresco in its oval dome. The bust of Cardinal Frederick above the entrance, along with numerous other sculptures and frescoes, came from the studio of Bernini. The **Elector's Chapel,** in the northwestern corner of the cathedral, dates from the early 18th century and was designed by the baroque architect Johann Fischer von Erlach of Vienna. As these chapels are often closed, check at the sacristy for an update as well as for admission costs. The **Archdiocesan Museum** lies north of St. John's Cathedral on Otrów Tumski; it has a collection of medieval Silesian art. ⊠ *Ul. Kanonia 12,* ☎ *071/22–17–55.* ⊒ *Zł 2.* ☾ *Daily 10–3.*

Dining and Lodging

$$$ ✕ **Dwór Wazów.** This beautifully decorated establishment in the heart
★ of Wrocław is divided into two parts: restaurant-nightclub and café–wine cellar. The restaurant offers a Polish and international menu. The shashlik (grilled beef and peppers) served with brown rice is particularly tasty. The service is discreet and professional; most waiters speak both English and German. The atmospheric Renaissance-style wine cellar is a good place for conversation or relaxation on a hot summer's day. Try one of the Hungarian or Bulgarian reds, which are far better than the selection of French or Italian labels offered here. ⊠ *Ul. Kiełbaśnicza 2,* ☎ *071/44–16–33. Jacket required. AE, DC, MC, V.*

$$ ✕ **Grunwaldzka.** This is the place to try in Wrocław if you want a menu full of typical Polish fare. Heading the menu are *schabowy* (pork cutlet) with mashed potatoes and sauerkraut, fried liver with onions and rice, *zrazy wołowe* (stuffed and rolled beef), *kasza* (kasha: buckwheat groats), and *golonka* (pig's knuckle). ⊠ *Pl. Grunwaldzki 6,* ☎ *071/21– 98–21. No credit cards.*

$$$ 🏨 **Dwór Wazów.** This hotel has now been expensively renovated and the rooms are well-lighted and attractively furnished in soft, pastel colors. There is a limited number of rooms, so book early. ⊠ *Ul. Kiełbaśnicza 2, 50–108,* ☎ FAX *071/44–16–33. 54 rooms. Restaurant. AE, MC, V.*

$$ 🏨 **Hotel Europejski.** Renovations in this hotel have been sporadic, leaving half-old and half-new elements. Though the refurbished rooms are up to Western standards, they have Western prices to match. The small and simple older rooms are more reasonably priced, and guests can still gawk at the exquisitely redone lobby. ⊠ *Ul. Józefa Piłsudskiego 88, 50–017,* ☎ *071/310–71. 40 rooms, most with bath. Restaurant. AE, MC, V.*

Nightlife and the Arts

Kalambur (⊠ Ul. Kuźnicza 29A, ☎ 071/44–75–28) is an art-nouveau café-bar attached to a well-known small theater; there is sometimes live music.

Teatr Polski (⊠ Ul. G. Zapolskiej 3, ☎ 071/386–53) is the occasional home of the Wrocław Pantomime Theater. **Wrocławski Teatr Lalek** (Puppet Theater; ⊠ Pl. Teatralny 4, ☎ 071/44–12–17) is widely regarded as the best puppet theater in Poland.

The most renowned of Wrocław's festivals are June's **Jazz on the Odra,** which has attracted an international group of performers for the past 25 years, and September's **Wratislavia Cantans,** a series of 24 concerts featuring Gregorian chants, German oratorios, operas, cantatas, and other choral performances. Concerts take place at the cathedral, the Ratusz, and Wrocław University's Aula Leopoldina; ask Almatur,

IT, or Orbis (☞ Visitor Information *in* Western Poland A to Z, *below*) for the latest schedules.

The **Opera** (⊠ Ul. Świdnicka 35, ☎ 071/35–652) has performances Tuesday–Sunday in the Grand Opera House on plac Teatralny, south of the Rynek. Both **Operetka** (⊠ Ul. Piłsudskiego 67, ☎ 071/35–6521) and the **Philharmonic** (⊠ Ul. Piłsudskiego 19, ☎ 071/442–001) host classical performances several nights a week.

Poznań

92 *300 km (186 mi) west of Warsaw, 170 km (105 mi) north of Wrocław.*

Halfway between Warsaw and Berlin, in the middle of the monotonously flat Polish lowlands, Poznań has been an east–west trading center for more than 1,000 years. In the Middle Ages, merchants made a great point of bringing their wares here on St. John's Day (June 23), and the annual tradition has continued. (The markets have now been superseded by the important International Trade Fair, which has been held here since 1922.) Until the 13th century, Poznań was (on and off) the capital of Poland, and in 968 the first Polish bishopric was founded here by Mieszko I. It still remains the capital of the **Wielkopolska** (Great Poland) region.

Despite its somewhat grim industrial environs, Poznań has one of the country's most charming old towns; consider making the trek through western Poland if only to visit Poznań's majestic market square. Poznań may be only the fifth-largest city in Poland, but to a tourist it will feel larger than that. While the majority of sights are near the Old Town's impressive Stary Rynek, other attractions are far off in the sprawling maze of ancillary streets. Walking is not recommended here. Invest in some tram tickets and a city map with the transit routes marked; your feet will thank you.

Poznań's **Stary Rynek** (Old Market Square) mainly dates from the 16th century. It has a rather cluttered feeling, since the center is heavily built up, with both 20th-century additions and Renaissance structures. (Poznań residents will proudly tell you that the imposing, arcaded Renaissance

★ **Ratusz** (town hall) at the center of the Old Market Square is the most splendid building in Poland. Its clock tower is famous for the goats that appear every day at noon to butt heads before disappearing inside. Legend has it that the clock maker who installed the timepiece planned to give a party on the occasion. He ordered two goats for the feast, but the goats escaped and started fighting on the tower. The mayor was so amused by the event that he ordered the clock maker to construct a mechanism to commemorate the goat fight. The Ratusz now houses a **Museum of City History**, which contains a room dedicated to Chopin and a beautiful vaulted ceiling in the Great Hall. ⊠ *Stary Rynek 1*, ☎ *061/52–56–13*. ⊡ *Zł 2.5.* ☉ *Sun.–Fri. 10–4.*

NEED A BREAK?	**Eliksir** (⊠ Stary Rynek 61) is a cool and elegant café with white-marble floors. Its tables afford fine views of the adjacent square.

The tiny arcaded shopkeepers' houses in Poznań's Old Market Square date to the mid-16th century. Some of them now provide a home for the **Museum of Musical Instruments,** where you can see Chopin's piano and a plaster cast of the maestro's hands. ⊠ *Stary Rynek 45*, ☎ *061/52–08–57.* ⊡ *Zł 2.* ☉ *Tues. and Sat. noon–6, Wed. and Fri. 10–4, Thurs. and Sun. 10–3.*

One of the large 16th-century mansions on the Old Market Square is now the **Historical Museum,** which features temporary exhibitions on the history of Poznań and, recently, the Solidarity movement. ⊠ *Stary Rynek 3,* ☎ *061/52–94–64.* ⊡ *Free.* ⊙ *Tues.–Sat. 10–6, Sun. 10–3.*

On Góra Przemysława (Przemyslaw's Hill), just west of the Stary Rynek, is the neoclassical **Zamek Przemysława** (Przemysław Castle), which now houses the **Museum of Decorative Arts.** Among its holdings are unusual examples of wrought gold, Venetian glass, and Dutch porcelain; particularly interesting is its collection of woven sashes worn by Polish noblemen during the 18th century. The castle itself has been restored after being half destroyed during World War II. ⊠ *Góra Przemysława 1.* ⊡ *Zł 3.* ⊙ *Tues. and Sat. noon–6, Wed. and Fri. 10– 4, Thurs. and Sun. 10–3.*

Ostrów Tumski (Cathedral Island), an islet in the Warta River east of the Old Town, is the historic cradle of Poznań. This is where the Polanie tribe built their first fortified settlement and their first basilica in the 10th century. The present **Poznań Cathedral** was rebuilt after World War II in pseudo-Gothic style, but 10th- and 11th-century remains can be seen in some interior details. Directly behind the main altar is the heptagonal **Golden Chapel,** which is worth seeing for the sheer opulence of its romantic-Byzantine decor (1840). Within the chapel is the **mausoleum** of the first rulers of Poland, Mieszko I and Bolesław the Great. ⊠ *Ul. Mieszka I.*

Dining and Lodging

$$$ ✕ **Shogun.** This restaurant serves a small range of Japanese dishes— the smoked cod is particularly good—and also a European menu. It is thickly carpeted and decorated Japanese style with light wooden screens to separate tables. This is the smart place to be seen in Poznań, as the expensive cars in the parking lot testify. ⊠ *Ul. Wspólna 58,* ☎ *061/32– 20–14. AE, DC, MC, V.*

$$–$$$ ✕ **Poznań.** This hotel restaurant is large and slightly cavernous, though
★   the tables are discreetly separated by banks of plants, and the food and service are considered by many to be the best in Poznań. The menu includes Polish dishes common to western Poland; try the roast pork and potatoes with sour cream and dill. There is also a reasonable wine list. ⊠ *Pl. Dąbrowskiego 1,* ☎ *061/33–20–81. AE, DC, MC, V.*

$$ ✕ **Pod Koroną.** This recently renovated restaurant on the edge of Poznań's Old Town specializes in traditional Polish dishes like pig's knuckle (golonka) cooked in beer and honey, or veal with bacon and prunes. There's also a range of lighter entrées—steak and grilled salmon, among them—and a good selection of desserts. ⊠ *Ul. Zamkowa 7,* ☎ *061/52–20–47. AE, DC, MC, V.*

$$ ⊞ **Merkury.** This five-story, glass-front hotel is a standard Orbis product from the 1960s. Identical brown doors lead from long corridors into nearly identical rooms, which either look out onto the noisy intersection by the rail station or onto a quieter courtyard at the back. Furnishings are in dark and somewhat gloomy shades but are well up to the usual Orbis standard of comfort. Besides the Merkury's excellent location, with easy access to the station and town center, the other big plus is its parking facilities. ⊠ *Ul. Roosevelta 20, 60–829,* ☎ *061/ 47–08–01,* 𝔽𝔸𝕏 *061/47–31–41. 351 rooms, 42 suites. Restaurant, bar, café. AE, DC, MC, V.*

$ ⊞ **Dom Turysty PTTK.** This hotel has only a small number of rooms, but its location, right at the center of the Old Town, makes it an attractive option—if you can get in. Rooms are comfortably furnished, with Polish folk elements, and the staff is friendly and well informed about the city and current cultural events. ⊠ *Stary Rynek 91, 61–001,*

☎ 𝖥𝖠𝖷 061/52–88–93. *18 rooms; 8 singles, 10 doubles, some with bath. Restaurant, café. AE, DC, MC, V.*

$ 🏨 **Lech.** This older hotel stands in the center of town, near the university, and is a good base for exploring Poznań by foot. Rooms are on the small side but comfortably and cheerfully furnished. There is no restaurant service apart from breakfast, and the hotel bar sometimes attracts a rather rowdy crowd in the evenings. ⊠ *Ul. Św. Marcin 4, 61–809,* ☎ *061/53–01–51,* 𝖥𝖠𝖷 *061/53–08–80. 79 rooms; 34 singles, 44 doubles, 1 suite, all with bath. Bar. AE, DC, MC, V.*

Nightlife and the Arts

Stefan Stuligrosz's Boys Choir, the *Słowiki poznańskie* (Poznań nightingales), is one of Poznań's best-known musical attractions. ⊠ *Teatr Wielki, ul. Fredry 9,* ☎ *061/52–21–52.*

All the big hotels in Poznań have nightclubs with floor shows; the **Black Club** in the Hotel Merkury (⊠ Ul. Roosevelta 20, ☎ 061/47–08–01) is always crowded.

Filharmonia Poznańska (⊠ Ul. św. Marcina 81) holds concerts in the beautifully restored Aula of the university, where the acoustics are excellent.

OFF THE BEATEN PATH

WIELKOPOLSKI NATIONAL PARK – Twenty-five kilometers (15 miles) southwest of Poznań) is this pleasurable place for nature lovers and the sports-minded. It has 16 lakes set in pine forests full of many different types of birds and game. Lake Rusałka and Lake Strzeszynek have long beaches, tourist accommodations, and water-sports equipment for hire. Splendid legends abound here. At the bottom of Lake Góreckie, for example, there is supposed to be a submerged town, and on still nights if you're very lucky, you can hear the faint ringing of the town bells, although it's probably nothing more eerie than the call of water birds. *Take Hwy. 44 south from Poznań, and turn north for Nowy Tomyśl at Grodzisk Wielkopolski. A good point to enter the park is at Bukowiec. If you want to penetrate further into the park and visit Lake Zbąszyńskie, continue 12 km (7½ mi) farther along Hwy. 44 to Wolsztyn and then turn north for Zbąszyn.*

Kórnik

93 *20 km (12 mi) southeast of Poznań, Kórnik can be reached by PKS bus from Poznań.*

In the old town of Kórnik there is an 18th-century **neo-Gothic castle** surrounded by a moat. It now houses a museum full of hunting trophies and furnishings, as well as an enormous library of incunabula and rare books (more than 150,000 volumes, including manuscripts by Mickiewicz and Słowacki). Be sure to look down while you're viewing the exhibits—you'll be walking on some truly magnificent wood-inlay floors. The castle is surrounded by Poland's largest **arboretum,** with more than 2,000 varieties of trees and shrubs. ☎ *061/17–00–81.* 🎫 *Zł 5.* ☉ *Mar.–Nov., Tues.–Fri. and Sun. 9–3, Sat. 9–2; closed day after holidays.*

Gniezno

94 *50 km (31 mi) northeast of Poznań.*

The original capital of Poland, Gniezno owes this honor (according to myth) to some white eagles spotted nesting on the site by Lech, the legendary founder of the country, who named the town Gniezno (nesting site) and proclaimed the white eagle the nation's emblem. On a more historical note, King Mieszko I brought Catholicism to the Polish people during the 10th century and made Gniezno the seat of the country's first bishop, St. Wojciech. Lying along the Piast Route, Poland's historic memory lane running from Poznań to Kruszwica, Gniezno is surrounded by towns whose monuments date to the origins of the Polish state. The highlight of the area is Biskupin (☞ *below*). In Gniezno itself, the cathedral, with the remains of the bishop, and the Museum of the Original Polish State attract some visitors to this small, industrial town today.

★ The first **cathedral** in Gniezno was built by King Mieszko I before AD 977. The 14th-century building is considered the most imposing Gothic cathedral in Poland. On the altar a silver sarcophagus, supported by four silver pallbearers, bears the remains of St. Wojciech (Adalbert), the first bishop of Poland. At the back of the church the famous 12th-century bronze-cast **Doors of Gniezno** have intricate bas-relief scenes depicting the life of St. Wojciech, a Czech missionary commissioned to bring Christianity to the Prussians in northeastern Poland. Not everyone appreciated his message: He was killed by pagans. It is said that his body was ransomed from its murderers by its weight in gold, which the Poles paid ungrudgingly. ☉ *Cathedral Mon.–Sat. 10–5, Sun. and holidays 1:30–5:30.*

NEED A BREAK? | **Café Gwarna** (✉ Ul. Mieszka I 16), just off the market square, is a great place to relax after a morning of sightseeing.

Housed in a characterless concrete school building in Gniezno, the **Museum of the Original Polish State** shows multimedia exhibitions (in five languages, including English) on medieval Poland. ✉ *Ul. Kostrzewskiego 6,* ☎ *066/26–46–41.* ☉ *Tue.–Sun. 10–5.*

En Route Step back in time by wandering along the wood-paved streets and peering into the small wooden huts at the fortified settlement at **Biskupin,** 30 kilometers (18½ miles) north of Gniezno on the road to Bydgoszcz. This 100-acre Polish Pompeii is one of the most fascinating archaeological sites in Europe. It was discovered in 1933, when a local school principal and his students noticed some wood stakes protruding from the water during an excursion to Lake Biskupieńskie. The lake was later drained, revealing a settlement largely preserved over the centuries by the lake waters. Dating to 550 BC, the settlement was surrounded by defensive ramparts of oak and clay, and a breakwater formed from stakes that were driven into the ground at a 45° angle. A wooden plaque at the entrance shows a plan of the original settlement. An English-language pamphlet is available. ▱ *Zł 5.* ☉ *Daily 8–6.*

Toruń

★ ❾❺ *210 km (130 mi) northwest of Warsaw, 150 km (93 mi) east of Poznań.*

The birthplace of Nicolas Copernicus, the medieval astronomer who first postulated that the earth travels around the sun, Toruń is a beautiful medieval city, although pollution has taken its toll. Fortunately, because Toruń was left relatively undamaged in World War II, most of its ancient buildings are still intact. The **Stare Miasto** (Old Town) brims with ancient churches, civic buildings, and residences.

★ The **Copernicus Museum,** one block south of the Old Town Square, commemorates Toruń's most famous native son. It consists of two houses: the house at ulica Kopernika 17, where Copernicus was born and lived until he was 17 years old, and the adjoining one. The rooms have been restored with period furnishings, some of which belonged to the Copernicus family. You can view his research equipment and exhibits associated with him and his findings. In addition, collections of stamps, badges, coins, and other trinkets pay homage to this stargazing Pole. For a small fee, you can view a scale model of Toruń while listening to a recorded dialogue (available in English) that tells the story of the city from its founding to the present. While the story is narrated, slides simultaneously flash on the wall behind the scene, and lights direct your attention to relevant areas of the city. This entertaining and informative presentation provides you with a good feel for both the geography and the history of the city. ⊠ *Ul. Kopernika 17,* ☎ *058/267–48.* ▦ *Zł 3.5.* ☉ *Thurs.–Tues. 10–4.*

<table>
<tr><td>NEED A
BREAK?</td><td>A few steps down from the museum, at ulica Ducha Świętego 3, is the atmospheric café Kawiarnia Pod Atlantem (☎ 056/267–39). Waitresses in floor-length gowns serve decadent pastries and delicious lody (ice cream) at the antique dark-wood booths and tables.</td></tr>
</table>

Toruń's **Rynek Staromiejski** (Old Town Square) is dominated by the 14th-century **Ratusz** (town hall), one of the largest buildings of its kind in northern Poland. There are 365 windows in the Ratusz, and the hall's four pinnacles are meant to represent the four seasons of the year. Concerts and poetry readings are occasionally held in the hall. Information on such events, as well as on all of the museums of Toruń, can be obtained at the office inside.

Built in 1274, the Ratusz's **tower** is the oldest in Poland, although it did receive some later Dutch Renaissance additions. For a small fee, you can go up into the tower for a spectacular view. Traces of the wall that once divided the Stare Miasto from the Nowe Miasto are still visible. In the square outside the Ratusz is a **statue of Nicolaus Copernicus.**

Inside the Ratusz is the **historical museum,** which houses a collection of fine works from the region's craftsmen. The collection includes painted glass, paintings, and sculptures. Look for the gingerbread molds, which have been used since the 14th century to create the delicious treats for which Toruń is famous. ⊠ *Rynek Staromiejski 1,* ☎ *056/270–38.* ▦ *Free.* ☉ *Wed.–Sun. 10–4.*

In a building known as **Pod Gwiazdą** (House under the Stars), on Toruń's Old Town Square, the **Far Eastern Art Museum** houses collections from China, India, Japan, Korea, and Vietnam. The house itself may, however, be the most interesting feature of the museum. Built in the 15th century, it was remodeled in the 17th century in the baroque style by a wealthy Italian. Notice the carved-wood staircase. ⊠ *Rynek Staromiejski 35,* ☎ *056/211–33.* ▦ *Zł 2.* ☉ *Fri.–Tues. 10–4.*

Kościół świelej Jana (St. John's Church) was built in the 13th–15th centuries. This is where Toruń's most famous native son, Copernicus, was baptized. Special care has been taken in recent years to preserve the church, and regional artists are painstakingly restoring the Gothic frescoes. The **tuba Dei,** a 15th-century bell in the church's tower, is one of the largest and most impressive in Poland. ⊠ *South of the Rynek on ul. Żeglarska.*

In a pleasant park northeast of Toruń's Old Town stands the local **Ethnographic Museum,** one of the most interesting you'll find in Poland. Its collections include tools of the fisherman's trade—nets, rods, and boats—from Kashubia and other parts of northwestern Poland, folk architecture, and arts and crafts. Outside the museum are brightly decorated farmhouses that have been restored and filled with antique furnishings and art pieces. The grounds have been designed to replicate life in the Bydgoszcz region (west of Toruń) in the 19th and early 20th centuries. You can see 19th-century gardens and barns and an 1896 windmill removed from the nearby village of Wójtówka. ⊠ *Wały Sikorskiego 19*, ☎ *056/280–91.* ⊒ *Zł 2.5.* ☉ *May–Sept., Tues.–Sat. 10–2, Sun. noon–4; closed day after holidays.*

NEED A
BREAK?

In a restored thatched-roof farmhouse on the north side of the Ethnographic Museum, **Kawiarnia u Damroki** offers phenomenal coffee and pastries. The entrance is on ulica Juliana Nowickiego.

Dining and Lodging

$$ ✕ **Trzy Korony.** In one of the old houses on the square, this restaurant has been given a major face-lift in the 1990s. It specializes in regional dishes, including many varieties of meat-filled dumplings (*pyzy*) and thick bean soup (*zupa fasolowa*). The waitresses are friendly and willing to try some English. ⊠ *Rynek Staromiejski 21*, ☎ *056/260–31. AE, DC, MC, V.*

$$ ✕ **Zajazd Staropolski.** This traditional Polish restaurant features ex-
★   cellent meat dishes and soups in a restored 17th-century interior. ⊠ *Ul. Żeglarska 10–14*, ☎ *056/260–60. AE, DC, MC, V.*

$ ✕ **Hotel Helios Restaurant.** As at most other Orbis hotel restaurants, the food here is good and moderately priced, with an emphasis on Polish and Continental dishes. Clean and with decent service, it is a short walk from Rynek Staromiejski. Some of its tastier items are the pork and veal cutlets and the omelets. ⊠ *Ul. Kraszewskiego 1–3*, ☎ *056/ 235–65. AE, DC, MC, V.*

$ ✕ **Restauracja Staromiejska.** This is one of the best deals in town. The
★   new Italian owner renovated this restaurant's old wine cellar, restored the polished wood and stone floors, whitewashed the walls, and repaired the brick-ribbed, vaulted ceilings. Enjoy the excellent pizza as well as Polish fare. Coffee lovers will have to be dragged kicking and screaming out the door—an imported espresso maker whips up one of the best cappuccinos north of Italy. The restaurant also has an extensive wine list. ⊠ *Ul. Szczytna 2–4, no phone. Reservations not accepted. No credit cards.*

$$ ▥ **Helios.** This friendly, medium-size hotel is situated in the city center and offers a good restaurant (☞ *above*). ⊠ *Ul. Kraszewskiego 1, 87–100*, ☎ *856/250–33*, ⅏ *856/235–65. 140 rooms, all with bath or shower. Restaurant, beauty parlor, sauna, nightclub. AE, DC, MC, V.*

$$ ▥ **Hotel Polonia.** A favorite of Polish families, this antiquated hotel is just across the street from the Municipal Theater near the Rynek. The friendly new owner is renovating the place, and he plans to put in Swiss furnishings. The rooms are large, with high ceilings—unusual for Polish hotels. ⊠ *Pl. Teatralny 5, 87–100*, ☎ *856/230–28. 46 rooms, some with bath. Restaurant. AE, MC, V.*

$ ▥ **Kosmos.** A functional 1960s hotel, Kosmos is beginning to show signs of wear and tear—from the shabby furniture to the somewhat dank rooms. It is near the river, in the city center. ⊠ *Ul. Portowa 2, 87–100*, ☎ *056/270–85. 180 rooms, most with bath or shower. AE, DC, MC, V.*

$ ▥ **Zajazd Staropolski.** Cheaper than the two Orbis hotels in Toruń (He-
★   lios and Kosmos, *above*), this central hotel off Rynek Staromiejski is well maintained and has a friendly staff, most of whom speak either English or German. The hotel has a good, moderately priced restaurant, open until 10 PM. ⊠ *Ul. Żeglarska 10–14, 87–100*, ☎ *056/260– 61*, ⅏ *056/253–84. 33 rooms, all with bath. Restaurant. AE, MC, V.*

Western Poland A to Z

Arriving and Departing

BY BUS

Long-distance PKS services from other Polish cities arrive at **Dworzec Centralny PKS** (⊠ Ul. Kościuszki 135, ☎ 071/44–44–61 or 071/385–22), diagonally opposite the main train station in Wrocław.

The **Dworzec PKS** bus station in Poznań (☎ 061/33–12–12) is on ulica Towarowa 17–19, a short walk from the train station. Frequent bus service is available to and from Kornik, Łódź, and Gniezno.

Toruń's **PKS** bus station (⊠ Ul. Dąbrowskiego, ☎ 056/228–42) is east of the medieval Old Town. Take local Bus 22 to and from the station.

BY CAR

From the west, a full-fledged highway links Wrocław with the German border at Cottbus and provides a very smooth entry to the city. From Warsaw, the best route is to take the E16 to Częstochowa, and then travel by Highways 35 and 34 via Opole to Wrocław.

Poznań, on the main east–west route from Berlin to Moscow, is easily accessed by car. The E8, which leads from the border at Frankfurt an der Oder through Poznań and Warsaw to the eastern border at Breść Litewski (better known to Westerners as Brest Litovsk) is already a fullscale highway for most of its length; at press time is was being widened and upgraded.

BY PLANE

LOT offers daily flights from Warsaw to Wrocław. Special LOT buses shuttle passengers from Starachowice Airport to the LOT office (⊠ Ul. Józefa Piłsudskiego 77, ☎ 071/343–90–31), and buses leave from the same point for the airport one hour before each flight. City Bus 106 will also take you the 10 kilometers (6 miles) from the city to the airport.

Poznań's **Ławice Airport** is to the west of the city in the Wola district; buses run regularly to and from the LOT office at Świelej Marcina 69 (☎ 058/52–28–47); allow about an hour for the journey.

BY TRAIN

Wrocław Główny PKP (⊠ Ul. Józefa Piłsudskiego, ☎ 071/360–31, reservations ☎ 071/44–31–13) connects Wrocław by rail to most major cities in Poland, with frequent service to and from Kraków (five hours), Warsaw (six hours), Gdańsk (seven hours), and Rzeszów (7½ hours). Trains also leave here for many cities in Western and Eastern Europe: Dresden, Berlin, Prague, Budapest, and Frankfurt. The station is in the city center, a 30-minute walk south of the Rynek. It offers more services and all-night facilities than any other station in Poland, including a bus-ticket office, a pharmacy, a snack bar, and a movie theater.

The **Wrocław Nadodrze** (⊠ Pl. Powstańców Wielkopolskich) station is the hub for local routes to the east and southeast, including those going to Kluczbork, Kępno, Opole, Trzebnica, and Gniezno.

Trains run frequently from the modern **Poznań Główny** (☎ 061/69–38–11) station to Szczecin (three hours), Toruń (2½ hours), Wrocław (three hours), Kraków (eight hours), and Warsaw (four hours). International destinations include Berlin (5½ hours), Budapest (15 hours), and Paris (20 hours). The train station has a secure luggage-storage office, 24-hour post office, map store, snack bar, and a quiet café upstairs. From the central platform in front of the station, the best way into the city center is to take a bus up the long station approach road to ulica Świelej Marcina and turn right, or take steps up to ulica Towarowa, turn back over the railway bridge, and keep walking (the city center and bus station are straight ahead).

The **PKP** train station (☎ 056/272–22) in Toruń is south of the city, across the Wisła River. Take Bus 22 (follow the little bus signs from the station) to reach the city center. There's daily service to and from Poznań (three hours), Gdańsk (four hours), Warsaw (three hours), and Kraków (nine hours).

Getting Around

BY BUS

PKS offers comprehensive service in the region. Diagonally opposite the main train station in Wrocław, **Dworzec Centralny PKS** (⊠ Ul. Kościuszki 135, ☎ 071/44–44–61 or 071/385–22) serves local routes, with frequent service to Jelenia Góra, Trzebnica, Częstochowa, Łódź, and the spas of Kudowa, Duszniki, and Polanica.

BY CAR

The west of Poland has one of the best road networks in the country, and the largest number of gas and service stations per mile.

BY TRAIN

You might want to come to the **Wrocław Świebodzki** (⊠ Pl. Orląt Lwowskich) station just to admire the station building, which dates from 1848. Otherwise, you can catch local trains here to Głogów, Węgliniec, Bogatynia, Legnica, and Jelenia Góra.

Contacts and Resources

EMERGENCIES

Wrocław (☎ 999). **Poznań** (☎ 999).

LATE-NIGHT PHARMACIES

Wrocław (⊠ Pl. Kościuszki 17–18, ☎ 071/343–67–24). **Poznań** (⊠ Ul. 23 lutego 18, ☎ 061/52–26–25).

VISITOR INFORMATION

Wrocław: Two **IT** offices offer general tourist information in English (⊠ Rynek 29, ☎ 071/44–31–11; in PTTK office, Rynek 38, ☎ 071/44–39–23), both open weekdays 9–5, Saturday 10–2; **Orbis** offers maps and information in English (⊠ Rynek 45, ☎ 071/44–76–79). **Poznań: IT** (⊠ Stary Rynek 77, ☎ 061/52–61–56) sells excellent town maps and is open weekdays 9–5, Saturday 10–2; **Orbis** (⊠ Ul. Marcinkowskiego 21, ☎ 061/53–20–52) sells train and bus tickets. **Toruń: Orbis** (⊠ Ul. Żeglarska 31, ☎ 056/261–30) has maps and pamphlets, an exchange desk, the occasional English-speaking staff person, and a complete train timetable for all cities.

SZCZECIN AND THE COAST

Visitors from Germany and Scandinavia seeking some sun predominate at the towns along the Baltic, once home to fishermen. In summer, duck the droves of foreign tourists and set yourself up in one of the smaller fishing villages, where you'll be able to get to know Poles at close range.

Szczecin

96 *340 km (215 mi) west of Gdańsk, 515 km (325 mi) northwest of Warsaw, 240 km (150 mi) north of Poznań.*

The large port of Szczecin is on the Odra River just 48 kilometers (30 miles) from the German border. Despite its somewhat industrial atmosphere, Szczecin's location and the overall friendliness of its inhabitants (maybe it's that healthy sea air) make it a pleasant stop on your way to Germany or the towns on the Baltic coast. Ruled by several countries over the centuries, Szczecin (or Stettin in German) finally ended up as part of Poland after the Potsdam Conference of 1945. Although not on the coast, Szczecin is separated from the Baltic Sea only by the Szczecin Lagoon (Zalew Szczecinski). Szczecin was remodeled during the 19th century on the Parisian system of radiating streets and is particularly pretty in spring, when the avenues along the Odra River glow with flowering magnolias.

Though it is no longer the most important German Baltic port, Szczecin still carries many reminders of its Teutonic heritage, including the grandiose **Pomeranian Princes' Castle.** Originally built during the 13th and 14th centuries, the castle reached the height of its glory under a series of Pomeranian princes during the Renaissance. The past 300 years have not been kind to the castle, which fell into the hands of the Swedes, Prussians, and French only to be ruined by carpet bombing near the end of World War II. Today the reconstructed castle is a cultural center housing an art gallery, photographic exhibits, an opera hall, an open-air concert hall, a cinema, a café, and the music department of the university. ⊠ *Ul. Rycerska 1,* ☎ *091/34–78–35.*

Housed in a baroque palace and in an annex that faces it across the street, the **National Museum** in Szczecin is devoted mainly to art—older paintings, sculpture, and antiques (13th- to 16th-century Pomeranian), and some Polish pieces from the 17th century. The annex, devoted to modern Polish art, brings a welcome respite when you've seen one too many representations of the *Annunciation* or old pewter cups. It contains works by a diverse collection of internationally known artists—another way to gain insight into the culture of modern Poland. ⊠ *Ul. Staromłyńska 27–28,* ☎ *091/33–60–53.* ☐ *Both museums zł 4.* ☉ *Tues. and Thurs. 10–5; Wed. and Fri. 9–3:30; weekends and holidays 10–4; closed day after holidays.*

Dining and Lodging

$$ ✕ **Restauracja Balaton.** Named for the largest lake in Hungary, Balaton specializes in Hungarian cuisine at reasonable prices. The goulash soup served with bread is especially tasty and filling. The rustic wood-paneled atmosphere helps to ease the wait of the often slow service. ⊠ *Pl. Lotników 3,* ☎ *091/34–68–73. AE, DC, MC, V.*

$ ✕ **Restauracja Chief.** This quasi-elegant seafood restaurant, in the more modern area of town, is cleverly decorated with stuffed fish, lobsters, and turtles on the walls; aquariums with live fish and turtles fill the corners of the two main rooms. The courteous staff serves such fish dishes as halibut, as well as beef Stroganoff and the mandatory pork cutlet. ⊠ *Ul. Rajskiego 16,* ☎ *091/34–37–65. No credit cards.*

$$ 🏨 **Neptun.** This hotel offers comfortable rooms, each outfitted with
★ color TV, a large bathroom, and modern furniture. A favorite with German and Scandinavian businesspeople, the Neptun is one of the most cosmopolitan hotels in Szczecin. ⊠ *Ul. Matejki 18, 70–530,* ☎ *091/24–01–11,* 🖷 *091/22–57–01. Restaurant, 2 bars. AE, MC, V.*

$ 🏨 **Hotel Gryf.** The best feature of this large, weathered hotel is its central downtown location. A standard buffet breakfast, free to guests, partially makes up for the lack of decoration in the small but clean rooms. ⊠ *Al. Wojska Polskiego 49, 70–473,* ☎ *091/33–45–66,* 🖷 *091/33–40–30. 64 rooms with bath. Restaurant. AE, MC, V.*

$ 🏨 **Hotel Pomorski.** Though this is your average inexpensive Polish hotel, its central location makes it a good base for exploring Szczecin. The rooms (singles to quads) are nothing to rave about, but you'll survive.

✉ *Brama Portowa 4, 870–225,* ☏ *091/33–61–51. 38 rooms, some with bath. No credit cards.*

Kamień Pomorski

(97) *90 km (55 mi) north of Szczecin.*

On the mainland, across the mouth of the bay from Świnoujście, sits the small town of Kamień Pomorski. Mysterious carved-wood idols can be found along its beaches, a reminder of the Slavic settlements that once existed here. The old walls that originally encircled the town are no longer complete, but portions have survived, including the gateway, **Brama Wolińska,** on the west end of the **Rynek.** Also on the Rynek is a well-preserved **town hall,** but the town's most impressive structure is its **late-Romanesque cathedral,** with a splendid baroque organ. Free organ concerts take place in the cathedral every Friday night at 7 in summer, and there's even an International Organ Festival in June.

Lodging

$ **Nad Zalewem.** As its name—On the Bay—tells you, this small, clean pension has views over the water. Full board is possible, but meals have to be arranged beforehand. ✉ *Ul. Zaułek Rybackich 1,* ☏ *0928/20–817. 32 rooms. No credit cards.*

Kołobrzeg

(98) *150 km (93 mi) north west of Szczecin.*

Every summer the coastal town of Kołobrzeg attracts thousands of vacationers, mostly Poles and Germans, to lie on its beaches and stroll along its promenade. Aside from the **beach,** there's not much else of interest; the **Collegiate Church of St. Mary** near the station was severely damaged during the war but has been fairly well reconstructed. At the western end of the beach stands **Pomnik Zaślubin,** a monument to "Poland's reunion with the sea" after World War II, not far from the lighthouse near the mouth of the Parsęta River.

Dining and Lodging

$$$ ✕ **U Jana Rewińskiego.** This is the place to go for really fresh fish. There is a large terrace for outdoor dining in summer. ✉ *Ul. Morska 6, no phone. No credit cards.*

$$$ **Hotel Solny.** This 1970s Orbis hotel has fine sea views and comfortable accommodations. The restaurant is very large and specializes in sea food. ✉ *Ul. Fredry 4, 78–100,* ☏ *0965/22–401,* FAX *0965/25–924. 110 rooms with bath. Restaurant, café. AC, MC, V.*

Szczecin and the Coast A to Z

Szczecin is the gateway to Poland's Baltic coast.

Arriving and Departing

BY BUS

The **PKS** bus station (✉ Pl. Grodnicki, ☏ 091/469–80) is right behind the train station. Check here for service to obscure towns along the Baltic coast. The bus to Gorzów takes two hours, the one to Międzyzdroje, 2½ hours.

BY CAR

To reach Szczecin and Świnoujście from western and southern Poland, take the E65 from Wrocław and Świebodzin via Gorzów wielkopolski. From eastern and central Poland take the E75 to Toruń and then travel via Bydgoszcz, Piła, and Stargard szczeciński.

Passengers arriving by air in Szczecin are taken by bus to the **LOT** office at Aleje Wyzwolenia 17 (☎ 091/33–99–26), which takes about 45 minutes.

BY TRAIN
Dworzec Główny (✉ Ul. Kolumba, ☎ 091/395) has service to and from the following cities: Warsaw (five hours), Gdańsk (six hours), Berlin (three hours), and the small towns along the Baltic coast. The station is just south of the city on the river; take Tram 3 to reach the city center.

Getting Around
BY CAR
Generally the roads in this part of Poland are reasonably good, although stretches of secondary roads can be poorly surfaced and occasionally trail off into dirt tracks. The secondary road running nearest to the sea along the coast from Świnoujście through Kołobrzeg to Koszalin and beyond is generally good and has picturesque views. In the summer season, almost every small town and village has a 24-hour gas station.

Contacts and Resources
EMERGENCIES
Police (☎ 997). **Ambulance** (☎ 998). **Emergency** (☎ 999).

LATE-NIGHT PHARMACIES
Kołobrzeg (✉ Ul. Koszalińska 31, ☎ 0965/213–06). **Szczecin** (✉ Pl. Wolności 5, ☎ 61–28–20).

VISITOR INFORMATION
Kołobrzeg: Informacja Turystyczna (✉ Ul. Dubois 20, ☎ 0965/223–11). **Szczecin: Centralny Ośrodek Informacji Turystycznej** (✉ Ul. Tkacka 55, ☎ 379–18); **Orbis** (✉ Ul. Bolesława Krzywoustego 13/14, ☎ 451–54).

POLAND A TO Z

Arriving and Departing

By Bus
A number of new companies are operating bus services from Glasgow, Birmingham, Manchester, and London to Poznań, Warsaw, and Kraków. Most travel nonstop and take about 36 hours. What you lose in comfort you make up for in cost: The bus fare is roughly half the train fare. Contact **Fregata Travel** (✉ 100 Dean St., London, W1, ☎ 0171/734–5101; ✉ 117A Withington Rd., Manchester, ☎ 061/226–7227) or **Mazurkas Travel** (✉ Ul. Długa 8/14, 00–238 Warszawa, ☎ 022/635–16–93).

Regular bus service also runs from Warsaw and other major Polish cities to most Eastern and Central European capitals. Contact **Polski Express** (☎ 022/630–29–67) or **PKS** (☎ 022/22–48–11).

By Car
In summer, the border crossing points into Poland from Germany can still involve long queues, while queues at Poland's eastern borders are notoriously lengthy. Green card insurance is necessary if you are bringing your own car.

By Ferry
Polske Linie Oceaniczne (Polish Ocean Lines, ✉ Informacja Morskiego Biura Podróży, Chałubińskiego 4–6, Room 1308, ☎ 022/629–28–95) no longer operates a regular ferry service from London to Świnoujście or Gdańsk, though PLO offers occasional crossings during high sea-

son; it will also book you (and your car) onto cargo boats. The port city of Świnoujście is convenient if you plan to tour Poland's north coast. For destinations in central and southern Poland, it's more sensible to take the ferry from Harwich to Hamburg and then drive across northern Germany.

By Plane

FROM NORTH AMERICA

All flights from North America arrive at Terminal 1 of Warsaw's Okęcie Airport (Port Lotniczy), just southwest of the city. **LOT** Polish Airlines offers direct service from the United States.

FLYING TIME

The flying time from New York is 7 hours, 40 minutes; from Chicago, 9 hours, 25 minutes; from Los Angeles, 12 hours, 30 minutes.

LOT (☎ 022/630–50–07) and **British Airways** (☎ 022/628–94–31) operate flights from London's Heathrow Airport to Warsaw's Okęcie Airport. In the summer LOT also offers flights to Kraków and Gdańsk. Flying time is 2½ hours to Warsaw; 2 hours, 40 minutes to Kraków; and 2 hours, 20 minutes to Gdańsk.

Discount Fares: Certain travel agents charter seats on scheduled British Airways and LOT flights and offer budget fares on an Apex basis if you are staying for less than a month. Contact **Fregata Travel** (✉ 100 Dean St., London, W1, ☎ 0171/734–5101; ✉ Ul. Zielna 39, Warsaw, ☎ 022/620–78–20).

By Train

Direct trains to Warsaw run either from Victoria Station via Dover and Oostende or from Liverpool Street Station via Harwich and Hoek van Holland; their routes converge in Germany and enter Poland via Kunowice and Poznań. You can change at Poznań for Kraków and Gdańsk. Travel time direct to Warsaw is approximately 33 hours; to Kraków, approximately 37 hours; and to Gdańsk, 39 hours. In Poland, Orbis and other travel agents deal with the purchase of international rail tickets, as do all main city stations.

Getting Around

By Bus

PKS, the national bus company, offers long-distance service to most cities. Express buses, on which you can reserve seats, are somewhat more expensive than trains but often—except in the case of a few major intercity routes—get to their destination more quickly. For really out-of-the-way destinations, the bus is often the only means of transportation.There are also new private operators in the 1990s, some of whom undercut PKS prices on major intercity routes. For example, **Polski Express** (information and reservations, ☎ 022/630–29–67) runs services to seven major cities.

By Car

Poland has no full-blown highways, although new east–west international highways are under construction and some major roads (e.g., Warsaw–Katowice) are now entirely two-lane. This is still the exception rather than the rule, however, and traffic conditions can be difficult on long-distance routes. Horse-drawn traffic can still cause congestion even on major roads, and carts are particularly dangerous at night, when they often have inadequate lighting. Poles drive on the right, and there is an overall speed limit of 100 kilometers per hour (62 miles per hour). The speed limit in built-up areas is 50 kmh (30 mph); the beginning and end of these are marked by a sign bearing the name of the town in a white rectangle. At press time, the price of gas is between zł 8.5 and zł 12 for 10 liters of high octane. Filling stations appear about every 40 kilometers (25 miles) on major roads but can be difficult to find when you travel on side roads. They are usually open from 6 AM to 10 PM, although there are some 24-hour stations, usually in cities. For emergency road help, dial 981. The **Polish Motoring Association** (**PZMot**) provides free breakdown and repair services for members of affiliated organizations. Check details with Orbis. It is a good idea to carry spare parts, which can still be difficult to get for Western models. If you break down in a really remote area, you can usually find a local farmer who will help with a tractor tow and some mechanical skills.

By Ferry

You can take ferries or hydrofoils between various points on the Baltic coast; two of the more popular routes are Szczecin to Świnoujście, near the German border on the coast, and Sopot to Hel, farther east near Gdańsk.

By Plane

LOT Polish Airlines has domestic services linking many major Polish cities: **Warsaw, Gdańsk, Katowice, Kraków, Poznań, Rzeszów, Szczecin,** and **Wrocław.** Most days there is at least one flight between Warsaw and each of the other cities; flying time in each case is about 40–50 minutes. Compared with rail travel, flying is expensive (two to three times the price of a first-class rail ticket), and most airports are some distance from the city center. However, for Wrocław and Rzeszów, rail connections with Warsaw are so poor (Wrocław–Warsaw can take seven hours) that flying is a real time-saver.

By Train

Polish trains run at three speeds: *ekspresowy* (express), *pośpieszny* (fast), and (the much cheaper) *osobowy* (slow). Intercity expresses have been introduced on major routes; these provide high-standard accommodations, and coffee and sandwiches are included in the price of the ticket. Only the first two categories can be guaranteed to have first-class accommodations, and it is only on express trains that you can reserve a seat (indeed, these are by reservation only, although the conductor usually comes up with something at the last moment). *Couchettes* and sleeping cars (three berths to a car in second class, two berths in first class) are available on long-distance routes (e.g., Warsaw–Zakopane or Warsaw–Wrocław). Though buffet cars are usually available on express trains, it is a good idea to take along some food on a long trip; the buffet is quite likely to be canceled at the last moment, and its food can be unappetizing. Lines for tickets have sped up thanks to the introduction of computers at ticket windows. Tickets are issued for a given date, after which you get only two days' leeway to travel; thereafter they are invalid. Rail tickets are also available through Orbis and at other travel agents.

Contacts and Resources

B&B Reservation Agencies

Ogólnopolska Informacja Noclegowa (☞ Warsaw A to Z, *above*).

Camping

In theory, you are allowed to camp only at recognized sites, but there are plenty of these. Standards vary; local branches of PTTK are a good place to seek information.

Car Rentals

A valid driver's license issued in the United States, Canada, or Britain, or indeed in almost any other country, will enable you to drive without a special permit. You do, however, need green-card insurance if you are driving your own car.

You can rent a car through **Orbis** (☞ Visitor Information, *below*), which is affiliated with Hertz. Cars with both manual and automatic transmissions are available, starting at about $500 a week (including insurance and unlimited mileage). All the major car rental firms have offices at local and international airports and in towns and cities throughout Poland.

Avis Poland (⊠ Pl. Powstańców Warszawy 2, ☎ 022/625–08–55). **Hertz** (⊠ Ul. Nowogrodzka 27, ☎ 022/621–02–38). **Europcar** (⊠ Ul. Moliera 4/6, ☎ 022/022/26–33–44).

Customs and Duties

You may bring into Poland duty-free: personal belongings, including musical instruments; a typewriter or laptop computer; a radio; up to two cameras and 24 rolls of film; up to 250 cigarettes or 50 cigars; ½ liter of spirits and 2 liters of wine, together with goods that are not for your personal use up to the value of $200. Although customs checks have relaxed greatly since 1990, antique jewelry or books published before 1945 should be declared on arrival to avoid possible problems in taking them out of the country. Further information can be obtained from Customs Information, ☎ 022/650–28–73.

Government Tourist Offices

Orbis (☞ Visitor Information, *below*) is in the process of privatization, though it is still the main Polish tourist information office, with the largest number of branches throughout the country. It currently deals mainly with booking reservations in its own hotels (a policy that is certain to change) and with selling tickets for both domestic and overseas travel of all kinds.

IN CANADA

Poland has no travel office in Canada; for information, contact the Polish Consulate in Toronto (⊠ 2603 Lakeshore Blvd. W, Ontario MAV 1GS, ☎ 416/252–5471).

IN THE U.K.

Polorbis Travel Ltd. (⊠ 82 Mortimer St., London, W1N 7DE, ☎ 071/637–4971).

Guided Tours

SPECIAL-INTEREST TOURS

Orbis Special Interest Travel (⊠ Ul. Świętokrzyska 20, 00–113 Warsaw, ☎ 022/26–20–11) arranges customized tours built around particular themes, primarily for preorganized groups. Recent excursions have focused on music, opera houses, the castles and palaces of Poland, regional folklore and cuisine, Polish Judaica, beekeeping, farming, and gardening.

Language

Polish is a Slavic language that uses the Roman alphabet but has several additional characters and diacritics. Because it has a much higher incidence of consonant clusters than English, most English speakers find that it's a difficult language to decipher, much less pronounce (when you try to speak Polish, your mouth may feel as if it's full of wet cement, at least in the early stages). Bring a phrase book and a pocket dictionary with you (they can be hard to find in Poland), and the people you're trying to communicate with will appreciate the effort. The

BBC Polish Phrase Book, which contains a mini-dictionary, is a good starting point.

Older Poles are more likely to know French or German—and, of course, Russian, which they will not admit to—than English. Educated people under 40 are likely to have learned some English; everyone, at least in the cities, is apparently attending classes. You will almost always find an English speaker in hotels—even in small, out-of-the-way places; but away from the cities you will rarely be able to use English in shops, post offices, or other everyday situations. Although it is now chic to give shops an English name, this does not necessarily mean they will speak your language inside.

Mail

For information on postal services in Poland, ☎ 022/26–75–11. You can reach the DHL office at ☎ 022/606–89–00.

POSTAL RATES

Airmail letters to the United States and Canada at press time cost zł 1.50; postcards, zł 1. Airmail letters to the United Kingdom or Europe cost zł 1.20; postcards, gr 90. Airmail Express costs an extra zł 2.5 flat charge and cuts the travel time in half. Post offices are open weekdays 8–8. At least one post office is open 24 hours in every major city.

RECEIVING MAIL

The main post office in every town has *poste restante* (general delivery) facilities. Friends and family who send you mail should write "No. 1" (signifying the main post office) after the name of the city.

TELEGRAMS AND FAXES

You can send telegrams from any post office, or dial 905. The cost to the United States is about zł 1.5 per word, half that to points in Europe. Fax machines are available in most hotels and main post offices.

Money and Expenses

POLISH CURRENCY

The monetary unit in Poland is the *złoty,* which is subdivided into 100 groszy (gr). Since the currency reform of 1995, there are notes of 10, 20, 50, 100, and 200 złotys, and coins in values of 1, 2 and 5 złoty and 1, 2, 5, 10, and 50 groszys. However, the old, inflated banknotes— the highest of which represented 2 million złoty—remained in circulation until December 1996, and many Poles still prefer to use the old denominations when they talk about money and prices, continuing to refer to zł 2.5 as zł 25,000. This can cause confusion among Poles and visitors alike. At press time, the bank exchange rate was about zł 2.5 to the U.S. dollar, zł 1.8 to the Canadian dollar, and zł 3.8 to the pound sterling. Foreign currency can be exchanged for złotys at banks or at private change bureaus (*Kantor Wymiany Walut*), where the rate offered can be slightly higher than the bank rate, but the service is swifter. Currency-exchange controls are still officially in force, although they are progressively being relaxed and for tourists are now largely ignored. However, you are still required by law to declare all foreign currency when you enter Poland. Technically speaking, you also cannot export a larger sum of currency than you brought in, and you are legally forbidden to export złotys.

WHAT IT WILL COST

At press time, the annual rate of inflation, which was very high indeed in the early 1990s, was running at about 30% and was predicted to fall to 15% in 1996. The złoty has therefore become stronger and the exchange rate against Western currencies has stabilized. The days when you could exchange $50 on the black market and feel like a million-aire have gone forever. Even though most goods and services are still cheaper than in the West, they are creeping up to recognizably European levels. On the other hand, the deregulation of hotel prices offers visitors a greater range of options in selecting appropriate accommodations. Though the top hotels have retained the old fixed-dollar price, many others have dropped their charges; and in the provinces it is not a problem to find a decent hotel room for as little as $10. Overall, you can still get very good value for your money in Poland, and the farther you venture off the beaten track, the cheaper your vacation becomes.

SAMPLE COSTS
A cup of coffee will cost about zł 1.5–zł 5; a bottle of beer, zł 2–zł 4.5; a soft drink, zł 1–zł 4.5; a 1½-kilometer (1-mile) taxi ride, zł 4; a 240-kilometer (150-mile) train trip (first-class single), zł 40.

TAXES
A value-added tax (VAT) is applied to hotel and restaurant services at a level ranging from 20% in the top categories to 7% in the lower. Hotel and restaurant taxes apply only in the Zakopane region, where the local authorities have imposed a 10% tax on all goods and services for non-residents (locals produce their identity card, if necessary, in shops). There are no airport taxes.

National Holidays
January 1; March 30, 31 (Easter Sunday and Monday); May 1 (Labor Day); May 3 (Constitution Day); May 29 (Corpus Christi); August 15 (Assumption); November 1 (All Saints Day); November 11 (rebirth of the Polish state, 1918); December 25, 26.

Opening and Closing Times
In the 1990s, all the old rules about opening hours have been broken, and there is much greater variation across the country and even within cities. On the whole, the farther you get from the capital and the bigger cities, the earlier shops will open and close: 11–7 is standard in Warsaw, 10–6 in provincial towns. On Saturday, shops are now usually open until 1 PM or 2 PM. Banks are generally open weekdays 8–3 or 8–6. Museum hours, which have always been highly unpredictable, remain so. There is a very general rule that museums are closed Monday and the day after public holidays, but even this is far from universal. Apart from that, hours vary from day to day, so it's best to check each case separately.

Passports and Visas
U.S. citizens as well as British and other EU citizens are no longer required to obtain visas for entry to Poland (a valid passport will suffice). Canadian citizens must pay C$40 or C$80 for a single- or double-entry visa. Apply at any Orbis office (☞ Visitor Information, *below*), an affiliated travel agent, or at the Polish Consulate General in any country. Each visitor must complete three application forms and provide two passport-size photographs. Allow about two weeks for processing. Visas are issued for 90 days but can be extended in Poland, either through the local police headquarters or through Orbis.

Rail Passes
The Eurailpass has been accepted in Poland since 1995. The InterRail pass (☞ Rail Travel *in* Important Contacts A to Z), available exclusively to residents of the European Community, entitles travelers to unlimited second-class rail travel throughout Poland.

The **European East Pass** covers Poland, Czechoslovakia, Hungary, and Austria. Passes (first class only) cost $169 for five days' travel (spread over a 15-day period) and $275 for 10 days' travel (spread over a 30-day period). If Austria is not on your itinerary, this isn't much of a bargain. For more information, contact Orbis.

Student and Youth Travel

Almatur (✉ Pl. Politechniki 1, Room 135, ☎ 022/25–01–53), the Polish student-travel organization, can provide information on LOT airlines' volunteer work camps through CCIVS (Coordinating Committee of International Voluntary Service), study programs, and home stays through the Experiment in International Living. The group may also be able to help you find inexpensive accommodations, either in a youth hostel or a student hotel; but don't expect comprehensive budget-lodging information.

Telephones

The country code for Poland is 48; the Warsaw city code is 22.

LOCAL CALLS

Public phones vary in type. Older-type public phone booths take *żetony* (tokens) for gr 50 for local calls and zł 1 or zł 2 for long-distance calls, which must be made from special booths, usually in post offices. Place a token in the groove on the side or top of the phone, lift the receiver, and dial the number. Many phones automatically accept the token; in others you must push it into the machine when the call is answered. A 50-gr token buys you three minutes for a local call, after which you will be cut off without warning; avoid this by feeding the slot with as many tokens as you like at the beginning of your call or during your conversation. Phone booths taking cards are now widespread and can be used for both local and long-distance calls. Cards, which cost zł 7.5 or zł 15, are available at post offices and most newspaper kiosks. When making a long-distance call, first dial 0, wait for the dial tone, then dial the rest of your number. To place a domestic long-distance call to a number without a direct dial facility, dial 900.

INTERNATIONAL CALLS

If you can't find a card-operated pay phone, international calls are best made from post offices, where the counter clerk connects you and collects your payment; you'll avoid having to shovel large numbers of tokens into the pay phone. You can dial direct to almost all European countries and to the United States. For international collect and credit-card calls, dial an English-speaking operator at 0–0104–800222 (MCI). Or call 010–480–0111 (AT&T) from within Warsaw or 0–010–480–0111 (AT&T) from outside Warsaw.

OPERATORS AND INFORMATION

International Operator: Dial 901 (international operators speak English). For information on international codes dial 930. **Local Inquiries:** Dial 913. **Long-Distance Inquiries:** Dial 912.

Tipping

Inflation has brought disorientation to Poland, but one thing for sure is that people expect higher tips in Warsaw than in the provinces. Service charges are added to bills in more expensive restaurants, but it is still customary to leave something, usually another 10%, for the waiter. Taxi drivers are not usually tipped, although you can round up to the nearest złoty if you wish. A tip of zł 2 is in order for porters carrying bags or for room service, although in very expensive hotels you could raise this to zł 5. Concierges and tour guides should also get at least zł 5.

Narodowej 49a, Warsaw, ☎ 091/33–58–32).
Pomerania (✉ Pl. Brama Portowa 4, Warsaw, ☎ 091/34–72–08 or 091/34–28–61) can provide maps and brochures as well as information on a range of accommodations from hotels to private lodgings to campgrounds throughout the region; it's open in the summer, daily 8–4. **Orbis** (✉ Pl. Zwycięstwa 1, Warsaw, ☎ 091/34–51–54) is primarily concerned with domestic and international train travel, though it has some local tourist information. The office is open daily 8–5.

6 Bulgaria

Slightly smaller than the state of Tennessee, Bulgaria is "a land as big as the palm of one's hand," as its poets have often said. At the crossroads of Europe and Asia, once ruled by the Turks, the "Jewel of the Balkans" offers a unique mix of Eastern and Slavic cultures. It is home to towering mountains with rugged hilltop monasteries, the colorful farmland of the fertile Danube plains, and a coastline strewn with miles of golden beaches and peaceful waterfront towns.

BULGARIA, A LAND OF MOUNTAINS AND SEASCAPES, of austerity and rustic beauty, lies in the eastern half of the Balkan Peninsula. From the end of World

Updated by
Ivanka Tomova

War II until recently, it was the closest ally of the former Soviet Union and presented a rather mysterious image to the Western world. This era ended in 1989 with the overthrow of Communist Party head Todor Zhivkov. Since then, Bulgaria has gradually opened itself to the West as it struggles along the path toward democracy and a free-market economy. Many Bulgarians believed the "miracle" of Westernization would bring prosperity overnight. But as time wears on, it's obvious that meaningful reform may take years to implement, perhaps decades to succeed. Although you may still feel some lingering Communistic characteristics when traveling (for example, at all times you must carry, on your person, a *Carte Statistique,* which must be stamped at every place you stay), it is becoming easier to get around Bulgaria. The tourist industry is quite well developed and is being restructured to shield visitors from shortages of goods and services and the other legacies of rigid central planning.

Founded in 681, Bulgaria was a crossroads of civilization even before that date. Archaeological finds in Varna, on the Black Sea coast, give proof of civilization from as early as 4600 BC. Bulgaria was part of the Byzantine Empire from AD 1018 to 1185 and was occupied by the Turks from 1396 until 1878. The combined influences are reflected in Bulgarian architecture, which has a truly Eastern feel. Five hundred years of Muslim occupation and nearly half a century of Communist rule did not wipe out Christianity, and there are many lovely, icon-filled churches to see. Some 120 monasteries, with their icons and many frescoes, provide a chronicle of the development of Bulgarian cultural and national identity, and several merit special stops on any tourist's itinerary.

The Black Sea coast along the country's eastern border is particularly attractive, with secluded coves and old fishing villages, as well as wide stretches of shallow beaches that have been developed into self-contained resorts. The interior landscape offers magnificent scenic beauty, with a tranquil world of forested ridges, spectacular valleys, and rural communities where folklore is a colorful part of village life.

The capital, Sofia, is in a valley at the base of Mt. Vitosha. You may be pleasantly surprised at the amount of cultural activity in this thriving city too often overlooked by travelers. Other main towns are Veliko Târnovo, the capital from the 12th to the 14th centuries; Plovdiv, southeast of Sofia, which has a particularly interesting old quarter; and Varna, Bulgaria's most important port.

Pleasures and Pastimes

Architecture

Old Bulgarian architecture is best seen in the country's towns and villages with cobbled streets, stone-vaulted bridges, and wooden houses. The houses you see in Bansko may seem inaccessible with their solid walls, latticed windows, and heavy gates, but the rooms inside provide a lively contrast, with carved ceilings and colorful handmade rugs. Other architectural gems can be seen in Melnik, Nesebar, Sozopol, Koprivstitsa, and in the Old Town of Plovdiv.

Churches, Monasteries, and Icon Paintings

Most Bulgarian churches and monasteries are monuments of the Bulgarian National Revival period (18th and early 19th centuries), a time

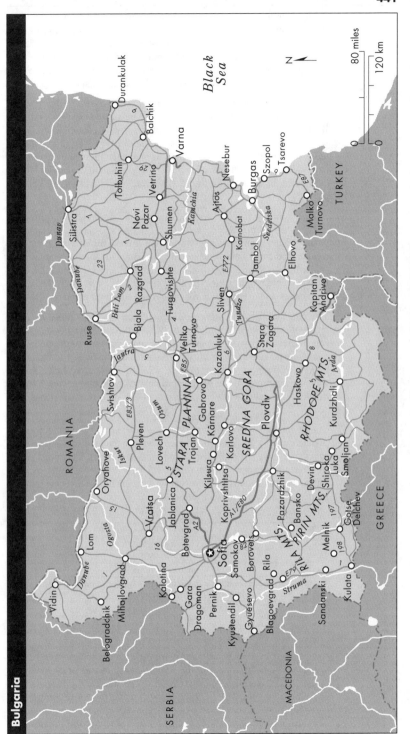

Bulgaria

of vigorous cultural activity and increased awareness of a national identity. The churches and monasteries have guarded the spirit and language of the country. The famous Rila Monastery is included on the UNESCO list of World Heritage Sites. The Bachkovo and Trojan monasteries are both well known for their splendid murals and icons, painted by Zahari Zograph and other great National Revival artists.

The tradition of the Bulgarian icon goes back to the 9th century, when the Bulgarians converted to Christianity. During and after the National Revival period of the 18th and 19th centuries, many icon-painting schools were formed. The schools of Bansko, Samokov, and Trojan produced icons for the newly built churches and private homes. The biggest collections of icons are displayed in the Crypt Museum of Alexander Nevski Cathedral in Sofia and in the Museum of Art and History in Varna.

Dining

Balkan cooking revolves around lamb, pork, sheep cheese, potatoes, peppers, eggplant, tomatoes, onions, carrots, and spices. Typical Bulgarian dishes include peppers and vine leaves stuffed with meat and rice, grilled meat balls, and kebabs. Bulgaria invented yogurt (*kiselo mleko*), with its promise of good health and longevity, and there are excellent cold yogurt soups (*tarator*) served in summer. Rich cheese and fruit cakes and syrupy *baklava* are served to round out a meal.

The national drink is *rakia*—plum or grape brandy, *slivova* or *grosdova*—but vodka is popular, too. Bulgarian wines are good, usually full-bodied, dry, and inexpensive. You may want to try the Bulgarian chardonnay, *traminer*, or muscat. As for the red wines, the Bulgarian cabernet sauvignon and merlot are excellent choices. Coffee is strong and is often drunk along with a cold beverage, such as cola or a lemon drink. Tea is taken with lemon instead of milk.

There is a choice of: hotel restaurants with international menus, Balkantourist restaurants, or the less expensive restaurants and cafeterias run privately and by cooperatives. The best bets are the small folk-style restaurants that serve national dishes and local specialties. The word *picnic* in a restaurant name means the tables are outdoors. Standards have improved, but food is still rarely served piping hot, and visitors should be prepared for loud background music.

CATEGORY	COST*
$$$$	over 1,000 leva
$$$	600 leva–1,000 leva
$$	300 leva–600 leva
$	under 300 leva

per person for a three-course meal, including tip but not alcohol

Hiking and Walking

The mountains of Vitosha, Rila and Pirin, and the Rhodopes are good for walking. Nature lovers will appreciate Vitosha for its beautiful moraines, Rila and Pirin for their clear blue lakes, and the Rhodopes for their green slopes and rare plants (the country has over 12,000 species). The higher slopes of the Rhodopes are covered with pines and spruce, and under these ancient trees grow wintergreen, twinleaf squill, and coral root. The Balkan range, which crosses the entire country, has splendid rocks and caves. Two of the most interesting are Ledenika and Magura, with their veritable scuptures of stalactites and stalagmites.

Lodging

There is a wide choice of accommodations, ranging from hotels—most of them dating from the '60s and '70s—to apartment rentals, rooms in private homes, and campsites. Although hotels are improving, they still tend to suffer from temperamental wiring and erratic plumbing, and it is a good idea to pack a universal drain plug, as plugs are often missing in hotel bathrooms. In moderate and inexpensive hotels, bathrooms often look unusual. Don't be surprised if strangely placed plumbing turns the entire bathroom into a shower. Flashlights and other battery-powered utilities are strongly recommended, as there are likely to be power outages in winter. However, quirks like these in accommodations give you a sense of the real Bulgaria.

Until recently, most hotels used by Western visitors were owned by Balkantourist and Interhotels. At press time many of the government-owned or -operated hotels were on the verge of privatization. The conversion is expected to take up to five years. Hotels may be closed for renovation for extended periods or may be permanently shut down. We strongly urge you to contact hotels in advance to get the latest information. Most have restaurants and bars; the large, modern ones have swimming pools, shops, and other facilities. Some coastal resorts have complexes where different categories of hotels are grouped, each with its own facilities. Popping up all along the coast are new private hotels, which have lots of personality, as opposed to the ever-so-common large, nondescript hotels. Most of these small hotels are family houses in small towns and villages south of Burgas.

CATEGORY	SOFIA*	OTHER AREAS*
$$$$	over $200	over $75
$$$	$75–$200	$55–$75
$$	$40–$75	$30–$55
$	under $40	under $30

All prices are for two people in a double room with half board (breakfast and a main meal). You can pay in either Western or local currency, but if you pay in leva, you must show your exchange slips to prove that the money was changed legally.

Music
You can hear Bulgarian folk music at numerous folk festivals around the country, including two important ones held in Koprivstitsa and near Pamporovo. Bulgarian folk dances are performed to traditional music by dancers in brightly colored costumes, which differ according to the region of the country.

The opera companies of Sofia, Varna, and Ruse keep the glorious tradition of vocal singing alive. International festivals of symphonic music are held throughout the country—Sofia has Sofia Music Weeks in May and June, Ruse has March Music Days, and Varna has Varna's Summer in June and July.

Skiing
Vitosha, Borovec, Pamporovo, and Bansko—all with both beginner and expert slopes—are Bulgaria's best skiing resorts. Bansko is one of Bulgaria's winter hot spots.

Spa Resorts
There are hundreds of mineral springs in Bulgaria. Their healing properties were well known to the ancient Romans. The spa hotels in the resorts of Sandanski and Velingrad have various traditional and new prophylactic and treatment methods including manual therapy, acupuncture, phytobalneology, phytotherapy, and slimmimg cures. The Black Sea hydrotherapy centers in Sveti Konstantin, Albena, and Pomorie are famous for their healing mud. The mineral waters along the northern Black Sea coast turn the sea resorts into year-round spas.

Exploring Bulgaria

Bordered by Romania to the north (the Danube River forms the border), Serbia and the former Yugoslav Republic of Macedonia to the west, Greece and Turkey to the south, and the Black Sea to the east, Bulgaria is in the southeastern corner of Europe in the heart of the Balkan Peninsula. Sofia, Bulgaria's capital, lies in the western part of the country. Geographically, Bulgaria can be divided into two basic regions: the Inland and the Black Sea Golden Coast. Inland you'll find one of Bulgaria's two chief attractions—its towering mountains—and on the Black Sea you'll find the other—its glittering seacoast.

Great Itineraries

Bulgaria is small, but its nature and landscapes are so diverse that it may take some time to absorb and appreciate its singular beauty. If you have more than a week to tour the country, you'll be able to see most of it. If you have less than a week, you'll still get to see some major sights and get an impression of the country and its people. If two or three days are all you have, you'll unfortunately have to choose between the mountains and the sea.

Numbers in the text correspond to numbers in the margin and on the maps.

IF YOU HAVE 3 DAYS

Begin in **Sofia** and spend the day in the central part of the city—be sure to visit the magnificent Alexander Nevski Cathedral, the rich collections of the National History Museum, and some of the new art galleries. On the second day, head for ⊞ **Plovdiv.** Spend the morning walking around in Plovdiv's Old Town. You'll see the museum houses, which will give you a feeling for the history of the country. This old Thracien town is more ancient than Bulgaria itself. In 342 BC it was conquered by Philip II of Macedonia, and not until AD 815 did the city become part of Bulgaria. Overnight here in Plovdiv and on the third day, pass through the town of **Karlovo** to ⊞ **Koprivstitsa,** where you can see some of the finest examples of typical old Bulgarian architecture. Or, instead of heading toward Koprivstitsa, you can go to ⊞ **Borovec,** the oldest and the biggest mountain resort in Bulgaria, at the foot of the highest peak on the Balkan Peninsula.

IF YOU HAVE 5 DAYS

Spend a day in **Sofia,** and from there travel to ⊞ **Rila Monastery,** founded in the 10th century by St. Ivan Rilski, a prophet and healer. Spend the night there and leave the next morning for ⊞ **Bansko** by way of **Blagoevgrad.** In Blagoevgrad, spend some time walking around in the center of town. Next, continue on to Bansko, another museum town with charming National Revival houses. Here you can spend the night. The third day, go hiking in the Pirin Mountains. You'll find gorgeous flower-covered slopes in spring and early summer; in winter, you'll find the slopes covered with snow. Return back to Bansko and spend the night. The fourth day you can visit ⊞ **Sandanski,** southwest of Bansko, and bathe in the area's warm mineral waters. Overnight in Sandanski and continue to **Melnik,** the smallest Bulgarian town, with a population of 417, famous for its architecture, sandstone-rock formations, and red wine. From Melnik, before going back to Sofia, you can visit the Rozhen Monastery, most of it decorated by unknown painters.

When to Tour

Summers here are warm, and winters are crisp and cold. If you're looking for sun, head to Bulgaria in July or August. Although this is Bulgaria's "high season," the only places you'll find crowds are the Black Sea coast and Sofia. Even when the temperature climbs in summer, the Black Sea breezes and the cooler mountain air prevent the heat from being overpowering.

Don't limit yourself to summer for a visit to Bulgaria though—the coastal areas get considerable sunshine year-round. The inland areas, however, are wet during most of March and April. If you're planning to ski, the season is mid-December through March; the coldest month is January.

May and September are two of the country's most enjoyable months. Fruit trees blossom in April and May; in May and early June the blossoms are gathered in the Valley of Roses (you have to get up early to watch the harvest); fruit is picked in September, and in October the fall colors are at their best.

SOFIA

Exploring Sofia

Sofia is set on the high Sofia Plain, ringed by mountain ranges: the Balkan range to the north; the Lyulin Mountains to the west; part of the Sredna Gora Mountains to the southeast; and, to the southwest, Mt. Vitosha, the city's playground, 7,500 feet high. The area has been inhabited for about 7,000 years, but the visitor's first impression is of a modern city with broad streets, heavy traffic, spacious parks, and open-air cafés. As recently as the 1870s it was part of the Turkish Empire, and one mosque still remains. Most of the city, however, was planned after 1880. The city's colorful atmosphere is both old and new, with well-preserved architectural monuments and modern administrative buildings.

Numbers in the text correspond to numbers in the margin and on the Sofia map.

A Good Walk

Begin your tour in the heart of Sofia at the crowded and lively Ploshtad Sveta Nedelya (St. Nedelya Square), named after the church, **Tzarkva Sveta Nedelya** ①, that dominates its south side. Behind the church, on the west side of Vitosha Boulevard, is the **Natzionalen Istoricheski Musei** (National History Museum) ②. On the north side of St. Nedelya Square is the **Rotonda Sveti Georgi** (Rotunda of St. George) ③, the oldest archaeolgical monument in Sofia. Heading east from here, you'll enter Alexander Batenberg Square and see the huge **Partiyniyat Dom** (the former headquarters of the Bulgarian Communist Party)—its architecture is reminiscent of the country's recent communist history.

Near the southwestern corner of the square is the **Natzionalen Archeologicheski Musei** (National Archeological Museum) ④. Next to the museum is the **Mavsolei Georgi Dimitrov** (Georgi Dimitrov Mausoleum) ⑤. Across from the mausoleum is the former royal palace, which today houses the **Natzionalen Etnografski Musei** (National Ethnographical Museum) ⑥ and the **Natzionalna Hudozhestvena Galeria** (National Art Gallery) ⑦. One block away on the left side of the street is **Tzarkva Sveti Nikolai** (Church of St. Nicholas) ⑧. From here, walk down Tsar Osvoboditel Boulevard, with its monument to the Russians, topped by the equestrian statue of Russia's Czar Alexander II. It stands in front of the National Assembly. Behind the National Assembly, just beyond Shipka Street, you'll be confronted by the **Hram-pametnik Alexander Nevski** (Alexander Nevski Memorial Church) ⑨. Here you should also take a look at the Crypt Museum inside. Across the square

Sofia

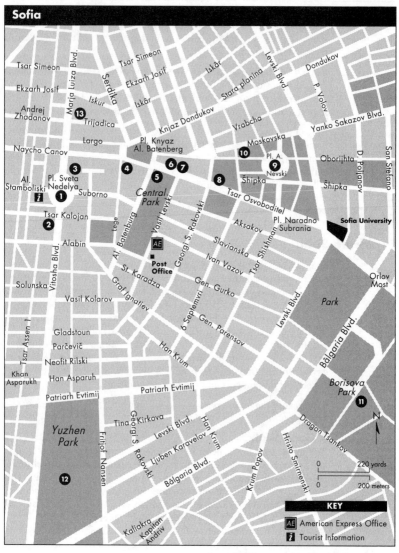

Banya Bashi
Djamiya, **13**

Borisova Gradina, **11**

Former Mavsolei
Georgi Dimitrov, **5**

Hram-pametnik
Alexander Nevski, **9**

Natzionalen
Archeologicheski
Musei, **4**

Nacionalen Dvoretz
na Kulturata
(NDK) **12**

Natzionalen
Etnografski Musei, **6**

Natzionalen
Istoricheski Musei, **2**

Natzionalna
Hudozhestvena
Galeria, **7**

Rotonda Sveti
Georgi, **3**

Tzarkva Sveta
Nedelya, **1**

Tzarkva Sveta
Sofia, **10**

Tzarkva Sveti
Nikolai, **8**

from the memorial church is the much older **Tzarkva Sveta Sofia** (Church of St. Sofia) ⑩. Return to Tsar Osvoboditel Boulevard through Alexander Nevski Square. If you continue east, you'll reach **Borisova Gradina** (Boris's Garden) ⑪.

From the park, walk south past the big sports stadium until you come to Dragan Tsankov Boulevard. Next, turn down Graf Ignatiev Street and head west to the monument of Patriarh Evtimij. Take the boulevard of the same name until you reach the **Natzionalen Dvoretz na Kulturata** (National Palace of Culture) ⑫.

Next, walk along Vitosha Boulevard back to St. Nedelya Square, and then follow Knyaginya Maria-Luiza Boulevard to the train station. On the right is the Tsentralen Universalen Magazin (Central Department Store). Just beyond this big store is the **Banya Bashi Djamiya** (Banya Bashi Mosque) ⑬ and across the boulevard from the mosque is Tsentralni Hali (Central Market Hall), which is unfortunately closed for renovations but is in the city center, so it's a good place to end your tour.

Timing

This walking tour covers a distance of about 5 to 6 kilometers (3 to 4 miles) and will take about four hours to complete. If you visit the National History Museum, you'll need to allow one or more extra hours because there's so much to see. You can also combine a tour of Sofia with a short walk on Mt. Vitosha. To do this, you'll need six to seven hours. It's best to head for Vitosha during the week, as it's much less crowded than on weekends. If you like to ski, Vitosha is usually covered with snow in winter (December–March). There are several ski lifts on the mountain, and rental skis are available.

Sights to See

⑬ **Banya Bashi Djamiya** (Banya Bashi Mosque). A legacy of Turkish domination, this 16th-century mosque is one of the most noteworthy sights in Sofia, with its imposing dome and elegant minaret. Built in 1576 by the Turkish architect Sinan, the mosque was named (*banya* means baths) for its proximity to mineral baths. The interior is closed to the non-Islamic public. ⊠ *Bul. Maria Luiza, across from Central Market Hall.*

⑪ **Borisova Gradina** (Boris's Garden). This spacious park is a veritable oasis in the middle of the city. With a lake, fountains, woods, and lawns, it's a beautiful place for walking. It has a huge sports stadium and an open-air theater. ⊠ *Bâlgaria Blvd. and Dragan Cankov.*

★ ⑨ **Hram-pametnik Alexander Nevski** (Alexander Nevski Memorial Church). You may recognize this neo-Byzantine structure with glittering onion domes from the pictures that appear on almost every piece of tourist literature. It was built by the Bulgarian people at the beginning of the 20th century as a mark of gratitude to their Russian liberators. Inside are alabaster and onyx, Italian marble and Venetian mosaics, magnificent frescoes, and space for a congregation of 5,000. There's a fine collection of icons and religious artifacts in the **Crypt Museum**. The works represent important periods in Bulgarian history—Byzantine influence, Ottoman rule, and the National Revival period. On Sunday morning you can attend a service to hear the superb choir. In the area near and around the church, you may be harassed by one of the many ladies selling lace tablecloths. ⊠ *Alexander Nevski Sq.*, ☎ *2/87–76–97.* ▨ *50 leva.* ☉ *Wed.–Mon. 10:30–5.*

⑤ **Former Mavsolei Georgi Dimitrov** (Georgi Dimitrov Mausoleum). A reminder of the recent communist past, this building contained, until 1990, the embalmed body of the first general secretary of the Bulgarian Communist Party, who died in Moscow in 1949 and was known as the "Father of the Nation." His remains have been moved to the Central Cemetery, and there is talk of either converting the mausoleum into a museum or destroying it. ⊠ *Alexander Batenberg Sq.*

★ ❹ **Natzionalen Archeologicheski Musei** (National Archaeological Museum). This museum is housed in the former Great Mosque. The 15th-century building itself is as fascinating as its contents, which illustrate the cultural history of the country up through the 19th century. ⊠ *Alexander Batenberg Sq., behind the Sheraton Hotel,* ☎ *2/88–24–06.* ⊙ *Tues.–Sun. 10–noon and 2–6.*

⑫ **Natzionalen Dvoretz na Kulturata** (National Palace of Culture). This large modern building, filled with a complex of halls for conventions and cultural activities, is the main focus of **Yuzhen Park.** Its underpass, on several levels, is equipped with a tourist information office, shops, restaurants, discos, and a bowling alley. The park itself is a great place for people-watching. ⊠ *Yuzhen Park, off Vitosha Blvd.,* ☎ *2/5–15–01.*

❻ **Natzionalen Etnografski Musei** (National Ethnographical Museum). Collections of costumes, handicrafts, and tools exhibited here in the former palace of the Bulgarian czar illustrate the agricultural way of life of rural people until the 19th century. ⊠ *1 Alexander Batenberg Sq.,* ☎ *2/87–41–91.* ⊙ *Wed.–Sun. 10–noon and 1:30–5:30.*

❷ **Natzionalen Istoricheski Musei** (National History Museum). Priceless Thracian treasures, Roman mosaics, enameled jewelry from the First Bulgarian Kingdom, and glowing religious art that survived the years of Ottoman oppression vividly illustrate the art history of Bulgaria. Considered the most important museum in the city, it occupies the former Courts of Justice. The courts are due to return to this location as soon as a new home is found for the National History Museum collection. ⊠ *2 Vitosha Blvd.,* ☎ *2/88–41–60.* ▣ *150 leva.* ⊙ *Weekdays 9:30–4:30.*

❼ **Natzionalna Hudozhestvena Galeria** (National Art Gallery). Here, in the west wing of the former royal palace are paintings by the best Bulgarian artists as well as representative works—notably prints—from the various European schools. ⊠ *Alexander Batenberg Sq.,* ☎ *2/89– 28–41.* ⊙ *Tues.–Sun. 10:30–6.*

❸ **Rotonda Sveti Georgi** (Rotunda of St. George). These ancient remains are at the northeast side of St. Nedelya Square in the courtyard of the Sheraton Sofia Balkan Hotel. The rotunda was built in the 4th century as a Roman temple, destroyed by the Huns, rebuilt by Justinian, and turned into a mosque by the Turks before being restored as a church. Recent restoration has revealed medieval frescoes. It is not open to the public. ⊠ *Off St. Nedelya Sq.*

❶ **Tzarkva Sveta Nedelya** (St. Nedelya Church). This impressive church was built during 1856–1863. The structure was later altered by a Russian architect and, in 1925, was destroyed by terrorist action. The church was rebuilt in 1931. Today it's open to visitors, and services are held on Sunday. You may even get a peek at a bride—this is one of the most popular wedding spots in the city. ⊠ *St. Nedyla Sq.*

❿ **Tzarkva Sveta Sofia** (Church of St. Sofia). One of the oldest churches in the city, it dates to the 6th century, though excavations have uncovered the remains of even older structures on the site. Because of its great age and its simplicity, the church provides a dramatic contrast to the showy Alexander Nevski Memorial Church nearby. While the church undergoes seemingly endless renovation, it's open to visitors, and services are held daily at 9:30 AM. ⊠ *Moskovska St.*

⑧ Tzarkva Sveti Nikolai (Church of St. Nicholas). This small and very ornate Russian church—it has five gold-plated domes and a green spire—was erected in 1912–14. Inside, mosaics depict favored Russian saints and czars. It's open for worship and to visitors daily. ⊠ *Tsar Osvoboditel Blvd.*

NEED A BREAK? You can stop in at one of the several eateries on the northern stretch of Vitosha Boulevard. If you're in the mood for ice cream, try **Café Espresso** (⊠ Vitosha Blvd. 37). Another favorite is **Café Magura** (⊠ Vitosha Blvd. 80).

Dining

Eating in Sofia can be enjoyable and even entertaining if the restaurant has a nightclub or folklore program. Be prepared to be patient and make an evening of it, as service can be slow at times. Or try a *mehana*, or tavern, where the atmosphere is informal and the service sometimes a bit quicker.

$$$$ ✕ **Deva Helios.** Expect no epicurean revolutions, just fine service and traditional Bulgarian, Italian, and Spanish food. Across from Alexander Nevski Memorial Church, this is one of the more elegant establishments in Sofia—an orchestra serenades diners most evenings. ⊠ *95 Vasil Levski Blvd.,* ☎ *2/88–03–85. No credit cards. Closed Sun.*

$$$$ ✕ **Dionyssos Vip.** You'll find a rich selection of international and Bulgarian dishes spiced with a three-hour floor show at this restaurant above the Central Department Store (Tsum). ⊠ *2 Knyaginya Maria-Luiza Blvd.,* ☎ *2/81–37–26. DC, MC, V.*

$$$$ ✕ **Krim.** The best beef Stroganoff in town is served at this Russian restaurant. ⊠ *17 Slavjanska St.,* ☎ *2/87–01–31. AE.*

$$$$ ✕ **Valimpex.** This restaurant, partially owned by the Hunting and Fishing Union, has an excellent menu of game, fish, and fowl. ⊠ *31–33 Vitosha Blvd.,* ☎ *2/87–94–65. Reservations essential. AE, DC, MC, V.*

$$$ ✕ **Berlin.** German food is the specialty at this quiet restaurant in the Serdika Hotel. ⊠ *2 Yanko Sakazov Blvd.,* ☎ *2/44–12–58. AE, DC, MC, V.*

$$$ ✕ **Budapest.** As the name suggests, Hungarian food takes center stage here. One of the older restaurants in Sofia, this eatery enjoys a fine reputation for good food, wine, and live music. ⊠ *145 G. S. Rakovski St.,* ☎ *2/87–27–50. No credit cards.*

$$$ ✕ **Club-Restaurant.** Bulgarian and European cuisine at its best is served in this elegant place. ⊠ *15 Dimitar Nestorov Blvd.,* ☎ *2/59–50–21. No credit cards.*

$$$ ✕ **Mexicano (Casa del Arquitecto).** Mexican food and music make this place popular. However, you'll also find traditional Bulgarian items on the menu, including a spicy moussaka (baked minced meat, eggplant, and potatoes). ⊠ *11 Krakra St.,* ☎ *2/44–65–98 or 2/44–17–24. No credit cards.*

$$$ ✕ **Party Club.** This restaurant features international fare, and some dishes with a Chinese flair. ⊠ *3 Vasil Levski Blvd.,* ☎ *2/81–05–44 or 2/81–43–43. AE, DC, MC, V.*

$$ ✕ **Golden Dragon.** This restaurant across from the National Opera House is very popular for its wide selection of Chinese dishes. ⊠ *86 Rakovski St.,* ☎ *2/87–34–00. No credit cards.*

$ ✕ **Zheravna.** This small, cozy place with a homey atmosphere serves tasty Bulgarian food. ⊠ *67 Levski Blvd.,* ☎ *2/87–21–86. Reservations not accepted. No credit cards.*

Lodging

The following hotels maintain a high standard of cleanliness and are open year-round unless otherwise stated. If you arrive in Sofia without reservations, go to Interhotels Central Office (⊠ 4 Sveta Sofia St.), the Bureau of Tourist Information and Reservations (⊠ 27 Stambolijski Blvd.), Balkantourist, the National Palace of Culture, or the central rail station for help finding a room.

$$$$ 🏨 **Novotel Europa.** This member of the French Novotel chain is near the train station and the city center. ⊠ *131 Knyaginya Maria-Luiza Blvd.,* ☎ *2/3–12–61,* FAX *2/32–00–11. 600 rooms with bath. 2 restaurants, bar, coffee shop, AE, DC, MC, V.*

$$$$ 🏨 **Sheraton Sofia Hotel Balkan.** This is a first-class hotel with a cen-
★ tral location that is hard to match. It also has excellent restaurants. ⊠ *5 St. Nedelya Sq.,* ☎ *2/87–65–41,* FAX *2/87–10–38. 188 rooms with bath. 3 restaurants, 2 bars, coffee shop, hot tub, health club, nightclub. AE, DC, MC, V.*

$$$$ 🏨 **Vitosha.** Designed by the Japanese, there is a distinct Asian flavor
★ to this towering, trim Interhotel. There's a large range of services and activities available here—and a superb Japanese restaurant. ⊠ *100 James Boucher Blvd.,* ☎ *2/6–25–18,* FAX *2/68–12–25. 454 rooms with bath. 5 restaurants, 6 bars, pool, sauna, 2 tennis courts, health club, shops, casino, nightclub. AE, DC, MC, V.*

$$$ 🏨 **Grand Hotel Sofia.** This five-story, centrally located Interhotel conveys an atmosphere of relative intimacy compared with some of its larger rivals in the capital. ⊠ *4 Narodno Sobranie Sq.,* ☎ *2/87–88–21,* FAX *2/88–13–08. 204 rooms with bath. 3 restaurants, bar, coffee shop, tavern, shops, nightclub. AE, DC, MC, V.*

$$$ 🏨 **Park Hotel Moskva.** The pleasant park setting makes up for this hotel's less central location compared to similar hotels. The excellent Panorama Restaurant is hidden away on the rooftop. ⊠ *25 Nezabravka St.,* ☎ *2/7–12–61,* FAX *2/65–67–45. 390 rooms with bath. 4 restaurants, bar, coffee shop, nightclub. AE, DC, MC, V.*

$$$ 🏨 **Rodina.** Sofia's tallest building is not far from the city center and has the latest in modern facilities, including a sports center and satellite television. ⊠ *8 Tsar Boris III Blvd.,* ☎ *2/5–16–31,* FAX *2/54–32–25. 536 rooms with bath. 3 restaurants, bar, coffee shop, pool, beauty salon, health club, nightclub. AE, DC, MC, V.*

$$ 🏨 **Bulgaria.** Despite its central location, this small hotel is quiet. The interior here, with turn-of-the century architectural elements, is charming. ⊠ *4 Tsar Osvoboditel Blvd.,* ☎ *2/87–19–77 or 2/87–01–91,* FAX *2/88–05–85. 85 rooms, some with bath or shower. Restaurant, bar, coffee shop, tavern, AE, DC, MC, V.*

$$ 🏨 **Deva-Spartak.** This small hotel, behind the National Palace of Culture, has excellent sports facilities, including aerobics. ⊠ *4 Arsenalski Blvd.,* ☎ *2/66–12–61,* FAX *2/66–25–37. 16 rooms with bath. Restaurant, indoor-outdoor pool, health club. No credit cards.*

$$ 🏨 **Hemus.** This is a smaller place near the Vitosha Hotel. Guests can take advantage of the facilities of its larger neighbor while saving money for the casino or nightclub. ⊠ *31 Cherni Vrah Blvd.,* ☎ *2/6–39–51,* FAX *2/66–13–18. 240 rooms, most with bath or shower. Restaurant, tavern, nightclub. AE, DC, MC, V.*

$$ 🏨 **Rila.** A convenient, central downtown location makes this establishment a low-cost alternative to the Sheraton. Contemporary Bulgarian paintings, which are for sale, hang in the hotel lobby. ⊠ *6 Kaloyan St.,* ☎ *2/980–88–65,* FAX *2/65–01–06. 120 rooms with bath or shower. Restaurant, coffee shop, tavern, health club. AE, DC, MC, V.*

$ 🏨 **Serdika.** This centrally located hotel is clean and comfortable. Ask for one of the newer rooms, which have enclosed shower stalls. The Old Berlin–style restaurant serves German specialties. ✉ *2 Yanko Sakazov Blvd.,* ☎ *2/44–34–11,* FAX *2/46–52–96. 140 rooms, most with shower. Restaurant. DC, MC, V.*

Nightlife and the Arts

Nightlife

DISCOS

There is a disco, nightclub, and bowling alley at the **National Palace of Culture** (✉ 1 Bulgaria Sq.). Check out **Orbylux,** known as the classiest disco in town (✉ 76 James Boucher Blvd., ☎ 2/63–939); **Excalibur,** a popular disco in the underpass of Sofia University; and **Yalta Club** (✉ 21 Aksakov St., ☎ 2/88–12–97).

NIGHTCLUBS

The following hotel bars have floor shows and a lively atmosphere: **Bar Sofia** (Grand Hotel Sofia); **Bar Variety Ambassador** (Vitosha Hotel); **Bar Variety** (Park Hotel Moskva); **Bar Fantasy** (Sheraton Sofia Hotel Balkan).

The Arts

The standard of music in Bulgaria is high, whether it takes the form of opera, symphonic, or folk music, which has just broken into the international scene with its close harmonies and colorful stage displays. Contact **Balkantourist** or the **Concert Office** (✉ 2 Tsar Osvoboditel Blvd., ☎ 2/87–15–88) for general information.

You don't need to understand Bulgarian to enjoy a performance at the **Central Puppet Theater** (✉ 14 Gen. Gurko St., ☎ 2/87–38–15), the **National Folk Ensemble** (check with the tourist office for details), or the **National Opera** (✉ 1 Vrabcha St., ☎ 2/87–13–16).

There are a number of fine-art galleries. The art gallery of the **Sts. Cyril and Methodius International Foundation** (✉ Alexander Nevski Sq., ☎ 2/88–49–22) has a collection of Indian, African, Japanese, and Western European paintings and sculptures. It's closed Tuesdays. The **Union of Bulgarian Artists** (✉ 6 Shipka St., ☎ 2/44–61–15) has exhibitions of contemporary Bulgarian art. **City Art Gallery** (✉ 1 Gen. Gurko St., ☎ 2/87–21–81) has permanent exhibits of 19th-century and modern Bulgarian paintings as well as changing exhibits by contemporary artists. There are also many private art galleries and fine antiques shops in the central part of the city.

The **Odeon, Serdika,** and **Vitosha cinemas** show recent foreign films in their original languages with Bulgarian subtitles.

Shopping

Department Stores

Sofia's biggest department store is the **Tsentralen Universalen Magazin** (Central Department Store), called TSUM for short. Here you'll find everything from cosmetics to furniture and gardening tools. ✉ *2 Knyaginya Maria-Luiza Blvd.*

Gift and Souvenir Shops

There are good selections of arts and crafts at the shop of the **Union of Bulgarian Artists** (✉ 6 Shipka St.) and the **Bulgarian Folk Art Shop** (✉ 14 Vitosha Blvd.). You'll find a range of souvenirs at **Sredec** (✉ 7 Lege St.) and **Prizma Store** (✉ 2 Tsar Osvoboditel Blvd.). For recordings of Bulgarian music, go to the **National Palace of Culture.**

If you're interested in furs or leather, try the shops along **Vitosha, Levski,** and **Tsar Osvoboditel boulevards.** You can buy handmade Bulgarian souvenirs—wood carvings, embroidery, lace tablecloths, jewelry, icons—in the streets surrounding Alexander Nevski Memorial Church. The colorful small shops along **Graf Ignatiev Street** also merit a visit.

Sofia A to Z

Arriving and Departing

BY CAR

Heading to Sofia from Serbia, the main routes are E80, going through the border checkpoint at Kalotina on the Niš-Sofia Road, or E871, going through the checkpoint at Gyueshevo. Traveling from Greece, take E79, passing through the checkpoint at Kulata; from Turkey, take E80, passing through checkpoint Kapitan-Andreevo. Border crossings to Romania are at Vidin on E79 and at Ruse on E70 and E85.

BY PLANE

All international flights arrive at **Sofia Airport.** For information on international flights, call 2/79–80–35 or 2/72–06–72; for domestic flights, ☎ 2/72–24–14 or 2/79–32–21–16.

Between the Airport and Downtown: Bus 84 serves the airport. Fares for taxis taken from the airport taxi stand run about 150 leva–200 leva for the 10-kilometer (6-mile) ride into Sofia. Avoid those soliciting you to take a taxi; they tend to overcharge or to insist on payment in hard currency.

BY TRAIN

The central station (☎ 2/3–11–11 or 2/843–33–33) is at the northern edge of the city. The ticket offices in Sofia are in the underpass of the **National Palace of Culture** (✉ 1 Bulgaria Sq., ☎ 2/843–42–92) or at the **Rila International Travel Agency** (✉ 5 Gen. Gurko St., ☎ 2/87–07–77 or 2/87–59–35). There is a taxi stand at the station.

Getting Around

BY BUS

Buses, trolleys, and trams run fairly often. Buy a ticket (a single fare is 5 leva–10 leva) from the ticket stand near the streetcar stop and punch it into the machine as you board (watch how the person in front of you does it). You can also pay the driver. Persons traveling with baggage or large backpacks are required by law to have both a ticket for themselves *and* a ticket for their baggage. If caught without a baggage ticket, an on-the-spot fine will be issued. Trams and trolleys tend to get crowded, so keep an eye on your belongings and be alert at all times. The tourist information offices have full details of routes and times. For information, call 2/312–42–63 or 2/88–13–53.

BY CAR

If you're staying near the city center, there's really no need for a car. Besides, driving in Sofia is no easy task—traffic is heavy and there are potholes everywhere.

ON FOOT

The main sites are centrally located, so the best way to see the city is on foot.

BY TAXI

Since private taxi drivers were given permission to operate in 1990, it has become easier to find cabs in Sofia. Hail them in the street or at a stand—or ask the hotel to call one. Daytime taxi rates (at press time) run 12 leva per kilometer, and 14 leva per kilometer after 10 PM. There is a 10-leva surcharge for taxis ordered by phone. To order by phone, call 21–21, 12–80, 12–82, or 12–84. To tip, round out the fare 5%–10%.

Contacts and Resources

B&B RESERVATION AGENCIES

Staying in private homes is becoming a popular alternative to hotels as a means of not only cutting costs but of offering increased contact with Bulgarians. Some private homes offer bed-and-breakfast or bed only; some provide full board. In Sofia, contact **Balkantourist** (☞ Visitor Information, *below*).

CAR RENTALS

The **Balkan Holidays/Hertz Rent-a-Car** organization (✉ 8 Pozitano St., ☎ 2/86–08–64 or 2/31–80–45) has offices in most of the major hotels and at Sofia Airport (☎ 2/72–01–57). **Avis** (☎ 2/73–80–23), **Intercar** (☎ 2/79–14–77), and **Europe Car** (☎ 2/72–01–57) also have offices in Sofia. Rental cars and fly/drive arrangements can be prebooked through Balkantourist agents abroad. These agents can also provide you with a driver for a small extra charge.

EMBASSIES

United States: (✉ 1 Suborna St., ☎ 2/88–48–01); consulate (✉ Captain Andreyev 1, ☎ 2/963–2022). **United Kingdom:** (✉ 38 Levski Blvd., ☎ 2/88–53–61).

EMERGENCIES

Ambulance: (☎ 150). **Doctor:** Clinic for Foreign Citizens (✉ Mladost 1, 1 Eugeni Pavlovski St., ☎ 2/75–361). **Fire:** (☎ 160). **Pirogov Emergency Hospital:** (☎ 2/5–15–31). **Police:** Sofia City Constabulary (☎ 166). **Pharmacies:** (☎ 178 for information about all-night pharmacies).

GUIDED TOURS

Orientation Tours. Guided tours of Sofia and environs are arranged by Balkantourist.

Evening Tours. Balkantourist has a number of evening tours, from a night out eating local food and watching folk dances to an evening at the National Opera.

Excursions. Balkantourist offers 23 types of special-interest tours (monasteries, spas, sports, etc.) of various lengths, using Sofia as the point of departure.

Visitor Information

Balkantourist Head Office (✉ 1 Vitosha Blvd., ☎ 2/43–331) is a travel agency as well as an information office, with offices in most major hotels. Also contact **Balkantour** (✉ 27 Stambolijski Blvd., ☎ 2/88–52–56), **Pirin** (✉ 30 Stambolijski Blvd., ☎ 2/88–41–22), **TIR** (Tourist Information and Reservations, ✉ Sofia 1000, 22 Lavele St., ☎ 2/88–01–39), or **SunShineTours** (✉ Sofia 1113, 6 Al. Zhendov St., ☎ 2/72–35–79).

SIDE TRIPS FROM SOFIA

Boyana

10 km (6 mi) south of the city center. Hire a taxi or take Tram 19 from ulista Graf Ignatiev in central Sofia to the southwestern part of Sofia, where you can catch Bus 63 or 64. The trip takes less than an hour.

At the foot of Vitosha Mountain, this settlement was a medieval fortress near the beginning of the 11th century. Today it is one of Sofia's wealthiest residential areas. In this area is one of Bulgaria's most precious monuments, the little, medieval **Boyana Church.** Unfortunately at press time it was closed for restoration, but a replica, complete with copies of the exquisite 13th-century frescoes, is open to visitors.

Dining

$$ ✕ **Boyansko Khanche.** Local and national specialties are served in a typical Bulgaria setting with live folk music. ✉ *Near Boyana Church,* ☎ *2/56–30–16. AE, DC, MC, V.*

$ ✕ **Chepishev.** You can try Bulgarian specialties and listen to live folk music at this spot at the foot of Mt. Vitosha. ✉ *Boyana District, 23 Kumata St.,* ☎ *2/55–08–88. No credit cards.*

Dragalevci

Hire a taxi or take Tram 19 from ulista Graf Ignatievto in central Sofia to the last stop, and switch to the Dragalevci Bus 63. You can also take Bus 66 or 93 from Hladilnika.

If you're ready for a little relaxation outside the city's hustle and bustle, make an effort to visit this village. Shepherds can often be seen tending their flocks in the beech forests surrounding the town. In the woods above the village is the nearby **Dragalevci Monastery.** It's currently a convent, but you can visit the 14th-century church with its outdoor frescoes. From Dragalevci, take the chairlift to the delightful resort complex of **Aleko,** and another nearby chairlift to the top of Malak Rezen. There are well-marked walking and ski trails in the area.

Dining

$$ ✕ **Vodeničarski Mehani.** The name Miller's Tavern is appropriate, since this spot is made up of three old mills linked together. Here, at the foot of Mt. Vitosha, you can see a folklore show while dining on Bulgarian specialties. ✉ *Dragalevci District,* ☎ *2/67–10–21 or 2/67–10–01. AE, DC, MC, V.*

THE BLACK SEA GOLDEN COAST

The Black Sea, contrary to its name, is a brilliant blue and is warm and calm most of the time. Its sunny, sandy beaches are backed by the easternmost slopes of the Balkan range and by the Strandja Mountains. The mild climate of this coastal region makes it a year-round destination for many European visitors. Although the tourist centers tend to be huge state-built complexes with a somewhat lean feel, they have modern amenities. Sunny Beach, the largest of the resorts, with more than 100 hotels, has plenty of children's amusements and play areas; babysitters are also available.

To truly experience the Bulgarian coast, you should visit the resorts north of Varna—Sveti Konstantin, Golden Sands, Balčik, and Albena.

Begin your exploration of the southern Black Sea coast, famous for its sheltered bays and cliffs, in the industrial port of Burgas. From Burgas, you can visit the fishing villages of Nesebâr (with Sunny Beach), Sozopol, and Djuni. Lodgings tend to be scarce in these villages, so private accommodations, arranged on the spot or through Balkantourist, are a good option. Whatever resort you choose, all offer facilities for water sports.

Varna

470 km (282 mi) east of Sofia. It's easily reached by rail (about 7½ hours by express) or by road from the capital.

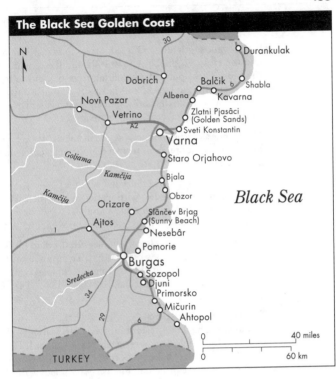

The Black Sea Golden Coast

N

Durankulak

Dobrich

Balčik   Shabla
6

Albena   Kavarna

Novi Pazar
Vetrino   Zlatni Pjasâci
A2   (Golden Sands)

Sveti Konstantin

Varna

Goljama

Staro Orjahovo

Kamčija

Bjala

Kamčija

Obzor

Black Sea

Orizare

Slånčev Brjag
(Sunny Beach)

Ajtos

Nesebâr

1

Pomorie

Burgas

Sredecka

Sozopol
Djuni
Primorsko

34

Mičurin

29   6   Ahtopol

0   40 miles

0   60 km

TURKEY

The ancient city, named Odessos by the Greeks, became a major Roman trading center and is now an important shipbuilding and industrial city. (Varna is Bulgaria's third-largest city.) If you plan to drive from Sofia to Varna, allow time to see the **Stone Forest** (Pobiti Kammani) just off the Sofia–Varna road between Devnya and Varna. The unexpected groups of monumental sandstone pillars are thought to have been formed when the area was the bed of the Lutsian Sea.

The **Museum of Art and History** is one of the great—if lesser known—museums of Europe. The splendid collection includes the world's oldest gold treasures, from the Varna necropolis of the 4th millennium BC, discovered in 1972, as well as Thracian, Greek, and Roman treasures and richly painted icons. ⊠ *41 Osmi Primorski Polk Blvd.,* ☎ *052/23–70–57.* ⊗ *Tues.–Sat. 10–5.*

Near the northeastern end of Osmi Primorski Polk Boulevard are numerous shops and cafés; the same street leads west to Mitropolit Simeon Square and the **cathedral** (1880–86). Take a look inside at the lavish murals.

Running north from the cathedral is Vladislav Varnenchik Street, with shops, movie theaters, and eateries. Opposite the cathedral, in the City Gardens, is the **Old Clock Tower,** which was built in 1880 by the Varna Guild Association. In the very city center on the south side of the City Gardens and on Nezavisimost Square stands **Stoyan Buchvarov National Theater,** a magnificent baroque building. The theater was founded in 1921 and showcased some of Bulgaria's greatest actors in a repertoire of distinguished plays.

On the corner of Knyaz Boris I Boulevard and Shipka Street you will see the remains of the **Roman Fortress Wall** of Odessos. Knyaz Boris I

Boulevard is another of Varna's shopping streets where you can buy handcrafted souvenirs.

If you walk south along Odessos Street to Han Krum Street you will find the Holy Virgin Church of 1602 and the remains of the **Roman Thermae.** These public baths dating from the 2nd to the 3rd century AD are among the largest and most substantial Roman ruins in Bulgaria. Not far from the baths, moving west, is Old Drăzki Street, lined with restaurants, taverns, and coffeehouses.

The **Archaeological Museum,** housed in an old prison building, exhibits Roman and other remains from a region with a colorful, multicultural past. ⊠ *5 November 8 St.* ۞ *Tues.–Sun. 10–5.*

If you follow Primorski Boulevard with the sea on your right, you will reach the **Naval Museum,** with its displays of the early days of navigation on the Black Sea and the Danube. ⊠ *2 Primorski Blvd., at the edge of the Marine Gardens,* ☎ *052/22–26–55.* ۞ *Weekdays 8–5.*

From the extensive and luxuriant **Morska Gradina** (Seaside Gardens), you can catch a great view over the bay. There are restaurants, an open-air theater, and a fascinating astronomy complex with a natural science museum, an observatory, and a planetarium. ⊠ *Off Graf Ignatiev.* ☎ *052/22–28–90.*

Dining and Lodging

$$ ✕ **Odessa.** This hotel restaurant has patio seating with good views, especially for people-watching on Slivnitza Boulevard. The *shopska* salad and cheese omelet make a good combination. Avoid the overpriced drinks. Menus are printed in English. ⊠ *1 Slivnitza Blvd.,* ☎ *052/22–53–14. No credit cards.*

$$ ✕ **Orbita.** Don't come here for the ambience (it's a dark room with tables) but to experience the typical Eastern European food in vast quantities. This cheap hole-in-the-wall is extremely popular with the locals, who come here for the lentil soup, grilled kebabs with potatoes, and Bulgarian sausage in a pot. ⊠ *25 Tsar Osvoboditel, off Knyaz Boris I, in Hotel Orbita,* ☎ *052/22–52–75. No credit cards.*

$ ✕ **Horizont.** This restaurant in Seaside Gardens has a good selection of seafood as well as a view of the Black Sea from its outside tables. It's not too busy during the day, but at night the live music draws a crowd. ⊠ *Morska Gradina,* ☎ *052/88–45–30. No credit cards.*

$$$ ▤ **Černo More.** One of the best things about this modern Interhotel is
★ the panoramic view from its 22nd floor. ⊠ *33 Slivnitza Blvd.,* ☎ *052/23–60–91 or 052/25–30–91. 230 rooms with bath or shower. 3 restaurants, bar, outdoor café, nightclub. AE, DC, MC, V.*

Sveti Konstantin

8 km (5 mi) north along the coast from Varna.

Sveti Konstantin, Bulgaria's oldest Black Sea resort, is small and intimate, spreading through a wooded park near a series of sandy coves. Warm mineral springs were discovered here in 1947.

Dining and Lodging

$$ ✕ **Bulgarska Svatba.** This folk-style restaurant with dancing is on the outskirts of the resort; charcoal-grilled meats are especially recommended. ⊠ *Sveti Konstantin Resort,* ☎ *052/86–12–83. No credit cards.*

$$ ✕ **Manastirska Izba.** This eatery is modest but pleasant, with a sunny terrace. Try the meatball and shopska salad. ⊠ *Sveti Konstantin Resort,* ☎ *052/86–20–36. No credit cards.*

$$$ 🏨 **Grand Hotel Varna.** This Swedish-built hotel has a reputation for
★ being the best hotel on the coast. It is only 139 meters (150 yards) from
the beach and offers a wide range of hydrotherapeutic treatments fea-
turing the natural warm mineral springs. ⊠ *Sveti Konstantin Resort*,
☎ *052/86–14–91*, FAX *052/86–19–20. 325 rooms with bath. 3 restau-
rants, 6 bars, coffee shop, 2 pools, 2 tennis courts, bowling, health club,
squash, nightclub. AE, DC, MC, V.*

$$ 🏨 **Čajka.** Čajka means "sea gull" in Bulgarian, and this hotel has a
bird's-eye view of the entire resort from its perch above the northern
end of the beach. ⊠ *Sveti Konstantin Resort*, ☎ *052/86–13–32. 130
rooms, most with bath or shower. No credit cards.*

Zlatni Pjasâci

8 km (5 mi) north of Sveti Konstantin.

In contrast to the sedate atmosphere of Sveti Konstantin, Zlatni Pjasâci
(Golden Sands) is lively, with extensive leisure-time amenities, mineral-
spring medical centers, and sports and entertainment facilities. Just over
4 kilometers (2½ miles) inland from Golden Sands is **Aladja Rock
Monastery,** one of Bulgaria's oldest, cut out of the cliff face and made
accessible to visitors by sturdy iron stairways.

Albena

10 km (6 mi) north of Zlatni Pjasâci.

Albena, the newest Black Sea resort, is between Balčik and Golden Sands.
It is well known for its long, wide beach and clean sea. The most luxurious of its 35 hotels is the Dobrudja, with extensive hydrotherapy
facilities.

Dining and Lodging

$$ ✕ **Bambuka** (Bamboo Tree). This open-air restaurant serves seafood
as well as international and Bulgarian fare. ⊠ *Albena Resort*, ☎
05722/24–04. No credit cards.

$$ 🏨 **Dobrudja Hotel.** This is a large, comfortable hotel with a mineral-
water health spa where you can relax in healing mud, enjoy a mas-
sage, or indulge in a curative bath. ⊠ *Albena Resort*, ☎ *05722/20–20,
FAX 05722/22–16. 272 rooms with bath. 3 restaurants, 2 bars, coffee
shops, indoor and outdoor pools, health club. DC, MC, V.*

Balčik

35 km (22 mi) north of Sveti Konstantin, 8 km (5 mi) north of Albena.

Part of Romania until just before World War II, Balčik is now a relaxed haven for Bulgaria's writers, artists, and scientists. On its white
cliffs are crescent-shaped tiers populated with houses, and by the
Balčik Palace, the beautiful **Botanical Gardens** are dotted with curious
buildings, including a small Byzantine-style church.

En Route About 25 kilometers (15 miles) east of Balčik on the north Black Sea
coastline is the steep rocky promontory of **Cape Kaliakra,** with a magnificent view of the sea. Its cliffs rise higher than 60 meters (200 feet).

Slânčev Brjag

95 km (60 mi) south of Varna and 140 km (87½ mi) south of Balčik.

The enormous Slânčev Brjag (Sunny Beach) is especially popular with
families because of its safe beaches, gentle tides, and playgrounds for

children. During the summer there are kindergartens for young vacationers, children's concerts, and even a children's discotheque. Sunny Beach has a variety of beachside restaurants and kiosks.

Dining and Lodging

$$ ✕ **Hanska Šatra.** In the coastal hills behind the sea, this combination restaurant and nightclub has been built to resemble the tents of the Bulgarian rulers of old. It has entertainment well into the night. ⊠ *5 km (3 mi) west of Slânčev Brjag,* ☎ *0554/28–11. No credit cards.*

$ ✕ **Ribarska Hiza.** This lively beachside restaurant specializes in fish and has music until 1 AM. ⊠ *Northern end of Slânčev Brjag Resort,* ☎ *0554/21–86. No credit cards.*

$$ 🏨 **Burgas.** Large and comfortable, this hotel lies at the southern end of the resort. ⊠ *Slânčev Brjag Resort,* ☎ *0554/23–58 or 0554/27–21,* ℻ *0554/25–24 or 0554/29–21. 250 rooms with bath or shower. Restaurant, bar, coffee shop, 2 pools, exercise room. AE, DC, MC, V.*

$$ 🏨 **Globus.** Considered by many to be the best in the resort, this hotel
★   combines a central location with modern facilities. ⊠ *Slânčev Brjag Resort,* ☎ *0554/22–45 or 0554/20–18,* ℻ *0554/25–24 or 0554/29–21. 100 rooms with bath or shower. Restaurant, bar, coffee shop, indoor pool, exercise room. AE, DC, MC, V.*

$$ 🏨 **Kuban.** Near the center of the resort, this large establishment is just a short stroll from the beach. ⊠ *Slânčev Brjag Resort,* ☎ *0554/23–09,* ℻ *0554/25–24 or 0554/29-21. 216 rooms, most with bath or shower. 2 restaurants, 2 coffee shops. AE, DC, MC, V.*

$ 🏨 **Čajka.** This hotel offers the best location at a low cost. ⊠ *Slânčev Brjag Resort,* ☎ *0554/23–08. 36 rooms, some with bath or shower. No credit cards.*

Nesebâr

5 km (3 mi) south of Slânčev Brjag (Sunny Beach) and accessible by regular excursion buses.

It would be hard to find a town that exudes a greater sense of age than this ancient settlement, founded by the Greeks 25 centuries ago on a rocky peninsula reached by a narrow causeway. Among its vine-covered houses are richly decorated medieval churches. There are dozens of small, private, cozy pubs all over Nesebâr.

Burgas

38 km (24 mi) south of Nesebâr.

The next place of any size south along the coast from Nesebâr is Burgas, Bulgaria's second main port on the Black Sea. Burgas is rather industrial, with several oil refineries, though it does have a pleasant **Maritime Park** with an extensive beach.

Dining and Lodging

$$ ✕ **Starata Gemia.** This restaurant's name is Old Boat, appropriate for a beachfront restaurant featuring fish specialties. ⊠ *Next to Primorets Hotel,* ☎ *056/4–57–08. No credit cards.*

$$ 🏨 **Bulgaria.** The Bulgaria is a high-rise Interhotel in the center of town. ⊠ *21 Aleksandrovska St.,* ☎ *056/4–28–20 or 056/4–26–10,* ℻ *056/4–72–91. 200 rooms, most with bath or shower. Restaurant, nightclub. DC, MC, V.*

Sozopol

32 km (20 mi) south of Burgas.

This was Apollonia, the oldest of the Greek colonies in Bulgaria. It is now a fishing port and popular haunt for Bulgarian and, increasingly, foreign writers and artists, who find private accommodations in the rustic Black Sea–style houses, so picturesque with their rough stone foundations and unpainted wood slats on the upper stories. Charming, narrow cobbled streets lead down to the harbor. The area is also famous for the Apollonia Arts Festival, held each September.

The Black Sea Golden Coast A to Z

Arriving and Departing

BY PLANE

There are daily 50-minute flights from Sofia and Plovdiv to Varna and Burgas.

BY TRAIN

It's a six- to eight-hour train ride from Sofia to Varna or Burgas.

Getting Around

Buses make frequent runs up and down the coast and are inexpensive. Buy your ticket in advance from the kiosks near the bus stops. **Cars** and **bicycles** can be rented; bikes are particularly useful for getting around such sprawling resorts as Sunny Beach. A **hydrofoil** service links Varna, Nesebâr, Burgas, and Sozopol. A regular **boat service** travels the Varna–Sveti Konstantin–Golden Sands–Albena–Balčik route.

Contacts and Resources

GUIDED TOURS

A wide range of excursions are arranged from all resorts. There are bus excursions to Sofia; a one-day bus and boat trip along the Danube; and a three-day bus tour of Bulgaria departing from Golden Sands, Sveti Konstantin, and Albena. All tours are run by Balkantourist.

VISITOR INFORMATION

There is a Balkantourist office in most towns and resorts. **Albena** (☎ 05722/27–21, 05722/21–41, or 05722/28–34). **Burgas** (Hotel Primorets, ⊠ 1 Knyaz Batenberg St., ☎ 056/4–54–96; ⊠ 2a Svoboda Blvd., ☎ 056/4–81–11). **Nesebâr** (☎ 0554/58–30 or 0554/58–33). **Sunny Beach** (☎ 0554/21–06, 0554/23–12, or 0554/25–10). **Sveti Konstantin** (☎ 052/86–10–45 or 052/86–14–91). **Varna** (main office, ⊠ 3 Moussala St., ☎ 052/22–55–24 or 052/22–22–72; private accommodations office, ⊠ Slaveikov Sq., ☎ 052/22–22–06). **Golden Sands** (☎ 052/85–53–02 or 052/85–54–14).

INLAND BULGARIA

Inland Bulgaria is not as well known to tourists as the capital and the coast, but an adventurous traveler willing to put up with limited hotel facilities and unreliable transportation will find plenty to photograph, paint, or simply savor. Wooded and mountainous, the interior is dotted with attractive "museum" villages (entire settlements listed for preservation because of their historic cultural value) and ancient towns; the folk culture is a strong survivor from the past, not a tourist-inspired re-creation of it. The foothills of the Balkan range, marked *stara planina* (old mountains) on most maps, lie parallel with the lower Sredna Gora Mountains, with the verdant Valley of Roses between them. In the Balkan range is the ancient capital of Veliko Târnovo; south of the Sredna Gora stretches the fertile Thracian Plain and Bulgaria's second-

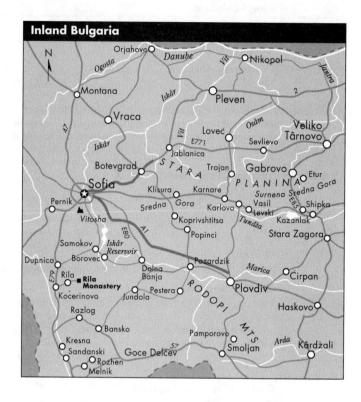

Inland Bulgaria

largest city, Plovdiv. Between Sofia and Plovdiv is the enchanting old town of Koprivshtitsa. To the south, in the Rila Mountains, is Borovec, first of the mountain resorts.

Koprivshtitsa

★ *105 km (65 mi) from Sofia, reached by a minor road south from the Sofia–Kazanlak expressway.*

One of Bulgaria's showplace villages, Koprivshtitsa is set amid mountain pastures and pine forests, about 3,000 feet up in the Sredna Gora range. Founded in the 14th century, it became a prosperous trading center with close ties to Venice during the National Revival period 400 years later. The architecture of this period, also called the Bulgarian Renaissance, features carved woodwork on broad verandas and overhanging eaves, brilliant colors, and courtyards with studded wooden gates. Throughout the centuries, artists, poets, and wealthy merchants have made their homes here, and you can visit many of the historic houses. The town has been well preserved and is revered by Bulgarians as a symbol of freedom, for it was here in April 1876 that the rebellion was sparked that led to the end of Turkish occupation two years later.

Dining and Lodging

\$\$ ✕ **Djedo Liben Inn.** This attractive folk restaurant with a nightclub is built in the traditional style of the area—with half-timbered, high stone walls. ☎ 07184/21–09. *No credit cards.*

\$ ⊞ **Barikadite.** This small hotel is on a hill 15 kilometers (9 miles) from Koprivshtitsa. The local residents will willingly give directions and probably offer to show you the way. *20 rooms with shower. Restaurant, bar, nightclub. No credit cards.*

$ 🏨 Koprivshtitsa. This good-value hotel is popular with Bulgarians. ⊠ *Just over the river from the center of town,* ☎ *07184/21–82. 30 rooms. No credit cards.*

En Route From Koprivshtitsa, return to the Sofia–Kazanlak Expressway and head east. After 15 kilometers (9 miles) you'll pass through **Klisura** and the beginning of the **Rozova Dolina** (Valley of Roses). Here the famous Bulgarian rose water and attar, or essence, are produced. Each May and June, the entire valley is awash in fragrance and color.

Trojan

At the village of Karnare, which is 17 km (11 mi) east of Klisura, take the winding scenic road north over the Balkan range to the town of Trojan, which is 93 km (58 mi) from Koprivshtitsa.

The **Trojan Monastery,** built during the 1600s, is in the heart of the mountains. The church was painstakingly remodeled during the 19th century, and its icons, wood carvings, and frescoes are classic examples of National Revival art.

Veliko Târnovo

Travel north on the mountain road from Trojan until it meets Highway E772, where you turn right for Veliko Târnovo, 82 km (50 mi) from Karnare; 240 km (144 mi) from Sofia.

In the 13th and 14th centuries, Veliko Târnovo was the capital of the Second Bulgarian Kingdom. Damaged by repeated Ottoman attack and again by an earthquake in 1913, it has been reconstructed and is now a museum city of marvelous relics with panoramic vistas of steep mountain slopes through which the river Jantra runs its jagged course.

This town ideally warrants one or two days of exploration. Try to begin at a vantage point above the town in order to get an overview of its design and character. **Tsarevec** (Carevec on some maps), protected by a river loop, is the hill where medieval czars and patriarchs had their palaces. The area is under restoration, and steep paths and stairways now provide opportunities to view the extensive ruins of the Patriarchate and the royal palace. In summer there is a spectacular sound-and-light show presented at night, which can be seen from the surrounding pubs.

Baldwin's Tower, to the south of Tsarevec, is the 13th-century prison of Baldwin of Flanders, onetime Latin emperor of Constantinople.

On the Tsarevec and Trapezitsa hills are three important churches: the **Church of the Forty Martyrs,** a 13th-century structure with frescoes of the Târnovo school and with two inscribed columns, one dating from the 9th century; the **Church of Sts. Peter and Paul,** from the 14th century, with vigorous murals both inside and out; and the **Church of St. Dimitrius,** from the 12th century, reached by a bridge near the Forty Martyrs, built on the spot where the Second Bulgarian Kingdom was proclaimed in 1185.

In the center of the town near Yantra Hotel is Samovodene Street, lined with restored crafts workshops—a good place to find souvenirs, Turkish candy, or a charming café.

On Rakovski Street is the **Hadji Nicoli Museum** in what was once an inn. Part of a cluster of buildings from the National Revival period, this is one of the finest structures in town. ⊠ *17 Georgi Sava Rakovski. At press time the museum was closed for renovations.*

OFF THE
BEATEN PATH
ŠUMEN – Moving east from Veliko Târnovo toward Varna on E772, you can go back farther in time by visiting the ruins of the two capitals of the First Bulgarian Kingdom in the vicinity of Šumen (spelled Shoumen in some English translations). The first ruins are the fortifications at **Pliska,** 23 kilometers (14 miles) southeast of Šumen, which date from 681. At **Veliki Preslav,** 21 kilometers (13 miles) southwest of Šumen, there are ruins from the second capital that date from 893 to 927. The 8th- to 9th-century **Madara Horseman,** a bas-relief of a horseman slaying a lion, appears 18 kilometers (11 miles) east of town on a sheer cliff face.

Dining and Lodging

$$ ✕ **Boljarska Izba.** In the center of the busy district just north of the river, this place is a folk tavern. ⊠ *St. Stambolov St., no phone. No credit cards.*

$$$ ⊟ **Veliko Târnovo.** Right in the middle of the most historic part of the town, this modern Interhotel has good facilities. ⊠ *2 Al. Penchev St.,* ☎ *062/3–05–71,* 🖷 *062/3–98–59. 195 rooms with bath or shower. 2 restaurants, bar, coffee shop, indoor pool, health club, nightclub. AE, DC, MC, V.*

$$ ⊟ **Yantra.** The Yantra has some of the best views in town, looking across the river to Tsaravec. ⊠ *1 Velchova Zavera Sq.,* ☎ *062/2–03–91,* 🖷 *062/2–18–07. 60 rooms, most with shower. Restaurant, bar, coffee shop. DC, MC, V.*

$ ⊟ **Etur.** This medium-size hotel, with an address near the more expensive Veliko Târnovo, makes it a good base for sightseeing within town. ⊠ *I. Ivailo St.,* ☎ *062/2–18–38. 80 rooms, most with shower. Restaurant, bar, coffee shop. AE, DC, MC, V.*

En Route
If you leave Veliko Târnovo by E85 and head south toward Plovdiv, you can make three interesting stops en route. The first, near the industrial center of Gabrovo—interesting in itself for its House of Humor Museum—is the museum village of **Etur,** 8 kilometers (5 miles) to the southeast. Its mill is still powered by a stream, and local craftsmen continue to be trained in traditional skills. The second is the **Shipka Pass,** with its mighty monument on the peak to the 200,000 Russian soldiers and Bulgarian volunteers who died here in 1877, during the Russian-Turkish Wars. The third is **Kazanlak,** at the eastern end of the Valley of Roses, where you can trace the history of rose production, Bulgaria's oldest industry. Here, in early June, young rose pickers dress in traditional costumes for rose parades and other carnival processions. There is also a highly decorated replica of a Thracian tomb of the 3rd or 4th century BC, set near the original, which remains closed for preservation. From Kazanlak take the road west through the Valley of Roses to either Vasil Levski or Karlovo, another Rose Festival town. Then turn south for Plovdiv.

Plovdiv

174 km (104 mi) southeast of Sofia, 197 km (123 mi) southwest of Veliko Târnovo.

Plovdiv, a major industrial center, is Bulgaria's second-largest city and one of the oldest cities in Europe. The Old Town is on the hillier south bank of the Marica River.

The **National Ethnographical Museum** is in the House of Arghir Koyumdjioglu, an elegant example of the National Revival style that made its first impact in Plovdiv. ⊠ *2 Čomakov St.* ☉ *Tues.–Sun. 9–noon and 1:30–5.*

If you walk below the medieval gateway of Hissar Kapiya, you'll see the Georgiadi House on Starina Street. Next, walk along steep, narrow Strumna Street, lined with workshops and boutiques, some reached through little courtyards. Follow Saborna Street westward to its junction with the pedestrians-only Knyaz Alexander I Street; here you'll find the remains of a **Roman stadium.** Turn east off Knyaz Alexander I Street and walk to the fine hilltop **Roman amphitheater,** a big open theater, sensitively renovated and frequently used for dramatic and musical performances. You may want to spend some time in the **Kapana district,** which has many restored and traditional shops and restaurants.

On the right side of the Old Town toward the river is the **National Archaeological Museum.** One of its displays is a replica of the 4th-century BC Panagjuriste Gold Treasure, the original of which is in Sofia. ⊠ *1 Suedinie Sq.,* ⊘ *Tues.–Sun. 9–12:30 and 2–5:30.*

Dining and Lodging

$$$ ✕ **Puldin.** This traditional restaurant in the center of town has a video presentation that highlights the city's past. ⊠ *3 Knyaz Tseretelev St.,* ☎ *032/23–17–20. AE, DC, MC, V.*

$$ ✕ **Alafrangite.** This charming folk-style restaurant is in a restored 19th-century house with carved-wood ceilings and a vine-covered courtyard. ⊠ *17 Nektariev St.,* ☎ *032/22–98–09 or 032/26–95–95. No credit cards.*

$$ ✕ **Filipopol.** This is an elegant restaurant with a menu that combines Bulgarian and Greek cuisines, served by candlelight and accompanied by jazz piano music. ⊠ *56 Stamat Matanov St.,* ☎ *032/22–52–96. No credit cards.*

$$ ✕ **Rhetora.** This coffee bar is in a beautifully restored old house near the Roman amphitheater in the old part of the city. ⊠ *8A T. Samodoumov St.,* ☎ *032/22–20–93. No credit cards.*

$$$ 🏨 **Novotel Plovdiv.** The large and modern Novotel is across the river from the center of town, near the fairgrounds. ⊠ *2 Zlatju Boyadjiev St.,* ☎ *032/55–51–71 or 032/5–58–92. 322 rooms with bath. Restaurant, bar, tavern, indoor and outdoor pools, bowling, exercise room, nightclub. AE, DC, MC, V.*

$$$ 🏨 **Trimontium.** This comfortable Interhotel built in the 1950s has the ideal location for exploring the Old Town. ⊠ *2 Kapitan Raico St.,* ☎ *032/2–34–91. 163 rooms with bath or shower. Restaurant, bar, tavern. AE, DC, MC, V.*

$ 🏨 **Marica.** This is a large, modern hotel that offers a less expensive alternative to its neighbor, the Novotel. ⊠ *5 Vazrazhdane St.,* ☎ *032/55–27–35. 171 rooms with bath or shower. Restaurant, bar. AE, MC, DC, V.*

Borovec

Travel west along the E80 Sofia Road. At Dolna Banja, turn off to Borovec, about 4,300 feet up the northern slopes of the Rila Mountains; 109 km (68 mi) from Plovdiv.

This is an excellent walking center and winter-sports resort, well equipped with hotels, folk taverns, and ski schools. The winding mountain road leads back to Sofia, 70 kilometers (44 miles) from here, past Lake Iskar, the largest in the country.

En Route On the way back to Sofia you should consider a visit to the **Rila**
★ **Monastery,** founded by Ivan of Rila in the 10th century. Cut across to E79, travel south to Kočerinovo, and turn east to follow the steep forested valley past the village of Rila. The monastery has suffered so fre-

quently from fire that most of it is now a grand National Revival reconstruction, although a rugged 14th-century tower has survived. The atmosphere in this mountain retreat, populated by many storks, is still heavy with a sense of the past—although part of the complex has been turned into a museum and some of the monks' cells are now guest rooms. Here you can see 14 small chapels with frescoes from the 15th and 17th centuries, a lavishly carved altarpiece in the new Assumption Church, the sarcophagus of Ivan of Rila, icons, and ancient manuscripts—a reminder that this was a stronghold of art and learning during the centuries of Ottoman rule.

Bansko

150 km (93 mi) south of Sofia via Blagoevgrad.

This small, picturesque town at the foot of the Pirin Mountains is an old Bulgarian settlement. The **Holy Trinity Church,** built in 1835, along with the tower and the town clock, is part of the architectural complex in the center of the town.

Dining and Lodging

$$ **Pirin Hotel.** This is a popular hotel in the area. ⊠ *Tsar Simeon 68,* ☎ *07443/2536,* **FAX** *07443/4244. 55 double rooms and 7 suites. Restaurant, bar, coffee shop, exercise room.*

Melnik

From Sandanski, head south down E79 about 8 km (5 mi); Melnick is west of E79.

Near fertile grape orchards, Melnik is most famous for the wine aged in its deep cellars. This area was an important Byzantine fortress during the 12th through the 14th centuries. It developed rapidly again during the 18th century due to wine and tobacco trade but declined by the end of the following century. Today Melnik retains well-preserved houses of the National Revival Period.

Rozhen Monastery, rising above the town, dates to 12th century, but was rebuilt in the 16th century after being ravaged by fire. Within these protective walls is the church, dating from 1600.

Inland Bulgaria A to Z

Getting Around

Rail and bus services cover all parts of inland Bulgaria, but the timetables are not easy to follow, and there are frequent delays. Your best bet is to rent a car. You may also prefer to hire a driver; Balkantourist can arrange this.

Contacts and Resources

VISITOR INFORMATION

Plovdiv (⊠ 106 Bulgaria Blvd., ☎ 032/55–38–48 or 032/55–28–07). **Veliko Târnovo** (⊠ 2 Al. Penchev St., ☎ 062/30–571 or 062/33–971).

BULGARIA A TO Z

Arriving and Departing

By Boat

Modern luxury vessels cruise the Danube from Vienna to Ruse in Bulgaria. Hydrofoils link main communities along the Bulgarian stretches of the Danube and the Black Sea.

By Bus

Some Bulgarian tourist agencies have regular round-trip bus service from Sofia to Victoria Coach Station in London. **ALMA TOUR -BG** bus service (✉ Sofia 1000, 83 V. Levski Blvd., ☎ 2/87–51–87 or 2/80–8–86) leaves London on Friday night, stops in Amsterdam the following morning, and reaches Sofia Monday morning. There is regular bus service from Sofia to most major Eastern European cities. Contact **DARIKOMM Tourist Agency** (✉ Sofia 1000, 171 Evlogi Georgiev St., ☎ 2/44–22–12 or 2/46–74–46), which offers direct bus services to Warsaw and to many cities and towns of the Czech Republic and Slovakia.

By Plane

The major gateway to Bulgaria is Sofia Airport, about 10 kilometers (6 miles) northeast of the city.

FROM NORTH AMERICA

Balkanair, also called Balkan Bulgarian Airlines (✉ 437 Madison Ave., 32nd floor, New York, NY 10022, ☎ 212/371–2047), flies from New York to Sofia twice weekly.

WITHIN EUROPE

You can fly from the capital cities of many Eastern European countries directly to Sofia. **Balkanair** flies from Budapest, Prague, and Warsaw. **Hemus Air** flies to Bratislava and Bucharest from Sofia. Transfer flights from these cities can be arranged through Balkanair with **CSA** (✉ 9 Saborna St., ☎ 2/88–55–58), **LOT Poland Airways** (✉ 27 Al. Stamolijski Blvd., ☎ 2/87–45–62), and **Malev** (☎ 2/88–40–61).

Lufthansa German Airlines (✉ 9 Saborna St., ☎ 2/88–23–10; airport, ☎ 2/72–07–58) flies from Frankfurt to Sofia. **British Airways** (✉ 56 Alabin St., ☎ 2/98–16–999 or 2/98–17–000) has nonstop service from London to Sofia three days a week.

Getting Around

By Car

Driving in Bulgaria can be difficult. Traffic jams are common, and you should always be on the lookout for dangerous potholes and aggressive drivers. In winter you'll need snow tires for all roads.

Drive on the right, as in the United States. The speed limits are 50 or 60 kilometers per hour (31 or 37 miles per hour) in built-up areas, 80 kilometers per hour (50 miles per hour) elsewhere, except on highways, where it is 120 kilometers per hour (70 miles per hour). You are required to carry a first-aid kit, fire extinguisher, and breakdown triangle in the vehicle, and you must not sound the horn in towns. Seat belts must be worn in front.

Gas stations are spaced at regular intervals on main roads but may be few and far between off the beaten track. All are marked on Balkantourist's free driving map. At press time, service stations were still selling unlimited quantities of fuel, supplies permitting, in leva (in summer 1996, 45 per liter, or $1.60 per gallon, for regular leaded). For motorist information contact the automobile club **Shipka** (✉ 18 Lavele St., Sofia, ☎ 2/88–38–56).

By Plane

Balkanair has regular services to Varna and Burgas, the biggest ports on the Black Sea. Book through Balkantourist offices; this can take time, however, and overbooking is not unusual. Business flights to other destinations in the country are also arranged by Hemus Air.

By Train

From Sofia there are six main routes—to Varna and Burgas on the Black Sea coast (overnight trains between Sofia and Black Sea resorts have first- and second-class sleeping cars and second-class *couchettes*); to Plovdiv and on to the Turkish border; to Dragoman and the Serbian border; to Kulata and the Greek border; and to Ruse on the Romanian border. The main lines are powered by electricity. When in Bulgaria, obtain any railway information you need from **Rila International Travel Agency** (⊠ Sofia 1000, 5 Gen. Gurko St., ☎ 2/87–07–77 or 2/87–59–35).

Contacts and Resources

Car Rentals

Orbita Tours (⊠ 76 James Boucher Blvd., Sofia, ☎ 2/65–51–46), a local travel agency, has rental cars. **Intercar Bulgaria** has offices at Sofia Airport (☎ 2/79–14–7), the Vitosha Hotel and Grand Hotel Sofia in Sofia, and in Varna, Plovdiv, and Burgas. **Balkan Holidays/Hertz** (⊠ 8 Pozitano St., Sofia, ☎ 2/86–08–64 or 2/31–80–45) has offices at the airport (☎ 2/72–01–57) and in most major hotels. Also try **Budget** (⊠ Sofia 1000, 1 Vitosha Blvd., ☎ 2/87–16–82). Rates in Sofia for an economy car with unlimited mileage begin at $22 per day. Rates do not include VAT.

You must obtain a Green Card from your car insurance company, as recognized international proof that your car is covered by International Civil Liability (third-party) Insurance. You may be required to show this card at the border. Balkantourist recommends that you also take out collision, or Casco, insurance.

Road maps can be found at some hotels, at most tourist offices, and can be bought at book stalls in the streets. Before buying a map, make sure that the names on it are in the Roman alphabet and not in Cyrillic.

Customs and Duties

You may import duty-free into Bulgaria 250 grams of tobacco products, plus 1 liter of hard liquor and 2 liters of wine. Items intended for personal use during your stay are also duty-free. Travelers are advised to declare items of greater value—cameras, tape recorders, etc.—so there will be no problems with Bulgarian customs officials on departure.

It is prohibited to take works of art, church icons, and coins of particular historical or cultural value out of the country. All international restrictive regulations apply.

Emergencies

Ambulance (☎ 150). **Fire** (☎ 160). **Police** (☎ 166). In case of breakdown on the road, dial 146.

Guided Tours

SunShineTours (⊠ Sofia 1113, 6 Al. Zhendov St., ☎ 2/72–35–79) offers special-interest tours for people of all ages.

Language

The official language, Bulgarian, is written in Cyrillic and is very close to Old Church Slavonic, the root of all Slavic languages.

In some resorts, railway stations, and airports, names and directions are spelled in the Roman alphabet. English is spoken in major hotels and restaurants, but is unlikely to be heard elsewhere. It is essential to remember that in Bulgaria, a nod of the head means "no" and a shake of the head means "yes." But there are people who are adopting the Western way, so you have to be careful.

Mail

Post offices in all cities and in most resorts and small towns offer postal and telephone services. Mail to Europe can take two weeks and to the United States up to three weeks.

POSTAL RATES

Letters and postcards to the United States cost 70 leva; to the United Kingdom, 60 leva.

RECEIVING MAIL

You can receive your mail through **Sofia Central Post Office** (⊠ Sofia 1000, 6 Gen. Gurko St.) if your letters are marked *Poste Restante*. You can also use the services of **DHL International** (⊠ 8 Tsar Osvoboditel Blvd., ☎ 2/88–23–09) or **International Post** (⊠ 11 Gen. Gurko St., ☎ 2/81–32–96). To collect your mail, you will be asked to present your passport.

Money and Expenses

Prices in Bulgaria have been low for years, but this is changing as the government tries to revive the economy and open it up to the West. It is possible to cut costs even more by staying in a private hotel or private room in a Bulgarian house or apartment—also arranged by Balkantourist or other tourism companies—or by camping. The favorable exchange rate, linked to foreign-currency fluctuations, makes such expenses as taxi, museum and theater admissions, and meals in most restaurants seem comparatively low by international standards. A little hard currency, exchanged at this rate, goes a long way.

CREDIT CARDS

The major international credit cards are accepted in the larger stores, hotels, and restaurants. Increasingly, even restaurants in the moderate category are accepting credit cards, although the list of cards accepted may not always be posted correctly. Before you place an order, check to see whether you can pay with your card.

CURRENCY

The unit of currency in Bulgaria is the lev (plural leva), divided into 100 stotinki. There are bills of 1, 2, 5, 10, 20, 50, 100, 200 , 500, 1000, and 2000 leva; coins of 1, 2, 5 , and 10 leva; and coins of 10, 20, and 50 stotinki. At press time, as part of efforts at economic reform, hard-currency payments for goods and services were no longer permitted. The only legal tender for commercial transactions and tourist services in Bulgaria is the lev. These services include air, train, long-distance bus travel, and all accommodations. You may import any amount of foreign currency, including traveler's checks, and exchange it at branches of the Bulgarian State Bank, commercial banks, Balkantourist hotels, airports, border posts, and other exchange offices, which quote their daily selling and buying rates. The rate quoted by the Bulgarian State Bank at press time was 140 leva to the U.S. dollar, and 214 leva to the pound sterling.

It is forbidden to import or export Bulgarian currency. Unspent leva must be exchanged on departure before you go through passport control. You will need to present your official exchange slips to prove that the currency was legally purchased.

SAMPLE COSTS

The following price list, based on costs at press time, can only be used as a rough guide. Trip on a tram, trolley, or bus, 10 leva; theater ticket, 80 leva–150 leva; coffee, 10 leva–20 leva; bottle of wine in a moderate restaurant, 150 leva–250 leva. Museum admission, 50 leva (less than 50¢), except at the National History Museum where it is 150 leva.

TAXES

Bulgaria has value-added tax (VAT). Its rate is 18%.

National Holidays

January 1 (New Year's Day); March 3 (Independence Day); April 27 and 28 (Easter Sunday and Monday; the date is determined by the Eastern Orthodox Church every year); May 1 (Labor Day); May 24 (Bulgarian Culture Day); November 1 (Day of the Leaders of the Bulgarian Revival); December 24, 25, 26 (Christmas).

Opening and Closing Times

Banks are open weekdays 8:30–3. **Museums** are usually open 9–6:30 but are often closed Monday or Tuesday. **Shops** are open Monday–Saturday 9–7. Some grocery stores are open Sunday until noon.

Passports and Visas

All visitors need a valid passport with an entry or transit visa. Those traveling in groups of six or more do not require visas, and many package tours are exempt from the visa requirement. No entry visa is required of citizens of the countries with which Bulgaria has visa-free agreements. Americans do not need visas when traveling as tourists. British and Canadian citizens do require visas, which permit stays of up to 30 days. Visas can be obtained at the Bulgarian border but it is better to apply for one in advance. Since regulations are subject to change, check before you travel. There is, however, a border tax of approximately $20 that must be paid upon entry into Bulgaria. For visa information and applications, contact the nearest Bulgarian consulate.

Telephones

The country code for Bulgaria is 359. To place a call in Sofia you need a 2-leva coin. Telephone booths in the streets are often in very bad condition. There is a new system of international telephones—modern, direct-dial phones with no coin slots—that operate only with special cards paid for in leva. Directions for buying the cards are given, often in English, on the phones.

Dial ☎ 00–1800–0010 (AT&T) or ☎ 00–800–0877 (Sprint Express) to reach an English-speaking operator who can effortlessly connect your direct, collect, or credit-card call to the United States.

Tipping

Tipping is expected especially by waiters, taxi drivers, and barbers, who usually get about 10%.

Visitor Information

Balkantourist (✉ Sofia 1040, 1 Vitosha Blvd., ☎ 2/43–331), the leading Bulgarian travel company and **Balkan Holidays International** (✉ Sofia 1000, 5 Triaditsa St., ☎ 2/88–37–39 or 2/83–25–45) provide information in English about lodging.

7 Romania

Bucharest, poised between Europe and the East, has begun to reawaken as a lively capital city. The pride of the nation's citizens, the Romanian countryside—among the most unspoiled in all of Europe—ranges from the forested Carpathian Mountains to the Danube Delta, with its abundant waterfowl and wildlife, to the Black Sea coastline, dotted with sandy beaches and resort hotels. Transylvania, the mysterious Land of Dracula, is home to traditional towns and rural villages out of a medieval painting, while the Bucovina's beautifully frescoed churches and monasteries are unique cultural treasures in Romania's remote, northern reaches.

Updated by
Gregory A.
Hedger

H

ISTORICALLY, ROMANIA has not been the easiest
place to visit as a tourist, but it is perhaps the most
beautiful country in Eastern Europe, a last bastion of a medieval past long since lost elsewhere. The overthrow of the
Ceauşescu regime in December 1989 started a continuing process of
reform toward Western-style democracy and a market economy. These
reforms are making for substantive changes for travelers: new, private,
service-oriented hotels and restaurants, greater access to sights and cultural attractions, and the ability to interact directly with native Romanians. Bread lines, food shortages, empty store shelves, no stores at
all—these are becoming a thing of the past. New stores sell both imported and locally made items. The problems and inefficiencies that
tourists may still encounter are often offset by the traditional hospitality and generosity that the Romanian people, once forbidden to speak
with foreigners, are now free to express.

Comparable in size to the state of Oregon, Romania is made up of three
provinces: Walachia, Moldova, and Transylvania. With a population
of 23 million, Romania is a Latin island in a sea of Slavs and Magyars
(it borders Ukraine, Moldova, Bulgaria, Serbia, and Hungary). Its people are the descendants of the Dacian tribe and of Roman soldiers who
garrisoned what was the easternmost province of the Roman Empire.
As a land, it has been repeatedly shuffled by history: constant Barbaric
invasions, struggles against the Turks, the Austro-Hungarian domination
of Transylvania, a once large and still extant Gypsy population (also
referred to as the Romany), and a strong French cultural influence all
contribute to present-day Romania's rich cultural stew.

It's easy to understand why Bucharest, with its wide, tree-lined avenues,
Arcul de Triumf, and lively café life, was once known as the "Paris of
the East." The mythic land of Transylvania is the region of Vlad Ţepeş,
the real-life prince upon whom the legend of Dracula was based. Its intact medieval villages are a trip back in time, with their town squares,
churches, and surrounding Bavarian-style homes and shops reflecting the
region's Hungarian and German ancestry. Many enchanting Orthodox
monasteries, including some from medieval times with colorful frescoes
on their outside walls, characterize the remote and mountainous region
of the Bucovina. To the northeast of Bucharest lies the Danube Delta, a
watery wilderness populated by fishermen (many of Ukrainian origin)
and visited by hundreds of rare bird species. The rugged Carpathian Mountains, which form a crown in the center of the country, offer double pleasures: skiing in winter and hiking in summer. The unattractive effects of
industrialization are generally confined to the cities, with life in the
countryside remaining picturesquely simple. Horse and cart are a popular means of transportation, horse-drawn plows a common sight, and
folk costume everyday wear in the northern regions of Maramures and
the Bucovina.

Ironically, Romania enjoyed a period of comparative prosperity during the 1970s, but it is currently the poorest country in Europe after
Albania. Petty theft is a widespread problem, although the streets are
fairly safe at night. Romanians still have limited experience in dealing
with foreigners and are sometimes envious of Westerners' wealth.
Their efforts on your behalf may charm you, but they could also be
cheating you. Tips, gifts, and even bribes are often expected, but use
discretion or you may be regarded as patronizing.

Today you may roam as you wish and should feel free to wander through the beautiful countryside or discover old churches and buildings, museums, and crafts workshops. Be aware, though, that it is illegal to enter or photograph any bridge, building, transportation facility, or other site that would be considered of military importance. These sites are usually, but not always, marked.

Romania is a bargain for package tourists. Prepaid package holidays to ski, spa, and seaside resorts offer the best available standards at a very reasonable cost, though tourists must be aware that Romanian standards may not be as high as they are in the West. Independent travelers often pay much more overall for their visit and find wide variations in quality. They must also be aware that there is a dual price system, apparently encouraged by the government, in which foreigners are charged a much higher price then Romanian tourists; this higher price is usually not displayed. The country is now in the throes of privatization of its state monopolies, including its tourism industry. Much chaos has resulted from the restructuring, and visitors are likely to experience changes in prices, unreliable amenities, and varying quality of services. Nevertheless, conditions for visitors are constantly improving. More and better restaurants, cafés, and shops are opening in many of the larger towns.

Romania is likely to remain underexplored until its serious economic difficulties are resolved, but in the meantime, the package tourist is still assured a good price, while the intrepid independent traveler will experience a part of Europe rich in tradition, one that has in part escaped the pressures, complexities, and aesthetics of modern times.

Pleasures and Pastimes

Dining

Bucharest is in the throes of a restaurant renaissance: French, German, Asian, and Middle Eastern restaurants are now thriving. Outside the capital, options are limited, and you should expect poorly cooked dishes based on pork or beef. Vegetables and salads may be canned or pickled. Traditional Romanian main courses are not always offered, but you might try *gustare*, a platter of hot or cold mixed hors d'oeuvres, or *ciorbă*, a soup stock that is slightly spicy and sour. Overcharging is a hazard outside the bigger restaurants with printed menus. You can insist on seeing the prices, but small establishments don't prepare a menu if they serve only one or two dishes. Creamy cakes are available at the better *cofetarie* (coffee shops). Try to avoid less expensive *bufet expres*, *lacto vegetarian* snack bars, and *autoservire*. Romanian coffee is served with grounds; instant coffee is called *nes*. Cappuccino is the closest to Western-style coffee.

If you are traveling independently, you may wish to take some food supplies with you. Vegetarians should know that there is a limited range of produce available outside Bucharest, especially in winter. But most towns have markets where local farmers sell produce at very reasonable prices (at least during summer and fall). Outside Bucharest and the Black Sea and Carpathian resorts, many restaurants stop serving by 9 PM, although an increasing number have begun to stay open until 11 PM or later. Restaurants usually open at midday. There are no dress rules as such, but Romanians themselves usually wear smart, informal clothes for an expensive evening out. Casual dress is appropriate elsewhere.

Tap water should be considered unsafe. Old piping contributes to a high lead content in the water in many areas of Bucharest. Outside

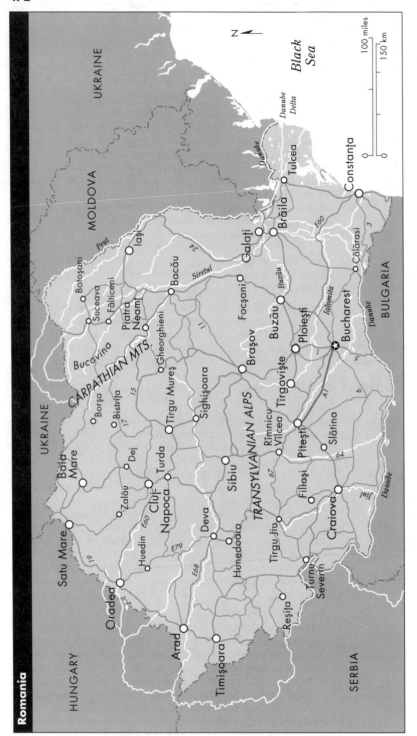

Romania

Bucharest there have been cases of cholera and hepatitis resulting from water consumption. Bottled water, referred to as *apa minerala,* is available in most restaurants and shops.

CATEGORY	COST*
$$$$	over $25
$$$	$15–$25
$$	$8–$15
$	under $8

*All prices are per person for a three-course meal, including wine and tip. Because high inflation means local prices change frequently, ratings are given in dollars, which remain reasonably constant. Your bill will be in lei.

Lodging

Lodging is, to put it simply, not Romania's forte. In general a night in a hotel will give you a chance to sleep in a decent bed and to shower, but don't look for style or ambience and don't be upset if you discover you are paying five or more times what a Romanian pays for a similar room. A star system of hotel classification is just being introduced, which takes the place of a system with categories including deluxe A and B (five-star or very expensive), first-class A (three-star or moderate), and first-class B (two-star or inexpensive), and so on. Facilities, including plumbing and hot water, can be poor even in the top hotels and deteriorate rapidly as the overall level of the establishment falls. Ask to see your room first, and always ask at the front desk when hot water will be available. In principle, at least, all hotels leave a certain quota of rooms unoccupied until 8 PM for unexpected foreign visitors.

Book accommodations through private agencies, directly with hotels, or through tourism agencies. Discounted prices are usually available if you make prepaid arrangements through a travel agency abroad. Fly-drive holidays and other package deals often provide bed-and-breakfast accommodation vouchers. Most state-run places take vouchers; in deluxe hotels, you have to pay a little extra. Rooms in private homes can be booked through the ONT office (☞ Visitor Information *in* Romania A to Z, *below*) and are a good alternative to hotels. Private citizens come to railway stations and offer spare rooms in their homes, but use discretion and be prepared to bargain. Inexpensive accommodations such as pensions or hostels are almost nonexistent, and student hostels are not available to foreigners. A few delightfully rustic cottages may be rented at ski resorts like Sinaia and Predeal. Details are available from Romanian tourist offices abroad.

CATEGORY	BUCHAREST*	OTHER AREAS*
$$$$	over $200	over $80
$$$	$125–$200	$50–$80
$$	$70–$125	$30–$50
$	under $70	under $30

*All prices are for two people in a double room. Guests staying in single rooms are charged a supplement. Prices are estimates for the high season. Because of inflation, ratings are given according to hard-currency equivalents— but you must pay in lei. (Note that hotels may insist on your buying lei from them to pay your bill, unless you can produce an exchange receipt to prove that you changed your money legally.)

Shopping

Romania has experienced a dramatic increase in imported goods in the last few years. These items tend to be fairly expensive by Romanian standards and more expensive than they are elsewhere. For real bargains look for items produced in Romania, including hand-woven

rugs, sweaters, crystal and porcelain, and folk art like masks, embroidered decorations, painted eggs, and wooden statuettes.

Open-air markets exist in every town and consist of food items as well
as merchandise being sold by local people, including unwanted home
furnishings and crafts. *Artizant* stores, found in most shopping areas
and museums, sell local folk art. Keep all receipts, as tight customs restrictions prohibit exporting many items, even bric-a-brac, unless proof
of purchase can be provided.

Walking and Hiking

The best way to explore the country is walking. Wherever you go, take
the time to walk to the various sites: Stroll through museums and shops
and admire the simplicity of the lives of many of the people here.

Hiking and backpacking are two of the best recreational activities in
Romania. During the Communist era, Romanians were discouraged
from vacationing outside Romania; as a result, a well-organized hiking system was developed. There are marked hiking trails throughout
most of the mountains and villages in the countryside. Cabanas where
you can stop for a drink and a hot meal can often be found along the
trails. Hiking maps are available through the tourism office (ONT),
from street vendors in Bucharest, and in some bookstores.

Exploring Romania

Great Itineraries

*Numbers in the text correspond to numbers in the margin and on the
maps.*

IF YOU HAVE 3 DAYS

Spend two days touring ⊠ **Bucharest** ①–⑭: on the first, follow the walking tour, exploring the museums and sights noted, and sign up for a
tour of **Cotroceni Palace Museum** ⑬ or **Ceaușescu's Palace** (Parliament
Palace) ① for your second day. If you have time, make the quick trip
to **Snagov,** where you can picnic at the monastery. On your third day,
journey to ⊠ **Sinaia,** the former summer retreat of the aristocracy, located within the Transylvanian Alps. Traveling here takes you through
the area of Ploiești—once the center of Romania's oil industry—which
was heavily bombed by the allies during World War II. Rebuilt as a
model communist city with centralized heating, plumbing, and other
utilities, it serves as an interesting contrast to the more remote towns
and villages that you will encounter if you have time for further explorations. In Sinaia take in the **Peles Palace,** one of the best-preserved royal palaces in Europe. If you have time, you might also visit
the **Pelisor** and **Sinaia Monastery** and ride the cable car above the town
for a breathtaking view of the surrounding mountainside.

IF YOU HAVE 5 DAYS

Follow the itinerary above during your first three days, and after visiting ⊠ **Sinaia,** continue north toward Brașov, taking a side trip to **Castle Bran,** once a major trading point during the Middle Ages. Along the
way you'll see traditional Romanian villages. At **Brașov,** your final destination, explore the center of the city, an exquisite example of a medieval frontier town, as well as the **Black Church** and **Piata Sfatului.** The
old section of the city is surrounded by fortified walls, while the town
itself is built with picturesque Bavarian-style architecture that evokes
the region's Germanic ancestry. ⊠ **Poiana Brașov,** in the mountains above
Brașov, is a resort area with a better selection of restaurants and hotels;
you can take an evening ride in a horse-drawn wagon here. If you have
time on your fifth day, hike the mountain trails around Poiana Brașov.

Follow trails from Poiana Braşov down to Braşov for a scenic hike, and take the bus back up at the end of the day.

When to Tour

Bucharest is at its best in the spring. The Black Sea resorts open in mid- to late May and close at the end of September. Winter ski resorts in the Carpathians are now well developed and increasingly popular, while the best time for touring the interior is late spring to fall. The Romanian climate is temperate and generally free of extremes, but snow as late as April is not unknown, and the lowlands can be very hot in midsummer.

BUCHAREST

The old story goes that a simple peasant named Bucur settled on the site where the city now stands. True or not, the name Bucureşti was first officially used only in 1459, by none other than Vlad Ţepeş, the real-life Dracula (sometimes known as Vlad the Impaler for his bloodthirsty habit of impaling unfortunate victims on wooden stakes). Two centuries later, this citadel on the Dimboviţa River became the capital of Walachia, and after another 200 years, it was named the capital of Romania. The city gradually developed into a place of bustling trade and gracious living, with ornate and varied architecture, landscaped parks, busy, winding streets, and wide boulevards. Today only hints of its past glory remain.

Exploring Bucharest

The high-rise Intercontinental Hotel dominates Bucharest's main intersection at Piaţa Universiţăţii. Northward up the main shopping streets of Bulevardul Nicolae Bălcescu, Bulevardul General Magheru, and Bulevardul Ana Ipătescu, only an occasional older building survives. However, along Calea Victoriei, something of Bucharest's grander past can be savored, especially at the former royal palace opposite the Romanian senate (formerly Communist Party headquarters) in Piaţa Revoluţiei. Here one also sees reminders of the December 1989 revolution, including the slow restoration of the domed National Library, gutted by fire, and the bullet holes on nearby walls. Modest, touching monuments to the more than 1,000 people killed in the revolution can be found here, and Piaţa Universiţăţii has a wall still festooned with protest posters.

South along Calea Victoriei is the busy Lipscani trading district, a remnant of the old city that sprawled farther southward before it was bulldozed in Nicolae Ceauşescu's megalomaniacal drive to redevelop the capital. Piaţa Unirii is the hub of his enormously expensive and impractical vision, which involved the forced displacement of thousands of people and the demolition of many houses, churches, and synagogues. Cranes now stand eerily idle above unfinished tower blocks with colonnaded, white-marble facades. They flank a lengthy boulevard leading to the enormous, empty, and unfinished Ceauşescu's Palace (now called Palatul Parlamentului, or Parliament Palace), second in size only to the Pentagon. With such a massive diversion of resources, it is not surprising that Bucharest is potholed and faded. But happily, the city continues to offer many places of historic interest, as well as cinemas, theaters, concert halls, and an opera house.

A Good Walk

Numbers in the text correspond to numbers in the margin and on the Bucharest map.

A tour of Bucharest should start with its most infamous point of interest, **Ceauşescu's Palace** (Palatul Parlamentului) ①. From here it is just a short walk north, across the Damboviţa River, to Strada I. Maniu to the historical core of the city, the **Curtea Veche** (old Princely Court) ② and the **Lipscani** district. The Princely Court now houses **Muzeul Curtea Veche-Palatul Voievodal.** The **Biserica din Curtea Veche** (Curtea Veche Church), founded in the 16th century and the oldest church in Bucharest, stands beside the Princely Court and remains an important center of worship in the city. Just across the road is **Hanul lui Manuc** (Manuc's Inn) ③. Nearby, **Lipscani** is a bustling area of narrow streets, open stalls, and small artisans' shops, which combine to create the atmosphere of a bazaar. At Strada Selari 11–13, you'll find glassblowers hard at work; glassware is sold next door. In **Hanul cu Tei,** off Strada Lipscani, are many galleries, crafts boutiques, and gift shops. On Strada Stavreopolos, there is a small but exquisite **Biserica Ortodoxă** (Orthodox church) ④. At the end of the street is the **Muzeul Naţional de Istorie** (Romanian History Museum) ⑤, which also houses the National Treasury. Opposite the Treasury is a full-size replica of the **Columna Traiană** (Trajan's Column) in Rome, which commemorates a Roman victory over Dacia in 2 AD.

Turning north along the Calea Victoriei, you'll pass a military club and academy before reaching the pretty little **Creţulescu Church** ⑥ on your left. Immediately north is a massive building, once the royal palace and now the Palace of the Republic. The **Muzeul de Artă al României** (National Art Museum) ⑦ is housed here. Opposite the palace, in Piaţa Revoluţiei, was the former headquarters of the Romanian Communist Party. Before the revolution in December 1989, no one was allowed to walk in front of this building. During the uprising the square was a major site of the fighting that destroyed the National Library, parts of the palace, and the Cina restaurant next to the **Ateneul Român** (Romanian Athenaeum Concert Hall) ⑧.

Follow Calea Victoriei as far as the Piaţa Victoriei. Opposite is the **Muzeul de Ştiinţe Naturale "Grigore Antipa"** (Natural History Museum) ⑨. Next door, in an imposing redbrick building, is the impressive **Muzeul Tăranalui Român** (Museum of the Romanian Peasant) ⑩.

Şoseaua Kiseleff, a pleasant tree-lined avenue, brings you to the **Arcul de Triumf** ⑪. Still farther north lies Herăstrău Park, accommodating the fascinating **Muzeul Satului Romanesc** (Village Museum) ⑫ and Herăstrău Lake.

TIMING

This walking tour of Bucharest could be done in as little as three to four hours, though you'll need to allow more time if you want to browse through the various museums. To have enough time to explore some of the museums, plan a full day. Keep in mind that most tourist sites don't open until 10 AM and close at 4 PM. On Saturday, most shops close between 2 PM and 4 PM, while on Sunday all state-owned stores are closed. Museums are closed on Monday; some on Tuesday as well.

Sights to See

⑪ Arcul de Triumf. A copy of the Paris landmark, the Arcul de Triumf was originally constructed of wood and stucco in 1922, to commemorate the Allied victory in World War I. It was then rebuilt during the 1930s, when it was carved by some of Romania's most talented sculptors. ⊠ *At the head of Sos. Kiseleff.*

⑧ Ateneul Român. Dating from 1888 and resembling a sort of Parthenon topped by a baroque dome, the Ateneul survived the revolution of 1989 and is still home to the George Enescu Philharmonic Orchestra. There is a large fresco in the concert hall, 9 feet (3 meters) high and 75 yards (70 meters) long. that depicts the history of the Romanian people from AD 100 to the end of World War II. ✉ *Piaţa Revoluţiei.*

❹ **Biserica Ortodoxă.** This Orthodox church combines late-Renaissance and Byzantine styles with elements of the Romanian folk-art style. Inside are superb wood and stone carvings and a richly ornate iconostasis, the painted screen that partitions off the altar. Boxes on either side of the entrance contain votive candles—for the living on the left, for the "sleeping" on the right. ✉ *Str. Stavreopolos.*

★ ❶ **Ceauşescu's Palace** (Palatul Parlamentului). It is claimed this is the second-largest building in the world, exceeded only by the Pentagon in Washington, D.C. As deep as it is tall, this mammoth building was originally meant to house the Communist dictator, Ceauşescu, and his government offices. Construction began in 1984, was interrupted by the revolution in 1989, and resumed again in 1991. The building is still unfinished, but is presently the home of the Romanian parliament. Tours can be arranged through a travel agent (☞ Guided Tours *and* Travel Agencies *in* Bucharest A to Z, *below*). ✉ *Blvd. Unirii.*

★ ⑬ **Cotroceni Palace Museum.** The former royal residence, one wing is now used by the Romanian president and is off-limits to visitors. The remainder of the palace offers a wealth of history about the intimate lives of Romania's former royalty. Reservations are required for tours. ✉ *Blvd. Geniului 1,* ☎ *01/4100581.* 🎫 *8,000 lei.*

❻ **Creţulescu Church.** Built in 1722 by the *boyar* (aristocrats) Iordache Creţulescu, this church is notable for its ornate carvings over the entrance and its decorative arches. The walls are adorned with frescoes by Tattarescu, a Romanian artist, which are a bit battered but still worth seeing. Parts of the church were restored during the 1930s. ✉ *Piaţa Revoluţiei.*

NEED A BREAK? Down the road, at Strada Stavreopolos 3, is the **Carul cu Bere** (☎ 01/6137560), serving half-liter tankards of beer, appetizers, and Turkish coffee. This is the oldest surviving beer hall in Bucharest.

❷ **Curtea Veche** and **Muzeul Curtea Veche-Palatul Voievodal.** The museum exhibits the remains of the palace built by Vlad Ţepeş in the 15th century. One section of the cellar wall presents the palace's history from the 15th century onward. You can see the rounded river stones used in the early construction, later alternating with red brick, and later still in plain brick. Prisoners were once kept in these cellars, which extend far into the surrounding city; a pair of ancient skulls belonging to two young boyars, decapitated at the end of the 17th century, will interest some. At press time, the museum was temporarily closed for restoration. ✉ *Str. Iuliu Maniu 31, no phone.* ☉ *Tues.–Sun. 10–6.*

❸ **Hanul lui Manuc** (Manuc's Inn). A renovated 19th-century inn, arranged in the traditional Romanian fashion around a courtyard, this now houses a hotel and restaurant (which is not recommended). Manuc was a wealthy Armenian merchant who died in Russia by poisoning—at the hand of a famous French fortune-teller who, having forecast Manuc's death on a certain day, could not risk ruining her reputation. The 1812 Russian-Turkish Peace Treaty was signed here. ✉ *Str. Iuliu Maniu 62–64,* ☎ *01/6131415.* 🎫 *Free.* ☉ *Daily 7:30–12:30.*

★ ⑭ **Jewish Community Museum.** The Jewish Museum traces the history of the Jewish people in Romania from AD 1000 through World War II. During the war, more than half of Romania's 750,000 Jews were killed in concentration camps established by Romania's police and military.

Bucharest

N

Str. Icoanei

Bdul. Dacia

Str. Galati

Str. Maria Rosetti

Banu Mămuleanu

Str. Tunari

Str. Aurel Vlaicu

B-dul Dacia

Str. Icoanei

Eminescu

Piaţa Al. Sahia

Şoseaua Ştefan Cel Mare

Str. Polonă

Str. Mihai

Str. Dionisie Lupu

Str. Pictor Verona

C. Dorobantilor

Piaţa Lahovari

...etti

Str. Roma

Str. Căderea Bastiliei

Piaţa Romană

B-dul G-ral Magheru

AE

i

8

Str. Londra

Str. Biserica Amzei

C. Victoriei

B-dul Iancu de Hunedoara

Str. Grigore Alexandrescu

B-dul Ana Ipătescu

Piaţa Amzei

Calea

Victoriei

B-dul Aviatorilor

Str. Occidentului

C. Grivitei

Şos. Kiseleff

Piaţa Victoriei

10 9

12 11

B-dul 1 Mai

Str. Buzeşti

Şos. Nicolae Titulescu

B-dul Alex Ioan Cuza

Str. Ştefan Furtună

Piaţa Matache

To Gara de Nord

Str. General Berth...

Str. Berz...

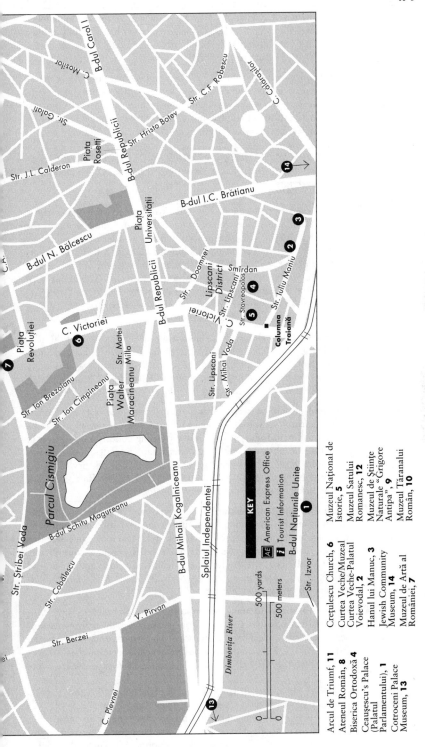

KEY

AE American Express Office

🇮 Tourist Information

Arcul de Triumf, **11**
Ateneul Român, **8**
Biserica Ortodoxă **4**
Ceauşescu's Palace
(Palatul
Parlamentului), **1**
Cotroceni Palace
Museum, **13**

Cretulescu Church, **6**
Curtea Veche/Muzeal
Curtea Veche–Palatul
Voievodal, **2**
Hanul lui Manuc, **3**
Jewish Community
Museum, **14**
Muzeul de Artă al
României, **7**

Muzeul National de
Istorie, **5**
Muzeul Satului
Romanesc, **12**
Muzeul de Ştiinţe
Naturale "Grigore
Antipa", **9**
Muzeul Ţăranalui
Român, **10**

Today many of Romania's 14,000 Jews feel compelled to practice their religion in secret, although the government has officially banned anti-Semitic sentiment in the press and in public. ⊠ *Str. Mamulari 3,* ☎ *01/6150837.* ☞ *Free.* ⊙ *Wed.–Sun. 9–1.*

Lipscani. Developed around 1750, Lipscani is one of the oldest streets in Bucharest. It has retained much of its appearance since then; it continues to be filled with shops, cafés, open stalls, and artists' displays. Of particular note is **Hanul cu tei,** an artists' alley near Boulevard Bratianu, where a variety of paintings and crafts can be found.

NEED A
BREAK?
Le Café de la Joie (⊠ Str. Lipscani 80–82, ☎ 01/3122910), an appealing French bistro, serves Romanian wine and gourmet coffee along with light French fare.

❼ Muzeul de Artă al României. Once the royal palace, the National Art Museum has a fine collection of Romanian art, including works by the sculptor Brâncuşi. The foreign section has a wonderful Brueghel collection. Much of this beautiful building was damaged during the events of December 1989, and it is now undergoing restoration; as a result, there are now only a few small exhibits on display. The majority of the original collection can be seen just down the road at Str. Calea Victoriei 111. ⊠ *Str. Stribei Voda 1,* ☎ *01/6133030 or 01/6155193.* ☞ *1,500 lei, free Wed.* ⊙ *Wed.–Sun. 10–6.*

❾ Muzeul de Ştiinţe Naturale "Grigore Antipa." The exhibits at this natural history museum include an exceptional butterfly collection and a skeleton of the dinosaur *Dinotherium gigantissimum,* as well as many exhibits depicting wildlife from around the world. ⊠ *Şoseaua Kiseleff 1,* ☎ *01/6504710.* ☞ *1,000 lei; 500 lei Wed.* ⊙ *Tues.–Sun. 10–5.*

❺ Muzeul Naţional de Istorie. This museum contains a vast collection of exhibits from Neolithic to modern times. The Treasury, which can be visited and paid for separately, has a startling collection of objects in gold and precious stones—royal crowns, weapons, plates, and jewelry—dating from the 4th millennium BC up to the 20th century. ⊠ *Calea Victoriei 12,* ☎ *01/6157056.* ☞ *3,000 lei.* ⊙ *Treasury Tues.–Sun. 10–5 (last tickets sold at 4); museum Wed.–Sun. 10–4.*

★ **⓬ Muzeul Satului Romanesc.** An open-air museum near Herăstrău Lake, this museum is outstanding, with more than 300 authentic, fully furnished peasant houses representing folk styles taken from all over Romania. The gift store sells crafts from the Romanian countryside. Occasionally concerts are held here, featuring traditional music and dance. ⊠ *Şoseaua Kiseleff 28,* ☎ *01/2229110.* ☞ *1,000 lei.* ⊙ *Winter, daily 8–4; summer, daily 10–7.*

❿ Muzeul Ţăranului Român. This imposing redbrick building is the Museum of the Romanian Peasant. Reopened in 1993, this impressive museum has a fine collection of costumes, icons, carpets, and other artifacts from rural life, including two 19th-century wooden churches. ⊠ *Şoseana Kiseleff 3,* ☎ *01/6505360.* ☞ *1,000 lei.* ⊙ *Tues.–Sun. 10–6.*

OFF THE
BEATEN PATH
SNAGOV – 40 kilometers (29 miles) north of Bucharest, Snagov Monastery, a small rustic cloister on a small island in the middle of Snagov Lake, is the reputed burial place of Vlad Ţepeş, also known as Dracula, who, it is claimed, lies beneath the floor of the church. To get there, go north out of Bucharest on E60 for about 20 minutes. Watch for a sign reading SNAGOV SAT. Turn right here and travel another 10 minutes, through the town of Snagov, until you reach the park area called Snagov Sat. You can rent a small rowboat here for the short ride out to

the island. Simply row out of the canal into the lake and take a quick left. Both Snagov Sat and Snagov Island are great places for a picnic. (A picnic is your best bet for food; though if you don't bring your own, there are small kiosks and a restaurant with a limited menu at Snagov Sat). ⊙ *Boat rentals daily 8–4.*

Dining

New restaurants featuring a variety of cuisines open in Bucharest almost daily, while McDonald's and Pizza Hut lead the fast-food incursion. Food kiosks, cafés, grills, and restaurants can now be found throughout the city. Some of these smaller kiosks should be avoided, but good, inexpensive meals can be found in many of the newer cafés. Always check your bill, as it is not uncommon for restaurants to try to overcharge foreigners. Note that most places will serve wine and water only by the bottle and not by the glass.

$$$$ ✕ **Darclee.** The Darclee, in the new Hotel Sofitel (☞ Lodging, *below*), ★ was the first French restaurant to arrive in Bucharest. Like the hotel, the restaurant is intended to be an outpost of French excellence. The menu includes a variety of dishes based on both French and Romanian cuisines. Choices include mussels in cream sauce, salmon, broiled chicken, and lamb roll. There is also a broad array of tempting desserts to choose from. The ambience is cozy and sophisticated. ⊠ *Expoziţiei Blvd. 2,* ☎ *01/2122998. AE, MC, V, DC.*

$$$$ ✕ **Golden Falcon.** One of many Middle Eastern restaurants in Bucharest, the Golden Falcon is distinguished by its Turkish cuisine. Entrees are presented on a tray at your table, from which you select your meal. Choices include a variety of kabobs, fish, and vegetables in spicy sauces. Hot, fresh flat bread complements all the dishes. The decor is very simple, and as is often the case in Romanian restaurants, it can be very smoky during busy hours. The staff is friendly and quick to help. ⊠ *Str. Histro Botev 20,* ☎ *01/6142825. No credit cards.*

$$$$ ✕ **Korea House.** The newest of Bucharest's many Asian restaurants. Upon entering you are asked to remove your shoes and put on slippers. You then have a choice between chairs at a Western-style table or cushions at a lower one. The food is spicy and very Asian-influenced, beginning with a variety of appetizers, presented at your table for you to choose from. Main course items are presented in a similar fashion. The fish are a particular specialty, especially the squid, which is prepared in a spicy brown sauce. The pleasant, service-oriented staff helps to keep this establishment busy. ⊠ *Str. Cimpina 53,* ☎ *01/6665283. No credit cards.*

$$$$ ✕ **Velvet.** One of the first deluxe restaurants to arrive in Bucharest, the Velvet offers an excellent mix of good service and a variety of food. Menu items include lobster, shrimp dipped in sauces, duck, pheasant, and lamb. Particularly notable is the chateaubriand. There is no official dress code here, but you will definitely feel out of place in travel wear. ⊠ *Str. Ştirbei Voda 2–4,* ☎ *01/6159241,* FAX *01/3127001. AE, MC, V, DC.*

$$$ ✕ **Casa Doina.** Recently refurbished, this historic restaurant, popular with the Bucharest elite between the wars, is once again one of the best in town. The decor, with many traditional colors and crafts on display, is inspired by the Romanian countryside. Romanian and international cuisines are served in a relaxing atmosphere; the menu includes seafood, stuffed cabbage rolls, and a variety of meats. In summer you can enjoy the terrace, which backs onto Kiseleff Park. In the evening there are often bands playing traditional music. Try to request seating in the lower restaurant, which has a more traditional feel. ⊠ *B-dul. Kiseleff 4,* ☎ *01/2223179. AE, DC, MC, V.*

$$$ ✕ **La Premiera.** In the center of the city, just behind the National The-
★ ater, La Premiera is a superb mix of German and Romanian cuisines,
served by one of the friendliest staffs in Bucharest. A variety of gourmet
Romanian fare is served, including stuffed grape leaves, liver in cream
sauce, and pork cutlets. The walls are decorated with scenes of Bucharest
in the 1920s and 1930s. In the summer you can enjoy the outdoor ter-
race. ⊠ *Blvd. Nicolae Balcescu 2,* ☎ *01/3124397. AE, MC, V, DC.*

$$$ ✕ **Piccolo Mondo.** Piccolo Mondo, a Lebanese restaurant, was one of
★ the first restaurants to open in Bucharest after the revolution in 1989.
Specialties include kabobs, hummus, tabouleh, *fettouche* (a flavorful Middle Eastern salad), and chicken; there's also as a sampling of Italian and
Romanian items. During warm weather meals can be served in the front
garden area. ⊠ *Str. Clucerului,* ☎ *01/2229046. No credit cards.*

$$$ ✕ **Sydney.** Just off Piața Victoriei, the Sydney has the ambience of an
Australian pub. The menu is very basic, offering a variety of grilled
meats and a salad bar. There is a wide choice of drinks, including many
imported beers. The staff is friendly and helpful; this is a good choice
for a late-night dinner. ⊠ *Calea Victoriei 222,* ☎ *01/6594207. V.*

$$ ✕ **Bistro Atheneum.** Just off Piața Revoluției, focal point of the 1989
★ revolution and former site of the official residence of the Romanian
royal family, this charming restaurant offers gourmet Romanian cuisine such as liver in mushroom sauce, steak, and grilled chicken. The
atmosphere is reminiscent of a traditional Paris bistro. Live classical
music performed by small troupes of local musicians adds to the charm.
⊠ *Str. Episcopiei 3,* ☎ *01/6134900. No credit cards.*

$$ ✕ **Boema.** Don't be disappointed by your first impression of this cen-
trally located restaurant: The walls are painted dark blue and plastic
palm trees are everywhere. But the food and service more then make
up for appearances. The extensive menu includes lobster, frogs' legs,
chicken, and red meat. Particularly impressive are sour soups, which
are homemade and very thick. The variety of schnitzels is particularly
impressive; all are served with a full plate of potatoes and a vegetable.
The staff here is attentive and helpful. ⊠ *Str. C. A. Rosetti,* ☎ *01/
6133783. No credit cards.*

$$ ✕ **Quatro Stagioni.** Two restaurants under the same proprietor, both
offer some of Bucharest's best pizza as well as a variety of Italian dishes.
The first, recently renovated, has large windows looking out onto
Boulevard Aviatorilor out front. The second is just off Piața Victorei.
⊠ *Blvd. Aviatorilor 19,* ☎ *01/2227230;* ⊠ *Str. Buzești 55,* ☎ *01/
2123064. No credit cards.*

$$ ✕ **Tandoori.** On a small side street, this Indian restaurant offers a
slightly dismal face, though don't be put off. When you enter, you are
met at the door by staff dressed in Indian garb who bow and show
you to your table. The menu features a variety of chicken and vegetable
dishes prepared in spicy sauces. The *riata*, a cucumber and yogurt salad,
is especially good. This is one of a handful of restaurants that have both
a smoking and no-smoking section. ⊠ *Str. Budai Deleanu 4,* ☎ *01/
6234147. No credit cards.*

$ ✕ **Mimi's Cafe.** Mimi's is an unusual mix of TexMex and Romanian
food: The owner is a Romanian who immigrated to California and has
now returned to open this restaurant. But the hybrid cuisine seems to
work well; be sure to ask about the daily specials for the best offer-
ings. The decor features stuffed parrots hanging from the ceiling and
bright colors everywhere. The staff is friendly and helpful. ⊠ *Blvd. Carol
I 27,* ☎ *01/6422705. No credit cards.*

Lodging

See Lodging *in* Pleasures and Pastimes, *above,* for general lodging information.

$$$$ ☷ **Helveția.** Bucharest's first privately constructed hotel since World War II, the Helveția has established itself as one of the capital's better establishments since opening in mid-1993. This is a small, quiet hotel with an emphasis on individual service and comfort. It is a little north of the city center but is easily accessible by metro or taxi. All rooms include cable television. ⊠ *Str. Uruguay 29,* ☎ *01/2228120,* ℻ *01/2230567. 30 rooms with bath. Restaurant, bar, café. AE, DC, MC, V.*

$$$$ ☷ **Intercontinental.** Designed principally for business clients, the Intercontinental offers American-style accommodations in the city's tallest building. Each room is air-conditioned and has a balcony and cable television. All rooms have a view of the city. ⊠ *B-dul N. Bălcescu 4–6,* ☎ *01/2107330,* ℻ *01/3120486. 423 rooms with bath. 7 bars and restaurants, pool, health club, nightclub, minicasino. AE, DC, MC, V.*

$$$$ ☷ **Lido.** Conveniently situated in the center of the city, this prewar hotel has recently been privatized and renovated to offer comfortable rooms and good facilities, including an outdoor swimming pool and terrace. Rooms are very clean and include air-conditioning and cable television. ⊠ *B-dul Magheru 5,* ☎ *01/6144930,* ℻ *01/3126544. 92 rooms with bath. Restaurant, bar, pool, nightclub. AE, DC, MC, V.*

$$$$ ☷ **Sofitel.** On the edge of the city on the way to the airport, the Sofi-
★   tel is a Western oasis in Bucharest. Every room is immaculate. Rooms on the front side of the hotel have a beautiful view of Herăstrău Park. ⊠ *Blvd. Expozitiei 2,* ☎ *01/2234000 or 01/2122998,* ℻ *01/2224650. 203 single and double rooms and apartments with bath. 2 restaurants, bar, local health club membership. AE, DC, MC, V.*

$$$ ☷ **Ambassador.** The 13-story Ambassador was built in 1937 and enjoys a fine central location. Although a little shabby, its rooms are comfortably furnished. The restaurant is not recommended, but there is a good café. ⊠ *B-dul General Magheru 6–8,* ☎ *01/6159080,* ℻ *01/3123595. 233 rooms with bath. Restaurant, café. AE, DC, MC, V.*

$$$ ☷ **Capitol.** The circa 1900 Capitol is situated in a lively part of town near the Cişmigiu Gardens. In days gone by, it was the stomping ground of Bucharest's major artists and writers. Today the Capitol is modernized and offers comfortable rooms—though the literati have long since moved on. ⊠ *Calea Victoriei 29,* ☎ *01/6139440,* ℻ *01/3124169. 70 rooms with bath. Restaurant. No credit cards.*

$$ ☷ **Casa Victor.** Though very simple, this is one of the better inexpen-
★   sive alternatives to the drab, government-run hotels left over from the Communist era or expensive newer hotels. Each room includes cable television, a refrigerator, and an ample breakfast (served at any hour). Within walking distance of the Arcul de Triumf, Herăstrău Park, and the metro, the hotel is conveniently situated. ⊠ *Str. Campia Turzii 44,* ☎ *01/2225723,* ℻ *01/2229436. 7 singles, doubles, and apartments with bath. Restaurant. No credit cards.*

$$ ☷ **Minerva.** Renovated in 1992 and near the center of the city, this is
★   one of the few state-run hotels that makes service a priority. The staff is very friendly and helpful. Rooms are comfortable and clean and come with air-conditioning and television. The restaurant here serves very good Chinese food. ⊠ *Str. Gheorghe Manu 2–4,* ☎ *01/3111550 or 01/3111551,* ℻ *01/3123963. 83 single and double rooms and apartments with bath. Restaurant, bar. AE, DC, MC, V.*

$$ ⊡ **Triumf.** Set on its own grounds slightly outside the city center near
★ the Arcul de Triumf, this is a beautiful building with comfortable
rooms. Formerly the President, it used to serve only the Communist
elite. The more expensive rooms are miniapartments. ⊠ *Şoseaua Kise-
leff 12,* ☎ *01/2223172,* 𝔽𝔸𝕏 *01/2232411. 98 rooms, 49 with bath.
Restaurant, bar, tennis court. V.*

Nightlife and the Arts

Bars and Nightclubs

Only a few years ago, Bucharest shut down completely at night. Street-
lights were scarce (traffic lights were even shut off early), and a decent
bar or nightclub was difficult to find. But all this has changed: It now
seems as though Bucharest never sleeps. Small bars are commonplace,
several nightclubs have opened, and new hot spots burn brightly for a
time, then flare out. Some caveats: Bars that serve alcohol may not meet
Western sanitary requirements, and be sure to check prices ahead of time
and look over your bill—it is common for foreigners to be overcharged.

Dubliner. This is a hot spot for the local expatriate community. Its Irish
pub atmosphere is comfortable, and the people here are always friendly.
A variety of imported beers are available; the two dart boards are a
draw. ⊠ *Blvd. N. Titulescu 18,* ☎ *01/2229473.*

Laptaria Enache (Milk Bar). Live jazz and blues, now popular in
Bucharest, can be enjoyed at this bar in the National Theater, which
moves outdoors onto the roof terrace in warm weather. There is a mod-
est, 5,000-lei cover charge; the live music doesn't start until around
11 PM. ⊠ *Teatrul Naţional,* ☎ *01/6158508.*

Manhattan Club. If you enjoy being an active participant in the evening's
entertainment, the Manhattan Club offers a great bar atmosphere and
a karaoke show. In the new World Trade Center (☞ Shopping, *below*),
the decor is Western and chic. Prices are three or four times what you'll
pay elsewhere. ⊠ *Blvd. Expozitiei 2,* ☎ *01/6686290.*

Casinos

With 16 casinos at last count, Bucharest offers plenty of opportunity
for those who want to try their hand at gambling. One of the older
and better known is the **Casino Victoria,** which also offers a dinner show
in their theater. There is gambling available in both dollars and lei. Drinks
are free. No admission. ⊠ *Calea Victoriei 174,* ☎ *01/6505865, 01/
6594913, or 01/3129516.*

Music

George Enescu Philharmonic Orchestra. Featured in Bucharest's famous
concert hall, the Romanian Athenaeum, this orchestra plays a variety
of classical favorites. The music is top quality at inexpensive prices.
Performances begin at 6:30 PM daily. Tickets can be purchased from
the concert hall or from your hotel, with a slight commission added.
⊠ *Str. Franklin 1,* ☎ *01/6195987.*

Radio Hall. A popular spot to hear the perennial classical music favorites
performed by a variety of local and foreign musicians. Tickets can be
purchased from the concert hall or from your hotel, with a slight com-
mission added. Performances begin at 7 PM. ⊠ *Str. General Berthelot
62–64,* ☎ *01/6146800.*

Opera and Ballet

Opera Română. The opera house has some good productions, though
not of the same quality you might find in Prague or Budapest. Tickets
can be purchased from the opera house or from your hotel, with a slight

commission added. ⊠ *Blvd. Mihail Kogălniceanu 70,* ☎ *01/6156812.* ⊙ *Performances Wed.–Sun. at 6:30 PM.*

Theater

Ion Dacian Operetta Theatre. Inside the National Theatre, this house has seen productions of many popular musicals (such as *My Fair Lady* and *King of the Gypsies*). Tickets can be purchased from the theatre or from your hotel, with a slight commission added. ⊠ *Piata Universitatii,* ☎ *01/6151502.*

Shopping

If you are interested in Western-style shopping, the new **World Trade Center** (⊠ Blvd. Expozitiei 2), next to the Sofitel is a small version of a Western shopping mall. There are several import stores here providing the latest in men's and women's fashions, a music store, a hair salon, and a rather expensive *artizanat* selling Romanian folk wares.

Art and Crafts

The **Apollo gallery** in the National Theater building (☞ Theater, *above*) next to the Intercontinental Hotel and the galleries in the **Hanul cu Tei** off Strada Lipscani sell art that you may legally take home with you.

For local folklore arts and crafts watch for the **artizanat** stores throughout the city. These specialize in crafts made by Romanian peasants, including embroidered decorations, dolls, masks, and other items. Both the **Peasant Museum** (⊠ Sos. Kieseleff 3, ☎ 01/6505360) and the **Village Museum** (⊠ Sos. Kieseleff 28–30, ☎ 01/2229110) have on-site artizanat shops.

Carpets

Romania is well known for its handmade woven carpets. It is often difficult to take these out of the country unless purchased from an authorized retailer, such as **Covorul** (⊠ Blvd. Unirii, ☎ 01/3112196). Be sure to hang on to your receipts.

China, Crystal, and Porcelain

Romanian china, crystal, and porcelain tend to be fairly inexpensive and of good quality. Two shops that specialize in these items are **Camina** (⊠ Calea Victoriei 16–20, ☎ 01/6136716) and **Leu** (⊠ Blvd. Unirii 11, ☎ 01/6149414). Be sure to hang on to your receipts in case you are questioned at the airport.

Food

The main food market is in **Piaţa Amzei,** open seven days a week and best visited during the morning. It sells a limited variety of cheese, fruit, and flowers. If you decide to visit outlying flea markets such as Piaţa Obor, take a guide to avoid being hassled and ripped off.

Bucharest A to Z

Arriving and Departing

BY CAR

There are three main access routes into and out of the city—E70 west from the Hungarian border, E60 north via Braşov, and E70/E85 south to Bulgaria. Bucharest has poor signposting and many tortuous one-way systems: Knowing how to say *Unde este centrul* (*oon*-day *yes*-tay *tchen*-trul—"Where's the town center?") is essential.

BY PLANE

All international flights to Romania land at Bucharest's **Otopeni Airport** (☎ 01/2120138 or 01/2120142), 16 kilometers (9 miles) north of the city.

Bus 783 leaves the airport every 30 minutes between 7 AM and 10 PM, stopping in the main squares before terminating in Piata Unirii. The journey takes an hour. Your hotel can arrange transport by car from the airport. Taxi drivers at the airport seek business aggressively and charge outrageously in dollars. Note that the "official" fare is in lei, the equivalent of about $12 with tip, so bargain.

BY TRAIN
There are five main stations in Bucharest, though international lines operate from Gara de Nord (☎ 01/952). For tickets and information, go to the Advance Booking Office (✉ Str. Brezoianu 10, ☎ 01/6132642). For international trains, go to CFR International (✉ B-dul I. C. Brătianu 44, ☎ 01/6134008). Arrival and departure information is available by calling 01/3110857.

Getting Around
Bucharest is spacious and sprawling. Though the old heart of the city and the two main arteries running the length of it are best explored on foot, long, wide avenues and vast squares make some form of transportation necessary. New tourist maps are being printed and can be found in bookstores; they may also be available at tourism agencies, hotels, and from street vendors. It is generally safe on the streets at night, but watch out for vehicles and hidden potholes.

BY BUS, TRAM, AND TROLLEY BUS
These are uncomfortable, crowded, and infrequent, but service is extensive. A ticket valid for two trips of any length can be purchased from kiosks near bus stops or from tobacconists; validate your ticket when you board. There are also day and week passes (*abonaments*), but more expensive *maxi taxis* (minibuses that stop on request) and express buses take fares on board. The system shuts down at midnight.

BY SUBWAY
The metro system recently received a face-lift and is now (by far) the best way to reach the city center from outlying areas. While the four subway lines—blue (M2), orange (M3), and red and yellow (both known as M1)—are fairly comprehensive, only three stations—**Piaţa Unirii, Universităţii,** and **Piaţa Romană,** all on the blue M2 line—serve the downtown area. Subway trains usually arrive about 10 minutes apart and run 5 AM–11 PM. Try to get on at the rear of the train; the front section is like an express class, meaning the doors don't open at every station. Fares run about 500 lei for one round-trip ticket; change is available from kiosks inside stations, and you may travel any distance.

BY TAXI
Need a cab? Hail a moving cab (parked ones tend to charge more to make up for money lost while sitting idle), or phone ☎ 01/953, 945, 956, or 941 (dispatchers speak English). A taxi is relatively inexpensive, but be sure to check that there is a meter or negotiate a price before getting in.

Contacts and Resources
DOCTORS AND DENTISTS
Medical care in Bucharest is still not up to Western expectations. You should look into evacuation insurance when traveling in Romania; your private health provider can usually make a recommendation. For minor difficulties your embassy or consulate may be able to help you. Two very good Western dental facilities have opened recently: **Novident** (☎ 01/4101222), and **Dent-America** (☎ 01/2122608). In an emergency you can get help by dialing ☎ 01/961.

EMBASSIES AND CONSULATES
United Kingdom (✉ Str. Jules Michelep 24, ☎ 01/3120303), open weekdays 9–noon. **Canada** (✉ Str. Nicolae Iorga 36, ☎ 01/2229845), open weekdays 2–4. **United States** (✉ Str. Nicolae Filipescu, ☎ 01/2104042), open weekdays 8:30–11:30 and Monday–Thursday 1–3.

GUIDED TOURS AND TRAVEL AGENCIES
Magellan Tourism (✉ Blvd. Magheru 12–14, ☎ 01/2119650, ℻ 01/2104903). **Medair Travel and Tourism** (✉ Str. Nicolae Balcescu, ☎ 01/3113190, ℻ 01/3127033). **Office of National Tourism (ONT)** (✉ Blvd. Magheru 7, ☎ 01/6141922, ℻ 01/3123907). **Realini Ionescu Tourism** (mobile ☎ 01/078600762). **Transylvanian Society of Dracula** (✉ Blvd. Primaverii 47, ☎ 01/6666195, ℻ 01/3123056).

LATE-NIGHT PHARMACIES
Farmacia 14 (✉ Sos. Iancului 57, ☎ 01/2502172). **Farmacia 20** (✉ Calea Serban Voda 43, ☎ 01/6237647). **Farmacia 26** (✉ Sos. Colentina 1, ☎ 01/6355010). **Farmacia Magheru** (✉ Blvd. Magheru 18, ☎ 01/6596115).

THE BLACK SEA COAST AND DANUBE DELTA

The **Delta Dunării** (Danube Delta) is Europe's largest wetlands reserve, covering 2,681 square kilometers (1,676 square miles), with a sprawling, watery wilderness that stretches from the Ukrainian border to a series of lakes north of the Black Sea resorts. It is Europe's youngest land—more than 43.7 square meters (47 square yards) are added each year by normal silting action. As it approaches its delta, the great Danube divides into three channels. The northernmost branch forms the border with Ukraine, the middle arm leads to the busy port of Sulina, and the southernmost arm meanders gently toward the little port of Sfintu Gheorghe. From these channels, countless canals widen into tree-fringed lakes, reed islands, and pools covered with water lilies; there are sand dunes and pockets of lush forest.

More than 80% of the delta area is water. Over 300 bird species visit the area, 70 of them from as far away as China and India. The delta is a natural stopover for migratory birds, but the most characteristic bird is the common pelican, the featured star of this bird-watchers' paradise. Fishing provides most of the area's inhabitants, many of whom are of Ukrainian origin, with a livelihood. One of the most common sights is a long line of fishing boats strung together to be towed by motorboat to remote fishing grounds. Smaller communities, such as Independenţa on the southern arm and Crişan on the middle arm, rent out the services of a fisherman and his boat to foreigners. The waters here are particularly rich in catfish, perch, carp, and caviar-bearing sturgeon.

Tulcea

277 km (172 mi) northeast of Bucharest.

The main town of the Danube Delta, Tulcea is the gateway to the splendors of the region. Built on seven hills and influenced by Turkish styles, this former market town is now an important sea and river port, as well as the center of the Romanian fish industry. The **Muzeul Deltei Dunării** (Danube Delta Museum) provides a good introduction to the flora, fauna, and way of life of the communities in the area. ✉ *Str. Progresului 32, ☎ 40/514330. ⊡ 2,000 lei. ☉ Daily 10–6.*

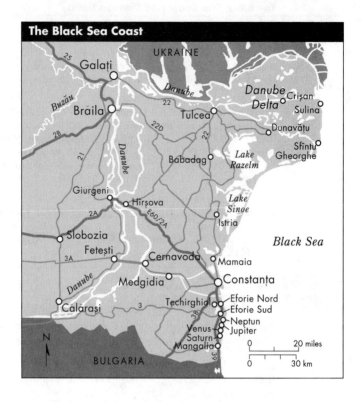

The Black Sea Coast

Lodging

$$ 🏨 **Delta.** A large, modern hotel on the bank of the Danube, the Delta currently has a mixed reputation. ✉ *Str. Isaacei 2, Tulcea,* ☎ *040/514720,* FAX *040/616260. 117 rooms with bath. Restaurant, bar. No credit cards.*

En Route There are good roads to the Black Sea resorts from Tulcea that take you to **Babadag** via the strange, eroded Măcin Hills. It was here, according to local legend, that Jason and his Argonauts cast anchor in their search for the mythical golden fleece. Farther south is **Istria,** with impressive ruins of the settlement founded in 6 BC by Greek merchants from Miletus. There are traces of early Christian churches and baths and even residential, commercial, and industrial districts. A useful English-language booklet, available on the spot, will help make sense of the remains of several cultures.

Mamaia

60 km (37 mi) south of Istria, 235 km (146 mi) east of Bucharest.

The largest of the Black Sea resorts, Mamaia is situated on a strip of land bordered by the Black Sea and fine beaches on one side and the fresh waters of Mamaia Lake on the other. All the resorts along this stretch of the coast have modern high-rise apartments, villas, restaurants, nightclubs, and discos. There are cruises down the coast to Mangalia and along the new channel linking the Danube with the Black Sea near Constanţa. Sea-fishing expeditions can also be arranged for early risers, with all equipment provided. These resorts offer everything necessary for a complete vacation by the sea.

Dining and Lodging

$$ ✕ **Insula lui Ovidiu.** This is a reed-thatched complex of rustic-style buildings with lively music every evening. A relaxed, informal atmosphere provides a good setting for well-prepared seafood dishes. ⊠ *Lake Siurghiol, Mamaia, no phone. No credit cards.*

$$$$ 🏨 **Rex.** One of King Carol's former residences, this is the largest and
★ grandest of all the hotels in Mamaia. The rooms are spacious and clean, and the staff is very attentive. ⊠ *Mamaia,* ☎ *041/831595,* 𝔽𝔸𝕏 *041/831690. 102 rooms with bath. Restaurant, bar, pool, exercise room. AE, DC, MC, V.*

$ 🏨 **Lido.** One of many newly built and moderately priced hotels. They are grouped in a horseshoe around open-air pools near the beach at the north end of the resort area of Mamaia. ⊠ *Mamaia,* ☎ *041/831555. 129 rooms with bath. Restaurant. No credit cards.*

Constanţa

10 km (6 mi) south of Mamaia (a trolley connects the two), 225 km (140 mi) east of Bucharest.

Romania's second-largest city and one steeped in history, Constanţa has the polyglot flavor characteristic of so many seaports. The famous Roman poet Ovid was exiled here from Rome in 8 AD, probably for his part in court scandals and for the amorality of his poem *Ars amandi* (*The Art of Love*). A city square named for him provides a fine backdrop for a statue of the poet by the sculptor Ettore Ferrari. Behind the statue, in the former town hall, is one of the best museums in Europe, the **Muzuel Naţional de Istorie şi Arheologie** (National History and Archaeological Museum). Of special interest here are the statuettes of the *Thinker* and the *Seated Woman,* from the Neolithic Hamangian culture (4000 to 3000 BC). Collections from the Greek, Roman, and Daco-Roman cultures are generally outstanding. ⊠ *Piaţa Ovidiu 12,* ☎ *41/618763.* 🎫 *3,000 lei.* ⊙ *Tues.–Sun. 10–6.*

Near the Muzuel Naţional de Istorie şi Arheologie is the **Edificiu Roman cu Mozaic,** a complex of Roman warehouses and shops from the 4th century AD, including a magnificent mosaic floor over 6,510 square meters (21,000 square feet) in area (⊠ Piaţa Ovidiu 1). The **Parcul Arheologic** (Archaeology Park) on Boulevard Republicii contains fragments of buildings dating from the 3rd and 4th centuries AD and a 6th-century tower. One of the modern-day attractions is an aquarium (⊠ Str. Februarie 16). Another is the dolphinarium (⊠ B-dul Mamaia 265), which offers aquatic displays by trained dolphins.

Dining and Lodging

$$$$ ✕ **Cazinou.** A turn-of-the-century former casino situated close to the aquarium, the Cazinou is decorated in an ornate 20th-century style; there's an adjoining bar by the sea. Seafood dishes are the house specialties. ⊠ *Str. Februarie 16,* ☎ *041/617416. No credit cards.*

$$ ✕ **Veneţia.** This Italian restaurant right off Ovidiu Square is very
★ quaint, and the staff is friendly. The walls are decorated with Venetian scenes. A number of pasta dishes is served. ⊠ *Str. Mircea cel Batrin 5,* ☎ *041/617390. No credit cards.*

$$$ 🏨 **Palace.** Near the city's historic center, the large and gracious old Palace has recently been renovated. It has a good restaurant and a terrace overlooking the sea and the tourist port of Tomis. ⊠ *Str. Remus Opreanu 5–7,* ☎ *041/614696,* 𝔽𝔸𝕏 *041/617532. 132 rooms with bath. Restaurant. No credit cards.*

En Route   A string of seaside resorts lies just south of Constanţa. **Eforie Nord** is an up-to-date thermal treatment center. A number of resorts built in the 1960s were given names evoking the coast's Greco-Roman past— **Neptune, Jupiter, Venus,** and **Saturn.** Not in any way typically Romanian, these resorts offer good amenities for relaxed seaside vacations. There are many inexpensive hotels near these beaches. Try **Moldova** (✉ Olimp–Neptune, ☎ 041/731916), where the rooms, though a bit run down, are clean and the staff is friendly. Right on the beach, **Panoramic** (✉ Olimp–Neptun, ☎ 041/731356) is one of the nicer hotels in the area. Sea-facing rooms have a magnificent view, and the restaurant offers very good Romanian cuisine. The old port of **Mangalia** is the southernmost resort. There are regular excursions from the seaside resorts of the Black Sea to the Istria, the Podgoriile Murfatlar (Murfatlar vineyards) for wine tastings, and the ruins of the Roman town at Tropaeum Trajani.

The Black Sea Coast and Danube Delta A to Z

Arriving and Departing

BY CAR

The Black Sea is only 210 kilometers (130 miles) from Bucharest. To get there follow 3 out of Bucharest until you hook up to 3A, following this the remainder of the way to Constanţa.

BY PLANE

Tarom, the Romanian national airline, flies regularly to Constanţa. The flight takes only 45 minutes (☎ 01/6594125 or 01/6594185).

BY TRAIN

There is regular train service to Constanţa, departing from Gara de Nord in Bucharest (☎ 01/3110857).

Getting Around

BY BOAT

Regular passenger and sightseeing boats operate along the middle and southern arms of the Danube Delta. Motorboats are available for hire, or rent one of the more restful fishermen's boats.

BY BUS

Bus trips from the Black Sea resorts and Constanţa to the Danube Delta, the Murfatlar vineyards, Istria, and the sunken city of Adamclisi are arranged by tourism agencies.

BY CAR

Rental cars, with or without drivers, are available through rental agencies in Bucharest.

Contacts and Resources

LATE-NIGHT PHARMACIES

Farmacia 6 (✉ Blvd. Ferdinand 97, Constanţa, ☎ 041/616821).

VISITOR INFORMATION

Constanţa: Danubius (✉ Blvd. Ferdinand 36, ☎ 041/615836, 041/619481, or 041/613103). **Mamaia: ONT—Carpaţi** (✉ Blvd. Tomis 46, ☎ 041/614861 or 041/617127). **Tulcea: Agency BTT** (✉ Str. Babadag, Bloc 1, Scara (stairway) A, ☎ 040/512496).

BUCOVINA

Moldova is the section of Romania in the extreme northeast of the country. During World War II, portions of Moldova were annexed by the Soviet Union and still remain separate from Romania to this day. Throughout history Moldova has been home to some of Romania's

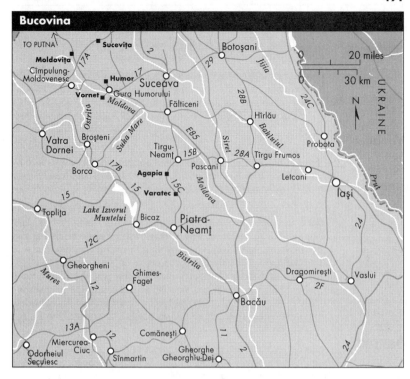

Bucovina

greatest poets, writers, and composers, including Mihai Eminescu, the national poet, and George Enescu, the national composer.

Bucovina—an area within Moldova that is west of Suceava and north of Piatra Neamt—is a remote region that did not suffer the deleterious suppression felt by the rest of the country under communism—in large part because the hilly land could not support large-scale agriculture. As a result, a visit to this area is like a step back in time: Farmers still use handmade hoes and ploughs, and homes are adorned with intricately carved wooden gables. The name Bucovina was first given to the area in the 18th century, when it was a part of the Austro–Hungarian Empire. It means "beech-covered land," and indeed there are large numbers of beech trees in the area still adding to its rustic beauty.

But the beech trees are only one element of the Bucovina's magnificent beauty. It is also home to splendid medieval monasteries nestled in small valleys and on hillsides. Many date to the 15th century, when Moldova was ruled by Prince Stefan Cel Mare, or Stefan the Great. During his rule, Stefan was engaged in ongoing battles with the infidel Ottoman Turks. He was often successful in battle, and many of these monasteries were built in thanks to God for his achievements. A number of them are noteworthy not only for their historical interest, but also for the vivid frescoes that were painted on both interior and exterior walls in an effort to educate the illiterate Romanians of that period about their political and national history. Even after centuries these frescoes are impeccably preserved—colorful and detailed (UNESCO has added them to its "Catalogue of the World's Great Monuments").

There are more than 15 monasteries in Bucovina, so it would be difficult to see them all. But visits to a few—most notably, Agapia, Humor, Moldovita, Putna, Sucevita, and Vornet—will give you an idea of their exceptional beauty. There is yet another reason to visit the Bucovina monasteries; in this remote region, they offer the best—and in some cases the only—available dining and lodging (☞ *below*). There is no official charge for these services, although a donation in dollars is appreciated. There are also small admission fees.

If you desire more conventional lodging, consider spending the night in **Suceava** before beginning your journey to the monasteries. Two inexpensive hotels here are the **Suceava** (☎ 030/521079, ℻ 030/520052) and the **Bucovina** (☎ 030/214700, ℻ 030/217048).

Varatec

94 km (58 mi) south of Suceava. From Suceava, follow E85 south to the turnoff to Tirgu-Neamţ on 15B. Follow 15B to Tirgu-Neamţ, then take 15C to the turnoff to Varatec.

Founded in the 18th century, the quaint, whitewashed monastery at Varatec was built later then most of the others in the Bucovina. And unlike most of the others it was neither fortified nor intended as the center of village life. Nor does it contain beautiful frescoes, but it is still worth a visit—if only because it is one of the monasteries offering lodging and meals. The surrounding forest was the setting for a poem by the Romanian national poet Mihai Eminescu. The poet Veronica Micle, who was an unobtainable love of Eminescu's, is buried within the monastery walls. ☎ *033/661141. Lodging and meals.*

Agapia

10 km (6 mi) north of Varatec, 84 km (52 mi) south of Suceava. From Varatec, return to 15C and travel roughly 10 km (6 mi) north to the turn off for Agapia.

Unlike the other monasteries, Agapia is notable not for its frescoes but for being the largest convent in Romania, with around 400 nuns in residence. The nuns make gorgeous handmade wool rugs and embroidery, much of which is on display covering the walls of the church. Set against the Carpathian Mountains in a valley surrounded by heavy forests, the monastery was built during the 16th and 17th centuries. It was almost completely destroyed by the Turks in 1821 and rebuilt in 1823. Its monastery provides an extraordinary opportunity to witness the traditional peasant way of life, for the nuns here farm, spin wool, weave, and build in much the same ways that people in this area have been doing for centuries. ☎ *033/662136. Lodging and meals.*

Vornet

★ *125 km (78 mi) northwest of Agapia, 41 km (25 mi) west of Suceava. From Suceava, travel west on E576 until you reach the turnoff for Vornet. From here it is about 5 km (3 mi).*

The blues in the frescoes on the walls of Vornet Monastery are so deep and penetrating that they have been given a color of their own: Vornet blue. Erected in 1488 by Stefan Cel Mare, Vornet is probably the most famous of all of the Bucovina monastic houses. Its frescoes include a detailed portrayal of the *Last Judgment,* in which Christ sits in judgment over those seeking entry into heaven. Among those turned away are Turks and Tartars, enemies of the Romanians during the medieval period. Another fresco is the *Fall,* which depicts Adam and Eve selling out to the Devil. There are also several frescoes depicting the lives of saints, as well as a *Tree of Jesse.* Vornet is uninhabited, and very little remains of the original structure other then the church and a bell tower.

Humor

8 km (5 mi) north of Vornet, 41 km (25 mi) north of Suceava. The turnoff for Humor Monastery is right across E576 from Vornet Monastery, making it a quick drive or a nice walk.

As with many of the monasteries in Bucovina, Humor is known for the vivid colors of its frescoes. Here it is the deep shades of red that stand out. Some of the frescoes here have begun to fade from the weather, but it is still possible to make out depictions of the *Return of the Prodigal Son* and the *Siege of Constantinople in 626*—only here the attacking Persians are revealed as Turks. Humor Monastery is also uninhabited, and it is surrounded by a wooden stockade.

Moldovita

★ *32 km (20 mi) northwest of Humor, 103 km (64 mi) west of Suceava. From Suceava, travel west on E576 to 17A. From here journey north to the Moldoviţa turnoff.*

Standing out as the focal point of the village, Moldovita was built in 1532 as a fortified monastery. It was to provide a place of refuge for the villagers in case of Turkish attack. Constructed completely of stone, the monastery is still home to a group of nuns. Both the interior and exterior are covered with exceptional frescoes. Two of the best-known are the *Defense of Constantinople* (in 626) and the *Last Judgment.* In both cases sinners and villains are depicted as Turks. The throne of Prince Petru Rares, who built the monastery, is on exhibit here. ☎ *030/336348. Lodging and meals.*

Sucevita

34 km (21 mi) northeast of Moldovita, 50 km (31 mi) northeast of Suceava. From Moldovita Monastery, return to 17A and traveling north to the Sucevita turnoff.

Another example of a fortified monastery, Sucevita was constructed between 1581 and 1601. It is best known for the frescoes that adorn its inner and outer walls, including the *Ladder of Virtue,* which shows the 30 steps from Hell to Paradise, and the *Tree of Jesse,* which acts as a symbol of the continuity between the Old and New Testaments. There are still nuns in the monastery, and it houses a **Museum of Monastic Treasures.**

Putna

55 km (34 mi) north of Suceviţa, 55 km (34 mi) northwest of Suceava. From Sucevita Monastery, travel north on 17a to Marginea; turn left and travel north to the Putna turnoff.

Notable for its stained-glass windows rather than frescoes, Putna is also the burial place of Stefan Cel Mare, the Romanian leader who was most successful at fighting against the Turks. In 1469, at the height of his success, Stefan had this monastery built with the purpose—apparent in the stone walls and battle tower—of providing a fortified refuge for the local populace. It is still inhabited by monks.

Bucovina A to Z

Arriving and Departing

BY BUS

Due to its remote location, Bucovina is best visited by bus on a tour arranged through an agency in Bucharest, which would provide a guide, as well as plan for lodging and dining. ☞ Guided Tours *and* Travel Agencies *in* Bucharest A to Z, *above.*

BY CAR

It is reasonable to travel to Bucovina by rented car from Bucharest. Travel time is about eight hours each way. From Bucharest you would go north on E60 to Ploiesti. Follow 1b to Buzau, then E85 to Suceava.

BY PLANE

There are regular flights between Bucharest and Suceava on **Tarom,** the Romanian national airline (☎ 01/6594125 or 01/6594185). This is not the best option for visiting Bucovina, as the monasteries are fairly spread out and difficult to reach except by car or bus.

BY TRAIN

Taking the train is a final option, though traveling this distance from Bucharest can be rather time-consuming and frustrating. If you do choose to take the train, try to get a sleeper car for part of the journey and try to travel by *expres* or *accelerat* service to help reduce the amount of time it takes. Taking the train does leave you without many options for transportation once you arrive in Bucovina. For domestic train information in Bucharest, call ☎ 01/3110857.

Getting Around

BY BUS

Bus service in this area of Romania is not very convenient or reliable. If you do choose to take a bus from Suceava or Piatra Neamt, you would be best off to shoot for one of the monasteries that is close to a few others and then hike from one to the other. Hiking trails are well marked, and trail maps can be picked up in Bucharest from street vendors or travel agencies.

BY CAR

Other then by tour, this is probably the best way to get around to the monasteries. It is possible to see them by traveling something of a loop from Agapia to Vornet, followed by Humor, Moldovita, Putna, and Sucevita.

BY TRAIN

Train access to the monasteries is fairly limited, though it is possible to travel by train to Putna and Moldovita from Suceava.

Contacts and Resources

VISITOR INFORMATION

Suceava: Bucovina Travel Office (✉ Str. N. Balceascu 4, ☎ 030/221297).

TRANSYLVANIA

Transylvania, Romania's western province, offers travelers the chance to explore some of Europe's most beautiful and unspoiled villages and rural landscapes. The Carpathian Mountains, which separate Transylvania from Wallachia and Moldavia, Romania's other two regions, shielded the province from the Turks and Mongols during the Middle Ages. Germans and Hungarians settled in Transylvania during this period, building many wonderful castles, towns, and churches. Since the 1980s many ethnic Germans have emigrated, but Transylvania, which was ruled by Hungary until 1920, is still home to a large Hungarian minority and to many of Romania's 2 million ethnic Gypsies. Many of the country's most beautiful tourist spots are found in Transylvania, but the lack of amenities outside the main towns makes traveling difficult. Although private entrepreneurs are developing tourism, hotels and restaurants of a reasonable standard are often difficult to find. One solution is to base yourself in a major town like Sibiu or Braşov and take day trips into the countryside. An alternative is to travel north out of Bucharest along E60 and follow a loop, traveling first to Sinaia, then to Braşov, Poiana Braşov, Sighişoara, and Sibiu. Another option is to join a guided tour.

Sinaia

127 km (79 mi) northwest of Bucharest.

Prior to World War II and the abdication of the royal family, Sinaia was a summer retreat for Romania's aristocracy. A walk up the mountainside reveals many grand summer homes from this period. The first point of importance to be encountered is the **Sinaia Minastire,** or monastery. This is still a working monastery, with buildings dating to 1695. Many of the monks living here are quite old, wear traditional garb, and are quite happy to show you around and answer any questions you might have. Most of them speak German as well as Romanian.

Just up the hill from Sinaia Minastire is **Peles Palace.** This is one of the best-preserved royal palaces in Europe. It served as the summer residence of the first Hohenzollern king of Romania, Carol I. Built in the latter half of the 19th century, it was the king's attempt to imitate the styles of his former homeland, creating a Bavarian setting in the mountains of Romania. The palace is ornately decorated, inside and out, with intricate wood carvings and paintings of scenes from Wagner operas. Tours in English are available upon request. ☎ *044/311151.* ⌛ *10,000 lei.* ⊙ *Wed.–Sun. 8–4.*

The **Pelisor** lies just above Peles Palace. This was the summer home of the second Hohenzollern king, Ferdinand. Though not as grand as the Peles Palace, Pelisor offered a more comfortable and less formal setting. Tours are available in English. ☎ *044/311151.* ⌛ *8,000 lei.* ⊙ *Wed.–Sun. 8–4.*

Beyond the Pelisor lies another palace built by the late dictator Ceauşescu. It is Spanish in style and was created as an attempt to place himself above the royal family. It is not possible to tour the palace, but it is interesting to view and then hike the mountain path that begins just beyond, which was created as a private path for Ceauşescu.

In the center of Sinaia, just south of the Hotel Montana, is the **teleferic.** Here, from 8 to 4 each day, you may ride a cable car to the top of the mountain. Once there, you can look out over the entire countryside, taking in the grandeur of the Transylvanian Alps. You can take the cable car back down, or it is also possible to hike down the approximately two-hour trail. ⌛ *3,000 lei.*

Dining and Lodging

$$ ✕ **Mont Banc.** The Mont Banc offers traditional French cuisine in a
★ very Germanic town. Here you can enjoy a hot drink made from a mixture of tea and rum, fondue, quiche, onion soup, and other delicious choices. Portions are very generous. Just across the street from the Palace Hotel, this restaurant is a convenient stop for a late lunch after touring sites higher up the mountain. ⊠ *Str. Octavian Goga 14,* ☎ *044/ 311151. No credit cards.*

$$$$ ✕▦ **Mara Sinaia.** Newly opened in 1996, the Mara Sinaia is easily the
★ grandest hotel in Romania outside Bucharest. Just south of Sinaia, it is within walking distance of the town and all tourist attractions. The service is superb, and all rooms are clean and spacious, with excellent views of the mountainside. The restaurant provides Romanian fare in

an elegant atmosphere. The menu ranges from seafood to pork, beef, and venison. A variety of salads is available. ⊠ *Str. Toporasilor 1A,* ☎ *044/110442,* FAX *044/110438. 142 single and double rooms or apartments with bath. Restaurant, bar, pool, health club, casino. AE, MC, V.*

$ ✕🏨 **Furnica.** With a location that makes up for a disappointing appearance, this hotel is surrounded by villas that once belonged to the Romanian aristocracy and is just a short walk from the major tourist attractions. The hotel is clean and comfortable. The restaurant provides a good opportunity to sample traditional Romanian dishes like *ciorbă,* a sour soup, fried cheese, and grilled meats. ⊠ *On the grounds of the Peles Palace,* ☎ *044/311850. 69 rooms with bath. Restaurant. No credit cards.*

$$ 🏨 **Palace.** The Palace Hotel is centrally located, right in Sinaia. It is a state-run hotel and appears somewhat shabby, although it is spacious and clean. ⊠ *Str. Octavian Goga 2,* ☎ *044/312051,* FAX *044/313555. 151 rooms with bath. Restaurant, bar, money exchange. No credit cards.*

$ 🏨 **Economat.** This hotel was built in the same Bavarian style as the nearby Peles Palace. Surrounded by mountains, it is very simple, comfortable, and ideally located. ⊠ *On the grounds of the Peles Palace,* ☎ *044/ 311151,* FAX *044/313555. 40 rooms with bath. Restaurant. No credit cards.*

OFF THE
BEATEN PATH
    CASTLE BRAN – Looming ominously in the shadow of Mt. Bucegi, Castle Bran is a dark and gloomy edifice towering over a bed of stone—a gruesome though beautifully preserved fortress, straight from an Edgar Allan Poe story. Bran was a trading point during the middle ages; now it's claimed this was the castle of Vlad Țepeș, but in fact his castle lies in ruins farther west in Transylvania in the Argeș Valley. Tours are available through the castle. In the parking area there is a market where local peasants sell handwoven sweaters and other crafts. ⊠ *Go north out of Sinaia for about 20 mins, take the turnoff for Rişnov and travel until the road comes to a T. Go left and drive to the town of Bran.* 🎫 *8,000 lei.* ☉ *Tues.–Sun. 8–4:30.*

Brașov and Poiana Brașov

43 km (27 mi) north of Sinaia, 127 km (79 mi) north of Bucharest.

Once an important medieval trading center and now largely industrial, Brașov is the third-largest city in Romania. Brașov's best sights can be found in the center of the city: **Piata Sfatului,** a large cobblestone square and the heart of the old Germanic town, is still surrounded in places by the original fortress walls; its buildings recall the region's German heritage. Built in 1420 and once the town hall, the large **Casa Sfatului** is in the center of the square and houses a historical museum open every day except Monday. The square is surrounded on all sides by shops, cafés, and restaurants; peddlers of different wares, an occasional musician, and colorful gypsies add to the square's liveliness.

Just off Piata Sfatului is the spiraling tower of the **Black Church.** This Gothic masterpiece was built in the early 15th century. It acquired its name after a fire in 1689 that left it with a black, charred appearance. It is usually possible to tour the church, though it is currently under renovation. The church also houses occasional classical-music concerts. Opposite the Black Church, and across Piata Sfatului, is **Strada Republicii.** This is a walking street that provides a wealth of opportunities for shoppers. There are many imported items here, but most important are the artizanat stores—shops that sell handmade Romanian wares including painted eggs, woven rugs, wooden toys, and carvings. The best view of Braşov can be attained by riding the **Telecabina Timpa,** a cable car that runs from 10 to 6 daily, except Monday, to the top of Timpa. To get to the cable car you can hike through the old section of the city. Leave Piata Sfatului on Strada Apollonia Hirscher. Stroll along to the end of the road, taking a left on Strada Castelului. The next right is Strada Romer. Follow this until it ends and climb the stairs to the cable car. Just below the entrance are remains of the old city wall. A stroll along the wall will take you to the **Weaver's Bastion.** This is a corner of the old walls dating from 1421–1436. It now holds a museum that is occasionally open to the public.

A 10-minute drive or bus ride outside Braşov brings you to **Poiana Braşov,** a mountaintop ski resort area that was originally developed for foreigners and top Communist officials. Still somewhat expensive by Romanian standards, it includes several good restaurants and hotels. During the winter months Poiana Braşov is home to some of the best skiing in Romania, though trails are not groomed and ski lifts are limited. In summer, well-marked hiking trails wind along the breathtaking mountainside, and there is a pleasant public swimming pool. Riding the cable car to the top of the mountain provides a view of the Transylvanian plains. Handmade wool sweaters are sold by local peasants in the central parking lot for low prices. Poiana Braşov is a better base for visiting Braşov and the surrounding area because its accommodations are superior.

Dining and Lodging

$$$$ ✕ **Coliba Haiducilor.** A rustic hunting lodge, the Coliba Haiducilor classically evokes the Romanian peasantry. The walls are decorated with hunting trophies, while a large fireplace, waiters dressed in peasant costume, and traditional singing and dancing take you back to an earlier era. The menu includes boar, bear, venison, and chicken. Be sure to request a view of the refrigerator, from which you can choose your own cut of meat. ✉ *Poiana Braşov,* ☎ *068/262137. No credit cards.*

$$$ ✕ **Sura Dacilor.** This restaurant was designed to resemble a traditional Romanian hunting lodge, with traditional peasant decor. Menu choices include garlic chicken, mixed grill, salad and *ciorbă,* a sour soup. A large central fireplace and local folk music add to the ambience. ✉ *Poiana Braşov,* ☎ *068/262327. No credit cards.*

$–$$$ ✕ **Stradivari.** This new Italian-owned establishment includes both a pizzeria and a more expensive restaurant that serves pasta and seafood dishes. The decor in the restaurant is fairly Romanian with very little effort made to make it attractive. The pizzeria, in a basement with a curved ceiling, resembles a wine cellar. ✉ *Piaţa Sfatului 1,* ☎ *068/ 151165. No credit cards. Closed Wed.*

$$ ✕ **Marele Zid China Restaurant.** The Great Wall, a large, privately run restaurant with a pleasant decor and ambience, serves reasonably priced Chinese food. The walls are painted with historic scenes of China. If you are traveling with a group, try one of their sample trays, which provide a taste of many different Asian dishes. ✉ *Piaţa Sfatului,* ☎ *068/144689. No credit cards.*

$ ✕ **Gustari.** This simple, bistro-type restaurant serves traditional Romanian dishes such as sour soup, fried cheese (*caşcaval pane*), and pancakes (*clătite*). This is one of the few restaurants in Romania that doesn't allow smoking anywhere. It is open from 9 AM to 9 PM. ✉ *Piaţa Sfatului 14,* ☎ *068/150857. No credit cards.*

$$$$ ✕▥ **Aro Palace.** Architecturally, a typical communist-era hotel built in the 1950s, the Aro Palace lacks charm but is comfortable, has good facilities, and is conveniently located in the center of town near the main tourist attractions. ⊠ *Bdul Eroilor 27, Braşov,* ☎ *068/142840,* FAX *068/150427. 262 double rooms, 30 singles, and 15 suites with bath. 3 restaurants, pool, barbershop, currency exchange. AE, DC, MC, V.*

$$$$ 🖭 **Alpin.** The Alpin is situated in the highest point in Poiana Braşov, provided breathtaking views from most rooms. It is very comfortable, clean, and service-oriented. ⊠ *Poiana Braşov,* ☎ *068/262343,* FAX *068/150427. 130 single and double rooms or apartments. Restaurant, bar, pool, exercise room, currency exchange. AE, MC, V.*

$$$ 🖭 **Capitol.** Standing at the edge of the old section of Braşov, the Capitol is convenient to most tourist attractions. It is a bit run down, but the rooms are clean and spacious. ⊠ *Bdul. Eroilor 19,* ☎ *068/118920,* FAX *068/151834. 184 double rooms with bath. Restaurant, bar, money exchange. AE, DC, MC, V.*

$$$ 🖭 **Centrul De Echitatie.** The Centrul De Echitatie has a stable, provid-
★   ing opportunities for wagon and sleigh rides and horseback riding through the mountainous countryside. Backwoods barbecues can also be arranged. A small number of clean villas are available for rent here. It is on the bus line to Braşov and within walking distance to all fa-cilities in Poiana Braşov. ⊠ *Poiana Braşov,* ☎ *068/262161. 11 1- and 2-bedroom villas. No credit cards.*

Sighişoara

★   *121 km (75 mi) northwest of Braşov, 248 km (154 mi) northwest of Bucharest.*

Long before you reach this enchanting place, you can see Sighişoara's towers and spires from a distance. Towering above the modern town is a medieval **citadel** that must be among the loveliest and least spoiled in Europe. Walking up from the city center of Sighişoara, one enters the citadel through the 60-meter-tall **clock tower,** which dates from the 14th century. The clock still works, complete with rotating painted wooden figures, one for each day of the week. The tower houses the town's **History Museum,** which includes some moving photographs of the 1989 revolution that led to the execution of dictator Nicolae Ceauşescu and his wife, Elena. From the wooden gallery at the top of the tower you can look out over the town with its terra-cotta roofs and painted houses. Opposite the clock tower is a small ocher-colored house where the father of Vlad Ţepes, better known as Dracula, once lived. It is now a pleasant restaurant. Walking uphill from the home of Dracula's father, along narrow, cobbled streets lined with faded pink, green, and ocher houses, you'll come to a covered staircase. This leads to a 14th-century Gothic church and a German cemetery.

Dining and Lodging

$$ ✕ **Casa Vlad Dracul.** In a house where the father of Vlad Ţepeş, bet-ter known as Dracula, once lived, this pleasant bar and restaurant is the best place in town for a meal. On the first floor you can drink draft beer from a tankard and sit at wooden tables. Upstairs, you'll find a cozy restaurant with fittingly Gothic-style furniture that serves good soups and traditional Romanian dishes. It has an early closing, how-ever—9 PM. ⊠ *Str. Cositorarilor 5,* ☎ *065/771596. No credit cards.*

$ 🖭 **Steaua.** This 19th-century hotel has seen better days. Though the lobby is shabby, the rooms are spacious and clean, and the staff is help-ful. The restaurant serves traditional Romanian dishes and is reason-ably priced. ⊠ *Str. 1 Decembrie 12,* ☎ *065/771954,* FAX *065/771932. 121 rooms with shower or bath. Restaurant, bar, nightclub. No credit cards.*

Sibiu

92 km (57 mi) southwest of Sighişoara, 271 km (168 mi) northwest of Bucharest.

Sibiu, known as Hermannstadt to the Germans, who founded the city in 1143, was the Saxons' chief settlement in Transylvania. Like Sighişoara and Braşov, the town still has a distinctly German or Central European feel to it, even though there are few ethnic Germans left. The old part of the town centers around the magnificent **Piaţa Mare** (Great Square) and **Piaţa Mica** (Small Square), with their painted 17th-century town houses. In Piaţa Mare is the **Roman Catholic church,** a splendid high-baroque structure. The **Brukenthal Museum,** housed in the palace of its founder, Samuel Brukenthal, Hapsburg governor from 1777 to 1787, is also on the Piaţa Mare. It has one of the most extensive collections of silver, paintings, and furniture in Romania. It also has an annex around the corner on Strada Mitropoliei. Next to Piaţa Mica you'll find the **Lutheran Cathedral,** a massive 14th- to 15th-century edifice with a simple, stark interior in total contrast to that of the Roman Catholic church just a couple hundred meters away. On the outskirts of the town there is a large Gypsy community, with the ornate homes of the Gypsies' self-proclaimed leaders King Cioba and Emperor Iulian.

Dining and Lodging

$$$ ✕🖪 **Continental.** Recently refinished, this hotel is the nicest Sibiu has
★ to offer. Rooms are clean and modern, and the staff is attentive. A large breakfast buffet is included with each night's stay; it includes eggs, sausages, meats, cheese, juice, and yogurt. The restaurant serves a variety of well-prepared dishes including trout, steaks, chicken, and a large fresh salad. ⊠ *Calea Dumbravii 2–4,* ☎ *069/218100,* 𝖥𝖠𝖷 *069/210125. 182 single and double rooms and apartments. Restaurant, bar, casino. No credit cards.*

$$$ ✕🖪 **Împăratul Romanilor.** This turn-of-the-century hotel, conveniently situated in the town center, is considered by some to be Romania's best provincial hotel. Rooms are attractively decorated with paintings and locally made furniture. The restaurant has a lively floor show and discotheque on weekends. ⊠ *Str. Nicolae Bălcescu 4,* ☎ *069/216500,* 𝖥𝖠𝖷 *069/413270. 175 rooms with bath. Restaurant, breakfast room, currency exchange. AE, DC, MC, V.*

$$ ✕🖪 **Bulevard.** At the end of Strada Nicolae Bălcescu, this hotel is a little dingy but offers comfortable accommodations at moderate prices and a reasonable restaurant. ⊠ *Piaţa Unirii 10,* ☎ *069/216060,* 𝖥𝖠𝖷 *069/413444. 129 rooms with bath. 2 restaurants, bar. V.*

Transylvania A to Z

Getting Around

BY BUS

Bus trips to Transylvania are arranged by an increasing number of tourist agencies in Bucharest, Budapest, and larger Transylvanian towns such as Braşov. There is an extensive network of local bus service in the region, but buses are often crowded, uncomfortable, and slow and should be used only for short distances, if at all.

BY CAR

Travel by car is perhaps the best way to explore Transylvania's rich rural life. Rental cars, with or without drivers, are available through tourist offices and major hotels. Hitchhiking is also common in Romania. Many Romanians cannot afford cars, and in remote areas they often rely on this form of transportation. It is customary to contribute to gas costs in return for a ride.

BY PLANE

There are regular flights from Bucharest to Braşov, Sibiu, and other major Transylvanian towns with **Tarom** (☎ 01/6594125 or 01/6594185), the Romanian national airline. Traveling by plane is a good option for those with limited time, given the slow speed of train and bus services and the relatively inexpensive cost of air travel.

BY TRAIN

Many Transylvanian towns are on international train routes, making train travel a good way to explore the region. Try to travel by *expres* or *accelerat* service, otherwise you may find that it takes several hours to cover just a couple of hundred kilometers. For domestic train information in Bucharest call ☎ *01/3110857.*

Contacts and Resources

VISITOR INFORMATION

Aro Palace Tourism Office (✉ Bdul Eroilor 27, Braşov, ☎ 068/142840). **Transylvanian Society of Dracula** (✉ Blvd. Primaverii 47, Bucharest, ☎ 01/6666195).

ROMANIA A TO Z

Arriving and Departing

By Car

You can drive into Romania from Hungary through the border towns of Satu Mare, Oradea, Varsand, and Arad. From Bulgaria you can enter through the boarder towns of Calafat, Giurgiu, Negru Voda, and Vama Veche. Driving into Romania can be a lengthy process. Border police are not very efficient, and the line to cross the border can sometimes take over 24 hours.

By Plane

Most international flights arrive at **Otopeni,** the international airport just outside Bucharest. **Tarom,** the Romanian national airline, offers some flights from other countries to Arad. To catch an internal flight requires transferring to **Baneasa Airport,** which is about a five-minute drive from Otopeni. Bus service is available regularly between both airports for a small fee. You can also catch a taxi; taxi fare should be no more than $5.

By Train

Train service is available from Budapest and Sofia to Bucharest and all sites in between. Try to travel on a night train and rent a *vagon de dormit,* or sleeper. First class is worth the extra cost.

Getting Around

By Bus

Bus stations, or *autogara,* are usually located near train stations. Buses are generally crowded and far from luxurious—in a word, horrible. Tickets are sold at stations up to two hours before departure. Local bus tickets can be bought at any stop; intercity bus tickets are only sold at the autogara.

By Car

An adequate network of main roads covers the country, though the great majority are still two lanes. Some roads are badly potholed, and a few have not been paved. Progress may be impeded by convoys of farm machinery or slow-moving trucks, by horses and carts, or by herds of animals. Night driving can be dangerous: Roads and vehicles are either poorly lighted or not lit at all.

Driving is on the right, as in the United States. Speed limits are 60 kilometers per hour (37 miles per hour) in built-up areas and 80–90 kilometers per hour (50–55 miles per hour) on all other roads. Driving after drinking any amount of alcohol is prohibited. Police are empowered to levy on-the-spot fines. Vehicle spot checks are frequent, but police are generally courteous to foreigners. Road signs are the same as those in Western Europe.

An International Driver's Permit is required for all drivers from outside the country (☞ Car Rental *in* Smart Travel Tips A to Z), as is national insurance. Insurance coverage costs $27 for a 15-day period and can be purchased at the border or when renting a car (☞ Car Rentals, *below*).

By Plane

Tarom operates daily flights to major Romanian cities from Bucharest's Baneasa Airport. During the summer, additional flights link Constanţa with major cities, including Cluj and Iaşi. Be prepared for delays and cancellations. Prices average $90 round-trip. International flights can be booked at the central reservations office (☒ Strada Brezoianu 10) and at some major hotels. For domestic flights go to Piaţa Victoriei 1, ☎ 01/6594185.

By Train

Romanian Railways (CFR) operates *expres, accelerat, rapide,* and *personal* trains; if possible, avoid the *personal* trains because they are very slow. Trains are inexpensive and often crowded, with cars in need of repair. First class is worth the extra cost. A *vagon de dormit* (sleeper) or a cheap *cuşeta*, with bunk beds, is available for longer journeys. It is always advisable to buy a seat reservation in advance, but you cannot buy the ticket itself at a train station more than one hour before departure. If your reserved seat is already occupied, it may have been sold twice. If you're in Bucharest and want to buy your ticket ahead of time, go to the Advance Booking Office (☒ Strada Brezoianu 10, ☎ 01/6132642/3/4, 01/6132643 or 01/6132644), or for international reservations, go to CFR International (☒ B-dul I. C., Brătianu 44, ☎ 1/6134008). You will be charged a small commission fee, but the process is less time-consuming than buying your ticket at the railway station.

Contacts and Resources

B&B Reservation Agencies

It is possible to rent rooms in Romanian homes in Bucharest and in the Romanian countryside. This can be arranged through most travel agencies in Bucharest and through the **Office of National Tourism** (ONT; ☞ Guided Tours *and* Travel Agencies *in* Bucharest A to Z, *above*).

Car Rentals

Budget, Avis, and Hertz have recently opened offices in Bucharest. There are also a few locally run operators, but they are largely undependable. Prices start at $100 per day plus mileage for an economy car, with lower rates available for longer periods. Car rental does require purchasing national automobile insurance, which is available from the rental agency (☞ Getting Around by Car, *above*).

Avis: Otopeni Airport, ☎ 401/212–0011; Hotel Bucharest, ☒ Calea Victoriei 29, ☎ 312–2043; Intercontinental, ☒ B-dul N. Bălcescu 4–6, ☎ 614–0400; Minerva Hotel, ☒ Str. Gheorghe Manu 2–4, ☎ 01/312–2738. **Budget:** Dorobanti Hotel, ☒ Calea Dorobanti 1–3, ☎ 01/210–2867. **Hertz:** Otopeni Airport, ☎ 401/212–0122; Dorobanti Hotel, ☒ Calea Dorobanti 1–3, ☎ 01/211–5450.

Customs and Duties

When you arrive, customs officials will usually give your bags the once-over to make sure you're not bringing anything like a video camera or a CD player into the country. If you have any expensive-looking electronic equipment, your passport will be stamped, and you'll have to show the item on your way out or pay a hefty fine. Upon arrival, you are allowed one carton of cigarettes, one liter of hard liquor, and two bottles of wine. Anything extra will be confiscated.

Emergencies

Police (☎ 955). **Titan Ambulance Service** (☎ 01/961), or contact your embassy or consulate.

Guided Tours and Travel Agencies

☞ Bucharest A to Z, *above*.

Language

Romanian is a Latin-based language that is very similar to Italian. Travelers who speak another Latin language will find that they can easily understand quite a bit of Romanian. Most Romanians also speak at least one other language. As a result, usually you can find someone who speaks English. Two resources for learning basic Romanian are *The Hippocrene Romanian Conversation Guide* and *Language/30 Romanian;* the latter is a cassette course created by Educational Services Teaching Cassettes.

Mail

In Romania, post offices can be identified by a yellow sign with the word **Posta.** The main post office in Bucharest is located at ⊠ Str. Matei Milo 10, ☎ 01/6144054 or 01/6145777.

POSTAL RATES

To send an average size letter to the United States or Canada from Romania costs 2150 lei (70¢). Within Europe the rate is 1550 (50¢).

RECEIVING MAIL

The safest way to receive mail in Romania is to have it sent to you at your hotel. First-class mail takes about two weeks from the United States and Canada.

Money and Expenses

CURRENCY

The unit of currency in Romania is the leu (plural lei). It is circulated in denominations of 500-, 1,000-, 5,000-, and 10,000-lei notes and 20-, 50-, and 100-lei coins. At press time, the exchange rate was approximately 3,000 lei to the dollar, though it can vary widely (in one recent three-month period, the exchange rate fluctuated between 700 and 2,500 lei to the U.S. dollar).

It is best to exchange money at local exchange houses, *Casa de Schimb Valutar* (ask for 500- and 1,000-lei notes). The exchange rates here tend to be higher then the official rate at banks, the airport, the train station, or in hotels. Be sure to hang on to your receipt to change your money back at the end of your trip, as it is needed to prove you didn't trade on the black market. Avoid trading on the black market, as it can be very dangerous.

When you are owed change from a purchase, do not expect change for amounts less then 100 lei. If you plan to stay long in Romania, it's imperative you bring American dollars in small denominations ($1, $5, and $10 bills); a couple of dollars can be useful in many situations. Also note that you must buy international train tickets in hard currency, so be sure to save at least US $50 for your trip out of the country.

WHAT IT WILL COST

Romania's post-1989 runaway inflation has calmed down considerably. The leu is now fairly stable, and prices do not fluctuate too much over a short period of time. Travelers may find that many imported items are much more expensive in Romania than at home due to the high import tax imposed by the government. Locally made items are still fairly inexpensive in comparison.

SAMPLE COSTS

A cup of coffee, 1,500 lei; museum entrance, 1,000–8,000 lei; a good theater seat, 3,000 lei; cinema seat 1,500 lei; a 1-kilometer (½-mile) taxi ride, 500 lei; a bottle of Romanian beer, 2,500 lei; imported beer, 7,000 lei; a bottle of Romanian wine in a good restaurant, 5,000 lei. Wine is not usually sold by the glass.

National Holidays

January 1; January 2; Orthodox Easter Monday; May 1 (Labor Day); December 1 (Greater Romania Day), December 25 and 26.

Opening and Closing Times

Most businesses open at 8 AM and close by 5 PM. On weekends most official businesses are closed. Shops are open Saturdays from 10 AM until 1:30 or 2 PM. An increasing number of private businesses stay open later.

TRAVELER'S CHECKS

Traveler's checks are mostly useless in Romania: They're accepted only at banks, tourist offices, Bucharest's major hotels, and some exchange shops in the area around the Hotel Intercontinental (look for signs in these shop windows). Banks usually charge a 5% commission, and tourist offices and hotels take a 5%–10% bite. Try to change a decent amount of traveler's checks into American dollars *before* you arrive, supplemented with a small bundle of traveler's checks in case of an emergency. Since you must travel in Romania with large sums of cash, it is absolutely imperative to stash your money in various safe places.

Passports and Visas

Americans need only a valid passport to enter Romania for up to 30 days, but border guards may try and extort money from you anyway: Be firm. If you're traveling on a British, Canadian, Australian, or New Zealand passport, you must pay $15 (if you arrive by train) or $22 (if you arrive by car) for a 30-day tourist card when you cross the border. There is no application, you don't need any photos—just hand the border guard your money. They prefer U.S. dollars but will accept British pounds or German marks.

Student and Youth Travel

Students can receive discounts to most museums and tourist attractions in Romania. Students are also able to take advantage of lower-priced student hotels in most larger cities, though these are usually in very poor condition. A student identification is required to take advantage of discounts. For more information, contact the Office of National Tourism (ONT; ☞ Guided Tours *and* Travel Agencies *in* Bucharest A to Z, *above*).

Telephones

The country code for Romania is 40. The city code for Bucharest is 01, and telephone numbers in the city have 2, 3, 6, or 7 as a prefix. To make a long-distance call within the country, first dial 0, then the area code and number. When calling to countries outside Romania, dial 00 followed by the country code of the country you are calling. For information dial the relevant area code, then 11515; in Bucharest, the information number is 931 (for A–L listings) and 932 (for M–Z listings). You may not always be able to speak to an operator who knows English.

Public telephones can be accessed using 20-, 50-, and 100-lei coins. Some phones now require a phone card, which can be purchased at the post office, some hotels, and some sidewalk kiosks. Post offices have a waiting system whereby you order your call and pay at the counter. When your call is ready, the name of the town or country you are phoning is announced, together with the number of the cabin you proceed to for your call.

To access AT&T from within Romania, dial toll free, 01–800–4288. To access MCI, dial toll free, 01–800–1800.

Tipping

Most Romanians are very poor tippers. Generally speaking though, services that cater to foreigners expect that you will tip 5%–10%.

Visitor Information

The **Romanian National Tourist Office (ONT)** (☞ Travel Agencies *in* Bucharest A to Z, *above*) has been officially disbanded, although most offices both in Romania and abroad continue to use the name. Try to obtain information before arriving in Romania from the office in New York or London (☞ Visitor Information *in* Important Contacts A to Z), for once you arrive in Romania it will be difficult (but not impossible) to find maps, pamphlets, helpful hints, and budget-hotel listings. You can usually find a small tourism office in the local train station. These offices have limited information, and the staff may not speak English. To find the train station, follow signs leading to the GARA; it is usually well marked.

INDEX

NOTES

Fodor's Travel Publications

Available at bookstores everywhere, or call 1–800–533–6478, 24 hours a day.

Gold Guides
U.S.

Alaska

Arizona

Boston

California

Cape Cod, Martha's Vineyard, Nantucket

The Carolinas & the Georgia Coast

Chicago

Colorado

Florida

Hawai'i

Las Vegas, Reno, Tahoe

Los Angeles

Maine, Vermont, New Hampshire

Maui & Lāna'i

Miami & the Keys

New England

New Orleans

New York City

Pacific North Coast

Philadelphia & the Pennsylvania Dutch Country

The Rockies

San Diego

San Francisco

Santa Fe, Taos, Albuquerque

Seattle & Vancouver

The South

U.S. & British Virgin Islands

USA

Virginia & Maryland

Washington, D.C.

Foreign

Australia

Austria

The Bahamas

Belize & Guatemala

Bermuda

Canada

Cancún, Cozumel, Yucatán Peninsula

Caribbean

China

Costa Rica

Cuba

The Czech Republic & Slovakia

Eastern & Central Europe

Europe

Florence, Tuscany & Umbria

France

Germany

Great Britain

Greece

Hong Kong

India

Ireland

Israel

Italy

Japan

London

Madrid & Barcelona

Mexico

Montréal & Québec City

Moscow, St. Petersburg, Kiev

The Netherlands, Belgium & Luxembourg

New Zealand

Norway

Nova Scotia, New Brunswick, Prince Edward Island

Paris

Portugal

Provence & the Riviera

Scandinavia

Scotland

Singapore

South Africa

South America

Southeast Asia

Spain

Sweden

Switzerland

Thailand

Tokyo

Toronto

Turkey

Vienna & the Danube

Fodor's Special-Interest Guides

Caribbean Ports of Call

The Complete Guide to America's National Parks

Family Adventures

Gay Guide to the USA

Halliday's New England Food Explorer

Halliday's New Orleans Food Explorer

Healthy Escapes

Kodak Guide to Shooting Great Travel Pictures

Net Travel

Nights to Imagine

Rock & Roll Traveler USA

Sunday in New York

Sunday in San Francisco

Walt Disney World, Universal Studios and Orlando

Walt Disney World for Adults

Where Should We Take the Kids? California

Where Should We Take the Kids? Northeast

Worldwide Cruises and Ports of Call

Special Series

Affordables

Caribbean
Europe
Florida
France
Germany
Great Britain
Italy
London
Paris

Fodor's Bed & Breakfasts and Country Inns

America
California
The Mid-Atlantic
New England
The Pacific Northwest
The South
The Southwest
The Upper Great Lakes

The Berkeley Guides

California
Central America
Eastern Europe
Europe
France
Germany & Austria
Great Britain & Ireland
Italy
London
Mexico
New York City
Pacific Northwest & Alaska
Paris
San Francisco

Compass American Guides

Arizona
Canada
Chicago
Colorado
Hawaii
Idaho
Hollywood
Las Vegas

Maine
Manhattan
Montana
New Mexico
New Orleans
Oregon
San Francisco
Santa Fe
South Carolina
South Dakota
Southwest
Texas
Utah
Virginia
Washington
Wine Country
Wisconsin
Wyoming

Fodor's Citypacks

Atlanta
Hong Kong
London
New York City
Paris
Rome
San Francisco
Washington, D.C.

Fodor's Español

California
Caribe Occidental
Caribe Oriental
Gran Bretaña
Londres
Mexico
Nueva York
Paris

Fodor's Exploring Guides

Australia
Boston & New England
Britain
California
Caribbean
China
Egypt
Florence & Tuscany
Florida

France
Germany
Ireland
Israel
Italy
Japan
London
Mexico
Moscow & St. Petersburg
New York City
Paris
Prague
Provence
Rome
San Francisco
Scotland
Singapore & Malaysia
Spain
Thailand
Turkey
Venice

Fodor's Flashmaps

Boston
New York
San Francisco
Washington, D.C.

Fodor's Pocket Guides

Acapulco
Atlanta
Barbados
Jamaica
London
New York City
Paris
Prague
Puerto Rico
Rome
San Francisco
Washington, D.C.

Mobil Travel Guides

America's Best Hotels & Restaurants
California & the West
Frequent Traveler's Guide to Major Cities
Great Lakes
Mid-Atlantic

Northeast
Northwest & Great Plains
Southeast
Southwest & South Central

Rivages Guides

Bed and Breakfasts of Character and Charm in France
Hotels and Country Inns of Character and Charm in France
Hotels and Country Inns of Character and Charm in Italy
Hotels and Country Inns of Character and Charm in Paris
Hotels and Country Inns of Character and Charm in Portugal
Hotels and Country Inns of Character and Charm in Spain

Short Escapes

Britain
France
New England
Near New York City

Fodor's Sports

Golf Digest's Best Places to Play
Skiing USA
USA Today The Complete Four Sport Stadium Guide

Fodor's Vacation Planners

Great American Learning Vacations
Great American Sports & Adventure Vacations
Great American Vacations
Great American Vacations for Travelers with Disabilities
National Parks and Seashores of the East
National Parks of the West

WHEREVER YOU TRAVEL, *H*ELP IS NEVER FAR AWAY.

From planning your trip to providing travel assistance along the way, American Express® Travel Service Offices are always there to help.

Eastern Europe

Megatours (R)
1 Levski Str.
Sofia, Bulgaria
2/80 04 19

American Express Ltd.
c/o Marriott Hotel
A1. Jerozolimskie 69/75
Warsaw, Poland
22/630-6952

American Express Hungary Ltd.
Deak Ferenc U. 10
Budapest, Hungary
1/266-8680

Tatratrou (R)
Marianske Namestie 21
Zilina, Slovak Republic
89/47-529

American Express Travel Service
Dom Bez Kantow
Krakowskie Przedmiescie 11
Warsaw, Poland
22/635-2002

Marshal Turism (R)
43 Magheru Blvd.
Bucharest, Rumania
1/223-1204

American Express Czech Republic Ltd.
Vaclavske Namesti 56
Prague, Czech Republic
2/24 219-992

Travel

http://www.americanexpress.com/travel

American Express Travel Service Offices are found in central locations throughout Eastern Europe.